AFRICA
2007

by
Les de Villiers

A publication of
The Corporate Council on Africa
and
Business Books International

AFRICA 2007
Africa - Reference

ISBN 0-916673-22-7
ISSN 1536-1454

The information in this book is furnished for informational use only and should not be construed as recommendations on investment and business transactions. It was developed largely on the basis of review of both secondary resources and first-hand advice and contains subjective opinion. While efforts were made to include the most recent and reliable sources of information, the accuracy of the content cannot be guaranteed. Investment and business decisions should only be made after proper further investigation and due diligence on the part of the reader.

Size	11,709,908 sq miles/30,328,662 sq. km	Island nations	Six, with Equatorial Guinea part landbased
	Second largest continent after Asia		Madagascar is world's 4th largest island
Distance	North-South 5,000 miles/8,000 km	Population	At 900 million 13% of world total
	East-West 4,700 miles/7,560 km		Speak more than 1,000 languages
Mountains	Highest: Mt. Kilimanjaro 19,340 ft/5,895 m	Density	Average of 105 people per sq. mile
	Ranks sixteenth worldwide		Well below world average of 105 and Asia's 205
Lakes	Lake Victoria is world's 3rd largest	Resources	8.2 % of world's oil, 7.7% of its natural gas
	Lake Tanganyika is 7th largest		11% to 45% of world's strategic minerals
Rivers	Longest: Nile is 4,180 miles/6,690 km	Economy	4.3% real GDP growth in 2005
	World's longest river		Per capita GDP in 2005 was $1,039
Countries	53 countries of which 15 landlocked	Investment	Returns on investment rarely dips below 10%
	Largest: Sudan, Algeria & DR of Congo		Highest returns in the world according to OPIC

We're developing much more than energy.

In over 50 African nations, we're creating new opportunities and building lasting relationships while working in the energy industry. And, in the next five years, Chevron is going even further, investing an additional $17 billion in energy-related projects to help support Africa's economies and the development of its people. Today, over 90 percent of our employees in Africa are Africans. For nearly 100 years, we've been honored to help turn promise into progress. And we'll be there in the years to come, more committed than ever.

Chevron

Human energy™

CONTENTS

CONTENTS

Global Neighbors

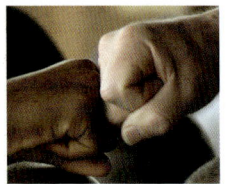

Dedicated to Business, Committed to Community

While Devon's roots are in North America, our operations — as well as our social investments — span the globe. We are committed to our role as an energy producer and to our partnership with communities where we do business. At Devon, being a good neighbor is not an ideal — it is an objective.

www.devonenergy.com

UNITED STATES   CANADA   GULF OF MEXICO   AZERBAIJAN   BRAZIL   CHINA   EGYPT   WEST AFRICA

CONTENTS

FOREWORD

CCA is once again very proud to be associated with AFRICA 2007 and its publisher, Business Books International. The Africa 2007 is a most readable and useful guide for any individual, institution or business beginning to explore the numerous and diverse opportunities offered by the countries of Africa.

We are equally proud that each year's edition captures the many positive developments and the changing business environments in Africa today. As you know, this continent is the most rapidly changing region in the world.

Many of its countries are adapting new economic models intended to accelerate development. Tanzania is booming. Mozambique is showing exceptional growth, as is Madagascar. So too are Benin and countries like Mali and Burkina Faso. Favorable change can be seen not solely in one region or country but spreading throughout the continent.

Each year the publisher of this series of books has been deeply committed to reflecting these positive changes in order to raise Africa's profile in the U.S. and elsewhere overseas—an objective shared and applauded by CCA.

There continues to be a need for fair and substantial information in the overseas media about Africa. AFRICA 2007 is one of the best introductory resources on Africa available today.

We hope that this book will motivate you to become involved in Africa, whether in business, academia, politics, or tourism. We urge you to use this guide as a valuable tool in beginning a close association with this rich and diverse continent.

Stephen Hayes
President
Corporate Council on Africa

GoodWorks International, LLC

GoodWorks
INTERNATIONAL, LLC
1996 - 2006

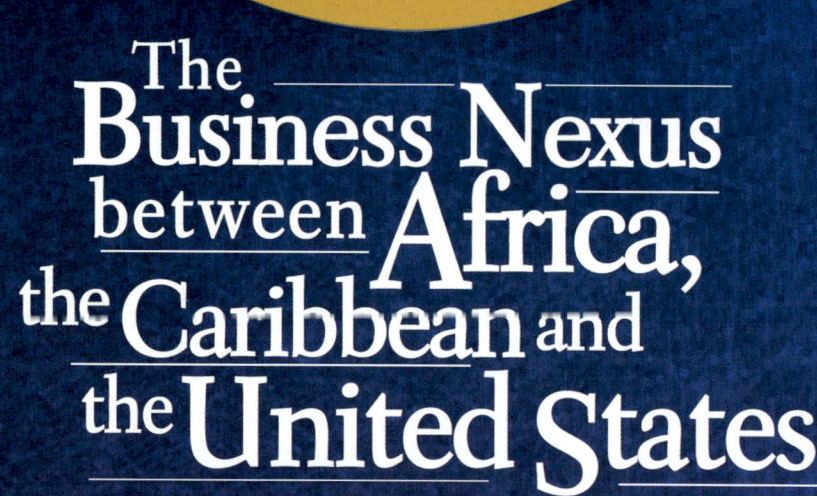

The Business Nexus between Africa, the Caribbean and the United States

303 PEACHTREE STREET, NE . SUITE . 4420 ATLANTA, GA. 30308 | TEL: 404.527.8484 | FAX: 404.527.3827

ATLANTA | WASHINGTON D.C | NEW YORK | ANGOLA | GHANA | COTE D' IVOIRE | NIGERIA | RWANDA | TANZANIA

PUBLISHER'S NOTE

When we published the first in this series seven years ago I pointed out that the presence of several thousand American, European and Asian companies in Africa is ample proof that pessimistic reports about this continent's ultimate demise were misplaced.

For too long, I pointed out, Africa had been portrayed purely in terms of acronyms such as HIPC, LDC and HIV/AIDS. These overseas firms, although many of them are taking their role as responsible partners seriously by supporting local communities in a variety of ways, are not there purely for altruistic reasons but for profit. Africa happened to have delivered the highest returns on foreign investment for more than a decade.

No one denies that the outlook in Africa (as in most other parts of the world) can best be described as partly cloudy or, I would contend, partly sunny. Even though since our first edition in 2000 much has happened in Africa to move it closer to reaching its full potential, there have also been, like elsewhere in the world, some serious setbacks.

Although Africa is falling short of the ambitious targets set in the UN-sponsored Millennium Development Goals at the time when we went into print with our first edition, it has shown remarkable progress in many respects since—enough to support our belief that it is set on the road to recovery. The Renaissance is happening.

Once again I am deeply indebted to the Washington-based Corporate Council on Africa for its outstanding partnership and to the advertisers who make it possible for us to produce a reference book praised by the American Library Association for being both "excellent" and "inexpensive." A special word of gratitude goes to the president of the Corporate Council, Steve Hayes, and his colleagues for their help and support.

Readers are invited to address any comments and suggestions regarding editorial content to me at *lesdv@businessbooksusa.com*. This feedback has been helpful in the past to steer us a little closer towards the every evasive "perfect" book.

Dr. Les de Villiers
Publisher/Editor
Email: *lesdv@businessbooksusa.com*

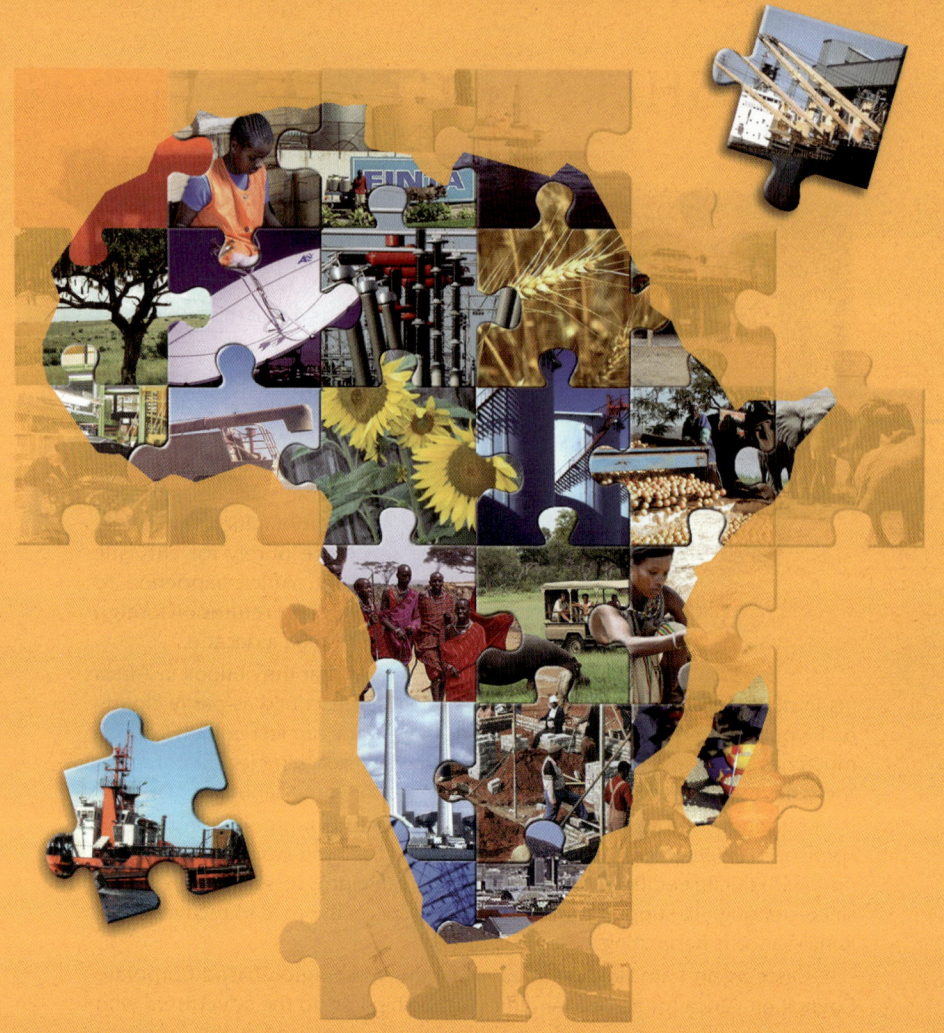

HELPING YOU FIND THE RIGHT FIT FOR YOUR BUSINESS IN AFRICA

CORPORATE COUNCIL ON AFRICA (CCA) MEMBERS REPRESENT NEARLY 85 PERCENT OF TOTAL U.S. PRIVATE SECTOR INVESTMENT IN AFRICA. SINCE 1993, CCA HAS BEEN THE LEADING AMERICAN ORGANIZATION DEDICATED TO ENHANCING TRADE AND INVESTMENT RELATIONS BETWEEN THE UNITED STATES AND THE 53 COUNTRIES OF AFRICA.

CCA IS YOUR PRIMARY SOURCE OF CONTINUOUS INFORMATION ON BUSINESS ACROSS THE CONTINENT, U.S. AND AFRICAN BUSINESS NETWORKS, TRADE AND INVESTMENT OPPORTUNITIES AND THE PROMOTION OF YOUR BUSINESS OPERATIONS IN AFRICA. JOIN CCA AND BENEFIT FROM SERVICES AND PROGRAMS THAT ARE AS DIVERSE AS OUR MEMBERSHIP.

FOR MORE INFORMATION ABOUT CCA MEMBERSHIP, CONTACT CHRISTOPHER MORE, DIRECTOR OF MEMBERSHIP AT CMORE@AFRICACNCL.ORG.

THE CORPORATE COUNCIL ON
AFRICA

PROMOTING TRADE AND INVESTMENT BETWEEN THE UNITED STATES AND AFRICA.

1100 17th Street, N.W. | Suite 1100 | Washington, D.C. 20036 | tel: 202-835-1115 | fax: 202-835-1117 | www.aficacncl.org

I AM AN AFRICAN

Pres. Thabo Mbeki

I am an African.

I owe my being to the hills and the valleys, the mountains and the glades, the rivers, the deserts, the trees, the flowers, the seas and the ever-changing seasons that define the face of our native land.

My body has frozen in our frosts and in our latter day snows. It has thawed in the warmth of our sunshine and melted in the heat of the midday sun. The crack and the rumble of the summer thunders, lashed by startling lightning, have been a cause both of trembling and of hope.

The fragrances of nature have been as pleasant to us as the sight of the wild blooms of the citizens of the veld.

The dramatic shapes of the Drakensberg, the soil-colored waters of the Lekoa, iGqili noThukela, and the sands of the Kgalagadi, have all been panels of the set on the natural stage on which we act out the foolish deeds of the theater of our day.

At times, and in fear, I have wondered whether I should concede equal citizenship of our country to the leopard and the lion, the elephant and the springbok, the hyena, the black mamba and the pestilential mosquito.

A human presence among all these, a feature on the face of our native land thus defined, I know that none dare challenge me when I say—I am an African!

I owe my being to the Khoi and the San whose desolate souls haunt the great expanses of the beautiful Cape—they who fell victim to the most merciless genocide our native land has ever seen, they who were the first to lose their lives in the struggle to defend our freedom and dependence and they who, as a people, perished in the result.

Today, as a country, we keep an audible silence about these ancestors of the generations that live, fearful to admit the horror of a former deed, seeking to obliterate from our memories a cruel occurrence which, in its remembering, should teach us not and never to be inhuman again.

I am formed of the migrants who left Europe to find a new home on our native land. Whatever their own actions, they remain still, part of me.

In my veins courses the blood of the Malay slaves who came from the East. Their proud dignity informs my bearing, their culture a part of my essence. The stripes they bore on their bodies from the lash of the slave master are a reminder embossed on my consciousness of what should not be done.

I am the grandchild of the warrior men and women that Hintsa and Sekhukhune led, the patriots that Cetshwayo and Mphephu took to battle, the soldiers Moshoeshoe and Ngungunyane taught never to dishonour the cause of freedom.

My mind and my knowledge of myself is formed by the victories that are the jewels in our African crown, the victories we earned from Isandhlwana to Khartoum, as Ethiopians and as the Ashanti of Ghana, as the Berbers of the desert.

I am the grandchild who lays fresh flowers on the Boer graves at St Helena and the Bahamas, who sees in the mind's eye and suffers the suffering of a simple peasant folk, death, concentration camps, destroyed homesteads, a dream in ruins.

I am the child of Nongqause. I am he who made it possible to trade in the world markets in diamonds, in gold, in the same food for which my stomach yearns.

I come of those who were transported from India and China, whose being resided in the fact, solely, that they were able to provide physical labor, who taught me that we could both be at home and be foreign, who taught me that human existence itself demanded that freedom was a necessary condition for that human existence.

Being part of all these people, and in the knowledge that none dare contest that assertion, I shall claim that—I am an African.

Extract from a speech by South African President Thabo Mbeki before the South African Parliament

THE YEAR IN REVIEW

IN THE PAST YEAR MOST OF AFRICA'S 53 COUNTRIES HAVE MADE GOOD PROGRESS TOWARDS LIFTING THEIR CITIZENS ABOVE THE POVERTY LINE. THE MAJORITY CONTINUED TO MAINTAIN GROWTH RATES IN EXCESS OF 4.5 PERCENT AND SEEM SET TO COMING CLOSE TO THE AMBITIOUS GOALS SET IN THE UNITED NATIONS MILLENNIUM DEVELOPMENT GOALS (MDG). ENCOURAGING ALSO WERE ORDERLY AND FREE ELECTIONS IN VARIOUS PARTS OF THE CONTINENT—MOST NOTABLY THE DEMOCRATIC REPUBLIC OF CONGO WITH ITS HISTORIC FIRST AFTER SEVERAL DECADES OF TYRANNY AND TURMOIL. IN 2006 AFRICA WON ITS FIRST OSCAR IN HOLLYWOOD AND WAS SELECTED TO STAGE THE SOCCER WORLD CUP IN 2010—AN EVENT THAT IS BOUND TO PROMOTE A GREATER GLOBAL AWARENESS OF THE BEAUTY AND SPLENDOR OF THIS CONTINENT.

GROWTH

The World Bank's African Development Indicators Report (ADI) depicts a diverse continent where several countries made notable strides, some stagnated and others lagged. The full spectrum for 2005 ranges from Zimbabwe, which recorded a negative growth rate of 2.4%—the only country to do so—to Equatorial Guinea with its 20.9% growth. According to the ADI report, most African countries had lifted their citizens above the poverty line by significant percentages. Annual GDP growth rates in excess of 4.5 percent have been attained in the majority of cases since the mid-nineties while inflation was down to historic lows, exchange rate distortions were being eliminated and fiscal deficits were dropping. Africa weathered higher oil prices better than before and its real GDP grew by 4.3 percent, compared to 5.4 percent in 2004. The report paints a picture of Zimbabwe as an island of decline amid growth across the continent. "Africa is today a continent on the move, making tangible progress on delivering better health, education, growth, trade and poverty-reduction outcomes," said Gobind Nankani, the World Bank Vice President for the Africa Region.

CAUTION

The World Bank's sister organization, the International Monetary Fund had a few words of caution for those who were ready to pop the champagne. While praising Africa's for attaining an eight year high in growth coupled with a drop in inflation to a 25 year low, the IMF warned that it was still not growing fast enough to reach the poverty reduction targets set in the UN Millennium Development Goals (MDG). It also cited several governments for restrictive business practices. Much of this growth, the IMF noted, came in the form of higher oil prices and had little to do with internal reforms. Disturbing, according to the IMF, is the fact that 16 of the world's 20 worst countries for business were in Sub-Saharan Africa.

CONGO ELECTION

Africa had nine elections during 2006. Most were declared free and fair by independent observers and conducted in a peaceful and orderly

World Bank President Paul Wolfowitz calling on Pres. Ellen Johnson-Sirleaf in Monrovia, Liberia *Official picture*

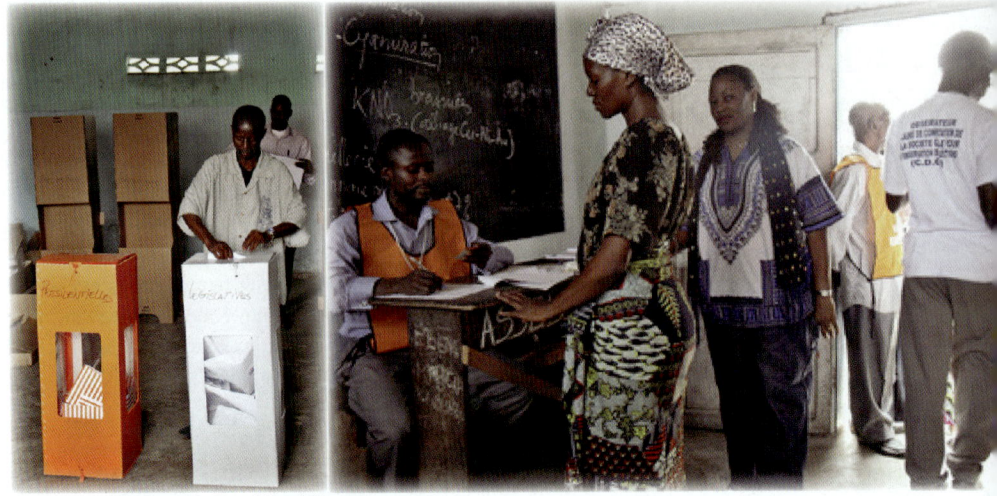
Voting in the Democratic Republic of Congo

Pictures: UNDPI

manner. The most significant was undoubtedly the drawn-out contest between Pres. Joseph Kabila and his main rival in the **Democratic Republic of Congo**, Jean-Pierre Bemba. In the first round in July, Kabila and Bemba emerged front-runners but neither could capture an outright majority. The second round resulted in a victory for Kabila. Although Bemba threatened to challenge the result in the courts he did dissuade his cadres from taking to the streets. There is hope that this election that cost the international community a hefty $500 million and involved UN and European peacekeeping troops might finally end a conflict which has since the late nineties taken 4 million lives through fighting and attendant hunger and disease—the most lethal combat since World War II. Neither Kabila's *Parti du peuple pour la reconstruction et la democratie* (PPRD) with its 111 seats nor Vice-President Jean-Pierre Bemba's *Mouvement pour la libération du Congo* (MLC) party with its 64 managed to win an outright majority in the 500 seat legislature.

OTHER ELECTIONS

In February 2006 Pedro Pires was reelected president of **Cape Verde** over rival Carlos Veiga. José Maria Pereira Neves was reappointed Prime Minister as leader of the victorious *Partido Africano da Independência de Cabo Verde* (PAICV). Also in February in the first multi-party election since Pres. Museveni became president of **Uganda** his National Resistance Movement (NRM) captured 205 seats against 37 for its nearest rival, the Forum for Democratic Change (FDC). In April, banker Yayi Boni succeeded Mathieu Kérékou as president

of **Benin** in a resounding victory over Assembly speaker Adrien Hounbendji. In May, Pres. Idriss Déby was reelected in **Chad**. In an election in **Comoros** that same month Ahmed Abdallah Sambi succeeded Azali Assoumani as president. Pres. Fradique de Menezes was reelected president of **São Tomé & Príncipe** in July and in September Pres. Yaya Jammeh was reelected president of **The Gambia.** That same month Pres. Levy Mwanawasa was reelected president of **Zambia.**

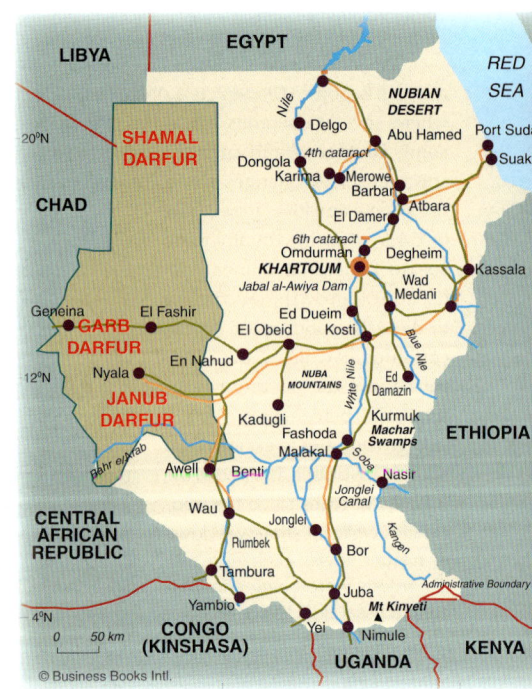

CONFLICT

Overshadowed in the world media by reports on the crisis in the Middle East, and especially Iraq, costly conflicts in Africa were neglected. Despite efforts on the part of some members of the United Nations and a signed peace agreement between Sudan and the rebels, the killings continued in the **Darfur** region. After initially agreeing to an assessment mission into the area to plan for UN troop deployment when it signed a peace accord with the main faction of the largest rebel group in Darfur, the Sudan Liberation Army, the government reneged. "Our position is against any foreign interference in Darfur. The U.N. troops will complicate rather than solve things," Elsamani Elwasila, Sudan's Foreign Minister told journalists. He insisted that 7,200 African Union troops currently deployed were sufficient to patrol this region—about the size of France. The Darfur conflict, which began in early 2003, has claimed tens of thousands of lives and uprooted more than two million people from their homes, according to UN figures. Abuses in Darfur are said to include widespread rape and the destruction of villages. US officials have termed attacks on the people of Darfur genocide.

There has been a spillover of the Darfur conflict into neighboring **Chad** and **Central African Republic (CAR)**. The Sudanese government has been accused by both Pres. François Bozizé of CAR and Pres. Idriss Déby of Chad of instigating unrest in their territory. This triangle of trouble seems destined to persist as both the governments of Chad and CAR failed to put a final end to the uprisings and Sudan seems unwilling to desist. In April 2006 the rebel offensive brought Chad to the brink of all-out civil war. When Déby ultimately stopped the Sudanese-backed United Front for Democracy and Change (FUCD) at the gates of the capital, N'Djamena, it retreated to find sanctuary

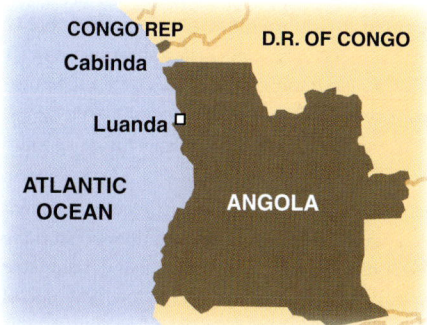

Darfur refugees   *UNDPI*

in Darfur to regroup and rearm. Rebels in the northeastern part of Central African Republic are allegedly supported by Chadian troops opposed to the current Chadian administration, as well as Sudanese mercenaries.

Even though government forces of **Côte d'Ivoire** and rebel fighters in its northern region agreed in June to start disarmament and dismantling of pro-government militias, the situation remains unsettled. In September President Laurent Gbagbo declared the UN roadmap to peace a failure and a farce and declined to attend fresh talks at the United Nations in New York. Côte d'Ivoire has been split in two since a failed coup in September 2002. Four years of negotiations failed to reunite the country. Rebel and pro-government fighters have not been disarmed and a key program to issue identity cards to some three million disenfranchised Ivorians hangs in the balance.

In August the government of **Angola** signed a peace treaty with António Bento Bembe, a former leader of the Front for the Liberation of the Enclave of **Cabinda** and the Armed Forces of Cabinda (FLEC-FAC). Bembe claims to represent the Cabinda Forum for Dialogue (FDC)—the representative body of the enclave's secessionist movements that include civil society groups, Catholic Church representatives and FLEC. But despite cliams by the Angolan Minister for Territorial Administration, Virgilio Fontes Pereira, who signed on behalf of the Luanda government, that this sealed the end of hostilities certain rebel factions insist that Bemba had no authority to sign on their behalf. Sandwiched between the Republic of the Congo (Congo-Brazzaville) and the Democratic Republic of the Congo (Congo-Kinshasa) rebels in this oil-rich enclave with its 300,000 inhabitants have been fighting for Cabinda's secession ever since Angola gained independence from Portugal in 1975. The Angolan government found it necessary to send 40,000 soldiers to Cabinda to prevent separatist guerrillas from taking power. Even though the deal signed by Bemba is said to be opposed by the majority of FDC and FLEC rank and file, Luanda hopes that it marks the end of a drawn-out struggle in this highly profitable province.

Another territorial dispute involving the resource-rich **Bakassi Peninsula** and the 1,600 kilometer border area between Cameroon and Nigeria extending from Lake Chad to the Gulf of Guinea has been settled by peaceful means. In 1994, Cameroon asked the International Court of Justice (ICJ) to settle the dispute. After eight years of adjudication, the Court delivered its judgment on the merits of the case in October 2002, deciding, in part, that sovereignty over the Bakassi Peninsula and in the disputed area in the Lake Chad region lies with Cameroon. On 13 June 2006, President Olusegun Obasanjo of Nigeria and President Paul Biya of Cameroon resolved the dispute in talks led by UN Secretary General Kofi Annan in New York City. Obasanjo agreed to withdraw Nigerian troops within 60 days and to

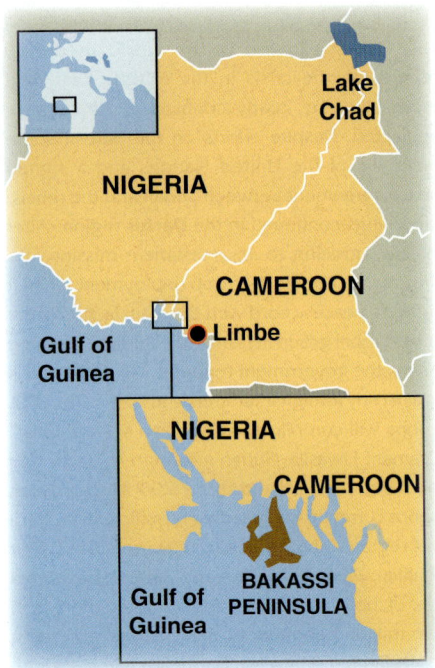

Chinese President Hu Jintao welcomes Kenyan President Kibaki to the conference in Beijing

leave the territory completely under Cameroon's control within the next two years. In August Nigeria began withdrawing its military, comprising some 3000 troops, marking the formal hand over of the northern part of the peninsula to Cameroon. The rest will remain under Nigerian civil authority for two more years.

New scramble

In 2006 **China** served notice that it was a serious contender in Africa and ready to compete with Europe and the US. Unencumbered by a colonial past or any inhibitions about the nature of the states with which they partner China swept into Sudan and Zimbabwe and several other countries with generous offers of development assistance and purchase orders for oil and other raw materials. China's total trade with the continent has grown from $10 billion in 1995 to $42 billion in 2005, helping Asia to become Africa's third largest trading partner (27%) after the European Union (32%) and the United States (29%). In November 2006 fifty African heads of state attended the Forum on China-Africa Co-operation (FOCAC) hosted in Beijing by Chinese President Hu Jintao. The purpose was to further boost trade relations between Africa and China. On the table were 2,500 new deals to add to the multitude of projects already in the pipeline. Speaking on this

Tsotsi stars Presley Chweneyagae and Terry Pheto celebrate the 2006 Oscar for best foreign film with former President Nelson Mandela at his Johannesburg home

best foreign movie at the 78th Annual Academy. This is a riveting portrayal by Director Gavin Hood of six days in the life of a ruthless young gang leader in the sprawling Johannesburg township of Soweto. Starring two young actors, Presley Chweneyagae and Terry Pheto, *Tsotsi* served to further underline the quality of productions coming out of Africa. (The word *tsotsi* means a black urban criminal, a street thug or gang member in the vernacular of black townships in South Africa). *Tsotsi's* top honor follows in the wake of another strong contender a year earlier—*Hotel Rwanda*, a joint South African-Italian production. In 2004, South African actress Charlize Theron won the Oscar for best actress in *Monster*.

occasion South Africa's Pres. Thabo Mbeki praised China's "commitment to Africa" as "demonstrated through tangible and concrete results" relating to "human source development, debt relief and investment." China, with nearly $1 trillion in reserves and a voracious appetite for natural resources, has evidently decided to spend a chunk of its billions of dollars in savings to secure access to the oil, gas, copper, coal and other mineral riches in African countries.

JOLLYWOOD

There have been numerous reports of a budding new film industry in Nigeria cashing in on an insatiable demand for local movies. Soon it earned the name Nollywood—as in Bollywood for films made in Bombay. Nollywood is bringing in big bucks, claiming to be third behind Hollywood and Bollywood in revenues. It claims to represent a unique turning point by finally telling African stories told by Africans themselves. Works by Tunde Kelani—the Francis Ford Coppola of Nollywood—and others, are increasingly touring international film festivals. The Montreal, Berlin, and Cannes festivals had Nollywood events and screenings this year. But top honors went to Jollywood (Johannesburg's film industry) instead when its production, *Tsotsi*, became the first ever African film to win an Oscar for

CELEBRITY POWER

In July 2005, musicians Bono and Geldof have shown how star power can help spur heads of state into action when they lobbied President George Bush and his colleagues at the G8 conference at Gleneagles to cancel Africa's debt. In 2006 actress Mia Farrow and actor George Clooney dedicated time and effort to highlight the atrocities in Darfur and trying to prod the world into taking action. In Washington Oscar winner Clooney joined two senators, Republican Sam Brownback of Kansas and Democrat Barack Obama, to appeal for greater action to stop the genocide in Sudan's Darfur region. Other activists included Holocaust survivor Elie Wiesel, *Hotel Rwanda* proprietor Paul Rusesabagina, entertainment mogul Russell Simmons, Olympics gold medalist speed skater

Actor George Clooney at the United Nations demanding action on Darfur

UNDPI

Immaculée Ilibagiza

Joey Cheek, and former NBA star Manute Bol, who was born in Sudan. "What we cannot do is turn our heads and look away and hope that this will somehow disappear," Clooney warned. He pointed to the massacres in Rwanda, Cambodia and the Balkans in recent years.

RWANDA RELIVED

In 2006 a book written by Immaculée Ilibagiza hit the best-seller list in the United States. *In Left to Tell* she shares the miraculous story of how she survived as a 22-year old during the Rwanda genocide in 1994 she and seven other women huddled silently together in the cramped bathroom of a local pastor's house for 91 days. In her captivating and inspiring book, Immaculée, a Tutsi, relates how the power of prayer and faith enabled her to forgive the Hutus who massacred most of her family. *Publisher's Weekly* described her book as "a precious addition to the literature

Coca-Cola Chief Executive Neville Isdell, left, celebrates with FIFA President Sepp Blatter, right, and World Cup trophy after signing a sponsorship agreement in Cape Town, South Africa.

that tries to make sense of humankind's seemingly bottomless depravity and counterbalancing hope in an all-powerful, loving God." Jeannette Kagame, First Lady of the Republic Rwanda, noted that she was "humbled by the extraordinary spirituality that shines throughout Immaculée Ilibagiza's story of terror, endurance, healing, and forgiveness," Ms Kagame urged "everyone [to] read this story—survivors as well as perpetrators" in the "hope that all can experience Immaculée's profound spiritual transformation and be inspired to work for a united and lasting nation."

2010 WORLD CUP

In 2006, Africa was selected to host World Cup Soccer for the first time in 2010. The venue will be South Africa where major projects are

Projected soccer stadium at Greenpoint, Cape Town

planned to transport and accommodate the hundreds of thousands expected to attend. Five new World Cup stadiums and the upgrading of existing ones are expected to cost close to R10 billion—about $1.5 billion. Additional outlays will be necessary for a rapid transit system around the Johannesburg complex and the upgrading of roads. In the meantime South Africa has engaged the services of South American supercoach Carlos Alberto Parreira to beef up its own team before the big event. Recent performances of Bafana Bafana—as the South African team is called—were disappointing. Coca-Cola which has had a long association with Africa in educational projects, community development, HIV/AIDS programs and sport has signed up again with FIFA as a major stadium advertiser for 2010. As arguably the single most recognizable brand name in Africa the company hardly needs to promote itself locally but it undoubtedly has its eyes on more than a billion soccer fans who will, for the first time, get their favorite event beamed from Africa.

African milestones[1]

BC

5,000,000	*Australapithecus africanus*—fossils found in eastern and southern Africa.
2,200,000	*Homo habilis* (emergent man and first toolmaker)—fossils found in East Africa.
1,600,000	*Homo erectus* (middle-period man)—expansion into Eurasia.
500,000	*Homo sapiens.*
100,000	Middle Stone Age (Neolithic era).
20,000	Late stone age and early agriculture.
4000	Stone and copper age. Settlement of the Nile Valley. Settlements in the Sahara.
3200	King Menes unites the kingdoms of the Delta and the Nile. Egypt invades Nubia.
2700	King Zoser, Imhotep and Step Pyramid at Sakara.
2600	Khufu (Cheops) and Great Pyramid at Giza.
2500	Egypt sends expeditions to land of Punt and into Sahara area.
2280	Old Kingdom ends. First Intermediate Period in Egypt.
2100	Middle Kingdom begins with Mentuhotep. Egypt expands southward into Nubia.
2000	Amenemhet I, founder of new Dynasty.
1780	Second Intermediate Period; Egypt has fifty rulers in slightly over a century.
1660	Asiatic invaders (Hyksos) conquer Lower and Middle Egypt.
1557	Ahmose I drives Hyksos out of Egypt and establishes XVIII Dynasty.
1511	Thutmose I reconquers Nubia. Egypt expands into Asia and Kush area.
1400	Amenophis III. Queen Tiy.
1360	Amarna Period in Egypt. Akhnaten, the heretic Pharaoh.
1340	Pharaoh Tutankhamen.
1300	Time of Moses. First horses in Africa.
1230	Exodus of Israelites from Egypt.
1000	Makeda of Axum (Queen of Sheba) visits Solomon.
751	Kush King Kashta conquers Upper Egypt. Piankhi conquers all of Egypt.
690	Pharaoh Taharqa.
650	Assyrians under Assurbanipal conquer Egypt. Capital of Kush moved to Meroë.
600	Greeks establish colony at Cyrene.
525	Persians, under Cambyses, conquer Egypt.
500	Axum begins to develop.
450	Herodotus visits Egypt and Kush. Earliest construction at Zimbabwe.
332	Alexander the Great conquers Egypt.
304	Ptolemy I establishes dynasty.
200	Height of Nok culture.
150	Cities of Zanj established.
100	Bantu introduce iron working into the area south of the Sudan.
146	Carthage conquered and razed by Rome.
31	Augustus Caesar conquers Egypt.

AD

1	Beginning of east African city states.
30	Lion Temple built in Kush.
100	Axum becomes capital of the major state of Eritrea.
200	Nok culture fades away; Ghana begins.
200	Roman Emperor Septimus Severus fortifies frontier in North Africa.
238	Revolt in Africa against Roman rule.
300-400	Bantu cereal cultivators begin to herd cattle.
333	King Ezana of Axum becomes a Christian.
350	Kingdom of Axum supercedes Kush.
354	St. Augustine born at Carthage.
429	Vandals invade North Africa.
534	Justinian's Byzantine expedition conquers North Africa.
571	Yoruba migration from Upper Egypt.

1. Some dates and events in the early years remain in dispute among scholars.

550	Nubians in Sudan become Christian.
600	Muslims start conquering North Africa.
640	Caliph Omar, successor to Mohammed as Islamic leader, conquers Egypt.
652	Christian Nubians and Arabs agree on Aswan as border on Nile.
700	So tribes settle Kanem (Lake Chad). Bantu peoples spread out.
788	Idris, Arab chief, ruler in Morocco.
790	First dynasty established in Benin. Ghana at its peak.
800s	Christian empire in Ethiopia continues after decline of Aksum.
800s	Arabs and Persians establish trading posts in East Africa.
950	Kilwa established. University of Cairo founded.
1000	Igbo-Ukwu culture thrives in Nigeria.
1100	Bantu-speaking peoples move into Southern Africa.
1054	Almoravid Moslems invade Ghana.
1061	Beni Halil Moslems invade North Africa.
1173	Muslim warrior Saladin becomes sultan of Egypt.
1200	King Lalibela of Ethiopia establishes churches cut from rock.
1220	City state of Kilwa in Tanzania prospers.
1235	Warrior Sun Diata founds Mali empire.
1250	Kanem kingdom in Lake Chad disintegrates; Mamelukes seize power in Egypt.
1300	Ife culture of West Africa produces famous brass objects.
1324	Emperor Mansa Musa of Mali travels on pilgrimage from Timbuktu to Mecca.
1348	Egypt devastated by Black Death plague.
1380	Kongo kingdom at river mouth.
1400	Mombasa becomes Swahili city state.
1445	Portuguese start slave trade on West Coast of Africa.
1450	Great Zimbabwe at its height; Oyo Empire is created.
1460	Songhai Empire established.
1479	Portuguese build Elmina Castle on West African coast.
1482	Portuguese explore Congo river estuary.
1488	Portuguese explorer Bartholomeu Dias sails around the southern tip of Africa.
1491	Ruler of Kongo kingdom baptized as Christian by Portuguese.
1497	Portuguese explorer Vasco da Gama sails around Africa to India.
1500	Songhai empire expands in West Africa. Hausa states grow through trade.
1502	First African slaves sent to the New World.
1505	Portuguese capture Sofala and settle in Mozambique on east coast.
1517	Ottomans defeat Mamelukes in Egypt.
1528	Portuguese capture Mombasa.
1529	Muslims defeat Ethiopian Christians.
1530	Beginning of trans-Atlantic slave trade by Portuguese.
1543	Portuguese help Christian Ethiopians to defeat Muslims.
1562	Sir John Hawkins starts English slave trade from West Africa to Americas.
1575	Portuguese start colonizing Angola.
1598	First Dutch trade posts on Guinea coast.
1619	First slaves arrive in colony of Virginia.
1640	Beginning of large-scale selling of slaves to Caribbean and Americas.
1650	Ethiopian ruler expels Portuguese missionaries.
1652	Dutch establish a settlement at the Cape of Good Hope.
1670	French settle in Senegal.
1680	Ashanti Kingdom is formed.
1686	Louis XIV of France officially annexes Madagascar.
1689	French Huguenots arrive at the Cape.
1701	Osei Tutu creates free Ashanti nation in West Africa.
1705	Bey Husain ibn Ali founds Tunis dynasty.
1727	Death of Mulai Ismail followed by 30 years of anarchy in Morocco.
1740	The Lunda create new kingdom.
1746	Mazrui dynasty in Mombasa becomes independent from Oman.
1750	Buganda becomes the leading Lake Kingdom.
1755	First outbreak of smallpox at Cape by sailors, decimating Khoisan tribesmen.
1768	Scottish explorer James Bruce travels to Ethiopia.

1770	Tukulor kingdom emerges in former Songhai region of West Africa.
1777	Sidi Mohammed, ruler of Morocco, abolishes slavery of Christians.
1779	First war between the Bantu and Boers in Cape border areas
1784	Yoruba civil wars.
1785	Omani rulers reassert rule over Zanzibar.
1787	British settlers, including slaves, establish colony at Sierra Leone.
1789	Spain opens slave trade to Cuba.
1794	French National Convention emancipates French colonial slaves.
1795	British occupy Dutch Cape Colony to preempt French until 1803.
1796	Scottish explorer Mungo Park reaches Niger.
1798	Napoleon takes Egypt.
1801	French troops withdraw after defeat by British at Alexandria.
1805	Mohammad Ali conquers Egypt.
1806	British wrest Cape Colony from Dutch.
1807	British parliament bans slave trade.
1807	Britain converts Sierra Leone into a crown colony.
1810	British negotiate elimination of slave trade in South Atlantic with Portugal.
1814	Cape colony finally ceded to Britain by Netherlands.
1815	British pressure Netherlands, Spain, Portugal and France to end slavery.
1816	Gambia occupied by British after French withdrawal.
1816-28	Shaka Zulu dominates eastern part of South Africa.
1817	American Colonization Society encourages return of slaves to Africa.
1820	Mohammad Ali captures Sudan in search of slaves and gold.
1820	British settlers land at Cape Colony.
1821	American Colonization Society establishes colony at Cape Mesurado—Liberia.
1822	Ex-slaves from America settle in Liberia.
1828	Egyptians found city of Khartoum in Sudan.
1830	French capture Algiers.
1832-47	Abd-al-Kadir directs resistance against French in Algeria.
1834-36	Great Trek begins in Cape as Boers migrate north away from British authority.
1838	Boers defeat Zulu leader Dingaan at Blood River in Natal.
1845	British annex Natal.
1847	Liberia declares itself an independent state.
1852	Independent Boer Transvaal Republic established.
1854	Independent Boer Republic of Orange Free State founded.
1852	Tukolor leader al-Hajj Umar launches Jihad along Niger and Senegal rivers.
1853-56	Livingstone discovers Victoria Falls.
1858-59	Burton and Speke discover Lake Tanganyika and Speke, Lake Victoria.
1858-61	Livingstone discovers Lake Nyasa.
1860	Speke identifies Lake Victoria as source of the White Nile.
1861	US recognizes the new state of Liberia founded by freed American slaves.
1862	US President Lincoln grants freedom to slaves after rebellion in the South.
1863	Al Hajj Umar captures Timbuktu.
1863	French establish protectorate over Porto Novo on coast of Dahomey.
1865-68	Wars between Orange Free State Republic and Basuto people.
1866	French establish posts on Guinea coast.
1867	Diamonds discovered at Hopetown in Cape colony of South Africa.
1868	French sign protectorate treaties for Ivory Coast.
1868	Britain annexes Basutoland at request of Basuto King Mosweshwe.
1870	Diamond rush starts at Kimberley South Africa.
1871	Stanley meets Livingstone at Ujiji and resupplies him.
1873	Livingstone dies at Chitambo's village, Ilala.
1879	Stanley begins operations in Congo on behalf of King Leopold.
1879	British defeated by Zulu at Ulundi in Natal.
1874	Britain occupies former Dutch colony of Gold Coast.
1880	Brazza signs treaty with King Makoko and establishes Brazzaville.
1881	Transvaal Republic defeats British in First Boer War.
1881-7	Stanley signs treaties with Congo chiefs and founds Leopoldville.
1881	French army invades Tunisia from Algeria and imposes protectorate.
1883	French establish protectorate over Dahomey.

1883	Paul Kruger elected president of Transvaal.
1884	German protectorate declared over Angra Pequena.
1884	Nachtigal takes over Togo on behalf of Bismarck.
1884	Carl Peters signs treaties with mainland chiefs in Zanzibar region.
1884	Britain signs protectorate treaties with Niger and Oil River chiefs.
1884	With assistance from Bismarck, Leopold gets recognition for Congo claims.
1885	Mahdi captures Khartoum and massacres Gordon and the British garrison.
1885	Bismarck declares German protectorate over part of East Africa.
1885	European powers divide Africa at the Berlin Conference.
1886	Gold discovered in the Transvaal.
1887	Britain signs conditional agreement with Turkey to withdraw from Egypt.
1887	British incorporate Zululand into Natal.
1888	Cecil Rhodes gets mining rights from Lobenguela north of Transvaal.
1888	Britain gives royal charter to Rhodes' British South Africa (BSA) in new region.
1889	France declares protectorate over Ivory Coast.
1889	Emperor Yohannes of Ethiopia killed by Menelik—supported by Italy.
1890	British-French agreement recognizes their respective interests in West Africa.
1890	Peters extends German influence in Uganda by treaty with Kabaka Mwanga.
1891	British recognize Italian protectorate over Ethiopia.
1891	Britain recognizes Rhodes BSA Company's control over Rhodesia.
1892	French defeat King Behanzin of Dahomey and extend protectorate.
1891-2	Harry Johnston secures British influence over Nyasaland.
1893	Guinea and Ivory Coast colonies established by France.
1894	French set up protectorate in Dahomey (Benin).
1895	Britain secures control over Uganda.
1895	Italians start invasion of Ethiopia from Eritrea.
1896-8	Kitchener and Anglo-Egyptian army recapture Sudan.
1896	British defeat Ashanti in West Africa.
1896	Menelik defeats Italians but allows them to keep Eritrea.
1897	Britain signs treaty with Ethiopia and concedes part of Somaliland.
1897	Slavery is banned in Zanzibar.
1899	British and Egyptian governments create condominium rule over Sudan.
1899	Anglo-Boer War ends in British supremacy in South Africa
1901-1902	British add Ashanti to Gold Coast.
1902	In treaty with Anglo-Egyptian authority Menelik abandons claims to Upper Nile.
1903-1905	Exposure of atrocities in the Belgian and French Congo by Morel and Brazza.
1904	France creates the Federation of French West Africa.
1910	Union of South Africa granted independence by Britain.
1916	South African leader Jan Smuts leads fight against Germans in East Africa.
1922	Egypt gains sovereignty from British under King Fuad.
1930	Ras Tafari crowned emperor of Ethiopia as Haile Selassie.
1931	First trans-African railroad from Angola to Mozambique completed.
1935-36	Italians under Mussolini invade and annex Ethiopia.
1936	Native Representation Act denies black South Africans chance of equality.
1939	South Africa under Smuts declares war against Germany.
1941	German army under Rommel campaigns in North Africa.
1941	Ethiopia liberated from Italy by South African and British troops.
1942	British Commonwealth troops defeat German army at El Alamein in Egypt.
1942	Germany and Italy driven from North Africa.
1948	National Party comes to power in South Africa and adopts apartheid.
1951	Libya gains independence under King Idris.
1952-59	Mau-Mau guerillas led by Kenyatta fight British in Kenya.
1952	King Farouk forced to abdicate by Colonel Naguib.
1954-62	War for independence in Algeria.
1954	Colonel Abdul Nasser succeeds Naguib and exiles King Farouk.
1956	Sudan receives independence from Egypt.
1956	Suez crisis erupts and British and French lose control of the canal.
1956	Morocco gains freedom from France and additional territory from Spain.
1956	Tunisia gains freedom from France.
1957	Ghana (former Gold Coast) granted independence by Britain.

1958	Guinea gains freedom from France.
1960	Civil war starts in South Sudan.
1960	Independence for Benin (former Dahomey), Burkina Faso (former Upper Volta).
1960	Central African Republic, Chad, Congo (Brazzaville), Côte d'Ivoire independent.
1960	Gabon, Madagascar, Mali, Mauritania, Niger, Senegal, and Togo independent.
1960	French Cameroon and part of British Cameroon form new nation of Cameroon.
1960	Belgian Congo becomes independent and civil war starts.
1960	Colonel Mobutu establishes rule over Zaire (former Belgian Congo).
1960	Nigeria gains independence from Britain.
1960	Former British and Italian Somaliland form independent Somalia.
1961	Sharpeville uprising in South Africa results in death of 69 black protesters.
1961	Sierra Leone independent from Britain.
1961	Tanzania (Tanganyika) gains independence from Britain.
1962	Algeria gains independence from France.
1962	Rwanda and Burundi (former Ruanda-Urundi) gain freedom from Belgium.
1962	Uganda becomes independent from Britain.
1963	Kenya gains independence from Britain.
1963	Organization of African Unity formed.
1964	Malawi (former Nyasaland) gains independence from Britain.
1964	United Republic of Tanzania and Zanzibar established.
1964	Zambia (Northern Rhodesia) gains independence from Britain.
1965	The Gambia granted independence by Britain.
1965	White-ruled Rhodesia declares unilateral independence from Britain.
1964	Nelson Mandela and other ANC leaders jailed at Robben Island, South Africa.
1966	Botswana (Bechuanaland) and Lesotho (Basutoland) independent from Britain.
1967-70	Biafran War in Nigeria.
1968	Equatorial Guinea granted independence by Spain.
1968	Mauritius gains freedom from Britain.
1968	Kingdom of Swaziland gains independence from Britain.
1968	Cape Town surgeon Christiaan Barnard performs world's first heart transplant.
1969	Muammar Qaddafi seizes power after coup in Libya.
1973	Guinea-Bissau granted freedom by Portugal.
1975	Angola, Mozambique, and Cape Verde independent from Portugal.
1975	São Tomé & Príncipe granted independence by Portugal.
1975	Comoros receives independence from France.
1976	Seychelles gains independence from Britain.
1976	Soweto uprising results in calls for further sanctions against South Africa.
1977	Former French Somaliland becomes independent Djibouti.
1980	Zimbabwe (Rhodesia) gains independence from Britain under Robert Mugabe.
1986	US Congress passes law requiring sanctions against South Africa.
1990	Nelson Mandela freed from jail.
1990	Namibia (former South West Africa) gains freedom from South Africa.
1991	Eritrea wins freedom from Ethiopia.
1994	ANC wins first multiracial election in South Africa.
1994	Nelson Mandela sworn in as president of South Africa.
1997	Democratic Republic of Congo replaces Zaire.
1997	Ghanaian diplomat Kofi Annan elected UN Secretary General.
2001	Organization of Africa Union disbanded in favor of new African Union.
2001	New Partnership for Africa's Development (NEPAD) launched.
2001	Kofi Annan reelected UN Secretary General.
2002	African Union inaugurated in Durban, South Africa.
2004	First meeting of the Pan African Parliament in South Africa.
2004	South African Charlize Theron becomes first African to win Oscar for best actress
2004	Ms. Wangari Maathai of Kenya awarded Nobel Peace Prize.
2005	G8 nations write off $40 billion in debt owed by 18 African nations
2005	Egypt's Mohamed ElBaradei receives Nobel Peace Prize
2005	Liberian Pres. Ellen Johnson-Sirleaf becomes Africa's first female head of state
2006	South African film Tsotsi is first African film to win Oscar for best foreign film

MAPPING AFRICA

Geographers in Africa maps
With Savage-Pictures fill their Gaps:
And o'er unhabitable Downs
Place Elephants for want of Towns.
Dean Swift

This old limerick summed up the efforts of early European cartographers to portray Africa. They depended on hearsay and fancy and the drawings of Claudius Ptolomy, who lived in Alexandria around 150 A.D. Referred to as the Aristotle of map-making, Ptolomy's influence extended well into the 16th Century.

The first printed map of Africa dates back to Milan in 1508 but it was Sebastian Munster who gained fame for his rendition of the Dark continent in 1540. Inspired by Ptolomy and the tales of Arab and Portuguese explorers, he drew an imaginary mountain range roping north Africa off from the rest and the Niger flowing in the wrong direction. And, of course, the elephant in the southern interior where both fact and fancy fell short.

When Munster drew his map, discoveries by Portuguese seafarers Dias (1486) and Da Gama (1497) had already dispelled the original notion of an Africa and Asia joined at the hip and enclosing the Indian ocean between them. Regular sea traffic around Africa brought new knowledge about the coastline but large portions of the interior remained a mystery for years to come.

Lack of information about the African interior obliged cartographers to innovate. Maps of Africa were often as ornate as they were inaccurate. French cartographer Bourguignon D'Anville was the exception. In the 18th Century he introduced—with limited success—the novel notion that unless there were reliable evidence, imaginary mountains and

First printed Africa map, Milan, Italy - 1508

hypothetical lakes should be left out. His stark rendition of Africa stuck out like a sore thumb in a profession where aesthetics ruled over fact.

Today the works of Ortelius, Bleau, Moll, Merian, Ogilby, Jaillot, Hondius, Visscher, Speed, Sandrart, and Seutter grace walls not to enlighten but to entertain—as works of art instead of representations of reality.

At the close of the 19th Century D'Anville finally prevailed. After extensive journeys by the likes of Livingstone and Stanley the Encyclopaedia Brittanica proudly introduced what it confidently proclaimed to be a true and final map of Africa. Little did it know how many borders and names would change in the next century.

Sebastian Munster - 1540

Africa's Nobel Laureates

Africa had a total of twelve Nobel laureates since 1901 when this prestigeous prize was first awarded in the name of Sweden's dynamite magnate, Alfred Nobel.

In 2005, Egyptian **Dr. Mohamed ElBaradei,** head of the International Atomic Energy Agency (IAEA), and the agency jointly received the Nobel peace prize for their efforts to prevent nuclear energy from being used for military purposes. A year earlier Kenya's **Wangari Maathai** was awarded the peace prize for her contribution to sustainable development, democracy and peace. In 2001, Secretary General **Kofi Annan** received the Nobel Peace Prize for his own and the UN's endeavors to promote world peace. In 1993, **Nelson Mandela** and **FW de Klerk** were joint recipients for their role in terminating apartheid and laying the foundation for a new non-racial South Africa. In 1984, Bishop **Desmond Tutu** was honored in his capacity as General Secretary of the South African Council of Churches for his role in the struggle against apartheid. In 1978, Egyptian President **Anwar Sadat** was recognized, together with Israeli Prime Minister Menachem Begin, for his contribution to peace in the Middle East. The first African recipient of the Nobel Peace Prize in 1960 was **Albert John Luthuli**, who led the non-violent campaign for civil rights in South Africa.

Four Africans won the Nobel prize for literature. Nigerian playwright, **Wole Soyinka**, was honored in 1986 for his poetical plays written in English. In 1988 Egyptian novelist **Naguib Mahfouz** won the prize for his short stories and novels and in 1991 South Africa's **Nadine Gordimer** received recognition for her novels and short stories. In 2003, another South African, **John Maxwell (JM) Coetzee** was the recipient of the literary prize.

Desmond Tutu

Albert Luthuli

Nelson Mandela

Anwar Sadat

FW de Klerk

Kofi Annan

Nadine Gordimer

Wole Soyinka

Courtesy: Nobel Museum

Mohamed ElBaradei

Wangari Maathai

Naquib Mahfouz

JM Coetzee

Behind the masks

"If sculpture is the projection of one's thoughts into three dimensions, then the African continent has produced many of the greatest sculptors of all time, even though no single name has ever been passed down," writes art critic Claude Rilly "The African mask is not an objet d'art in itself, but neither is it a simple cultural or theatrical accessory. At the same time, the sculptor is not an 'artist,' but his function goes much further than that of a simple craftsman."

From the beginning of civilization, masks have been part of tribal life—not only in Africa but in most other parts of the world. In Africa masks can instruct, discipline, warn, honor, protect and entertain. They depict deities, mythological beings, good and evil spirits, the spirits of ancestors and the dead, animal spirits, and a variety of other beings believed to have supernatural powers.

Rites

They are used in fertility and initiation rites, religious and funeral celebrations. And even when utilized as props in dramas and comedies they remain linked to ethnic myths. Sometimes a mask bestows on the wearer a certain social status or membership to closed societies or cults.

Most masks made for royalty were destroyed after the death of the emperor. Idia's mask is an exception. Carved from ivory, this 16th Century masterpiece represents Idia—mother of Oba Esigie, then king of Benin. The mask was worn by him at ceremonies commemorating his mother and eventually made its way to New York's Metropolitan Museum of Art via the Nelson

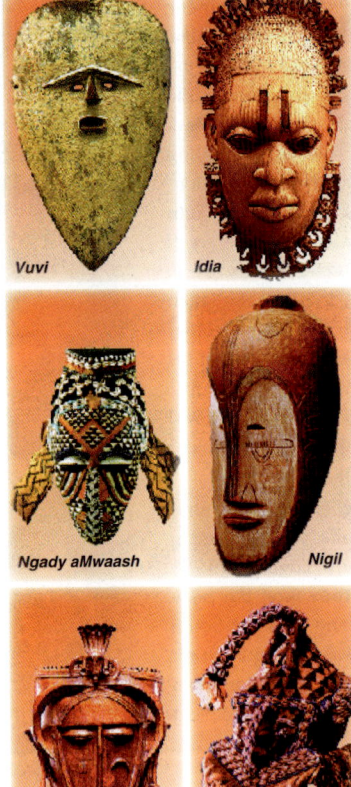

Vuvi

Idia

Ngady aMwaash

Nigil

Kpeliyehe

Mwaash aMbooy

D. Rockefeller private art collection. This ivory pendant mask is one of a pair of nearly identical works; its counterpart is on exhibit at the British Museum in London.

Royalty

African royalty has also left behind masks sculpted from gold, brass and copper, but most were carved from wood and sometimes decorated with shells, beads, animal skins and raffia. They vary in size, from the 6 inch (15 cm) lukwakongo masks of the Lega people to the 3 ft. (almost 1 meter) high kakuunga half-helmet mask of the Suku tribe. The Vuvi people in the Gabon region are masters of abstraction and simplicity as exemplified in a painted wooden mask from the collection of the Detroit Institute of Arts.

Much more elaborate is a Ngady aMwaash mask from the Peabody Museum at Harvard University. Originating with the Kuba tribe in Central Africa this mask—consisting of wood, raffia cloth, beads and cowrie shells— symbolizes links between the royal family and mythic characters.

The Nigil hardwood dance mask from the Fang tribe, on display in Geneva's Musée Barbier-Mueller, is intended to intimidate and enforce obedience. The same collection shows a Kpeliyehe mask made from brass, used by the Senufo people in West Africa for rituals inspired by jungle spirits. Also in the museum is a specimen of the elaborate Mwaash aMbooy masks made for royalty from vegetable fibers adorned with beads and cowries as a symbol of wisdom and authority.

CHAPTER 2

THE AFRICAN CONTINENT

AFRICA IS THE SECOND LARGEST CONTINENT. THE FARTHEST POINT NORTH—RAS BEN SEKKA, NEAR BIZERTE IN TUNISIA, AND THE SOUTHERNMOST POINT, CAPE AGULHAS IN SOUTH AFRICA—ARE ALMOST EQUIDISTANT FROM THE EQUATOR AT AROUND 2,500 MILES (4,000 KM). THE FARTHEST EASTERN EXTREMITY, RAS HAFUN PENINSULA IN SOMALIA, AND THE WESTERNMOST POINT, CAPE VERDE IN SENEGAL—ARE ABOUT 4,700 MILES (7,560 KM) APART. THE SAHARA DESERT IS THE WORLD'S LARGEST AND MT. KILIMANJARO IN TANZANIA IS AFRICA'S HIGHEST PEAK. THE NILE RIVER FLOWING NORTHWARDS TO THE MEDITERRANEAN SEA, IS THE WORLD'S LONGEST.

TOPOGRAPHY

Africa is basically one enormous plateau modified in part by erosion and earth movements. It resembles, in the words of explorer David Livingstone, "a wide awake hat with the crown a little depressed." Another explorer, John Speke, described it as "a dish turned upside down." Africa consists of three major regions: the Northern Plateau, the Central and Southern Plateau, and the Eastern Highlands. Elevation increases across the continent from the northwest to southeast reaching an average of 1,900 ft (600 m). The main feature of the Northern Plateau is the Sahara desert, occupying more than one-quarter of the continent.

At the fringes of the Northern Plateau are the Atlas Mountains, which extend from Morocco into Tunisia. The higher Central and Southern Plateaus contain several major depressions, notably the Congo River Basin and the Kalahari Desert, as well as the peaks of the Drakensberg mountains.

The Eastern Highlands, extending from the Red Sea to the Zambezi River, averages more than 5,000 ft (2,000 m) and reaches 15,157 ft (4,620 m) at Ras Dashen in northern Ethiopia. South of the Ethiopian Plateau are a number of towering volcanic peaks, including Kilimanjaro, Mount Kenya, and Mount Elgon. A distinctive feature of the Eastern Highlands is the Great Rift Valley—a vast geologic fault system.

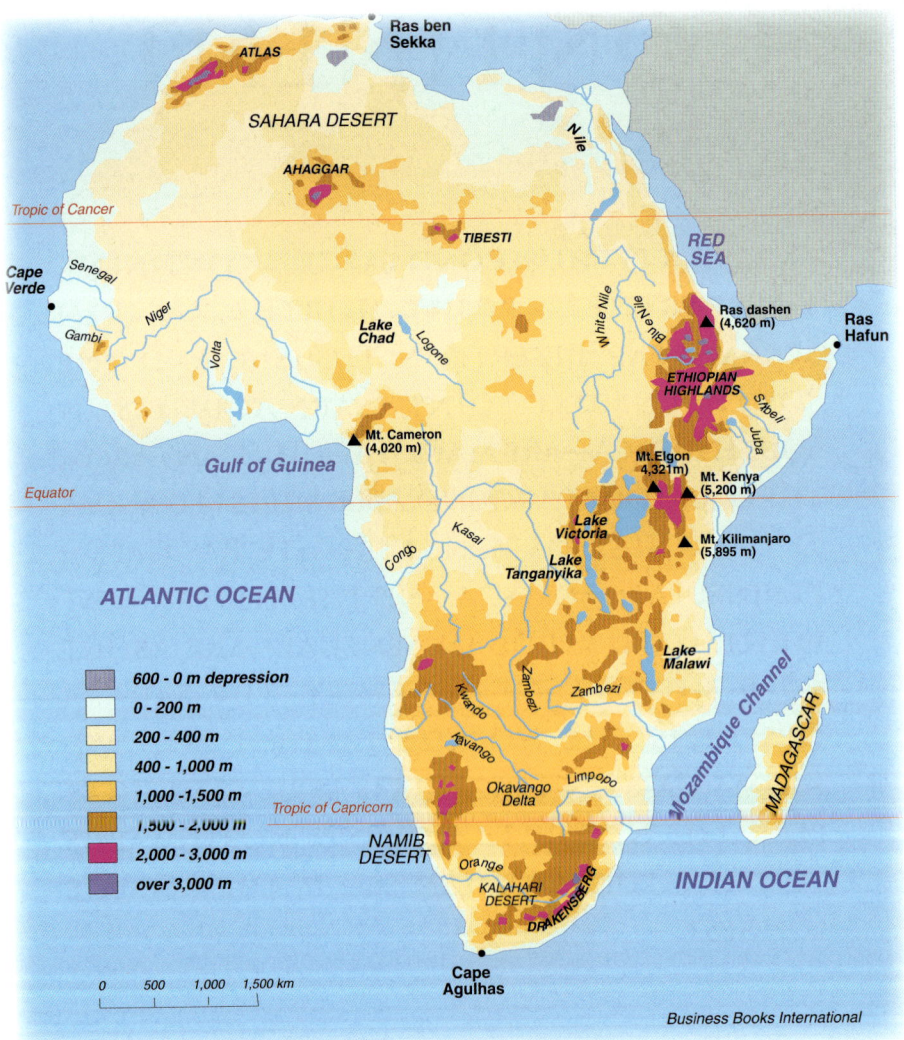

Business Books International

Africa's Natural Vegetation

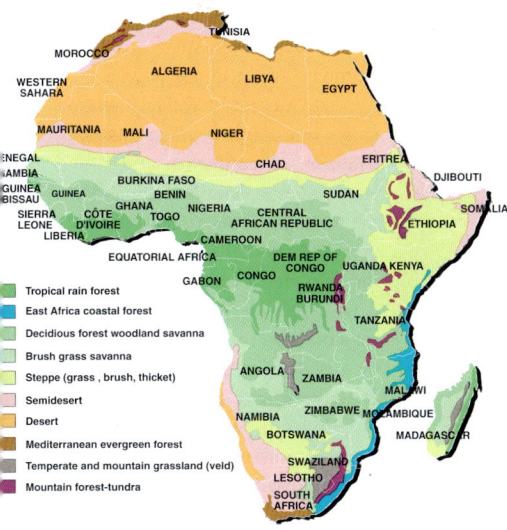

- Tropical rain forest
- East Africa coastal forest
- Decidious forest woodland savanna
- Brush grass savanna
- Steppe (grass , brush, thicket)
- Semidesert
- Desert
- Mediterranean evergreen forest
- Temperate and mountain grassland (veld)
- Mountain forest-tundra

CLIMATE

With three-quarters of its landmass situated between the Tropic of Cancer and Capricorn Africa is mostly tropical—hot summers and brief, mild winters. In some regions altitude has a moderating influence, and mountains near the equator such as Mt. Kilimanjaro and Mt. Kenya are covered with snow.

Beyond the equatorial zone rainfall is unreliable and large parts of the continent are prone to

Major European languages

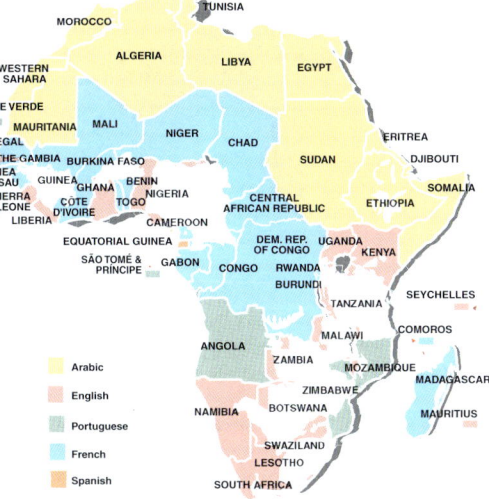

- Arabic
- English
- Portuguese
- French
- Spanish

droughts. Some 40 per cent of Africa is classified as desert or semidesert. Even in high rainfall areas, downpours are strictly seasonal and unpredictable in both volume and timing, making farming a gamble. Both the Namib and Sahara Desert get less than 2 inches (50 mm) of rain per year.

VEGETATION

With its average annual rainfall of more than 50 inches (1,300 mm), Africa's tropical rain forest is densely covered tropical hardwood trees, oil palms and a thick undergrowth of shrubs, ferns, and mosses. In the mountain forest zones of Cameroon, Angola, eastern Africa, and parts of Ethiopia, where the rainfall average is only slightly less, a ground covering of shrubs gives way to oil palms, hardwood trees, and primitive conifers. The savanna woodland zone, with an annual rainfall of 35 to 55 inches (900 to 1,400 mm), consists of deciduous and leguminous fire-resistant trees and undergrowth of grass and shrubs. The savanna grassland zone, with an annual rainfall of 20 to 35 inches (500 to 900 mm), is covered with low grass and shrubs and widely spaced, small deciduous trees. The so-called thornbush zone with its annual rainfall of 12 to 20 inches (300 to 500 mm), has a sparser grass covering and scattered succulent and semi-succulent trees. The sub-desert scrub zone, with an annual rainfall of 5 to 12 inches (130 to 300 mm) is covered with grasses and scattered low shrubs. In the desert zones, with an annual rainfall of less than 5 inches (130 mm), vegetation varies from sparse to none.

PEOPLES & LANGUAGES

In 2000, some 13% of the world's population lived in 53 African countries. Africa tops the world not only with the number of countries within one continent but also the diversity of its 800 million peoples and the number of languages spoken. Rural cultures where foods, religions, life-styles, dress and daily life have remained unchanged for hundreds of years, continue to thrive despite the rapid intrusion of bustling modern cities. More than 1,000 languages and dialects are spoken. Arabic in northern Africa, Mandinke, Igbo, Yoruba and Hausa in western Africa, Swahili in eastern Africa, Amharic and Oromo in the Horn of Africa, and Zulu, Sotho and Xhosa in southern Africa, are spoken by millions. Most of Africa's languages are, however, spoken by less than a million people and some, such as Kw'adza in Tanzania used by only a few older people, are close to extinction. Many

Cape Point at the southern tip of the Continent   Courtesy: SA Tourism

at the Cape and 19th Century missionaries. Islam spread from the Arabian Peninsula through Northern Africa in the course of the 17th Century. Today, Christianity dominates in 19 countries, Islam in 13 countries, and the Hindu faith in one (Mauritius). In the rest, ethnic beliefs still largely prevail and other faiths remain in the minority. Even though there is no single unifying and distinct religious code set out in a Koran or a Bible, indigenous religions continue to exert a strong influence on family life, rulers and the justice system in parts of the continent. What ethnologists refer to as Naturism, Animism, and Fetishism are all aspects of a deep-seated belief in a Creator that defies definition. Indigenous African religions—practiced under the guidance of priests, elders, rainmakers, diviners and prophets—are concerned with the origin of tribes and their cultures, the nature of society, the relationship of men and women and of the living and dead. Social values are frequently expounded in myths, legends, folktales, and riddles are passed along by word-of-mouth. *Voodoo (juju)* and other forms of witchcraft have mistakenly come to represent in the minds of foreigners the essence of African religion and tribal bel;iefs.

countries have selected the languages of former colonial powers for official and business purposes. Arabic is the official language in 12 countries, English in 20, and French in 21. Cameroon and Mauritius have both English and French as official languages. Portuguese is official in five countries and Spanish and French enjoy equal status in Equatorial Guinea. Spanish is spoken in Morocco and some Italian in Libya, Eritrea and Somalia.

RELIGIONS

Christianity at its very beginning spread from the north to Nubia (northern Sudan) and Ethiopia. Much later it was introduced elsewhere by Portuguese and other seafarers, early Dutch settlers

Christianity in Africa

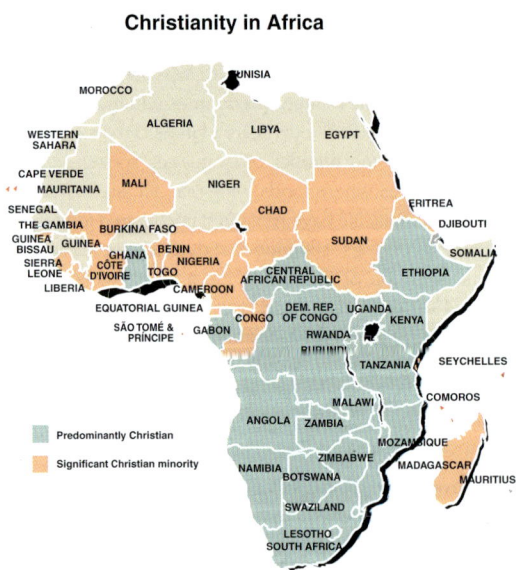

Islam in Africa

EARLY HISTORY

Several scientific discoveries of the remains of what seems to be early man in South Africa's Sterkfontein area and Tanzania's Olduvai Gorge lend strong support to Africa's claim of being the cradle of mankind. Less contentious is Egypt's claim to be among the world's first civilizations. A number of city states in the lower Nile Valley were united some 5,000 years ago under Menes, the first pharaoh. To the south in the Nubian desert (today's northern Sudan) another kingdom developed some 3,000 years ago that equalled Egypt in both splendor and achievement. The Semitic Phoenicians became the first colonizers of Africa when they set out from today's Lebanon to establish the city state of Carthage along the Mediterranean in what eventually became Tunis. Centuries of struggle in North Africa involving Romans and Germanic Vandals, and Christians and Muslims, left the rest of the continent largely free from outside influences. It was only about 1,000 AD that black Africans from the Sahel region first entered the North African theater—even though the kingdoms of Ghana, Mali, and Kanem (on the shores of Lake Chad) had existed for centuries. Inhabitants of the tropical forest regions originated in the north and were exclusively Negroid.

Ancient Africa

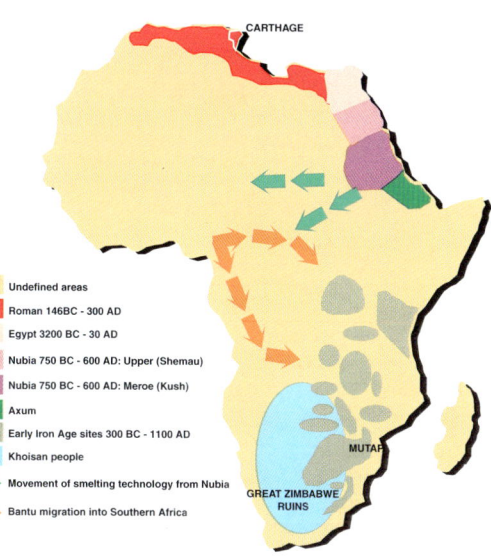

Undefined areas
Roman 146BC - 300 AD
Egypt 3200 BC - 30 AD
Nubia 750 BC - 600 AD: Upper (Shemau)
Nubia 750 BC - 600 AD: Meroe (Kush)
Axum
Early Iron Age sites 300 BC - 1100 AD
Khoisan people
Movement of smelting technology from Nubia
Bantu migration into Southern Africa

More than 2,000 years ago some of them migrated from West Africa to settle around the great lakes and on the savannah plains in East Africa and the Congo Basin. Bantu-speaking, they were crop cultivators and livestock breeders. To the north of Lake Victoria (in today's Uganda) the Nilotes (or Nilotic people), migrating from the north, ruled for centuries over various Bantu-speaking groups. Some Bantu-speakers moved south and reached South Africa about 1,500 years ago.

FIRST EUROPEANS

Toward the end of the 15th Century Portugal had established trade relations with the kingdoms of Benin and Kongo and built a fort at Elmina (Ghana). Barter items included gold, palm oil, cocoa, ivory and human cargo—consisting of slaves supplied by African kingdoms to a ready market in the Americas and elsewhere. In their search for a sea route to the Far East, Portuguese explorers rounded the Cape and extended trade to the east coast where the Arabs were already active. The Dutch, English, French and Spanish soon followed and for the next four centuries established spheres of influence along the coast of Africa.

SLAVERY

For most of the 18th Century the relationship between Europe and Africa was dominated by the slave trade. Before the middle of the 19th Century,

35

the slave trade had been declared illegal in the northern hemisphere by all the former European and North American slave-trading nations. That did not completely deter profit seekers from moving human cargo in bondage wherever the opportunity presented itself, and at towards the end of the 19th Century explorer David Livingstone still encountered a flourishing slave trade on his exploration routes.

FIRST SETTLEMENT

In 1652 the Dutch established a small settlement at the southern tip of the African continent. Originally intended as a supply station for its ships enroute to the Far East, the Cape settlement soon developed into a full-fledged colony. After the British took over, the Dutch descendants (Boers)

Libyan desert

trekked north to establish independent republics in the 1850s. The Cape was, however, the exception. Until the latter part of the 19th Century European powers had no desire for colonial possessions in Africa. Instead, they were content with mere trading stations. The British had enclaves along the West African coastline to protect the palm oil trade. They also maintained a presence in Freetown, Sierra Leone, established in 1787 as a haven for freed slaves. The French had a modest toehold in Libreville (Gabon) and freed American slaves settled in Liberia in 1822. The Portuguese had occupied the coast of Mozambique and the Arabs continued to pursue the slave trade in the East African interior.

COLONIALISM

Encouraged by explorers such as Livingstone, Burton, De Brazza, Nachtigal and Stanley, and spurred on by the growing need for raw materials and new markets, the Europeans started their scramble for Africa in the 1870s. It was Livingstone's vision of bringing Christianity, Civilization and Commerce to Africa that prompted Belgium's King Leopold to establish a personal colony in the Congo basin. Soon the European superpowers were tripping over each other in their quest for colonies all over Africa. The Berlin Conference of 1884-1885, convened by the German government to determine the fate of Leopold's Congo

Africa in 1876

Madeira (Port)
Canaries (Sp)
MOROCCO
ALGIERS
TUNIS
TRIPOLI
EGYPT
SENEGAL
GAMBIA
PORT. GUINEA
SIERRA LEONE
TUKOLOR EMPIRE
SAMORI
GOLD COAST
ASHANTI
DAHOMEY
BORNU
LAGOS
Fernando Po (Sp.)
TURKISH SUZERAINITY
ABYSSINIAN EMPIRE (ETHIOPIA)
Grand Bassam (Fr.)
Assinia (Fr.)
Cotonou (Fr.)
Porto Novo (Fr.)
Sao Tome (Port.)
TEKE
GABON
RWANDA
KARAGWE
BURUNDI
BUGANDA KINGDOM
SULTINATE OF ZANZIBAR
KATANGA
LOZI
ANGOLA
MATABELELAND
HERERO
BECHUANA LAND
TRANSVAAL
SWAZI LAND
ORANGE FREE STATE
BASUTOLAND
CAPE COLONY
NATAL
MOZAMBIQUE
MADAGASCAR

British
French
Portuguese
Turkish
Spanish

Africa in 1914

SP. MOROCCO
MOROCCO
RIO DE ORO
ALGERIA
LIBYA
EGYPT
FRENCH WEST AFRICA
ANGLO EGYPTIAN SUDAN
ERITREA
PORT. GUINEA
SIERRA LEONE
GOLD COAST
TOGOLAND
NIGERIA
GERMAN KAMERUN
BR. SOMALILAND
ETHIOPIA
LIBERIA
SP. GUINEA
ATLANTIC OCEAN
CABINDA (Portugal)
BELGIAN CONGO
BR. EAST AFRICA
GERMAN EAST AFRICA
IT. SOMA
ZANZIB
ANGOLA
N. RHODESIA
NYASALAND
SOUTH WEST AFRICA (GER.)
S. RHODESIA
BECHUANA LAND
SWAZI LAND
BASUTOLAND
SOUTH AFRICA
MOCAMBIQUE
MADAGASCAR

British
French
German
Portuguese
Italian
Belgian
Spanish
Independent

African Independence

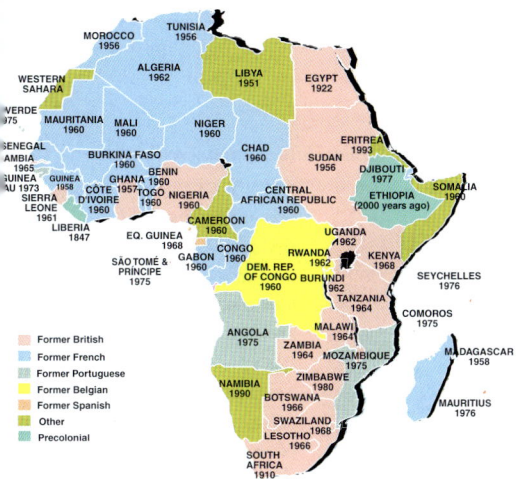

- Former British
- Former French
- Former Portuguese
- Former Belgian
- Former Spanish
- Other
- Precolonial

MOROCCO 1956
TUNISIA 1956
WESTERN SAHARA
ALGERIA 1962
LIBYA 1951
EGYPT 1922
MAURITANIA 1975
VERDE 975
MALI 1960
NIGER 1960
CHAD 1960
SUDAN 1956
ERITREA 1993
DJIBOUTI 1977
AMBIA
ENEGAL
BURKINA FASO 1960
GUINEA 1965
GUINEA 1958
GHANA 1960
BENIN 1960
NIGERIA 1960
CENTRAL AFRICAN REPUBLIC 1960
SOMALIA 1960
ETHIOPIA (2000 years ago)
IU 1973
SIERRA LEONE 1961
CÔTE D'IVOIRE 1960
TOGO 1960
CAMEROON 1960
LIBERIA 1847
EQ. GUINEA 1968
CONGO 1960
UGANDA 1962
RWANDA 1962
KENYA 1968
SÃO TOMÉ & PRÍNCIPE 1975
GABON 1960
DEM. REP. OF CONGO 1960
BURUNDI 1962
SEYCHELLES 1976
TANZANIA 1964
COMOROS 1975
ANGOLA 1975
MALAWI 1964
ZAMBIA 1964
MOZAMBIQUE 1975
MADAGASCAR 1958
NAMIBIA 1990
ZIMBABWE 1980
BOTSWANA 1966
MAURITIUS 1976
SWAZILAND 1968
LESOTHO 1966
SOUTH AFRICA 1910

...1951, Libya was granted independence by France and Britain which were in ...nt control after Italy's defeat during World War II; in 1960, when the French ...rmer German) Cameroun received its independence, part of British Cameroon ...ned in while the rest merged with Nigeria; in 1960, the former Italian (then un- ...French control) and British Somalia joined to become independent Somalia; ...orporated into Ethiopia after World War II, the former Italian colony of Eritrea ...ined its freedom in 1991; a mandate under South African control since the ...d of World War I, the former German colony of South West Africa gained its ...ependence as Namibia in 1990; administered by Morocco since 1976, West- ...Sahara is still an area under dispute, awaiting a final UN referendum.

cousin King Wilhelm could have the mountain. "Willie likes big things," she explained.

DECOLONIZATION

After the First World War Germany's possessions were confiscated and passed along to the victors. In the wake of a Second World War (fought with the help of thousands of African soldiers in colonial armies) came a revulsion against colonial rule that led to armed uprisings in many of the colonies. This "wind of change" swept across Africa, forcing first Belgium and Britain, then France, and eventually Portugal to grant freedom to all their former colonies. In some cases the departure of the former colonial rulers had some dignity and style while in others it was a frantic scramble to escape the consequences of mismanagement. The initial euphoria of the 1960s soon made way for pessimism and despair as military rulers and despots took the place of former colonial rulers. In many instances, the root of the problem was the artificially drawn colonial borders grouping together diverse peoples. By using Africa as a surrogate battleground the new superpowers, the United States and the Soviet Union added fuel to the fire. Oppressive dictatorships were tolerated and supported from both sides in a struggle for ideological supremacy in Africa. For many years, South Africa, despite its apartheid policies, received the support of the US and its allies because of its strategic importance at the tip of the continent and supplies of strategic minerals.

REFORM & HOPE

Coinciding with the collapse of the Soviet bloc and the end of the Cold War, a wave of democratic reform swept over Africa in the early 1990s. A new breed of leaders came to the fore intent on arresting the decline in living standards by introducing true democratic rule and far-reaching economic reforms. These leaders are no longer driven by ideological conflict at the behest of outside powers but by the imperatives set by internal economic and social conditions. Despite ongoing unrest and frequent warfare between ethnic groups boxed into entities created in 19th Century Europe, there has been enough growth and development in recent years to raise hopes of a resurgent Africa in the new millennium. World organizations and governments such as the US, Britain, Germany, Japan, France, Canada, Norway, Denmark and Sweden have placed Africa on their priority list. Recently, China has joined their ranks.

and to set the rules of the game, further turned up the heat. The Germans established enclaves in Togo, Cameroon, German West Africa (Namibia) and German East Africa (Tanzania) while the French expanded their territorial holdings inland from Senegal and Gabon across West Africa and parts of Equatorial Africa. Britain spread its rule over Nigeria, Ghana and Sierra Leone and retained The Gambia. Its major focus was, however, on Egypt and South Africa. At the turn of the century, Cecil John Rhodes' dream of a British Africa from the Cape to Cairo was well underway with Rhodesia, Nyasaland (Malawi), Kenya, and Uganda flying the Union Jack. Portugal acquired two major overseas possessions, Angola and Portuguese East Africa (Mozambique), which it ran as provinces. The scramble for Africa—completed in under 30 years—repainted the continent in bright colonial colors without any consideration for the peoples or their homelands. Italy and Spain had their own designs in North Africa. In one celebrated instance Queen Victoria decided to indent the straight border drawn between British East Africa and German East Africa (today's Kenya and Tanzania) to make a detour around Mt. Kilimanjaro so her German

37

DR. LIVINGSTONE, I PRESUME

Ask anyone to name an explorer and the name David Livingstone jumps to the fore. Even that other famous explorer, Henry Stanley, was in such awe when he caught up with the famous Scottish missionary at Ujiji in darkest Africa that he lost his eloquence and muttered: "Dr. Livingstone, I presume?"

But few know that it was Verney Lovett Cameron who first crossed the continent from east to west. This accomplished British officer was doomed to obscurity much in the same way as Norwegian Roald Amundsen who beat Captain Robert Scott to the South Pole.

FAME

Before Livingstone there were Scottish, English, French and German explorers such as Brue, Bruce, Park, Clapperton, Caillie, Krapf and Rebmann, and after him came the Grants and Brazzas. Few of them were humanitarians such as David Livingstone. Most were in it for fame and other more selfish reasons. There was Baker the hunter, Burton the intellectual and writer, and Henry Stanley, writer-adventurer and colonial agent.

Even though the search for the source of the Nile and the course of the Niger were major themes for early exploration, Africa is hardly a continent of waterways. With the exception of these two major rivers and a few other partly navigable ones such as the Senegal, Gambia, and Zambezi, most consist of forbidding swamps or seasonal swirling waters.

Few explorers could claim that they "discovered" new territory. Friendly local folks often served as guides and facilitators while hostile tribesmen at times added to the dangers already posed by wildlife and debilitating tropical diseases.

RIPPING

But by "ripping Africa open," as Englishman John Speke dramatically described the process, these explorers sparked an interest in Europe that turned into a scramble for land and the stripping of Africa's newly-discovered wealth. Some explorers actually became agents of imperialism. Stanley was employed by Belgian King Leopold as his agent in the Congo while De Brazza helped found the French Congo, and Karl Peters helped launch the German Protectorate of East Africa.

Livingstone painting at the Royal Geographic Society in London

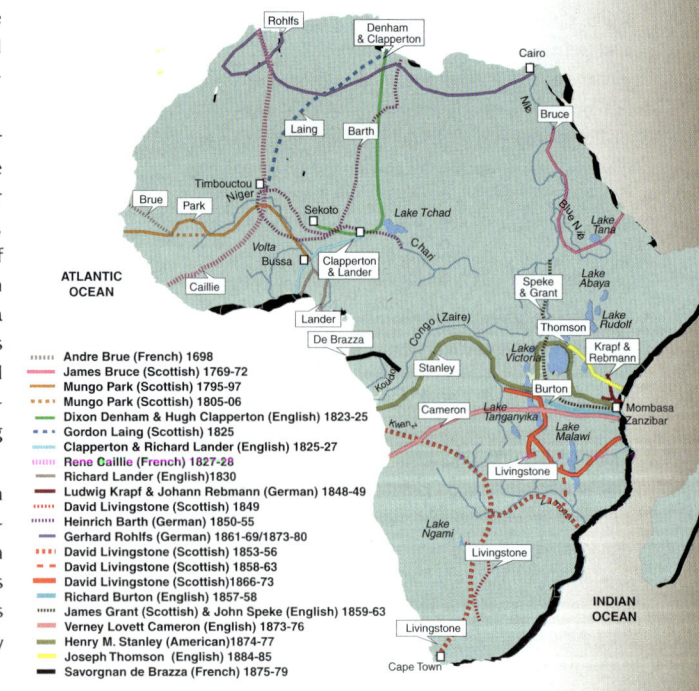

Andre Brue (French) 1698
James Bruce (Scottish) 1769-72
Mungo Park (Scottish) 1795-97
Mungo Park (Scottish) 1805-06
Dixon Denham & Hugh Clapperton (English) 1823-25
Gordon Laing (Scottish) 1825
Clapperton & Richard Lander (English) 1825-27
Rene Caillie (French) 1827-28
Richard Lander (English)1830
David Livingstone (Scottish) 1849
Ludwig Krapf & Johann Rebmann (German) 1848-49
Heinrich Barth (German) 1850-55
Gerhard Rohlfs (German) 1861-69/1873-80
David Livingstone (Scottish) 1853-56
David Livingstone (Scottish) 1858-63
David Livingstone (Scottish)1866-73
Richard Burton (English) 1857-58
James Grant (Scottish) & John Speke (English) 1859-63
Verney Lovett Cameron (English) 1873-76
Henry M. Stanley (American)1874-77
Joseph Thomson (English) 1884-85
Savorgnan de Brazza (French) 1875-79

THE AFRICAN DIASPORA

In 1977 more than 80 million Americans tuned in to an eight-part ABC-TV miniseries on slavery. Roots, based on a book by African American author Alex Haley traced his family history back to his enslaved ancestors in Africa. This stark depiction of the suffering inflicted on these unfortunate souls came as a shock to many.

Haley was not the first to take up this theme. As early as 1852 New Englander Harriet Beecher Stowe wrote Uncle Tom's Cabin. This sentimental work about an escaped slave was based on her superficial, brief encounter with life on a Kentucky plantation. It was seen in by fellow Southerners as an attack on their constitutional rights and hailed in the north as a timely exposure of a cancer in the

Slave House at Goreé Island

body of the United States. During the Civil War, President Abraham Lincoln described Mrs. Stowe as "the little woman who made this Great War."

Exactly how many men, women and children were sent in slavery from Africa across the Atlantic to the Caribbean islands and North and South America will never be known. Estimates vary, but there seems general agreement that there might have been as many as ten million who were shipped from the western shores of Africa and reached the markets while another 5 million perished during the arduous journey in cramped and unhygienic quarters.

Even though the abolition of slavery by the British—largely as a result of the efforts of William Wilberforce and his friend William Pitt—might have reduced the numbers, it did not stop the trade altogether. It simply made the journey more perilous as smugglers hid their human cargo in the even more unaccommodating holds of small, new craft, fast enough to outrun the British naval patrol ships along the African coast. When in danger of capture, these smugglers would readily jettison their contraband human cargo to prevent their expensive craft from being confiscated. Slaves were cheaper to replace than these new craft. Records show slaves selling at about two for the price of three lengths of woolen cloth or at an exchange of 3 muskets for one young robust male slave.

Most of the slaves who were sold into the United States came directly from the West African region stretching from the Senegal River through the Congo region. About a tenth arrived via the West Indies, after a "seasoning" period. The first "shipments" arrived in the American Colonies during the early 1600s. The transfer station at Goreé Island, off the coast of Senegal, today stands as a grim reminder.

The bulk of the slaves sold in the United States were settled in the South where they worked on rice, tobacco, sugar cane, and eventually, cotton plantations. The invention of the cotton gin by Eli Whitney of Massachusetts in 1793 caused a rapid expansion in the Southern cotton industry and a rising demand for plantation slaves. Others were craft workers, messengers, and servants.

Slaves at times resorted to mutiny and armed rebellion. In 1839 mutineers aboard the Amistad, off the coast of Cuba, diverted the vessel to New York where they won their freedom. Sixty people died in a revolt led by slave preacher Nat Turner in 1831 in Virginia.

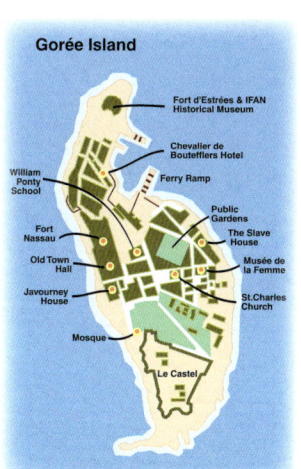

Gorée Island

Fort d'Estrées & IFAN Historical Museum
Chevalier de Boutefliers Hotel
William Ponty School
Ferry Ramp
Fort Nassau
Public Gardens
The Slave House
Old Town Hall
Musée de la Femme
Javourney House
St.Charles Church
Mosque
Le Castel

Today, the African Diaspora in the New World numbers close to 80 million. African Americans represent more than 12% of the total population of the US and 30% of Brazil are descendants of slaves.

In both countries and the Caribbean, the descendants of African slaves have reached prominence in all professions and count among their ranks celebrities in the arts, politics and sports.

RIVERS, LAKES AND MOUNTAINS

Several major lakes are situated in the Great Rift region of East Africa, including Lake Turkana, Lake Albert, Lake Tanganyika, and Lake Malawi. Although it forms part of the so-called Great lakes region Lake Victoria—the largest lake in Africa and the third largest in the world—is not part of this system. (Victoria is sometimes ranked second only after Lake Superior in North America but purists put the Caspian Sea first as it is considered landlocked despite its saltiness). Lake Tanganyika, the least accessible of Africa's great lakes, is Africa's deepest with depths up to almost a mile (1.5 km) and ranks second in the world in depth after Lake Baikal in Russia.

While fish life at Lake Victoria is under threat of pollution from motorized vehicles, fertilizers and pesticides, water hyacinths, and algae blooms, early intervention has provided protection for the natural wealth in Lake Malawi. With between 500 and 1,00 species of the family Cichlidae and a multitude of other species, the lake is the source of over 70 percent of animal protein in Malawi.

Mount Kilimanjaro is Africa's highest mountain and ranks sixteenth in the world. It is, however, the highest among the world's free-standing mountains. Africa's five highest mountains—Kilimanjaro (19,340ft/5,895m); Mount Kenya (17,057ft/5,199m); Mt. Stanley (16,765ft/5,110m); Ras Dashen Terara (15,157ft/4,620m); and Volcan Karisimbi (14,826ft/4,519m)—are all situated in the so-called Great Rift region.

Even though Africa's 4,160 mile long (6,695 km) Nile is the world's longest river, it is hardly a continent known for abundant navigable rivers. Africa offers few reliable waterways to and from its interior. Some rivers are very short and have no outlet to the sea. Many are dependent on seasonal rains that transform dry riverbeds into raging torrents for a short while. Sandbars and muddy deltas and cataracts and falls complicate navigation on the Nile, Congo, Niger, and Zambezi rivers. Some rivers such as the Sudd in the Upper Nile region disappear in swamps while others terminate in enclosed pools. Still these major rivers as well as the Senegal, Gambia and others serve not only as important water sources for communities along their banks but as local traffic routes.

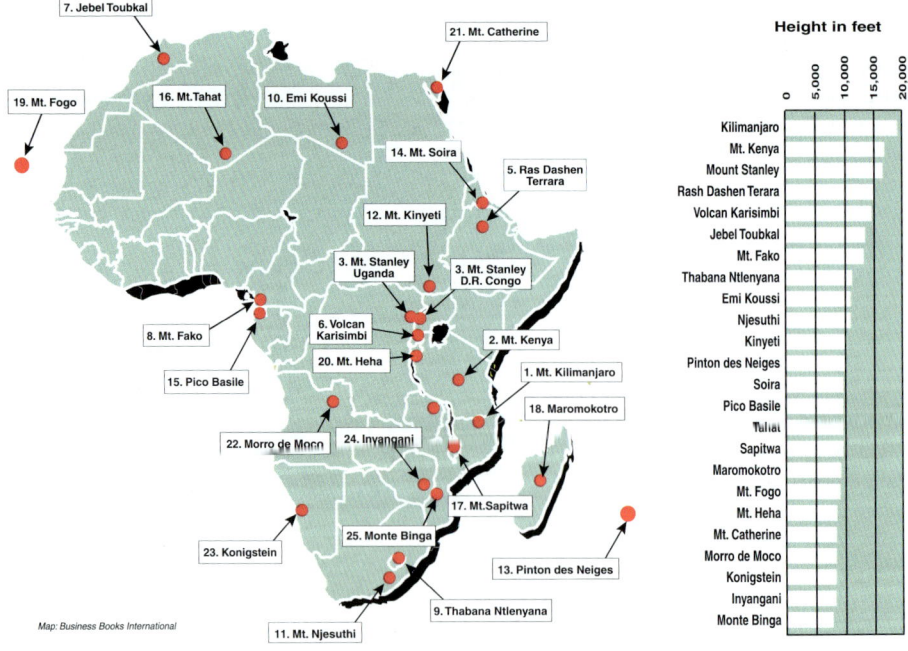

Map: Business Books International

LENGTH

The actual length of the Nile remains in dispute, depending on where the starting point is drawn. It measures 3,470 miles (5,584 km) from its principal source, Lake Victoria, and 4,160 miles (6,695 km) from its remotest headstream in Burundi—a branch of the Kagera River that feeds into the lake. Indeed, it was the search for the origin of the Nile that lured 19th Century explorers such as Baker, Speke, Burton, Livingstone and Stanley, who in turn whetted the appetite of European powers for acquisitions in the region. Much of the tumultuous colonial period involved the independent nations that today feed off the Nile and its tributaries—Tanzania, Burundi, Rwanda, Democratic Republic of Congo, Kenya, Uganda, Ethiopia, Sudan, and Egypt. The terrain along the Nile and its tributaries changes from rain forests and mountains in the south to savanna and swamps halfway, and ultimately to desert along its northern section.

ORIGIN

Starting in the mountains of Burundi, the waters flow via Lake Victoria into the Victoria Nile in Uganda and follow a northwest course for about 300 miles (500 km) through Lake Kyoga and across rapids and the famous Murchison Falls before entering Lake Albert. Continuing northwards as the Albert Nile, it becomes the Bahr al Jabal in Sudan and slows down in the As Sudd swamps, changing its name once again to the White Nile. At Sudan's capital, Khartoum, the White Nile is joined by the Blue Nile that originates 850 miles (1,370 km) southeast at Lake Tana in the Ethiopian highlands. Now known as the Nile, this river is joined further north by the Atbara River before it takes an S-shape turn through the Nubian desert. After passing through five cataracts in Sudan and one in Egypt, near Aswan, the Nile takes a course past Cairo, splitting into the Rosetta and Dalmietta branches before entering the Mediterranean Sea along a 160 mile (250 km) wide delta. Irrigation from the river supports

NILE RIVER

The Nile is the world's longest river and its fertile basin covers one-tenth of the African continent. It is the umbilical cord to world's oldest civilization. Starting at about 5,000 BC, the Egyptian pharaohs spread their influence south along the river as far as northern Sudan, leaving along its banks magnificent pyramids, temples and burial sites.

Greek historian Herodotus saw Egypt as "the gift of the River Nile." The Nile derives its current name from the Greek word Neilos (valley or river) but originally the Egyptians called it Ar or Aur (black) after the seasonal deposits of fertile black sediment along its banks. This is where the art of agriculture was perfected in ancient times with the first use of the hand plow.

41

large-scale cultivation of cotton, wheat, sorghum, citrus fruit, sugar, dates and a variety of legumes along the Nile River Basin. An abundance of Nile perch and tilapia underpins commercial fishing. Tourism, concentrated around the river with its historical sites and interesting wildlife, is a major revenue source. The river is navigable in parts.

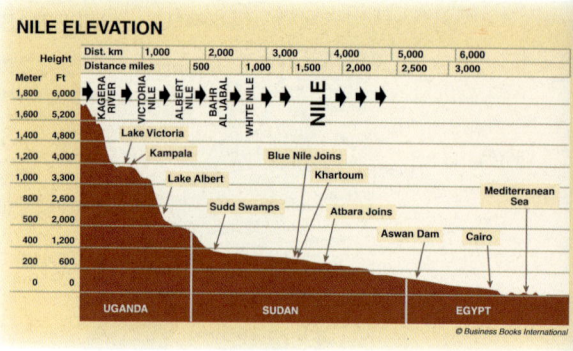

DAMS

During the 20th Century several dams were built to control the flow of the Nile and to generate power. Egypt's Aswan Dam was completed in 1902 and further extended in 1936. In 1919, Sudan built the Sennar Dam to supply water for its cotton industry. The Jabal Aulia Dam on Sudan's White Nile (1937), Owen Falls on Uganda's Victoria Nile (1954), Roseires Dam on the Sudanese Blue Nile (1962) and Egypt's High Aswan Dam (1970) generate hydroelectricity. While most experts agree that the pros of these dam projects far outweigh the cons, critics are not slow to point out the negatives. Controlling and reducing the flow of the river deny farmers deposits of fertile sediment along the river banks that came with summer floods. A decrease in flow towards the ocean has caused a greater salt content in the delta region. Lake Nasser, formed upstream from High Aswan Dam, submerged several once thriving communities and historical sites.

CONGO RIVER

The 2,900 mi (4,667 km) Congo River is Africa's second longest, flowing in a northern and western direction from the interior plains of the Democratic Republic of Congo (DRC) towards Moanda where spills into the Atlantic Ocean with such force that its murky waters can be detected 100 miles offshore. For several hundred miles it serves as the border between the DRC and the Republic of Congo, touching both the capitals of Kinshasa and Brazzaville.

Known during President Mobutu's rule from 1971 as the Zaïre River (a corruption of the local name Mzadi, meaning "great water"), the Congo River (named after the Kongo kingdom located near its mouth) reverted to its original name when the dictator was deposed in 1997. Through a multitude of tributaries the Congo drains a heavy rainfall region of 1,425,000 sq mi (3,690,750 sq km), comprising most of the DRC and parts of Congo (Brazzaville), Cameroon, the Central African Republic, Burundi, Tanzania, Zambia, and Angola.

However, its main source is Lake Mweru, situated on the DRC's border with Zambia,

which serves as a receptacle for the waters of the Chambeshi River. First the Luvua and subsequently the Lualaba River carry water northwards from Lake Mweru to Kisangani, where they join the Congo River. The Lualaba River, regarded as the upper Congo River, forms a deep and narrow gorge (the Gates of Hell) below Kongolo. A short navigable stretch from Kasongo to Kibombo switches to rapids and falls from Kibombo to Kindu, before reaching a shallow but navigable section from Kindu to Ubundu. The final section between Ubundu and Kisangani contains seven cataracts—known as Boyoma Falls.

LIFELINE

The Congo River serves as a lifeline for humans, animals, and plant life along its banks. It has great potential for hydroelectric power but aside from the partly completed Inga Power Project at Livingstone Falls little has been done.

In the 1870s, explorers David Livingstone and Henry M. Stanley travelled throughout the Congo basin. Joseph Conrad sailed along the Congo and immortalized the river in his novel, Heart of Darkness. The river was heavily used by Belgian King Leopold II to move tons of rubber, ivory, gold and other treasures to Europe in an era of unbridled colonial exploitation. Today, utilizing railroads to bypass major falls such as Matadi-Kinshasa, Kisangani-Ubundu and Kindu-Kongolo, the Congo River and its tributaries offer a 9,000 mi (14,480 km) transport system to move central

Africa's copper, palm-oil kernels, cotton, sugar, and coffee to the coast. Below Matadi (83 mi/134 km inland) the Congo accommodates oceangoing vessels. Despite the hazardous whirlpools of the Devil's Cauldron, shifting sandbars, and sharp bends in the river, Matadi offers one of the largest natural harbors in Africa. Dredging is, however, necessary to preserve a 4,000 ft (1,220 m) deep, 500-mi-long (800-km) navigation channel in the Atlantic Ocean at the mouth of the Congo near Moanda, between Banana Point in the DRC and Sharks Point, in Angola.

NIGER RIVER

The 2,504 m. (4,030 km) Niger River is Africa's third longest and impacts four West African nations—Guinea, Mali, Niger and Nigeria. More than twenty tribes rely on it for their livelihood. It is a major source of fish such as Nile perch, carp and tiger fish. Below Lokoja in Nigeria it is navigable year round. Its vast oil-rich delta region on the Nigerian Atlantic coastline has yielded billions of dollars in foreign exchange earnings. Wildlife includes crocodiles, hippos and a wide variety of exotic birds.

The horseshoe-shaped Niger River originates on the Fouta Djallon plateau in Guinea and flows in a northeasterly direction to Timbuktu in Mali before swinging in a southeastern direction through Niger and Nigeria, where it spills into the ocean in the vast Niger Delta region. At one time

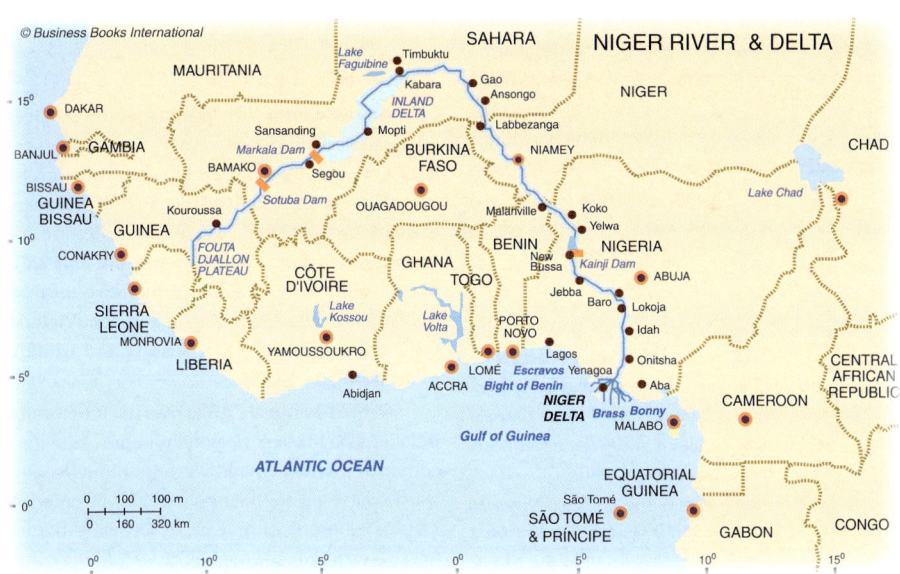

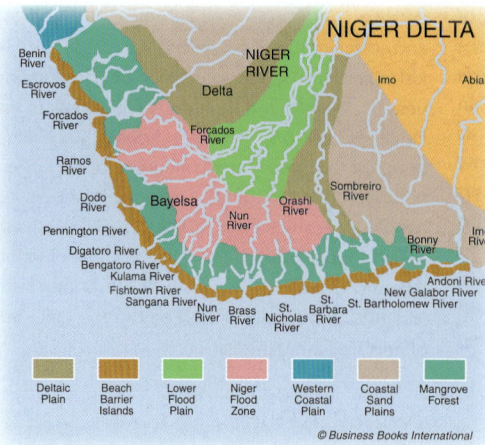

NIGER DELTA

NIGER RIVER

Benin River
Escrovos River
Forcados River
Ramos River
Dodo River
Pennington River
Digatoro River
Bengatoro River
Kulama River
Fishtown River
Sangana River

Delta

Forcados River

Bayelsa

Nun River

Orashi River

Sombreiro River

Imo

Abia

Bonny River

Imo River

Andoni River
New Galabor River
St. Bartholomew River

Nun River   Brass River   St. Nicholas River   St. Barbara River

| Deltaic Plain | Beach Barrier Islands | Lower Flood Plain | Niger Flood Zone | Western Coastal Plain | Coastal Sand Plains | Mangrove Forest |

© Business Books International

the main artery for the ancient Malian empire, the Niger is believed to have been named by the Greeks. The Malinke tribe calls it Joliba, meaning Great River, while others have come up with names such as Mayo Balleo, Isa Eghirren, Kwarra, Kworra and Quorra.

SOURCE

It is not surprising that early inhabitants and explorers searching for the source of the Niger, were baffled. Starting barely 150 miles inland from the Atlantic Ocean, the Niger takes a big loop through the interior before turning south and emptying in the same ocean. The Tembi ravine, 2,800 feet (850 meters) above sea level in the Fouta Djallon region of Guinea, is the origin of the Niger. Spring rains in these tropical highlands feed northeast into Mali where the Sotuba Dam at the capital of Bamako serves as a catchment area. From there the river flows towards the Markala Dam near Sansanding. At the town of Mopti the Niger is joined by a major tributary, the Bani River, before entering a region of lakes, creeks and backwaters, known as the Internal Delta. It sustains a vast crops, mostly rice and sorghum, covering than 100,000 acres (40,470 hectares).

TIMBUKTU

At the historic Timbuktu, nestled on the edge of the Sahara Desert, the Niger reaches its northernmost point, turns due east and continues for 250 miles through rocky ridges and a narrow gorge. At Gao it once again widens into a flood-plain between three to six miles wide.

The River Niger enters the country Niger at Labbezanga, taking a southeasterly course past capital Niamey before pressing on to Jebba where

it is joined by the Kaduna River. It is, however, at Lokoja where the Niger River links with its greatest tributary, the Benue River—more than doubling its water capacity in the process. (The Niger is estimated to drain a total of more than 730,000 sq. miles). Together the Niger and the Benue form a lake-sized slow-moving body of water flowing towards Idah through a restricted valley, flanked by sandstone cliffs that flatten out at Onitsha.

NIGER DELTA

South of Onitsha the river empties through the vast Niger Delta—the largest of its kind in the world—into the Atlantic Ocean at the Gulf of Guinea, splitting into a vein-like network of channels and rivers. The Nun River is considered to be a direct continuation of the Niger. Other major offsprings include the Forcados river, the Brass, the Sombreiro and the Bonny. Many of these channels and rivers are obstructed by sandbars fed continually by silt and sediment carried from the interior.

Once a major supplier of palm oil the 14,000 sq. m. (36,260 sq. km) Niger Delta has since become one of Africa's and the world's most important sources of petroleum and gas. Sadly, this windfall came at a stiff price for the locals. While the major oil companies are actively seeking to minimise the effect of oil drilling and pollution on farms, fisheries and the wetlands, they have little say over the way in which the government spends its billions in earnings.

ZAMBEZI RIVER

At 1,646 mi (2,649 km), the Zambezi River (also spelled Zambesi) is Africa's fourth largest river system. Touching on five countries on its journey from Central Africa to the Indian Ocean, the Zambezi not only serves as a lifeline for communities and abundant wildlife but as a major source of electricity. A lucrative tourism industry is built around the magnificent Victoria Falls and numerous water resorts and wildlife areas along its banks.

Named Zambezi ("great river) by the Batonka tribe it has a modest beginning in the northwest corner of Zambia, gaining strength in its southward course through Angola before re-entering Zambia where it turns east to form the border between Zambia and Namibia. It joins up with

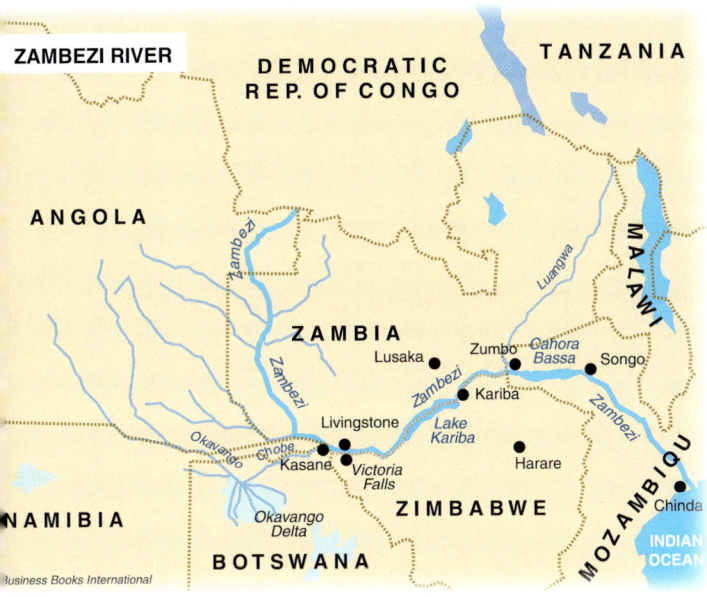

ZAMBEZI RIVER

important navigable stretch along the Zambezi. Completed in 1959 with a surface area of 2,124 sq mi (5,500 sq km), Kariba is one of the largest human-made lakes in the world with an installed generation capacity of 1300 megawatts.

KAFUE

After Zambia gained independence in 1964 and relations soured with the white government of Rhodesia (today's Zimbabwe), Zambia built two dams of its own near Kafue. Today these two, together Kariba, provide 50 per cent of the two nations' total electricity need. In the 1970s when the Portuguese colonial rulers and South Africa jointly constructed the Cahora Bassa Dam it won accolades for bringing the world's fifth largest hydroelectric power installation to a backward corner of Mozambique.

The dam was intended as a source of additional electricity for power-hungry industrial South Africa, and much-needed hard currency for impoverished Mozambique.

However, continuing rebel wars have rendered Cahora Bassa inoperative and it is only after the departure of the Portuguese rulers that the project was restored and fulfilled its initial promise.

CRITICISM

As in the case of Aswan and other major dams along the Nile, both the Kariba and Cahora Bassa dams have attracted criticism from environmentalists for their displacement of small farmers and intrusion on wildlife and nature in general. While conceding their important contribution to the economies of Zambia, Zimbabwe and Mozambique, purists maintain that these projects came at too heavy a price. Kariba alone, they pointed out, displaced a tribe of more than 50,000 along the Zambezi shores. The Lesotho Highlands Project has also been under fire from displaced farmers even though it earns much-needed currency for this impoverished land-locked country. (Also read *Dams in Africa*).

the Chobe River in the Caprivi Swamps, to briefly form a border with Botswana.

For the next 310 mi (500 km) the Zambezi serves as a border between Zambia and Zimbabwe, thundering over the Victoria Falls and through the narrow, steadily deepening Batoka Gorge that flattens out at the broad Gwembe Valley.

KARIBA DAM

From here it flows into the Kariba dam for 175 mi (281 km)—reaching a width of 25 mi (40 km). From Kariba the river travels due north, heading east again at Chirundu where it is flanked by the Lower Zambezi National Park on the Zambian side and Mana Pools National Park on the Zimbabwean side. Strengthened by the Luangwa confluence, the Zambezi flows into Mozambique where it is slowed down once again by the Cahora Bassa dam before emptying into the Indian Ocean at Chinde.

VICTORIA FALLS

Rapids interrupt the river's flow, including the world-renowned Victoria Falls, making it unsuited for continuous navigation. Long before Scottish missionary and explorer, Dr. David Livingstone, "discovered" the falls on November 16, 1855, and named it Victoria in deference to his queen, the Batonga people had dubbed it, perhaps more appropriately, Mosi-Oa-Tunya—"the smoke that thunders". The Kariba Dam offers the single most

HOW AFRICA MEASURES UP

SEVEN BIGGEST ISLANDS

	Sq. miles	Sq. km.
Greenland	839,000	2,175,597
New Guinea	316,515	820,033
Borneo	286,914	743,107
Madagascar	226,657	476,068
Baffin (Canada)	183,810	476,068
Honshu (Japan)	88,925	230,316
Great Britain	88,758	229,883

THE SEVEN LONGEST RIVERS

	Miles	Km
Nile (Africa)	4,180	6,690
Amazon (South America)	3.912	6,296
Mississippi (USA)	3,170	5.970
Yangtze Kiang (China)	3,602	5,797
Ob (Russia)	3,459	5,567
Huang Ho (China)	2.900	4,667
Yenisei (Russia)	2,800	4,506

THE SEVEN SUMMITS[1]

	Feet	Meters
Mt. Everest (Asia)	29,035	8,850
Mt. Aconcagua (Sth.Am.)	22,834	6,960
Mt. McKinley (Nth. Am.)	20,320	6,194
Mt Kilimanjaro (Africa)[2]	19,340	5,895
Mt. Elbrus (Europe)	18,510	5,642
Vinson Massif (Antarctica)	16,066	4,897
Kosciusko (Australia)	7,316	2,230

1. Highest peaks on each of the 7 continents.
2. The world's highest "free standing" mountain.

THE SEVEN BIGGEST LAKES

	Sq. miles	Sq. km
Caspian Sea (Russia etc)[1]	152,239	394,299
Superior (US-Canada)	31,820	82,414
Victoria (Tanz.-Uganda)	26,828	69,485
Huron (US-Canada)	23,010	59,596
Michigan (USA)	22,400	58,016
Aral (Kazakhstan-Uzbeki.)	13,000	33,800
Tanganyika (Tanz.-Congo)	12,700	32,893

1. Considered landlocked lake even though Romans
   called Mare Caspian a sea because of its saltiness.

THE SEVEN CONTINENTS

	Sq. miles	Sq. km
Asia[1]	17,212,041	44,579,000
Africa	11,065,000	30,065,000
North America	9,465,290	24,256,000
South America[2]	6,879,952	17,819,000
Antarctica	5,100,021	13,209,000
Europe[3]	3,837,082	9,938,000
Australia[4]	2,967,966	7,687,000

1. Includes the Middle East.
2. Includes Central America and the Caribbean.
3. Includes the recently-independent states of the former
   Soviet Union.
4. Includes Oceania.

THE SEVEN LARGEST DESERTS[1]

	Sq. miles	Sq. km
Sahara (Africa)[2]	3,500,000	9,065,000
Arabian (M. East)	1,000,000	2,590,000
Gt.Victoria (Australia)	250,000	647,500
Kalahari (Africa)[3]	220,000	569,800
Gt. Sandy (Australia)[4]	150,000	388,500
Gibson (Australia)	120,000	310,800
Simpson (Australia)	56,000	145,040

1. Subtropical deserts are the hottest, consisting of
   parched terrain with rapid evaporation. The Namib in
   Namibia (13,000 sq. miles/33,600 sq. km) is a cool
   coastal desert region).
2. Covers parts of Algeria, Chad, Egypt, Eritrea, Ethiopia,
   Libya, Mali, Mauritania, Morocco & Western Sahara,
   Niger, Somalia and Tunisia.
3. Spans parts of Botswana, Namibia and South
   Africa.
4. Also known as The Outback.

Sources: Columbia Encyclopedia, Time Almanac and Internet.

Chapter 2

The Economy of Africa

Agriculture accounts for one third of the Continent's GDP, two-thirds of its employment and 40% of its export revenues but most foreign economic activity is concentrated in the exploitation of the continent's abundant mineral resources. Multinationals are prominent in petroleum and gas, and minerals extraction ranging from gold to copper, uranium, manganese and phosphate rock to platinum and bauxite. Increasingly, however, foreign investors are becoming engaged in manufacturing for both local and regional as well as international markets where African nations enjoy special duty free status.

Economy

THE AFRICA THAT EMERGED AFTER THE SECOND WORLD WAR AS THE WINDS OF CHANGE SWEPT AWAY COLONIAL RULE WAS LARGELY UNPREPARED FOR NEW ECONOMIC CHALLENGES. BELGIAN, BRITISH, FRENCH, PORTUGUESE, SPANISH, GERMAN AND ITALIAN POSSESSIONS PRIMARILY SERVED THE INTERESTS OF THEIR COLONIAL MASTERS, NOT LOCAL POPULATIONS. EDUCATION, TRAINING AND LOCAL DEVELOPMENT—INADEQUATE AS THEY WERE—WERE THERE TO SATISFY IMPERIALISTIC GREED, NOT LOCAL NEED. EUPHORIA SOON MADE WAY FOR CHAOS AND DESPAIR AS ILL-EQUIPPED INDEPENDENT GOVERNMENTS FAILED TO SUSTAIN MULTI-ETHNIC STATES WITH ARTIFICIAL BORDERS DRAWN IN 19TH CENTURY IMPERIAL EUROPE. NEWLY INDEPENDENT STATES WERE LEFT SHORT OF BOTH ADMINISTRATIVE AND ENTREPRENEURIAL SKILLS.

A World Bank publication—Can Africa Claim the 21st Century?—sponsored by several agencies observed: "Explaining Africa's slow growth in the second half of the 20th Century remains a major challenge to economists and other analysts." There is no simple answer as to why a continent that stood at roughly one-third of Europe's income level at the beginning of the 19th Century fell so far behind and was totally eclipsed by Asia. In the 1960s, Gunnar Myrdal saw an Africa poised for steady growth in contrast to an Asia doomed to stagnation. The opposite happened.

Structural Adjustment

During the 1970s and the 1980s, the IMF and the World Bank extended loans to African countries in terms of structural adjustment programs (SAPs) conditioned on balanced budgets, devaluation of currencies, a cutback in state employment and privatization of state enterprises. While these programs in most cases played a positive role in arresting economic decline and increased economic growth they had negative side effects on the population in some cases. Even though countries with structural adjustment programs showed growth rates double those of nonparticipants, the austere and at times harsh conditions remained contentious.

Debt

Equally heated has been the debate on foreign debt and aid. Little of the borrowed money found its way into real development and productive programs. The bulk was used to cover budget deficits and imports, quite often from the lending countries. An undetermined amount found its way into the private foreign bank accounts. According to a recent estimate by the UN Industrial Development Organization (UNIDO) about $107 billion of Nigeria's money is held in private accounts in Europe and the US while the country's foreign debt stood at $35bn.

Aid

During the Cold War, aid to Africa was quite often based not by development considerations but by ideology. Today aid is by and large driven by a genuine effort to stimulate real growth instead of buying favors from rulers. Despite criticisms, USAID and other programs have had many successes to show in Africa where they funded health, educational, agricultural, infrastructural and manufacturing projects, in many instances in cooperation with NGOs. The consensus is that Africa will need significant aid until at least 2015 to attain preset *Millennium Development Goals* aimed at reducing extreme poverty around the world by half in 2015.

Major Economic Development Areas

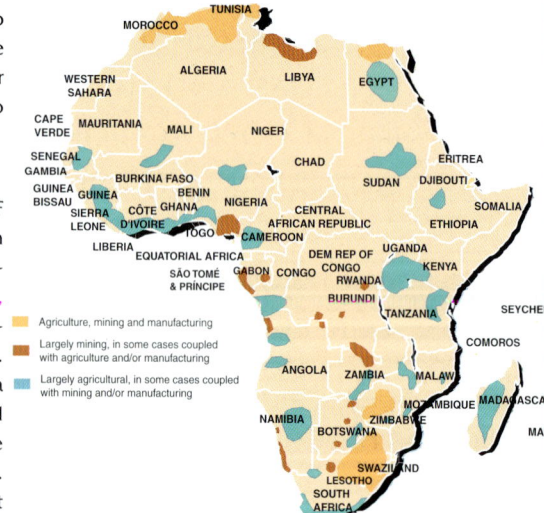

Agriculture, mining and manufacturing

Largely mining, in some cases coupled with agriculture and/or manufacturing

Largely agricultural, in some cases coupled with mining and/or manufacturing

DEBT RELIEF

In July 2005 the Group of Eight Industrialized Nations gathering in Gleneagles, Scotland, agreed to full cancellation of the $40 billion debt of 18 African Heavily Indebted Poor Countries (HIPCs). There was also an agreement to boost aid for developing countries by $50 billion over the next ten years.

NEW LEADERSHIP

More significant than foreign assistance or economic discipline imposed from abroad has been the emergence in Africa in the mid-1990s of a new breed of enlightened leaders imbued with a determination to make the so-called African Renaissance a reality. Often obscured by continuing headlines about crises and conflicts, disease and disaster, are the accomplishments of this cadre of new professionals in building democratic rule, developing sound macro-economic policies and opening their economies to international markets and influences.

GROWTH

Africa recorded a 5 percent growth in GDP, slightly down from the previous year but considerably higher than performances in previous years. The solid growth rate is attributed to the recovery of nations previously plagued by conflict; higher oil revenues; increased agricultural output due to favorable weather conditions; higher commodity prices; and to a lesser extent resumption of industrial growth. Inflation stabilized at an average of 10 percent. The GNI per capita rose from $675 in 2000 to $811 in 2004. According to the African Development Bank (ADB), the continent's aggregate GDP at current prices reached $672.4 billion in 2003—up by almost 21 percent from $555.4 billion in 2002.

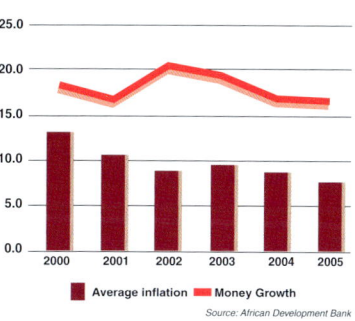

Africa: Real GDP/Real Per Capita GDP Growth (%)

Real GDP Growth ■ Real per Capita GDP Growth

Source: African Development Bank

Africa: Inflation and Growth of money supply (%)

■ Average inflation ■ Money Growth

Source: African Development Bank

POVERTY

Serious challenges remain. While the average per capita GNI stood at $811 in 2005—considerably higher than previous years it simply equals the level of $810 reached in 1981. This national average is, of course, somewhat misleading. African countries range in per capita GNI from barely $100 in Burundi to $8,000 in the Seychelles. More than half of the African population, the ADB reports, still live in countries where the per capita GNI is below than $350 or less than a dollar a day. In its 2005 progress report on poverty reduction under the *Millennium Development Goals*, the United Nations found that while the proportion of people living on less than a dollar a day were dramatically reduced in Asia, it actually rose in Africa from 44.6 to 46.4 percent.

HIV/AIDS

HIV/AIDS still threatens communities on the continent with extinction and impacts negatively on economic stability and growth. At the end of 2005 UNAIDS reported 25.8 million people living with HIV in Sub-Saharan Africa. This constituted two-thirds of the world total. A staggering 2.4 million died of HIV-related illnesses while a further 3.2 were infected during the year. The full impact of this disease on the economies of Africa has yet to be determined but it has already become abundantly clear that unless the spread of this disease can be arrested or contained, hopes of economic resurgence might well become a dream deferred.

RESOURCES

Originally the Europeans were lured to Africa with tales of gold. Today foreign investors are still mostly drawn to the continent by its vast reserves of mineral resources, ranging from gold and diamonds to platinum, chrome, cobalt, copper and a host of other precious, strategic and base metals. While South Africa has long been the focus of major mining houses, the World Bank has identified 25 other African nations with a vast potential for future mineral exploration. Ghana, Angola, Namibia and Congo (Kinshasa) top the list. For more than

49

a century, foreign mining companies have been active in Africa both as independent operators and in partnership. Oil and energy companies are involved in the extraction of oil and natural gas in countries such as Algeria, Nigeria, Gabon, Angola and Mozambique.

AGRICULTURE

Despite the importance of minerals, Africa's people remain largely dependent on farming for jobs and survival. In 2005 agriculture accounted for 14.0 percent of Africa's total output—slightly below its 17.2 percent share during the period from 1998-2000. The share of agriculture in individual economies range from a mere 2.6 percent in Botswana to 58.7 percent in the Democratic Republic of Congo. Eleven countries recorded shares below 10 percent while five countries showed agriculture topping 50 percent of their GDP. Major food crops include cassava, maze, millet, rice and sorghum. Prime exports are cocoa and coffee beans, palm oil, groundnuts, cotton, tea, sisal and tobacco. With food production steadily falling behind population growth during the past 30 years, Africa has become a net importer of food. Even though cattle herds in Ethiopia, Sudan and Nigeria exceed its own, South Africa has traditionally been the largest meat producer. In 2003 Africa recorded a 3.8 percent growth in agricultural production, largely as a result of favorable weather after severe droughts.

Africa: GNI Per Capita US$

2000	2001	2002	2003	2004
675	673	664	708	811

Source: African Development Bank

MANUFACTURING

Apart from South Africa, which ranks among the world's industrialized nations, manufacturing in Africa is underdeveloped but it also contributes significantly to the overall economic activity of countries such as Zimbabwe, Morocco, Algeria and Egypt. Most manufacturing activity in Africa is, however, limited to import-substitution of consumer goods such as clothes, footwear, soap, cigarettes, liquor, soft drinks and basic tools. Manufacturing's share of GDP on the continent stood at slightly more than 15% towards the end in 2003. Oil is a major foreign exchange earner. Industry accounted for 35 percent of Africa's GDP in 2003.

SERVICES

As in most other parts of the world, the service sector—comprising banking, insurance and other financial services, as well as wholesale and retail trade, tourism, transport and communications—is the single largest contributor to the African economy. Foreign financial institutions have been particularly active in recent times.

FOREIGN BANKS

According to the World Bank, Africa has the highest penetration by foreign banks of any region. Despite this extensive foreign involvement and widespread restructuring of state services, governments continue to play an inordinately large role in many countries. Reforms are expected to continue, opening up not only state utilities in telecommunications and power generation but to make it possible for local and foreign entrepreneurs to become partners in air, road and rail transport and shipping.

POPULATION

During the past half a century Africa's total population increased from 280 million to 905 million in 2005, representing an average annual growth rate of almost 3%. At this rate the population of the continent is expected to double itself every 25 years. There are indications, however,

African Incomes

GNP per capita

$3001 - $9000 (6 countries)
Upper middle income economies

$1000 - $3,000 (5 countries)
Lower middle-income economies

$500-$999 (10 countries)
Low income economies

Less than $500 (32 countries)
Low income economies

that the continent's population growth might have peaked. The high incidence of HIV/AIDS may also prompt futurists to revise their forecasts. Nonetheless, the US Census Bureau projects a population of 1.34 billion on the African continent in 2025. The African Development Bank's *Population Clock* for 2005 reveals the following dynamics of demographic change in Africa: an average of 4,125 people born per hour, 69 per minute, 1.1 persons per second. At the same time 235 infants die every hour, 4 every minute. In 2004-2005 six countries accounted for almost half of Africa's total population growth—Nigeria (14.9%), Ethiopia (9.5%), the Democratic Republic of Congo (8%), Egypt (7.2%), Uganda (4.8%) and Tanzania (3.8%). At an average of 65 persons per sq. mile Africa has a population density well below the world average of 105 people per sq. mile. (If Antarctica is eliminated—since it has zero population density—the world population density rises to 115). In Asia population density runs as high as 203 and in Europe tit is 134. Australia is a mere 6.4. The United States has a density of 76 people per square mile—slightly higher than Africa.

Africa's urban areas

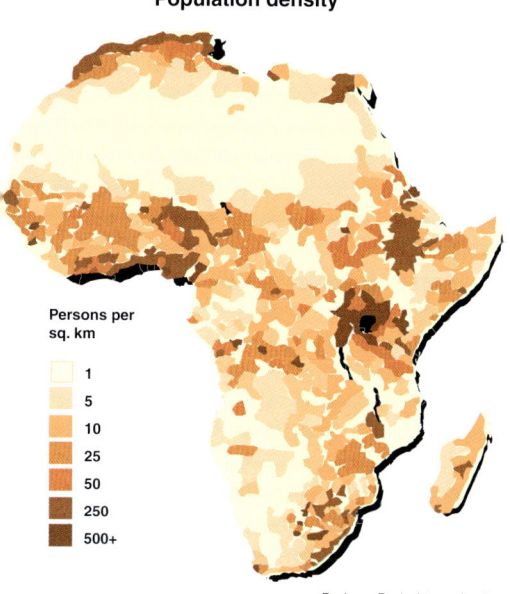

Population density

Persons per sq. km

- 1
- 5
- 10
- 25
- 50
- 250
- 500+

URBAN POPULATION

Although there has been a move towards the cities, Africa is still the world's least urbanized continent with more than 60 percent of its population living in rural areas. At latest count there were more than 60 urban areas with a population of more than a half a million, including 30 cities with more than one million. The largest metropolitan center in Africa is Lagos at 15 million. With an annual growth of 6 percent—the fastest growing in the world—it is expected to reach 24 million by 2010. Cairo is second with more than 12 million inhabitants in its metropolitan area. However, Africa's single most affluent urbanized region is, the Pretoria/Witwatersrand/Vereeniging or PWV complex around Johannesburg, South Africa, with more than 7 million people. In the 5 million plus range are Kinshasa/Brazzaville spanning across the Congo River and the Casablanca/Rabat complex in Morocco. Next in line at 3.5 million is the Durban/Pietermaritzburg complex in South Africa, and the city of Algiers. The Cape Peninsula leads in the 2 million plus league, which includes Maputo, Zambia's Copperbelt region, Luanda, Abidjan, Khartoum, Addis Ababa, Tripoli, Nairobi, and Dar es Salaam. A common problem faced by most of these cities is the uncontrolled squatting of migrants lured by hopes of jobs and newfound wealth.

INTERNATIONAL & REGIONAL LINKS

THE UNITED NATIONS HAS BEEN A VALUABLE FORUM FOR AFRICAN NATIONS IN THEIR STRUGGLE TO END COLONIALISM AND APARTHEID ON THE CONTINENT. TO-DAY, AFRICA'S 53 NATIONS PLAY A STRONG ROLE IN THE WORLD ORGANIZATION ITSELF AND ITS AGENCIES. THERE HAS BEEN A CONCERTED EFFORT IN AFRICA TO ESTABLISH ECONOMIC REGIONS ABLE TO COMPETE MORE EFFECTIVELY IN WORLD MARKETS. WHILE GROUPINGS SUCH AS ECOWAS, COMESA, SADC, UDEAC, UAM AND SACU ARE DETERMINED BY GEOGRAPHICAL FACTORS, COMMON CUR-RENCY AND HISTORICAL TIES, THERE HAS BEEN A TENDENCY OF LATE TO BE MORE PRAGMATIC. ONE RECENTLY FORMED GROUPING, IOARC, AIMS AT PROMOTING TRADE AND ECONOMIC COOPERATION AMONG AFRICAN, ARAB, ASIAN AND AUS-TRALASIAN NATIONS ALONG THE RIM OF THE INDIAN OCEAN. AMBITIOUS PLANS FOR THE AFRICAN UNION WHICH RE-PLACED THE ORGANIZATION FOR AFRICAN UNITY IN 2002 INCLUDE AN AFRICAN PAR-LIAMENT AND A COMMON CURRENCY FOR THE CONTINENT. FRANCE AND BRITAIN HAVE MAINTAINED A FORMAL RELATION-SHIP WITH THEIR FORMER COLONIES IN THE FRANC ZONE AND COMMONWEALTH, RESPECTIVELY. THE EUROPEAN UNION HAS CULTIVATED A SPECIAL TRADE RE-LATIONSHIP WITH AFRICAN, CARIBBEAN AND PACIFIC NATIONS UNDER THE LOMÉ CONVENTION—RECENTLY REVITALIZED AND REARRANGED UNDER THE COTONOU ACCORD. THE US HAS SPECIAL BILATERAL RELATIONSHIPS WITH SOUTH AFRICA, EGYPT AND NIGERIA AND IS IN THE PRO-CESS OF FORGING STRONGER ECONOMIC TIES WITH SUB-SAHARAN AFRICA. JAPAN, CHINA AND TAIWAN HAVE ALSO BECOME ACTIVE SUITORS.

UN SYSTEM

United Nations (UN)
United Nations
New York NY 10017, USA
Tel: [1] (212) 963 1234
Fax: [1] (212) 963 4879
Established on 26 June 1945, and starting operations on October 1945, the United Nations has witnessed the growth of a formidable and active African bloc since the sixties.

Economic Commission for Africa (ECA)
P. O. Box 3001-3005
Addis Ababa, Ethiopia
Tel: [251] (1) 51 72 00 Fax: [251] (1) 51 44 16
Web: *www.un.org/depts/eca/*
Established on 29 April 1958 to promote economic development as a regional commission of the UN's Economic and Social Council. All African nations are members. France and Britain serve as associate members.

Food and Agriculture Organization (FAO)
Viale delle Terme di Caracalla
00100 Rome, Italy
Tel: [39] (6) 57051 Fax:[39] (6) 5705 3152
Web: *www.fao.org*
Established on 16 October 1945 to raise living standards and increase availability of agricultural products.

International Atomic Energy Agency (IAEA)
Wagramerstrasse 5
P. O. Box 100
A-1400 , Vienna, Austria
Tel: [43] (1) 26000
Fax: [43] (1) 26007
Established on 26 October 1956, and operating since 29 July 1957, to promote peaceful uses of atomic energy among 129 members, including 25 from Africa: Algeria, Benin, Burkina Faso, Cameroon, Democratic Republic of Congo, Cote d'Ivoire, Egypt, Gabon, Kenya, Liberia, Libya, Madagascar, Mali, Mauritius, Morocco, Namibia, Niger, Nigeria, Senegal, Sierra Leone, South Africa, Tanzania, Uganda, Zambia, Zimbabwe.

International Development Association (IDA)
1818 H Street NW
Washington DC 20433
Tel: [1] (202) 477 1234
Fax: [1] (202) 477 6391
Established on 26 January 1960, as a specialized UN agency and part of the World Bank affiliate to provide financing on highly concessional terms to low coun-tries among its 160 members. South Africa is classified among the 26 developed countries and the rest of the continent among less developed countries.

AFRICAN UNION

In 2002, the African Union (AU) replaced the Organization of African Unity (OAU). Styled in part on the European Union, the AU is intended to be a more powerful and cohesive and effective body than its precursor. There is talk of closer economic cooperation and peacekeeping—even an African parliament and a common currency for the continent.

Founded in 1963 with the expressed purpose to promote solidarity in the struggle to eradicate colonialism and apartheid the OAU was ready for retrenchment after seeing the last vestige of white rule disappear in South Africa and its membership expanding from 31 to 53.

Foremost among those who felt that the OAU was ripe for retirement and replacement by something new was Col. Muammar Qaddafi of Libya, who pushed for the creation of a United States of Africa. Despite initial skepticism on the part of those who saw this as a mere ploy on his part to gain stature and influence in Africa, the required number of OAU member states ratified the formation of the African Union to make it a reality.

South African President Thabo Mbeki was elected the African Union's first chairman. The current chairman, elected in January 2006, is President Denis Sassou-Nguesso of the Republic of Congo. To date the AU has shown some success in brokering peace but it has yet to show meaningful progress in other areas.

NEPAD

The New Partnership for Africa's Development (NEPAD) was officially launched in October 2001 and adopted by the African Union as its vehicle to mobilize the concept of an African renaissance. It followed in the wake of Mbeki's Millennium African Recovery Plan (MAP) and Senegal President Wade's Omega Plan (OP) which were jointly adopted under the so-called New African Initiative (NAI). All these plans that came together in NEPAD have one common goal, namely, to integrate Africa into a globalizing world through responsive and responsible leadership. NEPAD is premised on the assumption that AU member states will make firm commitments towards good governance, democracy and human rights, while endeavoring to resolve conflicts in a peaceful manner.

While the African Union has moved into OAU headquarters in Addis Ababa in Ethiopia, NEPAD has opened offices in Pretoria. It is headed by President Mbeki's economic advisor, Dr. Wiseman Nkhulu. The Washington-based Corporate Council on Africa (CCA) was named US Representative for the Steering Committee of NEPAD. In September 2004 the African Union's newly formed Pan African Parliament (PAP) held its first session at a MidRand facility near Johannesburg, South Africa. More than forty nations attended. Recognizing the important role of women, an internationally known Tanzanian gender activist, Gertrude Mongella, was elected to preside over this first Africa-wide parliament.

CHALLENGES

Much more needs to be done to convince the skeptics that MAP, OP, NAI, NEPAD and AU are not merely meaningless mantras. Speaking at the African Union's inaugural, Ghanaian-born UN Secretary General Kofi Annan cautioned his compatriots in Africa to "guard against taking our hope as reality." To build a successful union, he pointed out, "will require great stamina and iron political will."

African Union President Denis Sassou-Nguesso of the Republic of Congo addresses the UN Security Council in September 2006.

International Finance Corporation (IFC)
2121 Pennsylvania Avenue NW
Washington, DC 20433, USA
Tel: [1] (202) 477 1234
Fax: [1] (202) 974 4384
Established on 25 May 1955, and starting operations on 24 July 1956, as a support mechanism for private enterprise in international economic development. It is a UN specialized agency and World Bank affiliate. All African countries are members by virtue of their Wolrd Bank membership.

International Fund for Agricultural Development (IFAD)
Via del Serafico 107
I-00142 Rome
Italy
Tel: [39] (6) 54591 Fax:[39] (6) 5043463
Web: www.ifad.org
Established in December 1977 to promote agricultural development.

International Labour Organization (ILO)
4 route des Morillons
CH-1211 Geneva 22
Switzerland
Tel: [41] (22) 799 61 11
Fax: [41] (22) 798 86 85
Web: www.ilo.org
The ILO was founded in 1919 and is the only surviving major creation of the Treaty of Versailles which brought the League of Nations into being and became the first specialized agency of the UN in 1946. The ILO formulates international labor standards and set minimum standards of basic labor rights: freedom of association, the right to organize, collective bargaining, abolition of forced labour, equality of opportunity and treatment, and other standards regulating conditions across the entire field of work-related issues. The ILO has a unique tripartite structure with workers and employers participating as equal partners with governments. All African nations and other UN members belong.

International Maritime Organization (IMO)
4 Albert Embankment
London SE1 7SR, UK
Tel: [44] (171) 735 7611
Fax: [44] (171) 587 3210
Web: www.imo.org
Established on 6 March 1948, as the Intergovernmental Maritime Consultative Organization (IMCO) and changed to the IMO on 22 May 1982, this specialized UN agency deals with international maritime affairs. Its 157 members include 39 African countries: Algeria, Angola, Benin, Cameroon, Cape Verde, Democratic Republic of Congo, Republic of the Congo, Côte d'Ivoire, Djibouti, Egypt, Equatorial Guinea, Eritrea, Ethiopia, Gabon, The Gambia, Ghana, Guinea, Guinea-Bissau, Kenya, Liberia, Libya, Madagascar, Malawi, Mauritania, Mauritius, Morocco, Mozambique, Namibia, Nigeria, São Tomé & Príncipe, Senegal, Seychelles, Sierra Leone, Somalia, South Africa, Sudan, Tanzania, Togo, Tunisia.
International

Monetary Fund (IMF)
700 19th Street NW
Washington DC 20431, USA
Tel: [1] (202) 623 7000 Fax: [1] (202) 623 4661
Web: www.imf.org
Established on 22 July 1944, and operative since 27 December 1945, the IMF, a specialized UN agency, works towards world monetary stability and economic development. All African countries are represented in the 182-member organization.

International Telecommunication Union (ITU)
Place des Nations
CH-1211 Geneva 20, Switzerland
Tel: [41] (22) 730 5111
Fax: [41] (22) 733 7256
Web: www.itu.int
Established on17 May 1865 and affiliated with the UN since 1947, the ITU handles world telecommunications issues among members.

United Nations Conference on Trade and Development (UNCTAD)
Palais des Nations
CH-1211 Geneva 10, Switzerland
Tel: [41] (22) 907 12 34 Fax: [41] (22) 907 00 57
Web: www.unctad.org
Established on 30 December 1964 to facilitate the integration of developing countries into the world economy and international trading system.

United Nations Educational, Scientific, and Cultural Organization (UNESCO)
7 place de Fontenoy
F-75352 Paris 07SP, France
Tel: [33] (1) 45 68 10 00
Fax: [33] (1) 45 67 16 90
Web: www.unseco.org
Established on in 1946 to promote cooperation in education, science, and culture among UN members.

African Union Chairman, Pres. Denis Sassou Nguesso of the C at press conference after briefing the Security Council—2006.

UND

**United Nations High Commissioner
for Refugees (UNHCR)**
Case Postale 2500 Depot
CH-1211 Geneva 2, Switzerland
Tel: [41] (22) 739 81 11
Fax: [41] (22) 731 95 46
Web: *www.unhcr.ch*
Established on in1951, UNHCR seeks to ensure the humanitarian treatment of refugees and to find permanent solutions to refugee problems. A significant part of its operations, which now aid internally-displaced persons as well as cross-border refugees, are geared to Africa, which has more than its fair share of refugees from warfare, oppression and hunger.

**United Nations Industrial
Development Organization (UNIDO)**
Vienna International Center
PO Box 300
A-1400 Vienna, Austria
Tel: [43] (1) 260 260 Fax:[43] (1) 269 2669
Web: *www.unido.org*
This United States agency was established in 1966, to promote industrial development among UN member nations. All African nations are members.

**Universal Postal
Union (UPU)**
Bureau International de l'UPU
Weltpoststrasse 4
CH-3000 Berne 15
Switzerland
Tel: [41] (31) 350 31 11
Fax: [41] (31) 350 31 10
Established in 1874, and became a UN specialized agency in 1948, Its role is to promote international postal cooperation among UN member states. All African states are members.

**World Bank
The International Bank
for Reconstruction
and Development or IBRD)**
1818 H Street NW
Washington DC 20433

Tel: [1] (202) 477 1234
Fax: [1] (202) 477 6391
Web: *www.worldbank.org*
Established on 22 July 1944 and operative since 27 December 1945, this UN specialized agency provides economic development loans to its membership of 181 members, including all 53 African countries. It is an active key participant in development programs geared to stimulate growth in Africa.

World Health Organization (WHO)
20, Avenue Appia
CH-1211 , Geneva 27, Switzerland
Tel: [41] (22) 791 21 11 Fax: [41] (22) 791 07 46
Web: *www.who.org*
The World Health Organization was established on 22 July 1946, as a specialized UN agency and started on 7 April 1948. It deals with health matters worldwide. All African states are members.

**World Intellectual Property
Organization (WIPO)**
34 Chemin des Colombettes
CH-1211 Geneva 20, Switzerland
Tel: [41] (22) 338 9111
Fax: [41] (22) 733 5428
Web: *www.wipo.int*
Established on 14 July 1967 and operative since 26 April 1970, WIPO as a specialized UN agency furnishes protection for literary, artistic, and scientific works. Its 171 members include all 53 African countries.

**World Meteorological
Organization (WMO)**
41 Avenue Giuseppe-Motta
CH-1211 Geneva 2, Switzerland
Tel: [41] (22) 730 81 11
Fax: [41] (22) 734 23 26
Web: *www.wmo.ch*
Established in 1947 and became a UN specialized agency in 1951. Its aims at providing authoritative scientific meterological information on a global basis. All African nations are members.

*s Briefing at UN by the Foreign Minister of Ghana
a Addo Dankwa Akufo-Addo in August 06*

World Tourism Organization (UNWTO)
Calle Capitan Haya 42
28020 Madrid, Spain
Tel: [34] (1) 567 81 00
Fax: [34] (1) 571 37 33
Established on 2 January 1975, to promote tourism as a means of contributing to economic development, international understanding, and peace. Its 131 members include 47 African countries: Algeria, Angola, Benin, Botswana, Burkina Faso, Burundi, Cameroon, Central African Republic, Chad, Democratic Republic of the Congo, Republic of Congo, Côte d'Ivoire, Djibouti, Egypt, Equatorial Guinea, Ethiopia, Gabon, The Gambia, Ghana, Guinea, Guinea-Bissau, Kenya, Lesotho, Libya, Madagascar, Malawi, Mali, Mauritania, Mauritius, Morocco,Mozambique, Namibia, Niger, Nigeria, Rwanda, São Tomé & Príncipe, Senegal, Seychelles, Sierra Leone, South Africa, Sudan, Tanzania, Togo, Tunisia, Uganda, Zambia, Zimbabwe.

**World Trade
Organization (WTO)**
Centre William Rappard
154 Rue de Lausanne
CH-1211 Geneva 21, Switzerland
Tel :[41] (22) 739 51 11
Fax: [41] (22) 739 54 58
Web: *www.wto.org*
Established on 15 April 1994, and operating since 1 January 1995, as a successor to the General Agreement on Tariff and Trade (GATT), the WTO provides the mechanism to resolve trade conflicts between members and to carry on negotiations with the goal of further lowering and/or eliminating tariffs and other trade barriers. Its 140 members include 41 African members: Angola, Benin, Botswana, Burkina Faso, Burundi, Cameroon, Central African Republic, Chad, Democratic Republic

of the Congo, Republic of Congo, Côte d'Ivoire, Djibouti, Egypt, Gabon, The Gambia, Ghana, Guinea, Guinea-Bissau, Kenya, Lesotho, Madagascar, Malawi, Mali, Mauritania, Mauritius, Morocco, Mozambique, Namibia, Niger, Nigeria, Rwanda, Senegal, Sierra Leone, South Africa, Swaziland, Tanzania, Togo, Tunisia, Uganda, Zambia, Zimbabwe. Two African nations have observer status: Somalia, Sudan. Another five have applications pending: Cape Verde, Comoros, Equatorial Guinea, São Tomé & Príncipe, and Seychelles.

OTHER ORGANIZATIONS

Following are other significant world and regional organizations to which all or some of Africa's nations belong:

**African, Caribbean, and Pacific
Group of States (ACP Group)**
Avenue Georges Henri 451
B-1200 Brussels, Belgium
Tel: [32] (2) 743 06 00
Fax [32] (2) 735 55 73
Established on 6 June 1975 to manage preferential economic and aid relationships with the EU. All Sub-Saharan African countries belong to the group of 71 less-developed African, Caribbean and Pacific (ACP) countries associated with the European Union (EU) under the Lomé Convention. Under this treaty the EU grants ACP exports access to its markets on either a low or zero tariff basis. The EU also provides financial and technical aid to Lomé signatories, including the Stabex and Sysmin stabilization funds. The Stabex scheme was designed to compensate the ACP countries for fluctuations in the price of their agricultural exports. Similarly, Sysmin safeguards exports of minerals. Four Conventions have been concluded since 1975 when the first treaty was signed in Lomé, the capital of Togo. When it became a signatory in 1997, South Africa did not

qualify for all the provisions of the convention as it was considered too highly developed for full membership. Other African member states are Angola, Benin, Botswana, Burkina Faso, Burundi, Cameroon, Cape Verde, Central African Republic, Chad, Comoros, Democratic Republic of the Congo, Republic of the Congo, Côte d'Ivoire, Djibouti, Equatorial Guinea, Eritrea, Ethiopia, Gabon, The Gambia, Ghana, Guinea, Guinea-Bissau, Kenya, Lesotho, Liberia, Madagascar, Malawi, Mali, Mauritania, Mauritius, Mozambique, Namibia, Niger, Nigeria, Rwanda, São Tomé & Príncipe, Senegal, Seychelles, Sierra Leone, Somalia, Sudan, Swaziland, Tanzania, Togo, Uganda, Zambia, Zimbabwe. The Cotonou Agreement, signed in Benin in June 2000, replaces the Lomé agreement. Discussions are underway to thrash out details among the 15 European signatories and the African and other ACP member nations. Considered are not only changed circumstances in Europe and Africa but WTO requirements.

**African Development
Bank (ADB)**
*Banque Africaine
de Developpement*
01 BP 1387
Abidjan 01
Côte d'Ivoire
Tel: [225] 20 44 44
Fax: [225] 21 77 53
Established on 4 August 1963 to promote economic and social development in Africa. All African countries are are regional members regional members. There are 25 non-regional members: Argentina, Austria, Belgium, Brazil, Canada, China, Denmark, Finland, France, Germany, India, Italy, Japan, South Korea, Kuwait, Netherlands, Norway, Portugal, Saudi Arabia, Spain, Sweden, Switzerland, UAE, UK, US.

African Union (AU)
PO Box 3243
Addis Ababa, Ethiopia
Tel: [251] (1) 517700
Fax: [251] (1) 512622, 517844
On 2 March 2001 the African Union was approved by a required two-thirds of Africa's 53 nations as a successor to the Organization of African Unity. Until its inauguration on 8 July 2002 at a special ceremony in Durban, South Africa, the African Union (AU) was given the opportunity to phase itself into OAU headquarters, which it inherited together with other assets and liabilities—including arrears of $42 million in membership dues. It was felt that the OAU, established on 25 May 1963, to promote unity and cooperation among African states in their fight against colonialism and apartheid had served its purpose and needed to be replaced. As in the case of the OAU, all 53 African nations are members of the AU. The general concensus among is that the African Union should be different from its predecessor to be able to meet new and changed circumstances. Priorities have changed from pure political activism to closer economic cooperation, globalization and peacekeeping in Africa. The aim is to eventually duplicate and adapt the the European Union model, replete with a common parliament, monetary system and currency. The ultimate goal is to enhance the economic and political future of the continent and find African solutions to local problems. The African Union's economic revival

mandate is closely linked to the so-called New African Initiative and the New Partnership for Africa's Development (NEPAD) plan.

Arab Bank for Economic Development in Africa (ABEDA)
[A.k.a. Banque Arabe de Developpement Economique en Afrique or BADEA]
Abdel Rahman El Mahdi Avenue
P. O. Box 2640
Khartoum, Sudan
Tel: [249] (11) 770498
Fax: [249] (11) 770600
Established on 18 February 1974, and started operations on 16 September 1974, to promote economic development. Its 17 members include: Algeria, Egypt, Libya, Mauritania, Morocco, Sudan, Tunisia. Other Arab members: Bahrain, Iraq, Jordan, Kuwait, Lebanon, Oman, Qatar, Saudi Arabia, Syria, UAE.

Arab Maghreb Union (AMU)
27 Avenue Okba Agdal
Rabat, Morocco
Tel: [212] (7) 77 26 82
Fax: [212] (7) 77 26 93
Established on 17 February 1989, to promote cooperation and integration among the Arab states of northern Africa. The Union du Maghreb Arabe (UMA), aims at safeguarding the region's economic interests, fostering and promoting economic and cultural cooperation,

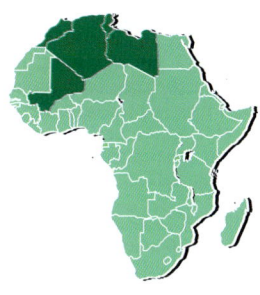

and intensifying mutual commercial exchanges as a precursor for integration and the creation of a North African Common Market . The secretariat is based in Rabat, Morocco. It has a membership of 5: Algeria, Libya, Mauritania, Morocco, Tunisia.

Central African States Development Bank (BDEAC)
[Acronym for *Banque de Developpement des Etats de l'Afrique Centrale*]
Place du Gouvernement
BP 1177, Brazzaville
Republic of the Congo
Tel: [242] 81 18 85
Fax: [242] 81 18 80
Established on 3 December 1975, to provide loans for economic development in African countries. The BDEAC's African members are Cameroon, Central African Republic, Chad, Republic of Congo, Equatorial Guinea, and Gabon. Other members are France, Germany, and Kuwait.

Commonwealth (CWLTH)
[A.k.a. Commonwealth of Nations]
Commonwealth Secretariat
Marlborough House
London SW1Y 5HX
United Kingdom
Tel: [44] (171) 839 3411, 747 6535
Fax: [44] (171) 930 0827, 839 9081
The Commonwealth was established on 31 December 1931 as a voluntary association evolving from the British Empire, to foster multinational cooperation and provide assistance to members where needed. The Commonwealth functions as an association of independent states—most of them, but not all, former British colonies. More affluent members such as Australia, Canada, New Zealand and the United Kingdom channel a substantial portion of their foreign aid into less developed fellow Commonwealth nations. There are also special trade and investment agreements. Links between governments are complemented by the activities of a large number of non-governmental Commonwealth organizations active in a variety of community building projects. Its membership of 53 includes 18 from Africa: Botswana, Cameroon, The Gambia, Ghana, Kenya, Lesotho, Malawi, Mauritius, Mozambique, Namibia, Nigeria, Seychelles, Sierra Leone, South Africa, Swaziland, Tanzania, Uganda, Zambia, Zimbabwe. The other members are: Antigua and Barbuda, Australia,

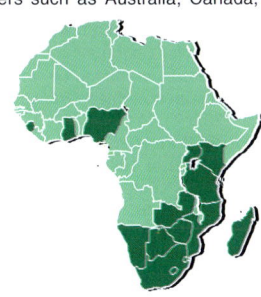

UN Secretary General Kofi Annan addresses the African Union Summit in The Gambia in September 2006.

The Bahamas, Bangladesh, Barbados, Belize, Brunei, Canada, Cyprus, Dominica, Fiji, Grenada, Guyana, India, Jamaica, Kiribati, Malaysia, Maldives, Malta, Nauru, New Zealand, Pakistan, Papua New Guinea, Saint Kitts and Nevis, Saint Lucia, Saint Vincent and the Grenadines, Samoa, Singapore, Solomon Islands, Tonga, Trinidad and Tobago, Sri Lanka, United Kingdom, Vanuatu.

Common Market for Eastern and Southern Africa (COMESA)

Tel: [260] 1 229-726
Fax: [260] 1 225-107
PO Box 30051
Lusaka 10101, Zambia

In November 1993, the member states of the Preferential Trade Area for Eastern and Southern Africa (PTA) signed a treaty transforming the PTA into the Common Market for Eastern and Southern Africa (COMESA). It aims at a fully integrated free trade area, a customs

union with a common external tariff, free movement of capital and finance, a payments union, and free movement of people. It aims at promoting cooperation in the development and rationalization of basic and strategic industries, agricultural development, the improvement of transport links, and the development of technical and professional skills. COMESA has 21 members: Angola, Burundi,Comoros, Djibouti, Eritrea, Ethiopia, Kenya, Madagascar, Ma-lawi, Mauritius, Namibia, Rwanda, Seychelles, Somalia, Sudan, Swaziland, Tanzania, Uganda, Democratic Republic of Congo, Zambia and Zimbabwe.

Customs and Economic Union of Central Africa (CEMAC)

[Acronym for *Communauté économique et monétaire en Afrique Centrale*].
Bangui, Central African Republic
Tel: [237] 21 44 15
Fax: [237] 21 44 88

Established in 1966 under the Brazzaville Treaty of 1964 as a customs union, the *Union douanière et économique de l'Afnique Centrale* (UDEAC) allowed

duty-free trade between French- and Spanish-speaking countries in Central Africa. A common external tariff applied to imports from third countries. In 1994 the members of UDEAC entered into a second agreement, the Economic and Monetary Com-

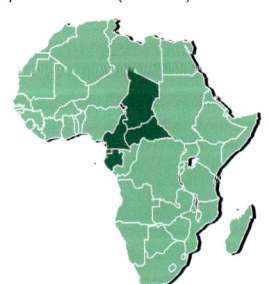

munity in Central Africa or *Communauté économique et monétaire en Afrique Centrale* (CEMAC), replacing the UDEAC. Members are: Cameroon, Central African Republic, Chad, Congo, Equatorial Guinea and Gabon. CEMAC's secretariat is in Bangui, Central African Republic. CEMAC members share as a central bank the *Banque des états de l'Afrique centrale (BEAC)* in Yaoundé, Cameroon.

Customs Cooperation Council (CCC)

[World Customs Organization (WCO)]
Rue du Marche 30
B-1210, Brussels, Belgium
Tel: [32] (2) 209 92 11
Fax: [32] (2) 109 92 92

Established on15 December 1950 to promote international cooperation in customs matters. Its 145 signatories include 44 African nations: Algeria, Angola, Botswana, Burkina Faso, Burundi, Cameroon, Cape Verde, Central African Republic, Comoros, Democratic Republic of Congo, Republic of the Congo, Côte d'Ivoire, Egypt, Eritrea, Ethiopia, Gabon, The Gambia, Ghana, Guinea, Kenya, Lesotho, Liberia, Libya, Madagascar, Malawi, Mali, Mauritania, Mauritius, Morocco, Mozambique, Namibia, Niger, Nigeria, Rwanda, Senegal, Sierra Leone, South Africa, Sudan, Swaziland, Tanzania, Togo, Tunisia, Zambia, Zimbabwe.

Commission for East African Co-operation (EAC)

P.O. Box 1096
Arusha, Tanzania
Tel: [225] 57 4253/8
Fax: [225] 57 4255

The Tripartite Commission for East African Cooperation (EAC) was formed by Kenya, Tanzania and Uganda in July 1999. It aims at eliminating all tariff rates between the member states and issuing a single passport for the region. Both Rwanda and Burundi are expected to join.

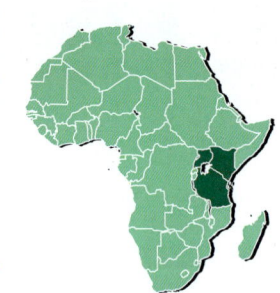

East African Development Bank (EADB)

4 Nile Avenue
P. O. Box 7128
Kampala
Uganda
Tel: [256] (41) 230021, 230825
Fax: [256] (41) 259763

Established on 6 June 1967, and started operations on 1 December 1967, promoting economic development among its three members—Kenya, Tanzania, and Uganda.

Economic Community of Central African States (CEEAC)

[Acronym derived from
*Communaute Economique
des Etats de l'Afrique Centrale*]
BP 2112
Libreville
Gabon
Tel: [241] 73 35 47, 73 35 48
Established on 18 October 1983, to promote regional economic cooperation and develop a Central African Common Market. Its eleven members are: Angola, Burundi, Cameroon, Central African Republic, Chad, Democratic Republic of Congo, Republic of the Congo, Equatorial Guinea, Gabon, Rwanda, São Tomé & Príncipe.

Economic Community of the Great Lakes Countries (CEPGL)

[Acronym—CEPGL—derived from *Communaute Economique des Pays des Grands Lacs*]
BP 91, Gitega
Burundi
Established on 20 September 1976, to promote regional economic cooperation and integration of its 3 members: Burundi, Democratic Republic of Congo, Rwanda.

Economic Community of West African States (ECOWAS)

6 King George V Road
PMB 12745, Lagos, Nigeria
Tel: [234] (1) 636839, 636841, 636064, 630398
Fax: [234] (1) 636822
Established in May 1975, the Economic Community of West African States (ECOWAS) is a common market striving towards uniform lower tariff rates. Poorer members are to be compensated from a common fund.

ECOWAS also promotes the free movement of people, services and capital, harmonization of agricultural policies, joint development of economic and industrial policies, common monetary policies, and the elimination of disparities in levels of development.
It has a membership of 16: Benin, Burkina Faso, Cape Verde, Côte d'Ivoire, The Gambia, Ghana, Guinea, Guinea-Bissau, Liberia, Mali, Mauritania, Niger, Nigeria, Senegal, Sierra Leone and Togo.

Franc Zone (CFA)

[Officially known as the Communauté Financière Africaine or CFA]
Direction Generale des Service
Etrangers (Service de la Zone Franc)
Banque de France
Paris, France
Tel: [33] 42 92 31 26

Established in December 1945, the Franc Zone is a union of African countries with currencies linked to the French franc at a fixed rate of exchange. The *Communauté Financière Africaine* (CFA) franc is ensured by the French Treasury, and remains readily convertible. In 1994, the exchange rate parity was reduced by 50 percent to a fixed parity of 100 CFA francs to one French franc. Under mutual agreement members hold their reserves mainly in French francs and undertake to exchange them on the French market. With the exception of

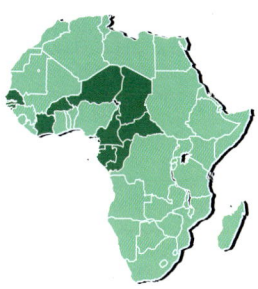

Guinea and Mauritania, all former members of French West Africa and French Equatorial Africa joined this monetary union. So did the former French island possession of Comoros. Equatorial Guinea, a former Spanish colony, joined in 1985, and in 1997, Guinea Bissau, a former Portuguese Guinea, in 1997. There are two Franc Zone groupings, one in Western and one in Central Africa. A separate agreement applies to Comoros. Apart from Guinea and Mauritania, other African francophone nations who opted not to join the monetary union are Madagascar, Djibouti, the Democratic Republic of Congo, Rwanda and Burundi. The CFA franc has been useful in facilitating international payments and foreign trade. Francophone countries received assistance from France in the form of development and technical, budget and military support, as well as subsidies on commodity exports.

International Chamber of Commerce (ICC)

38 Cours Albert 1st
F-75008 Paris, France
Tel: [33] (1) 49 53 28 28
Fax: [33] (1) 49 53 29 42
Established in 1919 to promote free trade and private enterprise and to represent business interests at national and international levels. Its 62 national councils represented include 11 from African countries: Burkina Faso, Cameroon, Côte d'Ivoire, Egypt, Madagascar, Morocco, Nigeria, Senegal, South Africa, Togo, Tunisia.

International Confederation of Free Trade Unions (ICFTU)

International Trade Union House
Boulevard Emile Jacqmain 155
B-1210 , Brussels, Belgium
Tel: [32] (2) 224 02 11
Established in December 1949, to promote trade union movements. More than 200 organizations representing 141 countries, are affiliated. Movements from 38 African countries are represented: Algeria, Benin, Botswana, Burkina Faso, Cameroon, Cape Verde, Central African Republic, Chad, Democratic Republic of the Congo, Republic of Congo, Côte d'Ivoire, Djibouti, Eritrea, Gabon, The Gambia, Ghana, Guinea, Guinea-Bissau, Kenya, Liberia, Madagascar, Malawi, Mali, Mauritius, Morocco, Mozambique, Rwanda, Senegal, Seychelles, Sierra Leone, South Africa, Swaziland, Tanzania, Togo, Tunisia, Uganda, Zambia, Zimbabwe.

59

International Criminal Police Organization (Interpol)
BP 6041, F-69411
Lyon CEDEX 06, France
Tel: [33] (4) 72 44 70 00
Fax: [33] (4) 72 44 71 63
Established in 1923 as the International Criminal Police Commission and modified on 13 June 1956, under its current name to promote international cooperation among police authorities in combating crime. Among its 177 members, 51 African countries are represented: Algeria, Angola, Benin, Botswana, Burkina Faso, Burundi, Cameroon, Cape Verde, Central African Republic, Chad, Democratic Republic of the Congo, Republic of the Congo, Côte d'Ivoire, Djibouti, Egypt, Equatorial Guinea, Ethiopia, Gabon, The Gambia, Ghana, Guinea, Guinea-Bissau, Kenya, Lesotho, Liberia, Libya, Madagascar, Malawi, Mali, Mauritania, Mauritius, Morocco, Mozambique, Namibia, Niger, Nigeria, Rwanda, São Tomé & Príncipe, Senegal, Seychelles, Sierra Leone, Somalia, South Africa, Sudan, Swaziland, Tanzania, Togo, Tunisia, Uganda, Zambia, Zimbabwe.

Intergovernmental Authority for Development (IGAD)
BP 2653, Djibouti
Djibouti
Tel : [253] 354050, (253) 352880
Fax : [253] 356994
Signatories to the Intergovernmental Authority on Development (IGAD) are Djibouti, Eritrea, Ethiopia, Kenya, Somalia and Uganda. The group focuses on economic cooperation and regional integration to combat the effects of drought and to help solve regional conflicts. The focus has also been on transportation and communications infrastructure building.

There is a possibility that in the long term, the membership could increase as countries such as Egypt might join.

International Organization for Migration (IOM)
17 route des Morillons CP 71
CH-1211 Geneva 19, Switzerland
Tel: [41] (22) 717 91 11
Fax: [41] (22) 798 61 50
Established on 5 December 1951, to facilitate orderly international emigration and immigration. Among its 69 members are the following 13 African countries: Angola, Egypt, Guinea-Bissau, Kenya, Mali, Morocco, Senegal, South Africa, Sudan, Tanzania, Tunisia, Uganda, Zambia. Fourteen African countries are among the 47 hat have observer status: Algeria, Cape Verde, Democratic Republic of Congo, Republic of the Congo, Ethiopia, Ghana, Guinea, Madagascar, Mozambique, Namibia, Rwanda, São Tomé & Príncipe, Somalia, Zimbabwe.

International Mobile Satellite Organization (Inmarsat)
99 City Road
London EC1Y 1AX, UK
Tel: [44] (171) 728 1000 Fax: [44] (171) 728 1044
Established on 3 September 1976 as the International Maritime Satellite Organization, the renamed Inmarsat, it promotes cooperation in worldwide communications for commercial, distress, and safety applications at sea, in the air, and on land. Its membership of 86 includes 12 from Africa: Algeria, Egypt, Gabon, Ghana, Kenya, Liberia, Mauritius, Mozambique, Nigeria, Senegal, South Africa, Tanzania.

Indian Ocean Commission (IOC)
Commission de l'Océan Indien
Q4 Avenue Sir Guy Forget
Quatre Bornes
Ile Maurice
Fax: [230] 425.12.09
The Indian Ocean Commission (IOC) was formed by Comoros, Madagascar, Mauritius, Seychelles and France (Reunion), in 1999 to represent members' interests in other regional and international organizations. It also aims at tariff reduction among members and joint trade promotion.

International Organization for Standardization (ISO)
CP 56, 1 Rue de Varembe
CH-1211 Geneva 20
Switzerland
Tel: [41] (22) 749 01 11
Fax:- [41] (22) 733 34 30
Established in February 1947, to further the development of international standards in the exchange of goods and services and to develop cooperation in the sphere of intellectual, scientific, technological and economic activity among members. There are 14 African countries among the 88 members: Algeria, Botswana, Egypt, Ethiopia, Ghana, Kenya, Libya, Mauritius, Morocco, Nigeria, South Africa, Tanzania, Tunisia, Zimbabwe. Eleven African nations are among the 44 correspondent and subscriber members: Benin, Democratic Republic of Congo, Côte d'Ivoire, Guinea, Madagascar, Malawi, Mozambique, Namibia, Seychelles, Sudan, Uganda.

International Telecommunications Satellite Organization (Intelsat)
3400 International Drive NW
Washington
DC 20008-3098
Tel: [1] (202) 944 7500
Fax: [1] (202) 944 7890
Established on 20 August 1964, as the Telecommunications Satellite Consortium and changed to Intelsat on 12 February 1973, the International Telecommunications Satellite Organization aims at developing and operating a global commercial telecommunications satellite system. Forty- three of its 143 members are African: Algeria, Angola, Benin, Botswana, Burkina Faso, Cameroon, Cape Verde, Central African Republic, Chad, Comoros, Democratic Republic of Congo, Republic of the Congo, Côte d'Ivoire, Egypt, Equatorial

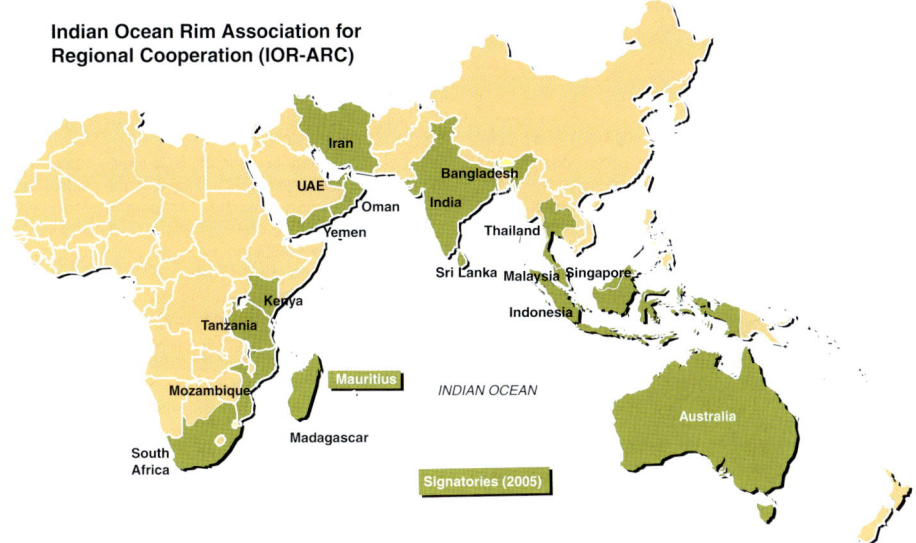

Indian Ocean Rim Association for Regional Cooperation (IOR-ARC)

Labels on map: Iran, UAE, Oman, Yemen, Bangladesh, India, Thailand, Sri Lanka, Malaysia, Singapore, Indonesia, Kenya, Tanzania, Mozambique, Mauritius, Madagascar, South Africa, Australia, INDIAN OCEAN, Signatories (2005)

Guinea, Ethiopia, Gabon, Ghana, Guinea, Kenya, Libya, Madagascar, Malawi, Mali, Mauritania, Mauritius, Morocco, Mozambique, Namibia, Niger, Nigeria, Rwanda, Senegal, Somalia, South Africa, Sudan, Swaziland, Tanzania, Togo, Tunisia, Uganda, Zambia, Zimbabwe. A further 10 African countries are among the non-signatory users: Burundi, Djibouti, Eritrea, The Gambia, Guinea-Bissau, Lesotho, Liberia, São Tomé & Príncipe, Seychelles, Sierra Leone.

Indian Ocean Rim Association for Regional Cooperation (IOR-ARC)
Port Louis, Mauritius

Launched in Mauritius in March 1997, the Indian Ocean Rim Organization for Regional Cooperation aspires to be a regional economic grouping such as ASEAN and APEC. It involves the business community, academia and governments in the promotion of wide-ranging co-operation among member states. Similar trading blocs elsewhere prompted a movement towards closer economic ties among the countries bordering the Indian Ocean. The focus is on trade and investment and the exchange of technical know-how, research and training. The following 18 countries are signatories: Australia, Bangladesh, India, Indonesia, Iran, Kenya, Madagascar, Malaysia, Mauritius, Mozambique, Oman, Singapore, South Africa, Sri Lanka, Tanzania, Thailand, UAE and Yemen. Seychelles withdrew as a member in July 2003. The nations of the IOR-ARC have a combined population of more than 1.3 billion or 23% of the world's population—with India and Indonesia accounting for 85% of the Association's total population. The Association represents a GNP of $1,184 billion or 4% of the world total. The GNP per capita for the region as a whole amounted to about $892 in 1995, which qualified it as lower middle income area in terms of the World Bank's classification. At the beginning of 2000 a Working Group on Trade and Investment (WGTI) met formally for the first time in Muscat to formulate an Action Plan to liberalize trade and promote investment in the Indian Ocean Rim Region. Egypt, Japan, China, France and the United Kingdom are "dialogue partners."

International Red Cross and Red Crescent Movement (ICRM)
International Conference of the Red Cross
19 Avenue de la Paix
CH-1202 Geneva
Switzerland
Tel: [41] (22) 734 60 01
Fax: [41] (22) 733 20 57

Established in 1928 to promote worldwide humanitarian aid through the International Committee of the Red Cross (ICRC) in wartime, and in peacetime through the International Federation of Red Cross and Red Crescent Societies (IFRCS). Of the 175 national societies 50 African: Algeria, Angola, Benin, Botswana, Burkina Faso, Burundi, Cameroon, Cape Verde, Central African Republic, Chad, Democratic Republic of the Congo, Republic of Congo, Côte d'Ivoire, Djibouti, Egypt, Equatorial Guinea, Ethiopia, The Gambia, Ghana, Guinea, Guinea-Bissau, Kenya, Lesotho, Liberia, Libya, Madagascar, Malawi, Mali, Mauritania, Mauritius, Morocco, Mozambique, Namibia, Niger, Nigeria, Rwanda, São Tomé & Príncipe, Senegal, Seychelles, Sierra Leone, Somalia, South Africa, Sudan, Swaziland, Tanzania, Togo, Tunisia, Uganda, Zambia, Zimbabwe.

Organization of Petroleum Exporting Countries (OPEC)
Obere Donaustrasse 93
A-1020 Vienna
Austria
Tel: [43] (1) 21 11 20
Fax: [43] (1) 216 43 20

Established on 14 September 1960 to coordinate petroleum policies among major oil producers. Algeria, Libya and Nigeria are members of the eleven-member body. Other members include Indonesia, Iran, Iraq, Kuwait, Qatar, Saudi Arabia, UAE, Venezuela.

Southern African Customs Union (SACU)
Director of Customs and Excise
Ministry of Finance
Private Bag 13295
Windhoek
Namibia

A Southern African Customs Union (SACU) was established in 1969 between South Africa, Botswana, Lesotho and Swaziland. Namibia became a member in 1990.

Goods move freely between members, unhampered by tariffs or quantitative constraints, and there is a common customs tariff on goods imported from outside. All duties are paid into a common pool administered and disbursed annually by the South African Reserve Bank. Smaller countries receive a 42 percent allowance to compensate for the disadvantage of sharing with the much larger South Africa. Except for Botswana, all members of the Southern African Customs Union are also in a common monetary area arrangement (CMA), under which the currencies of Lesotho, Namibia and Swaziland are backed by the South African rand.

Southern African Development Community (SADC)
Private Bag 0095
Gaborone
Botswana
Tel: [267] (31) 351863
Fax: [267] (31) 372848

The Southern African Development Community (SADC) is an outgrowth of the Southern African Development Coordination Conference (SADCC). It was established in July 1979 by 11 nations in an effort to reduce the region's economic dependence on apartheid-ruled South Africa. On 17 August 1992, ten SADCC member states signed

a treaty establishing the Southern African Development Community (SADC) with South Africa as the eleventh member. Mauritius joined in 1995, followed by the Democratic Republic of Congo and the Seychelles in 1997. All the members of the SADC—with the exception of Botswana, South Africa, Lesotho and Mozambique—are also members of COMESA. The Southern African Development Community promotes cross-border economic cooperation, investment and trade, and freer movement of goods and services, free enterprise, competitiveness, democracy and good governance, respect for the rule of law and human rights, popular participation and the alleviation of poverty. A tribunal was established to arbitrate disputes between member states arising from the treaty. To avoid an unwieldy bureaucracy at the SADC secretariat in Gaborone, Botswana, organizational responsibilities are shared by the various member states: Angola—energy; Botswana—economic affairs, agricultural research, animal disease control and livestock production; Lesotho— tourism, environment and land management; Malawi—inland fisheries, wildlife and forestry; Mozambique—transport and communication, culture and information; Namibia—marine fisheries and resources; Swaziland—human resources development; Tanzania—trade and industry; Zambia—mining; Zimbabwe—food security. When South Africa became the eleventh member in August 1994, it was given responsibility for finance and investment. The sector for tourism was allocated to Mauritius after the island nation it joined the Southern African Development Community in August 1995.

West African Development Bank (WADB)
[A.k.a. Banque Ouest-Africaine de Developpement or BOAD]
68 Avenue de la Liberation
BP 1172 Lome
Togo
Tel: [228] 21 59 06, 21 42 44
Fax: [228] 21 52 67, 21 72 69

Established on 14 November 1973, as a financial institution of WAEMU, the WADB promotes regional economic development and integration among its 8 regional members: Benin, Burkina Faso, Cote d'Ivoire, Guinea-Bissau, Mali, Niger, Senegal, and Togo. Also represented are 5 international/nonregional members: African Development Bank, Belgium, European Investment Bank, France, and Germany.

West African Economic and Monetary Union (WAEMU)
[A.k.a. Union Economique et Monetaire Ouest Africaine or UEMOA]
01 BP 543
Ouadgadougou
Burkina Faso
Tel: [226] 31 88 73

Established on 1 August 1994, to increase the competitiveness of its 8 members' economic markets. The West African Economic and Monetary Union (WAEMU) promotes closer cooperation between West African

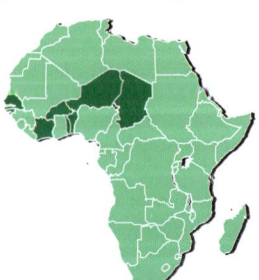

states, the establishment of a common market and coordination of monetary policies. Tariff reduction is high on the priority list. Members are: Benin, Burkina Faso, Côte d'Ivoire, Guinea Bissau, Mali, Niger, Senegal and Togo. A secretariat is planned at Bamako in Mali.

CHAPTER 3

TRADE AND INVESTMENT

AFRICA RELIES HEAVILY ON THE EXPORT OF PETROLEUM AND OTHER NATURAL RESOURCES SUCH AS GOLD, DIAMONDS AND OTHER STRATEGICALLY IMPORTANT MINERALS, INCLUDING CHROME, PLATINUM AND MANGANESE. THE TREND IS, HOWEVER, TOWARDS DIVERSIFICATION AND EXPECTATIONS ARE THAT AFRICA WILL INCREASINGLY BECOME A SOURCE FOR MANUFACTURED GOODS. PRIVATIZATION OF LARGE STATE-OWNED TELECOMMUNICATIONS, MANUFACTURING AND TRANSPORT FACILITIES CONTINUES TO LURE SIZEABLE INVESTMENTS FROM ABROAD.

TRADE

OVER THE PAST TEN YEARS AFRICA'S SHARE OF GLOBAL EXPORTS AND IMPORTS RANGED BETWEEN 2% AND 3%. THE SHARE OF AFRICA IN WORLD MERCHANDISE EXPORTS REACHED 2.9% IN 2005 WHILE IMPORTS WERE AT 2.4%. AFRICA'S PRINCIPAL TRADING PARTNERS ARE, IN ORDER OF RANK, THE UNITED STATES, FRANCE, BRITAIN, GERMANY, JAPAN AND ITALY. IN 2004, IN 2004 AFRICA'S MERCHANDISE EXPORTS INCREASED BY ONE THIRD TO ALMOST $226 BILLION SHOWED A TRADE SURPLUS WITH IMPORTS TOTALING $199 BILLION.

While the continent still relies heavily on its rich natural resources, including gold, diamonds, petroleum and a whole range of strategic minerals, foreign firms have found that trade preferences for African-made products and a growing number of export free zones on the continent make it profitable to move factories there. Textile exports from Mauritius and automobiles and other sophisticated equipment from South Africa to the rest of the world are part of this trend.

In 2004 South Africa's merchandise trade growth was particularly buoyant on the import side while the seven major African oil exporters continued to experience a surge in their exports. Primary products accounted for three quarters of Africa's merchandise exports.

US TRADE

U.S. total trade with Sub-Saharan Africa (exports plus imports) continued to grow in 2005, as both exports and imports increased. According to the US Department of Commerce two-way trade was $60.6 billion, up 36.7% from 2004. U.S. exports to Sub-Saharan Africa rose 22.2 percent to $10.3 billion, due to increased sales of oil field equipment and parts, aircraft, vehicles, wheat, and electrical machinery (including telecommunications equipment)—the same set of products which drove U.S. exports in 2004. U.S. imports rose 40.2 percent from 2004 to $50.3 billion, in 2005 due to a large increase in imports of crude oil (mainly driven by rising demand and high oil prices) as well as smaller increases in imports of platinum, diamonds, and cocoa. Trade between

the United States and Sub-Saharan Africa is highly concentrated, with a small number of African countries accounting for an overwhelming share of the total for both imports and exports. U.S. exports to South Africa grew by 22.1%, to Nigeria by 3.9%, to Angola by 56.2%, to Kenya by 60.5%, and to Ethiopia by 45.1%. The large increases in Kenya and Ethiopia resulted from aircraft sales to both countries. U.S. imports continued to increase from all of the oil producing countries with imports from Nigeria growing by 48.9%, from Angola by 87.7%, from Gabon by 14.1%, from the Republic of Congo by 89.5%, from Equatorial Guinea by 33.5%, and from Chad by 97.6%. Imports from South Africa declined a little more than one percent, caused by declines in the imports of manganese and vehicles.

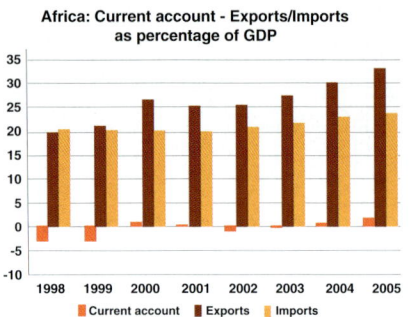

Africa: Current account - Exports/Imports as percentage of GDP

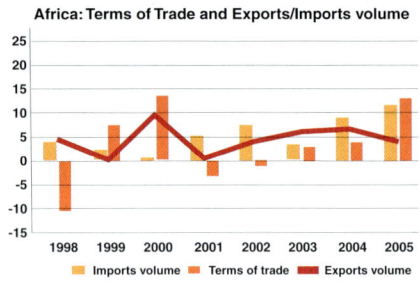

Africa: Terms of Trade and Exports/Imports volume

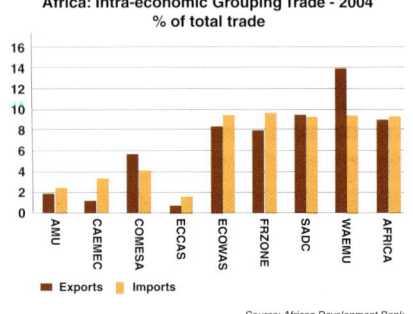

Africa: Intra-economic Grouping Trade - 2004 % of total trade

Source: African Development Bank

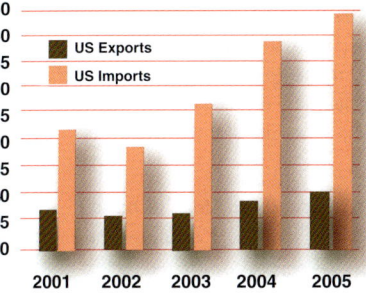

US Trade with Sub-Saharan Africa
($US billions)

- US Exports
- US Imports

2001 2002 2003 2004 2005

Source: US Department of Commerce

DEMAND

Agricultural products find a ready market in most of Africa, with Egypt, Algeria, Morocco, Nigeria, South Africa and Ghana among the biggest buyers. The market for forest products is limited. The sale of chemicals and related products averages a billion dollars per year, consisting primarily of miscellaneous organic chemicals used as feedstock, downstream specialty chemicals and pharmaceuticals, plastics in primary and semi-primary forms, and various finished chemical products such as soaps, detergents, and cosmetics and toiletries. Imports of chemicals and related products from Africa consist largely of miscellaneous organic and inorganic chemicals. In recent times the strongest growth in exports to Africa was in electronic products as improvement of telecommunications and computer networks created an ongoing need for a whole range of sophisticated equipment. There is also a growing demand for transportation equipment, consisting of construction and mining equipment, general aviation aircraft, motor vehicles, and automotive parts. With the emphasis on infrastructure development there will be an increasing demand for construction equipment.

AFRICAN MERCHANDISE TRADE

	2003		2004	
	Exports US$m	Imports US$m	Exports US$m	Imports US$m
Algeria	14,105	12,916	32,297	18,199
Angola	10,330	4,136	13,550	4,970
Benin	541	757	671	881
Botswana	2,480	2,085	2,778	2,300
Burkina Faso	326	940	445	1,070
Burundi	38	157	47	176
Cameroon	2,840	2,020	3,200	2,235
Cape Verde	14	344	112	346
Central African Republic	140	105	151	120
Chad	387	1,283	1,548	1,180
Comoros	13	105	14	116
Congo, Dem. Rep. of	1,281	1,404	1,413	1,873
Congo, Republic of	2,645	1,110	3,115	1,450
Côte d'Ivoire	5,844	3,3206	6,546	3,784
Djibouti	37	238	41	274
Egypt	6,311	11,139	7,530	12,606
Equatorial Guinea	2,095	874	2,908	847
Eritrea	57	750	50	1,052
Ethiopia	504	2,685	593	3,750
Gabon	2,998	834	3,970	1,112
Gambia, The	13	190	20	235
Ghana	1,945	3,225	2,200	4,030
Guinea	609	757	631	765
Guinea-Bissau	69	69	81	86
Kenya	2,411	3,725	2,641	4,418
Lesotho	480	1,113	595	1,280
Liberia	300	580	220	600
Libya	14,344	6,292	20,200	7,504
Madagascar	856	1,109	931	1,065
Malawi	459	702	452	791
Mali	929	1,130	1,123	1,300
Mauritania	306	387	315	420
Mauritius	1,898	2,363	2,004	2,778
Morocco	8,771	14,230	9,660	17,620
Mozambique	880	1,228	925	1,400
Namibia	1,260	1,428	1,507	1,640
Niger	339	490	371	525
Nigeria	24,047	14,873	31,147	14,164
Rwanda	58	245	98	284
São Tomé and Principe	7	42	9	47
Senegal	1,312	2,270	1,530	2,630
Seychelles	277	429	286	467
Sierra Leone	92	303	139	286
Somalia	223	517	225	700
South Africa	36,481	41,083	46,029	47,794
Sudan	2,542	2,898	3,778	4,100
Swaziland	1,030	1,030	1,140	1,100
Tanzania	1,218	12,189	1338	2,500
Togo	616	844	771	1,024
Tunisia	8,027	10,910	9,685	12,738
Uganda	562	1,251	639	1,657
Zambia	1,044	11,460	1,180	1,780
Zimbabwe	2,450	2,835	2,800	3,220
AFRICA	**168,841**	**219,285**	**225,649**	**199,289**

Source: UNCTAD

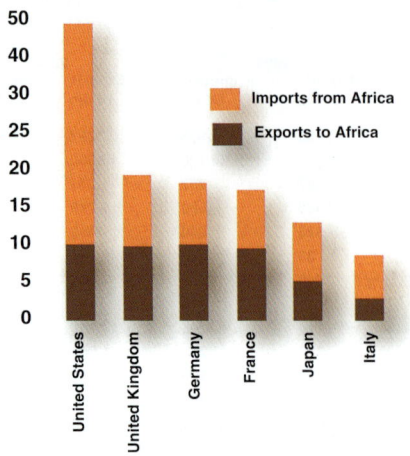

Africa's Principal Trading Partners - 2004

Imports from Africa

Exports to Africa

TARIFFS

High tariffs and duties on imports aimed at protecting domestic industry, corrupt practices, inadequate transport and marketing facilities, relatively small markets and low consumer bases have hampered trade in some parts of the continent. Lack of infrastructure has left valuable mineral and other natural resources untouched in countries that are in great need of additional revenues. Fifteen countries are landlocked, paying a premium on transport.

REFORMS

Duty reduction and other reforms, a move towards greater transparency, the creation of free trade zones and the formation of regional trade groupings have addressed some of these concerns. Infrastructural projects including road, rail and pipeline construction, airport improvement and the expansion of air links and telecommunications, widening use of radio and television and the Internet, and the refurbishing of harbors and expansion of shipping links should place Africa closer to the trading lanes of the world.

LIBERALIZATION

Until 1990, when reforms started, much of Africa was closed to trade except in minerals, oil and other natural resource exports. In the past decade, however, Africa has become part of the process of globalization, offering ample opportunity for both exporters of products ranging from consumer goods to high technology equipment and importers not only of minerals, oil and raw ma-

terials, but food, textiles and other manufactures. A variety of tax incentives and lowered tariffs encourage both trade and investment. Export Processing Zones (EPZs) have become a convenient springboard for foreign manufacturers taking advantage of special trade quotas and privileges for African goods in other parts of the world.

REGIONAL MARKETS

The growing tendency in Africa to bolster markets by combining individual countries into regional groupings has been a boon to foreign exporters in recent years. By lowering or eliminating tariffs among the member states, these economic groupings facilitate crossborder marketing and distribution to an extended market. The Southern African Development Community (SADC), the Common Market for Eastern and Southern Africa (COMESA), and the Economic Community of West African States (ECOWAS) are all in the process of becoming common markets. Intra-Africa trade is largely boosted by these regional entities.

AGOA

The US African Growth and Opportunity Act (AGOA), introduced in 2000 and renewed in 2004, has served to boost trade with Africa. This nonreciprocal preference allowance for exporters from selected African countries has shown encouraging results in the past five years. In 2003, US imports from 37 eligible African countries rose by 43 per cent to nearly $25 billion. Although 70 per cent of these imports came from five oil-exporting countries (Nigeria, Angola, Gabon, Congo and Cameroon), substantial increases were also reported for imports from nations such as Kenya, Lesotho and Swaziland.

African % of world merchandise trade

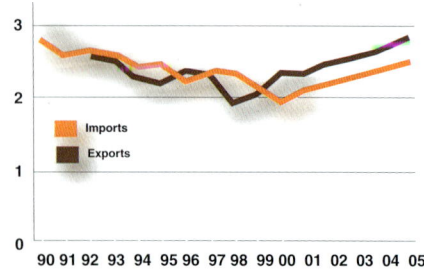

Imports

Exports

DIRECT INVESTMENT

FROM THE SEVENTIES TO THE EIGHT-IES THE YEARLY FOREIGN DIRECT INVEST-MENT (FDI) INFLOWS TO AFRICA DOUBLED TO $2.2 BILLION. DURING THE NINETIES IT INCREASED SIGNIFICANTLY AND IN A SINGLE YEAR FROM 2004 TO 2005 IT SHOT UP FROM $17 BILLION TO AN UNPREC-EDENTED $31 BILLION. NONETHELESS, THE REGION'S SHARE IN GLOBAL FDI CONTINUED TO BE LOW, AT JUST OVER 3%. SOUTH AFRICA WAS THE LEADING RECIPI-ENT, WITH ABOUT 21% ($6.4 BILLION) OF THE REGION'S TOTAL INFLOWS, MAINLY AS A RESULT OF THE ACQUISITION OF ABSA (SOUTH AFRICA) BY BARCLAYS BANK (UNITED KINGDOM). EGYPT WAS THE SECOND LARGEST RECIPIENT, FOLLOWED BY NIGERIA. WITH A FEW EXCEPTIONS SUCH AS SUDAN, AFRICA'S 34 LEAST DE-VELOPED COUNTRIES (LDCS) ATTRACTED VERY LITTLE FDI. IN 2005 THE LEADING SOURCES OF FOREIGN CAPITAL WERE THE US AND THE UK, ALONG WITH FRANCE AND GERMANY. HOWEVER, IN 2006 CHINA EMERGED AS A SERIOUS CONTENDER. FDI FLOWS TO AFRICA IN 2005 WENT MAINLY INTO NATURAL RESOURCES, ESPECIALLY OIL, ALTHOUGH SERVICES ALSO FIGURED PROMINENTLY.

UNCTAD's *World Investment Report 2006* lists Algeria, Egypt, Equatorial Guinea, Libya, Mauritania, Nigeria and Sudan as countries that benefited largely from an increase of foreign exploration activities spurred on by high prices and strong demand for petroleum. TNCs from the United States and the EU continued to dominate the industry, but a number of developing coun-try TNCs, such as CNOOC from China, Petronas from Malaysia and ONGC Videsh from India, are increasing their share in Africa. Total FDI into six African oil-producing countries—Algeria, Chad, Egypt, Equatorial Guinea, Nigeria and Sudan —amounted to $15 billion, representing about 48% of inflows into the region in 2005. Although outward FDI from Africa declined in 2005, several African TNCs deepened their internationalization, in part through cross-border M&As.

HISTORIC GROWTH

Total FDI inflows into Africa surged to reach $31 billion in 2005. According to UNCTAD this represented a historic growth rate of 78%—con-siderably higher than the global FDI growth rate of 29% and that of developing economies as a whole. Nonetheless, Africa's share in global FDI was much lower than it used to be in the 1970s and early 1980s. UNCTAD ascribes the decline in Africa's share in global FDI over the past two decades to slow progress in increasing production capacity and diversification, or creating larger regional markets. Africa's per capita inflows were only $34 in 2005, compared with $64 for developing economies as a whole.

FDI in Africa has traditionally been geo-graphically and industrially concentrated, and 2005 was no exception. Five countries—South

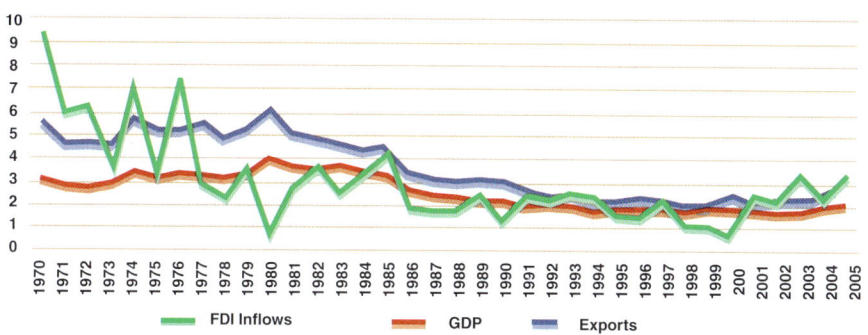

Africa's share in world FDI inflows, GDP and world exports, 1970-2005 (Per cent)

FDI Inflows   GDP   Exports

Source: UNCTAD, FDI/TNC database (www.unctad.org/fdistatistics)

67

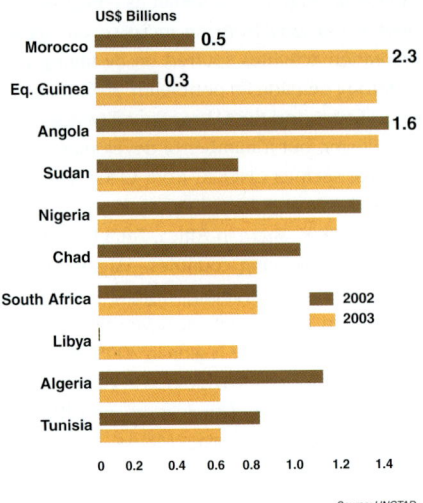

FDI Inflows in Africa: Top Ten Countries 2003

US$ Billions

- Morocco **0.5** / **2.3**
- Eq. Guinea **0.3**
- Angola **1.6**
- Sudan
- Nigeria
- Chad
- South Africa — 2002 / 2003
- Libya
- Algeria
- Tunisia

0 0.2 0.4 0.6 0.8 1.0 1.2 1.4

Source: UNCTAD

are still considerably less than those from more traditional sources such as the United Kingdom (with a total FDI stock of $30 billion in 2003), the United States ($19.0 billion), Germany ($5.5 billion) and France ($4.4 billion). Among developed countries, Japan, incidentally, has relatively little FDI in Africa ($2 billion).

ASSISTANCE

UNCTAD undertakes investment policy reviews in African countries and, together with International Chamber of Commerce (ICC) manages a project on investment guidelines and capacity-building. The Multilateral Investment Guarantee Agency (MIGA) carries out assessments for a number of investment promotion agencies (IPAs) and, primarily through its Promote Africa field functions, assists them in formulating effective strategies to attract FDI.

LIBERALIZATION

African countries continue to liberalize their investment environments. In 2005, UNCTAD approved of 42 of the 53 new regulations introduced as favorable to foreign direct investment, while it considered 11 as less favorable. The trend towards privatization continued across Africa. Algeria, Angola, Comoros, Congo, Côte d'Ivoire, Kenya, Libya, Mauritius, Morocco, Nigeria, Sierra Leone and Tunisia either privatized specific sectors or introduced plans to enhance cross-sectoral liberalization. The industries affected included utilities, telecommunications and tourism. Much of this privatization is related to infrastructure.

Africa, Egypt, Nigeria, Morocco and Sudan—in descending order of value of FDI, accounted for 66% of the region's inflows.

LARGEST RECIPIENTS

South Africa registered the largest inflows, with a sharp increase to $6.4 billion from only $0.8 billion in 2004, or about 21% of the region's total. This was the result of the acquisition of Amalgamated Bank of South Africa (ABSA) by Barclays Bank (United Kingdom) for $5 billion. Among the other leading recipients in 2005 were Chad, Equatorial Guinea and Sudan, along with Algeria, the Democratic Republic of the Congo and Tunisia—mostly in their oil and gas sectors. FDI in South Africa and, interestingly, the Democratic Republic of the Congo, were the most diversified. It ranged from energy, machinery and mining to banking. Always a significant investor in the rest of Africa, South Africa's outward FDI dropped by 95% in 2005, to only $0.07 billion.

LARGEST INVESTORS

Driven by an increasing demand for petroleum and other raw materials, China has come to the fore as a serious player on the continent. *(See THE NEW SCRAMBLE FOR AFRICA)*. China is currently engaged in multi-billion dollar projects in Algeria, Angola, Nigeria, South Africa and Sudan. Other Asian participants are India, Malaysia, Pakistan, and Taiwan. As of now, however, Asian investments in Africa

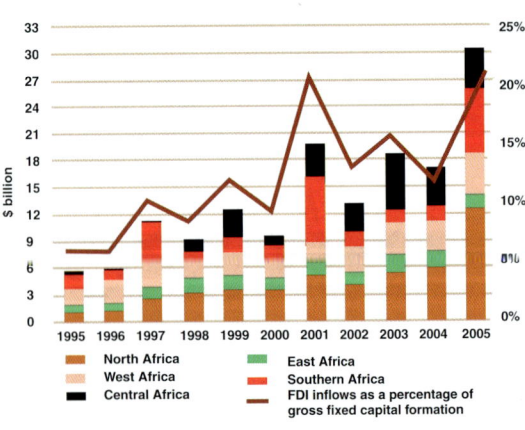

FDI inflows and their share in gross fixed capital formation - 1995-2005

North Africa · West Africa · Central Africa · East Africa · Southern Africa · FDI inflows as a percentage of gross fixed capital formation

Source: UNCTAD, FDI/TNC database (www.unctad.org/fdistatistics)

© *Business Books International*

INDIRECT INVESTMENT

IN RECENT YEARS A NUMBER OF NEW EXCHANGES HAVE SPRUNG UP IN AFRICA TO JOIN WELL ESTABLISHED BOURSES IN SOUTH AFRICA, EGYPT AND ZIMBABWE. THE CAIRO EXCHANGE WAS FOUNDED IN 1883, THE JOHANNESBURG SECURITIES EXCHANGE IN 1887 AND ZIMBABWE'S EXCHANGE IN 1896. NEWCOMERS INCLUDE BOTSWANA GHANA, KENYA, MALAWI, MAURITIUS, CÔTE D'IVOIRE, MOROCCO, NAMIBIA, NIGERIA, TANZANIA, TUNISIA, UGANDA AND ZAMBIA.

Over the past decade nine new exchanges have been created on the continent, bringing the total to 17—including one regional bourse and the South African Futures Exchange. Africa company trading volume has increased by 700 percent between 1999 and 2003. Companies listed on Africa's exchanges have grown from 1,771 in 1992 to more than 2,200 in 2003. The UNDP lists 58 capital-raising transactions between January 2001 and January 2003 on 15 exchanges—excluding the largest, the Johannesburg Securities Exchange (JSE). These transactions, comprising both initial and secondary offerings, totaled more than $3.6 billion. However, most of Africa's exchanges remain severely restricted by lack of liquidity.

ASEA

The African Stock Exchange Association (ASEA) was formed in the early nineties to provide a formal framework for co-operation between all African stock exchanges. It has concentrated its efforts on four main regions: East Africa, including Kenya, Tanzania and Uganda; Southern Africa, led by the world-ranking JSE in South Africa, and including Namibia, Botswana, Zambia and Zimbabwe; North Africa, led by the Cairo and Alexandria Exchanges; and West Africa, including Nigeria, Ghana and the Francophone countries.

REGIONAL

Apart from introducing economic reforms and seeking credit rating certification to reassure and attract investors, smaller countries have joined forces to present a more cohesive and attractive

African Stock Exchanges

AFRICAN STOCK EXCHANGES

COUNTRY	EXCHANGE	CITY	Website
BOTSWANA	Botswana Stock Exchange	GABERONE	www.bse.co.bw
WEST AFRICA	BRVM (REGIONAL)[1]	ABIDJAN	www.brvm.org
EGYPT	Cairo & Alexandria SE (CASE)	CAIRO	www.egyptse.com
GHANA	Ghana Stock Exchange	ACCRA	www.gse.com.gh
KENYA	Nairobi Stock Exchange	NAIROBI	www.nse.co.ke
MALAWI	Malawi Stock Exchange	BLANTYRE	www.mse.co.mw
MAURITIUS	Mauritius Stock Exchange	PORT LOUIS	www.semdex.com
MOROCCO	Casablanca Stock Exchange	CASABLANCA	www.casablanca-bourse.com
NAMIBIA	Namibian Stock Exchange	WINDHOEK	www.nsx.com.na
NIGERIA	Nigerian Stock Exchange	LAGOS	www.nigerianstockexchange.com
SOUTH AFRICA	JSE Securities Exchange	JOHANNESBURG	www.jse.co.za
SOUTH AFRICA	SA Futures Exchange	JOHANNESBURG	www.safex.co.za
SWAZILAND	Swaziland Stock Exchange	MBABANE	www.ssx.org.sz
TUNISIA	Tunis Stock Exchange	TUNIS	www.darstockexchange.com
UGANDA	Uganda Securities Exchange	KAMPALA	www.ugandacapitalmarkets.co.ug
ZAMBIA	Lusaka Stock Exchange	LUSAKA	www.luse.com.zm
ZIMBABWE	Zimbabwe Stock Exchange	HARARE	www.zse.co.zw

1. Bourse Régionale des Valuers Mobilières (BRVM)

equity market to outsiders. In 1998 the Abidjan Stock Exchange in Côte d'Ivoire was replaced by the first regional exchange, *Bourse Régionale des Valeurs Mobilières (BRVM)*, serving the members of the West African Economic and Monetary Union (WAEMU)—Benin, Burkina Faso, Côte d'Ivoire, Guinea Bissau, Mali, Niger, Senegal and Togo. It opened with a listing of 35 companies. There has been talk of closer cooperation between the equity markets of Ghana and Nigeria in the Economic Com-

Johannesburg Securities Exchange

munity of West African States (ECOWAS) and WAEMU. These plans are, however, hampered by a lack of common currency. The SADC Committee of Stock Exchanges was formed in January 1997 with South Africa, Namibia, Botswana, Mauritius, Swaziland, Tanzania, Malawi, Zambia and Zimbabwe as members. These exchanges have agreed to adopt the JSE Securities Exchange's (JSE) listing requirements. The ultimate aim is to have an integrated real-time network among all the exchanges in the region by 2006, each offering automated trading in a wide range of financial instruments from a single desktop workstation with settlement and central depository facilities conforming to international standards.

JSE

As Africa's premier stock market, the Johannesburg Securities Exchange (JSE) ranks with the world's major bourses in both volume and sophistication. Its open-outcry trading floor gave way to fully electronic trading. Listing requirements and the trading system are similar to those of the London Stock Exchange. New products such as derivative trading have been introduced. Over 30,000 trades now take place daily, compared with 5,000 a decade ago. Liquidity, measured by the ratio of trading volume to market capitalization, has risen from 7% to about 40%. The value of listed companies is now 4.2 trillion rand ($650 billion), making the JSE the world's 17th largest exchange, as well as Africa's biggest. In 2005 the main share-price index rose by

43%, after 22% in 2004. The JSE, which accounts for 93% of the region's market capitalization, has not only helped financial markets in South Africa but the rest of the continent. Although the South African exchange encourages dual listings, it is not trying to lure companies away from their home exchanges. In November 2005, Oando, a Nigerian energy group listed in Lagos, became the first company from another African country to be listed on the JSE as well. This foreign listing has helped boost Oando's credibility with international investors and gave it access to a deeper pool of money. With 25 foreign companies listed on the JSE at the end of 2006, it is actively seeking listings from companies beyond Africa. The JSE offers screen trading through its Johannesburg Equities Trading (JET) system. Its Share Transactions Totally Electronic (STRATE) system eliminates paper transactions by making settlement and the transfer of ownership of scrip possible through electronic book entry.

AFRICA INDEX

The launch of the FTSE/JSE Africa Index Series together with Britain's FTSE (Footsie) in

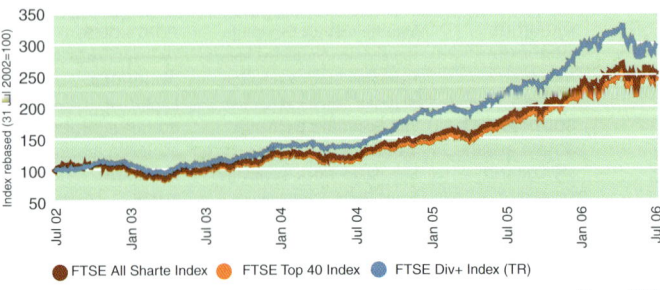

FOUR YEAR TOTAL RETURN PERFORMANCE FTSE/JSE DIVIDEND+ INDEX

Source: FTSE

2002 represented another step in the JSE's drive to provide new products and services. It came shortly after the implementation of the JSE's new trading system, JSE SETS, and its new information dissemination system, InfoWiz. This move made the JSE more transparent to investors and particularly to foreigners who are able to track the movement of the JSE's market using indices with which they are familiar. More recently the JSE launched the FTSE/JSE Dividend+ Index, a yield-weighted index designed to measure the performance of higher yielding stocks within the large and mid-cap universe of the FTSE/JSE All-Share Index. The new index selects the top 30 stocks by one-year forecast dividend yield. The constituents' weightings within the index are determined by their dividend yield as opposed to market capitalization.

CAPITAL GROWTH

Both foreign and local capital market experts are advocating better utilization of the continent's exchanges to attract overseas funds for industrial and social projects. The JSE has for many years been successful in attracting huge foreign involvement through the issuance of bonds in state and semi-government expansion projects. "The future of Africa's stock markets is the future of the poor in Africa," says the administrator of the UN Development Program (UNDP). Not only South Africa but Morocco, Egypt and Ghana have utilized their stock markets to privatize state-owned enterprises through IPOs.

RETURNS

During nineties African stock exchanges produced attractive returns, averaging around 40%. Nigeria's stock exchange rose 144%, the Côte d'Ivoire index was up 57%. Averages on the exchanges in Namibia and Zimbabwe rose more than 50%. In recent years discerning and well-informed investors continued to reap benefits that far outstripped gains at the Dow, FTSE and NASDAQ. While Africa's most sophisticated market, the Johannesburg Securities Exchange, tends to follow trends at the other world markets, lesser known African markets do buck the trend and yield surprisingly high profits. The best performer in Africa during 2005 was the Cairo and Alexandria Stock Exchange (CASE) with an average yield of 130 percent. Venturing on some of these markets is, however, only for the well-informed with ample local input and information. The Ghana Stock Exchange that topped Africa from 2000 to 2004 and attracted substantial foreign interest before it dropped to the bottom to take 16th place in 2005.

ANALYSIS

Apart from South Africa where brokerage houses maintain research teams and foreign banks have a strong presence, authoritative and reliable analysis of African investment prospects is hard to obtain. There are, however, a growing number of international and local research groups that include Africa in their studies.

TRENDS ON AFRICAN MARKETS IN 2006

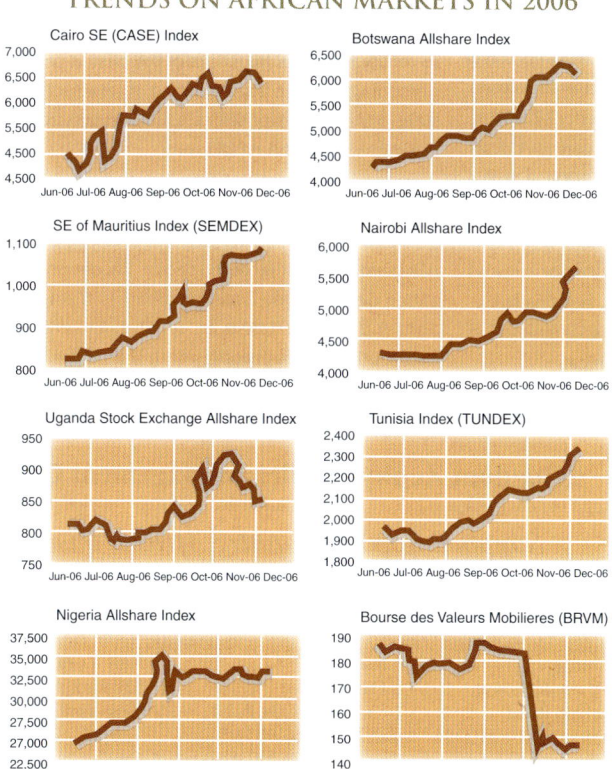

© Business Books International

71

ADRs

American Depositary Receipts (ADRs) and Global Depositary Receipts (GDRs) offer a convenient way for Americans who wish to invest in about 100 African companies listed by major US banks and institutions. All but four—Ashanti Goldfields of Ghana (now listed on the NYSE), Botswana RST Ltd., Mangura Copper Mines and Nigeria's United Bank for Africa PLC—are South African companies. An ADR is a negotiable certificate held in a US bank representing a specific number of shares of a foreign stock traded on an American stock exchange. The widespread availability of dollar-denominated price information, lower transaction costs, and timely dividend distributions, make many American investors opt for ADRs. Several South African companies—including Sappi, SA Breweries, Anglogold, Telkom, Sasol, Old Mutual and Anglo-American—are listed on the London, Frankfurt and New York Exchanges.

AFRICA FUNDS

Few of the world's more than 1300 emerging market equity funds focus on Africa. Recent political and economic and structural reforms and impressive gains from African markets have stimulated new interest among foreign investors. Kingdom Zephyr Africa Management (KZAM) is among the leaders in focusing on worthy African investment prospects. Formed in 2004 it manages Pan-African Investment Partners (PAIP) and Pan-Commonwealth African Partners (PCAP), two private equity funds that seek superior returns from investments in high growth, regionally expanding companies with proven management and established revenue streams in Africa.

PRIVATIZATION

PRIVATIZATION, WHICH FIRST GAINED ACCEPTANCE AND POPULARITY IN CONSERVATIVE BRITAIN IN THE EARLY 1980s, BECAME AN INEXTRICABLE PART OF THE ECONOMIC DEVELOPMENT PLANS OF MOST AFRICAN NATIONS. ALTHOUGH STILL A MERE MANTRA FOR SOME, MOST OF THEM ARE SET ON SELLING OFF OR LIQUIDATING STATE ASSETS IN A VARIETY OF SECTORS RANGING FROM POWER UTILITIES TO RAILROADS, TELECOMS, HOTELS AND FACTORIES. PRIVATIZATION COMES IN A VARIETY OF CONFIGURATIONS, RANGING FROM OUTRIGHT SALES TO PARTIAL MINORITY SHARE-HOLDINGS AND JOINT VENTURE OWNERSHIP.

Some African governments still seem reluctant to release control altogether, while others find it politically expedient to restructure in stages. In South Africa, where the government is committed to rectify the racial injustices of the past, a certain percentage of the shareholding in restructured state-owned enterprises is usually reserved for black investors and employees.

Favorite sectors in the privatization process are manufacturing, services and agricultural products and processing. To date the financial sector has been the least targeted sector. Recent privatization deals include water distribution in Angola; agro-industries, transport, mining, beverages, and tourism in Cameroon; more than a hundred

private firms established in the two Congos; palm oil industries in Côte d'Ivoire: electricity and water in Gabon; breweries, mines, resorts, and land in Mozambique; game reserves, breweries, tour operations, and hotels in Tanzania; retail stores, flour mills and pharmaceutical companies in Lesotho; and telecommunications, hotels, airlines, banks, and coffee marketing in Uganda.

Major multi-million dollar deals in the past include South Africa's sale of a 30 percent share in its huge telecommunications monopoly, Telkom, to US and Malaysian investors; Morocco's sale of a 30 percent stake in its state refinery, SAMIR, to Swedish investors and a 35% share in Maroc-Telecom to the French; Ghana's sale of its gold mining company, Ashanti Goldfields, through an international placement of shares; and Kenya and South Africa's partial sale of their respective national airlines.

OBJECTIVES

The **objectives** are usually one or more of the following: 1) raising revenue for the state; 2) raising investment capital for the industry or company being privatized; 3) reducing government's role in the economy; 4) promoting wider share ownership; 5) increasing efficiency; 6) introducing greater competition; and 7) exposing firms to market discipline.

SOUTH AFRICA

Privatization came to South Africa first. It started in the eighties with the highly successful sale of Sasol's assets on the Johannesburg Stock Exchange and broadened in the post-apartheid era to include state-owned iron, steel industries, toll roads, agricultural marketing, transport, broadcasting and telecommunications. The process is expected to continue despite continued fierce opposition from powerful trade union groupings. Not only South Africa but other governments in Africa frequently experience opposition from some quarters who see it simply as the transfer of state monopolies to private conglomerates, thereby enriching a small elite class at the expense of the masses. Another recurring concern

African Privatization by sector

Other 13%
Agricultural 21%
Trade 9%
Financial 4%
Services 22%
Manufacturing 31%

Sources: IMF, ADB, UNCTAD

on the part of organized labor is that it will result in job retrenchment as the private sector tries to accomplish greater efficiency and profitability with fewer people. Still the trend towards privatization continues across Africa. In 2005 Algeria, Angola, Comoros, Congo, Côte d'Ivoire, Kenya, Libya, Mauritius, Morocco, Nigeria, Sierra Leone and Tunisia either privatized specific sectors or introduced plans to enhance cross-sectoral liberalization. The industries affected included utilities, telecommunications and tourism.

METHODS

"Privatization" has been defined in a number of ways. Most observers, however, see it simply as the reduction of the role of government or increasing the role of the private sector through the sale of part or all of a state enterprise. As such "privatization" is the opposite of "nationalization," where governments take over the ownership of private enterprise, with or without payment or compensation. Other terms often found in the privatization stable are devolution, corporatization, commercialization, deregulation and restructuring of state assets. The removal of a state subsidy can also be viewed as a form of privatization. Privatization can be implemented in varying degrees. It could be comprehensive—with the private investors taking over a major portion of the state entity—or partial. Private participation comes in many forms: the purchase of a shareholding, directly or in a competitive bid, or via preemptory rights or a public offering; the purchase of assets, directly or through a competitive bid or in a liquidation procedure; through a debt/equity swap; leasing; joint venture; a management or employee buyout; management contract; or a trusteeship arrangement. It can be a combination of several of these. One innovative financing method growing in popularity in Africa involves a foreign investor who builds and operates a plant for a prescribed period, and then transfers it to the host company or country (BOOT). This has been a popular means of encouraging foreign investment in power projects. In some African countries foreign investment commitments have been restricted to a joint venture with a domestic company, especially in strategic industries. Africa has utilized most of these methods.

African Growth and Opportunity Act (AGOA)

Underpinning the African Growth and Opportunity Act (AGOA) is the belief that trade incentives and preferences are preferable to mere aid. Introduced in the House of Representatives by liberal Democrat Jim McDermott and driven forward by conservative Republican Phil Crane with the help of Democrat Charles Rangel, AGOA's adoption was a truly bipartisan affair. It was signed into law by former President Bill Clinton in 2000 and in July 2004, President George Bush signed into law the AGOA Acceleration Act of 2004 extending AGOA's authorization until 2015.

In terms of AGOA and General Sales Preferences (GSP) products from qualifying African countries in Sub-Saharan Africa are allowed into the United States duty free. In 2004, over 98 percent of US imports from AGOA beneficiary countries entered duty-free. Products are eligible for preferential access to the US market under AGOA in three ways:

Firstly, AGOA extends the GSP program (which covers 4,650 products) for beneficiary countries through September 30, 2015. AGOA also eliminates the GSP's competitive need limitation for beneficiary countries in Sub-Saharan Africa.

Secondly, AGOA grants the President the authority to provide duty-free treatment for certain goods not covered under the existing GSP program. Using his authority to expand GSP, on December 21, 2000, the President proclaimed duty-free treatment for an additional 1,835 items.

Thirdly, separate AGOA provisions grant duty-free treatment to qualifying apparel articles of beneficiary sub-Saharan African countries and to textile or apparel articles that are determined to be handloomed, handmade or folklore items, or ethnic printed fabrics.

As a result of these provisions, very few products of beneficiary countries are not eligible for duty-free treatment under AGOA.

To qualify for duty free access to the lucrative US market, Sub-Saharan countries have to show a firm commitment to economic and political reform, respect for human rights, tear down trade barriers, and strengthen property rights and the rule of law. The United States maintains an ongoing dialogue with Sub-Saharan African countries on topics related to the AGOA eligibility criteria and continues to encourage progress in those countries not yet eligible for AGOA.

Eligible nations

As of November 2006, thirty-seven of the 48 sub-Saharan African countries were eligible under AGOA. In December 2004, Burkina Faso was added to the list of eligible countries, and Côte d'Ivoire was removed. In April 2005, twenty four of these 37 nations were eligible to receive AGOA's apparel benefits as well.

US President Bush in a joint press conference at the White House with the presidents of several AGOA eligible nations. From left to right with him are Pres. Guebuza of Mozambique, Pres. Kufuor of Ghana, Pres. Mogae of Botswana, Pres. Tandja of Niger, and Pres. Pohamba of Namibia (partly obscured).

Picture: Eric Draper, White House

WTO

With the end of country quotas at the WTO, however, competition in the textile and apparel sector has sharpened worldwide. Many analysts believe that the heightened competition will force some of the marginal AGOA producers out of the market, and there are reports that factories in some African countries have already closed. There are those who insist that AGOA's tariff advantage will help some African producers to remain competitive and retain their market share in certain apparel products.

STUDY

As part of the implementation of the AGOA Acceleration Act of 2004, the US Administration has commissioned a major study to identify potentially competitive sectors in each of the 37 AGOA-eligible countries, barriers that are impeding growth in these sectors, and to provide recommendations for reducing or eliminating these barriers. The study was completed in July 2005 and presented at the AGOA Forum in Dakar, Senegal. It provides an opportunity for African and US government and private sector officials to jointly plan a future strategy for Africa's apparel sector, and promote the tripartite alliance among US and African businesses, civil society organizations, and governments that is essential for realizing the full potential of the US-Sub-Saharan African trade and economic relationship. In the post-quota environment, AGOA is expected to continue to play an important role in diversifying US.-Africa trade and supporting sub-Saharan African countries' efforts to address poverty, boost economic development, and participate more fully in the global economy.

RESULTS

Results attained under AGOA so far are encouraging. Since its inception in 2000, AGOA has helped increase our two-way trade with Africa and diversify the range of products being traded. Two-way total trade (exports plus imports) between the United States and sub-Saharan Africa increased by 37% to just over $60.6 billion in 2005. U.S. total exports to Africa rose 22 percent to $10.3 billion, with notable gains in agricultural goods, machinery, and transportation equipment. U.S. total imports (AGOA and non-AGOA) from Africa increased by 40% to $50.3 billion, largely due to an increase in oil imports. U.S. imports from sub-Saharan African countries under AGOA (including its GSP provisions) totaled $38.1 billion in 2005, up 44% over 2004, primarily due to an increase in oil imports. Non-oil AGOA trade declined by 16%, to $2.9 billion in 2005, mainly due to declines in AGOA apparel imports ($1.4 billion, down 12%), minerals and metals ($493.9 million, down 32%), and transportation equipment ($273.6 million, down 49%).These declines were due in part to increased global competition in the apparel sector, resulting in part from the end of global apparel quotas and the anticipated end of AGOA third country fabric provisions; an appreciation of key currencies such as the South African rand; decreased demand for key minerals and metals such as manganese; and production shifts in the South African automotive sector. There were also some gains in AGOA trade in 2005. Thirty-three countries exported products to the United States under AGOA in 2005. Several countries expanded their AGOA exports including Malawi, Botswana, Mozambique, Tanzania, Mali, Niger, Guinea, and Rwanda. Several non-oil sectors experienced increases, including footwear, toys, sportswear, fruits, nuts and cut flowers. Despite the overall decline in apparel exports, some countries (including Botswana, Uganda, Ethiopia, Tanzania and Mozambique) experienced increases in their apparel exports to the United States.

AGOA Beneficiary Countries

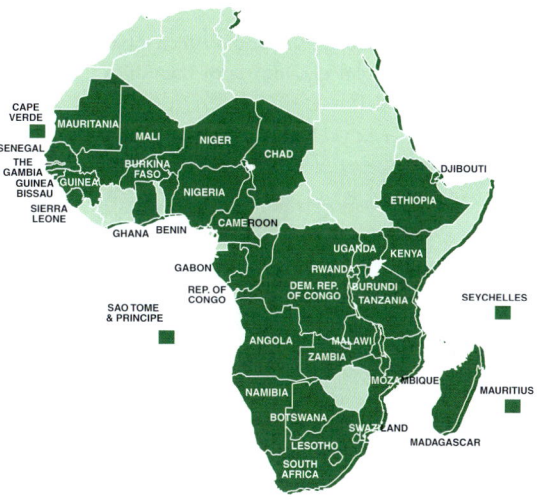

75

NEPAD

Early in the new millennium four African leaders saw the need for Africa to pull itself up by its own bootstraps instead of merely relying on foreign assistance to kick start sagging economies and reduce poverty. President Thabo Mbeki of South Africa—a strong proponent of the African Renaissance—together with Senegal's President Abdoulaye Wade, Nigerian President Olusegun Obasanjo and Algerian President Abdelaziz Bouteflika conceived an action plan called NEPAD.

NEPAD, the acronym for the New Partnership for African Development, was Formalized at the 37th Summit of the Organization of African Unity (OAU) in July 2001, It has since been adopted by the African Union (AU) as the OAU's successor.

NEPAD (www.nepad.org) is a strategy to eradicate poverty and to place African countries on a path of sustainable growth and development; to halt Africa's marginalization in the globalization process and facilitate beneficial integration into the world economy. It also plans to accelerate the empowerment of women on the continent.

SCOPE

Since its inception in 2001 NEPAD has broadened its scope to include conflict resolution and peacekeeping as well as good governance in both the public and private sector. It has also added to its expanding list of priorities human resource development and regional infrastructure and trade expansion.

From its headquarters in South Africa it has been cooperating closely with both the Africa Union and the United Nations in trying to move the continent closer to the ambitious target set under the Millennium Development Goals (MDG).

While critics point out that Africa is still well below the required 7 percent growth rate envisaged under the MDG and NEPAD plans to eradiacte extreme poverty in Africa by 2015, the 4.4 percent recorded in 2003 was a marked improvement on the previous year's 3.5 percent.

What seemed improbable only a few years ago now has become reality with NEPAD's so-called African Peer Review (APR) which allows African leaders to monitor and pressure their peers into aaccepting and implementing reforms.

GRASSROOTS

At grassroots level NEPAD has promoted the growth of e-schools to bring education to remote peoples with the help of the private sector, foundations, development agencies and civil society organizations. Broadband information and communication technology is seen as an important building block in the process of pulling up Africa's poor—at latest count still more than half languishing at less than a dollar a day.

Despite notable accomplishments on both a macro and micro level since it started, NEPAD still has to prove that it is not just another acronym for the archives. In April 2005 senior NEPAD secretariat official David Nalo lamented that those living in rural parts of the continent still did not know what it does. "We cannot say we are moving ahead when the people do not know what we are doing."

FOUNDING FATHERS

South African Pres. Mbeki   Algerian Pres. Bouteflika   Nigerian Pres. Obasanjo   Senegalese Pres.

CHAPTER 4

KEY SECTORS IN AFRICA

IN THE PAST COFFEE, COCOA AND COTTON AND A WHOLE RANGE OF OTHER CASH CROPS FROM THE CONTINENT HAVE MADE MILLIONAIRES OUT OF FOREIGN INVESTORS AND TRADERS. THEN CAME GOLD AND DIAMONDS AND A SLEW OF HIGH PRICED STRATEGIC MINERALS. THIS WAS FOLLOWED BY MAJOR OIL DISCOVERIES. IN RECENT TIMES RESTRUCTURING AND REFORM HAVE OPENED UP LUCRATIVE NEW AVENUES FOR ENTREPRENEURS IN AREAS SUCH AS TELECOMMUNICATIONS, TRANSPORT, TOURISM, HEALTH SERVICES AND BANKING.

PETROLEUM & ENERGY

AFRICA'S ABUNDANT ENERGY PRODUCTS ARE MAJOR SOURCES OF EXPORT REVENUES AND THE ENGINE FOR LOCAL DEVELOPMENT AND GROWTH IN A NUMBER OF COUNTRIES. WITH 9.5% OF THE WORLD'S PROVEN OIL RESERVES, 8.0% OF ITS NATURAL GAS RESERVES AND 5.6% OF ITS COAL SUPPLY, THE CONTINENT IS A SIGNIFICANT PLAYER IN THE FIELD OF ENERGY EXPORTS. PARTICIPATION OF MAJOR OVERSEAS FIRMS IN PARTNERSHIP WITH GOVERNMENTS AND DOMESTIC FIRMS IN THE EXPLORATION AND EXPLOITATION OF THESE ASSETS HAS HAD CONSIDERABLE SPIN-OFFS ASIDE FROM EARNING MUCH-NEEDED FOREIGN RESERVES.

The African continent produces an average of 9.8 million barrels per day (bbl/day) and is currently the third largest crude oil exporter to the United States. African countries with the largest proven crude oil reserves are Libya with 39.1 billion barrels, Nigeria with 35.3, Algeria with 12.2, Angola with 9.0 and Egypt with 3.7 billion barrels).

Nigeria is the continent's largest producer at 2.58 million bbl/day, followed by Algeria with 2.0 million, Libya with 1.7 million, Angola with 1.2 million and Egypt with 696,000. Other significant producers are Sudan with 379,000, Equatorial Guinea with 355,000, Republic of Congo with 253,000, and Gabon with 234,000 bbl/day.

Nigeria leads Africa in natural gas reserves with 184.6 trillion cubic feet (Tcf), followed by Algeria (161.7), Egypt (66.7), and Libya (52.6). Algeria accounts for about 69% of Africa's total gas production with Egypt a distant second.

Tunisia and South Africa, with substantial recent offshore finds, and Tunisia, have the potential to become significant producers in the forseeable future. Proven coal reserves of more than 48.75 billion tons in South Africa compensate in part for its lack of oil. With 5.4% of the world's total coal reserves, South Africa, accounting for 4.8% of the world's total production, has become the third largest exporter of this solid fuel. Coal is also used by South Africa to manufacture oil with a locally developed process which is now also also utilized abroad.

North Africa is the continent's most developed oil region. It contains 56% of Africa's proven reserves, has 54% of its refining capacity and represents 49% of its total production. Algeria, Libya and Egypt dominate the region's oil sector while Morocco and Tunisia are actively seeking to expand their upstream facilities.

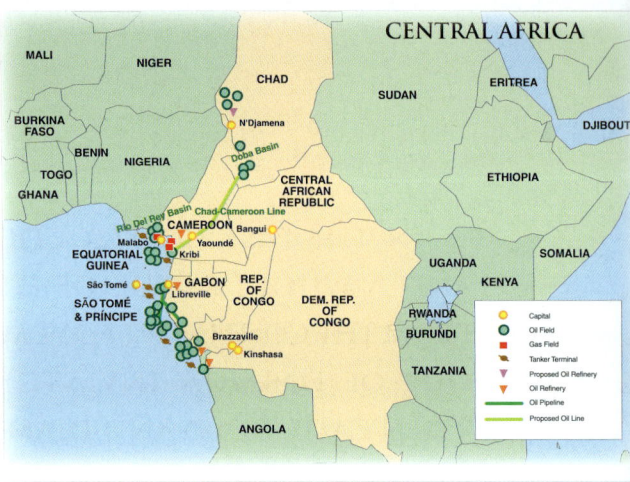

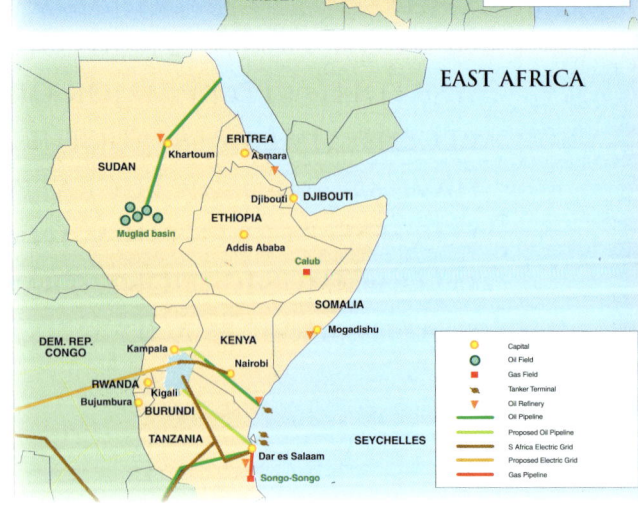

West Africa is Africa's second largest oil producing region and ranks third in terms of oil consumption. Nigeria, with more than 90 percent of West Africa's proven oil reserves, is the continent's largest oil producer. Benin produces a small amount. Togo, Gambia, Ghana, Mauritania and Senegal have granted offshore exploration rights to foreign firms. West Africa is also the second largest gas producer and consumer in Africa.

Central Africa has seen has seen crude oil production rise considerably in recent years. Largest increases were in Equatorial Guinea, the Congo and Gabon. Equatorial Guineau has become the focus of many multinationals and is referred to as Africa's Kuwait. Production from Chad's Doba Basin fields has reached 250,000 bbl/d after the completion of a pipeline to Cameroon's coast—constructed by a consortium of major oil companies. Successful exploration and production activities throughout Central Africa have encouraged several other countries in the region to issue new leases in the hope of joining the swelling ranks of oil producers in the region.

East Africa, with the exception of Sudan, has little proven oil reserves. Sudan, however, has become a significant producer and lured massive commitments from China. Kenya is the region's largest oil consumer (overall, Africa's 9th largest) and net importer. East Africa's refining capacity (5 plants) of 155,000 bbl/d represents 5.1% of Africa's total capacity.

Southern Africa's oil production is dominated by Angola while most of the refineries are situated in South Africa. As Africa's second largest oil consumer, South Africa is also the continent's largest oil importer. It manages only in part to fill its own need with synthetic oil from coal and natural gas.

MAJOR PRODUCERS

Petroleum and other energy products make a major contribution to the economies of several African nations. Algeria's oil and gas export revenues account for some 90% of its total export revenues, and more than half of total fiscal revenues. Oil export revenues account for about 98% of Libya's hard currency earnings and half its fiscal receipts. Crude oil exports generate over 90% of Nigeria's foreign exchange earnings. Recently Chad joined the list of major producers after the completion of the Chad-Cameroon pipeline. Of special significance is South Africa which has developed into a major player in the energy field despite its hitherto limited proven reserves of oil. Aside from the processing of recent impressive discoveries of offshore gas, South Africa became the first country to commercially extract oil-from-coal in with a state-run operation established in the fifties. Privatized since, Sasol is not only a significant producer of synfuels but a major producer and exporter of chemicals, polymers and plastics.

NORTH AFRICA

Legend:
- Capital
- Oil Field
- Gas Field
- Tanker Terminal
- Coal Field
- LNG Plant
- Proposed LNG Plant
- Oil Refinery
- Oil Pipeline
- Gas/Condensate Line
- Proposed Oil Line
- Proposed Gas Line

WEST AFRICA

Legend:
- Capital
- Oil Field
- Gas Field
- Tanker Terminal
- LNG Plant
- Coal Field
- Oil Refinery
- Oil Pipeline
- Gas/Condensate
- Proposed Gas

ALGERIA

A member of OPEC and an important energy source of oil for Europe, Algeria should see a sharp increase in crude oil exports over the next few years due to a rapid shift towards domestic natural gas consumption and planned increases in oil production by state-owned Sonatrach and its foreign partners. Approximately 90% of Algeria's crude oil exports go to Western Europe. Algeria's Saharan Blend oil, 45% API with 0.05% sulfur and negligible metal content, is among the best in the world. By far the largest oil field in Algeria is Hassi Messaoud, located in the center of the coun-

try, with a production of about 400,000 bbl/d of 46° API crude. Algeria opened its oil sector to foreign investment more than a decade ago. There are 25 foreign firms from 19 countries operating in Algeria including ConocoPhillips, Exxon-Mobil, Anadarko, BP, Lasmo, Burlington Resources and Occidental Petroleum Corporation. Four oil refineries are capable of meeting most domestic requirements. Algeria's 4.58 trillion cubic meters (Tcm) of proven natural gas reserves place it among the top 10 worldwide. It provides about 25% of Europe's needs. Algeria became the world's first producer of liquefied natural gas (LNG).

ANGOLA

Angola is Sub-Saharan Africa's second largest oil producer after Nigeria. It is seen as the single country with the greatest increase in production capacity over the next 10 years. Tens of billions of dollars are being invested by the majors into deepwater and ultra deepwater projects along the shores of Angola. ChevronTexaco alone will invest $4 billion in Angolan upstream projects over the next decade. Angolan exports to Asian countries have also grown rapidly in recent years. China's growing demand for Angolan crude is primarily a result of its adoption of stricter environmental standards that place a premium on lower-sulfur West African crudes. Although reserves have been located north of Luanda, most of its crude production is in the Cabinda exclave. Crude reserves are also located onshore around the city of Soyo, offshore in the Kwanza Basin north of Luanda, and offshore along the northern coast. The oil sector

accounts for almost half of GDP and four-fifths of the country's revenues. Crude oil production has increased by nearly 400% since 1980. Arrangements between the state-owned Sonangol and foreign companies are either joint ventures (JVs) with investment costs and production divided according to shareholding in the venture, or production-sharing agreements (PSAs) with the foreign partners acting as contractors, financing all investment costs, and recovering their investment when production begins. Natural gas reserves are estimated at 1.6 trillion cubic feet (Tcf). New discoveries could, however, push Angola's proven gas reserves as high as 25 Tcf. More than 85% of the gas produced in Angola is flared and the remainder is reinjected to aid in oil recovery or processed in the production of LPG. Foreign companies involved in Angola include Chevron-Texaco, ConocoPhillips, ExxonMobil, Shell and Elf Aquitane. Angola is not a member of OPEC.

CAMEROON

Despite rapidly declining reserves Cameroon is still one of sub-Saharan Africa's significant oil producers. Its refinery capacity and its role as the terminal for the 200,000 barrels-per-day export pipeline from Chad is expected to make up in part for the decline in oil reserves. In 2004 a 650 mile (1,050 km) oil pipeline from the Doba oilfields in landlocked neighboring Chad to Kribi in Cameroon was completed by a consortium including ChevronTexaco, Esso-Mobil and Malaysia's Petronas. Both Cameroon and Nigeria have laid claims to the 1,000 sq km oil-rich Bakassi Peninsula in the Gulf of Guinea. Development of several discoveries remained on hold awaiting a ruling by the

International Court of Justice (ICJ). The recent ruling in favor of Cameroon should boost its oil reserves. Cameroon's gas reserves top 3.9 Tcf. The state-owned *Société Nationale de Raffinage* (SONARA) refinery in Limbé supplies the local market. Petroleum products constitute more than half of Cameroon's exports. Until 1965, Elf Aquitaine was the sole explorer but since then ChevronTexaco, Phillips Petroleum, ExxonMobil, Shell and several others have joined in.

CHAD

In 2004 650 mile/1,070 km pipeline to Kribi in Cameroon was completed by a World bank supported consortium including CevronTexaco, EssoMobil and Petronas to transport oil from Chad's Doba fields that remained dormant for 30 years. The transportation of 200,000 barrels-per-day along this pipeline to Cameroon's Kribi port boosted Chad's revenues by between 45 and 50 percent per year.

400 km
400 miles
CHAD
SUDAN
NIGERIA
Doba
Oil
Pipeline
CENTRAL AFRICAN
REPUBLIC
CAMEROON
Kribi
Gulf of
Guinea
GABON
CONGO

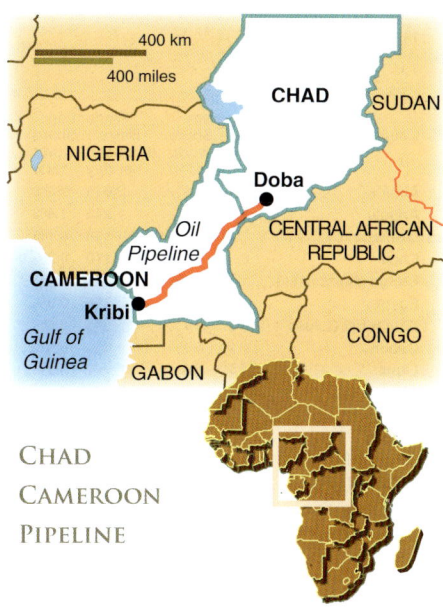

CHAD CAMEROON PIPELINE

CONGO

Most of its crude in Republic of Congo (Brazzaville) is located offshore. The official *Société Nationale des Pétroles du Congo* (SNPC) prefers production-sharing agreements (PSAs) with foreign firms to carry out exploration and development within a pre-determined time (usually three years for each phase), finance all investment costs and recover their investments when production begins. Congo gas reserves are mostly found with oil and vented or flared. TotalFinaElf operates the majority of Congo's crude oil producing fields.

oved reserves at the end of 2005

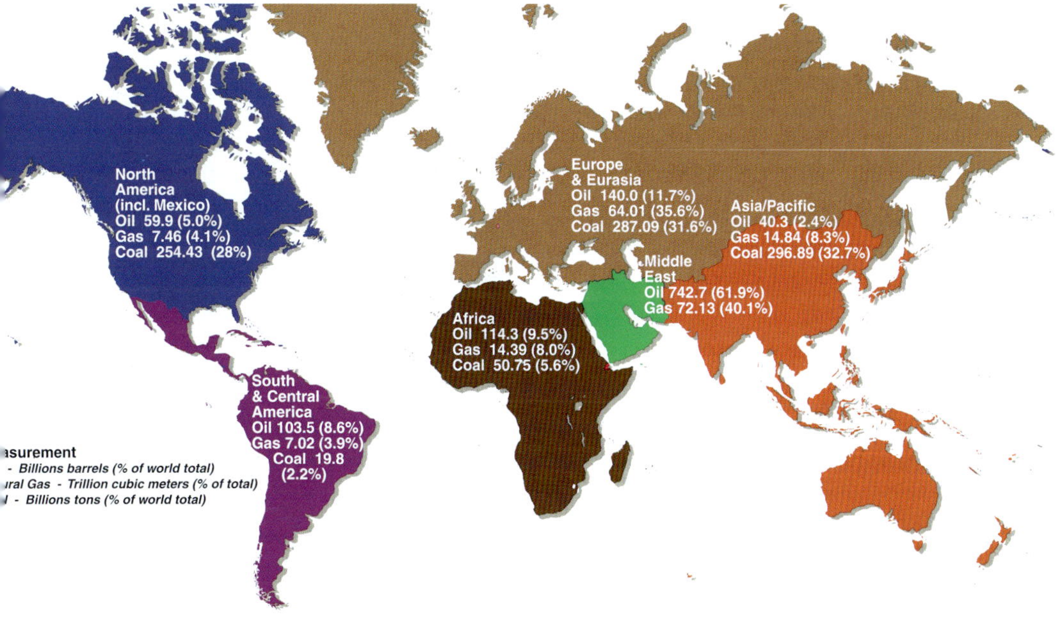

North
America
(incl. Mexico)
Oil 59.9 (5.0%)
Gas 7.46 (4.1%)
Coal 254.43 (28%)
Europe
& Eurasia
Oil 140.0 (11.7%)
Gas 64.01 (35.6%)
Coal 287.09 (31.6%)
Asia/Pacific
Oil 40.3 (2.4%)
Gas 14.84 (8.3%)
Coal 296.89 (32.7%)
Middle
East
Oil 742.7 (61.9%)
Gas 72.13 (40.1%)
Africa
Oil 114.3 (9.5%)
Gas 14.39 (8.0%)
Coal 50.75 (5.6%)
South
& Central
America
Oil 103.5 (8.6%)
Gas 7.02 (3.9%)
Coal 19.8
(2.2%)
asurement
- Billions barrels (% of world total)
ural Gas - Trillion cubic meters (% of total)
l - Billions tons (% of world total)

Map: Business Books Intl.

AFRICA'S SHARE

OIL - END 2005

Country	Reserves		Production	
	Barrels billion	Share world total	Barrels thousand per day	Share world total
Algeria	12.2	1.0%	2,015	2.2%
Angola	9.0	0.8%	1,242	1.6%
Cameroon	#	#	58	0.1%
Chad	0.9	0.1%	173	0.2%
Congo (Brazzaville)	1.8	0.1%	253	0.3%
Egypt	3.7	0.3%	696	0.9%
Equatorial Guinea	1.8	0.1%	355	0.5%
Gabon	2.2	0.2%	234	0.3%
Libya	39.1	3.3%	1,702	2.1%
Nigeria	35.9	3.0%	2,580	3.2%
Sudan	6.4	0.5%	379	0.5%
Tunisia	0.7	0.1%	74	0.1%
Other Africa	0.6	#	72	0.1%
AFRICA TOTAL	114.3	9.5%	9,835	12.0%

NATURAL GAS - END 2005

Country	Reserves		Production	
	Trillion cubic meters	Share world total	Billion cubic meters	Share world total
Algeria	4.58	2.5%	87.7	3.2%
Egypt	1.89	1.1%	34.7	1.3%
Libya	1.49	0.8%	11.7	0.4%
Nigeria	5.23	2.9%	21.8	0.8%
Other Africa	1.20	0.7%	7.0	0.3%
AFRICA TOTAL	508.1	8.0%	163.0	5.9%

COAL - END 2005

Country	Reserves		Production	
	Million tonnes	Share world total	Million tonnes	Share world total
South Africa	48,750	5.4%	138.9	4.8%
Zimbabwe	502	0.1%	2.6	0.1%
Other Africa & ME	1,503	0.1%	1.3	#
AFRICA & ME	50,755	5.6%	142.8	4.9%

Less than 0.05

Source: BP Statistical Review 2006

Also involved are ChevronTexaco and Marathon. Most of Congo's crude oil exports go to Western Europe and the United States of crude oil.

CÔTE D'IVOIRE

Recent offshore oil discoveries in the Gulf of Guinea as well as gas finds in its territorial waters, make Côte d'Ivoire a popular area for hydrocarbon exploration in Sub-Saharan Africa. This renewed interest followed almost a decade of relative inactivity. During the twenty-year period from 1970 to 1990 over 100 wells were drilled offshore Côte d'Ivoire, and several commercial oil and gas fields developed. Some of these were in production for a limited period. In recent years Houston-based Devon Energy has developed into a dominant force both in exploration and production, working in partnership in some areas with the government-owned Petroci and Shell. Other participants include TotalFina Elf and ExxonMobil.

EGYPT

Egyptian crude oil production peaked in 1996. Since then there has been a rapid rise in domestic consumption due to strong economic growth. Unless Egypt can find new reserves it is likely to become a net oil importer in the next decade. There are hopes that increased exploration activity might slow the decline in output. Currently oil is produced in four main areas: the Gulf of Suez (about 70%), the Western Desert, the Eastern Desert, and the Sinai Peninsula. A discovery in 2001 by Devon Energy in the East Zeit Gulf of Suez concession doubled reserves from that province. The company is also active in several other concession blocks. Other major foreign companies involved in gas exploration and production include British Gas, BP and Shell. Egypt also serves as a conduit for oil supplies from other Middle Eastern producers to Europe. The 200 mile Sumed pipeline carries 2.2 million barrels-per-day from the Persian Gulf

Devon Energy's platform at East Zeit field, Gulf of Suez, Egypt

region to the Mediterranean. Newly discovered natural gas reserves has led to a search for export opportunities, to compensate in part for the decline in oil exports.

EQUATORIAL GUINEA

Referred to as the "Kuwait of Africa," Equatorial Guinea overtook Gabon and the Republic of Congo and become the fourth largest oil producing country in Sub-Saharan Africa. Production from Equatorial Guinea averaged 355,000 bbl/day in 2005—a twentyfold increase since 1996. Production comes from offshore fields located offshore Bioko and the mainland enclave of Rio Muni. Equatorial Guinea's recent emergence as an important oil producer has not been without controversy. Regional relations between Equatorial Guinea, Cameroon, São Tomé & Príncipe and Nigeria have been strained over maritime border demarcation in the Gulf of Guinea. Equatorial Guinea and Nigeria have signed a treaty on joint exploration of crude oil at the Zafiro-Ekanga oilfield located at the maritime boundary between the two. The state-owned Petroguinea, created in 2000, is plays an important role in the upstream hydrocarbon sector. Among the foreign participants the Houston-based Devon Energy has been particularly prominent. Others include ExxonMobil, Marathon and Energy Africa.

GABON

Crude oil accounts for about 80% of Gabon's total export revenues, 60% of its revenues, and over 40% of its GDP. Even though Gabon's proven oil reserves have nearly doubled since 1996, its government has expressed fears about a longer-term trend of diminishing oil reserves. In an effort to boost reserves and production, Gabon's oil ministry has revised its production-sharing contracts to attract new investors. Oil exploration and production are undertaken by Shell, Elf, Kerr McGee and several others. Gabon's natural gas reserves total 1.2 trillion cubic feet.

GHANA

In the seventies discoveries were made offshore near western and central Ghana by US-based Santa Fe Energy Resources, Hunt Oil and Nuevo Energy, as well Yukong of South Korea and United Kingdom's Dana Petroleum and Seafield Resources. Significant gas reserves were considered commercially nonviable and relinquished. Ghana's estimated 16.5 million barrels of recoverable oil reserves are located in five sedimentary basins. The Ghana National Petroleum Company (GNPC)

Devon Energy operation at Zafiro field, Equatorial Guinea

produces 6,000 bbl/d. The Tema Oil Refinery (TOR) near Accra primarily processes imported Bonny Light/Brass River crude from Nigeria for domestic consumption and export. Ghana is the terminal of the West African Gas Pipeline, which will deliver natural gas from Nigeria to markets in Benin, Togo and Ghana.

LIBYA

Libya, an OPEC member, has Africa's largest proven oil reserves and is a major oil exporter to Europe of high-quality, low-sulphur crude oil. Oil export revenues, which account for about 95% of Libya's hard currency earnings, declined as a result of US and UN sanctions. Two US oil companies (Exxon and Mobil) withdrew from Libya in 1982, following a US trade embargo that began in 1981 but five others (Amarada Hess, Conoco, Grace Petroleum, Marathon, and Occidental) remained until 1986, when President Reagan ordered them to cease all activity. After the 1988 bombing of Pan Am flight 103 over Lockerbie, Scotland, by Libyan nationals, the UN Security Council also adopted mandatory sanctions. While UN sanctions were suspended after the extradition of two suspects United States sanctions remained in place until April 2004 when the Bush administration lifted most of the trade restrictions, allowing American firms to reestablish relations. Since 1968, Libya's oil industry has been run by the state-owned National Oil Corporation (NOC) together with several foreign firms, including Italy's Agip-ENI, which has been operating in the country since 1959. There are three refineries with a combined capacity nearly twice domestic oil consumption. Libya distributes refined products in Italy, Germany, Switzerland, and Egypt. Expansion of gas production is encouraged both for domestic use and export. In 1971, Libya became the second country after Algeria to export liquefied natural gas (LNG).

Oil Production
millions of barrels per day

Legend:
- Asia Pacific
- Africa
- Middle East
- Europe & Eurasia
- South & Central America
- North America

Source: BP Annual Report 2e

MOROCCO

Although it has only a small supply of natural gas, Morocco is a major transit center for Algerian gas exports across the Strait of Gibraltar to Spain via the Maghreb-Europe Gas (MEG) pipeline. Morocco has insignificant proven oil reserves. Still, most sedimentary basins offshore on the Atlantic continental shelf or in deep waters have not been explored and Morocco is actively pursuing expansion of its upstream oil and natural gas sector. Morocco produces small volumes of natural gas from the Gharb Basin in the north, and appears to have a considerable gas field at Meskala. Coal production from its one mine at Jerada is insufficient and has to be augmented with imports.

MOZAMBIQUE

South African synthetic fuels and chemicals producer Sasol purchased the Pande gas exploration and production rights and constructed a 373-mile (610-km) pipeline transporting natural gas to the Maputo Iron and Steel Project. This agreement with Mozambique's state oil firm, *Empresa Nacional Hydrocarbonetos* (ENH), gave Sasol operating control of both the onshore Pande and Temane blocks, as well as the offshore M10 and Sofala blocks. Two small power stations, utilizing gas from the Pande gas field, came online and in October 2000, Sasol signed the first of several agreements with the governments of Mozambique and South Africa outlining a timetable for the further development of the Temane and Pande fields. A gas pipeline stretching from Mozambique's southern Inhambane province to Secunda in South Africa has been completed.

NIGERIA

Nigeria, a member of OPEC, is one of the world's largest oil exporters. It is a major seller to Western Europe and the fifth largest supplier of crude oil to the US, oil accounts for nearly 50% of its GDP and 95% of the country's foreign exchange earnings. Nigeria's proven oil reserves of 35.9 billion barrels place it second in Africa after Libya. Most reserves are found along the coastal Niger River Delta. Foreign participation in offshore exploration and production activities is usually through joint ventures (JVs) while deepwater exploration is on a basis of production-sharing contracts (PSCs). In a typical PSC the operator covers all exploration and development costs and pays tax and royalties to the government once production commences. In late September 2000, Nigeria and Equatorial Guinea signed an

ChevronTexaco personnel in West Africa

agreement regarding their maritime boundaries. Nigeria has also reached agreement with São Tomé and Príncipe to jointly exploit petroleum reserves in a disputed offshore region and in February 2001, the two countries signed a shared offshore oil exploration deal, ending the dispute over their maritime border. ChevronTexaco, Phillips Petroleum, ExxonMobil, Shell, ENI/Agip (Agip) and Elf Aquitaine (Elf) have a long-standing presence in Nigeria.

SÃO TOMÉ AND PRÍNCIPE

This small island nation is poised to benefit from exploration in its part of the lucrative Gulf of Guinea basin.

SOUTH AFRICA

With the exception of meaningful offshore gas reserves at Mossel Bay and the Kudu field off the west coast, South Africa has yet to show meaningful reserves of oil. Exploration continues on South Africa's West and South coasts. The Oribi gas field 87 miles (140 km) off the Mossel Bay coast produces 25,000 bbl/d through a liquefaction process run by Mossgas. This operation and most exploration is under control of the national oil company, Petroleum Oil and Gas Corporation of SA (Pty) Limited (PetroSA). Opertaing as a non-listed commercial entity, PetroSA owns, operates and manages the South African government's commercial assets in the petroleum industry as a subsidiary of the Central Energy Fund (CEF).The first privatization in South Africa's gas distribution sector was completed in December 1999, when a consortium led by the US-based Cinergy acquired Johannesburg's Metro Gas Company. South Africa is one of the major oil refining nations in Africa with a total refining capacity (excluding synfuel) of around 500,000 bbl/d. Multinational companies (including BP, Shell, Caltex, and Total) are major participants in South Africa's downstream petroleum markets. With proven reserves of more than 49.5 billion tons, South Africa compensates for the lack of oil and gas with coal. It is the third biggest coal exporter in the world and uses substantial quantities to produce synfuel. In the fifties the government established the South African Coal, Oil and Gas Corporation Limited (Sasol) to develop the world's first and largest commercially viable oil-from-coal extraction operation. Today Sasol is a diversified private oil and chemical enterprise.

SUDAN

Sudan exports oil through a terminal in the Red Sea along a 930 mile (1,500 km) pipeline from the oil fields of the Muglad Basin. The pipeline is an undertaking of the Greater Nile Petroleum Operating Company (GNPOC), consisting of the China National Petroleum Corporation (CNPC)(40%), Petronas of Malaysia (30%), the Sudanese national firm Sudapet (5%), and Canadian-based Arakis (25%). Sudan also became an exporter of refined petroleum products following the inauguration of the Khartoum Oil Refinery in June 2000. With a production of 379,000 bbl/day Sudan has become one of Africa's significant suppliers.

TUNISIA

Tunisia has over 700 million barrels in proven oil reserves and significantly higher estimated recoverable reserves. It produces modest volumes of oil and gas—expected to increase with investment. The state-owned oil company, *Enterprises Tunisienne d'Activites Petrolieres* (ETAP) encourages foreign exploration, especially in the northern region. A Tunisian-Libyan joint venture is exploring an oilfield straddling the border between their territorial waters. Tunisia has 2.8 trillion cubic feet (Tcf) of proven natural gas reserves and British Gas engineered a $450 million expansion in the southeastern region.

ChevronTexaco offshore platform in the Gulf of Guinea

Committed to Africa

Devon Energy Corp. is one of the world's leading independent oil and natural gas producers with a solid portfolio of exploration and production assets worldwide. The Fortune 500 company is committed to innovation as it works to find new reserves needed to keep pace with the world's growing demand for energy.

Devon is a rapidly expanding company with worldwide reserves comprising more than 2 billion barrels of oil equivalent. The 35-year-old producer's solid platform of oil and natural gas reserves in North America and the Gulf of Mexico is balanced with key international operations.

Much of Devon's expansion into West Africa and Egypt was facilitated by the company's 2003 merger with Ocean Energy Corp. Several of its African subsidiaries continue to do business under the Ocean name.

Centerpiece

The centerpiece of Devon's West African oil production is the Zafiro Field in Equatorial Guinea. The company is also evaluating future development opportunities at two 2005 discoveries offshore Equatorial Guinea.

The company has additional oil output from Gabon, as well as oil and natural gas production from Cote d'Ivoire. Devon is engaged in exploration activities in Nigeria, where it is the operator of substantial lease acreage in the deepwater. It also is continuing to evaluate opportunities in Angola.

In Egypt, the company's production and exploration operations have included the Gulf of Suez and the country's western desert.

Devon's long history of strong performance as an energy producer is complimented by its solid record of safety and environmental stewardship.

If an operation cannot be done safely and in an environmentally responsible way, then Devon does not do it. Devon's philosophy is illustrated by its safety record, which is consistently among the industry's finest.

Devon's proactive approach to safety identifies risks before accidents occur. The company continuously develops safer procedures and strives to maintain injury rates below the industry average.

As a production company, Devon's success has come through the application of new ideas. The company extends that same spirit of innovation to environmental initiatives as well.

In Egypt, Devon became the first energy company to successfully establish a bioremediation program for oil-based drill cuttings. Since 2001, the company has treated about 500 cubic meters of the material by spreading it over the ground with a mixture of fertilizer and straw. The procedure allows the waste to decompose in a way that is safe for the environment.

As a multi-national company with operations that touch thousands of lives, Devon is dedicated to community involvement because healthy communities allow businesses and their employees to grow and prosper. Devon's support for education and community

Young students benefit from a Devon-sponsored school construction and renovation effort in Nigeria

Devon's natural gas production and processing operations provide jobs in Côte d'Ivoire

education as well as funding for traffic safety projects, such as construction of a crosswalk over Cairo's busiest road. Other safety initiatives have included a training program for school bus drivers in Cairo. In addition to safety initiatives,

Orphans

Devon has provided food, blankets and medicine for poor families and orphans in Cairo and the Central Nile Delta region. The company also has raised money for education, water management, health services and agricultural development.

While Devon is committed to promoting a better quality of life through support of community initiatives, its primary goal is to be a successful enterprise, promoting international investment and creating jobs and economic growth in communities where it operates.

projects is at the foundation of the company's effort to be a valued corporate citizen.

Devon's community support has coincided with the company's exploration and production programs in West Africa and Egypt. From educational projects in Nigeria to orphanage refurbishment in Cote d'Ivoire and a variety of community projects in Egypt, Devon looks for opportunities to be a good neighbor.

Scholarships

Under its scholarship program in Nigeria, Devon invests $1 million annually to provide students opportunities to study at Nigerian universities as well as higher educational institutions in the United States and Europe. Through the program, Devon sponsors students pursuing degrees in petroleum engineering, petroleum law, geology and geophysics. Also under its education program, Devon funds renovation and construction projects at primary and secondary schools in Nigeria. Since implementation of this program in 2004, Devon has refurbished four schools, providing safe, clean and modern learning facilities for 4,100 students.

In Côte d'Ivoire, Devon has funded renovations and purchased furniture, new appliances, computers and office equipment for the Bingerville orphanage. Devon employees in nearby Abidjan also volunteer time to help at the 53-year-old home for more than 200 boys. In Egypt, Devon has been a key member of the "Society for Road Safety." The program provides

Devon operates a natural gas processing plant in Lion, Côte d'Ivoire

ELECTRICITY IN AFRICA

	Supply Installed capacity Megawatts 2000-4	Consumption Electric power consumption kWh per capita 2000-4	Access to electricity		
			Total (% of total population) 2000-4	Urban access (% of urban population) 2000-4	Rural access (% of rural population) 2000-4
Algeria	6,400.0	913.5	98.0	..	..
Angola	618.0	103.5	12.0	..	..
Benin	120.6	12.2	22.0	49.6	5.5
Botswana	132.0	538.5	22.0	..	..
Burkina Faso	121.0	36.6	13.0	39.7	0.2
Burundi	43.0	18.0	5.0	45.1	0.4
Cameroon	880.0	212.2	20.0	84.6	21.0
Cape Verde	7.0	87.3	..	..	..
Central Afr. Rep.	39.9	..	5.0	8.0	0.3
Chad	29.0	10.9	3.0	9.4	0.1
Comoros	5.0	34.2		51.8	19.6
Congo, Dem. Rep.	2,515.5	109.9	6.7	..	..
Congo, Rep.	121.0	77.3	20.9	..	..
Côte d'Ivoire	915.0	219.4	38.5	85.9	22.5
Djibouti	..				
Egypt, Arab Rep.	..	1,337.4	93.8	..	..
Equatorial Guinea	12.0	45.4	..	..	..
Eritrea	..	44.4	17.0	80.6	2.1
Ethiopia	533.8	25.7	4.7	76.2	0.4
Gabon	403.3	957.3	31.0	..	..
Gambia, The	29.0	162.2	5.0	..	..
Ghana	1,227.5	334.1	50.0	82.4	20.9
Guinea	261.3	97.4	5.0	53.8	1.5
Guinea-Bissau	21.0	63.9	7.9	..	..
Kenya	1,084.3	119.7	7.9	47.5	4.3
Lesotho	75.8	173.6	5.0	..	..
Liberia	330.0	112.2	..	..	..
Libya	4,700.0	3,338.5	99.8	..	..
Madagascar	285.0	48.5	8.0	47.8	5.2
Malawi	272.5	68.8	5.0	28.7	1.0
Mali	208.5	46.7	7.6	37.0	2.2
Mauritania	114.5	65.4	50.0	49.7	2.5
Mauritius	582.6	1,487.6	100.0	..	..
Morocco	17,600.0	592.1	71.1	..	..
Mozambique	2,378.0	462.6	7.2	25.8	2.1
Namibia	..	695.4	34.0	..	..
Niger	105.0	26.7	7.9	36.5	0.2
Nigeria	5,888.0	140.2	40.0	84.3	27.9
Rwanda	34.3	19.9	5.0	38.9	0.9
São Tomé & Principe	10.1	105.9	..	..	..
Senegal	237.5	166.3	30.1	68.9	6.0
Seychelles	28.0	2,573.9	..	..	..
Sierra Leone	124.0	33.8	5.0	..	..
Somalia	79.5	24.2	..	..	..
South Africa	41,365.5	4,559.5	66.1	..	..
Sudan	727.3	71.3	30.0	..	..
Swaziland	127.5	359.0	20.0	..	..
Tanzania	847.3	67.8	10.5	27.3	1.1
Togo	35.5	9.1	9.0	41.2	2.4
Tunisia	2,900.0	1,239.6	94.6	..	..
Uganda	291.5	68.5	3.7	43.9	2.4
Zambia	1,786.0	739.4	12.0	45.1	2.9
Zimbabwe	1,942.0	532.0	39.7	87.4	8.3

Source: African Development Bank

ELECTRICITY

TOGETHER NORTH AND SOUTHERN AFRICA ACCOUNT FOR MORE THAN 80 PERCENT OF TOTAL POWER GENERATING CAPACITY ON THE CONTINENT. THE DEMOCRATIC REPUBLIC OF CONGO (CENTRAL), KENYA (EAST), AND NIGERIA (WEST) ARE LEADING IN POWER GENERATION ELSEWHERE. SOUTH AFRICA'S UTILITY, ESKOM, IS NOT ONLY AFRICA'S BIGGEST, BUT THE WORLD'S FIFTH LARGEST UTILITY BOTH IN TERMS OF ELECTRICITY SALES AND GENERATING CAPACITY. ESKOM ALSO OPERATES AFRICA'S ONLY NUCLEAR POWER GENERATION FACILITY AT KOEBERG, NEAR CAPE TOWN. SOUTH AFRICA WITH 6.6 TERAWATT HOURS (TWH) OF POWER, ZAMBIA WITH 1.2 TWH AND GHANA WITH 0.3 TWH ARE THE THREE LARGEST NET EXPORTERS OF ELECTRICITY IN AFRICA.

But globally, Africa lags far behind both in terms of production and consumption of electricity. At the end of the nineties Africa's total electricity generating capacity of 94 gigawatts represented about 3 percent of the world total. Even though commercial energy production in Africa has nearly doubled since 1970, and is expected to increase another 68% by 2020, its share of the world's total remained at around 7%. The continent's share of world commercial energy consumption is also small due to low per capita incomes, low levels of industrialization and ownership of electric appliances. Underdeveloped commercial energy resources and insufficient energy delivery systems, coupled with widespread and severe poverty, force rural populations to rely heavily on biomass. Firewood and charcoal is both the most common and the most environmentally detrimental biomass energy source. The resulting deforestation has become one of the most pressing environmental problems faced by African nations. In many countries three-quarters of the forest cover has already been depleted.

INVESTMENT

Africa's energy sector has, however, begun to light up the radar screens of international investors. Interest is growing in new construction projects and a number of privatization prospects. International agencies are helping to accelerate the privatization process. Among current major projects is the Lesotho Highlands Water Project that will provide additional power to the Witwatersrand complex around Johannesburg. Even utilities that are expected to remain state-owned have been targeted for overhaul with the help of private expertise.

OVERVIEW

In its overview, the US Energy Information Administration (EIA) summarizes electricity generation in Africa as follows:

NORTH AFRICA

A newly constructed Hamma 450-megawatt (MW) natural gas-fired facility provides power to **Algeria**'s capital city, Algiers. Nedw projects include a 1,200-MW plant near Tipasa, the 2X600-MW Terga plant near Oran Tipasa and a 2X600-MW plant near Annaba. **Egypt**'s first Build Own Operate Transfer (BOOT) power project became operational in 2002. The complex, Sidi Kerir 3 and 4, consists of two 325-MW gas-fired units which and forms the largest private power station in North Africa and the Middle East. The Egyptian Electric Authority (EEA) has entered into two additional BOOT agreements with *Electricite de France* (EDF) for 650-MW gas-fired facilities at each end of Egypt's Suez Canal at an estimated total cost of $900 million. **Morocco**'s state-owned *Office Nationale d'Electricite* (ONE) is a major investor in the country's power generation sector. Additions to generating

Johannesburg—one of Africa's largest electricity consumers

capacity include the Kouida al Baida 50-MW wind farm overlooking the Strait of Gibraltar, a 470-MW station located near Tangiers at Tahaddart, a 200-MW hydroelectric facility at Dchar el Oued, and

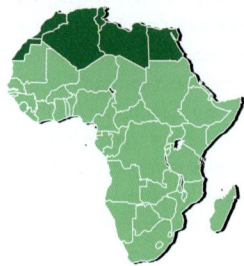

a 300-MW pumped storage hydroelectric facility near Afourar. Morocco also added two 330-MW units on a build-oper-ate-transfer (BOT) basis to the Jorf Las-far plant. Another $200-million 180-MW hybrid solar-gas power plant is to be built in the northeastern Jerada province. More than 70 percent of Morocco's total population has access to electricity. The US-based PSEG is led a consortium that developed **Tunisia**'s first privately-run generating facility. The 470-MW combined cycle gas-fired plant, Rades II, is located outside the capital of Tunis. More than 94 percent of the population has access to electricity.

CENTRAL AFRICA

A Canadian firm, Ocelot Energy, and the *Societe Nationale des Hydrocarbures* (SNH), **Cameroon**'s state-owned oil firm, cooperated in the construction of a 175-MW gas-powered facility

utilizing the Sanaga Sud field in offshore southern Camer-oon. The **Demo-cratic Republic of Congo** undertook expansion at the Inga hydroelec-tric facility on the Congo River. The combined capacity of the 2,000-MW Inga II plant and the 40,000-MW Grand Inga facility will be almost as large as all of Southern Africa's current installed capacity. EEF (Switzerland), Infra-Consult (Germany) and Medis (Belgium) have signed an agreement to re-habilitate the DRC's *Societe Nationale d'Electricite* (SNEL) electricity system, including work on generating facilities in the capital, Kinshasa, and production and distribution in the North and South Kivu provinces. In **Equatorial Guinea** the diesel plant on the island of Bioko was replaced with a 6-MW to 8-MW thermal power plant to utilize flared gas from the Alba field.

EAST AFRICA

Electricite de Djibouti (EDD) increased its generating capacity by 20 MW with the purchase of four 5-MW diesel-powered generators with assistance from the Kuwaiti Fund. EDD also con-structed an 18-MW facility in Marabout. Studies are underway to evaluate the geothermal poten-tial of **Eritrea**'s Alid region. Initial results indicated that temperature and permeability conditions were favorable for an electrical-grade geothermal resource. **Djibouti** and **Uganda** are also exploring the possibility of utilizing geothermal resources for power generation. The **Ethiopian** Electric Power Corporation (EEPC) increased the country's electric generating capacity with the upgrading of facilities on the Koka and Tis Abay rivers and the comple-tion of a 34-MW hydroelectric plant on the Fincha

river in its western region. The EEPC is also constructing hydroelectric facili-ties on Ethiopia's Gilgel-Gibe (184 MW) and Blue Nile (73 MW) rivers. A 150-MW hydro-electric facility on the Gojeb river became operational in 2003. Additional hydro-electric facilities are envisaged on the Tekeze, Tana, Beles, and Halele Werabisa rivers. **Kenya** has several independent power projects (IPPs) underway. Recently completed are coal-fired plants at Nairobi South and the 75-MW Kipevu II. **Kenya** plans to generate 25% of its electricity from geothermal energy by 2017 as the Olkaria III project enters its second phase. It already has the highest penetration rate of photovoltaic systems in the world, with over 100,000 systems in place and annual sales of 20,000. Two Chinese firms financed 75% of the Kajbar hydroelectric facility in northern **Sudan**. The $200 million project is locat-ed on the Nile and have a generating capacity of 300 MW. The 180-MW Owens Falls hydroelectric facility, located in southern **Uganda** on the Nile, was expanded to provide an additional 200 MW of generating capacity. US-based AES developed a 250-MW Bujagali Falls hydroelectric facility on the Nile at $450-$500 million. Norway's Norpak headed a consortium in the construction of the 180-MW Karuma Falls hydroelectric project in northwestern Uganda.

West Africa

US-based firms negotiated with the government of **Benin** to develop, construct and operate an 80-MW power generation facility. The proposed project includes building a 20-mile (30-km) pipeline to feed natural gas to a plant south of Porto Novo. **Côte d'Ivoire's** *Compagnie Ivoirienne de Production d'Electricite* (CIPREL) project was one of the first to be undertaken in Sub-Saharan Africa. The 210 MW gas-fired plant is a joint development of the French firms EDF and *Saur-Bouygues* (SAUR). The Cinergy consortium won a 23-year BOOT concession to build a thermal power plant at Azito outside of Abidjan, Côte d'Ivoire. Plans called for a $223-million, 420-MW gas-fired facility. Cinergy includes the Swiss-based Asea Brown Boveri (ABB), Industrial Promotion Services (IPS) and EDF. The government of **Burkina Faso** plans to provide electricity to 48 of its 350 communities in the country by 2010. **Ghana** has developed plans for an additional hydroelectric facility to be located on the Black Volta River at Bui with a generating capacity of 400 MW for exporting to Burkina Faso, Côte d'Ivoire and Mali.

A consortium of American and Japanese firms participated in the construction of a 220-MW power station in Tema, Ghana. The 75-MW Garafi hydroelectric facility was inaugurated in **Guinea** seven years ago. It is the country's largest hydroelectric facility and will supply power to Conakry. **Nigeria** developed several IPP projects. ExxonMobil, for example, generates power from a 350-MW, gas-fired facility located at Bonny in southeastern Rivers State for the state-owned National Electric Power Authority (NEPA). Nigeria also rehabilitated six generating facilities in an effort to meet the rapidly expanding need for power. Less than half of the population have access to electricity. **Senegal's** SENELEC plans to electrify over 150 rural towns bringing electricity to all villages with a population of 3,000 or more. Currently only 30 percent of the population have access to electricity.

Southern Africa

The Southern African Power Pool (SAPP) was created in the nineties by the 12 countries in the Southern African Development Community (SADC). Participating utilities include Angola's ENE, the Botswana Power Corporation (BPC), the Democratic Republic of Congo's SNEL, Lesotho Electricity Corporation (LEC), Malawi's Electricity Supply Commission (ESCOM), Mozambique's EDM, Namibia's Nampower, South Africa's Eskom, Swaziland Electricity Board (SEB), Tanzania Electric Supply Company (TANESCO),

Electricity flows into a remote village   Picture: Eskom

Eskom power station at Matimba

91

Zambia's ZESCO and Zimbabwe's ZESA. The power grids of Angola, Malawi and Tanzania are in the process of being connected. **Angola**'s generating capacity doubled with the completion of the 520-MW Capanda hydroelectric facility. Its state-owned utility, *Empresa Nacional de Electricidade* (ENE), plans to construct an oil-fired power plant in the city of Lubango. On completion the **Lesotho** Highlands Water Project, involving the construction of dams, tunnels and pipelines, will have a power generating capacity of 274 MW. The Compagnie Thermique de Belle Vue (CTBV), a joint-venture between Harel Freres (51%) of **Mauritius**, France's Cidec (27%), the Sugar Investment Trust of Mauritius (14%) and the State Investment Fund (8%), constructed a 70-MW IPP facility north of the Mauritian capital of Port Louis. The CTBV plant utilizes bagasse (biomass refuse from the processing of sugar cane) as its primary fuel. *Electricidade de Mocambique,* **Mozambique**'s state utility, and *Hidro-electrica de Cahora Bassa* (HCB)—a joint venture involving Portugal—have restored the link between the Cahora Bassa dam and **South Africa**, by replacing over 2,000 pylons that were damaged during the civil war. Cahora Bassa, with a nominal capacity of 2,000 MW, also supplies power to neighboring Zimbabwe. There are plans

for a second dam on the Zambezi River, with capacity of 2,000 to 2,500 MW. The **Zambia** Electricity Supply Corporation (ZESCO) is in the process of rehabilitating the generating facilities at Victoria Falls. ZESCO also undertook rehabilitation work on its main generation facility, the Kafue Gorge hydroelectric station. National Power of Britain, in conjunction with the **Zimbabwe** Electricity Supply Authority (ZESA), is developing a 1,400-MW coal-fired plant at Gowke North to supply one-third of Zimbabwe's electricity requirements. Since the 1920s, **South Africa's** state utility, Eskom, has developed into the world's fifth largest, supplying over 95% of the country's electricity needs and over 50% of the electricity needs of the continent. It is leading the effort to expand power generation across the continent and to implement the goals set out in the so-called New Partnership for Africa's Development (NEPAD). Eskom's 35,060 megawatts (MW) of nominal generating capacity, which is primarily coal-fired (34,532 MW), includes one nuclear power station at Koeberg (1,930 MW), two gas turbine facilities (342 MW), six conventional hydroelectric plants (600 MW), and two hydroelectric pumped-storage stations (1,400 MW). It produces adequate electricity for domestic use and exports power to Botswana, Lesotho, Mozambique, Namibia, Swaziland, and Zimbabwe but has experienced problems in serving the Cape Peninsula area in 2006 due to inadequate feed from its nuclear powered station at Koeberg. Eskom announced plans in June 2004 to bring its three mothballed power stations back into service at a cost of $1.96 billion. The company sought overseas partners to assist. South African municipalities own and operate 2,436 MW of generating capacity, and an additional 836 MW of generating capacity is privately held. In October 2004, the South African government announced that it would spend $26 billion on its power and transport sector over the next five years. South Africa's National Electricity Regulator (NER) oversees the restructuring of South Africa's electricity supply industry (ESI).

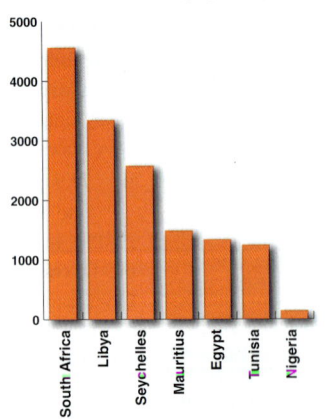

Percentage of the total population with access to electricity

(Bar chart with y-axis from 0% to 100%, categories: Mauritius, Libya, Algeria, Tunisia, Egypt, South Africa, Ghana, Nigeria, Zimbabwe)

Kilowatts usage per capita

(Bar chart with y-axis from 0 to 5000, categories: South Africa, Libya, Seychelles, Mauritius, Egypt, Tunisia, Nigeria)

© Business Books Intl.

MINERALS & MINING

AFRICA IS NOT ONLY ONE OF THE WORLD'S MAJOR SOURCES OF HYDROCARBON FUELS BUT ALSO OF HARD MINERALS. IT RANKS FIRST OR SECOND IN TERMS OF CONCENTRATION OF WORLD RESERVES OF GOLD, ANTIMONY, BAUXITE, CHROMITE, COBALT, DIAMONDS, FLUORSPAR, HAFNIUM, MANGANESE, PHOSPHATE ROCK, THE PLATINUM GROUP, TITANIUM, VANADIUM, VERMICULITE, AND ZIRCONIUM. THE CONTINENT ACCOUNTS FOR BETWEEN 1% TO 6% OF THE WORLD'S SUPPLIES OF ALUMINUM, CEMENT, COAL, COPPER, GRAPHITE, IRON ORE, LEAD, STEEL, AND ZINC; FROM 11% TO 31% OF THE TOTAL GLOBAL SUPPLIES OF BAUXITE, COBALT, GOLD, MANGANESE, PHOSPHATE, AND URANIUM; AND FROM 50% TO 57% OF THE WORLD'S CHROMIUM AND DIAMONDS.

South Africa alone accounts for 76% of the world supply of vermiculite, 62% of vanadium, 59% of its alumino–silicates, 43% of its platinum-group of metals, 26% of all zirconium minerals, and 23% of the world's titanium.

These natural resources continue to be vital to the economies of African nations as earners of foreign exchange, providers of employment and stimulants for the development of transportation, energy and other infrastructure projects. Trade in fuel and hard minerals in countries such as Algeria, Angola, Botswana, Gabon, Guinea, Libya, Namibia, Niger, Nigeria, and Zambia accounts for between 50% and 95% of their export earnings, and represents between 50% and 66% of the export earnings of South Africa, Ghana and Egypt. West and North Africa dominate in oil and gas and subequatorial Africa (especially the southern portion) leads in the production of hard minerals.

KEY SECTOR

Mining is seen as key to economic development in Africa. Mining operators, who are often pioneer foreign investors in African countries, generate substantial amounts of foreign exchange that significantly boost government revenues. Unlike other infrastructural projects, the immediate foreign exchange earnings of mines minimize currency risk, one of the main bugbears of investment in Africa.

INVESTMENT

Mining, unlike manufacturing, does not bring the same level of competition from other low-wage countries. In recent years, mining transformed the economies of several countries. Botswana's earnings from its diamond mining industry enabled it to record impressive growth rates. Foreign direct investment (FDI) in Zambia's copper mines revived a stagnant sector and the economy at large while in Zimbabwe foreign mining investment gave a shot in the arm to a sagging economy. Mozambique's economic revival was greatly accelerated by a $1 billion aluminum smelter and renewed exploration interest. FDI in Tanzania's mining sector during the turn of the millennium followed the discovery of promising gold ore bodies. Mining's contribution to these economies involves not only the mining operation itself but upstream and downstream activities. In a recent survey the US Geological Survey outlines multi-billion dollar investment plans in mining and mineral processing projects. Investment in newly committed mineral-related projects in South Africa totaled $9.37 billion in 2004. The platinum group of minerals (PGM)

Headgear at Witwatersrand mine, South Africa
© South African Tourism

93

accounted for 57% of the newly committed investment; gold, 24%; other primary minerals, 12%; and processed minerals, 7%. An additional $8.33 billion was earmarked for potential mineral-related projects (feasibility-level projects. Gold accounted for 55% of the potential mineral projects); PGM, 37%, and other primary minerals, 8%. By 2008, capital expenditures on heavy mineral sands projects are expected to be $840 million at Corridor Sands and Moma in Mozambique, $120 million at Kwale in Kenya, and $70 million at Imperri Hills in Sierra Leone. By 2009, capital expenditures for bauxite and alumina in Guinea are likely to be more than $2.35 billion; nickel in Madagascar, $2.25 billion; and coal in Mozambique, $1 billion. Substantial capital expenditures are also likely for aluminum in Mozambique and South Africa, copper in Congo (Kinshasa) and Zambia, and iron ore in Mauritania and Senegal.

REFORMS

Reforms to mining legislation have been introduced in Algeria, the Central African Republic, the Democratic Republic of Congo, Gabon, Madagascar, Mali, Mauritania, Namibia, South Africa and Tanzania to level the playing field between local and foreign investors; lighten the tax burden and reduce the government's role in mining. In most cases they serve to encourage foreign participation and greater private involvement. Unfortunately civil wars, political conflicts and refugee displacements in some mineral-rich regions have hampered the process.

SOUTH AFRICA

In South Africa—Africa's and the world's foremost mineral giant—mining still accounts for half of all exports and continues to be the single most important earner of foreign exchange. Even though the gold index has been playing second fiddle to the industrial index for some time in the weighting of the mining industry on the Johannesburg Securities Exchange it is still an important indicator of the economic health of this country. Numerous large-scale investment projects are at varying stages of design and implementation. Sectors such as coal, platinum group metals (PGM) and chrome have doubled in size in the past twenty years while iron ore production has increased by more than half. Major projects were launched in ferrochrome, zinc and other minerals and new investment in mines and smelters has grown at a rate of 5 to 7 per cent per year. A recent surge in the price of gold has not only reinvigorated the South African mining industry but encouraged its leaders to seek gold fortunes further afield in Africa.

EXPLORATION

South African companies are leading the resurgence of mining activity on the continent, frequently in partnership with foreign mining operations. Anglo American, Randgold and JCI have invested heavily in exploration. Billiton built an aluminum smelter in Mozambique and Anglo American and Gold Fields are involved in gold projects in West Africa. Both Anglo American and Anglovaal Mining have invested in copper and cobalt operations in Zambia. Today Johannesburg is the global headquarters for mining technology, specialist services and supplies. South African firms are among world's leaders in the manufacturing of mining explosives, drilling equipment and abrasives, the establishment of metallurgical processing plants, and provision of knowledge-based services to mines around the world. African countries that experienced the highest levels of exploration activity in 2004 were, in descending order based on the number of exploration sites: South Africa, Ghana, Mali, Tanzania, Burkina Faso, Congo (Kinshasa), Zambia, Namibia, and Botswana. Gold accounted for approximately 54% of these exploration projects; diamonds, 14%; PGM, 11%; and base metals, 10%.

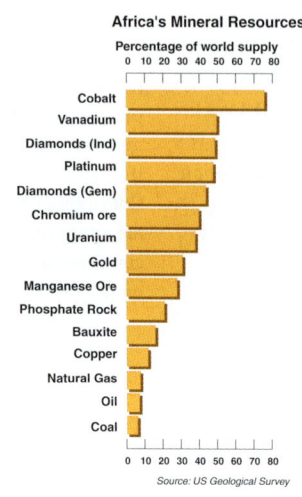

Africa's Mineral Resources
Percentage of world supply

Cobalt, Vanadium, Diamonds (Ind), Platinum, Diamonds (Gem), Chromium ore, Uranium, Gold, Manganese Ore, Phosphate Rock, Bauxite, Copper, Natural Gas, Oil, Coal

Source: US Geological Survey

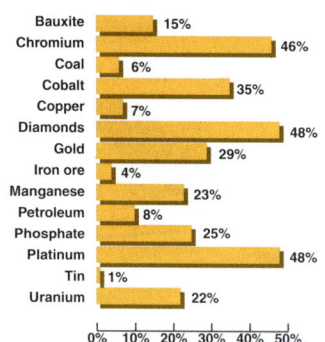

Africa's Share of World Mineral Production

Bauxite 15%
Chromium 46%
Coal 6%
Cobalt 35%
Copper 7%
Diamonds 48%
Gold 29%
Iron ore 4%
Manganese 23%
Petroleum 8%
Phosphate 25%
Platinum 48%
Tin 1%
Uranium 22%

Source: US Geological Survey

Legend:

- Asbestos
- Bauxite
- Coal
- Copper
- Copper Cobalt
- Chrome
- Diamonds
- Gold
- Graphite
- Natural Gas
- Iron
- Lead-Zinc
- Lithium
- Manganese
- Petroleum
- Phosphates
- Tin
- Tantalite
- Uranium

Priority zones for mineral development

☑ Africa is a major supplier of strategic minerals to the United States and other world markets.

☑ There has been a resurgence in mineral exploration in Africa in recent years involving major and US, Canadian and South African mining companies. For the period 2000 to 2007 more than $26 billion is earmarked for mining and mineral processing projects on the continent—including nonferrous metals investments of $9.55 billion; ferrous metals, $4.82 billion; gold, $4.55 billion; and PGM, $3.7 billion.

☑ The Multilateral Investment Guarantee Agency (MIGA) has worked with many African countries to develop more progressive mining and foreign investment laws to lure foreign capital and technology and reforms are underway in ten countries.

☑ Recent changes in the political climate made it possible to resume exploration in countries such as Mozambique and Angola.

☑ With the lifting of sanctions the mining giants of post-apartheid South Africa have been able to spread their wings over the rest of Africa, frequently in profitable partnership with other foreign entrepreneurs. South Africa has become a major player not only in mining on the rest of the continent but worldwide.

☑ Economic reforms in several African countries have widened the scope for private enterprise and led to greater efficiency and profitability in privatized former state mining enterprises. Both in Ghana and Zambia these reforms have led to greater efficiency and profitability in the mining sector.

☑ There is a high probability that much of Africa's mineral wealth still lies hidden in remote and high risk regions. As infrastructures improve and governments stabilize, these new opportunities are bound to attract mineral seekers from abroad.

AFRICAN PRODUCTION OF SELECTED MINERAL COMMODITIES 2004
(THOUSAND METRIC TONS GROSS WEIGHT UNLESS OTHERWISE SPECIFIED)

	Aluminum Bauxite	Cobalt output m.tons	Copper output cu. cnt.	Gold output kilograms	Iron & steel gross wt.	Manganese ore output Mn m. tons	Diamonds natural ,000 carats	Phos- phate rock gross wt.	Uranium U_3O_8 m. tons
Algeria	--	--	--	597	1,414	--	--	805	--
Angola	--	--	--	--	--	--	6,100	--	--
Benin	--	--	--	20	--	--	--	--	--
Botswana	--	--	29	162	--	--	31,125	--	--
Burkina Faso	--	--	--	1,125	--	--	--	2	--
Burundi	--	--	--	2,900	--	--	--	--	--
Cameroon	--	--	--	1,500	--	--	--	--	--
Cape Verde	--	--	--	--	--	--	--	--	--
C. African Rep.	--	--	--	7	--	--	350	--	--
Chad	--	--	--	150	--	--	--	--	--
Comoros	--	--	--	--	--	--	--	--	--
Congo Rep.	--	--	--	60	--	--	--	--	--
Congo D.R.	--	8,900	73	5,700	--	--	30,880	--	--
Cote d'Ivoire	--	--	--	1,219	--	--	230	--	--
Djibouti	--	--	--	--	--	--	--	--	--
Egypt	--	--	--	--	2,500	--	--	2,219	--
Eq. Guinea	--	--	--	500	--	--	--	--	--
Eritrea	--	--	--	33	--	--	--	--	--
Ethiopia	--	--	--	3,443	--	--	--	--	--
Gabon	--	--	--	70	--	--	1	--	--
Gambia, The	--	--	--	--	--	--	--	--	--
Ghana	498	--	--	63,139	--	--	905	--	--
Guinea	15,000	--	--	10,700	--	--	740	--	--
Guinea-Bissau	--	--	--	--	--	--	--	--	--
Kenya	--	--	--	1,600	1	--	--	--	--
Lesotho	--	--	--	--	--	--	4	--	--
Liberia	--	--	--	20	--	--	10	--	--
Libya	--	--	--	--	--	--	--	--	--
Madagascar	--	--	--	5	--	--	--	--	--
Malawi	--	--	--	--	--	--	--	--	--
Mali	--	--	--	37,974	--	--	--	--	--
Mauritania	--	--	--	--	11,000	--	--	--	--
Mauritius	--	--	--	--	--	--	--	--	--
Morocco	--	1,600	4	1,200	10	31,300	--	25,369	--
Mozambique	7	--	--	56	--	--	--	--	--
Namibia	--	--	11	2,205	--	14,338	2,004	--	3,583
Niger	--	--	--	684	--	--	--	--	3,870
Nigeria	--	--	--	30	--	200	--	--	--
Rwanda	--	--	--	--	--	--	--	--	--
Sao Tome & Pr.	--	--	--	--	--	--	--	--	--
Senegal	--	--	--	600	--	--	--	1,804	--
Sierra Leone	--	--	--	1,000	--	--	692	--	--
South Africa	--	280	103	340,500	39,322	37,485	14,293	2,735	888
Sudan	--	--	--	5,000	--	--	--	--	--
Swaziland	--	--	--	--	--	--	--	--	--
Tanzania	--	--	4	51,010	--	--	304	7	--
Togo	--	--	--	--	--	--	--	1,115	--
Tunisia	--	--	--	--	244	5,500	--	7,954	--
Uganda	--	--	--	178	--	--	--	--	--
Zambia	--	13,000	427	--	--	--	--	--	--
Zimbabwe	--	--	2	21,330	283	--	--	83	--
AFRICA	15,500	23,800	654	555,000	54,800	88,800	87,800	42,100	8,340
% SHARE	10.5%	44.7%	4.6%	22.8%	4.1%	2.9%	48.5%	30.1%	18.5%
WORLD	147,000	53,200	14,300	2,430,000	1,350,000	3,090,000	181,000	140,000	45,100

Source: US Geological Survey 2006

TELECOMMUNICATIONS

THE YEAR 2000 IS STILL CONSIDERED A MILESTONE IN AFRICAN TELECOMMUNICATION HISTORY. IT IS THE YEAR WHEN SUB-SAHARAN AFRICA FIRST ACHIEVED A TELEPHONE DENSITY OF ONE SUBSCRIBER PER 100 INHABITANTS. THOUGH MODEST CONSIDERING A WORLD AVERAGE AT THE TIME OF 1 IN 30 THIS WAS NEVERTHELESS AN IMPORTANT BREAKTHROUGH. SINCE THEN REMARKABLE PROGRESS HAS BEEN MADE. TODAY 16 OUT OF EVERY ONE HUNDRED AFRICANS HAVE ACCESS TO TELEPHONE SERVICES. TELEPHONE USERS HAVE INCREASED TO MORE THAN 138 MILLION IN 2005 FROM A MERE 10.8 MILLION IN 2000. THIS CAME AS NO SURPRISE TO ANALYSTS WHO HAVE BEEN TRACKING DEVELOPMENTS ON THE CONTINENT SINCE THE MID-NINETIES. TELECOMMUNICATIONS GROWTH IN AFRICA IN RECENT YEARS FAR OUTSTRIPPED ITS ECONOMIC GROWTH OF 5 PERCENT.

MILLENNIUM GOALS

The Millennium Declaration, adopted by 189 member states at the UN General Assembly in September 2000 acknowledges Information and Communication Technology (ICT) as an important tool to alleviate poverty, improve the delivery of education and health care, and make government services more accessible. It calls upon the private sector make available the benefits of new technologies, specifically information and communications. The International Telecommunications Union (ITU) was assigned to help measure progress. Three indicators were chosen to measure ICT availability in countries: total number of telephone subscribers per 100 inhabitants, personal computers per 100 inhabitants and Internet users per 100 inhabitants. The importance of ICT and the way it transforms the world, were reaffirmed by the UN's decision to hold a World Summit on the Information Society (WSIS).

PROGRESS

In 2004 alone, the African continent added almost 15 million new mobile cellular subscribers to its subscriber base—a figure equivalent to the total number of (fixed and mobile) telephone subscribers on the continent in 1996, just eight years earlier. Over the last decade, Information and Communication Technologies (ICT) have been growing at great speed, always exceeding global economic growth and changing the way people work, entertain, shop, communicate and organize their live. This growth has been driven by both demand-side factors such as the increasing popularity of mobile phones and the Internet and by supply-side factors such as regulatory reforms, falling costs, and technological innovation.

DISPARITY

There is, however, great disparity between countries and regions on the continent. The countries of the Sahel and Central Africa are lagging far behind the rest. Nations such as Niger, Eritrea and Chad have less than 2 subscribers for every 100 inhabitants, while Tunisia has a teledensity of 69 subscribers per 100, Botswana 54, South Africa 46, Morocco 43 and Egypt 32. It should be noted that small island nations (both in territory and population) such as Seychelles (97) and Mauritius (86) have less of a challenge in trying to connect everyone.

CHALLENGES

Despite impressive strides, Africa still faces great challenges. On average Africans pay much more than Americans and Europeans for both telephone services and access to the Internet.

Mobile market development in Africa
Number of countries

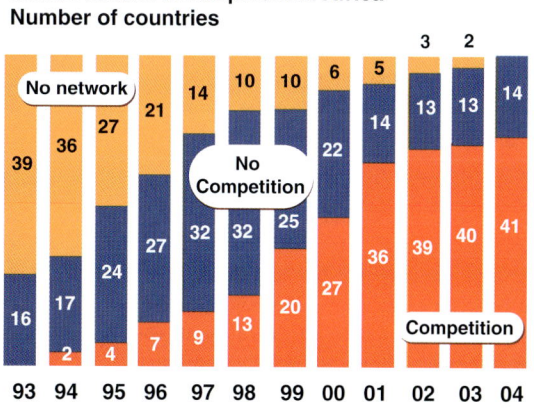

Source: ITU

International calls within Africa are often routed via Europe, adding an estimated US $600 million to the continent's annual phone bill. But most of the recent progress has not been and is unlikely in future to be in fixed lines. Sub-Saharan Africa with 10 percent of the world's population (899 million) still has less than 1 percent of its telephone lines. In fact, the continent as a whole has fewer fixed line telephones available than either New York or Tokyo. Africa's solution lies in mobile wireless services.

CELLULAR SERVICES

From 1993 until 2005 mobile cellular services have expanded from 16 countries to all 53, serving 135 million Africans—way beyond the originally estimated 100 million. By the end of 2005, cellular users represented 83 percent of the total of 138,000 subscribers. In Africa's most populous country, Nigeria, the number of mobile subscribers grew from a mere 1.6 million in 2002 to 18.5 million in 2005 while the number of mobile subscribers in South Africa almost tripled in the same period from 12 million to 34 million. South Africa—where the standard of cellphone services provided by three private entities match any worldwide— ranks 16th in the world in terms of number of users. It has become a formidable force in developments on the rest of the continent. Smart or scratch card and other PIN-based techniques have greatly enhanced usage of cellular phones on the continent.

COMPETITION

The International Telecommunications Union (ITU) points out that the majority of the countries on the African continent are allowing competition in mobile cellular networks. Growth in the number of mobile operators on the continent has been impressive. Today there are more than 100 mobile networks in operation compared to only 33 in 1995. With few exceptions these are not state-owned entities, multilateral donors or multinational giants but homegrown private telecommunication networks—often with overseas partners. With the participation of a number of foreign telecommunications companies, Africa has not only made significant progress in cellular services but also in fixed line installation and technology and trunk radio technology, very small aperture terminals (VSATs) and value-added services, including the Internet. By restructuring former monopolistic and inefficient state-owned telecommunications companies, entering into strategic partnerships with foreign entrepreneurs, and allowing others to compete, several African governments have indeed succeeded in narrowing the gap. There are a growing number of countries—including Botswana, Côte d'Ivoire, Egypt, Kenya, Ghana, Mauritius, Morocco, the

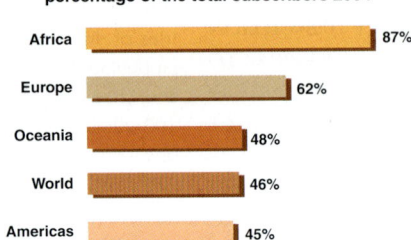

Mobile subscribers per 100 inhabitants 2004

Europe	71.4%
Oceania	62.8%
Americas	42.6%
World	27.6%
Asia	19.1%
Africa	9.1%
SS Africa	7.3%

Source: ITU

Prepaid mobile subscribers as percentage of the total subscribers 2004

Africa	87%
Europe	62%
Oceania	48%
World	46%
Americas	45%
Asia	31%

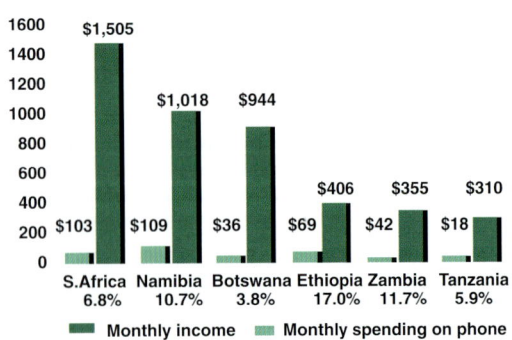

Spending on household telephones 2004 in US$

	S.Africa 6.8%	Namibia 10.7%	Botswana 3.8%	Ethiopia 17.0%	Zambia 11.7%	Tanzania 5.9%
Monthly income	$1,505	$1,018	$944	$406	$355	$310
Monthly spending on phone	$103	$109	$36	$69	$42	$18

■ Monthly income   ■ Monthly spending on phone

Source: ITU

TELECOMMUNICATIONS IN AFRICA 2005

	Population Total (M) 2005	Total number of Subscribers		Mobile Subscribers		As % of total Telephone subscribers 2005
		Total (000s) 2005	per 100 inhabitants 2005	Total 000 2005	per 100 inhabitants 2005	
Algeria	32.91	16,861.0	51.24	13,661.4	41.52	84.2
Angola	15.94	1,188.4	7.45	1'094.1	6.86	92.1
Benin	7.50	151.3	2.02	386.7	5.33	83.5
Botswana	1.76	955.1	54.11	823.1	46.63	86.2
Burkina Faso	13.23	669.6	5.06	572.2	4.33	85.5
Burundi	7.55	128.3	1.82	153.0	2.03	84.7
Cameroon	16.32	1,636.0	10.04	2,259.0	13.84	95.8
Cape Verde	0.51	153.1	30.20	81.7	16.12	53.4
Central African Rep.	4.04	70.0	1.79	60.0	1.53	85.7
Chad	9.75	136.0	1.54	210.0	2.15	94.2
Comoros	0.80	33.0	4.14	16.1	2.01	48.7
Congo	4.00	397.5	10.41	490.0	12.25	97.3
Congo (Dem. Rep.)	57.55	2,756.6	4.79	2,746.0	4.77	99.6
Côte d'Ivoire	18.15	1'518.7	9.13	2'190.0	12.06	89.5
Djibouti	0.69	45.6	6.70	34.5	5.07	75.6
Egypt	74.03	24,025.8	32.45	13,629.6	18.41	56.7
Equatorial Guinea	0.50	106.9	21.25	96.9	19.26	90.6
Eritrea	4.40	78.2	1.78	40.4	0.92	51.7
Ethiopia	77.43	532.8	0.77	410.6	0.53	40.2
Gabon	1.38	688.9	49.78	649.8	46.95	94.3
Gambia	1.52	291.5	19.21	247.5	16.31	84.9
Ghana	22.11	2,008.3	9.39	2,842.4	12.85	89.8
Guinea	8.00	137.7	1.78	189.0	2.36	87.8
Guinea-Bissau	1.34	11.8	0.92	67.0	5.01	86.4
Kenya	34.26	4,893.7	14.29	4,612.0	13.46	94.2
Lesotho	1.80	293.0	16.32	245.1	13.65	83.6
Liberia	3.28	-	...	160.0	4.87	100.0
Libya	5.85	877.0	15.86	234.8	4.15	23.8
Madagascar	18.61	571.6	3.07	504.7	2.71	88.3
Malawi	12.88	532.0	4.13	429.3	3.33	80.7
Mali	11.34	944.6	8.33	869.6	7.66	92.1
Mauritania	3.07	561.4	18.84	745.6	24.30	94.8
Mauritius	1.25	1,072.3	86.13	713.3	57.29	66.5
Morocco	31.48	13,734.0	43.63	12,392.8	39.37	90.2
Mozambique	19.79	777.7	4.10	1,220.0	6.16	94.6
Namibia	2.03	414.0	20.59	495.0	24.37	79.5
Niger	13.96	172.4	1.39	299.9	2.15	92.6
Nigeria	131.53	19,820.0	15.07	18,587.0	14.13	93.8
Rwanda	9.04	161.7	1.91	290.0	3.21	92.7
S. Tomé & Principe	0.16	11.8	7.89	12.0	7.67	63.0
Senegal	11.66	1'996.7	17.13	1,730.1	14.84	86.6
Seychelles	0.08	78.4	97.21	57.0	70.68	72.7
Sierra Leone	5.53	-	...	113.2	2.21	100.0
Somalia	8.23	600.0	7.29	500.0	6.08	83.3
South Africa	47.43	21,681.0	46.21	33,960.0	71.60	87.8
Sudan	36.23	2,077.5	6.02	1,827.9	5.04	73.2
Swaziland	1.03	235.0	22.75	200.0	19.36	85.1
Tanzania	38.33	2,090.4	5.56	1,942.0	5.16	92.9
Togo	6.14	280.6	5.61	443.6	7.22	88.3
Tunisia	10.09	6,937.7	68.79	5,680.7	56.32	81.9
Uganda	28.82	1,625.9	5.64	1,525.1	5.29	93.8
Zambia	11.67	556.1	4.84	946.6	8.11	90.9
Zimbabwe	11.90	1,027.0	8.63	699.0	5.87	68.1
AFRICA	899.82	138,605.6	15.93	135,014.5	15.03	83.2

Source: ITU

	Fixed line subscribers 2005	Mobile subscribers 2005	Mobile As % of total Telephone subscribers 2005
Algeria	2,572.0	13,661.4	84.2%
Angola	94.3	1,094.1	92.1%
Benin	76.3	386.7	83.5%
Botswana	132.0	823.1	86.2%
Burkina Faso	97.4	572.2	85.5%
Burundi	27.7	153.0	84.7%
Cameroon	99.4	2,259.0	95.8%
Cape Verde	71.4	81.7	53.4%
Ctral. African Rep.	10.0	60.0	85.7%
Chad	13.0	210.0	94.2%
Comoros	16.9	16.1	48.7%
Congo	13.8	490.0	97.3%
Congo (Dem. Rep.)	10.6	2'746.0	99.6%
Côte d'Ivoire	257.9	2,190.0	89.5%
Djibouti	11.1	34.5	75.6%
Egypt	10,396.1	13,629.6	56.7%
Equatorial Guinea	10.0	96.9	90.6%
Eritrea	37.7	40.4	51.7%
Ethiopia	610.3	410.6	40.2%
Gabon	39.1	649.8	94.3%
Gambia	44.0	247.5	84.9%
Ghana	321.5	2,842.4	89.8%
Guinea	26.2	189.0	87.8%
Guinea-Bissau	10.6	67.0	86.4%
Kenya	281.8	4,612.0	94.2%
Lesotho	48.0	245.1	83.6%
Liberia	...	160.0	100.0%
Libya	750.0	234.8	23.8%
Madagascar	66.9	504.7	88.3%
Malawi	102.7	429.3	80.7%
Mali	75.0	869.6	92.1%
Mauritania	41.0	745.6	94.8%
Mauritius	359.0	713.3	66.5%
Mayotte	...	48.1	100.0%
Morocco	1,341.2	12,392.8	90.2%
Mozambique	69.7	1,220.0	94.6%
Niger	24.0	299.9	92.6%
Nigeria	1,223.3	18,587.0	93.8%
Réunion	...	579.2	100.0%
Rwanda	23.0	290.0	92.7%
S. Tomé & Principe	7.0	12.0	63.0%
Senegal	266.6	1,730.1	86.6%
Seychelles	21.4	57.0	72.7%
Sierra Leone	...	113.2	100.0%
Somalia	100.0	500.0	83.3%
South Africa	4,729.0	33,960.0	87.8%
Sudan	670.0	1,827.9	73.2%
Swaziland	35.0	200.0	85.1%
Tanzania	148.4	1,942.0	92.9%
Togo	58.6	443.6	88.3%
Tunisia	1,257.5	5,680.7	81.9%
Uganda	100.8	1,525.1	93.8%
Zambia	94.7	946.6	90.9%
Zimbabwe	328.0	699.0	68.1%
AFRICA	27,349.9	135,014.5	83.2%

Seychelles, Sudan, Togo, Tunisia, South Africa and Uganda, where ISDN services have been introduced.

ORGANIZATIONS

International organizations involved in the coordination and promotion of telecommunications development in Africa range from the International Telecommunications Union (ITU) and the African Telecommunications Union (ATU) to the recently established African Connection Program. The ATU was created in December 1999 by the Organization of African Unity as a successor to the Pan African Telecommunications Union (PATU) to coordinate African telecommunications policy, establish a regulatory framework, and help arrange the financing of development programs. It has since transitioned into the African Union. The African Connection Program (ACP) was launched by African Ministers of Communication in October 2000 to fill the need for an African-led, regionally-focused, unified program.

REGIONAL INITIATIVES

Regional initiatives such as Pan-African Telecommunications (Panaftel)—covering some 39,000 kilometers of radio-relay systems, about 39 international telephone switches and 8,000 kilometers of submarine cable—aim at eliminating crossborder interconnection problems, such as those experienced between Kenya and Malawi; Kenya, Ethiopia and Djibouti; and Cameroon and Chad. Resulting tariff restructuring benefit major customers. The Common Market for Eastern and Southern Africa (COMESA) developed a regional telecommunications network to be built and managed by COMTEL Communications Ltd., a private company. The East African Community Digital Transmission Project involves Kenya, Uganda and Tanzania and aims at linking capital cities and major towns in the three countries by optical fiber cable. The Regional African Satellite Communications (RASCOM) project envisages the creation of a regional satellite system that will be cheaper than the existing International Telecommunications Satellite Organization circuits.

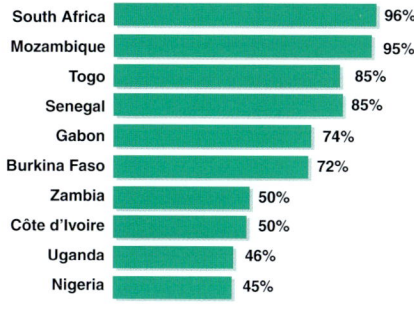

Percentage of population covered by mobile cellular signal in some African countries 2004

South Africa	96%
Mozambique	95%
Togo	85%
Senegal	85%
Gabon	74%
Burkina Faso	72%
Zambia	50%
Côte d'Ivoire	50%
Uganda	46%
Nigeria	45%

Source: ITU

PRIVATIZATION

More than 35 countries in Africa are in the process of privatizing telecommunications services. Proceeds to date top $5 billion with roll-out obligations by participating private investors totaling 3.8 million lines at a further estimated $4 to $6 billion. The rapidly-growing, largely private, cellular market already comprises about 20% of the total market. Deregulation, privatization, and regulatory reform are creating a robust telecommunications environment that stimulates demand for new services, especially on the Internet. Thirteen African countries have sold significant shareholdings in state telecommunications operations to private investors, mostly foreigners: Cape Verde, Central African Republic, Chad, Côte d'Ivoire, Equatorial Guinea, Gabon, Ghana, Guinea Bissau, Guinea, Morocco, São Tomé & Príncipe, South Africa, Sudan and Uganda. Ten countries have indicated plans to sell off part of their state telecommunications corporations to the private sector: Benin, Burundi, Cameroon, Egypt, Kenya, Mauritius, Nigeria, Senegal, Seychelles, and Tunisia. Seventeen countries licensed cellular service providers on a wholly-owned private basis or in partnership with state telecoms: Benin, Botswana, Burundi, Central African Republic, the Republic of Congo (Brazzaville), Egypt, Ghana, Madagascar, Malawi, Mauritius, Mozambique, Rwanda, South Africa, Tanzania, Uganda, Zambia, and Zimbabwe.

MEGADEALS

Until recently the single biggest privati-zation deal involving an African telecom was the purchase in 1997 of a 30% share in South Africa's Telkom by the American giant SBC and Telekom Malaysia for $1,260 million and a commitment to spend more than that amount on future expansion. In 2003 Telkom made an initial public offering on both the Johannesburg and New York Stock Exchanges to complete the privatization of the continent's largest telecom. That same year the sale of a 35% share in Morocco's Maroc-Telecom to France's Vivendi Universal for $2.3 billion topped the Telkom deal by a billion.

BUSINESS POTENTIAL

Foreign telecommunications firms are not only involved as partners in privatized former state telecoms but as independent new operators and suppliers of hardware, software, services and expertise. In many instances, the operation of cellular networks is licensed to local private operators with overseas partners. The United Nations Conference on Trade and Development (UNCTAD) cited telecommunications as one of the sectors in Africa with the greatest potential for foreigners. ITU estimates that this sector will grow by 40 percent over the next ten years.

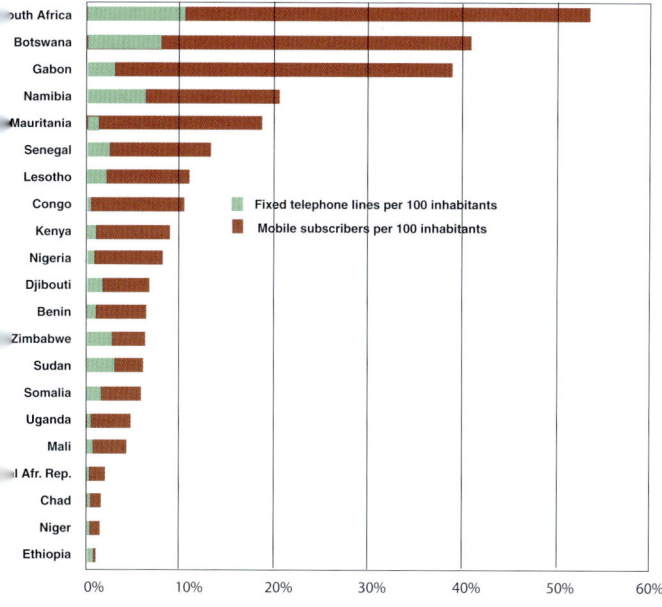

Comparison of fixed and mobile phone density in some African countries

South Africa, Botswana, Gabon, Namibia, Mauritania, Senegal, Lesotho, Congo, Kenya, Nigeria, Djibouti, Benin, Zimbabwe, Sudan, Somalia, Uganda, Mali, C. Afr. Rep., Chad, Niger, Ethiopia

Fixed telephone lines per 100 inhabitants
Mobile subscribers per 100 inhabitants

0%   10%   20%   30%   40%   50%   60%

Source: ITU

AFRICA ON THE INTERNET 2005

	INTERNET				PERS. COMPUTERS	
	Hosts Total 2005	Users per 10,000 inhabitants 2005	Users total '000 2005	Users per 100 inhabitants 2005	PCs Total '000 2005	PCs per 100 inhabitants 2005
Algeria	944	0.29	1,920.0	5.83	350	1.06
Angola	420	0.30	172.0	1.22	...	...
Benin	899	1.24	425.0	5.67	32	0.43
Botswana	2,097	11.85	60.0	3.39	80	4.52
Burkina Faso	436	0.33	64.6	0.49	31	0.24
Burundi	155	0.22	25.0	0.35	34	0.48
Cameroon	461	0.28	167.0	1.02	160	0.98
Cape Verde	228	4.88	25.0	5.35	48	10.27
Central African Rep.	12	-	9.0	0.23	11	0.28
Chad	6	-	35.0	0.40	15	0.17
Comoros	9	0.11	20.0	2.51	5	0.63
Congo	46	0.12	36.0	0.94	17	0.45
Congo (Dem. Rep.)	163	-	140.6	0.24	...	...
Côte d'Ivoire	3,801	2.25	160.0	0.95	262	1.55
Djibouti	772	11.35	9.0	1.32	21	3.09
Egypt	3,499	0.50	5,000.0	6.75	2,800	3.78
Equatorial Guinea	16	0.32	5.0	0.99	7	1.38
Eritrea	1,037	2.46	70.0	1.59	35	0.80
Ethiopia	38	-	113.0	0.16	225	0.31
Gabon	194	1.43	67.0	4.84	45	3.25
Gambia	784	5.36	49.0	3.35	23	1.57
Ghana	373	0.17	401.3	1.81	112	0.52
Guinea	385	0.49	46.0	0.59	44	0.56
Guinea-Bissau	2	-	26.0	1.99	...	...
Kenya	10,016	3.05	1,054.9	3.22	300	0.95
Lesotho	152	0.84	43.0	2.39	...	...
Liberia	17	0.05	...	...	...	...
Libya	67	0.12	205.0	3.62	...	...
Madagascar	883	0.49	90.0	0.50	91	0.50
Malawi	65	0.05	52.5	0.41	25	0.19
Mali	364	0.33	60.0	0.53	45	0.40
Mauritania	27	0.09	14.0	0.47	42	1.41
Mauritius	4,243	34.41	180.0	14.60	200	16.22
Morocco	4,118	1.38	4,600.0	14.61	740	2.35
Mozambique	7,167	3.78	138.0	0.73	112	0.59
Namibia	3,359	16.70	75.0	3.73	220	10.94
Niger	145	0.12	24.0	0.19	10	0.07
Nigeria	966	0.08	5,000.0	3.80	867	0.68
Rwanda	1,744	2.06	38.0	0.45	...	...
S. Tomé & Principe	1,025	67.01	20.0	13.07	...	...
Senegal	685	0.66	540.0	4.63	250	2.14
Seychelles	266	332.87	20.0	250.28	16	19.84
Sierra Leone	277	0.52	10.0	0.19	...	...
Somalia	1	-	90.0	1.09	50	0.63
South Africa	350,501	74.25	5,100.0	10.75	3,966	8.36
Sudan			3,000.0	7.70	3,250	8.97
Swaziland	2,642	24.40	36.0	3.32	36	3.32
Tanzania	5,908	1.57	333.0	0.89	278	0.74
Togo	81	0.16	300.0	4.88	185	3.01
Tunisia	373	0.37	953.8	9.46	568	5.63
Uganda	2,678	0.96	500.0	1.74	250	0.87
Zambia	2,342	2.04	231.0	2.01	113	0.98
Zimbabwe	8,055	6.77	1,000.0	8.40	1,200	10.08
AFRICA	424,968	4.92	32,753.7	3.72	17,450	2.24

Source: ITU

INTERNET

IN 1995, ONLY A HANDFUL OF AFRI-
CA'S COUNTRIES HAD INTERNET ACCESS.
FIVE YEARS LATER, ALL 53 NATIONS HAVE
ESTABLISHED PERMANENT CONNECTIV-
ITY AND FULL SERVICE DIALUP INTERNET
SERVICE PROVIDERS (ISPS). THE NUMBER
OF INTERNET USERS IN AFRICA HAS IN-
CREASED FROM 2.5 MILLION IN 2000 TO
NEARLY 33 MILLION IN 2006, REPRESENT-
ING A GROWTH OF MORE THAN 600%—BY
FAR THE HIGHEST IN THE WORLD. STILL,
AFRICA'S 3% OF THE WORLD'S INTERNET
USAGE AND A POPULATION PENETRA-
TION OF A MERE 3.6% COMPARED WITH A
WORLD AVERAGE OF 16.6% SHOWS THAT
IT STILL HAS A LONG WAY TO GO BEFORE
IT CAN CROSS THE DIGITAL DIVIDE.

DIGITAL DIVIDE

The full extent of this digital divide becomes
evident when Africa's Internet connectivity and
usage are compared not only with the industrialized world but other developing regions. North
America, with one third of Africa's population,
accounts for 21.5% of the world's total while Europe with roughly the same population as Africa
accounts for 35.2% of the world's total users. More
than 15 percent of Latin America's population is
connected to the Internet while Asia shows 10.3%
connected and the Middle East 10%.

DISPARITY

There is, of course, a wide disparity among the nations of Africa. In 2006
South Africa represented 15.6% of the
total number of Internet users in Africa,
followed by Egypt and Nigeria each with
15.3%, Morocco with 14%, Sudan with
8.5%, Algeria with 5.9%, Kenya with 3.2%
and Zimbabwe with 3.1%. The rankings
of percentage population connected to
the Internet show a similar disparity. Not
surprisingly, small island nations such
as Seychelles with its 23.8% Internet
penetration, Mauritius (14.1%) and São
Tomé & Principé (11.7%) feature among
the top ten. With a population ranging

from 80,000 in Seychelles to slightly more than
a million in Mauritius living on small islands the
task is much less formidable than in Sudan, Africa's
largest country (one-quarter the total size of the
USA) with a population of almost 36 million.
Nonetheless, Sudan finds itself among the top ten
with a penetration of 7.8%. In 2006 Morocco led
Africa's larger land-based nations with a 14.1%
penetration, followed by South Africa with 10.4%
and Tunisia with 9.3%. Although encouraging they
were all below the world average of 16.6%. Most
promising is the rate at which Internet connectivity
is spreading across certain parts of the continent.
Africa led the world with a 625% usage growth
between 2000 and 2006. The Middle East with
479% was second, followed by Latin America with
370%. World average usage growth during this
period was 198.1%.

IMPORTANCE

The importance to Africa of larger connectivity to the Internet has frequently been emphasized
by both its own leaders and international organizations. It goes way beyond faster and more convenient personal and business connections by email.
E-commerce, the availability of data and instant
exchanges between African and overseas government policy makers, academics, and medical and
other professionals, are vital in the promotion
of trade, investment, good governance, better
education and health services. The Small Islands
Developing States Network, or SIDSNet, enables
42 countries from Malta to Mauritius to Cuba and
the Comoros to share data on common concerns
ranging from energy options and sustainable
tourism to coastal and marine resources and bio-
diversity. PEOPLink, for example, links more than

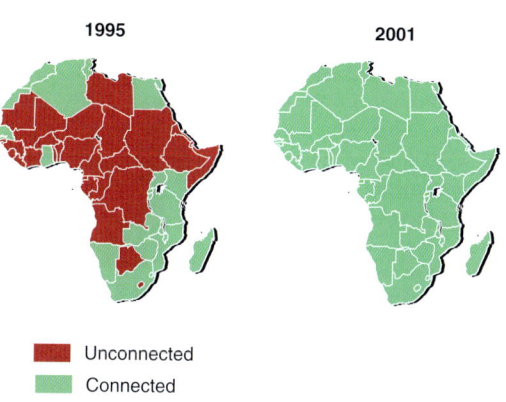

African countries with Internet connection

1995   2001

■ Unconnected
■ Connected

WORLD INTERNET USAGE AND POPULATION 2006

World Regions	Population 2006 est.	Population % of world	Internet Usage	% Population Penetration	Usage % of world	Usage Growth 2000-2006
AFRICA	915,210,926	14.1%	32,765,700	3.6%	3.0%	625.8%
ASIA	3,667,774,066	56.4%	378,593,457	10.3%	35.2%	231.2%
EUROPE	807,289,020	12.4%	311,406,751	38.6%	28.9%	479.3%
MIDDLE EAST	190,084,161	2.9%	19,028,400	10.0%	1.8%	479.3%
NORTH AMERICA	331,473,276	5.1%	231,001,921	69.7%	21.5%	113.7%
LATIN AMERICA[1]	553,908,632	8.5%	85,042,986	15.4%	7.9%	370.7%
OCEANIA/AUSTRALIA	33,956,977	0.5%	18,364,772	54.1%	1.7%	141.0%
WORLD TOTAL	6,499,697,060	100.0%	1,076,203,987	16.6%	100.0%	198.1%

1. Includes Caribbean

Source: Miniwatts Marketing Group—www.internetworldstats.com

130,000 artisans selling crafts across 14 countries in Africa, Asia and Latin America. As an example of the value of networking in the medical field, UNDP cites HealthNet which supports health care workers in more than 30 developing countries, including 22 in Africa. Using radio and telephone-based computer networks, this network provides summaries of the latest medical research, email connectivity and access to medical libraries. It was, for example, used in 1995 to share information on the outbreak of the Ebola virus. Burn surgeons in Mozambique, Tanzania and Uganda utilized the network for consultation on reconstructive surgery techniques while malaria researchers at remote regions in Ghana used it in daily communications with colleagues in London.

COST

The growth of the Internet in Africa at large has been inhibited by low incomes and the relatively steep cost of both computers and connectivity. The average cost in Africa of using a local dialup Internet account for 20 hours per month (including usage fees and local telephone time but not telephone line rental) is about $60. ISP subscriptions vary substantially between $10 and $80 a month, depending on the sophistication and level of maturity of the market.

By comparison figures recently released by the Organization for Economic Cooperation and Development (OECD), show 20 hours of Internet access per month at an average of $22, across the European Union, with Germany at the higher end with $33. All of these countries have per capita incomes at least 10 times the African average. Actually, $60 per month is more than the average African monthly salary. In his study Olof Hesselmark of Sweden points out that the nominal cost of Internet services varies from $158 per year in Mauritius to $1,000 in Uganda. The purchase value of one dollar varies a great deal between countries and the affordability of Internet services varies even more when the income level in different countries is taken into account. Uganda is poorer than Mauritius but pays more than five times as much for Internet connectivity. Calculated as the share of the average income in the countries, a Ugandan pays 77 times as much as the Mauritian. In about half the countries in Africa, one year of Internet service will cost more than the average annual income, Hesselmark found. Only in South Africa, Botswana, Tunisia, Mauritius and Libya is the annual cost less than 10% of the average income. By comparison, the ratio in Sweden is only 1%.

EMAIL

In response to the high cost of full Internet-based services lower-cost email-only services have been launched by many African ISPs. A large number of African email users have resorted to free US and other overseas services such as Hotmail and Yahoo. There is also a rapidly-growing market

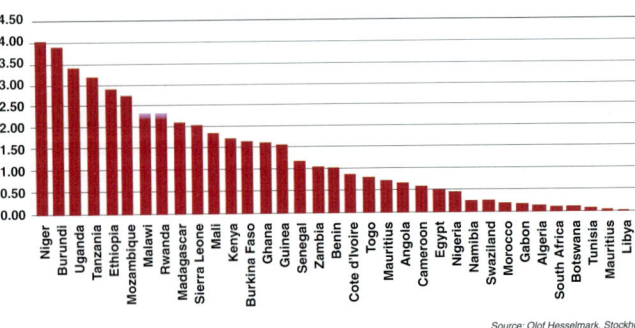

Cost of one year dial-up Internet supply expressed as part of GNP per capita

Source: Olof Hesselmark, Stockholm

for Internet kiosks, cyber cafés and other forms of public access. PCs have been installed for public use in phone shops, schools, police stations and clinics. Most hotels and business centers across the continent provide convenient Internet access for visitors. (In a recent study the UNDP points out that a 40-page document can be sent from Madagascar to Côte d'Ivoire by five-day courier for $75, by 30-minute fax for $45 or by two-minute email for less than 20 cents—and the email can go to hundreds of additional people at no extra cost). A study by the Economic Commission for Africa (ECA) puts the average level of Internet use per account in Africa at about one incoming and one outgoing email per day, averaging 3 to 4 pages in communications, mostly with correspondents abroad. Surveys also indicated that about 25 percent of the email traffic is in replacement of faxes, while 10 percent is instead of phone calls and the other 65 percent new communications.

CIRCUITS

Several of the international Internet circuits in Africa still connect to the USA, the United Kingdom, Italy and France, making it quite expensive. In contrast ISPs in South Africa's neighboring countries benefit from the low tariff policies instituted by its international telecom operator. South Africa acts as a hub for countries such as Lesotho, Namibia, and Swaziland. Major international Internet suppliers to other parts of Africa are AT&T, BT, Global One/Sprint, UUNET/AlterNet, MCI, NSN, BBN, Teleglobe, Verio and France Telecom/FCR. Roaming dialup Internet access is available to travelers in most African countries through the commercial division of the airline operative SITA-SCITOR, renamed Equant.

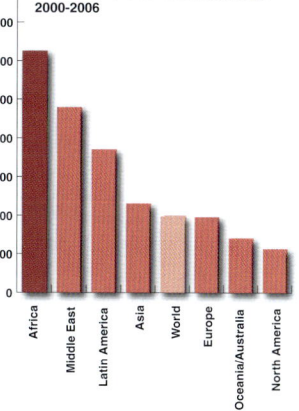

Africa's Leading Internet users
Percentage of total - 2006

(Bar chart with y-axis from 0% to 20% and categories: South Africa, Egypt, Nigeria, Morocco, Sudan, Algeria, Kenya, Zimbabwe)

World Internet Usage - Penetration
Percentage of the total population - 2006

(Bar chart with y-axis from 0% to 80% and categories: North America, Oceania/Australia, Europe, Latin America, World, Asia, Middle East, Africa)

Percentage Growth in Internet Usage
2000-2006

(Bar chart with y-axis from 0 to 800 and categories: Africa, Middle East, Latin America, Asia, World, Europe, Oceania/Australia, North America)

Source: Miniwatts Marketing Group

It operates dialup points of presence in 40 African countries. South Africa is the only country on the continent with X.400 service while ISDN services are also available in including Botswana, Côte d'Ivoire, Egypt, Kenya, Ghana, Mauritius, Morocco, the Seychelles, Sudan, Togo, Tunisia, and Uganda. The American Registry for Internet Numbers (ARIN) administers Internet IP address space for Africa (along with North America, South America, and the Caribbean).

USERS

Most of the users in a recent survey belonged to non-governmental organizations (NGOs), private companies and universities while the ratio of nationals to non-nationals varied sharply between different African countries. In Zambia, for example, only 44 percent of the users surveyed were nationals, compared to 90 percent in Ghana. Most users are male— 86 percent in Ethiopia, 83 percent in Senegal, and 64 percent in Zambia. The large majority of users are well educated—87 percent in Zambia and 98 percent of the respondents in Ethiopia had university degrees. Another recent survey limited to South Africa showed similar results: an average user that is male, between 26 and 30 years, speaking English with a high-school or university-level education.

DEVELOPMENT

The UN Economic Commission for Africa has launched several initiatives to upgrade Africa's information and communication technology (ICT) capability. The African Information Society Initiative (AISI) is working towards the development of a National Information and Communication Infrastructure (NICI) plan and closer regional co-operation.

TRANSPORT FACILITIES IN AFRICA

	Total Area (sq km)	Coastline (km)	Railroads (km) - total	Highways (km) Total	Paved Road	Unpaved or Gravel	Inland Water-ways (km)	Marine Ports	Runway Total
ALGERIA	2,381,740	998	4,733	95,576	57,346	38,230		13	139
ANGOLA	1,246,700	1,600	3,189	73,828	8,577	65,251	1,295	8	289
BENIN	112,620	121	578	8,432	1,038	7,397		2	7
BOTSWANA	600,370	LL	888	11,514	1,600	9,914		0	100
BURKINA FASO	274,200	LL	620	16,500	1,300	15,200		0	48
BURUNDI	27,830	LL	0	5,900	640	5,260		1	4
CAMEROON	475,440	402	1,111	65,000	2,682	60,318	2,090	5	60
CAPE VERDE	4,030	965	0	1,100	680	420		3	6
CENTRAL AFRICAN REP.	622,980	LL	0	22,000	458	21,542	800	2	61
CHAD	1,284,000	LL	0	31,322	263	31,059	2,000	0	66
COMOROS	2,545	525	0	792	228	564		4	5
CONGO (BRAZZAVILLE)	342,000	169	797	11,960	560	11,400	1,120	5	41
CONGO (KINSHASA)	2,345,410	37	5,138	146,500	2,800	143,700	15,000	11	270
CÔTE D'IVOIRE	322,460	515	660	46,600	3,600	43,300	980	4	40
DJIBOUTI	22,000	314	97	2,900	280	2,620		1	13
EGYPT	1,001,450	2,450	4,895	47,387	34,593	12,794	3,500	9	91
EQUATORIAL GUINEA	28,050	296	0	2,760	NA	NA		3	3
ERITREA	121,320	2,234	307	3,845	807	1,796		2	20
ETHIOPIA	1,127,127	LL	681	24,127	3,289	20,838		0	98
GABON	267,670	885	649	7,500	560	6,940	1,600	6	69
GAMBIA,THE	11,300	80	0	3,083	431	2,652	400	1	1
GHANA	238,540	539	953	32,250	6,084	26,166	1,293	2	12
GUINEA	245,860	320	1,048	30,100	1,145	23,455	1,295	3	15
GUINEA-BISSAU	36,120	350	0	3,218	2,698	520		1	32
KENYA	582,650	536	2,650	64,540	7,000	4,150		3	246
LESOTHO	30,350	LL	2.6	7,215	572	6,643		0	29
LIBERIA	111,370	579	490	10,087	603	9,484		4	59
LIBYA	1,759,540	1,770	0	19,300	10,800	8,500	0	9	146
MADAGASCAR	587,040	4,828	1,020	40,000	4,694	35,306		5	138
MALAWI	118,480	LL	789	13,135	2,364	10,771	144	4	47
MALI	1,240,000	LL	642	15,700	1,670	14,030	1,815	1	33
MAURITANIA	1,030,700	754	690	7,525	1,685	5,840		5	28
MAURITIUS	1,860	177	0	1,800	1,640	160		1	5
MOROCCO	446,550	1,835	1,893	59,474	29,440	30,034		12	74
MOZAMBIQUE	801,590	2,470	3,288	26,498	4,593	21,905	3,750	5	192
NAMIBIA	825,418	1,572	2,341	54,500	4,080	50,420		2	135
NIGER	1,267,000	LL	0	39,970	3,170	36,800	300	0	29
NIGERIA	923,770	853	3,567	107,990	30,019	77,971	8,575	6	80
RWANDA	26,340	LL	0	4,885	880	4,005		3	7
SÃO TOMÉ & PRÍNCIPE	960	209	0	300	200	100		2	2
SENEGAL	196,190	531	905	14,007	3,777	10,230	897	7	24
SEYCHELLES	455	491	0	260	160	100		1	14
SIERRA LEONE	71,740	402	84	7,400	1,150	6,250	800	3	11
SOMALIA	637,660	3,025	0	22,500	2,700	19,800		5	76
SOUTH AFRICA	1,219,912	2,798	20,638	188,309	54,013	134,296		7	853
SUDAN	2,505,810	853	5,516	20,703	2,000	18,703	5,310	7	70
SWAZILAND	17,360	LL	297	2,853	510	2,343		0	18
TANZANIA	945,090	1,424	2,600	81,900	3,600	78,300		11	108
TOGO	56,790	56	532	6,462	1,762	4,700	50	2	9
TUNISIA	163,610	1,148	2,260	29,183	17,510	11,673		7	31
UGANDA	236,040	LL	1,300	26,200	1,970	24,230		3	29
ZAMBIA	752,610	LL	1,273	36,370	6,500	29,870	2,250	1	113
ZIMBABWE	390,580	LL	2,745	85,237	15,800	69,437		2	471

LL: Landlocked

Source: US Department of Transport - World Directory of Transport

Transport

Africa is a vast, sparsely populated continent with only 19% of
its people within 100 kilometers of
the coast. With the exception of the
Nile, Niger and a few others, most of
Africa's rivers are seasonal or not
navigable. There are few natural
harbors. Rough terrain, varying
from deserts to mountain ranges
pose special challenges in rail and
road construction. Fiscal short-
falls and other priorities have led
to the decay of existing roads and
railways.

Rail & Road

Sub- Saharan Africa accounts for only 3 per
cent of the rail transport of developing countries,
but has 17 per cent of its population and 7 per
cent of its GDP. The OECD reports that less than a
fifth of Africa's road network is paved compared
to over a quarter in Latin America and over two
fifths in South Asia. Even the paved roads are severely affected by overloading of trucks and poor
drainage posing special hazards. In the nineties
about 10 per cent of global road deaths occurred
in sub-Saharan Africa even though it operted only
some 4 per cent of the total registered vehicles.
Only 16% of all roads are paved. While more than
80% of the unpaved roads are in fair condition,
85% of rural feed roads are in a poor state. Colonial
fragmentation and lack of regional coordination
left some adjoining states with incompatible rail
widths.

Africa's Railroads, Harbors and Rivers

© Business Books International

DENSITY

Although Africa fares better than East or South Asia in the length of roads per capita, it is worse off in terms of road density per square kilometer of land. Poor transport in many areas is considered one of the main reasons for Africa's low competitiveness. Road and maritime transport costs top those of other parts of the world. In recent years, for example, freight costs for imported goods shipped to West and East Africa were 70% higher and, to landlocked countries in Africa, twice as high as to Asian destinations. The cost of air freight between destinations in Africa (where such services are available) often runs as much as two to four times the rate for equivalent distances across the Atlantic. Experts have concluded that in many parts of Africa, transport costs are more of a barrier to free trade than tariffs.

MODES

Roads remain Africa's principal mode of moving people and freight—accounting for 80% of the total in almost every country. After heavy construction projects in the 1960s and 1970s on top of networks left by former colonial powers, Africa had nearly 2 million km of roads in the early 1990s, much of it in a state of neglect due to shortages in budgets for post-construction maintenance. Railroads, harbors and airports suffered the same fate. With few exceptions—notably South Africa where links are well maintained—large sections of Africa's rail transport needs upgrading. Many harbors and airports need to be enlarged and modernized to cope with larger freight demands. Southern Africa—where a sophisticated network of railroads and highways as well as efficient harbors and state-of-the-art airports support a rapidly expanding trade that benefits both South Africa and its neighbors—serves as a model for the continent as it moves towards globalization in the new millennium.

SEA PORTS

Only one African seaport is owned by one of the five largest global port operators known worldwide for their efficiency and most container terminals are reaching or have reached capacity limits, and are under-equipped. Even the very sophisticated Durban harbor in South Africa has had a congestion surcharge imposed by shipping lines for two years. Cargo-handling costs have, however, fallen where competition among service providers has been introduced. Currently charges are between $60-$75 per 20ft container in Dakar, Abidjan and Douala where private competition is allowed compared to $200 in Lagos.

AIR TRAVEL

Despite the importance of airports only a few airports (in Egypt, Cape Verde, Ethiopia, Morocco, Ghana and South Africa) have attained FAA Category I status in the United States, required for international flights. While several major airlines on the continent have managed good safety records the OECD notes that with only 4.5 per cent of global air traffic is in Africa its share of accidents reached 25 per cent in 2004.

FUTURE DEVELOPMENT

The World Bank estimates that African countries will need to spend the equivalent of 4 per cent of their GDP every year for the coming decade, just on roads. Yet, throughout the nineties infrastructure was largely overlooked in the allocation of official development assistance in favor of the social sectors. It is only recently, with the September 2005 UN Millennium plus

5 Summit and the Report of the Commission for Africa (so-called Blair Report), that infrastructure again became a top priority on the international development agenda.

MODEST GAINS

Nonetheless, there have been some modest gains in infrastructure construction and repair recent years in several countries where road and rail building and repair, harbor refurbishing and streamlining of air connections and airport facilities were undertaken. This is a costly affair. (For example, putting an all-weather road within 20 km reach of most of Ethiopia's population, will cost an estimated $4 billion). In the first twelve years since its inception in 1990 the UN Transport and Communications Decade for Africa (UNCTADA) raised almost $13 billion for projects. These included construction on the Trans-African Highway, railways in East and West Africa and liberalization of air transport. The Sub-Saharan African Transport Program (SSATP), administered by the World Bank, involves countries ranging from Burkina Faso in the northwest to Malawi in the East and Zimbabwe in the south. The US Overseas Private Investment Corporation (OPIC) underwrote an infrastructure fund to promote development in Africa. This is seen as a catalytic effort, contributing together with other private equity funds towards an estimated $100 billion required for African infrastructural development over the next twenty years. At the same time, these funds targeting Africa's infrastructural needs offer investors long-term appreciation in equity and overseas engineering and construction firms with plenty of work. In recent years the China, as part of its focus on Africa, has been particularly active in infrastructure development.

OPPORTUNITIES

The business opportunities presented by new construction and road repair have not been lost on large and medium-sized contractors and suppliers. One US-based company that has been actively engaged in supplying the African market with new and used heavy construction equipment, backed by Eximbank financing for purchasers, is Nationwide Equipment in Jacksonville, Florida. China has also entered the market and since early 2005 its Eximbank has extended $2 billion worth of loans to rehabilitate roads and railways in Angola. Chinese contractors are also involved in over one-third of Mozambique's road construction.

PRIVATIZATION

Various forms of public-private partnerships have been implemented at airports, seaports and railways, and some roads. Most private participation in transport infrastructure take the form of leases or concessions. Not only in South Africa but elsewhere on the continent airports and harbors have been entrusted to private management with immediate positive results. Several African governments have allowed private firms to build, own and operate (BOO) toll roads and privatized state-owned railroad companies, airlines and shipping lines. These public-private partnerships (PPPs) take many forms but most have resulted in more efficient and less costly services to consumers. The continent's largest single transport utility, South Africa's Transnet is being primed for restructuring while its national airline, South African Airways, was sold in part. At the end of the nineties 23 West and Central African nations have agreed to liberalize air transport in their region and make it more competitive.

: EssoChad and South Africa Tourism

AGRICULTURE

AFRICA HAS TRADITIONALLY BEEN SEEN AS THE CONTINENT OF COFFEE, COCOA AND COTTON. COMMERCIAL AND SUBSISTENCE FARMING ON AVERAGE CONTRIBUTE BETWEEN 30% AND 35% OF GDP AND PROVIDE EMPLOYMENT FOR SOME 70% OF THE CONTINENT'S WORK FORCE. IN RECENT YEARS, DESPITE ITS IMPORTANCE, AGRICULTURE HAS BEEN ALLOWED TO SLIP FAR BELOW ITS POTENTIAL. LESS THAN 7% OF THE CROP-GROWING AREAS ARE IRRIGATED, INPUTS ARE LIMITED AND MECHANIZATION OFTEN LACKING. MOST OF THE CONTINENT IS VULNERABLE TO DROUGHTS AND THERE IS LITTLE ACCESS TO IRRIGATION. SIX COUNTRIES—EGYPT, MADAGASCAR, MOROCCO, NIGERIA, SOUTH AFRICA AND SUDAN—ACCOUNT FOR NEARLY 75 PERCENT OF THE TOTAL IRRIGATED LAND IN AFRICA.

HIV/AIDS further undermines agricultural systems and threatens the food security of rural families. Global projections of food production show that although the world population growth rate will be matched by similar growth in food production and that food prices will continue to decline, Africa as a region will continue to be unable to meet its own food demand. The total annual shortfall is estimated to reach 150 million tons of grain by 2020. With some notable exceptions where nations actually manage not only to feed themselves but earn valuable foreign exchange through exports, agriculture in Africa at large has long been plagued by poor policies and institutional failures. In many parts of the continent not only stringent state control but under-capitalization, inadequate infrastructures and antiquated farming methods have inhibited growth.

POTENTIAL

Still, the UN Food and Agriculture Organization (FAO) maintains that sub-Saharan Africa has the potential to increase agricultural production and become self-reliant. World Bank and IMF-inspired programs encourage research and new strategies to raise productivity. In its analysis of the agricultural crisis in Sub-Saharan Africa, the FAO identified arable land expansion, increased yields and increased cropping intensity as potential sources of boosting production.

BIOTECHNOLOGY

Biotechnology has shown that it can increase crop yields but research to date has been largely geared to reduce input and labor costs for large scale production systems in developed nations. There have been no serious investments in sorghum, groundnuts, peas and other crops important to Africa and other less developed semi-arid tropical regions.

FOOD SHORTAGES

In April 2002 the Food and Agricultural Organization described the food outlook for sub-Saharan Africa in 2002 as mixed. Good cereal harvests in Eastern and West Africa coincided with disappointing harvests in drought-stricken southern African countries. In February 2002, the FAO issued a special warning of impending serious food shortages threatening the lives of some 4 million people in the sub-region. In Zimbabwe, where crop failures coincided with increased government pressure on white farmers to leave,

110

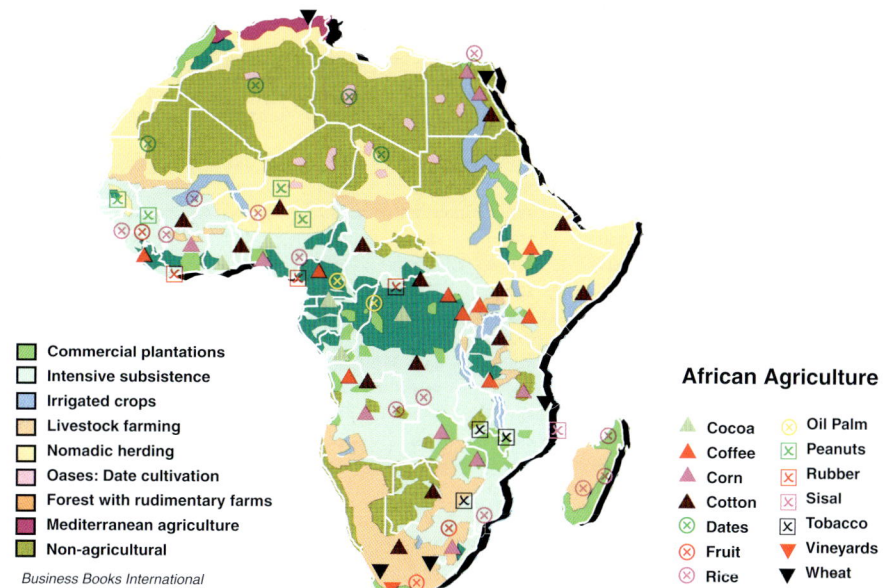

African Agriculture

Legend:
- Commercial plantations
- Intensive subsistence
- Irrigated crops
- Livestock farming
- Nomadic herding
- Oases: Date cultivation
- Forest with rudimentary farms
- Mediterranean agriculture
- Non-agricultural

Business Books International

- Cocoa
- Coffee
- Corn
- Cotton
- Dates
- Fruit
- Rice
- Oil Palm
- Peanuts
- Rubber
- Sisal
- Tobacco
- Vineyards
- Wheat

an appeal was made for international food assistance. Malawi also declared a state of emergency, appealing to the international community for food assistance to avert famine. In Zambia, the food supply was seen as extremely tight as a result of a poor cereal crops and delays in maize imports. Also in the southern provinces of Mozambique the food situation continued to be serious. The FAO listed another 15 countries that were facing food emergencies, ranging from Uganda to Somalia and Burundi to Sierra Leone.

EXPORTS

These widely publicized recurring food crises tend to obscure Africa's continued importance as a supplier of not only cocoa, cotton and coffee but tobacco, tea, sisal, sugar cane, fresh fruit, palm oil, wines and meat to the world market. There is foreign investment in agricultural production and processing across the continent from South Africa in the south to Tunisia in the north. As more countries are opening up their agricultural sectors to private entrepreneurs this involvement is bound to grow. In recent years, with improved air links, foreign firms have branched out from processing pyrethrum in Kenya to producing fresh cut flowers for the European and North American markets in countries such as Malawi and Tanzania. Not only large but several smaller overseas companies have involved themselves in farming projects in Africa ranging from providing irrigation systems to pesticides and solar power system in rural regions and to growing product for export ranging from flowers to fruit.

SECTORAL SHARE OF GDP IN AFRICA

Country	Area ('000 Km2)	GDP at market prices $m 2005	Per capita GDP in US$ 2005	% Share of GDP Agriculture 2005	% Share of GDP Industry 2005	% Share of GDP Services 2005	% Share Manufact. of Industry 2005	Protected land as % of total area 1995-2000
Algeria	2 382	104 935	3 194	7.8	55.4	36.8	5.1	2.5
Angola	1 247	28 475	1 786	8.3	65.4	26.3	4.0	6.6
Benin	113	4 328	513	38.7	15.7	45.5	9.8	7.0
Botswana	582	9 130	5 173	2.5	49.4	48.1	4.4	18.5
Burkina Faso	274	5 441	411	30.1	20.6	49.2	14.2	10.4
Burundi	28	799	106	47.3	19.8	32.9	11.9	5.7
Cameroon	475	16 895	1 035	20.7	30.3	49.1	19.3	4.5
Cape Verde	4	1 051	2 074	10.2	15.3	74.5	4.5	0.0
Cent. Afr. Rep.	623	1 382	342	60.8	23.9	15.3	5.7	8.2
Chad	1 284	5 225	536	21.5	49.2	29.3	4.8	9.1
Comoros	2	384	481	41.1	11.8	47.1	4.2	0.0
Congo	342	5 859	1 465	4.9	66.2	28.9	4.8	4.5
Congo (DRC)	2 345	6 922	120	46.5	24.3	29.2	5.5	4.5
Côte d'Ivoire	322	16 172	891	23.3	22.9	53.8	15.9	6.2
Djibouti	23	700	883	3.6	17.1	79.2	2.7	0.4
Egypt	1 001	90 917	1 228	15.4	37.2	47.4	18.6	0.8
Equat. Guinea	28	6 416	12 742	2.1	94.0	3.8	0.1	0.0
Eritrea	118	1 058	240	15.8	24.1	60.1	9.5	5.0
Ethiopia	1 104	11 078	143	43.6	15.3	41.1	5.9	5.5
Gabon	268	8 515	6 153	5.2	55.6	39.1	4.5	2.8
Gambia	11	458	302	37.1	13.2	49.7	5.1	2.3
Ghana	239	11 886	537	37.8	24.7	37.5	8.7	4.9
Guinea	246	3 292	350	20.6	30.7	48.7	3.5	0.7
Guinea Bissau	36	300	189	43.8	16.5	39.7	12.3	0.0
Kenya	580	19 041	556	25.9	17.7	56.4	11.0	6.2
Lesotho	30	1 467	817	16.9	43.3	39.8	20.3	0.2
Liberia	111	...	...	...	...	...	...	1.3
Libya	1 760	37 256	6 365	3.5	76.1	20.3	1.6	0.1
Madagascar	587	5 115	275	26.7	15.9	57.5	12.6	1.9
Malawi	118	1 979	154	35.8	17.6	46.6	11.6	11.3
Mali	1 240	5 117	379	35.3	25.1	39.6	10.3	3.7
Mauritania	1 026	1 823	594	12.9	20.9	66.3	5.9	1.7
Mauritius	2	6 386	5 131	5.6	27.6	66.9	19.8	7.70
Morocco	711	52 289	1 661	13.9	31.1	55.1	20.1	0.7
Mozambique	802	6 832	345	20.9	26.5	52.5	14.2	6.1
Namibia	824	6 345	3 124	9.8	31.6	58.6	13.5	12.9
Niger	1 267	3 025	217	36.9	12.0	51.0	6.2	7.7
Nigeria	924	94 757	720	23.2	55.7	21.1	3.9	3.3
Rwanda	26	2 092	231	40.7	21.7	37.6	10.3	14.7
São T. & Principe	1	79	504	17.1	15.0	67.9	3.7	0
Senegal	197	8 356	717	21.2	22.9	55.8	13.9	11.3
Seychelles	0.5	698	8 659	3.0	31.1	65.8	18.4	100
Sierra Leone	72	1 163	211	43.2	26.6	30.3	1.6	1.1
Somalia	638	...	...	...	...	...	...	0.3
South Africa	1 221	240 734	5 075	2.8	30.5	66.8	18.8	5.4
Sudan	2 506	28 112	776	29.1	29.4	41.5	7.5	3.6
Swaziland	17	2 685	2 601	12.3	46.7	41.0	38.3	2.0
Tanzania	945.1	12 207	318	43.7	17.0	39.4	6.8	15.6
Togo	57	2 174	354	41.5	22.9	35.6	9.6	7.9
Tunisia	164	29 353	2 906	11.5	27.7	60.7	17.7	0.3
Uganda	241	8 475	294	33.5	20.9	45.6	9.0	9.6
Zambia	753	6 782	581	22.2	44.0	33.8	18.5	8.6
Zimbabwe	391	5 792	445	18.5	15.1	66.4	11.6	7.9
AFRICA	30 307	933 776	1 032	14.0	39.5	46.5	12.1	

Source: African Development Bank

Opportunities

There is bound to be an ongoing market for food from abroad due to a general decline in the production of wheat, rice and corn in some regions, and droughts and other catastrophes in elsewhere. Suppliers from abroad are likely to find outlets for their surplus production either as part of a food aid program or through normal sales channels.

Commerce and conservation

South African paper giant, Sappi, combined agriculture and manufacturing, and commerce and conservation into a worldwide success story. Working on the principle of sustainable development that not only replaces but expands forests while utilizing pulp for paper it has taken the lead in education in conservation and funded the rescue and revival of endangered species, including the cheetahs at De Wildt. Sappi—with manufacturing operations on four continents and markets in more than a hundred countries—is the world's largest producer of coated fine paper used in quality publications.

Manufacturing

AFRICA'S SHARE OF GLOBAL MANU-FACTURED PRODUCTS IS MINIMAL. WITH THE EXCEPTION OF SOUTH AFRICA, WHICH OFFERS A BROAD RANGE OF MANU-FACTURED GOODS, MOST OTHER AFRICAN COUNTRIES ARE CURRENTLY RELYING LARGELY ON THE EXPORT OF RAW MATERI-ALS AND AGRICULTURAL PRODUCTS FOR MORE THAN ONE THIRD OF THEIR GDP AND ARE IN URGENT NEED OF DIVERSIFI-CATION. IN MANY INSTANCES INDUSTRIAL ACTIVITY IS BASED ON THE EXTRACTION OF A SINGLE PRODUCT SUCH AS OIL OR DIAMONDS OR, AS ONE ECONOMIST PUT IT, INDUSTRIALIZATION IS LIKELY TO BE LINKED TO NATURAL RESOURCE ENDOW-MENTS RATHER THAN "FOOT LOOSE" IN-DUSTRIES. THAT IS CHANGING AS COUN-TRIES COURT FOREIGN MANUFACTURERS WITH NEW INCENTIVES.

Sappi paper plant in South Africa

In Africa at large most major manufacturing activity came as a result of foreign involvement. Even South Africa, which currently counts among one of the world's top twenty five industrialized nations, early beginnings in colonial times can be traced back to infusion from abroad. Today the drive in Africa is towards beneficiation of its natural resources instead of allowing large-scale extraction and export of raw materials for utilization elsewhere.

MULTINATIONALS

Easily recognizable brand names such as Coca Cola, General Motors, Ford, Xerox, IBM, Kodak and Chrysler trace their African beginnings back to the early twentieth century. Today manufacturing multinationals from Europe and Asia and the United States compete for market share in Africa through wholly or partly-owned local manufacturing and assembly subsidiaries. Many are taking advantage of the trade preferences extended to Africa by the developed world by shifting manufacturing into the continent. The latest to enter the field are China and India.

FLYING GEESE

Africa has begun to experience what became known in the Far East as the "flying geese" phenomenon, with some of its more advanced countries opting for manufacturing in neighboring countries where wages are lower and incentives higher. Not only South Africa but even smaller nations such as Mauritius have, for economic reasons, shifted their manufac-

turing of garments and other textiles, handmade toys and other labor-intensive operations to less developed nations in Africa, thus duplicating the process with which Asia has become so familiar in recent years.

DEVELOPMENT BANK

In 1986, the African Development Bank (ADB), the International Finance Corporation (IFC), the United Nations Development Programme (UNDP) and 15 other donor countries jointly established the Africa Project Development Facility (APDF) to assist African entrepreneurs. APDF's objective is to accelerate the development of productive private enterprises sponsored and owned by African entrepreneurs as a means of stimulating sustainable economic growth and productive employment in Sub-Saharan Africa.

OPPORTUNITIES

Foreign direct investment in Africa is no longer concentrated in the traditional natural resources sector. Manufacturing has received considerable amounts of foreign capital in recent years. Multinational textile and apparel manufacturers have established themselves in African countries to take advantage of trade preferences and quotas in European and North American markets through legislation such as the African Growth and Opportunity Act (AGOA). Other light industries are now following their example by setting up plants in free trade zones across the continent from Mauritius to Cape Verde.

Industry as % of GDP

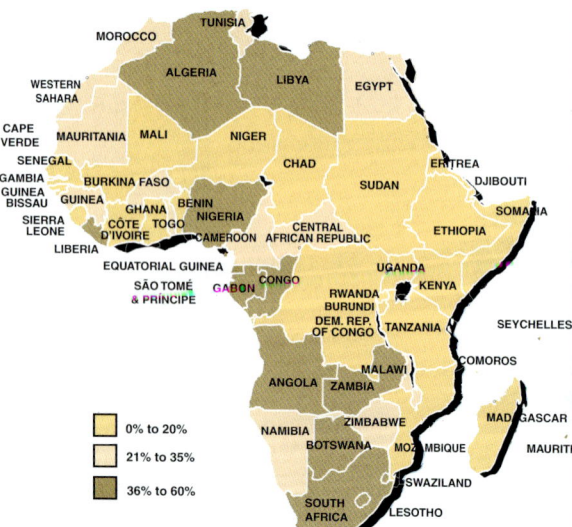

SOUTH AFRICA

South Africa's manufacturing sector growth has averaged 4 per cent per year since 1994 in terms of production volumes. The automobile industry has contributed significantly to this growth. More than 130,000 vehicles worth $2 billion were exported in 2003. This figure is expected to reach 200,000 per year in the year 2014. In 2004 South African-built Toyotas have gone to the European market while 45,000 of the 55,000 vehicles produced by Daimler Chrysler were exported. The auto industry provides employment to more than 100,000 people full-time,

Mozal aluminum smelter in Mozambique

with another 150,000 employed on a part-time or contract basis. Manufacturing for export in South Africa involving many major multinationals in North America, Europe and the Far East goes well beyond autos and parts. Today the list of exports from South Africa runs the gamut from beer to barley, wines to windmills, chemicals to computers, textiles to titanium, and artifacts to automobiles—setting an example for the rest of the continent in its desire to diversify.

GOING GLOBAL

Unleashed in the early 1990s when sanctions were scrapped, several of post-apartheid's South Africa's industrial giants have gone global, controlling markets abroad with their manufactures and buying out competitors. Starting with a dramatic takeover of the US-based Warren in the nineties, South Africa's Sappi has grown into the world's largest producer of coated fine paper and dissolving pulp. Headquartered in Johannesburg, with manufacturing operations on four continents and in nine countries, and customers in more than a hundred countries, the company employs over 16,000 people. The group now produces over 15% of the world's coated fine paper, used in high quality publications. De Beers has long been dominating the global diamond market while mining giants such as Anglogold and Billiton are rapidly taking over operations in other parts of the world. South African Breweries has established itself as one of the world's leading beer giants with acquisitions in Europe and the United States. In recent years South Africa has taken the lead in neighboring African countries as evidenced by the establishment of a giant aluminum smelter in Mozambique and numerous major mining and manufacturing projects elsewhere on the continent. Lately most of the foreign direct investment in manufacturing and mining in other parts of the continent originated in South Africa.

MINI MANUFACTURING

In the focus on large-scale production and revenues there is a tendency to lose sight of the significant combined contribution of small manufacturing and home industries to the welfare and well-being of the continent. Like most developed nations of the world, small business undertakings represent a major share of the job opportunities in Africa. Labor intensive activities ranging from leather processing, pottery to textiles and artifacts will undoubtedly remain important regardless of future growth in mega-industries.

Small enterprises in Burkina Faso and Central African Republic

PI

115

DAMS OF AFRICA

DAM IT AND BE DAMNED. THIS SEEMS TO BE THE CASE IN AFRICA WHERE SEVERAL LARGE-SCALE PROJECTS HAVE DISPLACED COMMUNITIES, FLOODED SACRED LAND AND WILDLIFE SANCTUARIES AND ADVERSELY AFFECTED THE LIVELIHOOD OF SOME WHILE BENEFITING THE POPULATION AS A WHOLE. IN A CONTINENT WHERE WATER IS A SCARCE COMMODITY AND ELECTRICITY NEEDS ARE GROWING LARGE HYDRO PROJECTS SEEM TO BE THE OBVIOUS ANSWER. BUT THEY COME AT A PRICE WAY BEYOND THE BILLIONS OF DOLLARS SPENT ON CONSTRUCTION.

The Lesotho Highlands Project followed the Aswan in Egypt, Volta in Ghana, Kariba in Zambia and Zimbabwe and Cahora Bassa in Mozambique as well as lesser known but equally impressive dams in Morocco and Côte d'Ivoire. On the drawing board is the Inga Rapids Project in the Democratic Republic of Congo that will generate enough electricity for all of Africa's industrialized needs and still have some left for export to Europe.

ASWAN

Aswan is the name that conjures up when anyone mentions dams in Africa. Completed in 1902 the first Aswan Dam was merely the precursor of a much larger construction further up the river Nile. The High Aswan Dam, built with financial and technological assistance from the Soviet Union, was completed in 1971. At a height

THERE ARE 1,272 LARGE DAMS IN AFRICA

80.8% are single purpose dams
66% were built for irrigation
25% for water supply
South Africa has 539 major dams
Zimbabwe (213) and Algeria (107)

THE 6 LARGEST DAMS BY HEIGHT

Cahora Bassa Dam, Mozambique, 171 meters
Katse Dam, Lesotho, 155 meters
Hassan 1 Dam, Lakhdar River, Morocco, 145 meters
Akosombo Dam, Ghana, 134 meters
Bine El Ouidane Dam, Morocco, 133 meters
Kariba Dam, Zambia/Zimbabwe, 128 meters

THE 5 LARGEST DAMS BY CAPACITY

Kariba Dam, Zambia/Zimbabwe, 180 bn cu. meter
High Aswan Dam, Egypt, 162 bn cu. meter
Akosombo Dam, Ghana, 150 bn cu. meter
Cahora Bassa Dam, Mozambique, 52 bn cu. meter
Kossou Dam, Côte d'Ivoire, 28 bn cu. meter

of 111 meters and a width of 3,800m it featured 180 watergates and 12 power-generating units supplying 2.1 million kw of electric power. Lake Nasser that swelled up behind this massive wall threatened to drown numerous priceless historic ruins, including the Abu Simbel shrine dedicated to Ramses II. With donations from across the world UNESCO assigned masterful Italian engineers to move these massive treasures in piecemeal fashion to higher ground. Less fortunate were the farmers downstream who are denied by the dam deposits of fertile sediment that used to flow seawards during the summer floods.

KARIBA

The story repeated itself at Kariba Dam on the Zambezi River between Zambia and Zimbabwe. Completed in 1977, it relegated High Aswan to second place and ranks as one of the largest dams

Abu Simbel shrine on high ground—after a UNESCO campaign that brought in assistance from around the world

Picture: Donna Eby Anders

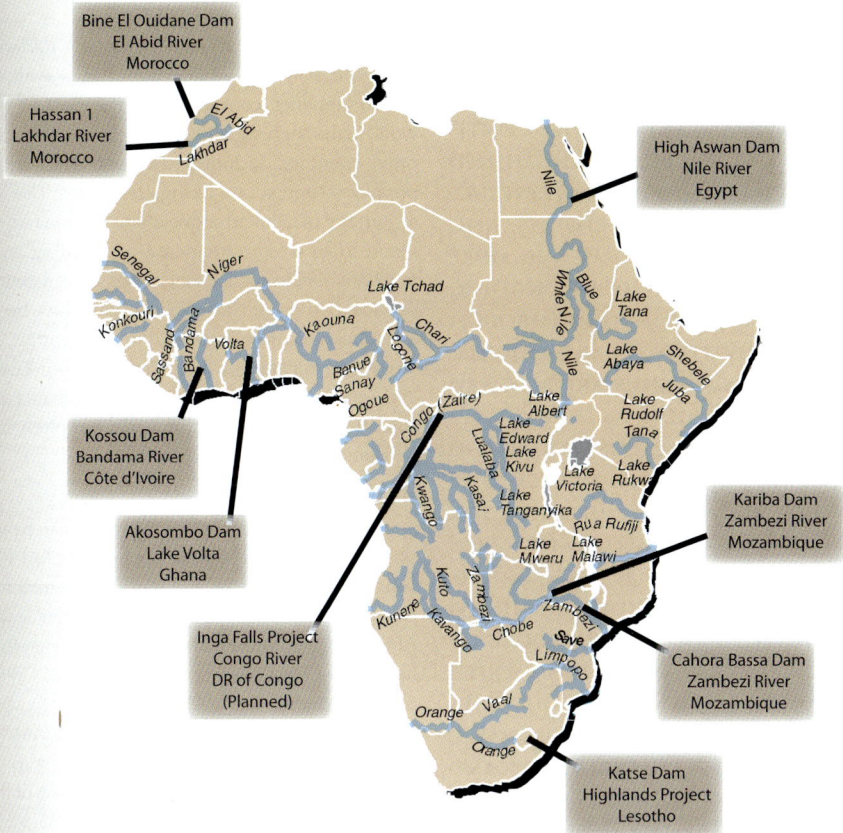

Bine El Ouidane Dam
El Abid River
Morocco

Hassan 1
Lakhdar River
Morocco

High Aswan Dam
Nile River
Egypt

Kossou Dam
Bandama River
Côte d'Ivoire

Akosombo Dam
Lake Volta
Ghana

Kariba Dam
Zambezi River
Mozambique

Inga Falls Project
Congo River
DR of Congo
(Planned)

Cahora Bassa Dam
Zambezi River
Mozambique

Katse Dam
Highlands Project
Lesotho

in the world. At a height of 128m and 579m wide Kariba dam supplies electricity to both Zambia (the Copperbelt) and Zimbabwe. But it also changed the downstream ecology dramatically and forced the resettlement of 57,000 Tonga people living upstream along the Zambezi. Operation Noah involved the rescue of around 6,000 large animals and numerous small ones threatened by the lake's rising waters. While the animals thrive in their new sanctuaries the displaced Tonga never seemed to have adjusted after the lands where they had farmed, fished, worshipped, raised their children and buried their dead, were flooded. They were resettled to poor lands with no development assistance. Downstream in the Zambezi River construction started on the Cahora Bassa dam in 1969. This joint effort between Portugal, the then ruler of Mozambique, and South Africa, resulted in a flood area 250 km long and 38 km wide covering an area of 2,700 sq. km with an average depth of 20.9m. South Africa buys the electricity and despite serious interruptions during the civil war Cahora Bassa has returned to full capacity.

LESOTHO

Power hungry South Africa also inspired the Lesotho Highlands Water Project. Construction commenced in the late nineties and is currently in its final phase. Electricity has already started to flow into South Africa's Pretoria Witwatersrand Vereeniging (PWV) industrial complex. Current sales account for 20% of Lesotho's national income. Once again, 30,000 of Lesotho's tribesmen had to be relocated.

INGA

There are plans on the drawing board to harness the mighty Congo River to generate more than 40,000 megawatts—enough to power most of Africa's industrialized areas and still have a lot left to sell to southern Europe via a proposed Mediterranean connector. The project will incorporate and upgrade the existing two dams, Inga I and Inga II, that fell into disrepair. The World Bank, among other groups, is said to have pledged as much as 500 million dollars. The plan also calls for the construction of Inga III, a massive hydroelectric station, at a cost of $6 billion.

BANKING

IN SEVERAL PARTS OF THE CONTI-
NENT BANKING HAS BEEN STRENGTHENED
BY FINANCIAL LIBERALIZATION, RESTRUC-
TURING, AND OTHER REFORMS, AND
BECAME MORE COMPETITIVE AND MORE
TRANSPARENT. THERE IS AN ONGOING
PROCESS OF CONSOLIDATION THROUGH
MERGERS, PRIVATIZATION AND LIQUIDA-
TIONS. FOREIGN BANKS ARE ALLOWED
IN COUNTRIES WHERE UNTIL RECENTLY
BANKING WAS TIGHTLY CONTROLLED AND
ALL OVERSEAS COMPETITION EXCLUDED.
IN COUNTRIES WHERE PUBLIC SECTOR
INSTITUTIONS ARE THE LARGEST USERS
OF BANKING SERVICES, REFORMS ARE AL-
LOWING THEM TO DECIDE WHETHER TO
BANK WITH PUBLIC, LOCAL PRIVATE OR
FOREIGN BANKS. BUT APART FROM SOUTH
AFRICA AND A FEW OTHER COUNTRIES
SUCH AS EGYPT, MOROCCO, ZIMBABWE,
MAURITIUS, CÔTE D'IVOIRE, KENYA AND
BOTSWANA, THE CONTINENT IS STILL LAG-
GING BEHIND IN SERVICES. .

In the immediate post-colonial era most
African governments interfered in their financial
sectors by nationalizing existing institutions and
creating state-owned banks. Credit was curtailed
and strict exchange controls introduced.

REFORMS

In the 1980s when it finally became apparent that this approach failed miserably, a wave
of reform spread across Africa. The
transformation to freer financial markets did not happen without cost.
In many instances the larger spread
between lending and deposit rates
led to higher local interest rates.
Some governments still cling to
failing state banks and a number
of undercapitalized institutions
spawned in the process of reform
are experiencing problems. In general, however, the freer financial environment has been a boon to both
domestic and foreign investors.

ELECTRONIC

African banks are making moving towards
electronic banking. While South Africa with its
ample landlines compete with the best in the
world in the sophistication of its electronic services
other countries, including the continent's most
populous Nigeria, are facing challenges. Due to
a shortage of landline connectivity Nigeria had to
resort to an off-line smartcard payment system.
In Ghana electronic banking relies on a satellite
service company. Internet banking has been
introduced to more than 15 African countries. In
emerging markets such as Nigeria, Ivory Coast
and Senegal where the majority of merchants are
still off-line, magnetic stripe cards are often still
rendered useless.

RANKINGS

Early 2006, the 'big five' South African banks
occupied the top positions in The Banker's Top 100
sub-Saharan African banks listing. The remaining
places in the top 10 were filled by another South
African bank, African Bank, at sixth and then four
banks from Nigeria: First Bank of Nigeria, Union
Bank of Nigeria, Zenith International Bank and
Intercontinental Bank. Five other South African
banks are represented in the Top 100, helping
that country to account for a massive 74.9% of the
aggregated Tier 1 capital of the Top 100, 83.5% of
the aggregate assets and 72.4% of the aggregate
pre-tax profits. Nigerian banks, of which there are
25 listed, accounted for 11.3% of aggregate Tier
1 capital, 5.9% of aggregate assets and 9.2% of
aggregate pre-tax profits. The third largest share
of the aggregate Tier 1 capital is by the group of 38
banks from 22 countries grouped under "others",
which account for 6.6%, 5.6% of aggregate assets
and 9.0% of aggregate pre-tax profit.

Profitability contributors in African banking

Southern Africa West Africa Central Africa East Africa

Source: KPMG Banking Survey 2004

NORTH AFRICA

In North Africa countries such as Egypt, Morocco, Tunisia and Algeria have gone through major structural adjustments. In Morocco, which has led the way in both reform and privatization in the region, Wafa Bank, with 12 per cent of total Moroccan deposits, is a prime example of successful diversification. The same trend is evident in Tunisia, albeit at a slower pace due to a higher degree of state ownership of banks and a paternalistic political system. Challenges in both Morocco and Tunisia are much less severe than those faced in Algeria where the state-run banking sector has had a difficult time adapting to economic reforms. Egyptian banking has undergone substantial liberalization in the past decade. Even though the privatization of Egypt's "big four" state banks was delayed, private banks such as Commercial International Bank (CIB), Misr International Bank (MIBank) and Egyptian American Bank (EAB) have made great strides in gaining market share. Today the private sector accounts for some 20% of the total and is by far the most profitable with a return on equity (ROE) ranging between 19% and 30%.

SOUTHERN AFRICA

Banking and financial services in South Africa are not only state-of-the-art by any world standards but lead in some respects. Most foreign banking institutions setting their sights on Africa start in South Africa where a sophisticated financial market presents no surprises and minimum risk. However, to make serious inroads in this market foreign enterprises have to spend substantial sums as opposed to relatively small outlays elsewhere on the continent. Competition is fierce among 30 local banking institutions—five of them rank among the top 300 worldwide—and 24 foreign-controlled banks. Another 30 foreign banking institutions have representatives stationed in the country. The largest South African banks not only have branch operations in neighboring countries but further afield in East Africa. In 2005 United Kingdom's Barclays Bank acquired 54% of one of South Africa's biggest banking groups, ABSA, for $5 billion.

REGIONAL

Cross border cooperation and greater cohesiveness in banking, insurance and stock market activity within groupings such as the Southern African Development Community, the Common Market for Eastern and Southern Africa (COMESA) and the Economic Community of West African States (ECOWAS) should make the market more attractive for prospective foreign participants.

ADB

The African Development Bank, headquartered in Abidjan, focus on rural development, human capital development and the private sector. Its shareholders are the 53 countries in Africa as well as 24 countries in the Americas, Europe and Asia. The financial resources of the Bank comprises subscribed capital, reserves, funds raised through borrowings, and accumulated net income.

FOREIGN BANKS

Foreign banks have provided know-how and much-needed support for African financial systems in need of a fresh inflow of capital to buttress economic reforms. They have been useful catalysts for inward investment and trading by offering financing and expertise and, in some cases, acting as go-betweens to clinch deals. Often foreigners prefer the comfort zone of a familiar bank when dealing with remote and unfamiliar countries. US, French and British banks have a presence across the continent. In fact, in its review of the world banking scene, the World Bank concluded that Africa had the world's highest penetration of foreign banks.

WIRELESS

Wireless and smart card technologies have been useful in the development of services in previously un-banked areas. South African banks and a local mobile phone companies joined forces to help the poor in remote areas who have never had access to banks, cash machines or credit cards. By simply pushing buttons on their cell phones it enables them to transfer funds and make payments at reasonable fees per transaction.

Africa's top 100 Banks by country

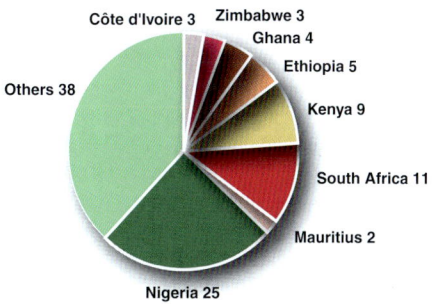

Source: The Banker

119

NEW SCRAMBLE FOR AFRICA

CHINA'S RISE AS A GLOBAL ECONOMIC POWER HAS HAD SERIOUS IMPLICATIONS FOR TRADE AND DEVELOPMENT IN AFRICA. ITS TOTAL TRADE WITH THE CONTINENT HAS GROWN FROM $10 BILLION IN 1995 TO $42 BILLION IN 2005, HELPING ASIA TO BECOME AFRICA'S THIRD LARGEST TRADING PARTNER (27%) AFTER THE EUROPEAN UNION (32%) AND THE UNITED STATES (29%). CHINA'S GROWING PRESENCE IN AFRICA IS LARGELY FUELED BY THE NEED TO SECURE ESSENTIAL RAW MATERIALS, PARTICULARLY OIL. CHINA ALSO VIEWS AFRICAN COUNTRIES AS STRATEGIC MARKETS FOR LOWER-END MANUFACTURED GOODS AND APPAREL AND TEXTILES EXPORTS—OFTEN THREATENING DOMESTIC AFRICAN MANUFACTURERS.

In November 2006 fifty African heads of state attended the Forum on China-Africa Co-operation (FOCAC) hosted in Beijing by Chinese President Hu Jintao. The purpose was to further boost trade relations between Africa and China. On the table were 2,500 new deals to add to the multitude of projects already in the pipeline.

Speaking on this occasion South Africa's Pres. Thabo Mbeki praised China's "commitment to Africa" as "demonstrated through tangible and concrete results" relating to "human source development, debt relief and investment." Africa's commitment to China's development, he said, was evidenced "through the supply of raw materials, other products and technology transfer."

OIL APPETITE

China, with nearly $1 trillion in reserves and a voracious appetite for natural resources, has decided to spend some of its billions of dollars in savings to secure access to the oil, gas, copper, coal and other mineral riches in African countries.

Its thirst is limitless and by 2020 it will be forced to supply 60% of its energy needs from abroad, even from nations such as Chad that have maintained diplomatic relations with Taiwan.

Africa is the only place left to go, as most of the world's other big oil reserves are already being developed by major Western energy companies.

Beijing has spent billions of dollars securing drilling rights in Nigeria, Sudan and Angola. It has also signed numerous exploration deals with various African countries from the Republic of Congo in West Africa to Ethiopia. China is now the world's second largest consumer of crude oil, bringing in more than 25% of its oil imports from the Gulf of Guinea and Sudan.

Driven by its own energy needs, China has been a major contributor to the reconstruction of Angola's cities and infrastructure, including the construction of a $3 billion oil refinery, and extension of a $2 billion loan in exchange for a contract for 10,000 barrels of crude oil per day;

Chinese President Hu Jintao with two of the 50 African Heads of State who attended the Forum on China-Africa Co-operation (FOCAC) in Beijing in November 2006. On the left is Pres. Ravalomanana of Madagascar on the right Pres. Kikwete of Tanzania.

China's $3 billion investment made it the single largest shareholder in the operating company that controls Sudan's oil fields; after failing to acquire American-owned Unocal, China purchased a 45% stake in a Nigerian offshore oil and gas field for $2.27 billion and set aside another $2.25 billion for field development; and even Gabon's declining oil industry saw massive investment from China National Petrochemical Corporation (SINOPEC), which plans to explore Gabon's onshore and offshore oil reserves. China has also snapped up the first production of crude oil in Mauritania, Africa's latest oil producer.

MARKET

Beijing denies that China's growing ties with Africa are purely about oil. Even though in 2004 only 2% of Chinese trade was with Africa, the continent has done particularly well. During the 1990s Sino-African trade grew by 700%.

Africa has undoubtedly benefited beyond the sale of raw materials. It looks at China as a source of cheap loans and merchandise. Beijing promised $3 billion in preferential loans and US$2 billion in export credits over the next three years.

China will train 15,000 African professionals and set up a development fund to help build schools and hospitals.

Africa is also a growing market for Chinese goods, but critics contend that in return Beijing is stifling African manufacturing.

According to the deputy chairman of the South African Institute of International Affairs, Moeletsi Mbeki—Pres. Thabo Mbeki's brother—China represents "both a tantalizing opportunity and a terrifying threat." It is a familiar story, he says. "We sell them

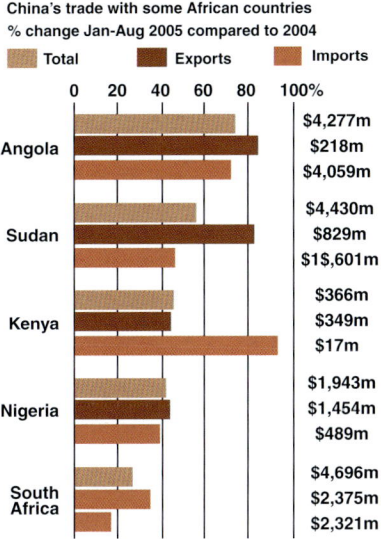

Scramble for Africa

China's trade with some African countries
% change Jan-Aug 2005 compared to 2004

Country		
Angola	$4,277m	$218m / $4,059m
Sudan	$4,430m	$829m / 1,601m
Kenya	$366m	$349m / $17m
Nigeria	$1,943m	$1,454m / $489m
South Africa	$4,696m	$2,375m / $2,321m

Sources: National Bureau of Statistics, China
General Administration of Customs

raw materials and they sell us manufactured goods with a predictable result—an unfavorable trade balance against South Africa." (South Africa's trade deficit with China has risen from $24m in 1992 to more than $400m).

In September 2004 the powerful Congress of South African Trade Unions (CO-SATU) threatened to boycott anyone selling Chinese products, which it blamed for rising unemployment. China has responded with a few promises and significant gestures. It has been, among other things, well ahead of the G8 with its cancellation in December 2003 of $10 billion owed it by African states.

THREAT?

American interests are not yet seen as seriously threatened. US oil companies still dominate in the offshore technology that is at the heart of West Africa's growing energy production and America still imports substantially from African oil and gas producers in a market controlled more by international price and demand than by individual country manipulations.

But it is clear that the US and other western nations have gained a serious contender in the scramble for Africa's riches.

Africa Exports to Asia in $ billion

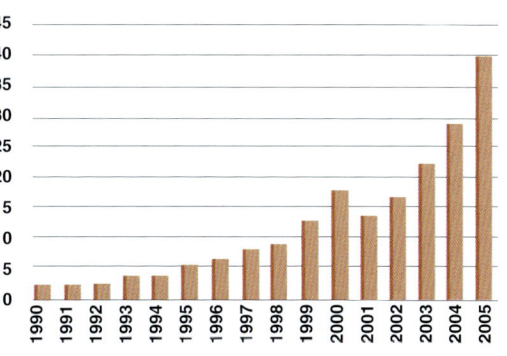

WRITER'S RETREAT

OVER THE YEARS AFRICA HAS NOT ONLY BEEN A RESOURCE FOR HOME-GROWN WRITERS BUT A RETREAT FOR AUTHORS FROM ABROAD. IT HAS BEEN A FOUNTAIN FOR PLENTY OF PROMISING LOCAL WRITERS AND AN INSPIRATION FOR WORLD-FAMOUS WORDSMITHS.

Out of Africa came a long list of accomplished authors, including Nobel laureates Nadine Gordimer, Wole Soyinka and Naquib Mahfouz and JM Coetzee. In recent years popular bestseller writer Wilbur Smith has entertained readers around the world with his South African novels.

Naturalists swear by Eugene Marais' writings about the *Soul of the Ape* and the *Soul of the Ant* as holy grail. But it was Olive Schreiner with her simple tale about a *South African Farm* that first caught the attention of Victorian England in the 19th Century. To those interested in delving into the spirit of Africa through the eyes of accomplished authors and poets there is much in store—especially, as translations from Afrikaans and other local languages become available.

JRR Tolkien, author of the *Lord of the Rings*, was born in the old Free State capital of Bloemfontein. Although he moved to England with his mother at a tender age, he later recounted a hairy encounter with a spider which might well have set him on course to the land of the Hobbits.

The list is long of famous foreign writers who came to Africa for nourishment and ideas. Among the early ones were Leo Africanus who wrote his famous *History and Description of Africa and the Notable Things Therein Contained* and Pliny who coined the phrase: *"Ex Africa semper aliquid novi"*—"Out of Africa always something new."

Rider Haggard (*King Solomon's Mines*), Arthur Conan Doyle (creator of Sherlock Homes) and Rudyard Kipling all came to South Africa during the Anglo-Boer War to see what kind of people would stand up to Her Majesty's forces in a David and Goliath struggle. In his Great War, Doyle speaks admiringly about the outnumbered Boers. So did Kipling, who later returned to Cape Town on a regular basis. Winston Churchill's earliest books were about Africa where he hunted and observed the Boer War as a correspondent. American President Teddy Roosevelt added to the African library with works about his own experiences on safari in East Africa. Other frequent visitors to the region were Ernest Hemingway, who wrote The *Macomber Affair* and *The Snows of Kilimanjaro*, and Robert Ruark with *Uhuru*. In the sixties James Michener spent a sabbatical in South Africa to write a historical novel—*The Covenant*—about the very people who once so intrigued the Haggards, Doyles and Kiplings. After him came Thomas Pakenham with *The Boer War* and *The Scramble for Africa*.

Out of Africa sprung many intriguing writings. There is no doubt much more to follow as others come along and fall under its spell. But Danish-born Baroness Karen Blixen (writing under her pen-name Isak Dinesen), is bound to retain first rights to the title *Out of Africa*—courtesy of a striking Hollywood movie rendition of her book about experiences on an African farm near Nairobi.

Rudyard Kipling

Ernest Hemingway

Isak Dinesen

TOURISM

In Henry IV Shakespeare spoke of "Africa and golden joys" and two thousand years ago Pliney the Elder coined the phrase "Out of Africa always something new." Foreigners who travel to the continent to go on safari or to get a close-up look at tribal life or the antiquities of Egypt find much else that is new in Africa's golden joys. There are breathtaking scenes, pristine beaches, gracious wine estates, world class hotels, elegant restaurants, challenging golf courses, white water rafting, fishing and other recreational pursuits.

TOURISM

TOURISM IS THE SINGLE BIGGEST INDUSTRY IN THE WORLD. CONSIDERING ITS WEALTH OF WILDLIFE, ANCIENT CIVILIZATIONS, CULTURAL DIVERSITY, SUPERB SCENERY, MAGNIFICENT BEACHES, AND SUNNY CLIMATE, AFRICA SHOULD BE GETTING A LION'S SHARE OF THE WORLD'S GROWING TOURIST TRAFFIC. HOWEVER, RECENT FIGURES SHOW AFRICA WITH A DISAPPOINTING 4.6% OF THE WORLD TOTAL. THE CONTINENT'S APPARENT INABILITY TO PULL IN LARGER NUMBERS OF VISITORS HAS BEEN ASCRIBED TO A VARIETY OF FACTORS INCLUDING LACK OF PROMOTION, INSUFFICIENT INFRASTRUCTURE, REMOTENESS AND WIDELY HELD PERCEPTIONS OF A CONTINENT RIFE WITH DISEASE, AND WAR AND CRIME. SOPHISTICATED AND DISCERNING TOURISTS WHO WILL NEVER ENTERTAIN THE THOUGHT OF CANCELLING A VISIT TO FRANCE OR GERMANY BECAUSE OF A WAR IN THE BALKANS OFTEN ESCHEW ALL OF AFRICA WHEN WAR BREAKS OUT IN AN AREA THOUSANDS OF MILES REMOVED FROM THE COUNTRY THAT THEY INTENDED TO VISIT. AT THE SAME TIME THERE ARE ENCOURAGING SIGNS OF INCREASED INVESTMENT FROM ABROAD IN INFRASTRUCTURE AND OTHER TOURIST-RELATED AMENITIES THAT SHOULD INCREASE AFRICA'S COMPETITIVENESS. AND AFRICA IS SLOWLY GAINING ON THE REST OF THE WORLD.

INTERNATIONAL ARRIVALS 2005

	Arrivals $ million 2005	Share % 2005	Change % 2005/4
WORLD	806	100	5.5
EUROPE	441.5	54.8	4.0
Northern Europe	52.9	6.6	6.5
Western Europe	142.7	17.7	2.6
Central/Eastern Europe	87.9	10.9	1.9
Southern/Mediter. Eu.	158.0	19.6	5.7
ASIA & PACIFIC	155.4	19.3	7.8
North-East Asia	87.6	10.9	10.3
South-East Asia	49.3	6.1	4.8
Oceania	10.5	1.3	3.8
South Asia	8.0	1.0	5.5
AMERICAS	133.5	16.6	6.2
North America	89.9	11.2	4.9
Caribbean	18.9	2.3	4.3
Central America	6.5	0.8	15.7
South America	18.2	2.3	12.2
AFRICA	36.7	4.6	8.5
North Africa	13.7	1.7	7.5
Subsaharan Africa	23.0	2.9	9.1
MIDDLE EAST	39.1	4.8	7.7

Source: World Tourism Organization

Statistics released by the UN World Tourism Organization (UNWTO) at the end of 2006 showed Africa recording the best growth in arrivals in 2005 (+9%), followed by the Asia and the Pacific (+8%), Middle East (+8%), the Americas (+6%) and Europe (+4%). Estimates for 2005 pointed to an increase by $2 billion to $21 billion in tourism receipts for Africa, representing 4.6% of the world total. In Africa growth was about as strong in Sub-Saharan Africa (+9%) as in North Africa (+8%). In 2005 Algeria reported 17% more arrivals, while Morocco increased arrivals by 7% and Tunisia by 6%. Among the Sub-Saharan destinations, particularly remarkable results were reported by the Democratic Republic of Congo (+103%), Swaziland (+83%), Gambia (+23%) and Senegal (+15%). Major destinations such as South Africa

AFRICAN TOURISM IN 2005

<table>
<tr><th colspan="6">INTERNATIONAL TOURIST ARRIVALS</th><th colspan="5">INTERNATIONAL TOURISM RECEIPTS</th></tr>
<tr><th></th><th colspan="2">1000</th><th colspan="2">Change %</th><th>Share %</th><th colspan="2">US$ million</th><th colspan="2">Change %</th><th>Share %</th></tr>
<tr><th></th><th>2004</th><th>2005</th><th>2004/3</th><th>2005/4</th><th>2005</th><th>2004</th><th>2005</th><th>2004/3</th><th>2005/4</th><th>2005</th></tr>
<tr><td>Africa</td><td>33,838</td><td>36,715</td><td>9.1</td><td>8.5</td><td>100</td><td>19,171</td><td>21,514</td><td>19.1</td><td>12.2</td><td>100</td></tr>
<tr><td>Algeria</td><td>1,234</td><td>1,443</td><td>5.8</td><td>16.9</td><td>3.9</td><td>178</td><td>–</td><td>58.9</td><td>–</td><td>–</td></tr>
<tr><td>Botswana</td><td>–</td><td>–</td><td>–</td><td>–</td><td>–</td><td>549</td><td>562</td><td>20.2</td><td>2.3</td><td>2.6</td></tr>
<tr><td>Egypt</td><td>7,795</td><td>8,244</td><td>35.7</td><td>5.8</td><td>21.1</td><td>6,125</td><td>6,851</td><td>33.6</td><td>11.8</td><td>24.9</td></tr>
<tr><td>Ghana</td><td>584</td><td>–</td><td>10.0</td><td>–</td><td>–</td><td>466</td><td>–</td><td>12.6</td><td>–</td><td>–</td></tr>
<tr><td>Kenya</td><td>1,199</td><td>–</td><td>29.3</td><td>–</td><td>–</td><td>486</td><td>579</td><td>39.8</td><td>19.2</td><td>2.7</td></tr>
<tr><td>Mauritius</td><td>719</td><td>761</td><td>2.4</td><td>5.9</td><td>2.1</td><td>853</td><td>871</td><td>22.5</td><td>2.2</td><td>4.1</td></tr>
<tr><td>Morocco</td><td>5,477</td><td>5,843</td><td>15.0</td><td>6.7</td><td>15.9</td><td>3,924</td><td>4,617</td><td>21.6</td><td>17.7</td><td>21.5</td></tr>
<tr><td>Namibia</td><td>–</td><td>–</td><td>–</td><td>–</td><td>–</td><td>403</td><td>348</td><td>22.1</td><td>-13.8</td><td>1.6</td></tr>
<tr><td>Reunion</td><td>430</td><td>409</td><td>-0.5</td><td>-4.9</td><td>1.1</td><td>448</td><td>384</td><td>8.5</td><td>-14.3</td><td>1.8</td></tr>
<tr><td>Senegal</td><td>667</td><td>769</td><td>34.7</td><td>15.3</td><td>2.1</td><td>–</td><td>–</td><td>–</td><td>–</td><td>–</td></tr>
<tr><td>Seychelles</td><td>121</td><td>129</td><td>-1.0</td><td>7.1</td><td>0.4</td><td>172</td><td>192</td><td>0.3</td><td>11.9</td><td>0.9</td></tr>
<tr><td>South Africa</td><td>6,815</td><td>7,518</td><td>2.6</td><td>10.3</td><td>20.5</td><td>6,282</td><td>7,327</td><td>13.7</td><td>16.6</td><td>34.1</td></tr>
<tr><td>Swaziland</td><td>459</td><td>839</td><td>-0.4</td><td>82.8</td><td>2.3</td><td>95</td><td>–</td><td>-5.9</td><td>–</td><td>–</td></tr>
<tr><td>Tanzania</td><td>566</td><td>–</td><td>2.5</td><td>–</td><td>–</td><td>746</td><td>796</td><td>15.4</td><td>6.7</td><td>3.7</td></tr>
<tr><td>Tunisia</td><td>5,998</td><td>6,378</td><td>17.3</td><td>6.3</td><td>17.4</td><td>1,970</td><td>2,063</td><td>24.5</td><td>4.7</td><td>9.6</td></tr>
<tr><td>Uganda</td><td>512</td><td>468</td><td>68.2</td><td>-8.7</td><td>1.3</td><td>266</td><td>–</td><td>44.6</td><td>–</td><td>–</td></tr>
<tr><td>Zambia</td><td>515</td><td>–</td><td>24.8</td><td>–</td><td>–</td><td>161</td><td>–</td><td>8.1</td><td>–</td><td>–</td></tr>
<tr><td>Zimbabwe</td><td>1,854</td><td>1,559</td><td>-17.8</td><td>-15.9</td><td>4.2</td><td>194</td><td>99</td><td>217.5</td><td>-48.9</td><td>0.5</td></tr>
</table>

Source: World Tourism Organization

(+10%), as well as the island destinations of Sey-chelles (+7%) and Mauritius (+6%) also improved on their 2004 results. Product improvement and diversification have been two of the main factors boosting tourism demand for African destinations. Investment in infrastructure has also been very positive and enhanced cooperation between the public and private sectors has helped to ensure increased benefits for all the participants.

In total numbers, however, African countries still remain well behind major tourist destinations such as France, Spain, the United States, Italy, China and the United Kingdom. There is, however, little doubt on the part of both economists and travel experts that with the proper planning and promotion Africa is bound to reap as much benefit from tourism as it has in the past from minerals.

The UNWTO envisages that Southern Africa will in the next two decades outstrip the rest of the continent in the number of tourists it attracts. The world organization forecasts that in 2020 the number of travelers to Southern Africa alone will increase to 36 million in comparison with a total of 19 million for North Africa. East Africa is projected to be a close third with 17 million.

In the WTO's most recent final statistics for 2005 places Egypt first with 8.2 million arrivals and a growth rate of 5.8 percent; South Africa ranks second with 7.5 million arrivals at a 10.3 percent growth rate; and Tunisia third with 6.3 million arrivals and a growth rate of 6.3 percent. Other significant tourist destinations included Morocco (5.8m), Zimbabwe (1.5m), Algeria (1.4m), Swazi-land (839,000) and Mauritius (761,000).

DISCOVERY

Ancient Egypt and other exotic North African destinations have long intrigued the European traveler. The discovery of Sub-Saharan Africa came much later. It was only through the personal accounts of Livingstone, Stanley and others that Europe and North America became aware of the unique attractions of this part of the continent. Tourists followed adventurers, hunters to the untamed hinterland in search of something new. They came from all corners of the world. The writers and the visionaries, the presidents and the princes, the rich and the regulars, the famous and the not so familiar.

UNDER-TRAVELED

Still, Africa remains surprisingly under-travelled. For a continent with all its offerings and charm. According to the experts, it should be getting a much larger chunk of the world's tourist traffic. Many countries on the continent stand to gain almost as much from tourism as they did in past years from the exploitation of other natural resources such as oil, gas, gold, platinum and other precious and strategic minerals. At a total of $12 billion in revenues tourism is already second only to oil as a source of revenue for Africa.

FEATURES

There is in the far north the mighty Nile, quietly flowing through the world's oldest civilization, and at the southern tip majestic Table Mountain that continued to impress the world's seafarers since the days of Vasco da Gama and Francis Drake. And in-between there are the likes of Lake Victoria, Victoria Falls, Mount Kilimanjaro and The Ngorongoro Crater. There are the Atlas mountains in the northeast, bordering the Sahara Desert, and there is a strip on the southwest coast aptly called the Skeleton Coast. There are tens of major animal kingdoms and literally hundreds of smaller wildlife estates where the exotic animals of the ark roam free for all to see. Africa offers visitors the treasures of Ancient Egypt and the throbbing excitement of the modern world.

OUT OF AFRICA

What is it that, since the time of Pliny and Leo Africanus, turned so many foreigners into Africa addicts? Writing as Isak Dinesen, Karen Blixen summed up her own experience as follows in *Out of Africa* : "Now, looking back on my life in Africa, I feel that it might altogether be described as the existence of a person who had come from a rushed and noisy world, into a still country."

GLIMPSE OF EDEN

In *A Glimpse of Eden*, Evelyn James declares: "Nothing can really prepare you for Africa. It is too full of extremes and contrasts, too immense, a spectrum of creation so much wider and more vivid than anywhere else that it seems to require a new set of senses, or the rediscovery of lost ones." Pres. Theodore Roosevelt, who spent considerable time on the continent, wrote from Khartoum on March 15, 1910: "There are no words that can tell the hidden spirit of the wilderness, that can reveal its mystery, its melancholy, and its charm." It is something in your blood, says Chris McBride, author of *The White Lions of Timbavati*. "A combination of the climate, the landscape, the wildlife, the whole atmosphere" that makes "you somehow feel that you're missing everything when you're not there." Author Vivienne de Wateville in *Out of The Blue* mused about the Nile river as one that "stands as a symbol of time itself, running down through the ages" and the patience of those who live along its banks. "There, perhaps, lay the solution. Africa is too mighty for anything so brittle as impatience, and one's strength lies not in pitting oneself against it, but in ranging oneself upon the same side."

Africanus

In 1550, a Moor by the adopted name of Joannes Leo Africanus—his real name was Al-Hassan Ibn Mohammed Al-Wezaz Al-Fasi—recorded his impressions of Africa. Originally written in Italian, it was later published in old English as *The History and Description of Africa and the Notable Things Therein Contained*. Here are some of his impressions: "The Hippopotamus or water-horse is somewhat tawnie, of the colour of a lion; in the night he comes on lands to feed upon the grasse, and keepeth in the water all the day time... the Zebra or Zabra of this country being about the bignes of a mule, is a beast of incomparable swiftnes, straked about the body, legges, eares, and other parts, with blacke, white and browne circles of three fingers broad; which do make a pleasant shew... Also here are infinite store of elephants of such monstrous bignes, that by the report of sundrie credible persons, some of their teeth do weigh two hundred pounds, at sixteene ounces the pound: upon the plaines this beast is swifter than any horse, by reason of his long steps; onely he cannot turne with such celeritie. Trees he overturneth with the strength of his backe, or breaketh them between his teeth; or standeth upright upon his hinder feete to browse upon the leaves and tender sprigs. The she elephants beare their brood in their wombes two years before they bring foorth yoong ones. This creature is saide to live 150 yeeres; hee is of a gentle disposition, and relying upon his great strength, he hurteth none but such as do him injurie; only he will in a sporting maner gently heave up with his snowte such persons as he meeteth." They are still all there for visitors to behold thanks to timely intervention of Africa-based and foreign conservationists. So are hundreds of other species, protected in pristine land set aside by African governments. Visitors have a choice of numerous destinations.

Cultures & Cuisines

Egypt has long fascinated travelers from abroad with its rich offerings in ancient architecture and artifacts. More recently other parts of Africa have also become choice destinations for foreigners in search of history and culture. Gorée Island draws hundreds of thousands of visitors who wish to step back into the days when millions of slaves were sorted and shipped like cargo from this little island near Dakar in Senegal to the New World. Heads of state, historians and ordinary folk include this island on their itinerary. While African Americans travel to Africa in search of their ancestral roots many more go simply to witness and experience the rich and diverse cultures of the continent. It comes replete with an array of local cuisines that appeals to every palate from mild to fiery spicy. Golfers, anglers, surfers and those inclined to spend their time indoors gambling all have a wide choice of venues—ranging from rustic to ultra-luxurious. Even though much of the continent's charm is in unspoiled nature, travelers are always assured of comfortable accommodation within easy distance from the most exotic parts. Hotels on the continent have received accolades for both service and style and several game lodges have earned high ratings among seasoned travelers. Both business and leisure travelers should also be reassured by the presence of the world's leading hotel groups in most major cities.

Going There

Air services are provided by a number of international and domestic airlines utilizing the latest long-haul aircraft between the US, Europe, the Far East, Australasia and Africa. Customs vary on a vast continent where thousands of cultures coexist and all major religions plus some indigenous beliefs. It makes for interesting travel but also requires proper preparation. Done right, Africa, makes for an unforgettable experience.

The Ultimate Safari

WWW.THEULTIMATESAFARI.COM

"Everything you arranged was #10, letter perfect. A superb, once in a life time, trip." N.F.

"We were overwhelmed by the efficiency of all the arrangements you made for our most delightful trip to Southern Africa." S.F.

"You planned the perfect trip for us. We truly enjoyed every aspect of our visit and can only describe it in superlatives!" L.S.

"Everything went so smoothly. It was a little like fantasy land! We all can't tell you enough how much we appreciate your arranging the most fabulous trip of a life time!" J.M.

We not only wrote the guide on how to get the most out of your African safari. We practice what we preach. At www.theultimatesafari.com you will find further detail about us and the clients we serve.

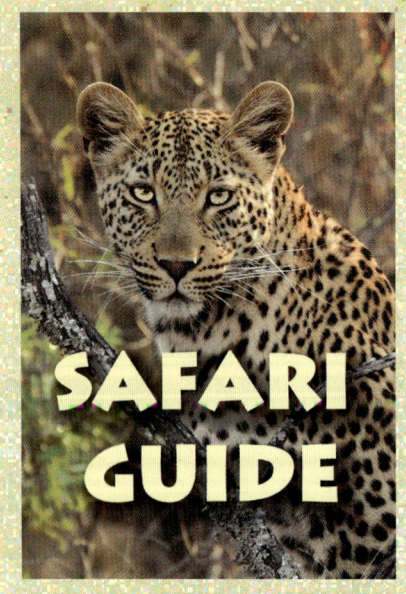

SAFARI

Major safari destinations in Southern and East Africa lure visitors from all parts of the world. National and private parks offer a wide variety of accommodations and services ranging from super de luxe to less extravagant. Regardless of the price tag the experience is guaranteed to be exquisite for all those who wish to view Africa's wildife in their natural habitat.

Giraffe and ox-pecker passenger

© Lorna Mack

SOUTH AFRICA, BOTSWANA, KENYA, MALAWI, NAMIBIA, UGANDA, ZAMBIA AND ZIMBABWE, HAVE A WHOLE RANGE OF NATIONAL PARKS AND GAME RESERVES, AS WELL AS A GROWING NUMBER OF PRIVATE GAME PARKS. AROUND SOUTH AFRICA'S KRUGER NATIONAL PARK NUMEROUS PRIVATE GAME PARKS HAVE SPRUNG UP WHERE ACCOMMODATIONS AND SERVICES ARE TAILORED TO SUIT THE TASTE OF THE MOST DEMANDING VISITORS. WHILE SOME MIGHT COMPLAIN ABOUT TOO MUCH LUXURY IN THE WILDS, OTHERS OBVIOUSLY WANT IT. THE OWNER OF ONE OF THE PRIVATE GAME PARKS EXPLAINS AS FOLLOWS: "TO VIEW THE ANIMALS YOU DON'T HAVE TO LIVE LIKE THEM." BUT FOR THOSE WHO LONG FOR SOMETHING MORE CLOSELY RESEMBLING THE EXPERIENCE OF LIVINGSTONE AND OTHER PIONEERS THERE IS STILL AMPLE OPPORTUNITY TO ROUGH IT.

Foreign interest is, however, not only in the enjoyment of the offerings but in the supply side as well. In recent years investors from abroad have increasingly become involved in the development of new private game parks and the upgrading of existing ones. Several governments have privatized parks and are actively seeking partners in both the development and management of facilities. There are no shortage of takers who anticipate a massive expansion in ecotourism to the world's foremost wildlife region. **Following are the major national parks (NP), game parks (GP), and game reserves (GR). Smaller private game parks are not listed:**

BOTSWANA:

Chobe National Park
At 4,247 sq. miles (11,000 sq km), this is Botswana's second largest park with varied wildlife including Africa's largest elephant population.

Okavango Delta
Referred to as *The Jewel of the Kalahari*, it covers an area of 6,178 sq. miles (16,000 sq. km). It is the largest inland delta in the world and home to abundant wildlife such as crocodile, hippo, water buck.

Moremi Game Reserve
The Moremi Game Reserve lies within the Okavango Delta, covers an area of over 1,351 sq. miles (3,500 sq.km) and has a wide variety of wildlife, including elephant, buffalo, giraffe, lion, leopard, cheetah, wild dog, hyena, jackal and antelope.

Central Kalahari Game Reserve
This is Africa's largest wildlife conservation area, covering an area of over 20,080 sq. miles (52,000 sq km). It is home to a wide variety of antelope including eland, gemsbok, kudu, red hartebeest and springbok as well as giraffe, lion, cheetah, leopard, wild dog and hyena.

Kgalagadi National Park
This is the first official *transfrontier* park, managed jointly by the Botswana and South African governments. Kagalagadi covers an area of 10,850 sq.

Leopard on lookout

© Les de

miles (28,105 sq. km) and has abundant wildlife including lion, leopard, cheetah, wildebeest, eland, hartebeest, gemsbok and springbok.

KENYA:

Aberdare National Park

Part of the Aberdare Mountain Range with wildlife that includes elephant, lion, black rhino, waterbuck, gazelle, giant forest hog, genet cats, leopard, buffalo and rare spiral-horned antelope known as bongo.

Amboseli National Park

Relatively small at approximately 153 sq. miles (395 sq. km), Amboseli is one of Kenya's most popular game parks with views of Mount Kilimanjaro and a wide variety of game, including large herds of elephants.

Lake Nakuru National Park

The main attraction is Lake Nakuru, a shallow alkaline, soda lake set beneath the high cliffs of the eastern Rift Valley, offering a spectacular view of up to 2 million flamingos at the same time (during the season) along with hundreds of other bird species.

Marsabit National Park

This park was famous for it's large tusker elephants before the poachers slaughtered most of the large ones. Elephants are, however, still present along with large herds of kudu and many birds of prey.

Masai Mara Game Reserve

This is Kenya's most popular game reserve. From July to September it experiences the annual influx of over a million wildebeest and zebra, migrating from the Serengeti across the Mara River. Masai Mara is also populated by lion, hippo, crocodile, elephant, cheetah, baboon, gazelle, giraffe, jackal, leopards, hyena, water buffalo, and antelope.

Meru National Park

This was the setting for Joy Adamson's book, *Born Free*. Meru offers varied scenery on the slopes of the Nyambeni Mountain Range and game ranging from lion, cheetah, leopard, elephant, antelope, and buffalo to hippo and crocodile.

Mount Kenya National Park

Mount Kenya is an extinct volcano on the equator and a favorite of both botanists and game viewers in search of unique plants and species such as the bongo and Black and White colobus and Sykes monkeys. Mt. Kenya park also has bushbuck, buffalo, elephant, baboon, black rhino, and leopard.

Nairobi National Park

Within easy distance from Kenya's capital, this park is inhabited by leopard, lion, buffalo, rhino, giraffe, hippo, crocodile, antelope, wildebeest, eland, zebra and Thompson's gazelle.

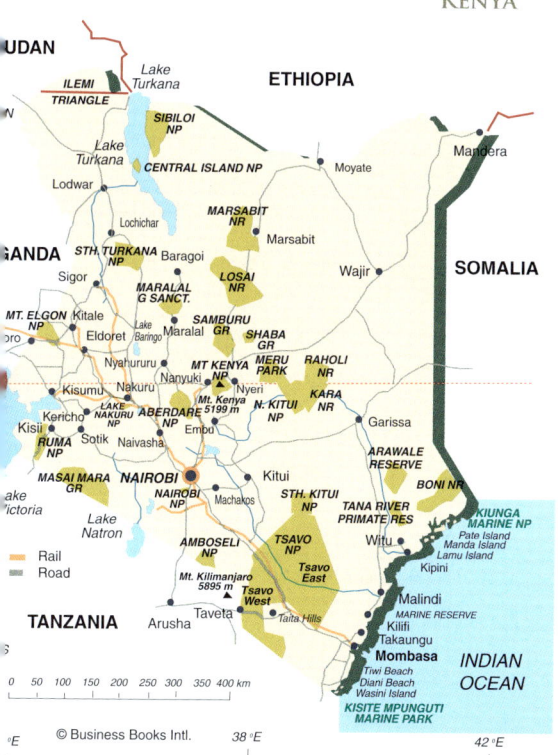

BOTSWANA

KENYA

131

Sambura Game Reserve

This is a semi-desert region with a large concentration of game including rare species such as the oryx, gerenuk, reticulated giraffe and Grevy's zebra.

Shaba Game Reserve

This semidesert region is the natural habitat for the Grevy zebra, reticulated giraffe, and gerenuk—unique to this part of Kenya. It also has elephants, lions, cheetah, crocodile, and hundreds of bird species.

Sibiloi National Park

Kenya's most remote national park. It is hot, dry and windswept, features a petrified forest and has a large variety of wildlife including Grevy's zebra, ostrich, gerenuk, oryx, tiang and a large population of Nile crocodile.

Tsavo National Park

This is Kenya's oldest and largest park with parts still inaccessible to the public. The southern region spans across the Kanderi Swamp and the Aruba Dam on the Voi river and has a large concentration of game, including hippo, crocodile, lion, leopard, waterbuck, kudu, zebra, ostrich, and the largest herd of elephant in the country.

Tsavo West National Park

Three rivers—the Galana, the Athi and the Tsavo—attract large concentrations of game including buffalo, rhino, giraffe, zebra, lion, leopard, cheetah, crocodile and many varieties of antelope.

MALAWI

Nyika National Park

At 1,158 sq. miles (3,000 sq. km) and with an average elevation of 5,906 ft (1,800 m) it is the largest and highest of Malawi's parks—settled by a few Aphoka people and populated by large herds of zebra, eland, roan antelope, sable, Lichtenstein's hartebeest, kudu reedbuck, bushbuck, duiker, and warthog, as well as 300 bird species.

Vwaza Marsh Game Reserve

This reserve contains large herds of buffalo and elephant, and a great variety of antelope, including roan, greater kudu, harte-beest, eland and impala, and has abundant and varied birdlife.

Kasungu National Park

At 772 sq. miles (2,000 sq. km), this is Malawi's second largest park. Kasungu is known for its elephants and hippo—resident in several rivers in the park—as well as sable, roan, kudu, impala and predators such as hyena, wild dog and serval.

Nkhotakota Game Reserve

The oldest established reserve in Malawi with elephant, buffalo, lion, leopard, hyena and 300 species of birds.

Lake Malawi Marine Park

This park is the most important freshwater fish sanctuary in Africa and the first worldwide to protect to the marine life of in tropical deep freshwater.

Liwonde National Park

On the banks of the Upper Shire River, vegetation ranges from swamps, lagoons and reed-beds to dense woodland. It is home to Malawi's largest elephant population, as well as sable antelope, kudu, duiker, oribi, hippo and lion. Birds are abundant.

Majete Game Reserve

Known for the Kapichira Falls in the Shire River, and its abundant bird life.

Lengwe National Park

Known for its nyala antelope and bushbuck, impala, duiker and kudu, warthogs, monkeys and baboons.

Mwabvu Game Reserve

At 135 sq. miles (350 sq. km), Malawi's smallest park with rugged terrain and various kinds of antelope, lion, baboons, monkeys, and a variety of birdlife.

NAMIBIA

Daan Viljoen Game Park

A small park close to Windhoek with kudu, red harte-beest, springbok, klipspringer, steenbok, eland, oryx, baboons, blouwildebeest, and giraffe, as well as 200 bird species.

Etosha National Park

Covering an area of 8,880 sq. miles (23,000 sq. km), Etosha is one of Africa's largest game reserves. It is home to elephant, zebra, giraffe, lion, leopard, black

MALAWI

Chitipa
Karonga
TANZANIA
ZAMBIA
NYIKA NP
Chilumba
Livingstone
VWAZA MARSH GR
Nyika Plateau
Lake Malawi
Rumphi
Mzuzu
Nkhata Bay
Mzimba
Likoma islands (Malawi)
VIPHYA MTS
Dwangwa
MOZAMBIQUE
KASUNGU NP
Bua
Kissungu
Nkhotakota
NKHOTAKOTA NP
Mponela
Namitete
LILONGWE
LAKE MALAWI MARINE PARK
Mchinji
Nathenji
Monkey Bay
Dedza
Mangochi
Lake Chiuta
Ntcheu
LIWONDE NP
Balaka
Lake Chilwa
Tedzani
Zomba
Mwanza
Blantyre
MAJETE GR
Limbe
Luchenza
Mt Mulanje
MOZAMBIQUE
LENGWE NP
Thyolo
Mulanje
Bangula
MWABVU GR
Nsanje

Rail
Roads
© Business Books Intl.
0 50 100 150 km
33°E
35°E

© Business Books Intl.

SAFARI CHIC

Safari has become synonymous with travel to Africa, fittingly so because that is what the word means in Swahili. In the old days the journey comprised a few men with guns, a string of carriers and a tent or two. Since then a few enterprising entrepreneurs have turned it into a luxurious experience.

President Teddy Roosevelt gave new meaning to the word *safari* when he embarked on a major expedition to East Africa with shipload of supplies sufficient for an army. He proudly sent out a card to friends showing his tent under the American flag with the inscription: "My boma where I was camped alone."

While author-hunter Ernest Hemingway did much of his writing in a tent in Africa actor William Holden and a friend bought a hotel in the shadow of Mount Kenya and turned it into an exotic Safari Club—complete with a bowling green and a nine hole golf course frequented by wildlife.

Proceeding on the principle that to enjoy animals in their natural habitat you don't have to live like them, entrepreneurs in southern Africa started developing private game reserves. There is certainly nothing unecological about the sumptious luxury lodges that blend in so well with the bush that they keep winning accolades from both conservationists and comfort seekers. Several of these game lodges have been voted best hotels in the world by Condé Nast, Tatler and Travel Leisure readers and there is a stampede of other private game reserves vying for the top spot.

Safari in today's world means waking up to the sound of drums in a luxurious private lodge in the wild; enjoying game tracking under the supervision of knowledgeable game rangers; feasting around a campfire in the boma on venision and other local dishes prepared by cullinary wizards; sipping the local wines while watching wildlife from the soft comfort of a lounge chair on a private veranda; or soaking in the plunge pool or your bathtub to the amusement of the monkeys and the ever-present flocks of exotic birds.

Incidentally, President Teddy Roosevelt had it wrong. *Boma* simply means a roofless brush enclosure, not a tent. Today some private game reserves provide luxury tented accommodation as well—the kind that puts Roosevelt's to shame with their finely appointed interiors and hot and cold showers.

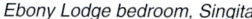

Ebony Lodge bedroom, Singita

Ivory Lodge bathroom, Lion Sands

Rhinos reflected   © Bill Schmitt

rhinoceros, red hartebees, wildebees, cheetah, hyena, eland, kudu, springbok, gemsbok, black-faced impala and many other types of antelope, as well as over 340 species of birds.

Fish River Canyon NP

The Grand Canyon of Southern Africa, situated on the lower parts of the Fish River near the southern border of Namibia. Its hiking trails are closed in summer when temperatures reach highs of 122°F (50°C).

Khaudom Game Reserve

This is a remote, medium-sized park situated in the Kalahari region, at the bottom of the Caprivi strip, accessible only with a convoy of four wheel drive vehicles. It offers a wide variety of wildlife including lion and hyena.

Mahango Game Reserve

This smallish park at the western end of the Caprivi strip along the gateway to Botswana's Okavango Delta, offers a wide range of wildlife.

Mamili & Mudumu Park

Referred to as the mini-Okavango Delta, the flooded marshy terrain of Mamili and Mudumu is accessible only in four wheel drive vehicles. It contains abundant wildlife, including large numbers of water buffalo and hippo.

Namib-Naukluft National Park

Interaction between the hot Namibian desert and the cold Atlantic ocean along a 1200 mile (1,930 km) strip of land provides a breeding ground for lizards, snakes, beetles and other creatures.

Skeleton Coast Park

Associated with famous shipwrecks and sailors who died in search of food and water and the topic of many an adventure novel, parts of the Skeleton Coast Park are inhabited by springbok, oryx, hyena, ostrich, the rare Desert Elephant, black rhino, lion and giraffe.

SOUTH AFRICA

Addo Elephant Park

This small park, near the harbor city of Port Elizabeth, was established to protect the huge herds of elephants that once roamed the area.

Augrabies Falls National Park

Features the Augrabies Falls, where the Orange River drops 56 meters into a solid granite ravine, and small mammals including klipspringer antelope, rock dassie, as well as black rhino, eland, springbok and kudu.

Bontebok Park

Established to protect the bontebok from extinction and provides shelter for other antelope thriving on fynbos such as grey rhebok, grysbok, red hartebeest and Cape mountain zebra.

Drakensberg National Park

The Afrikaans word, *Drakens-berge*, means *Dragon Mountains*. The peaks of this mountain range are covered with snow in winter and heavy clouds in summer. The lush slopes with a variety of African flora are home to grey rhebok, oribi, eland and a variety of large birds such as the lammergeyer.

Kalahari Gemsbok National Park

A semi-desert inhabited by gemsbok, springbok and the Kalahari lion as well as a variety of birds, reptiles and small mammals.

Karoo National Park

A semidesert with 60 species of mammal, including the dassie and bat-eared fox.

Kruger National Park

Established in 1898 by President Paul Kruger, this well-known park is home to a wealth of wildlife, including 147 species of mammals, 500 types of bird and 33 amphibian types. The flora is equally diverse. There are 300 difference types of trees. All the big game can be found here including lion, leopard, cheetah, elephant, hippo, giraffe, rhino and buffalo. It is the foremost wildlife research area in Africa and the world leader in the study of African wildlife conservation and protection.

Royal flush—Nigel Dennis   © South African Tourism

Mountain Zebra NP

This small park protects one of the rarest animals in the world, the mountain zebra, and is also home to other antelope.

St. Lucia Wetland

A lagoon separated from the sea by a chain of dunes with swamp forests and mangroves, inhabited by seabirds, crocodiles and hippo.

Tankwa Karoo Park

An arid region with natural springs and succulent vegetation, small mammals, birds and a variety of reptiles.

Umfolozi & Hluhluwe GR

A hilly savannah landscape, covering 425 sq. miles (1,100 sq km), with large herds of rhinos as well as elephants, buffalo, lion, leopard, and giraffe.

Vaalbos National Park

Situated along the Vaal River in a former alluvial diamond digging area near Kimberley, this park's wildlife includes black rhino, white rhino, buffalo, eland, red hartebeest and tsessebe .

TANZANIA

Arusha National Park

Contains a diverse population of herbivores, primates and predators, including black and white colobus monkey, baboon, elephant, giraffe, buffalo, hippo, leopard, hyena, waterbuck and other antelope.

Gombe Stream National Park

Among Tanzania's smallest parks, with a total area of 20 sq. miles (52 sq.km), Gombe Stream is also one of the most popular. It is known for chimpanzees in their natural habitat. The park is also home to several species of monkey including the red colobus, red-tail and blue monkey, as well as grey duiker, bushbuck and bushpig and numerous bird species.

135

Elephant greetings—Nigel Dennis

© South African Tourism

Katavi National Park

With an area of 870 sq. miles (2,253 sq km) Katavi is one the most natural sanctuaries in Africa, with minimal human interference. It has abundant wildlife, including big mammals.

Lake Manyara National Park

An area consisting of forest, woodland, grasslands, and swamps situated at the base of the Great Rift Valley escarpment with abundant wildlife including gazelle, impala, buffalo, wildebeest, lions, hyena, baboon, giraffe, hippo, a great number of smaller mammals and 350 bird species.

Mikumi National Park

Its wildlife includes giraffe, zebra, buffalo, hartebeest, wildebeest, elephant, wild dog and tree climbing lions, as well as smaller mammals and reptiles. The park is home to more than 300 species of birds.

Mkomazi Game Reserve

Together with Tsavo, Mkomazi forms part of one of East Africa's most important savannah ecosystems, characterized by the semi-arid climatic conditions of the Sahel. Most of the large mammal species found in Tsavo are also resident in Mkomazi or migrate here from the Kenyan game park. Wildlife includes lion, cheetah, elephant, giraffe, buffalo, zebra, impala, and leopard.

Mt. Kilimanjaro National Park

The area surrounding Africa's highest mountain has been a game reserve since 1921 and designated a national park in 1973. The rainforest is home to many species of animals, including leopard, rhino, elephant, buffalo. There are six different routes up the mountain with varying degrees of difficulty.

Mahale Mts. National Park

This remote park can be reached by air or boat. Chimpanzees still live here along with elephant, buffalo, antelope, giraffe, leopard and lion.

Ngorongoro Crater Conservation Area

This conservation area in the world's largest intact crater is a blend of landscapes and wildlife and contains Africa's main archaeological site. It teems with wildlife such as zebra, wildebeest, black rhino, antelope, elephants, giraffe, buffalo, lion, cheetah, and leopard. Thousands of flamingos are to be found.

Ruaha National Park

This is Tanzania's second largest park, covering an area of over 5,019 sq. miles (13,000 sq km). It is the world's largest elephant sanctuary. Wildlife includes elephant, buffalo, giraffe, cheetah, lion, leopard, a wide variety of antelope. There are 465 bird species.

Selous Game Reserve

Africa's largest game reserve and one of the largest protected wildlife areas in the world. With more than 120,000 elephants, 160,000 buffaloes and about 2,000 rhinos, Selous also tops the world in big game. It has the greatest concentration of hippo, crocodile and wild dogs.

Serengeti National Park

Tanzania's most popular game reserve. Named after the Masai word *Serengeti*, which means *endless plain*, the park consists of flat, treeless plains and

TANZANIA

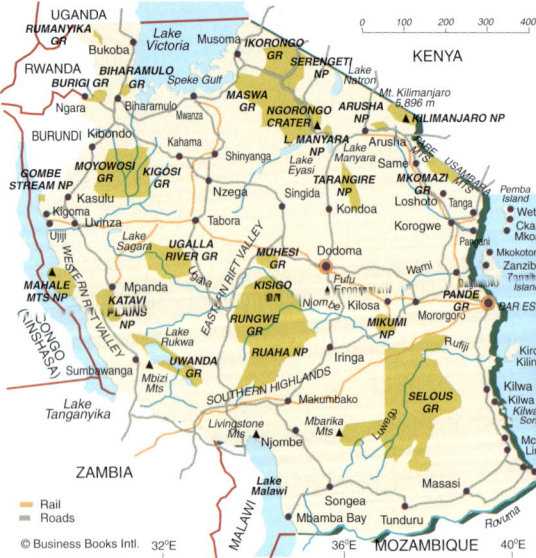

offers one of the highest concentrations of wildlife in Africa. Virtually every species in Africa can be found here but the park is known for its vast herds of wildebeest, zebra and antelope, and the *Serengeti lions.*

Tarangire National Park

During the dry season from June to October this park has a high concentration of wildlife, crowding along the Tarangire River. It has more than 300 bird species.

Uwanda Game Reserve

Its dominant feature is Lake Rukwa, a shallow alkaline lake with an extensive floodplain that attracts large herds after the rains. Mammals include the rare puku and albino giraffe.

Buffalo bronco

© Les de Villiers

UGANDA

Bwindi National Park

Known for its mountain gorilla, it has over 120 other species of mammals, including chimpanzee, black and white colobus, blue monkey, bushpig, duiker, leopard, jackal and elephant in the south east region of the park. There are over 350 bird species.

Kibale Forest National Park

Represents the vast diversity of wildlife and flora typical of a tropical rainforest. The park has the largest population of forest elephants in Uganda and is inhabited by the red-tailed money, blue monkey, olive baboon, chimpanzee, black, white and red colobus.

Kipedo Valley National Park

A mountainous region bordering Sudan with wildlife ranging from giraffe, ostrich, elephant, cheetah, and leopard, to kudu, zebra, and buffalo.

Lake Mburo National Park

Its terrain consists of savannah and includes four lakes that are frequented by large herds of elephants, buffalo, leopard, hyena, hippo and a variety of antelope and birds.

Mgahinga National Park

Uganda's smallest park, covering an area 13 sq. miles (34 sq km) on the Congolese border, Mgahinga is one of the last remaining habitats of the mountain gorilla along the slopes of the Virunga Mountains. Three extinct volcanos rise within the park—Mt. Muhuvura, Mt. Gahinga and Mt. Sabinyo.

Mt Rwenzori National Park

The mist-shrouded, snow-capped Rwenzori mountain peaks have been referred to as the *Mountains of the Moon.* At the center of the range is Africa's third highest mountain, Mt. Stanley at 16,765 ft. (5,110 m). Wildlife includes elephant, genet, Vervet monkey, Rwenzori colobus, chimpanzee and duiker.

Mt Elgon National Park

The park at Mt. Elgon, an extinct volcano, offers a variety of vegetation and wildlife including, duiker, hyena, leopard, chimpanzee, buffalo and elephant, as well as numerous species of birdlife.

Murchison Falls National Park

This is the largest park in Uganda. It covers an area of over 1,483 sq. miles (3,840 sq km) and is known for its scenic beauty, spectacular falls and varied wildlife. The Nile river that divides the park into the northern and southern sections, attracts large numbers of game including elephant, giraffe, hippo, lion, leopard, buffalo, Nile crocodiles, monkeys, and over 450 species of birds.

Zebra crossing   © South African Tourism

hippo, buffalo, zebra, lion, cheetah, leopard, various antelope species, and a large variety of birds.

Mosi-Oa-Tunya National Park

The country's smallest national park, with a name that means *the smoke that thunders*, it has as a centerpiece, the famous Victoria Falls, and offers game viewing along the riverbank. It is best known for its giraffe, but also contains sizeable numbers of sable, eland, wildebeest, lechwe, impala, warthog, baboon and monkey.

Nsumbu National Park

Situated in the remote north of Zambia, Nsumbu had to be restocked after severe poaching. Once it again offers a diverse range of wildlife including large herds of elephant, bushbuck, warthog, puku, roan antelope, sable, eland, hartebeest, buffalo and zebra.

North Luangwa National Park

Primarily a woodland area known for its huge herds of buffalo as well as leopard, wildcat, elephant, hyena, and blouwildebeest as well as oribi, hartebeest, reedbuck and eland.

South Luangwa National Park

Covers an area over 3,494 sq. miles (9,050 sq. km) and considered one of the prime sanctuaries in Zambia. Its wildlife include elephant, hippo, buffalo, black rhino, zebra, blouwildebeest, leopard, lion, and a wide variety of antelope as well as numerous bird species.

Queen Elizabeth National Park

This game area covers almost 772 sq. miles (2,000 sq. km) and is known for hippo, as well as elephant, buffalo, Uganda kob, antelope, baboons and chimpanzees, and tree-climbing lions.

ZAMBIA

Kafue National Park

The third largest park in Africa with over 40 species of wildlife including elephant, buffalo, zebra, kudu, sable, roan antelope, lion, leopard, hyena, hippo and crocodile. It is home to the rare lechwe antelope and has more than 400 varieties of bird life.

Kasanka National Park

This small park on the edge of the vast wetlands of Lake Bangweulu is privately managed. Its mammals include elephant, hippo, warthog, bushpig, baboon, leopard, and the rare blue monkey.

Liuwa Plain National Park

The Luambimba and Luanginga rivers run through the region and are flanked by a grass-covered flood plain in this remote park. It has large herds of blou-wildebeest, buffalo, and zebra. It also has red lechwe, oribi, steenbok, duiker, tsessebe, roan, jackal, serval, wildcat, wild dog, and hyena. Massive flocks of birds migrate through the park.

Lochinvar National Park

A small park with a wide variety of game including large herds of the lechwe antelope, buffalo, zebra, blouwildebeest, orbi, bushbuck, kudu, hippo and over 420 bird species.

Lower Zambezi National Park

A recently established area of over 1,544 sq. miles (4,000 sq. km) on the northern bank of the Zambezi river, downstream from the Victoria Falls. Wildlife includes elephant,

Chimanimani National Park

Animal life includes baboon, antelope, blue duiker, klipspringer and waterbuck as well as many bird species.

Chizarira National Park

Remote, wild, and rich in wildlife, with mammals including elephant, leopards, lions, warthog and numerous species of antelope. Chizarira consists of three regions—the Zambezi Escarpment, the Uplands and the Bush Valley.

Gonarezhou National Park

In Shona, the name of the park means *abode of elephants*, but poaching has taken its toll. Apart from elephant, the area contains buffalo, hippopotamus, hartebeest, zebra, giraffe, nyala and roan antelope, and black rhinoceros.

Hyper hippo   © Les de Villiers

Hwange National Park

Zimbabwe's largest park, covering 5,598 sq. miles (14,500 sq. km), it has the country's biggest variety of animals, including elephant, giraffe, zebra, buffalo, hyena, lion, leopard, cheetah, and antelope.

Lake Kariba

This man-made lake, covering an area of over 2,510 sq. miles (6,500 sq. km), does not only provide hydropower and irrigation but has become an important water playground and game region. After the construction of the dam when the water started rising, a rescue mission—dubbed Operation Noah—managed to save thousands of animals trapped on islands, from drowning.

Mana Pools National Park

The name *Mana* means four to indicate the number of pools situated around the park's headquarters. This World Heritage site is home to elephant, buffalo, zebra, kudu, waterbuck, hippo and crocodile.

Matopos National Park

Matopos or Matobo offers a combination of history, scenery and wildlife. British empire builder Cecil John Rhodes was buried at the top of Malindidzimu Mountain, to which he referred to as *View of the World*. A million years ago the first hunting and gathering societies appeared around the Matobo Hills.

Matusadona National Park

Situated on Lake Kariba's southern shore, two-thirds of this 579 sq. miles (1,500 km) park is only accessible on foot. It has herds of buffalo and elephants and varied birdlife. Matusadona is a melodic word for *constant dripping of dung*, in reference to the huge elephant population which took to these high grounds after they were rescued from Kariba's rising waters under Operation Noah.

Victoria Falls Park

Considered one of the world's most spectacular natural wonders, Victoria Falls is surrounded by a fair amount of wildlife including warthog, hippo, crocodile, antelope, elephants and buffalo.

Zambezi National Park

Game found within the park includes of hippo, elephant, giraffe, sable and other species of antelope, zebra, and buffalo.

139

Merck's Commitment to Health in Africa

At Merck & Co., Inc., our efforts to address health care challenges go beyond research and development of novel treatments to seek out and support initiatives that foster disease education, prevention and treatment and promote sustainable access to medicines, vaccines and quality health care. Examples of programs and partnerships supported by Merck and The Merck Company Foundation include:

The African Comprehensive HIV/AIDS Partnerships (ACHAP)

Established in 2000, ACHAP is a partnership among the Government of Botswana, Merck and The Merck Company Foundation and the Bill & Melinda Gates Foundation to support and enhance Botswana's national response to HIV/AIDS through a comprehensive approach to prevention, care, treatment and support. The Merck Company Foundation and the Bill & Melinda Gates Foundation are each providing $56.5 million to the effort. In addition, Merck is donating its two antiretroviral (ARV) medicines to Botswana's national ARV treatment program, known as "Masa" ("dawn"). The partnership has shown that treatment programs in Africa can and will produce sustainable results and save lives. As of July 2006, 62,185 people were receiving ARV treatment in the public sector in Botswana, making the program one of the largest ARV treatment programs in Africa.

The Merck Mectizan Donation Program

Since 1987, Merck has donated its drug MECTIZAN® (ivermectin), for the treatment of onchocerciasis (river blindness), to all who need it for as long as necessary until the disease is eliminated as a public health problem. In 1998, Merck expanded its commitment to include the prevention of lymphatic filariasis (LF) in African countries where LF co-exists with river blindness. The program currently reaches more than 70 million people each year.

The Merck Vaccine Network Africa (MVN-A)

Launched in 2003, MVN-A is a multi-year initiative to help increase the capacity of immunization programs to deliver vaccines effectively in Kenya and Mali through training of national and regional health care workers in vaccine management and immunization services.

Nursing Libraries for Refugee Health

Launched in February 2006, the Nursing Libraries for Refugee Health is a collaboration of the International Council of Nurses (ICN), United Nations High Commissioner for Refugees (UNHCR) and Merck to provide current health care information and training to nurses and health workers serving refugee populations in Africa. This program builds upon the work of the ICN Merck Mobile Library project, which launched in 2001 as a partnership of ICN, Merck, and Elsevier, the world's largest publisher of nursing titles. To date, the Mobile Libraries have reached thousands of people in more than 300 clinical settings in 15 countries.

The African Comprehensive HIV/AIDS Partnerships has established support and counseling services including faith-based services, pre- and post-test counseling and interventions targeting youth and other vulnerable groups in Botswana.

The National AIDS Control Program in Rwanda

The National Aids Control Program in Rwanda has been the recipient of continuous Merck support since 1998 with the goal to strengthen local HIV expertise and HIV-related care and services. Through this support, 12 Rwandan physicians received training on ARV therapy and HIV care. Today, these physicians serve as the referral physicians for ARV therapy in Rwanda at the tertiary level. Merck has also supported local workshops/conferences on HIV-related issues. The local capacity building enabled by Merck's support has played an instrumental role in improving HIV/AIDS care and treatment in Rwanda. Since 2002, the number of patients on ARV therapy has increased from 1,200 to more than 22,000 by early 2006.

To date, Merck has donated more than 1 billion tablets of MECTIZAN to combat the tropical diseases river blindness and lymphatic filariasis, helping to bring an end to the number of people afflicted by these two debilitating diseases.

The Regional AIDS Initiative of Southern Africa

For several years, Merck has supported the Regional AIDS Initiative of Southern Africa (RAISA), a project of the organization Voluntary Service Overseas (VSO). RAISA works with government institutions and civil society organizations to provide effective prevention, treatment, care and advocacy support for people affected by HIV/AIDS, and to mitigate the personal, social and economic impact of the pandemic. This regional initiative works in Malawi, Mozambique, Namibia, South Africa, Zambia and Zimbabwe.

Merck ANADER Partnership Program

Merck is working with the National Agency for the Support to Rural Development in Côte d'Ivoire (ANADER) to support Côte d'Ivoire's response to HIV/AIDS. The partnership initially began with an HIV prevention and workplace care program, including access to ARV treatment for ANADER's 2,500 employees. Since then, ANADER has extended its services to 3.8 million people living in rural areas.

IBANISE HIV/AIDS Initiative

Driven by expanding industrial development, Bonny Island in the Niger Delta region of Nigeria has become a hive of social activity and mobility, and is a focal point for the regional HIV epidemic in West Africa. Merck is providing technical guidance and is helping to facilitate a community-led, comprehensive HIV/AIDS and malaria program on Bonny Island. The program concentrates on several key areas: behavior modification among vulnerable groups; promoting safe sexual practices, awareness and education in schools; managing sexually transmitted infections; prevention and treatment of malaria; and access to ARV medicines.

More information on these and other programs supported by Merck & Co., Inc., and The Merck Company Foundation can be found at *www.merck.com/cr*

More than 200 health service providers have completed the Merck Vaccine Network—Africa training course, including these graduates in Kenya. The MVN-A Center in Kenya is a collaboration between Indiana University School of Medicine in Indianapolis and Moi University Faculty of Health Sciences in Eldoret.

CULTURES OF AFRICA

In Long Walk to Freedom Nelson Mandela vividly recalls the Xhosa circumcision ceremony at age sixteen that signalled his entry into manhood. Even though this *abakwetha*, **performed by an elder (***ingcibi***) with a spear or assegai and without any anaesthetic, caused excruciating pain, no one was to show any outward emotion. "A boy may cry; a man conceals pain," Mandela explains. "I had now taken the essential step in the life of every Xhosa man. Now I might marry, set up my own home and plough my own field."**

Until this day the *abakwetha* is performed in the Xhosa region of South Africa. So are numerous other unique ceremonies across the face of Africa, designed to build character and honor, solidify marriages and strengthen family and community ties. Everyone of these ceremonies—even those that might seem as bizarre to foreigners as certain customs in their world might appear to the Africans—have a definite purpose and a deeper meaning.

Today much of the travel to Africa is inspired by a desire to learn more about the cultures and customs of this continent with its diverse peoples. African-American author Henry Louis Gates has done much to educate the outside world about the hidden Wonders of Africa in a television series, revealing its rich cultures and ancient civilizations unknown to many in the Western world.

In Delgo, Gates was invited to participate in a traditional Nubian wedding, in Ethiopia he mingled with Christians whose faith predated that of England by several hundred years and whose icons were all in black, and in Dogon he was allowed a glimpse of the circumcision cave with its fascinating wall paintings—an area totally closed to women.

But it took two enterprising women to produce what could arguably be described as the most extensive and impressive photographic record of Africa's ceremonies. Accomplished Africanists and photographers Carol Beckwith and Angela Fisher collaborated in the production of a dramatic two volume presentation of African Ceremonies, published by Henry M. Abrams Inc., New York. (www.abramsbooks.com).

"Living in traditional African societies has made us aware of the value that rites of passage have for the individual and the community. Ceremonies that mark the stages of life from birth to death provide clear definitions of what is expected of the individual and give him or her a sense of identity and belonging," write Beckwith and Fisher. "Each rite begins with a gift or an offering and nothing is taken from the land without giving something back to it. Survival depends on this basic principle."

While no one can truly expect to experience more than a fraction of the magnificent rites, rituals and ceremonies which took Beckwith and Fisher ten years to record, a mere sampling of these magnificent color photographs is bound to wet the appetite to know more through travel.

Himba, Namibia   *Masaai, Kenya*   *Fulani, Mali*   *Ashanti, Ghana*

© Carol Beckwith & Angela Fish

CHAPTER 5

CHALLENGES OF AFRICA

REED-THIN REFUGEES FROM FIERCE FIGHTING THAT APPEAR ON TV SCREENS AND FEATURE IN NEWSPRINT ARE REAL. SO ARE THE GROWING MILLIONS OF HIV/AIDS INFECTED AFRICANS. AND SO ARE THE COUPS AND WARS THAT PERSIST IN AFRICA DESPITE ADMIRABLE EFFORTS BY NEW LEADERSHIP INTENT ON RESPONSIBLE AND TRANSPARENT GOVERNANCE. THE CONTINENT CARRIES A HEAVY DEBT BURDEN AND CORRUPTION STILL PREVAILS IN MANY PARTS. WHILE SOME MIGHT SEE THESE CHALLENGES AS INSURMOUNTABLE OTHERS ARE ACTUALLY MAKING SOME PROGRESS IN TRYING TO FIND SOLUTIONS.

WARS & REFUGEES

ACCORDING TO THE UNITED NATIONS MORE THAN 30 WARS HAVE BEEN FOUGHT IN AFRICA SINCE 1970—MOST OF THEM INTERNAL STRUGGLES. IN 1996, THE WORST SINGLE YEAR, 14 OF THE CONTINENT'S 53 COUNTRIES WERE AFFECTED BY ARMED CONFLICT, ACCOUNTING FOR MORE THAN HALF OF ALL WAR-RELATED DEATHS WORLDWIDE AND RESULTING IN MORE THAN 8 MILLION REFUGEES, RETURNEES AND DISPLACED PERSONS.

Deaths as the result of a 17-year civil war in the Sudan are estimated at 2 million while 500,000 have died in Angola over the past 25-years and a million in Rwanda over a six year period. Almost all of these conflicts involve power struggles within countries. Wars between states are rare.

UNHCR

According to the UN High Commissioner for Refugees (UNHCR) there are 21.8 million refugees worldwide (1 out of every 275 persons) and 25 million internally displaced people. Africa at 4.17 million refugees is second to Asia with 8.8 million. While there are no precise statistics, the

Refugees in Africa

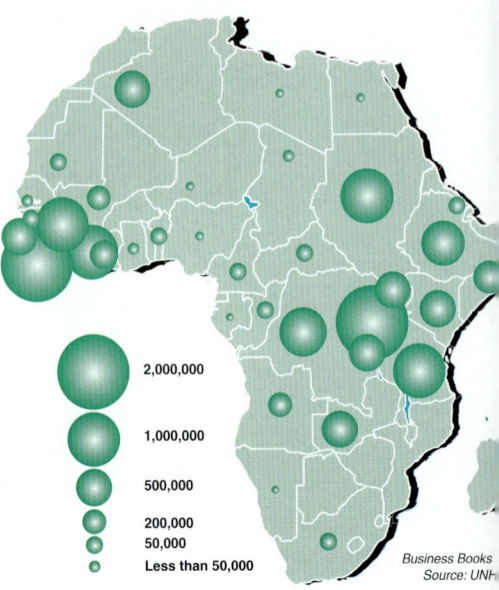

2,000,000
1,000,000
500,000
200,000
50,000
Less than 50,000

Business Books
Source: UNH

UNHCR believes that women and children constitute the majority of these refugee and displaced populations.

MAIN CAUSES

The legacy left by the Berlin Conference in 1885 when Africa was partitioned by European colonial powers without any regard for populations is undoubtedly a contributing factor. Some states accomplished a remarkable degree of peace and national unity among diverse peoples within their arbitrary borders. Others, however, are having a hard time to cope not only with internal divisions but attempts from people divided by these artificial borders to reunite with their kinsmen.

OTHER REASONS

Other reasons are greed, grievance against leadership, and desperation born out of poverty and hunger. One cynical view is that rebellion and war might in some instances be the only job opportunity. The warlords and the international arms merchants who gain handsomely from these small but devastating wars-for-profit have little interest in stopping the conflict.

War, Refugees and Famine

Chronic malnutrition
(less than 2 300 calories per year per person during 1995-97)

Food scarcity

Major famine during the past thirty years

Concentration of displaced persons and refugees during the nineties

Major conflicts during the nineties

Map: Business Books International
Source: United Nations

PEACEKEEPING

DESPITE CRITICISM THAT THE UNIT-
ED NATIONS HAS BEEN DERELICT IN ITS
PEACEKEEPING DUTY IN AFRICA, 24 OUT
OF A TOTAL OF 60 OPERATIONS LAUNCHED
SINCE 1948 WERE IN AFRICA. IT HAS DONE
SO WITH MIXED SUCCESS. STILL, WHILE
STRIFE CONTINUED IN SOMALIA AND SU-
DAN AFTER THE DEPARTURE OF THE UN
PEACEKEEPING FORCES, SEVERAL OPERA-
TIONS WERE BROUGHT TO A SUCCESSFUL
CONCLUSION. IN SIERRA LEONE, BURUNDI
LIBERIA AND, MOST RECENTLY, IN THE
DEMOCRATIC REPUBLIC OF CONGO THE
UN MANAGED TO OVERSEE FREE AND
FAIR ELECTIONS AND A TRANSITION TO
DEMOCRATIC RULE.

Africans themselves are becoming more active in finding solutions. The African Union has peacekeepers in Burundi, the DRC and the Darfur region of Sudan. The Economic Community for West African States (ECOWAS) participated in peace efforts in Liberia, Sierra Leone and more recently in Côte d'Ivoire. Encouraged by Africa's readiness to play an active part, the international community—including the G-8 and the European Union—has lent support by providing funds and logistics equipment. The African Union has in-dicated a resolve to take the lead in policing its own continent.

UN Peacekeeping missions currently under-taken in Africa are as follows:

**United Nations Mission
for the Referendum
in Western Sahara (MINURSO)**
Established in April 1991, MINURSO supervises a cease-fire and conduct a referendum in Western Sahara.

**United Nations Mission in
Sierra Leone (UNAMSIL)**
Established in October 1999 to cooperate with the Government of Sierra Leone and the other parties and implement the peace agreement; to monitor the military and security situation and disarm and demobilize combatants and the Civil Defense Forces (CDF); and to assist in promoting respect for international humanitarian law.

**United Nations Organization
Mission in the Democratic Republic
of the Congo (MONUC)**
Established in November 1999 to liaise with the signatories to the cease-fire agreement enforce the observation of the cease-fire.

MISSIONS IN AFRICA

Business Books International
Source: United Nations

CURRENT OPERATIONS

MINURSO	UN Mission for the Referendum in Western Sahara	Started Apr. 1991
MONUC	UN Mission in Dem. Rep. of Congo	Started Dec. 1999
ONUB	UN Operation in Burundi	Started May 2004
UNAMSIL	UN Mission in Sierra Leone	Started Oct. 1999
UNMEE	UN Mission in Ethiopia and Eritrea	Started Jul. 2000
UNMIL	UN Mission in Liberia	Started Sep. 2003
UNMIS	UN Mission in Sudan	Started Mar. 2005
UNOCI	UN Operation in Côte d'Ivoire	Started Apr. 2004

COMPLETED OPERATIONS

UNAVEM I	UN Angola Verification Mission	Dec.1988-Feb.1991
UNAVEM ii	UN Angola Verification Mission	May 1991-Feb.1995
UNAVEM iii	UN Angola Verification Mission	Feb. 1995-Jun.1997
MONUA	UN Observer Mission in Angola	Jun.1997-Feb. 1999
MINURCA	UN Mission in the Central African Republic	Apr. 1998-Feb. 2000
UNASOG	UN Aouzou Strip Observer Group (Chad/Libya)	May 1994-Jun. 1994
ONUC	UN Operation in the Congo	Jul. 1960-Jun. 1964
UNOMIL	UN Observer Mission in Liberia	Sep. 1993-Sep.1997
ONUMOZ	UN Operation in Mozambique	Dec. 1992-Dec. 1994
UNTAG	UN Transition Assistance Group (Namibia)	Apr. 1989-Mar. 1990
UNAMIR	UN Assistance Miss. for Rwanda	Oct. 1993-Mar. 1996
UNOMUR	UN Observer Mission Uganda/Rwanda	Jun. 1993-Sep. 1994
UNOMSIL	UN Observer Mission in Sierra Leone	Jul. 1998-Oct. 1999
UNOSOM I	UN Operations in Somalia I	Apr. 1992-Mar. 1993
UNOSOM II	UN Operations in Somalia I	Mar. 1993-Mar. 1995
MINUCI	UN Mission in Côte d'Ivoire	May 2003-Apr. 2004

145

United Nations Mission in
Ethiopia and Eritrea (UNMEE)

Established after Ethiopia and Eritrea signed a cease fire in December 2000 to guard a buffer zone between the two armies. UN personnel are deployed at key points along the 620 mile (1,000 km) frontier. An unique mission insofar as having the United Nations keep the troops of sovereign nations apart.

United Nations Mission in
Sudan (UNMIS)

EUNMIS supports the Comprehensive Peace Agreement signed by the Government of Sudan and the Sudan People's Liberation Movement/Army in Nairobi on 9 January 2005. It also provides support to the African Union Mission in Sudan (AMIS) which is operating in Darfur.

United Nations Operation in
Côte d'Ivoire (UNOCI)

In April 2004 MINUCI was replaced by UNOCI after the UN determined that the situation in Côte d'Ivoire continued to pose a threat to international peace and security in the region. Its mandate is implement the peace agreement signed by the Ivorian warring parties in January 2003.

United Nations Operation in
Burundi (ONUB)

Established in May 2004 to help to implement the efforts undertaken by Burundians to restore lasting peace and bring about national reconciliation, as provided under the Arusha Agreement.

United Nations Mission in
Liberia (UNMIL)

Established on 19 September 2003 to support the implementation of the ceasefire agreement and the peace process; protect United Nations staff, facilities and civilians; support humanitarian and human rights activities; as well as assist in national security reform.

Members of the South African peacekeeping force in DRC   UNDPI

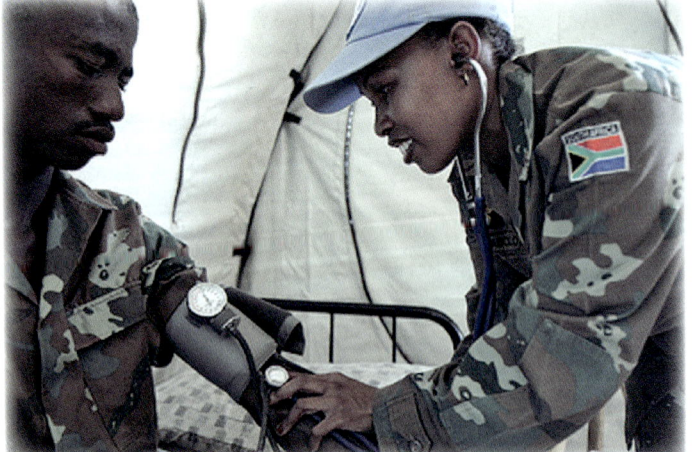

FAMINE

FAMINE IS NOT A PROBLEM PECULIAR TO AFRICA. IN 1958, BETWEEN 20 AND 30 MILLION CHINESE DIED IN THE WORST FAMINE OF THE TWENTIETH CENTURY. FAMINE AND MALNUTRITION, HOWEVER, PRESENT MAJOR CHALLENGES IN AFRICA WITH ITS LARGE EXPANSE OF ARID LAND. DROUGHT, CONFLICT, NATURAL DISASTERS, OVERPOPULATION, OVERGRAZING AND INADEQUATE FARMING METHODS HAVE ALL BEEN IDENTIFIED AS CONTRIBUTING FACTORS TO RECURRING FAMINE IN AFRICA. FAMINE IS THE RESULT OF BOTH WARFARE AND WEATHER.

The Brussels-based Center for Research on Epidemiology of Disasters (CRED) put the number of people affected by drought and famine in Africa since 1960 at over 245 million with nearly 2 million dying as a direct result.

DROUGHT

At the end of the nineties 36 African countries were affected by drought. Sometimes prolonged and extreme droughts are followed by equally devastating floods, as witnessed in Mozambique in recent times. Roughly 2 billion hectares or 65 percent of Africa's total land area, inhabited by more than half of the continent's total population, is arid land—one third of it hyper arid and the rest consisting of arid, semi-arid and dry land. Nineteen African countries are among 25 in the world identified as having the highest percentage of their population without access to drinking water. Precipitation ranges from almost zero over the Horn of Africa and the Namibian Desert to more than 158 inches (4,000 mm). Most of Africa's semi-arid landmass, however, depends on between

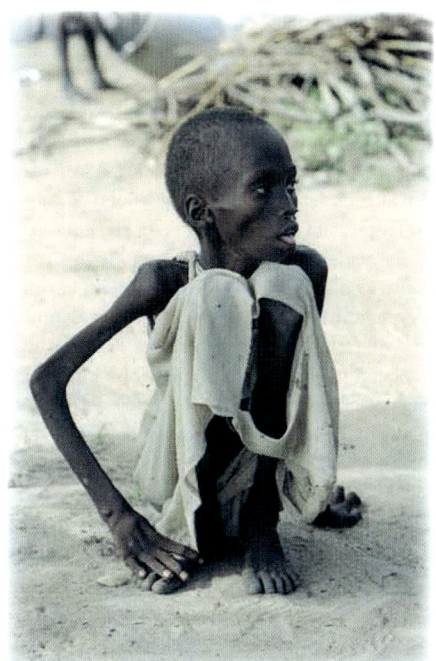

The face of famine   *UNDPI*

rivers and Lake Victoria. Recently several new large dam projects have been launched with the involvement of world organizations and large multinational corporations.

OVERGRAZING

Vegetation and soil degradation as a result of overgrazing, deforestation, and overcultivation, coupled with inappropriate agricultural technology, have also been identified as major problems. About 90 percent of Africa's soils are deficient in phosphorus and low in organic matter. There is low water infiltration and retention due to surface crusting.

RAIN FORESTS

Between 1980 and 1990 Africa's rain forests shrunk from 569 million to 530 million hectares—averaging an annual deforestation rate of 0.7 percent. Commercial logging, clearance for agricultural reasons and wood fuel are all contributing to the problem. In Sub-Saharan Africa, 70 percent of the total consumed and 90 percent of household energy are derived from wood fuel. The average African family uses an estimated 7 metric tons of wood per year.

CONFLICT

There is the fear that unless properly developed and managed on a regional basis, Africa's available water resources might trigger conflicts at local, national and regional levels as the demand increases.

8 and 16 inches (200-800 mm) per year. Due to inadequate infrastructure, only 4% of an estimated 5.2 trillion cubic yards (4 trillion cubic m) of Africa's renewable water is exploited. There is a lack of regional cooperation between countries in the development and exploitation of water resources offered by the Nile, Zambezi, Volta, and Niger

Agricultural environment

Crop failures rare

Periodic crop failures

Desert

African Hunger Map

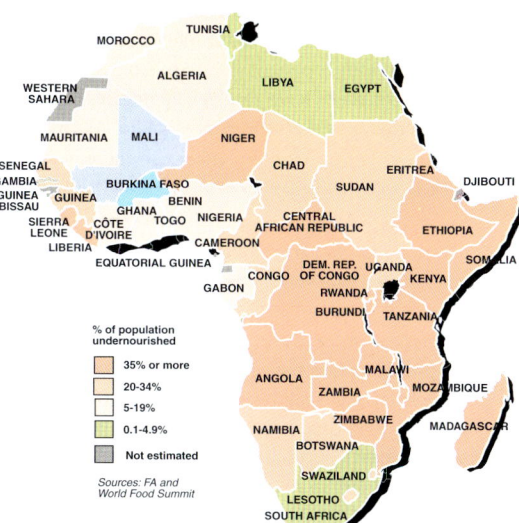

% of population undernourished

35% or more

20-34%

5-19%

0.1-4.9%

Not estimated

Sources: FA and World Food Summit

147

TROPICAL DISEASES

HIV/AIDS, TB AND MALARIA ARE THE LEADING KILLER DISEASES IN DEVELOPING REGIONS, INCLUDING AFRICA. BETWEEN THEM THESE THREE AFFECT 300 MILLION PEOPLE AND EACH YEAR CAUSE SOME 5 MILLION DEATHS WORLDWIDE. APART FROM HUMAN SUFFERING THE AFFECTED COUNTRIES PAY A HEAVY ECONOMIC TOLL. SOME EXPERTS CLAIM THAT AFRICA WOULD HAVE BEEN $100 BILLION BETTER OFF TODAY IF MALARIA HAD BEEN ELIMINATED YEARS AGO. OTHERS CLAIM THAT ANY AFRICAN NATION WITH AN HIV INFECTION RATE OF MORE THAN 20% COULD EXPECT A GDP DECLINE OF 1% PER YEAR.

With the public focus on HIV/AIDS not only malaria and an alarming resurgence of tuberculosis, but also a host of other deadly and costly tropics-related diseases have been largely ignored in recent years. While Africans are less prone to heart disease and cancer than the inhabitants of Europe and North America but they are exposed to a number of deadly and crippling tropical and subtropical diseases.

MALARIA

While malaria is endemic in 101 countries and regions, Africa is most seriously affected. More than 90 percent of all malaria cases are on the African continent. Many millions on the African continent have this debilitating disease, transmitted by the *Anopheles* mosquito. Malaria kills more people than any other communicable disease with the exception of tuberculosis. Deaths as a result of malaria are estimated at over 1 million per year, mostly among African youth. The disease also exacts an enormous toll in medical costs and in labor days. The geographical area affected by malaria has shrunk considerably over the past fifty years but control is becoming more difficult and gains are being eroded by the emergence of multi-drug resistant strains of the parasite and increased international travel. According to UNICEF, the average cost for each nation in Africa to implement malaria control programs is estimated to be at least $300,000 a year. This amounts to about six US cents ($.06) per person for a country of 5 million people. Mapping Malaria Risk in Africa (MARA) in conjunction with *Atlas du Risque de la Malaria en Afrique* (ARMA) undertook extensive studies on the incidence of malaria in Africa. Our map is based on MARA/ARMA data in which endemic regions are defined as "areas with significant annual transmission, be it seasonal or perennial" and epidemic regions as "areas prone to distinct inter-annual variation, in some years with no transmission taking place at all." The Multilateral Initiative on Malaria (MIM) was launched in Dakar in the nineties by public and private sectors and the WHO. Adding to several grants made by the Bill and Melinda Gates Foundation for the fight against HIV/AIDS in Africa, Microsoft's Bill Gates in October 2005 pledged $258.3 million for research and development to combat malaria and to test the world's first vaccine against the disease.

SLEEPING SICKNESS

Sleeping sickness (*African trypanosomiasis*) was first identified at the beginning of the twentieth century when an epidemic left half a million dead. The disease is caused by *trypanosomes* or protozoan parasites transmitted to humans through the bite of the Glossina tsetse fly. Through persistent research and with new tools and improved field strategies, the endemic disease was slowly brought under control but not eradicated. When a person becomes infected, the *trypanosome* multiplies in the blood and lymph glands, crossing the blood-brain barrier to invade the central nervous system, where it provokes major neurological disorders. Without treatment, the disease is fatal. Sleeping sickness is a daily threat to more than 60 million men, women and children in 36 countries of sub-Saharan Africa. With an estimated 300,000 to 500,000 people infected the disease has a major impact on the labor force.

EBOLA

Originating in the jungles of Africa and Asia, Ebola Haemorrhagic Fever (EHF) is one of the most virulent viral diseases known to humankind, causing death in 50% to 90% of all reported cases. The Ebola virus is transmitted by direct contact with the blood, secretions, and organs or semen of infected persons. Transmission of the Ebola virus has also occurred by handling sick or dead infected chimpanzees, as was documented in Côte d'Ivoire and Gabon. Health care workers have frequently been infected while attending patients. The Ebola virus was first identified in 1976 after significant epidemics in northern Zaire (Democratic Republic of Congo) and Nzara, in southern Sudan. Ebola-related filoviruses were also isolated from *cynomolgus* monkeys (*Macacca fascicularis*), imported into the United States from the Philippines in 1989.

YELLOW FEVER

Though largely associated with the tropics of Africa and South America, Yellow Fever has, until the beginning of the 20th Century, occurred in Europe and North America. The "yellow" in the name denotes jaundice that affects some patients. Although a safe and effective vaccine has been available for 60 years, the virus is still present with low levels of infection (i.e. endemic) in the African and South American tropical areas. In Africa thirty-three countries within a band from 15°N to 10°S of the equator and a combined population of 468 million are at risk. The virus is spread among animals and humans by mosquitos and to their offspring through infected eggs.

DENGUE

Dengue is another mosquito-borne infection in tropical and sub-tropical regions which became a major international public health concern. It is endemic in more than 100 countries in Africa, the Americas, the Eastern Mediterranean, South-East Asia and the Western Pacific. WHO estimates there may be as many as 50 million cases of dengue infection worldwide every year. The Dengue virus is transmitted by infected female *Aedes* mosquitoes. It causes a flu-like illness, which affects infants, young children and adults, but rarely causes death. Vaccine development for dengue and DHF is difficult because any of four different viruses may cause the disease, and at present the only method of controlling or preventing Dengue and DHF is to combat the vector mosquitoes.

RIVER BLINDNESS

Although also present in the Arabian Peninsula and South America, river blindness (*Onchocerciasis*) is most closely associated with Africa where it has become a serious public health problem. Of the 36 countries where the disease is endemic, 30 are in Sub-Saharan Africa and six are in the Americas. Close to 99 percent of the 18 million people infected are in Africa. Among those infected 6.5 million suffer from severe *dermatitis* and 270,000 are blind. *Onchocerciasis* is caused by *Onchocerca volvulus*, a parasitic worm that lives in the human body for up to 14 years. Each adult female worm, thin but more than 1/2 meter in length, produces millions of *microfilariae* (microscopic larvae) carried from one human to another by the blackfly (*Simulium damnosum*).

BILHARZIASIS

Among human parasitic diseases, *schistosomiasis* (a.k.a. *bilharziasis*) is second only to malaria as a public health threat in the world's tropical and subtropical areas. The disease is endemic in 74 developing countries, infecting more than 200 million people in rural agricultural and peri-urban areas. *Schistosomes* enter the body through contact with infested surface water. Three drugs—*praziquantel, oxamniquine* and *metrifonate*—are used to treat the disease.

MALARIA RISK IN AFRICA

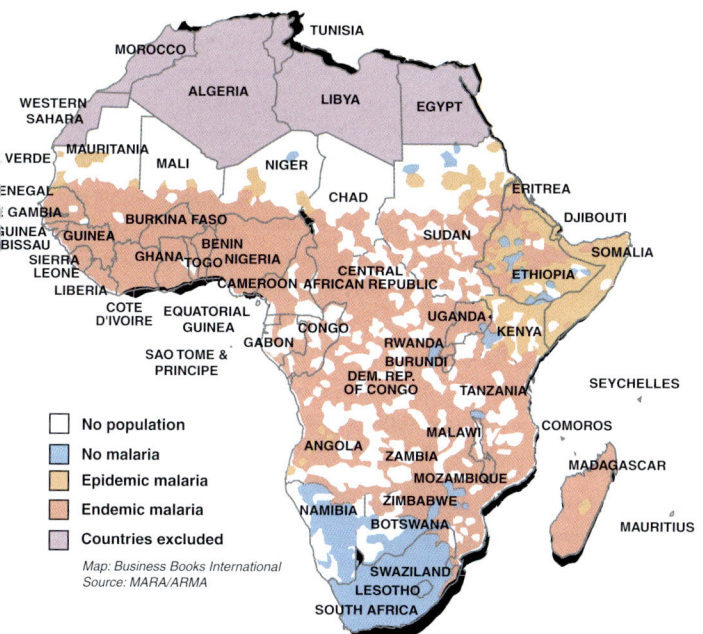

- No population
- No malaria
- Epidemic malaria
- Endemic malaria
- Countries excluded

Map: Business Books International
Source: MARA/ARMA

149

HIV/AIDS

HIV/AIDS (HUMAN IMMUNODEFI-
CIENCY VIRUS/ACQUIRED IMMUNE DEFI-
CIENCY SYNDROME) IS NOW THE NUMBER
ONE KILLER IN AFRICA AND AMONG THE
GREATEST THREATS TO THE CONTINENT'S
SOCIAL AND ECONOMIC DEVELOPMENT.
THE EPIDEMIC HAS SPREAD BEYOND
ALL PREDICTIONS AND THREATENS THE
FUTURE OF THE CONTINENT, WHERE IT
HAS ALREADY PERSONALLY AFFECTED ONE
QUARTER OF ALL AFRICANS. IN HARD-HIT
COUNTRIES, WHERE UP TO A QUARTER OF
ALL ADULTS ARE INFECTED, AIDS IS WIP-
ING OUT DEVELOPMENT GAINS ACHIEVED
OVER DECADES.

According to UNAIDS an estimated 38.6
million people worldwide were living with HIV
in 2005. An estimated 4.1 million became newly
infected with HIV and an estimated 2.8 million lost
their lives to AIDS. A little more than one-tenth of
the world's population live in sub-Saharan Africa
which is home to almost 64% of all people living
with HIV—24.5 million. Two million of them are
children younger than 15 years of age. Almost
nine in ten children (younger than 15 years) living
with HIV are in sub- Saharan Africa. An estimated
2.7 million people in the region became newly
infected, while 2.0 million adults and children died
of AIDS. *For obvious reasons UNAIDS predicates
every statistic with the word estimated and actually inserts a range within which the actual figure
might be. UNAIDS is, however, by far the world's
premier source of information on this subject.*

CATASTROPHE

HIV/AIDS in Sub-Saharan Africa, notes the
United Nations, is the "worst infectious disease
catastrophe" since the bubonic plague killed a
quarter of Europe in the 14th Century. Deaths due
to AIDS in the region, the UN predicts, will soon
surpass the 20 million people who perished in
Europe during the plague of 1347, and the more
than 20 million people worldwide who died in
the influenza epidemic of 1917. Over the next
decade, AIDS is expected to kill more people in
Sub-Saharan Africa than the total number of lives
lost in all wars during the 20th Century.

POSITIVE SIGN

One positive sign, according top UNAIDS,
is that during 2005 the HIV incidence rate has
peaked in most countries in sub-Saharan Africa.
However, UNAIDS cautions that the epidemics
in this region are highly diverse and in some
countries the epidemics are still expanding. A
new survey underlines the disproportionate impact of the AIDS epidemic on women, especially
in sub-Saharan Africa where, on average, three
women are HIV-infected for every two men.
Among young people (15–24 years), that ratio
widens even more—to three young women for
every young man.

ANTIRETROVIRAL

Another positive is that more than 1.3 million
people were receiving antiretroviral therapy in
low- and middle-income countries by December
2005—up from a mere 400,000 people two years
earlier. In sub-Saharan Africa treated patients
increased more than eight-fold (from 100 000 to
810 000) between 2003 and 2005. Most of this
trend is due to increased treatment access in a
few countries (notably Botswana, Kenya, South
Africa, Uganda and Zambia).

DEVELOPMENT CRISIS

Given the scale of the epidemic, it is no
longer just a public health problem. It is a development crisis that has been in the making for at least
10 years. HIV/AIDS has already reversed 30 years
of hard-won social progress in some countries and
has impacted on every level from the micro- to
the macroeconomic. Companies have begun to
realize that HIV/AIDS poses a genuine threat to
the workforce and the marketplace. Alarming new
costs are showing up on balance sheets. This is
especially the case in Africa, where the private
sector is feeling the cumulative impact of a severe,
long-standing and still-emerging epidemic. Many
businesses have started prevention programs at
the workplace to try to protect their investment in
human capital. They provide information and con-
doms to workers, often through peer education
programs. Forward-thinking companies in high
HIV/AIDS-prone countries, however, are looking
beyond prevention to the inevitable dent that
the disease will make in their workforce and their
profits. The Global Business Coalition on HIV/AIDS
was formed under UN auspices to mobilize the
private sector. Employee turnover related to the

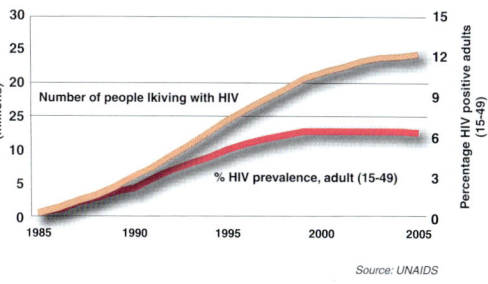

HIV Epidemic in Sub-Saharan Africa - 1985-2005

Source: UNAIDS

disease increases training and recruitment costs. The effect of HIV/AIDS on the macro-level is hard to judge but expert studies point to a likely loss of real GDP growth in some African countries in the order of one to two percent. The Southern Africa AIDS Information Dissemination Service estimates that over the next 20 years HIV/AIDS might reduce some economies in sub-Saharan Africa by a fourth. The disease undermines agricultural systems and threatens the food security of rural families. The UN Food and Agriculture Administration (FAO) has estimated that in the 25 most-affected African countries, AIDS has killed seven million agricultural workers since 1985. Rural communities bear a higher burden of the cost of the disease as urban dwellers and migrant laborers return to their village of origin when they

fall ill. Household expenditures rise as a result of medical bills and funeral expenses.

INCREASED COST

In Africa, the disease attacks educated urban professionals—the backbone of economic expansion—first. The loss of these people can rob the continent of much of its potential. The damage is immeasurable, economists say, because it appears in ways that cannot be seen—businesses that will never be founded, ideas that will never be pitched, university departments that will never be created. In eastern and southern Africa, where the epidemic is worst, the economically strongest countries—South Africa, Botswana, Zimbabwe, Kenya, Uganda and Zambia—have infection rates of between 10 percent and 25 percent. Virtually all of those infected will die within 10 years. West Africa's strongest economies such as Nigeria, Ghana and the Ivory Coast, have lower, but still alarming, infection rates. Increased benefits and training costs, and the disruption of regular production due to sick and bereavement leave, are seriously affecting both the private and public sectors. A study in South Africa found that at current levels of benefits per employee, as a result of HIV/AIDS costs rose from 7% of salaries and wages in 1995 to 19% by 2005. An employer survey conducted by Deloitte & Touche found

GLOBAL HIV INFECTION—38.6 MILLION PEOPLE LIVING WITH HIV IN 2005

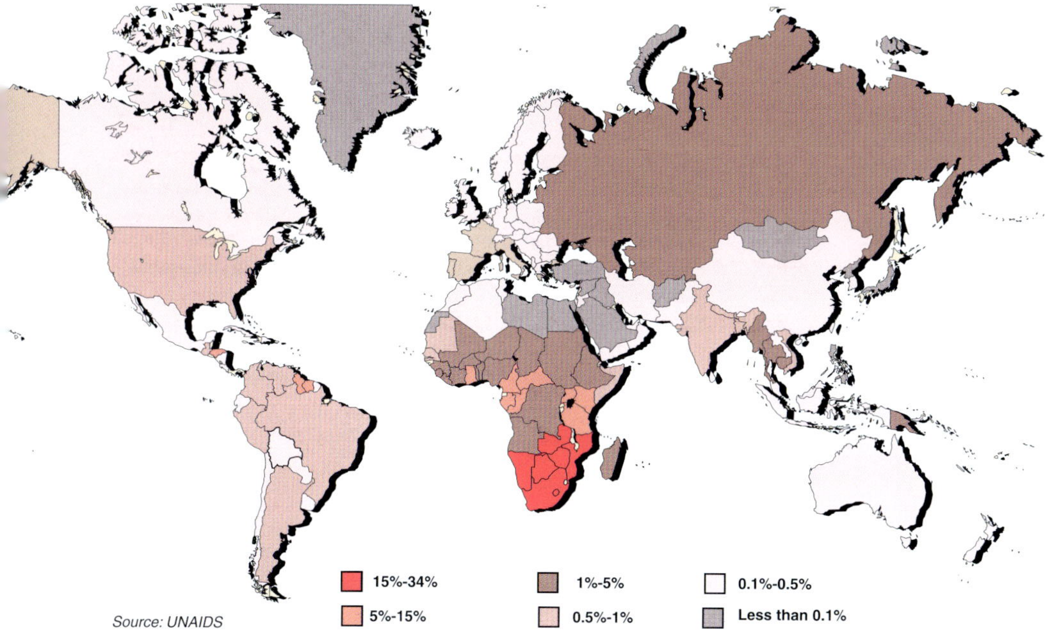

Source: UNAIDS

15%-34%	1%-5%	0.1%-0.5%
5%-15%	0.5%-1%	Less than 0.1%

151

that 70% of the respondent private companies already had a formal HIV/AIDS policy in place. About 80% of them expected that the disease will have "moderate" to "extreme" impact on their operations. A study released by the International Labor Organization claims that previous attempts by economists to measure the costs of HIV/AIDS in Sub-Saharan Africa "are likely to be significant underestimates of the social and economic value of the losses of human capital." The ILO found that it was becoming increasingly difficult to replace both skilled and unskilled labor lost to the disease. The epidemic is prevalent among working age people (between 15 and 49), each affecting the lives of at least five other people. In the public sector, according to the ILO study, overall mortality in some African countries has risen by ten times in the past decade due to AIDS. This might soon result in governments being unable to provide essential goods and services.

Aids orphan in Zambia   UNAIDS

PROJECTS

In 2002 UN Global Fund to Fight AIDS, Tuberculosis and Malaria was launched with $2.1 billion at its disposal—half the estimated amount needed to carry out its programs. The US has pledged to spend $15 billion over five years to fight AIDS in Africa. So have other governments. In 2006 the Bill and Melinda Gates Foundation donated $500 million. Among the large pharmaceutical companies Merck has been in the forefront in its combat of HIV/AIDS. In its efforts to address health care challenges in Africa Merck has gone beyond research and development of novel treatments to seek out and support initiatives that foster disease education, prevention and treatment and promote sustainable access to medicines, vaccines and quality health care.

ADULT (AGED 15–49 YEARS) HIV PREVALENCE (%) IN COUNTRIES IN SUB-SAHARAN AFRICA WHICH HAVE CONDUCTED POPULATION-BASED HIV SURVEYS IN RECENT YEARS

Country	Median HIV prevalence (%) among women attending antenatal clinics 2003–2004*	Population-based survey prevalence (%) (year) Report on the global AIDS epidemic	2003 HIV prevalence (%) reported in 2004 report	Adjusted 2003 HIV prevalence (%) in current	2005 HIV prevalence (%) in current report	Trend in prevalence
Botswana	38.5	25.2 (2004)	38.0	24.0	24.1	Stable
Burkina Faso	2.5	1.8 (2003)	4.2	2.1	2.0	Decline in urban areas
Burundi	4.8	3.6 (2002)	6.0	3.3	3.3	Decline in capital city
Cameroon	7.3†	5.5 (2004)	7.0	5.5	5.4	Stable
Ethiopia	8.5	1.6 (2005)	4.4	(1.0–3.5)	(0.9–3.5)	Decline in urban areas
Ghana	3.1	2.2 (2003)	3.1	2.3	2.3	Stable
Guinea	4.2	1.5 (2005)	2.8	1.6	1.5	Stable
Lesotho	28.4	23.5 (2004)	29.3	23.7	23.2	Stable
Rwanda	4.6	3.0 (2005)	5.1	3.8	3.1	Decline in urban areas
Senegal	1.9	0.7 (2005)	0.8	0.9	0.9	Stable
Sierra Leone	3.0	1.5 (2005)	–	1.6	1.6	Stable
South Africa	29.5	16.2 (2005)	20.9	18.6	18.8	Increasing
Tanzania	7.0	7.0 (2004)	9.0	6.6	6.5	Stable
Uganda	6.2‡	7.1 (2004–5)	4.1	6.8	6.7	Stable

*WHO Africa (2005). HIV/AIDS epidemiological surveillance report for the WHO African region, 2005 Update. Harare.
†Estimate based on country report for 2002 (2003). Ministry of Public Health Cameroon. HIV sentinel surveillance report 2002.
‡Estimate based on country report 2002 (2003). Ministry of Health Uganda. STD/HIV/AIDS surveillance report. Kampala.

Source: UNAIDS

Stark Stats - 2005

⇨ A little more than one-tenth of the world's population live in sub-Saharan Africa which is home to almost 64% of all people living with HIV—24.5 million.

⇨ Two million of them are children younger than 15 years of age. Almost nine in ten children (younger than 15 years) living with HIV are in sub-Saharan Africa.

⇨ An estimated 2.7 million people in the region became newly infected, while 2.0 million adults and children died of AIDS.

⇨ There were some 12.0 million HIV/AIDS orphans living in sub-Saharan Africa in 2005.

⇨ Three-quarters of all women (15 years and older) living with HIV are in sub-Saharan Africa.

⇨ An most of the region, women are disproportionately affected by AIDS, compared with men. Women comprise an estimated 13.2 million or 59%—of adults living with HIV in the region.

⇨ About 43% or 860 000 of all children (under 15 years) living with HIV are in southern Africa and approximately 52% (6.8 million) of all women (15 years and older) living with HIV are in this region.

⇨ An estimated 930,000 adults and children died of AIDS in southern Africa in 2005—one-third of all AIDS deaths.

⇨ Access to antiretroviral therapy increased more than eight-fold since 2003, with about 810,000 people on treatment in December 2005. About 1 in 6 (17%) of the 4.7 million people in need of this therapy in this region now receive it.

Source; UNAIDS

Corruption

MAJOR SCANDALS IN GERMANY, FRANCE, BRITAIN, ITALY, JAPAN AND THE UNITED STATES HAVE SHOWN THAT CORRUPTION IS HARDLY A PROBLEM CONFINED TO DEVELOPING COUNTRIES OR EMERGING MARKETS. BUT IN IMPOVERISHED AFRICA THE EFFECT OF CORRUPT PRACTICES IS MORE DEVASTATING. CORRUPTION NOT ONLY SIPHONS OFF FUNDS THAT COULD HAVE BEEN UTILIZED FOR INFRASTRUCTURE AND OTHER DEVELOPMENT. IT INFLATES THE COST OF DOING BUSINESS AND SCARES OFF FOREIGN INVESTORS.

Billions of dollars diverted into secret foreign bank accounts represent a significant share of the continent's stock of flight capital, totaling, according to the UN Economic Commission for Africa, around $148 billion. Economists estimate that in some African countries bribes, sales "commissions" and the diversion of funds add between 10% and 20% to the cost of development projects. No one believes that corruption, one of the world's oldest and most persistent sins, can be stamped out altogether. But serious efforts are needed in Africa to facilitate a business climate that is more conducive to foreign participation.

The Berlin-based *Transparency International (TI)* leads a number of NGOs and think-tanks intent on quantifying global corruption and pressuring UN agencies and governments to take remedial action. In its 2006 *Corruption Perceptions Index (CPI)* survey Transparency International seventy countries scored less than a 3 out of perfect 10 for a totally non-corrupt society. Corruption is perceived to be most acute in Haiti, Myanmar, Iraq, Guinea, Sudan, Democratic Republic of Congo, Chad, Bangladesh, Uzbekistan, Equatorial Guinea and Côte d'Ivoire. Countries with a score higher than 9 included Iceland, Finland, New Zealand, Denmark, Singapore, Sweden and Switzerland. In 2006 TI ranked 19 African countries among the top 100 nations with the least corruption. Scoring above 3 were Botswana, Mauritius, South Africa, Tunisia, Namibia, Seychelles, Egypt, Ghana, Senegal, Burkina Faso, Lesotho, Morocco, Algeria, Madagascar, Mauritania and Gabon.

POOR NATIONS

Sadly, according to TI, the poor nations that can least afford it as the monies are siphoned off important development projects, tend to be the greatest victims of corrupt practices and bribery. Levels of corruption in the public sector are recorded as perceived by business people, country analysts and ordinary citizens.

CONVENTION

In 1999 the Organization for Economic Cooperation and Development (OECD) adopted its own Convention on Combating Bribery, based on the US Foreign Corrupt Practices Act. Most industrialized nations have signed on and several African states have pledged to take further constructive steps to combat corruption. An African Convention on Preventing and Combating Corruption was initially approved by the African Union's Ministerial Conference in Addis Ababa in September 2002 and later adopted by its executive council. The new convention guarantees access to information and the participation of civil society and the media the monitoring process. It also outlaws the use of funds acquired through illicit and corrupt practices to finance political parties. African leaders have, with ample justification, laid part of the blame on foreign entrepreneurs who use bribes to beat their competition out of lucrative contracts. Corruption, they argue, can only be effectively contained if the leading industrial nations do their part in policing their own corporations doing business in Africa.

BRIBE PAYERS

While Transparency International's Corrupt Perception Index (CPI) focuses on officials in recipient countries, its Bribe Payers Index (BPI), conducted in 2002, focused on bribe paying governments and corporations, seeking to win business and other favors abroad. TI found that many governments in developed countries preferred to turn a blind eye to bribes paid out to win business in the developing world. The Bribe Payers Index (BPI) showed high levels of bribery in the developing world, not only by corporations from Russia, China, Taiwan and South Korea, but also by those from leading industrial nations. The US, for example, with a score of 5.3 out of a possible clean 10, ranked 13th with Japan, below France, Spain, Germany, Singapore and the United Kingdom. Most likely areas where bribes might be demanded, according to the survey, are firstly public works and construction, followed by arms and defense, oil and gas, real estate, telecommunications, power generation, mining and transportation. Oil revenues all too often vanish in the pockets of middlemen and local officials.

TRANSPARENCY INTERNATIONAL CORRUPTION PERCEPTION INDEX - 2006

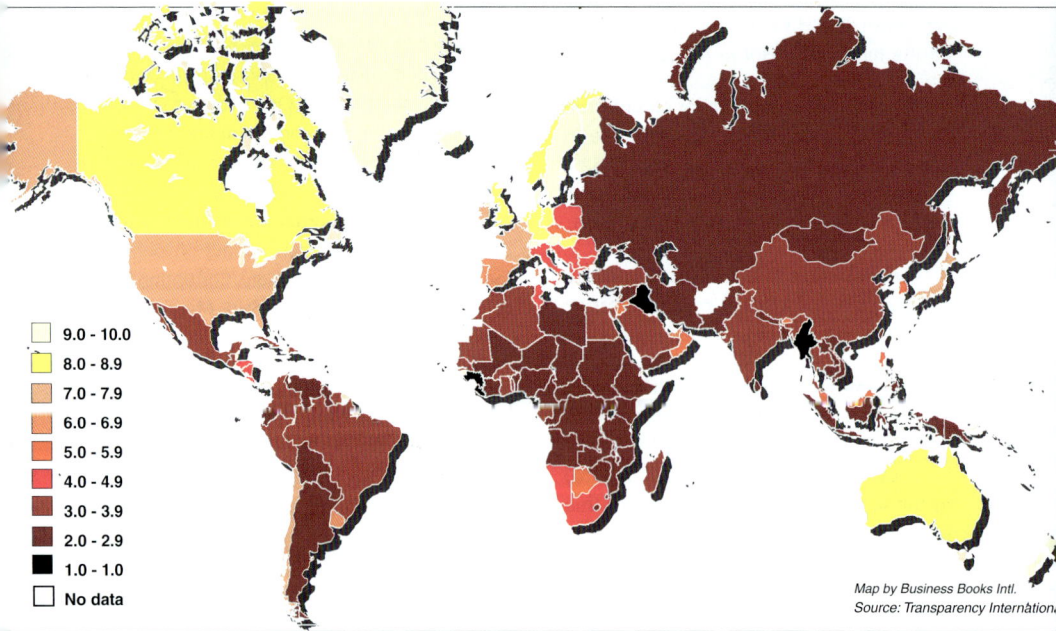

- 9.0 - 10.0
- 8.0 - 8.9
- 7.0 - 7.9
- 6.0 - 6.9
- 5.0 - 5.9
- 4.0 - 4.9
- 3.0 - 3.9
- 2.0 - 2.9
- 1.0 - 1.0
- No data

Map by Business Books Intl.
Source: Transparency International

DEBT BURDEN

THE MORE THAN $300 BILLION THAT AFRICA OWES ITS FOREIGN CREDITORS—AMOUNTING TO $375 FOR EVERY MAN, WOMAN AND CHILD ON THE CONTINENT—REPRESENTS A CRIPPLING BURDEN TO SOME OF ITS NATIONS. AFRICA CARRIES 11% OF THE DEVELOPING WORLD'S DEBT WITH ONLY 5% OF ITS INCOME. IN THE PAST 17 YEARS, AFRICA'S TOTAL DEBT ROSE BY 350%. IN MANY AFRICAN COUNTRIES UP TO 40% OF GOVERNMENT REVENUE IS ALLOCATED TO SERVICING FOREIGN DEBT, TO THE DETRIMENT OF HEALTH, EDUCATION AND OTHER ESSENTIAL SOCIAL SERVICES. SUB-SAHARAN AFRICA SPENDS OVER TWICE AS MUCH ON DEBT SERVICE AS IT DOES ON BASIC HEALTH CARE. IN THE PAST DECADE TOTAL DEBT SERVICE HAS RISEN BY 39%, FROM $10.9 BILLION TO $15.2 BILLION.

Altogether 33 of the 41 countries identified by the World Bank as "Heavily Indebted Poor Countries" (HIPC) are in Africa and even some countries in North Africa (none of which has been labeled as an HIPC country) are spending almost one-fourth of their export earnings on interest and debt repayments. Development aid, which has been in steep decline in recent years, does not close the gap. For example, Sub-Saharan African countries have been paying $1.51 on debt service for every $1 received in grant aid from foreign donors.

CAUSES

In the 1960s and 1970s, international lenders readily pushed a high volume of loans on many African states. Neither the lenders nor the borrowers anticipated these to balloon due to exchange rate fluctuation and interest rate hikes. Other factors that contributed to the debt crisis in Africa include poor government economic management, deteriorating terms of trade, shrinking market shares for major exports, and boom and bust cycles in recent years.

AFRICAN FOREIGN DEBT - 2005
(IN BILLIONS OF US$)

Country	Debt	% of GDP	% of Exports
Algeria	19.4	18.4	39.2
Angola	10.6	38.9	48.8
Benin	1.6	35.9	258.9
Botswana	1.1	11.1	23.0
Burkina Faso	1.9	33.6	353.4
Burundi	1.5	191.5	1 878.2
Cameroon	5.8	34.3	136.5
Cape Verde	0.8	75.2	235.8
Cent. Afr. Rep.	1.3	92.2	733.6
Chad	1.7	33.9	61.5
Comoros	0.3	75.9	506.3
Congo	5.8	98.7	112.9
Congo, Dem. Rep.	10.9	157.0	486.6
Côte d'Ivoire	10.5	64.4	133.6
Djibouti	0.5	67.2	182.3
Egypt	28.7	31.6	98.8
Equatorial Guinea	0.3	4.0	3.8
Eritrea	0.6	68.0	747.3
Ethiopia	6.6	70.6	351.3
Gabon	3.8	41.2	64.9
Gambia	0.6	138.2	287.1
Ghana	8.1	76.6	220.1
Guinea	3.1	87.7	343.3
Guinea-Bissau	0.8	282.4	743.8
Kenya	5.3	28.3	118.2
Lesotho	0.8	53.9	105.6
Liberia	...	...	...
Libya	6.0	15.8	19.7
Madagascar	4.9	99.8	320.3
Malawi	2.9	144.1	497.0
Mali	3.4	60.5	241.9
Mauritania	2.1	109.4	326.4
Mauritius	1.0	17.1	29.8
Morocco	15.6	30.2	91.4
Mozambique	4.7	66.4	224.2
Namibia	0.9	18.1	49.7
Niger	1.7	50.6	296.0
Nigeria	28.7	30.4	54.5
Rwanda	1.5	73.7	759.3
Sao T. & Principe	0.3	425.6	1 081.8
Senegal	3.6	42.7	155.4
Seychelles	0.6	81.8	84.5
Sierra Leone	1.2	105.8	425.4
Somalia	4.0	46.7	1 348.5
South Africa	44.7	19.1	70.5
Sudan	26.4	95.4	461.3
Swaziland	0.4	16.6	19.6
Tanzania	6.4	51.3	260.2
Togo	2.1	93.2	193.6
Tunisia	16.7	54.7	119.8
Uganda	4.3	49.8	402.3
Zambia	3.8	60.9	170.2
Zimbabwe	5.2	65.6	265.3
Africa	318.5	35.7	95.6

Sources: AFDB, IMF

HIPC Initiative

In 1996, the International Monetary Fund, together with the World Bank and major creditor nations, adopted the Heavily Indebted Poor Countries (HIPC) initiative that entitled 41 developing countries to assistance beyond mere rescheduling of debt. To qualify, debtor nations had to have a GNP per capita of US$695 or less in 1993, and a present value of debt to exports higher than 220%, or a present value of debt to GNP higher than 80%. The program envisages the cancellation of as much 80% of external debt—one third owed to multilateral institutions. With the adoption of the Enhanced HIPC program in 1999, the international community agreed to make the Initiative broader and faster by increasing the number of eligible countries, raising the amount of debt relief, and speeding up the process.

Two stages

Eligible countries qualify for debt relief in two stages. During the first stage, before reaching the so-called decision point—usually after three years—the debtor country needs to establish a satisfactory track record in terms of IMF and (International Development Agency (IDA) supported programs. During the second stage, after reaching the decision point, the country is required to implement a full-fledged poverty reduction strategy. During this stage, the IMF and IDA, the Paris Club creditors and others, are expected to grant interim relief. At the end of the second stage, when the floating completion point is reached, the IMF and IDA provide the remainder of the committed debt relief while Paris Club creditors enter into a highly concessional stock-of-debt operation with the country. Other multilateral and bilateral creditors will be required to contribute to the debt relief on comparable terms. Twenty five countries (Benin, Bolivia, Burkina Faso, Cameroon, Chad, Ethiopia, The Gambia, Ghana, Guinea, Guinea-Bissau, Guyana, Honduras, Madagascar, Malawi, Mali, Mauritania, Mozambique, Nicaragua, Niger, Rwanda, São Tomé and Príncipe, Senegal, Tanzania, Uganda, Zambia) have reached their decision point under the enhanced HIPC Initiative and four countries (Bolivia, Mozambique, Tanzania and Uganda) reached completion point under the original HIPC Initiative.

Forgiven Debt

In July 2005, the Group of Eight Industrialized Nations gathering in Gleneagles, Scotland, agreed to full cancellation of the $40 billion owed them by 18 African Heavily Indebted Poor Countries. This happened after considerable pressure from various quarters including the Commission on Africa set up British Prime Minister Tony Blair as well as public appeals by music stars Bob Geldof and Bono.

Debt service of HIPC countries 2003

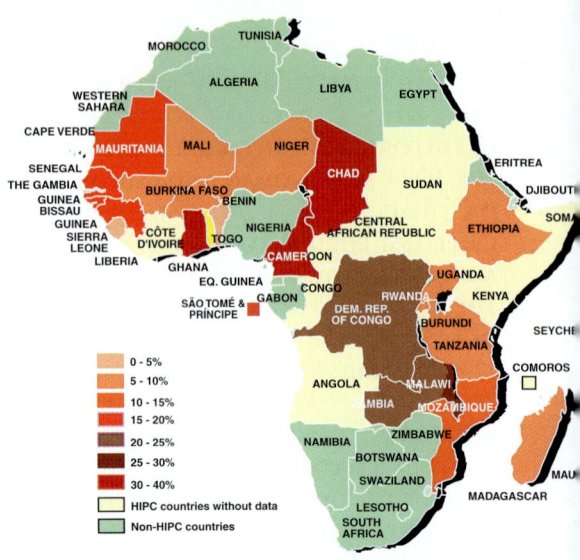

Legend:
- 0 - 5%
- 5 - 10%
- 10 - 15%
- 15 - 20%
- 20 - 25%
- 25 - 30%
- 30 - 40%
- HIPC countries without data
- Non-HIPC countries

Business Books International
Source: HIPC, IMF

Performer-activists Bono and Bob Geldof pushing for debt forgiveness for Africa before Pres. Bush goes into the Glengeagles G8 meeting

ILLITERACY

ALTHOUGH OUTSTRIPPED BY SOUTH ASIA (56.2%) IN TERMS OF IL-LITERACY, AFRICA WITH AN OVERALL 35% RATE POSES A SEVERE CHALLENGE TO A CONTINENT TRYING TO PROMOTE DEVELOPMENT AND REDUCE POVERTY. ILLITERACY IN 9 OF ITS 53 NATIONS EXCEED 50%—GOING AS HIGH AS 71.5% IN BURKINA FASO AND 81.3% IN NIGER. AFRICA'S MOST POPULOUS COUNTRY, NIGERIA, SHOWS A 30% ILLITERACY RATE. SOUTH AFRICA, AFRICA'S MOST ADVANCED NATION, HAS AN ILLITERA-CY RATE OF 13%—COMPARED TO RATES IN EUROPE AND NORTH AMERICA OF ABOUT 1%. ONE DISTURBING FACET OF ILLITERACY AND LOW SCHOOL ENROLL-MENT IS THE INABILITY TO EDUCATE YOUTH AND ADULTS THROUGH THE PRINTED WORD ABOUT THE DANGERS OF HIV/AIDS INFECTION.

CRITERIA

Statistics provided for adults aged 15 and older by UNESCO and the African Development Bank come with a disclaimer regarding their sources. "Different countries," UNESCO points out, "have different social and cultural contexts, different definitions and standards of literacy, different methodologies for collecting and compiling literacy data, as well as different quality of data collected." In some cases data may represent the whole country and in others only part. Some countries may identify literate persons by simply asking: "Are you literate or not" or "Can you read and write with under-standing, while others may ask more com-prehensive questions or administer literacy tests to identify different levels of literacy. The United Nations simply defines literacy as the inability to read and write a simple message in any language. Definitions and disclaimers aside, it is evident that large-scale illiteracy in Africa hinders poverty reduction, effective HIV/AIDS prevention education and general improvement of the human condition, and that massive input is required.

ILLITERACY & EDUCATION

Country	Adult Illiteracy Rate (%) 2005	% Primary achool enrollment 2002/3	% Secondary school enrollment 2002/3
Algeria	27.9	109	80
Angola	...	...	...
Benin	56.8	109	28
Botswana	18.6	103	73
Burkina Faso	71.5	46	11
Burundi	46.1	77	11
Cameroon	23.1	108	31
Cape Verde	22.0	121	70
Cent. Afr. Rep.	46.1	66	...
Chad	49.3	76	16
Comoros	43.2	90	31
Congo	14.2	80	...
Congo (DRC)	31.9	...	...
Côte d'Ivoire	46.3	78	...
Djibouti	29.7	40	20
Egypt	40.8	97	85
Equat. Guinea	12.9	...	...
Eritrea	39.5	63	28
Ethiopia	54.8	66	20
Gabon	...	132	...
Gambia	57.5	85	34
Ghana	23.0	79	39
Guinea	...	81	24
Guinea Bissau	55.2	...	...
Kenya	13.1	92	33
Lesotho	14.3	126	35
Liberia	41.1	...	...
Libya	15.9	114	105
Madagascar	29.5	120	...
Malawi	35.7	140	33
Mali	70.5	58	20
Mauritania	57.4	88	23
Mauritius	13.6	104	81
Morocco	46.5	110	45
Mozambique	49.6	103	16
Namibia	14.6	105	62
Niger	81.3	44	7
Nigeria	29.2	119	36
Rwanda	27.3	122	16
São T. & Principe	...	...	...
Senegal	57.9	80	19
Seychelles	...	114	111
Sierra Leone	...	...	...
Somalia	...	...	...
South Africa	12.9	106	89
Sudan	36.9	60	35
Swaziland	17.1	98	45
Tanzania	19.9	84	...
Togo	36.5	121	...
Tunisia	23.8	111	78
Uganda	28.4	141	20
Zambia	17.8	82	28
Zimbabwe	8.1	94	40
AFRICA	35.0	97	43

Sources: ADB, UNESCO

Primary school in Tanzania · *UNDPI*

HIV/AIDS Effect

Sadly, teachers in Sub-Saharan Africa have themselves fallen prey to the HIV/AIDS pandemic. It is estimated that more than 10% will die from the disease in the next five years.

Free education

In 2000 at World Education Forum at Dakar, Senegal, the nations in attendance pledged to provide free primary education for every child in the world by 2015. Despite limited progress in overall numbers at primary school level, girls, disabled children and orphans are still marginalized. Some 40 million children are still not in school. In recent years foreign governments, including the USA, UK, Germany and France, and a number of non-governmental organizations and private entrepreneurs have become involved in educational projects. Under NEPAD the private sector, including companies such as Hewlett-Packard and Oracle have been implementing e-classes to reach children and adults in remote areas electronically with basic education.

ILLITERACY BY REGION

REGION	% of Pop.
Africa (incl.North Africa)	35.0
Sub-Saharan Africa	39.9
East Asia & Pacific	14.2
Europe & Central Asia	1.0
Latin America & Caribbean	8.7
Middle East & North Africa	28.2
South Asia	56.2

Illiteracy rate in Africa

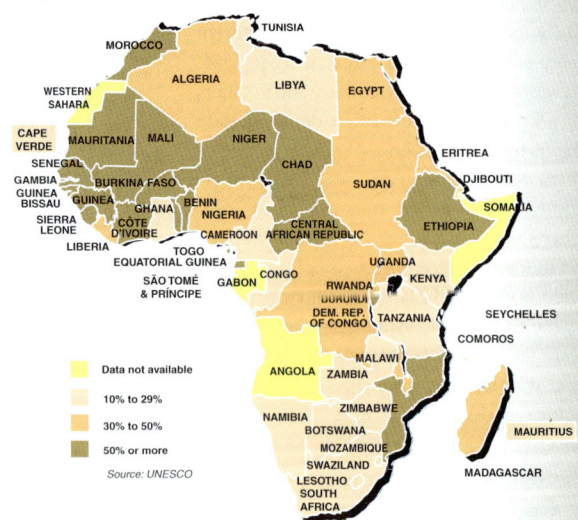

Data not available
10% to 29%
30% to 50%
50% or more

Source: UNESCO

158

CHAPTER 6

ADVICE AND ASSISTANCE

SOME OBSERVERS REMAIN TOTALLY FIXATED ON WAR, FAMINE, AND HIV/AIDS IN AFRICA. OTHERS ARE BENT ON GOING THE OPPOSITE DIRECTION— IGNORING ALL THAT IS NEGATIVE IN AN EFFORT TO COUNTER THE SO-CALLED AFRO-PESSIMISTS WITH AN OVERDOSE OF OPTIMISM. FEW STRIKE A BALANCE BETWEEN THE POSITIVE AND THE NEGATIVE, BREAKING AFRICA UP IN PARTS, AS THEY SHOULD, BEFORE WEIGHING THE PITFALLS AGAINST THE PROSPECTS.

ADVICE

THERE WAS A TIME WHEN THE OUT-
SIDE WORLD COULD BLAME ITS IGNO-
RANCE ABOUT THE REAL AFRICA ON A
LACK OF SOLID SOURCES. THAT IS NO LON-
GER THE CASE. STUDENTS, INVESTORS, EN-
TREPRENEURS AND TRAVELERS LOOKING
FOR DATA AND DETAIL ON ALL ASPECTS
OF THE CONTINENT HAVE A WEALTH OF
INFORMATION AT THEIR DISPOSAL. THOSE
WITH ACCESS TO THE INTERNET USING
THEIR FAVORITE SEARCH ENGINE WILL AT
THE ENTRY OF THE WORD "AFRICA" ELICIT
NOT HUNDREDS OR THOUSANDS BUT A
FEW MILLION "HITS." THE PROBLEM IS TO
SORT OUT THE CORN FROM THE CHAFF.

There are numerous non-governmental organizations (NGOs) in Washington and other world capitals that are dedicated to African causes and countries and able to assist members in their search for information. Several universities have developed Africa-related databases. World organizations such as the United Nations and its specialized agencies, including the UN Develop-ment Program (UNDP) and the Inter-national Monetary Fund (IMF), all maintain databases on Africa.

CONSULTANTS

Business executives who are seriously considering investment or dealings with any of Africa's 53 diverse and often complex nations, usually seek advice from experienced and trust-worthy consultants to help analyze and evaluate prospects. When sorting through the many investment and trade advisors that specialize in Africa it is prudent to ask for referrals and to take a close look at past performance. For example, establishments such as the Atlanta-based Goodworks Inter-national and Zephyr Management, headquartered in New York, have a long and proven record of active engagement in real and profitable projects in different parts of Africa where they maintain a network of branch offices and expert staff.

CORPORATE COUNCIL

For many in the United States a good starting point is the Washington-based Corporate Council on Africa (CCA)—the premier business-related non-governmental organization for US and other multinational and medium-sized corporations. With a membership of more than 250 representing some 87 percent of all US investment in Africa, the Council acts as a catalyst for business by introducing American firms not only to potential top-level partners in Africa but to like-minded firms in the United States that might become partners in new ventures. The CCA has hosted a large number of African heads of state in the US and organized trade missions to various parts of the continent. It has an ongoing African business development series that reaches into every facet of deal-making and maintains a database for its corporate membership. Its task forces on different regions and issues related to Africa range from HIV/AIDS to trade and investment. The CCA's biennial Africa summits are the occasion where several thousand business leaders and Africa experts rub shoulders with a host of African heads of state and key members of their government.

INTEREST

Since the early nineties decision makers in Washington, London, Paris, and the other capitals of the world started focusing on the long-forgotten and neglected African continent. This sudden interest in Africa was no mere coincidence. It followed in the wake of reform and change that swept across the continent after Communism crumbled in Eastern Europe. South Africa, which was isolated from the rest of the continent and shunned by the world, finally shed apartheid and

CCA head, Steve Hayes, and Pres. Bush at a Corporate Council Africa Sum.

became an engine for regional growth. Not only in Europe but in Africa a wind of change blew across the continent. Former autocrats who built a power base on the support of one of the superpowers in the Cold War and on their opposition to apartheid, were obliged to take note of the needs of their own citizens instead. Many were ousted by enlightened leaders and others remained and reformed. In the process, aggregate per capita incomes rose in most of the 48 Sub-Saharan African countries, reliance on the state as the engine for development declined, market economies started taking form, exchange rates were liberalized, budget deficits were reduced, protectionist trade policies gave way to liberalized trade. With ample justification many African leaders are today talking confidently about an African Renaissance in the making.

IGNORANCE

Despite the formidable presence of Fortune 500 companies and a growing number of small and medium-sized enterprises, the international business community at large remains blissfully unaware of the untapped potential for profit awaiting enterprising entrepreneurs.

NGOS

There are several hundred other NGOs situated in overseas capitals and active in Africa. Some of these offer databases and related information to the general public while others restrict services to their membership.

MEDIA

As is to be expected, overseas media usually cover only what could be termed as sensationally significant in Africa with little space devoted for in-depth analysis. Wars, famine, epidemics, HIV/AIDS, crime and corruption get ample press while ongoing progress towards political and economic freedom hardly receive mention. Africa-specific magazines are geared to fill this vacuum on a monthly basis while country-specific newspapers and magazines in both English and French are available in print and often on the Internet as well. A very useful sources to help observers stay abreast of developments across the continent on a daily basis is the comprehensive Washington-based online news service *www.allafrica.com* and Cape Town-based *www.africareport.com*. African Embassies may also serve as useful sources of information and advice. *(See the list at the end of this book)*

WHY AFRICA?

Why should business care about Africa beyond merely tapping its natural resources and making good profits. In a recent article Reuters chairman Niall Fitzgerald advanced interesting thoughts. Coming from a man who headed Unilever for many years, his words carry special weight. Following is an abridged version:

Niall Fitzgerald

"There is an exciting business opportunity. African leaders, increasingly elected democratically, know they must commit themselves to good governance, investment and economic growth. There have been big improvements in macroeconomic performance.

"Business has a responsibility to engage with Africa and its challenges. The ambitions for Africa cannot be achieved without widespread business partnership. We must be an active part of the communities where our consumers live. We must contribute to the wider society on whose goodwill we depend.

"For those who remain skeptical, not to say deeply cynical, and see only corrupt politicians, incompetent administrators and unskilled workers, let me give you three wholly selfish and self-centered reasons why you should care.

"Africa is the epicenter of a clash of religious beliefs: Islam and Christianity. Two communities that lived peacefully together for many centuries are in danger of slipping into mutual hatred and killing. Business needs to be a force for healing not horror, through engagement and investment; otherwise the ensuing chaos will eventually engulf our prosperous ghettos.

"Second, migration can unbalance societies and undermine security. Migration is most effectively dealt with at source, by helping to ensure there is opportunity and hope, bread and jobs, not hunger and guns. In sub-Saharan Africa, 450 million people live on $1 a day. They are right to look at our prosperity with envy and resentment.

"And then there is oil, the commodity on which our lives and lifestyle most depend. Most oil resources are concentrated in areas of greatest unrest and volatility. Africa is likely to be the most important source of new oil. We have a vested interest in helping to create a secure and stable environment through the growth and spread of prosperity in this oil-rich region.

"Put simply, if we want to protect our own prosperity we had better be part of the attack on poverty—poverty of resource, hope and opportunity.

"There has been lots of input, but the future of Africa depends on effective output.. . It will be essential to agree and define the specific nature and extent of the business opportunities, the way in which business can best make effective partnerships with governments, and the support that business can provide to help implement those opportunities.

ASSISTANCE

WITHIN THE WORLD BANK GROUP THERE ARE SEVERAL DIVISIONS THAT HAVE AID AND LOAN PROGRAMS SPECIFICALLY FOR AFRICA, WHILE IN THE UNITED STATES EXIMBANK, OPIC, USAID, FAS AND TDA ARE AMONG THE AGENCIES THAT OFFER PROGRAMS AIMED AT EXPANDING US BUSINESS INVOLVEMENT ON THE CONTINENT. SEVERAL INFRASTRUCTURAL AND OTHER DEVELOPMENT PROJECTS OF INTEREST TO US CONTRACTORS ARE FUNDED BY THE AFRICAN DEVELOPMENT BANK, THE WORLD BANK OR COUNTRY DONORS. THESE PROGRAMS PROVIDE OPPORTUNITIES NOT ONLY FOR MULTINATIONAL OR TRANSNATIONAL GIANTS BUT ALSO SMALL AND MEDIUM-SIZED FIRMS LOOKING FOR THE FIRST TIME AT THE POSSIBILITY OF DOING BUSINESS WITH AFRICA.

Africa has claimed an increasing share of funds allocated for special programs by major World Bank and United Nations development agencies. International agencies involved in funding and underwriting African projects include IDA, UNIDO and UNDP. MIGA helps to minimize risk by providing investment guarantees and technical assistance in member African countries. Especially in countries where foreigners are uncertain about their legal rights reliance on the ICSIP arbitration center is a good option.

American entrepreneurs who wish to do business with Africa have an array of possible sources of assistance in official Washington. These agencies are geared to give all possible assistance to help American businesses establish themselves in Africa. No project is too small or too big to run by these agencies. In fact, the Small Business Administration has been an active promoter of business between small and medium-sized US enterprises and their counterparts in Africa. Even though the Trade and Development Agency works on a small budget, its impact on expansion of business in Africa has been significant. Several of the feasibility studies which it funded eventually led to major projects financed by other agencies.

Following are some of the key international and US agencies involved in Africa:

INTERNATIONAL

The African Development Bank (ADB)
01 BP 1387 Abidjan 01
Côte d'Ivoire
Tel: (225) 20.20.44.44
Fax: (225) 20.20.40.06
Website: www.afdb.org
The ADB was established in the 1960s to make loans and equity investments for economic and social advancement in its 53 member countries.

WORLD BANK GROUP

International Development Association (IDA)
1818 H Street NW
Washington DC 20433
Tel: 202-477-1234
Fax: 202-477-6391
Website: www.worldbank.org/ida
The International Development Association (IDA) is the World Bank Group's concessional lending window. Half of its active projects are in Africa amounting to over $1 billion a year.

International Finance Corporation (IFC)
2121 Pennsylvania Avenue NW
Washington DC 20433
Tel: 202-473-7711
Fax: 202-974-4384
Website: www.if.org
Since its creation in 1989, the IFC's African Enterprise Fund (AEF) has provided a total of $206 million for 309 projects in 30 African countries. Projects are appraised, processed, and supervised by IFC representatives in Africa.

Multilateral Insurance Guarantee Agency (MIGA)
1800 K Street NW (Suite 1200)
Washington DC 20433
Tel: 202-473-6167
Fax: 202-522-2630
Website: www.miga.org
MIGA's mandate is to encourage the flow of foreign direct investment to developing and other member countries. Through its guarantee program it offers insurance to mitigate political risk and provides promotional and advisory services to member countries to help attract and retain direct investment.

International Center for Settlement of Investment Disputes (ICSID)
1818 H Street N W
Washington DC 20433
Tel: 202-458-1534
Fax: 202-522-2615
Website: www.worldbank.org/icsid
ICSID was established in 1966 as an autonomous international organization but maintains close links with the World Bank. All its members are also members of the

Bank. It provides facilities for the conciliation and arbitration of disputes between member countries and foreign investors. Recourse to ICSID arbitration is voluntary.
\

UNITED NATIONS

UN Industrial Development Organization (UNIDO)
Vienna International Center
A-1400 Vienna
Austria
Tel: (43) 1-26026
Fax: (43) 1-269-2269
Website: www.unido.org
UNIDO promotes and accelerates industrialization in developing countries by contracting with international consultants to provide technical assistance to local companies and organizations. Consultancy projects range from general surveys to transfer of manufacturing technology and the establishment of pilot plants.

UN Development Program (UNDP)
Bureau for Development Policy
United Nations, New York
Tel: 212-906-5200
Fax: 212-906-5857
Website: www.undp.org
The UNDP is the world's largest multilateral grant development and assistance organization with offices in 124 countries and drawing on the expertise of 40 specialized and technical UN agencies. It also works extensively with non-governmental organizations and the business sector.

US AGENCIES

Export-Import Bank of the US (Eximbank)
811 Vermont Ave NW
Washington DC 20571T
Toll free: 800-565-3946
Tel: 202-565-3946
Fax: 202-565-3380
Website: www.exim.gov
The Eximbank is an independent government agency that assists in the sale of US goods and services overseas by providing loans and other credit measures. Eximbank's loans, guarantees and insurance supported more than $150 million in US exports to Sub-Saharan Africa in the first half of 1999. The bank is open to consider project finance business in every African country with the exclusion of Sudan and Libya. Financing is available for projects that do not rely on typical export credit security but need long-term cash flow financing.

Foreign Agricultural Service (FAS)
Department of Agriculture, Africa & Middle East
Washington DC 20250-1000
Tel: 202-720-3222
Website: www.fas.usda.gov
FAS assists in the development and expansion of US agricultural exports to Africa and other regions. Assistance includes Export Credit Guarantee Programs (GSM-102 and GSM-103) to underwrite private bank credit for three or ten years, a Supplier Credit Guarantee Program (SCGP) that extends short term guarantees up to 180 days, and the Facility Guarantee Program (FGP) that provides payment guarantees to improve or establish agriculture-related facilities in emerging markets.

Overseas Private Investment Corporation (OPIC)
1100 New York Avenue
Washington DC 20527
Tel: 202-336-8799
Fax: 202-408-9859
Website: www.opic.gov
OPIC is a self-sustaining government agency that provides investment information, financing, and political risk insurance for US investors in African and other developing countries. It currently has four privately managed funds that support investment in Sub-Saharan Africa: the $120 million New Africa Opportunity Fund for Southern Africa, the $150 million Modern Africa Growth and Investment Fund, the $120 million Global Environment Emerging Markets Fund II, and the $300 million Aqua International Partners Fund.

Trade Information Center (TIC)
International Trade Administration
US Department of Commerce
Washington DC 20230
Tel: 1-800-USA-TRADE
Fax: 202-482-4473
Website: www.ita.doc.gov
The TIC, operated by the International Trade Administration of the US Department of Commerce for the 20 federal agencies comprising the Trade Promotion Coordinating Committee (TPCC), is the first stop for US exporters seeking government advice and assistance. It provides country-specific export counseling and assistance for Africa, including trade leads and suggestions on potential sources for export financing.

US Agency for International Aid and Development (USAID)
Ronald Reagan Building
Washington DC 20523-0016
Tel: 202-712-4320
Fax: 202-216-3524
Website: www.usaid.gov
USAID implements government foreign economic assistance programs ranging from health, education, economic growth, population, democracy, environment, and crisis prevention. In most of these programs the US private sector has an opportunity to participate. Regional programs offered by USAID include the following: the Leland Initiative, the Greater Horn of Africa Initiative (GHAI), the Initiative for Southern Africa (ISA), the Africa Food Security Initiative (AFSI), and the Africa Trade and Investment Policy (ATRIP). The Leland Initiative seeks to bring the benefits of the global information revolution to the people of Africa.

US Small Business Administration (SBA)
409 3rd Street SW
Washington DC 20416
Tel: 800-U-ASK-SBA
Website: www.sba.gov
The SBA has taken an active role in promoting American small business ventures in Africa. SBA's Export Working Capital Program (EWCP) provides short-term loans to small businesses for export-related transactions. Its International Trade (IT) Loan Program offers a combination of working capital and fixed asset financing to help small businesses compete more effectively in export markets. The SBA can guarantee up to $1 million for fixed assets and $750,000 for working capital.

Photo reproduced courtesy of Coca-Cola SABCO (CCS)

The Coca-Cola Company

The Coca-Cola Company is Africa's soft drinks leader. Every day, about 78 million servings of Coca-Cola products are consumed in Africa. These are produced and distributed by over 160 bottling and canning plants, and then sold by 900,000 retail partners selling our beverages in all 56 countries and territories on the continent, making the Coca-Cola Company, together with its bottling partners, Africa's largest consumer goods provider.

With over 55,000 employees, the Coca-Cola system in Africa is also the continent's largest private sector employer. It is estimated that for every person employed by the Coca-Cola system, a further 10 people are employed in related industries, through the sale of Coca-Cola products, or by supplying the Company and its associate bottlers with goods and services.

The Company actively supports small retailers and micro entrepreneurs. For example, in Kenya, the Company stimulates entrepreneurship and employment opportunities by providing people with the opportunity to run kiosks selling Coca-Cola products.

Servicing Coca-Cola's retail customers in remote African communities has also led to innovative approaches and new employment opportunities. The system has helped local people establish small-scale distribution centers to meet these customers' needs in Ethiopia, Kenya, Tanzania, and Uganda. The Company's partnership with the International Finance Corporation (IFC), part of the World Bank Group, has helped provide these entrepreneurs with access to funding. A similar program in Nigeria, West Africa has created a network of more than 550 small businesses, 70 percent of which are run by women.

Kenya: bottler Manual Distribution Centres (MDCs)

The program was established in 1990 in Nairobi and now extends nationwide.

Case study: the story of a Manual Distribution Centre operator

- Francis Mukoma Nyanzi has worked hard to provide his family with a better life. The 45-year old supports 20 dependants, including both his and his wife's parents and ten siblings. He started out as a driver to a wholesaler with a salary of US $40 per month, before becoming a route sales driver and salesman at a salary of approximately US $78, a position he held for 16 years. Between 1989 and 2002, Francis worked as a wholesaler in two areas, Umoja and Kibera, which averaged 50 cases in daily sales.

- Francis' life changed with the advent of Coca-Cola Manual Distribution Centres (MDC) Systems in 2002 when he was appointed an MDC operator for Nairobi Bottlers. Francis now sells an average 10,000 physical cases monthly, equating to turnover of approximately US $52,000. The financial security that the MDC program offers has meant more than just daily bread provision for Francis and his family. With the money he has made through the program, he has build a permanent house in Makueni, is educating two siblings on a full time basis and others when the need arises. He has also built his parents a house. Francis, who employs 12 people in total including his wife and himself, expresses the feeling of many MDC operators, "Coca-Cola has built me to where I am and I know that this partnership will mutually thrive to greater heights. I shall be forever grateful to Coca-Cola"

Through an innovative and unique distribution model, our bottler Coca-Cola Sabco (CCS) is creating entrepreneurs, who in turn, are creating jobs for others in their community. Since 2005, a public-private task force has been evaluating and evolving the program, enhancing its sustainability.

The IFC was looking for appropriate corporate partners interested in driving economic upliftment through small business development and identified CCS for this role in East Africa. The result is that not only has CCS created employment and entrepreneurship in these countries through its distribution model, but it has also, together with the IFC, assisted these entrepreneurs to receive favourable financing/loans to start their own businesses.

Our community responsibilities

Having operated in Africa for more than three quarters of a century, the Coca-Cola business has deep roots in local communities across the continent. It is committed to maintaining an open and constructive dialogue with people in its communities, understanding their needs and aspirations, and investing company time, expertise, and resources in collaborative initiatives that respond in a meaningful way to community needs and priorities.

The business rationale for tackling HIV/AIDS is straightforward – it is devastating communities, and will impact Coca-Cola Company employees and The Coca-Cola Company's business partners if left unchecked. Globally, nearly 40 million people are estimated to have HIV/AIDS. While the virus has no borders, more than 70 percent of people infected live in Africa. The epidemic increases costs, reduces productivity, and threatens the continent's burgeoning economic prosperity.

Since its establishment in 2001, the Coca-Cola Africa Foundation, based in Swaziland, has led the system's efforts to prevent and treat HIV/AIDS in Africa. Through education and awareness campaigns, as well as by making prevention programs and treatment available to approximately 55,000 system employees and their spouses and children, some 250,000 people are touched by the system's initiatives.

Ramadan Charity Campaign

Our Ramadan charity campaign, now in its third year has to date helped feed more than 2.4 million people in Morocco and Egypt through a free Iftar meal distribution initiative.

The Coca-Cola Company worked with its bottling partners; concentrate plant staff, community members, NGOs and employees to donate both cooked and dried foods to poor families in Muslim countries in North Africa.

Supporting orphans and children in the community

Beach cleaning in Ghana

Our Ramadan campaign offered free meals to orphanages, hospitals and underprivileged residents in both urban and rural areas, through a network of NGOs, employees and community members. During the holy time of Ramadan, Muslims fast from sunrise to sunset for one month, ending their daily fast with an Iftar. Unfortunately, many poor families cannot afford regular meals, or even one daily Iftar during Ramadan.

The Love Life Caravan

In 2006, the Coca-Cola system supported an innovative regional World Bank HIV/AIDS awareness campaign, designed to stop the spread of the disease in five West African countries. A highly visible caravan of specially equipped trucks staffed by health experts, volunteers, and artists ran the length of the most heavily trafficked corridor on the continent.

The corridor extends from Cote d'Ivoire through Ghana, Togo and Benin to Nigeria. The caravan staged music and drama productions, while providing education, counseling, and treatment to millions of people living and traveling along the 1,000-kilometer route. By the time the caravan – the first program of its kind – ended in Lagos, Nigeria, it had, through interactions with people and a media campaign, reached an estimated 50 million people.

The Iftar is often a shared meal, and The Coca-Cola Company's donated food helped reinforce community values by providing nourishment and volunteer opportunities for community members and employees. The campaign's success will encourage us to continue such initiatives in the years to come.

For more details about The Coca-Cola Company and The Coca-Cola Africa Foundation please visit:

www.africa.coca-cola.com
www.africacommunity.coca-cola.com

RATING AFRICA

MINDFUL OF THE IMPORTANT ROLE THAT CREDIT RATINGS PLAY IN THE GLOBAL CAPITAL MARKETS, AN INCREASING NUMBER OF AFRICAN COUNTRIES ARE SUBJECTING THEMSELVES TO ASSESSMENTS BY THE WORLD'S LEADING RATING AGENCIES. SO FAR NINETEEN AFRICAN NATIONS HAVE BEEN RATED.

MOODYS

Moody's (www.moodys.com) concedes that credit ratings are by their very nature subjective as they rely on the judgment of a diverse group of credit risk professionals weighing a number of pertinent factors. Moody's issues country ceiling ratings for foreign-currency bonds and notes (both long- and short-term), and country ceilings for foreign currency bank deposits (both long- and short-term). Using an Aaa-through-C rating, an Aaa signifies the best quality with the smallest degree of investment risk and is generally referred to as "gilt edged." Aa signifies high quality by all standards while A implies favorable investment at an upper-medium-grade level. Baa is considered as medium-grade, Ba has speculative elements, B generally lacks the characteristics of the desirable investment, Caa denotes poor standing, Ca is speculative to a high degree, and C shows extremely poor prospects of ever attaining investment grading. Moody's applies numerical modifiers 1, 2, and 3 in each generic rating classification from Aa through Caa. The modifier 1 indicates that the obligation ranks in the higher end of its generic rating category; a 2 indicates a mid-range ranking; and a 3 stipulates a ranking in the lower end of a specific category.

STANDARD & POOR'S

Standard & Poor's (www. standardpoor. com) cautions against interpretation of its sovereign ratings as "country ratings." Instead, it suggests that a sovereign credit rating should be seen as an assessment of a government's capacity and willingness to repay debt according to its terms. Sovereign ratings address the credit risks of national governments and is not a recommendation to invest, according to S&P. An AAA rating, the highest assigned by Standard & Poor's, indicates an extremely strong capacity to meet financial commitments. An AA shows a very strong capacity to meet obligations and an A rating a strong capacity to meet financial commitments. A BBB is assigned to those judged to have an adequate capacity to meet their commitments but with a greater likelihood being affected by adverse economic conditions. Sovereign debt rated BB, B, CCC, and CC are all seen as having significant speculative characteristics. The ratings from AA through CCC may be modified by the addition of a plus or minus sign to show relative gradings.

FITCH RATINGS

Fitch (www.fitchratings.com) draws for its sovereign rating on recent instances of default and near-default to establish a range of key leading indicators of distress. This information is incorporated in a risk model that gives a percentage score to sovereign borrowers, which is used in turn to determine the long-term rating. Sovereign borrowers usually enjoy the highest credit standing for obligations in their own currency. There is the risk, however, that a country may service its debt through excessive money creation, effectively eroding the value of its obligations through inflation. On the other hand, when a sovereign nation borrows in a foreign currency there is the even more serious risk of outright default since the sovereign borrower cannot print the means of servicing the debt. In long-term obligations, an AAA rating indicates the highest credit quality and lowest expectation of credit risk and is highly unlikely to be adversely affected by foreseeable events. AA denotes very high credit quality and very low expectation of credit risk. An A rating indicates high credit quality and a low expectation of credit risk. BBB assigns good credit quality and low expectation of credit risk. This is the lowest investment-grade category. For its short-term ratings F1 is the highest credit quality and the strongest capacity for timely payment of financial commitments. A plus sign may be added to denote exceptionally strong credit. F2 denotes good credit quality and a satisfactory capacity for timely payment of financial commitments, but with a lower margin of safety. F3 means fair credit quality and adequate capacity for timely payment of financial commitments with the possibility that near-term adverse changes could result in downgrading to below investment grade. While a B rating is speculative, C indicates high default risk and D actual or imminent payment default.

African sovereign credit ratings - Dec. 2006

BENIN

Standard & Poor's
Domestic currency	B/Negative/B
Foreign currency	B/Negative/B

Fitch ratings
Foreign currency long-term	B
Domestic currency long-term	B

BOTSWANA

Moody's Investors Service
Country ceiling for. currency	Ba3/STA
Country ceiling local currency	Aa3

Standard & Poor's
Domestic currency	A+/Stable/A-1
Foreign currency	A/Stable/A-1

BURKINA FASO

Standard & Poor's
Domestic currency	B/Positive/B
Foreign currency	B/Positive/B

CAMEROON

Standard & Poor's
Domestic currency	B-/Stable/C
Foreign currency	B-/Stable/C

Fitch ratings
Foreign currency long-term	B/Stable
Domestic currency long-term	CCC/Stable

CAPE VERDE

Fitch ratings
Foreign currency long-term	B+/Stable
Domestic currency long-term	BB-/Stable

EGYPT

Moody's Investors Service
Country ceiling for. currency	Baa2/STA
Country ceiling local currency	A3

Standard & Poor's
Domestic currency	BBB-/Stable/A-3
Foreign currency	BB+/Stable/B

Fitch Ratings
Foreign currency long-term	BB+/Stable
Domestic currency long-term	BBB/Stable

GAMBIA, THE

Fitch Ratings
Foreign currency long-term	CCC/Stable
Domestic currency long-term	CCC/Stable

GHANA

Fitch Ratings
Foreign currency long-term	B+/Positive
Domestic currency long-term	B/Positive

LESOTHO

Fitch Ratings
Foreign currency long-term	BB-/Stable
Domestic currency long-term	BB/Stable

MALAWI

Fitch Ratings
Foreign currency long-term	CCC/Stable
Domestic currency long-term	CCC/Stable

MALI

Fitch ratings
Foreign currency long-term	B-/Stable
Domestic currency long-term	B-/Stable

MAURITIUS

Moody's Investors Service
Country ceiling for. currency	Baa1/NEG
Country ceiling local currency	Aa2

MOROCCO

Moody's Investors Service
Country ceiling for. currency	Baa2/STA
Country ceiling local currency	A3

Standard & Poor's
Domestic currency	BBB/Stable/A-3
Foreign currency	BB+/Stable/B

MOZAMBIQUE

Standard & Poor's
Domestic currency	B/Positive/B
Foreign currency	B/Positive/B

Fitch Ratings
Foreign currency long-term	B/Stable
Domestic currency long-term	B+/Stable

NAMIBIA

Fitch Ratings
Foreign currency long-term	BBB-/Stable
Domestic currency long-term	BBB/Stable

SENEGAL

Standard & Poor's
Domestic currency	B+/Negative/B
Foreign currency	B+/Negative/B

NIGERIA

Fitch Ratings
Foreign currency long-term	BB-/Stable
Domestic currency long-term	BB-/Stable

SOUTH AFRICA

Moody's Investors Service
Country ceiling for. currency	A2/STA
Country ceiling local currency	Aaa

Standard & Poor's
Domestic currency	A+/Stable/A-
Foreign currency	BBB+/Stable/A-1

Fitch Ratings—Aug. 2005
Foreign currency long-term	BBB+
Domestic currency long-term	A

TUNISIA

Moody's Investors Service
Country ceiling for. currency	A3/STA
Country ceiling local currency	Aa2

Standard & Poor's
Domestic currency	A/Stable/A-
Foreign currency	BBB/Stable/A-3

Fitch Ratings
Foreign currency long-term	BBB
Domestic currency long-term	A-

AFRICA ON THE WEB

AFRICAN WEB-SPACE IS EXPANDING AND MOST COUNTRIES HAVE SOME FORM OF LOCAL OR INTERNATIONALLY HOSTED WEB SERVER, UNOFFICIALLY OR OFFICIALLY REPRESENTING THE COUNTRY—SOME OF THEM SPONSORED BY INTERNATIONAL DEVELOPMENT AGENCIES. WITH THE EXCEPTION OF SOUTH AFRICA, EGYPT AND KENYA, MOST AFRICAN SITES ARE HOSTED OFF-SHORE. THERE HAS BEEN A PROLIFERATION OF AFRICA-RELATED WEB-SITES IN BRITAIN AND THE US, OFFERING ANYTHING FROM THE ULTIMATE SAFARI TO TRADITIONAL FOODS, NEWS, DATA AND INVESTMENT SERVICES. ANY PHRASE WITH THE WORD AFRICA ENTERED ON A SEARCH ENGINE BRINGS UP MILLIONS OF WEBSITE ADDRESSES. OUR SELECTION OF WEBSITES DOES NOT IMPLY ENDORSEMENT OR RECOMMENDATION BUT MERELY SIGNIFIES USEFULNESS.

INTERNATIONAL ORGANIZATIONS

The following websites of international organizations provide useful data and special reports on Africa and its nations:
World Bank—*www.worldbank.org*
World Trade Organization—*www.wto.org*
UNCTAD—*www.unctad.org*
World Tourism—*www.world-tourism.org*
UNAIDS—*www.unaids.org*
UNESCO—*www.unesco.org*
Intl. Monetary Fund—*www.imf.org*

REGIONAL ORGANIZATIONS

The following websites of regional organizations provide useful data and special reports on Africa and its nations:
African Union—*www.africa-union.org*
African Dev. Bank—*www.afdb.org*
SADC—*www.sadc.int*
COMESA—*www.comesa.int*
ECOWAS—*www.ecowas.intport*

U.S. BASED ORGANIZATIONS

The following websites are key to any US company interested in developing meaningful business relations in Africa:
CCA—*www.africacncl.org*
Exim Bank—*www.exim.gov*
World Trade—*www.africareport*
Exim Bank—*www.exim.gov*

NEWS & INFORMATION

Daily news feed about and from Africa supplied by sources in Africa and abroad:.
All Africa News—*www.allafrica.com*
Africa Report—*www.africareport*

Specialized books about Africa's economy, history and tourism attractions:
BBI Pub.—*www.businessbooksusa.com*

TRAVEL & SAFARI
The following website offers specialized assistance on safari arrangements:
Ultimate Safari—*www.theultimatesafari.com*

WEATHER

The following websites offer regular updates on weather in Africa:
South Africa—*www.weathersa.co.za*
Africa—*www.weather.msn.com*

EXCHANGE RATES

The following website offers regular updates on exchange rates for all Africa's currencies:
Go Currency—*www.gocurrency.com*

STATISTICAL SOURCES

STATISTICS ON AFRICA ARE NOT DIF-
FICULT TO OBTAIN. TO VERIFY THE ACCU-
RACY OF THESE FIGURES IS ANOTHER MAT-
TER. NOT INFREQUENTLY DATA ON THE
SAME TOPIC FROM DIFFERENT SOURCES
VARY. MOST AFRICAN COUNTRIES HAVE
THEIR OWN STATISTICAL DEPARTMENTS
WITH SOME OF THEM PROVIDING THE
LATEST DATA ONLINE:

ALGERIA
Office National des Statistiques
8,10 Rue des moussebilines, Alger Algérie
Tel : (213) 21- 74-41-41

ANGOLA
Insituto Nacional de Estatistica (INE)
Rua Ho-Chi-Min, Edificio INE, Luanda
Tel: (244) 320 430 or 322 757

BENIN
Institut National de la Statistique
et de l'Analyse Economique, BP 323, Cotonou
Tel (229) 31.34.31
Web: http://planben.intnet.bj/13a/benin.htm

BOTSWANA
Central Statistics Office
Office P/B 0024, Gaborone, Botswana
Tel 267-352200 Web: www.cso.gov.bw

BURKINA FASO
Institut National de la Statistique
et de la Démographie (INSD)
01 BP 374 , Ouagadougou
Tel: (226) 32 42 69

BURUNDI
Institut de la Statistique et des Etudes
Economiques du Burundi (ISTEEBU)
BP 1156, Bujumbura
Tel: (257) 22 67 29

CAMEROON
Direction de la Statistique et
de la Comptabilité Nationale, Yaoundé
Tel: (237) 22 04 45

CAPE VERDE
Instituto Nacional de Estatistica (INE)
Avenida Amilcar Cabral, C.P. 116 Praia
Tel (238) 61 39 60 or 61 38 27

CENTRAL AFRICAN REPUBLIC
Division des Statistiques et
des Etudes Economiques, BP 696, Bangui
Tel: (236) 61 45 74 Fax: (236) 61 03 90

CHAD
Direction de la Statistique des Etudes
Economiques et Démographiques
BP 453, N'Djaména Tel: (235) 52 31 64

COMOROS
Direction de la Statistique,
BP 131, Moroni
Tel (269) 74 42 34

CONGO
Centre National de la
Statistique et des Etudes Economiques
BP 64, Brazzaville Tel: (242) 81 08 58

CÔTE D'IVOIRE
Institut National de la Statistique (INS)
01 BP V55, Abidjan 01 Tel: (225) (22) 21 05 38

DJIBOUTI
Direction Nationale de la
Statistique (DINAS), BP 1846, Djibouti
Tel: (253) 35 16 82

EQUATORIAL GUINEA
Direction Générale des Statistiques
A.C. 607, Malabo Tel: (240) 9 2884

ERITREA
National Statistics Office
2 Wollo Street, P.O. Box 5838, Asmara
Tel: (291) 1-12 00 91

ETHIOPIA
Central Statistical Authority
PO Box 1143, Addis Ababa
Tel: (251) (1) 11 51 31

GABON
Direction Générale de la Statistique
et des Etudes Economiques
BP 2119, Libreville Tel: (241) 76 06 71

GAMBIA
Central Statistics Department
32 Buckle Street, Banjul Tel: (220) 22.83.64

GHANA
Ghana Statistical Service (GSS)
PO Box 1098, Accra, Ghana
Tel: (233) (21) 68 26 92

GUINEA
Direction Nationale de la Statistique
BP 221 Conakry Tel: (224) 41 41 36

GUINEA-BISSAU
Instituto Nacional de
Estatistica e Censos
CP 6, Bissau Tel: (245) 22 20 54

KENYA
Central Bureau of Statistics
PO Box 30266, Nairobi
Tel: (254) (2) 33 39 70

LESOTHO
Bureau of Statistics, PO Box 455, Maseru
Tel: (266) 32 38 52 Fax: (266) 31 017

MADAGASCAR
Institut National de la Statistique
BP 485, Antananarivo 101
Tel: (261) (20) 22 357 03

MALAWI
National Statistical Office
P.O Box 333, Zomba
Tel: 265 524111 Web: www.nso.malawi.net

MALI
Direction Nationale de la Statistique et de
l'Informatique, BP 12, Bamako
Tel: (223) 22 24 55

MAURITANIA
Office National de la Statistique
BP 240, Nouakchott
Tel: (222) 25 50 31 Web: www.ons.mr

MAURITIUS
Central Statistical Office
Port Louis Tel (230) 212 2316
Web: ncb.intnet.mu/cso.htm

MOROCCO
Direction de la statistique
Avenue Al Haj Ahmed Cherkaoui
Agdal - BP. 826, 10004 Rabat

MOZAMBIQUE
Instituto Nacional de Estatística
Av.Ahmed Sekou Touré, nº 21, CP 493 Maputo
Tel: (258) (1) 49 10 54 / 5 Web: www.ine.gov.mz

NAMIBIA
Central Bureau of Statistics
Private Bag 13356, Windhoek
Tel: (264) (61) 283-4111\

NIGER
Direction de la Statistique
et des Comptes Nationaux, BP 862, Niamey
Tel: (227) 72 35 60 Fax: (227) 72 22 89

NIGERIA
Federal Office of Statistics
PO Box 52724, Falomo PO, Ikoyi, Lagos
Tel: (234) (1) 264 72 58

RWANDA
Direction de la Statistique
BP 46, Kigali Tel: (250) 78 937

SAO TOME AND PRINCIPE
Instituto Nacional de Estatistica
Tel: (239) (12) 21 313

SENEGAL
Direction de la Prévision et
de la Statistique (DPS), BP 116, Dakar
Tel: (221) 824 03 01 Fax: (221) 825 07 43

SEYCHELLES
Ministry of Information Technology
PO Box 206, Victoria Tel : (248) 38 31 81
Web: www.seychelles.net/misdstat

SIERRA LEONE
Central Statistics Office
Tower Hill, Box 595, Freetown
Tel: (232) (22) 22-3287

SOUTH AFRICA
Central Statistics Service (CSS)
PB X44, Pretoria 0001
Tel: (27) (12) 310-8911
Web: www.statssa.gov.za

SUDAN
Central Bureau of Statistics
Khartoum
Tel: (249) (11) 77 003

SWAZILAND
Central Statistics Office
PO Box 456
Mbabane
Tel: (268) 42 151
Fax: (268) 43 300

TANZANIA
Bureau of Statistics
PO Box 9242
Dar-es-Salaam
Tel: (255) (51) 11 26 81/82/83
Fax: (255) (51) 13 17 23
Email: nbs.dg@raha.com

TOGO
Direction de la Statistique
BP 118, Lomé
Tel: (228) 21 27 75
Fax: (228) 21 37 53
Email: edst2@cafe.tg

UGANDA
Uganda Bureau of Statistics (UBOS)
Plot 10/11 Airport Road
P.O. Box 13 Entebbe, Uganda
Tel: (256) 041-320165 / 320741 / 32164
Web: www.ubos.org

ZAMBIA
Central Statistical Office
PO Box 31908
Lusaka
Tel: (260) (1) 25 34 68
Fax: (260) (1) 25 25 75
Email: dpucso@zamnet.zm

ZIMBABWE
Central Statistical Office
Box CY 342, Causeway
Harare
Tel: (263) (4) 70 66 81 to 88
Fax: (263) (4) 70 88 54

AFRICA REPORT

Africa Report is a weekly programme that focuses on business and investment in Africa.

Broadcast on CNBC Europe, the world's leading business channel - Africa Report showcases the very best of Africa, covering market dynamics, economic reforms and rewarding investment opportunities.

Africa Report provides a unique platform reaching out to 117 millions homes in over 60 countries on CNBC Europe and an additional 250 million viewers in Africa.

Call Africa Report today and find out how you can be seen by 1,2 million of the top 20% income earners in Europe, every week.

View Africa Report on CNBC Europe at this time:

Saturday 20.30 CET before the Jay Leno show

In Africa, you can watch CNBC Europe on DSTV channel 54.

For more information on Africa Report and to find out show times on our broadcast partners in Africa:

www.africareport.com
info@africareport.com
www.cnbceurope.com

**Recommended by
NEPAD and COMESA**

BIKO INVESTMENTS

Supplier of programmes for

CNBC
EUROPE
a service of NBC and Dow Jones

Chapter 7
The Nations of Africa

Diversity should be expected on a continent of 800 million people consisting of hundreds of ethnic groupings and thousands of tribal affiliations, speaking 2,000 languages in 53 countries. Today business is conducted in English, French, Arabic, Portuguese, Spanish and Swahili, with English having an edge on the others.

AFRICA'S 53 NATIONS

174

COUNTRY PROFILES

PROFILING POLITICAL AND ECONOMIC CONDITIONS IN 53 DIVERSE COUNTRIES SPANNING ACROSS THE AFRICAN CONTINENT AND AN ARRAY OF ADJOINING ISLANDS WOULD HAVE BEEN IMPOSSIBLE WITHOUT THE KIND COOPERATION OF SEVERAL INSTITUTIONS, INCLUDING THE UNITED NATIONS AND THE IMF AND A NUMBER OF AFRICA-RELATED ORGANIZATIONS, INCLUDING THE AFRICAN DEVELOPMENT BANK AND THE UN ECONOMIC COMMISSION FOR AFRICA. WE HAVE ALSO RECEIVED STATISTICAL DATA FROM SEVERAL COUNTRY SOURCES.

In assessing business opportunities in specific countries, we are indebted to the US State Department (www.state.gov) and the US Department of Commerce (www.ita.doc.gov). We recommend that entrepreneurs who are seriously interested in conducting business in Africa consult with these departments.

DATA

While every effort was made to cross-check statistics and to provide the most recent data available, there will no doubt be areas of dispute. Not all nations apply the same criteria and some are unfortunately lacking in up-to-date figures. Even in this book you will find conflicts and variations depending on which source we quote.

MAPS

Our maps follow the official borders recognized by the United Nations. It is not within our power to adjudicate in border disputes and adjust maps to suit the preferences of either party in contested cases.

PPP

Apart from real GDP statistics based on current official dollar exchange rates, figures are also published based on purchasing power parity (PPP). The PPP method, considered by many economists as a more accurate measure of economic strength, weighs incomes against domestic costs and prices in specific countries. Exchange rates may suddenly go up or down by 10% or more as a result of market forces or official decisions while real output remains unchanged. On 12 January 1994, for example, the 14 countries of the Communauté Financière Africaine, or CFA, (whose currencies are tied to the French franc) devalued their currency by 50%. This did not, however, cut the real output of these countries by half as real GDP based on the new exchange rates would suggest. It should be noted that while PPP estimates for OECD countries are quite specific, the same estimates for developing countries are often mere approximations.

AFRICAN INDICATORS- 2005

	Area '000 Km²	Population '000	Adult Illiteracy Rate %	Life expectancy at birth	Population doubling date	GDP at market prices $m	Per capita GDP in US$	External debt US$ bn	Debt service % of GDP
Algeria	2,382	32,854	27.9	72	2048	104,935	3,194	19.4	4.7
Angola	1,247	15,941	...	41	2026	28,475	1,786	10.6	5.2
Benin	113	8,439	56.8	55	2024	4,328	513	1.6	1.0
Botswana	582	1,765	18.6	35	2705	9,130	5,173	1.1	8.4
Burkina Faso	274	13,228	71.5	49	2024	5,441	411	1.9	1.9
Burundi	28	7,548	46.1	45	2021	799	106	1.5	5.4
Cameroon	475	16,322	23.1	46	2041	16,895	1,035	5.8	2.2
Cape Verde	4	507	22.0	71	2032	1,051	2,074	0.8	5.8
Cent. Afr. Rep.	623	4,038	46.1	39	2056	1,382	342	1.3	0.0
Chad	1,284	9,749	49.3	44	2024	5,225	536	1.7	1.2
Comoros	2	798	43.2	64	2028	384	481	0.3	2.3
Congo	342	3,999	14.2	53	2026	5,859	1,465	5.8	8.5
Congo (DRC)	2,345	57,549	31.9	44	2025	6,922	120	10.9	2.1
Côte d'Ivoire	322	18,154	46.3	46	2046	16,172	891	10.5	0.0
Djibouti	23	793	29.7	53	2041	700	883	0.5	2.4
Egypt	1,001	74,033	40.8	71	2039	90,917	1 228	28.7	3.5
Equat. Guinea	28	504	12.9	42	2033	6,416	12,742	0.3	0.7
Eritrea	118	4,401	39.5	55	2020	1,058	240	0.6	2.9
Ethiopia	1,104	77,431	54.8	48	2031	11,078	143	6.6	0.7
Gabon	268	1,384	...	54	2046	8,515	6,153	3.8	5.5
Gambia	11	1,517	57.5	57	2028	458	302	0.6	15.3
Ghana	239	22,113	23.0	57	2036	11,886	537	8.1	2.0
Guinea	246	9,402	...	54	2034	3,292	350	3.1	3.3
Guinea Bissau	36	1,586	55.2	45	2025	300	189	0.8	5.4
Kenya	580	34,256	13.1	49	2032	19,041	556	5.3	0.3
Lesotho	30	1,795	14.3	35	2613	1,467	817	0.8	6.8
Liberia	111	3,283	41.1	42	2055	...	...	...	...
Libya	1,760	5,853	15.9	74	2037	37,256	6,365	6.0	0.0
Madagascar	587	18 606	29.5	56	2028	5,115	275	4.9	2.8
Malawi	118	12,884	35.7	41	2034	1,979	154	2.9	5.0
Mali	1,240	13,518	70.5	49	2025	5,117	379	3.4	1.8
Mauritania	1,026	3,069	57.4	54	2026	1,823	594	2.1	4.3
Mauritius	2	1,245	13.6	73	2077	6,386	5,131	1.0	3.2
Morocco	711	31,478	46.5	70	2049	52,289	1,661	15.6	4.7
Mozambique	802	19,792	49.6	42	2039	6,832	345	4.7	6.1
Namibia	824	2,031	14.6	47	2066	6,345	3,124	0.9	1.2
Niger	1,267	13,957	81.3	45	2023	3,025	217	1.7	2.3
Nigeria	924	131,530	29.2	44	2034	94,757	720	28.7	10.0
Rwanda	26	9 038	27.3	44	2042	2,092	231	1.5	0.7
São T. & Principe	1	157	...	64	2032	79	504	0.3	9.5
Senegal	197	11,658	57.9	57	2031	8,356	717	3.6	4.6
Seychelles	0.5	81	...	...	2077	698	8,659	0.6	5.7
Sierra Leone	72	5,525	...	41	2022	1,163	211	1.2	3.9
Somalia	638	8228	...	48	2023	...	...	4.0	2.9
South Africa	1,221	47,432	12.9	46	2148	240,734	5,075	44.7	2.2
Sudan	2,506	36,233	36.9	57	2037	28,112	776	26.4	2.3
Swaziland	17	1,032	17.1	31	2613	2,685	2,601	0.4	...
Tanzania	945	38,329	19.9	46	2040	12,207	318	6.4	2.2
Togo	57	6,145	36.5	55	2029	2,174	354	2.1	3.5
Tunisia	164	10,102	23.8	74	2067	29,353	2,906	16.7	7.1
Uganda	241	28,816	28.4	50	2022	8,475	294	4.3	1.9
Zambia	753	11,668	17.8	38	2044	6,782	581	3.8	2.4
Zimbabwe	391	13,010	8.1	37	2125	5,792	445	5.2	1.3
AFRICA	30,307	904,804	35.0	51	2034	933,776	1,032	318.5	2.3

Source: African Development Bank

ALGERIA

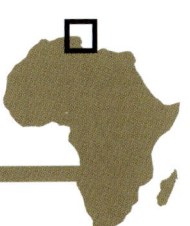

With more than 30 million inhabitants, ample oil resources and an economy in transition, formerly socialist Algeria offers great potential for foreign investment. Responding to IMF and the World Bank programs, Algeria has made remarkable economic and financial progress, improving its trade and budget balances, reducing inflation and foreign debt and bolstering foreign currency reserves. Currently the main focus of foreign investors is on oil and gas, but as privatization progresses, this is likely to change.

COUNTRY PROFILE

The Democratic and Popular Republic of Algeria (Aljumhuriyah aljaza'lriyah ad Dimuqratiyah ash Shabiyah) is the largest of the countries in the northwestern corner of Africa, known as the Maghreb. It is, after Sudan, the second largest country on the continent. Regions vary from coastal plains along the Mediterranean, to high plateaus, mountains and the Sahara Desert—with large reserves of oil and natural gas that are so important to the economy. About 80% of the

predominantly Muslim population speak Arabic. Berbers, including Kabyles, and the Tuaregs are major linguistic groups. A medium ranking on the United Nations Human Development Index reflects the comparatively high levels attained in education and health.

HISTORY

The Arab culture and Islam were introduced to the predominantly Berber peoples of Algeria in the 7th Century. It survived subsequent invasions by the Turks and the French, who came in 1830 and stayed until 1962 when the Algerians won their independence after a protracted war against France. President Ahmed Ben Bella and his successor, President Houari Boume-dienne, introduced various socialist reforms. In 1988 widespread strikes led to rioting and the killing of hundreds in Algiers and other cities. It also gave rise to the Islamic Salvation Front (FIS), an extremist fundamentalist movement bent on eradicating "European" influence in Algeria. As a result of violence backed by the FIS before the 1990 elections and pronouncements by its leaders that they intended to replace democracy with a theocracy, the rulers suspended the election. The FIS was dissolved by court order in 1992. In 1994 General Liamine Zeroual was appointed president to replace the High Council of State (HSC), which ruled in the interim. By mid-1994 some 4,000 Algerians and more than 30

177

FAST FACTS

Pres. Abdelaziz
Bouteflika
Born: March 2, 1937
Since 1999

POLITICAL

Head of State	Pres. Abdelaziz Bouteflika
Majority Party	FLN
Others major paties	RND, MRN, MSP, PT
Independence	5 July 1962
National capital	Algiers
Official language	Arabic

PHYSICAL

Total area	919,595 sq. miles 2,381,740 sq. km (3½ x Texas)
Arable land	3% of land area
Coastline	746 m/1200 km

POPULATION

Total	32.9 million
Av. yearly growth	1.22%
Population/sq.mile	34
Urban population	19.7 million
Adult literacy	65.0%

ECONOMY

Currency	Algerian dinar (DA)(US$1=72.37)
GDP (real)	$85.3 billion
GDP growth rate	6.0%
GDP per capita[1]	$3,194
GDP (ppp)[2]	$233.2 billion
GDP per cap. (ppp)	$7,200
Inflation rate	1.9%
Exports	$49.59 billion
Imports	$22.53 billion
External debt	$19.45 billion
Unemployment	17.1%

1. *Atlas method.*
2. *See page 175 for an explanation of purchasing power parity (ppp).*

foreigners had been killed by the FIS. General Zeroual held elections in 1997, which the Rassemblement national démocratique (RND) won. Following President Zeroual's resignation in 1999, Abdelaziz Bouteflika was elected as Algeria's first civilian president. After an amnesty agreement in 1999 with some of the armed Islamic fundamentalist groups, violence diminished and in 1999 referendum Bouteflika's peace plan was adopted by a landslide 98% of the vote. Boutreflika was reelected in April 2004 by a comfortable margin of the popular vote.

GOVERNMENT

A bicameral parliament consists of a 389-seat National People's Assembly (Al-Majlis Ech-Chaabi Al Watani) elected by popular vote for five years and a Council of Nations which serves as an upper chamber. One third of the 144 members of the Council are appointed by the President and the rest elected by indirect vote. Council members serve six years. In the May 2002 National Assembly elections, a voter turnout of 46.2% favored the Front de libération nationale (FLN). It gained 199 seats while 47 seats went to the Rassemblement national pour la démocratie (RND). The Movement for National Reform (MRN) came third with 43 seats. The rest of the seats were split between the Mouvement de la société pour la paix/Harakat Moudjtamaa As-Silm (Movement of the Society for Peace, Islamist—MSP) with 31, the Parti du Travail (Workers' Party—PT) with 21, and a number of smaller parties.

ECONOMIC POLICY

In the first two decades after independence Algeria, heavily influenced by socialism, maintained a government-controlled economy. The petroleum industry was nationalized and collective ownership introduced in the agricultural sector. Legislation allowing foreign-owned companies to become involved in the "reconstruction" of the national economy was adopted since and several reforms introduced. In recent years government regulatory pricing was relaxed and more liberal tax policies introduced as part of an ongoing reform program. Structural reform within the economy, such as development of the banking sector and the construction of infrastructure, is moving ahead.

SECTORS

Algeria has one of Africa's more advanced economies based on oil and natural gas. The oil production of 1.373 million bbl/day is of a high quality with a low sulphur content. The hydrocarbons sector accounts for roughly 60 percent of budget revenues, 30 percent of GDP, and over 95 percent of export earnings. Algeria has the world's seventh-largest reserves of natural gas and ranks second as a gas exporter. It is 14th in oil reserves. High oil prices along with macroeconomic policy reforms sanctioned by the IMF boosted the country's financial and macroeconomic indicators. Algeria's large trade surpluses helped it to build substantial foreign exchange reserves. A key player in this petroleum sector is the state oil company, SONATRACH, which has been courting overseas investors in recent years. There are four oil refineries and four natural gas liquefaction plants. Agriculture is confined to the Mediterranean coastal region where crops such as wheat, barley, vegetables, citrus fruits, dates, olives, peas, beans, lentils, tobacco and sugar beet are grown. Wine is the main agricultural export. Other mineral resources include iron ore, uranium, zinc, phosphates, gold, antimony, bituminous coal, tungsten, manganese, lead, mercury, gypsum and salt. Manufacturing largely consists of heavy industries such as iron and steel, and fertilizer and cement plants, but the emphasis is shifting towards textiles and the processing of food, tobacco and cigarettes.

PRIVATIZATION

The government has privatized or liquidated 1000 state enterprises since 1996. Insurance and banking have also been deregulated. The Algiers Stock Exchange started functioning in July 1999. The private sector accounts for all of the activity in agriculture, has minority representation in hydrocarbons, and leads the way in services (78%) and commerce (77%). Its share in transportation and communications has increased to close to half.

TRADE

About 95 percent of Algeria's export revenues come from oil and natural gas exports. Major buyers are Spain, Portugal and Morocco. Algeria produces only about one-third of its own food requirements and relies heavily on imports from the United States and Europe for the rest.

INVESTMENT

Following the example of the state-owned petroleum corporation, SONATRACH, various sectors in Algeria have been courting foreign investors in recent years. American interest has mainly been in the petroleum sector. Other significant entrants were Coca-Cola and Pepsi Cola. It is expected that in the next few years others will follow suit in the service, food processing and mining sectors.

FINANCIAL SECTOR

The Bank of Algeria controls monetary growth by setting bank lending limits. Interest rates are adjusted on a weekly basis by a government board. In 1998 the central bank opened a secondary market for government debt. Still, the lack of a modern financial services sector restricts growth of the private sector and has impeded foreign investment in Algeria. Reform efforts in the state-owned banking sector overall have progressed slowly. A few foreign banks have opened representational offices since the promulgation of the currency and credit law.

TAXES & TARIFFS

The government reformed its tax code to encourage business development, cutting rates in several categories. Corporate tax rates were reduced from 38 to 30 percent, and went as low as 18 percent in cases where profits are reinvested. A five year taxation vacation is allowed on profits derived from stock and bond sales.

BUSINESS ACTIVITY

AGRICULTURE
Wheat, barley, oats, grapes, citrus, fruit, olives, livestock.

INDUSTRIES
Petroleum, natural gas, light industries, mining, electrical, petrochemical, food processing.

NATURAL RESOURCES
Petroleum, natural gas, iron ore, phosphates, uranium, lead, zinc.

EXPORTS
$49.59 billion (2005 est.): petroleum, natural gas and petroleum products.

IMPORTS
$22.53 billion (2005 est.): capital goods, food and beverages, consumer goods.

MAJOR TRADING PARTNERS
Italy, US, France, Spain, Germany

Doing Business with Algeria

▶ **INVESTMENT**

Algeria, with its large proven oil and gas reserves and potential for new discoveries, offers significant commercial opportunities to foreign investors. Investments in the hydrocarbon sector involve a minority partnership with the state-owned SONATRACH . The same rules apply in telecommunications and national transportation, but in all other sectors foreign investors have unlimited scope. Repatriation of profits, interest, dividends or any other form of revenue is permitted.

▶ **TRADE**

Machinery for the exploration and exploitation of oil and gas offers the best potential for US exports. As the world's fifth largest and Africa's largest importer of wheat, this commodity, as well as other foodstuffs, present good opportunities. There is a strong demand for housing materials, consumer products, and equipment for water projects and telecommunications. Import licenses are no longer required for most of these items, but the government stipulates that imported products, particularly consumer goods, must be labeled in Arabic. Distribution is largely in private hands and can be done through legally authorized dealers.

▶ **TRADE FINANCE**

Eximbank programs apply to Algeria. The World Bank has assisted with loans for purchases relating to housing, water and sewage, and urban transport. The US-based Agricultural Mutual Bank, in partnership with a major insurance company and the private Union Bank, established a leasing corporation for agricultural equipment. Algerian state corporations have the reputation of honoring their purchase obligations, even though there may sometimes be bureaucratic delays.

▶ **SELLING TO THE GOVERNMENT**

Direct negotiation for contracts is only permitted in a few special cases. Tenders for primary raw materials, agricultural products, and construction are frequently limited to known suppliers. Public tenders are advertised in the dailies, the official weekly contract bulletin of the public agency (BOMOP) and sometimes in the international press. Algerian organizations rarely buy at the tendered price as further negotiation usually takes place with a short list of bidders. It is customary for companies to visit the state organizations beforehand and introduce their products and their company's capabilities. The use of agents or other intermediaries is strictly prohibited.

▶ **EXCHANGE CONTROLS**

A government board manages a float for the dinar, which is convertible for all current account transactions. Private and public importers may buy foreign exchange from five commercial banks for transactions on proof that they can pay for hard currency in dinars.

▶ **PARTNERSHIP**

The Algerian government is looking for outside resources to modernize its plants and encourages foreign investors to enter into joint ventures. In their search for partners Algerian companies usually look for technical expertise and financial assistance. Recent legislation gave foreign banks the freedom to establish in Algeria, paving the way for partnerships in the financial sector. Other state sectors are trying to emulate the success that the state-owned petroleum giant, SONATRACH, had in striking partnerships with major foreign investors both in the exploration and downstream processing of its oil and gas.

▶ **ESTABLISHING A PRESENCE**

To open a liaison office, foreign firms apply for an office leasing agreement at the Algerian Ministry of Commerce. They have to appoint a director and submit bank guarantee of $20,000.

▶ **LABOR**

Trade unions are allowed. The law mandates a 40-hour work week and the government has set a guaranteed monthly minimum wage of 6,000 Algerian dinars ($100). A decree regulates occupational and health standards. Working conditions are largely left at the discretion of employers in consultation with employees.

▶ **LEGAL RIGHTS**

Even though Algeria is a member of the Paris Industrial Property Convention and the 1952 Convention on Copyrights, its protection of intellectual property is less than satisfactory. There is recourse to international arbitration to settle possible legal disputes with investors.

▶ **BUSINESS CLIMATE**

Algerian organizations usually deal only with foreign partners who have developed their trust by personal visits, follow-up, and who have shown ability to honor commitments. It is sometimes necessary to spend large amounts on market development, especially when the contracts are substantial.

ANGOLA

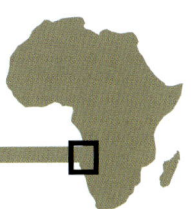

RICH IN OIL AND DIAMONDS AND OTHER NATURAL RESOURCES, ANGOLA IS A SPARSELY POPULATED COUNTRY ROUGHLY THE COMBINED SIZE OF TEXAS AND CALIFORNIA. THE COUNTRY IS REBUILDING AFTER THE END OF A CIVIL WAR LASTING TWENTY SEVEN YEARS. ITS HIGH GROWTH RATE IS DRIVEN BY ITS OIL SECTOR, BENEFITING FROM HIGH OIL PRICES COUPLED WITH RISING PRODUCTION. POSTWAR RECONSTRUCTION AND THE RESETTLEMENT OF DISPLACED CITIZENS HAVE FURTHER BOOSTED INCOME FROM CONSTRUCTION, AGRICULTURE, GOLD AND DIAMOND MINING, AND FISHING. REFORMS RECOMMENDED BY THE IMF AND GREATER TRANSPARENCY SERVE TO ENCOURAGE FOREIGN INVESTORS.

COUNTRY PROFILE

The Republic of Angola is slightly larger than South Africa and the combined size of Texas and California. The climate varies from tropical in the north to subtropical in the south. Major rivers are the Kunene, Zambezi and the Kwanza (after which the country's currency was named). The Bantu-speaking Ovimbundu, Kimbundu and Bakongo peoples are in the majority. Fifty-three percent are Christians (mostly Roman Catholic). The rest adhere to indigenous beliefs.

HISTORY

In the 16th Century, Portuguese interest in the region focused on the slave trade to supply the needs of its newfound colony, Brazil. Portuguese influence remained centered around Luanda (founded in 1575) and the kingdom of Ndongo ruled by chiefs referred to as ngola—which eventually served as an inspiration when naming independent Angola. It was not until the 1920s that Portugal managed to extend its influence to the borders of Angola, as defined by European treaties in the 1880s and 1890s. A protracted anti-colonial insurgent war ended in when Portugal granted independence to Angola in 1974 after army officers toppled the Salazar regime in Lisbon. Three movements were involved in the freedom struggle, largely divided on a regional and ethnic basis: The Popular Movement for the Liberation of Angola (MPLA) (receiving support from Cuba and the Soviet Union), the National Front for the Liberation of Angola (FNLA) and the National Union for the Total Independence of Angola (UNITA) (receiving assistance from the US and South Africa). On 11 November 1975, MPLA leader Agostinho Neto was sworn in as the first president of an independent Angola under Marxist one-party rule. Both FNLA and UNITA

FAST FACTS

Pres. José Eduoardo
dos Santos
Born: August 28, 1942
Since 1979

POLITICAL

Head of State	Pres. José Eduardo dos Santos (1979)
Ruling Party	MPLA
Main Opposition	UNITA
Independence	11 November 1975
National capital	Luanda
Official language	Portuguese

PHYSICAL

Total area	481,350 sq. miles 1,246,700 sq. km. (3 x California)
Arable land	3% of land area
Coastline	994 miles/1,600 km

POPULATION

Total	12.13 million
Av. yearly growth	2.45%
Population/sq. mile	21
Urban population	5.4 million
Adult literacy	66.8%

ECONOMY

Currency	New Kwanza (NKz) (US$1=81.65)
GDP (real)	$24.35 billion
GDP growth rate	19.1%
GDP per capita[1]	$1,786
GDP (ppp)[2]	$45.93 billion
GDP per cap. (ppp)	$3,200
Inflation rate	23%
Exports	$26.8 billion
Imports	$8.17 billion
External debt	$9.4 billion
Unemployment	23%

1. Atlas method.
2. See page 175 for an explanation of purchasing power parity (ppp).

turned their offensive against the new rulers. Even though US backing and South African support were eventually withdrawn, UNITA leader Jonas Savimbi continued the war. Dr. Neto died in 1979 and was succeeded as president by the new leader of the MPLA, José Eduardo dos Santos. President dos Santos has pledged to call an election before the end of 2007 but has not set a date, sparking repeated complaints from the opposition of dragging his feet.

GOVERNMENT

In 1992 President dos Santos received a plurality of votes against 122 other legally recognized parties in Angola's first round of elections, declared free and fair by UN observers. The second round never took place as UNITA, the other major party, repudiated the first as fraudulent. In 1994 MPLA and UNITA signed the Lusaka Protocol in an effort to end 20 years of civil war and in April 1997, UNITA joined MPLA and 10 smaller opposition parties in a Government of Unity and National Reconciliation (GURN). UNITA took up the 77 seats it won in the 220-member National Assembly against the MPLA's 129 seats during the 1992 election. Four ministers and seven deputies from UNITA ranks were included in the 78 member cabinet. In the second half of 1998, however, UNITA pulled out and resumed the war. Since the death in battle of its leader, Jonas Savimbi, in 2001 the party has been in disarray and the civil war ended. In 2006 the Launda government signed a Memorandum of Understanding for Peace and Reconciliation with rebels in the oil-rich Cabinda province.

ECONOMIC POLICY

Angola operated a Soviet-style centrally planned economy until 1991, but has since been making a transition to a market-based system. The country's high growth rate is driven by high oil prices and rising petroleum production. Increased oil production contributed to a 12% growth in 2004 and 19% in 2005. The postwar reconstruction boom and resettlement of displaced persons led to high rates of growth in construction and agriculture. The country's infrastructure is, however, still damaged or undeveloped from as a result of a 27-year-long civil war. Land mines still mar the countryside even though a durable peace seems to have been established after the death of rebel leader Jonas SAVIMBI in February 2002. In 2005, the government started using a $2 billion of credit line from China to rebuild the public infrastructure. Several large-scale projects are due for completion by 2006. The central bank in 2003 implemented an exchange rate stabilization program using foreign exchange reserves to buy kwanzas out of circulation, a policy that was more sustainable in 2005 because of strong oil export earnings. It has significantly reduced inflation. Consumer inflation declined from 325% in 2000 to about 18% in 2005. This stabilization policy has, however, placed pressure on international net liquidity. To take full advantage of its rich national resources—gold, diamonds, extensive forests, Atlantic fisheries, and large oil deposits—Angola will need to continue with reforms. Considerable progress are shown in terms of transparency in government spending suggested by the IMF.

PRIVATIZATION

A privatization program has been developed but a weak private sector in Angola seems to lack the financial and/or administrative capacity to pick up on offers. A few smaller state-run enterprises have been sold but some have turned out to be economically nonviable. Most large enterprises such as telecommunications firms, insurance companies, and banks, remain government monopolies.

SECTORS

Oil production and its supporting activities contribute about half of GDP and 90 percent of exports. Subsistence agriculture provides the main livelihood for half of the population. Half of the country's food must still be imported. Real gross domestic product (GDP) grew by 19.1 percent in 2005, largely driven by the petroleum sector which accounts for close to half of total GDP. Apart from significant diamond mining, the country also has deposits of iron ore, phosphates, copper, feldspar, gold, bauxite and uranium. Agricultural production continues to suffer from a degraded infrastructure, lack of funds for investment. Production is expected to increase once the infrastructure is repaired and upgraded with the assistance of foreign investors, notably China. The ports of Luanda, Lobito, and Namibe are all operational, but still require improvements.

TRADING

With a production of approximately 1.6 million bbl/day of crude, oil accounts for 93 percent of Angola's export revenues. Refined petroleum, natural gas, and raw timber are also important export items. Diamonds are another major export with sales estimated at $400-600 million per year, much of it through unofficial channels. Angola imports most consumer items, capital goods, and transport equipment. The US, South Africa, Germany, and Belgium are major partners. The US buys 75% of Angola's oil exports.

INVESTMENT

Precise foreign direct investment statistics are not available, but estimates place current US FDI at over $4 billion. Annual foreign investment exceeds $1 billion, mostly in the petroleum exploration and production sector.

FINANCIAL SECTOR

Owned and operated by the Ministry of Finance, the Caixa de Credito Agro-Pecuaria e Pescas (CAP) took over all commercial operations from Banco National de Angola (BNA). CAP loans, often on concessionary and sometimes interest-free terms, have been used by the government to provide off-budget financing for parastatal entities. The Banco de Comercio e Industria (BCI) is a semiprivate bank, with 40 percent of its shares owned by the government.

BUSINESS ACTIVITY

AGRICULTURE
Bananas, sugar cane, coffee, sisal, corn, cotton, manioc, tobacco, vegetables, plantains, livestock.

INDUSTRIES
Petroleum, diamonds, iron ore, phosphates, feldspar, bauxite, uranium, gold, cement, basic metal products, fish processing, food processing, brewing, tobacco products, sugar, textiles.

NATURAL RESOURCES
Petroleum, diamonds, iron ore, phosphates, copper, feldspar, gold, bauxite, uranium.

EXPORTS
$26.8 billion (2005 est.): crude oil, diamonds, refined petroleum products, gas, timber, cotton, fish products.

IMPORTS
$8.17 billion (2005 est.): machinery and electrical equipment, vehicles and spare parts, medicines, food, textiles, military supplies.

MAJOR TRADING PARTNERS
US, EU, China, Portugal, France, South Africa.

Doing Business with Angola

▶ Investment

The Foreign Investment Institute is the point of contact for investors and the Foreign Investment Code guarantees equal treatment for overseas entrepreneurs who are subject to the same tax regime as locals. Repatriation of profits is guaranteed, and prompt indemnification promised in cases of nationalization or expropriation. The country's rich resources—oil, diamonds and several other strategic minerals—have lured big foreign firms. Petroleum-related investments dominate but once the war ends, rebuilding and repair of roads and railways are expected to offer further opportunities, as will agribusiness and telecommunications.

▶ Trade

The best prospects for exports are in oil-field machinery and equipment, computers and parts, used clothing, cars and trucks, generators and parts, ships, and aircraft. Product distribution can be problematic as a result of poor infrastructure. Foreign companies may chose to sell through an established importer in Angola, by winning a tender, through investment, or by opening an office.

▶ Trade finance

In 1999 the US Eximbank resumed financing for US trade deals with Angola. Angola has in recent years been a recipient of US Department of Agriculture PL-480 Title I program foodstuffs.

▶ Selling to the government

The Angolan authorities solicit supplies and services in local and international publications. Bid documents are obtained from a specific government ministry, department or agency at a nonrefundable fee.

▶ Exchange controls

The government sets the official rate and has imposed limits on foreign exchange transactions. There are no restrictions on the total amount of foreign currency brought into Angola but it must be declared within 24 hours at an authorized agency. No national currency can be exported from Angola. It is legal to maintain accounts in dollars. All import payments must be made through the central bank, even if foreign exchange is held in another bank.

▶ Partnerships

Joint ventures are sanctioned under the foreign investment law, which also regulates the amount and form of capital invested. If an investment is valued at more than $50 million or involves activities that can only be carried out by concession (such as oil and diamond exploration and production), a contract must be established defining the project's objectives, the tax benefits and incentives to be granted, and providing for government monitoring. Such contracts are subject to the approval of the Ministry of Planning, the Prime Minister, and the Council of Ministers. Joint ventures must also be licensed by the Ministry of Commerce.

▶ Establishing a presence

A local attorney is needed to prepare the "Articles of Association" before registering a company and to conduct due diligence investigations prior to the conclusion of any purchase or other contractual agreement. The authorities assist foreign businesses interested in establishing agency, franchise, joint venture, or licensing relationships.

▶ Project financing

The country is experiencing difficulty in securing financing for projects other than those guaranteed by oil production. Under the Cabinda Trust arrangement, projects in the petroleum sector can receive financing secured by future oil production. Non-Cabinda Trust loans are often short term and at high interest rates.

▶ Labor

Labor is plentiful, but skills are scarce. The average level of education is sixth grade. There are two significant labor organizations in Angola.

▶ Legal rights

Under Angola's Foreign Investment Code all overseas investments are guaranteed protection and, in the event of expropriation, prompt compensation. Angola is a member of the World Intellectual Property Organization and makes use of its international classification of patents and products and services.

▶ Business climate

The buisness climate has improved drastically after the cessation of the war and several petroleum companies and other major foreign firms are involved in mining, banking and the service industry. Both domestic and international telecommunications can be problematic. Many large international corporations rely on high frequency radio transmissions for routine communication.

BENIN

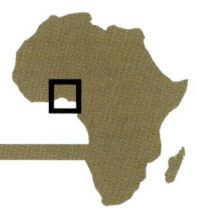

IN 1990 BENIN, FORMERLY KNOWN AS DAHOMEY, TURNED AWAY FROM A CEN-
TRALLY PLANNED ECONOMY UNDER ONE-PARTY MARXIST-LENINIST RULE. THE NEW
DEMOCRATICALLY-ELECTED GOVERNMENT ADOPTED REFORMS PROPOSED BY THE
WORLD BANK AND IMF AIMED AT DEVELOPING A FREE MARKET ECONOMY IN THIS
SMALL WEST AFRICAN COUNTRY. AFTER SEVERAL STRUCTURAL ADJUSTMENT PROGRAMS
(SAPS), BENIN HAS MANAGED A RECOVERY THAT HAS CAUGHT THE ATTENTION OF US
AND EUROPEAN INVESTORS AND TRADERS. POLITICAL AND ECONOMIC RELATIONS
WITH THE CAPITALIST WORLD—ONCE MARRED BY BENIN'S HARDLINE MARXISM—ARE
CLOSE AND CORDIAL.

COUNTRY PROFILE

The Republic of Benin (formerly Dahomey) extends about 650 km north from the Bight of Benin (part of the Gulf of Guinea) to the Niger River.

The southern equatorial region is covered with moist woodland savanna and oil palm trees along the coast. The poorer soil on the northern plateau is used for large-scale cotton cultivation and live-stock. Along its borders with Niger and Burkina Faso, Benin maintains several national parks which constitute West Africa's premier wildlife conserva-tion area. Most Beninese are related to peoples in neighboring countries. The Fon are closely related to the Ewe in Togo and the Yoruba are related to one of Nigeria's major ethnic groups. Also the Bariba (Borgu), Somba, Fulani, Dendi and Busa (Bussa) have relatives across the various borders. French is the official language and is spoken by groups of mixed descent and expatriates in the coastal towns and cities. Benin is one of only a few African countries where ethnic beliefs still hold sway over the Muslim and Christian faiths, with 70 percent adhering to indigenous beliefs and the rest evenly split between Christianity and Islam. The coastal regions of Benin and Togo practice voodoo (vodun or juju), a tribal ritual that spread to the Caribbean and the Americas during the slave trade era.

HISTORY

The Abomey kingdom of the Dahomey or Fon peoples was established in 1625. Its rich cultural life found expression in wooden masks, bronze statues, tapestries and pottery that have gained world renown in recent years. The Portu-guese and the Dutch conducted slave trade from Porto Novo until the mid-19th Century before the French, with the approval of Britain and Germany,

185

FAST FACTS

Pres. Yayi Boni
Born: 1952
Since April 2006

POLITICAL

Head of State	Pres. Yayi Boni
Ruling Party	PRB
Main Opposition	PRD, FARD
Independence	1 August 1960
National capital	Porto Novo[3]
Official language	French

PHYSICAL

Total area	43,483 sq. miles
	112,620 sq. km
	(± Tennessee)
Arable land	13% of land area
Coastline	75 miles/121 km

POPULATION

Total	7.86 million
Av. yearly growth	2.73%
Population/sq. miles	147
Urban population	3.3 million
Adult literacy	33.6%

ECONOMY

Currency	CFA franc (CFAF)(US$1=559.44)
GDP (real)	$4.34 billion
GDP growth rate	3.5%
GDP per capita[1]	$513
GDP (ppp)[2]	$8.56 billion
GDP per cap. (ppp)[2]	$1,100
Inflation rate	3.5%
Exports	$826.9 million
Imports	$1.04 billion
External debt	$1.6 billion
Unemployment	N/A

1. *Atlas method.*
2. *See page 175 for an explanation of purchasing power parity (ppp).*
3. *Official. Cotonou is the de facto capital.*

appropriated a colony extending from the Niger to the sea and named it Dahomey. Early in the 20th Century it became part of French West Africa and on 1 August 1960, was one of 14 former French African colonies granted independence. Several coups led to the assumption of power by Major Mathieu Kérékou in 1974. During his 17-year rule Kérékou turned Dahomey into the People's Republic of Benin under a Marxist dictatorship. In 1989, President Kérékou was forced by widespread opposition to his failed centralized economy to renounce Marxism-Leninism and implement a major privatization program. His cuts in the government payroll and reduction of social services promoted student and labor unrest. Fearing revolution Kérékou agreed to a new constitution and free elections in 1991. He lost to Nicéphore Soglo, who introduced economic reforms but failed to win reelection in 1996 when Kérékou made a dramatic comeback. Thus Benin became not only the first one-party state in Africa to vote an incumbent ruler out of office but also to return the same former authoritarian ruler to the presidency by popular vote. In the March 2001 presidential election Kérékou was re-elected. In April 2006, banker Dr. Yayi Boni succeeded Kérékou by defeating speaker Adrien Hounbendji by a 75 percent to 25 percernt margin.

GOVERNMENT

Under a Constitution adopted in 1990 by national referendum, an executive President is elected for a 5 year term, renewable once. The President appoints the Council of Ministers. The unicameral 83-member National Assembly is elected for four years. Coalition politics is common in Benin and any of the more than 30 splinter parties might swing the balance for any of the main contenders in close elections. In the March 2003 election the Mouvance présidentielle or Presidential Movement, a nine party coalition that supported the policies of President Mathieu Kérékou, captured 52 seats against the opposition's 31. He retired in 2006 when he reached the presidential age limit of 70.

ECONOMIC POLICY

Benin has implemented far-reaching changes in accordance with a structural adjustment program (SAP) sponsored by the World Bank and the IMF. This program aims at stabilizing public finances, reducing inflation, increasing domestic savings, and attracting investments. Marked progress has been made in all these areas and in July 2000 the World Bank and IMF announced that Benin qualified for $460 million in debt relief under the Heavily Indebted Poor Countries Initiative. (HIPC). Benin is actively courting foreign investors and encouraging tourism.

PRIVATIZATION

Despite opposition from the unions, the government has proceeded with the sale of state-owned companies. Apart from selling state enterprises such as SONACOP (oil company), Société Sucrière de Save (a sugar refinery), Société des Ciments d'Onigbolo (cement company), SONICOG (vegetable oil refineries), and SONAR and IARD (national insurance companies), the government has liquidated several other failing enterprises. In some cases foreign buyers are obliged to partner with Beninese nationals. Privatization continues in telecommunications, water utilities, electricity supply and agriculture.

SECTORS

Agriculture employs three-quarters of the population and accounts for 37% of GDP. Benin produces cotton, palm oil and kernels, coffee, and cocoa for export. It is generally self-sufficient in food production, though large quantities of foodstuffs, especially rice, are imported. Main food crops are millet, sorghum, maize, and root and tuber crops, such as cassava and yams. Livestock farming is important in the drier areas to the north. Fishing is popular in the rivers, lakes and lagoons. Timber production is negligible, but plans are underway to exploit the country's potential for forestry. Offshore oil is produced near Seme and further exploration is being undertaken. There are known deposits of phosphate, iron ore, chromium, gold and marble awaiting exploitation. Extensive limestone deposits are utilized for cement production. Manufacturing centers around the processing of agricultural products and consumer goods and construction materials. Tourism is a growing industry.

TRADING

A substantial part of Benin's trade consists of goods smuggled across its border with Nigeria and therefore not accounted for in official trade statistics. Oil and cotton are major export items while food, fuel, energy and capital goods top the list of import items. Exports are mainly to Portugal, Morocco and the United States while France, Thailand and China supply in most of Benin's needs.

INVESTMENT

Major foreign investors in Benin are France, Germany, and Canada, but US firms have become increasingly involved in the petroleum sector. Other recent foreign investment came through acquisition of state-owned enterprises in textiles, tobacco, cement, beer brewing, petroleum and public transportation.

FINANCIAL SECTOR

Five major commercial banks were established after the state-owned banking system failed, causing a serious liquidity crisis. With foreign assistance and guidance from the World Bank and IMF, Benin took measures to attract foreign banks back. The present financial system includes the Credit Promotion Benin (CCB), the postal checking accounts (CCP), the Savings Bank (CNE) and the Sonar, a state-owned insurance company.

TAXES AND TARIFFS

Tax reforms were introduced in recent years to attract investors. Benin adopted one of the most open trade regimes in Africa, reducing the maximum tariff rate from 63% to 20%.

LINKS

The United States has supported Benin's move towards democracy with several human rights fund grants. It has offered military training to the Beninese armed forces.

BUSINESS ACTIVITY

AGRICULTURE
Corn, sorghum, cassava (tapioca), yams, beans, rice, cotton, palm oil, peanuts, poultry, livestock.

INDUSTRIES
Textiles, cigarettes, beverages, food, construction materials, petroleum.

EXPORTS
$826.9 million (2005 est.): cotton, crude oil, palm products, cocoa.

IMPORTS
$1.04 billion (2005 est.): petroleum products, intermediate goods, capital goods, light consumer goods.

MAJOR TRADING PARTNERS
China, India, France, Ghana, Indonesia, Niger, Nigeria, Thailand.

DOING BUSINESS WITH BENIN

▶ INVESTMENT

Good investment opportunities stem from the privatization process, with the oil sector offering the best potential for foreign investors. The government is slowly, but not entirely, disengaging itself from the this sector. Further scope is offered by Benin's efforts to improve the infrastructure for telecommunications, electricity and roads. The country also holds potential for those who are able to offer modern techniques for cold storage, canning, and packing. Saltwater fishing is another area where foreign involvement is sought. Considerable cotton production and privatization of the textile industry open up further prospects.

▶ TRADE

Agricultural products, food processing machinery, consumer goods and gas powered turbines for electricity generation are good prospects. Large foreign firms often enter into exclusive contracts with an agent/distributor. Overseas firms are cautioned to deal only with Beninese companies that are registered with the government. Among the long-established distributors of consumer goods are French firms and Lebanese and Indian traders. The main types of outlets are open-air markets, street displays and street vendors, and European-style supermarkets and convenience stores with a wide range of local and imported products.

▶ TRADE FINANCE

Eximbank operates programs in support of US capital goods and services. With properly documented trade transactions, authorization for overseas payments is easily obtained. There is, however, no protection against currency fluctuations. Several banks have reliable and efficient correspondent relationships with overseas banks.

▶ SELLING TO THE GOVERNMENT

There has been a concerted effort on the part of the authorities to promote transparency and eliminate favoritism when considering bids. Bureaucratic red tape remains a problem.

▶ EXCHANGE CONTROLS

Any enterprise engaged in a commercial, industrial, agricultural, or artisan activity, or that provides services, is entitled to transfer capital, profits and dividends.

▶ ESTABLISHING A PRESENCE

A limited company (Inc.) is the most common form of entry. Its establishment is speedy and simple. Establishing of a company normally requires authorization by the relevant ministry after completion of specific forms. Some industrial firms may opt for preferential schemes under the Investment Code, offered by the Technical Investment Commission of the Ministry of Planning. In most cases overseas firms rely on the services of a local attorney.

▶ PROJECT FINANCING

Several infrastructure renovation contracts are funded by grants or loans from the World Bank or other International Development Banks. The Overseas Private Investment Corporation (OPIC) offers financial assistance to small US companies and provides political risk insurance, loans, and investment guarantees. Two World Bank-related institutions, FIAS (Foreign Investments Advisory Service) and MIGA (Multilateral Investment Guarantee Agency), are active in Benin. Potential development financing is also available through the African Development Bank, the West African Bank for Development (BOAD), the European Development Fund (FED), and the International Fund for Economic Development (FIDA).

▶ LABOR

A largely unskilled workforce is organized in four trade union confederations. Due to high unemployment (no official statistics) there is a substantial surplus of workers. A considerable number of skilled workers also continue to reenter the job market as privatization eliminates jobs in former state enterprises. Foreign firms have also had considerable success with in-house training and the government has established several technical schools. Salaries have not kept pace with the cost of living after devaluation. Labor reforms aiming at greater flexibility are underway.

▶ BUSINESS CLIMATE

There are guarantees against nationalization and the post-Marxist Benin is going out of its way to make the country investor friendly. In disputes between the state and a foreign firm, Benin recognizes the Hague Permanent Arbitration Court as the final authority. It also subscribes to the International Center for Settlement of Investment Disputes, which is part of the World Bank Group. Laws protect against IPR infringements. Benin is a signatory of the OAPI Convention of Yaounde (African Organization for Intellectual Property) and the World Intellectual Property Organization.

BOTSWANA

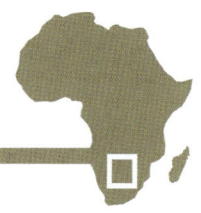

BOTSWANA HAS MAINTAINED A HIGH GROWTH RATE SINCE ITS INDEPENDENCE IN 1966 AS WELL AS FOUR DECADES OF EXEMPLARY DEMOCRATIC RULE. IT HAS TRANSFORMED ITSELF FROM ONE OF THE POOREST COUNTRIES IN THE WORLD TO A MIDDLE-INCOME COUNTRY WITH THE BEST CREDIT RATING IN AFRICA. DIAMOND MINING ACCOUNTS FOR MORE THAN ONE-THIRD OF GDP AND FOR BETWEEN SEVENTY AND EIGHTY PERCENT OF THE COUNTRY'S EXPORT EARNINGS. TOURISM, SUBSISTENCE FARMING, AND CATTLE ARE OTHER KEY SECTORS. BOTSWANA HAS ONE OF THE WORLD'S HIGHEST KNOWN RATES OF HIV/AIDS INFECTION BUT ALSO HAS IN PLACE ONE OF AFRICA'S MOST PROGRESSIVE AND COMPREHENSIVE PROGRAMS FOR DEALING WITH THE DISEASE.

COUNTRY PROFILE

The Republic of Botswana is a large, sparsely populated, landlocked country sharing borders with five other countries. Its terrain varies from the arid Kalahari Desert to the lush forests of the Okavango Delta and the dry savannah of the Limpopo Valley. Botswana is constantly in need of rain, hence the national motto, Pula or rain. More than 80% of its 1.6 million citizens are Tswana (plural Batswana, singular Motswana). They speak various dialects of the Sotho language, Setswana. The rest are Herero, Mbukushu, Subia and Fwe, apart from a few whites. Half of the population are Christians and the rest still adhere to traditional tribal beliefs.

HISTORY

The earliest inhabitants of the area were the San, followed by the Tswana. Bechuanaland, as it was known before independence, had been the crossroads for missionaries, merchants and migrants before Britain annexed and declared it a protectorate in 1885 in a preemptive strike to prevent the Boers of the Transvaal from taking possession. Independence for Bechuanaland under its new name, Botswana, came in 1966. The first elected president, Sir Seretse Khama, remained in power until his death in 1980. Khama was succeeded by Vice President and later Sir Ketumile Masire who remained in power for seventeen years. When Masire retired in 1998, his vice president—an Oxford-educated economist and former Finance Minister—Festus Mogae, was elected president. Mogae was reaffirmed in the post in 2004 and declared his intention

FAST FACTS

Pres. Festus Gonte-
banye Mogae
Born: August 21, 1939
Since 1998

POLITICAL

Head of State	Pres. Festus Mogae
Ruling Party	Botswana Democratic Party (BDP)
Main Opposition	Botswana National Front (BNF)
Independence	30 September 1966
National capital	Gaborone
Official languages	English, Tswana

PHYSICAL

Total area	231,800 sq. miles 600,370 sq. km. (± Texas)
Arable land	1% of land area
Coastline	Landlocked

POPULATION

Total	1.6 million
Av. yearly growth	-0.89%
Population/sq. mile	7
Urban population	0.9 million
Adult literacy	79.8%

ECONOMY

Currency	Pula (US$1=5.68)
GDP (real)	$9.05 billion
GDP growth rate	4.5%
GDP per capita[1]	$5,173
GDP (ppp)[2]	$17.24 billion
GDP per cap. (ppp)	$10,500
Inflation rate	8.6%
Exports	$3.68 billion
Imports	$3.37 billion
External debt	$519 million
Unemployment	23.8%

1. Atlas method.
2. See page 175 for an explanation of purchasing power parity (ppp).

to step down in favor of Vice President Seretse Ian Khama, son of Botswana's first president, after the completion of his second term.

GOVERNMENT

Held out as a model of democracy in Africa, Botswana continues to adhere strictly to its 1966 constitution requiring the election of a president and National Assembly for a period of five years. The President is limited to two terms. The unicameral Assembly is made up of 40 directly elected and four nominated members, a speaker and attorney general. In the October 2004 election the Botswana Democratic Party (BDP), which has been in power since independence, maintained its dominance over the Botswana National Front.

ECONOMIC POLICY

At independence in 1966, Botswana was one of the 20 poorest nations. The discovery of diamonds in 1971 and sound economic policies enabled it to attain one of the world's highest economic growth rates. Under its Industrial Development Policy the government utilized mineral wealth to develop human resources and infrastructure, communications facilities and utilities. Two major investment services rank Botswana as the best credit risk in Africa. The stock exchange sought new listings to attract business on the foreign capital markets. HIV/AIDS, however, presents a major threat to the country, with some estimates putting the infection rate at 36%—the highest in the world. Despite its great economic strides Botswana is still faced with the challenge of large scale unemployment.

PRIVATIZATION

The government has indicated that with the exception of Debswana (diamond mines) and the Diamond Valuing Agency, all parastatals will be privatized in the foreseeable future. In some instances, Botswana has resorted to a partial sale of equity to private investors. State enterprises in electricity, telecommunications, transportation, water, real estate, cattle and mining sectors have been "commercialized"—the elimination of government subsidies to enterprises run as private businesses with the state as a shareholder. In some instances Botswana citizens are given first rights to purchasing state enterprises.

SECTORS

Diamonds, discovered five years after Botswana became independent, account for most of the country's wealth, followed by cattle farming. Diamonds constitute close to 80% of total export earnings. Botswana also has significant deposits of coal, copper-nickel, soda ash, potash and sodium sulphate. Livestock—especially cattle farming—constitutes 80% of the total agricultural income. Sorghum, maize, millet, beans and other crops are cultivated on a subsistence basis. A developing manufacturing sector entails motor vehicle assembly, and pharmaceuticals, leather and textiles, food processing and furniture. Due to the small size of the domestic market, most of these industries are export-oriented. Tourism is a major industry. Botswana's national parks and private game lodges lure safari enthusiasts from around the world.

TRADING

Botswana's largest export market is the European Union (74%) with diamonds (70%) as the main commodity. South Africa is in second place with 21% of the total, purchasing mostly vehicles and beef and supplying 78% of Botswana's imports. Principal United States exports are manufactured goods, including heavy machinery, electrical appliances, data processing machines, radar appliances, communication and electrical equipment. US imports consists largely of textiles, clothing and handicrafts.

INVESTMENT

Foreign direct investment (FDI) forms a major portion of overseas capital flows into Botswana, followed by portfolio investments. The latter have grown considerably since the establishment of the Botswana Stock Exchange in the 1990s. Not surprisingly, mining draws the largest percentage of FDI. Significant foreign capital has also gone into the development of infrastructure and, in recent years, the manufacturing and tourist sectors. Most foreign equity and non-equity investments came from South Africa (80%). The remainder originated largely in the European Union (12.7%), with the U.K. and Luxembourg as major sources. Investments from the US constitute 3.3% of the total and went largely into the service, manufacturing and tourism sectors. The automobile industry remains a priority and vehicle assembly is now the country's second most important industry. By far the largest foreign investor in Botswana is South Africa's Anglo-American Corporation (De Beers), which has a multimillion dollar stake, along with the Government of Botswana, in the country's major diamond mining industry, Debswana.

FINANCIAL SECTOR

The central bank—the Bank of Botswana—has an impressive track record managing the commercial banking sector and monetary policies. Foreigners have access to credit at local market rates and often receive preferential treatment over local borrowers. There are four commercial banks and one investment bank, all with correspondent arrangements in the US. Nonresidents are no longer restricted from issuing bonds on the stock market and are able to hold bonds with maturity periods of over one year. This is designed to encourage inward portfolio investments. Dual listings are also permitted on the Botswana Stock Exchange. The establishment of an International Financial Services Center (IFSC) in the wake of progressive economic liberalization, the abolition of exchange controls, high foreign exchange reserves, and the maintenance of a favorable macroeconomic environment present a potentially lucrative business opportunity for foreigners interested in operating offshore banking, insurance and accounting.

TAXES AND TARIFFS

Taxes in Botswana are among the lowest in southern Africa. Corporate tax rates are 25%, including a 15% concessional rate for manufacturers and providers of financial services.

BUSINESS ACTIVITY

AGRICULTURE
Sorghum, maize, millet, pulses, groundnuts (peanuts), beans, cowpeas, sunflower seed, livestock.

INDUSTRIES
Diamonds, copper, nickel, coal, salt, soda ash, potash, livestock processing.

NATURAL RESOURCES
Diamonds, copper, nickel, salt, soda ash, potash, coal, iron ore, silver.

EXPORTS
$3.68 billion (2005 est.): diamonds , nickel, copper, meat.

IMPORTS
$3.37 billion (2005 est.): foodstuffs, vehicles and transport equipment, textiles, petroleum products.

MAJOR TRADING PARTNERS
EU, Southern African Customs Union (SACU), Zimbabwe.

DOING BUSINESS WITH BOTSWANA

▶ **INVESTMENT**

There is scope for investment in motor vehicle assembly, photovoltaic manufacturing, financial services and tourism. Investment incentives are offered. The Botswana Export Development and Investment Agency assists investors through all the preliminary stages and provides support services, such as purchasing or leasing of property, obtaining work and residence permits, licenses, and grants. The Botswana Development Corporation seeks out suitable partners for specific projects and the National Development Bank offers long-term loans. Under the Financial Assistance Policy, grants are extended to labor-intensive projects outside the cattle farming and diamond sectors.

▶ **TRADE**

State purchase of drugs (particularly to combat HIV/AIDS) and a growing need for computer hardware and software, mining, construction, telecommunications equipment, as well photovoltaic and water supply systems, offer trade opportunities. As a result of frequent droughts, there is often a need for corn, sorghum, wheat, and rice.

▶ **TRADE FINANCE**

Short-term finance, including pre-and-post-shipment credit, is available through the local commercial banking system and export credit insurance is offered by domestic insurance companies. Eximbank financing is available to US exporters.

▶ **SELLING TO THE GOVERNMENT**

The Central Tender Board (CTB) awards government tenders in an open process. Lobbying of the CTB is strictly prohibited. Occasionally preferential treatment is given to local participants. Firms are encouraged to make contact with the relevant government ministries or parastatals to ensure proper presentation of tenders for major projects.

▶ **EXCHANGE CONTROLS**

Botswana has abolished exchange controls but the authorities monitor capital flows for early warning signals of potentially destabilizing activity. Commercial banks require investors to fill out basic forms for outward and inward transactions.

▶ **PARTNERSHIPS**

Partnership with a local investor has occasionally been an unwritten requirement for winning government tenders. The government, however, does not impose any performance requirements or local participation on foreign enterprises.

▶ **ESTABLISHING A PRESENCE**

Foreign private entities may freely establish, acquire, and dispose of interests in local business enterprises. The government does not set any conditions regarding location, local content, local equity, import substitution, export targets, or financing. There is no restriction on the repatriation of profits and dividends, debt service, capital gains, returns on intellectual property, royalties, franchise fees and service fees. Upon disinvestment, foreigners are allowed to reclaim all proceeds.

▶ **PROJECT FINANCING**

OPIC finance and insurance programs apply to US operations in Botswana. Botswana is a member of the Multilateral Investment Guarantee Agency and all four major local commercial banks as well as an investment bank offer financing for new businesses. Six separate development financial institutions also offer specialized services. The borrowing provisions for US and other foreign firms are liberal.

▶ **LABOR**

With high unemployment, there is no shortage of workers. Due to the low skill base employers may have to undertake significant training, depending on the industry. Only a small portion of the formal sector—mostly mining and banking— is unionized and strikes are rare. An industrial court ensures impartial adjudication in labor disputes.

▶ **LEGAL RIGHTS**

Civil law is based on Roman-Dutch law and the English criminal legal system applies. Botswana is a member of the International Center for the Settlement of Investment Disputes (ICSID) and the Multilateral Investment Guarantee Agency. The Industrial Property Act and recently revamped Copyright Act brought the country in conformity with the WTO's Trade Related Aspects of International property Rights. The Constitution prohibits nationalization of private property.

▶ **BUSINESS CLIMATE**

Botswana's business and government community tend to be reserved and formal. English is the official language and used extensively in business, but Setswana is widely spoken. It is wise to reconfirm appointments 24 hours ahead. Meetings may start late and are sometimes interrupted by telephone conversations. Neither is an indication of disrespect or lack of interest.

BURKINA FASO

FORMERLY KNOWN AS UPPER VOLTA, BURKINA FASO IS THE SMALLEST OF WEST AFRICA'S LANDLOCKED STATES. DESPITE ITS RELATIVELY SMALL POPULATION OF TEN MILLION AND LIMITED NATURAL RESOURCES, BURKINA HAS MANAGED TO ATTRACT FOREIGN INTERESTS BY STREAMLINING ITS PUBLIC SECTOR, PRIVATIZING, LIFTING TRADE BARRIERS AND LIBERALIZING PRICES. SINCE THE EARLY NINETIES IT HAS WORKED CLOSELY WITH THE WORLD BANK AND THE IMF IN A STRUCTURAL ADJUSTMENT PROGRAM. BURKINA FASO DEPENDS ON GHANA AND CÔTE D'IVOIRE FOR OUTLETS TO THE SEA AND JOB OPPORTUNITIES FOR SOME OF ITS CITIZENS. FOREIGN ENTREPRENEURS, ESPECIALLY THOSE INVOLVED IN MINING AND MINERALS, ARE INCREASINGLY FOCUSING ON BURKINA FASO—"THE LAND OF THE HONORABLE."

COUNTRY PROFILE

The Democratic Republic of Burkina Faso (or Burkina), formerly known as Upper Volta, is the smallest of Western Africa's landlocked states. It spans the headwaters of the Great Volta River. Burkina is rich in historical relics but relatively poor in natural resources. The climate is tropical. The Gur (or Voltaic) peoples, who also inhabit northern parts of Togo, Ghana and Côte d'Ivoire, dominate Burkina. The largest group of Gur-speaking peoples is the Mossi (or Moore) around Ouaga-dougou, the nucleus of their ancient kingdom. The Mande-speaking Bobo and Dyula, found in the southwest around the town of Bobo-Dioulasso and the with the Bisa, who live further east, are related to the people of Mali. In the dry north are the pastoral Fulani. About half the population adhere to traditional ethnic faiths and the rest are predominantly Muslim.

HISTORY

Burkina Faso's original inhabitants were the Bobo, Lobi and Gurunsi peoples. The Mosi and Gurma peoples migrated to the region in the 14th Century. From the 15th to the 18th Century the Mossi successfully resisted incorporation into the Mali and Songhai empires as well as Fulani invasions. France conquered the territory between 1895 and 1904. Responding to insurrection in Upper Volta, the French introduced military rule until 1919, when it became a separate colony in the union of French West Africa. Upper Volta received self-government following a referendum in 1958 and full independence in 1960. Shortly after he won the first election, President Maurice Yameogo banned all opposition parties. He

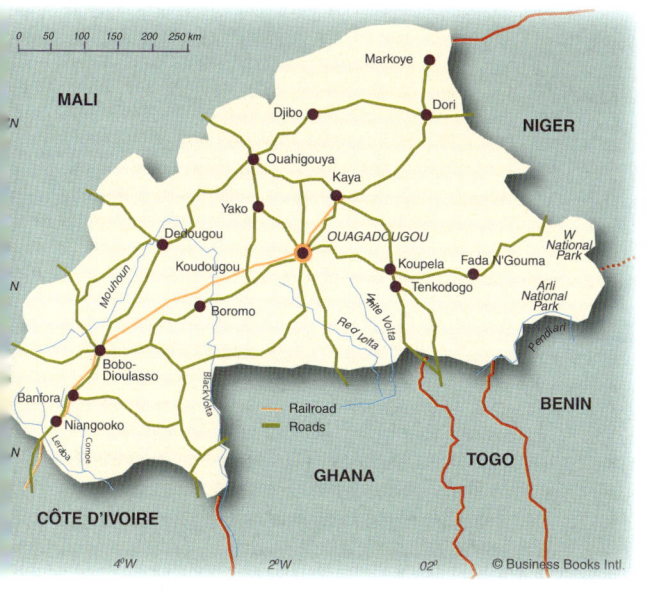

193

Fast Facts

Pres. Blaise Compaoré
Born: February 3, 1951
Since 1987

POLITICAL

Head of State	Pres. Blaise Compaoré
Ruling Party	CDP
Main Opposition	PDP
Independence	4 August 1960
National capital	Ouagadougou
Official languages	French

PHYSICAL

Total area	105,870 sq. miles
	274,122 sq. km.
	(± Colorado)
Arable land	13% of land area
Coastline	Landlocked

POPULATION

Total	13.9 million
Av. yearly growth	3%
Population/sq. mile	113
Urban population	2.6 million
Adult literacy	26.6%

ECONOMY

Currency	CFA franc
	(CFAF)(US$1=559.44)
GDP (real)	$5.4 billion
GDP growth rate	4.5%
GDP per capita[1]	$411
GDP (ppp)[2]	$16.95 billion
GDP per cap. (ppp)	$1,300
Inflation rate	6.4%
Exports	$395 million
Imports	$992 million
External debt	$1.85 billion
Unemployment	N/A

1. Atlas method.
2. See page 175 for an explanation of purchasing power parity (ppp).

was overthrown in 1966 and succeeded by Gen. Sangoule Lamizana, who, as promised, returned the country to civilian rule in 1970 but reverted to authoritarian rule four years later. Until the early 1980s, several further attempts to establish multiparty politics failed. In August 1983 Capt. Thomas Sankara, a 34-year admirer of Libya's Colonel Qaddafi, came to power. He changed the name of Upper Volta to Burkina Faso, a blend of local words meaning "the land of the honorable," and introduced a Libyan-style "Jamahiriya." After several failed attempts, Sankara was assassinated in 1987 and succeeded by Capt. Blaise Compaoré who reversed hardline socialist policies and introduced economic reforms in cooperation with international banks. Attempts by the opposition to have Compaoré excluded from the November 2005 presidential election on the grounds that it violated the two-term stipulation in the Constitution, failed. He won easily against a fractured opposition in a race deemed fair and free.

GOVERNMENT

In the May 2002 election for the National Assembly Pres. Compaoré's Congrès pour la Démocratie et le Progrès (CDP), captured 57 out of 111 seats. The main opposition party, the Alliance pour la démocratie et la féderation-Rassemblement démocratique africain (ADF-RDA) won 17 seats while the Parti pour la Démocratie et le Progrès (PDP) captured 10 seats. Smaller parties such as the Coalition des Forces Démocratiques (CFD) and the Parti Africain de l'Indépendance (PAI) won 5 seats each and the other eight parties 4 seats or less.

ECONOMIC POLICY

Once one of the world's poorest countries, Burkina Faso has been implementing a structural adjustment program (SAP) in close cooperation with the World Bank and the IMF. Starting from a mere 0.4% growth rate in 1989, the country averaged 2.3% between 1990 and 1994, reaching a growth rate of 4.5% in 2005. While an increase in agricultural output helped, the government is credited in large part for its diligent enforcement of reforms. Price liberalization and external tariff reduction coupled with banking and financial sector reform, as well as privatization, further enhanced the business environment. In July 2000, Burkina Faso qualified for $700 million in debt relief under the Heavily Indebted Poor Countries Initiative (HIPC).

PRIVATIZATION

In the nineties Burkina Faso's parliament approved the restructuring of 42 state-owned enterprises. These included 19 major corporations in banking, brewing, mining, medicine, manufacturing and advertising that have already been restructured. Since then several others have been liquidated or turned over to private control. Further privatization of the state-owned electricity, water and telecommunications utilities is underway.

SECTORS

Burkina has few natural resources and depends in part on foreign aid remittances by its citizens employed in neighboring countries such as Côte d'Ivoire and Ghana. The rural population is largely dependent on subsistence farming and nomadic stock raising. Main food crops are sorghum, millet, yams, maize, rice and beans. Cotton is grown for export. Mining activity is confined to gold, manganese, phosphates, marble and antimony. There are also viable deposits of zinc, silver, limestone, bauxite, nickel and lead. Small scale manufacturing entails flour milling, sugar refining, manufacture of cotton yarn and textiles and the production of consumer goods such as bicycles, footwear and soap.

TRADING

Importation of most consumer and other manufactured goods and equipment causes a chronic unfavorable trade balance. The largest exportee to Burkina is still France but imports from other countries and are growing. China has become the major buyers of goods from Burkina. Cotton, livestock and gold are principal exports. Abidjan's harbor in Côte d'Ivoire is used for bulk imports and exports.

INVESTMENT

Mining is the area of greatest interest for foreigners. The authorities have lured foreign mining companies by easing of regulatory laws, reducing taxes, adopting standard investment contracts, and improving the dissemination of geological data. American, Australian and South African corporations have obtained exploration and mining permits in recent times. French and Lebanese investors dominate in other sectors.

FINANCIAL SECTOR

The financial and banking sectors have been restructured during the past seven years. Non-performing banks have been liquidated or privatized with the help of foreign partners. Three large commercial banks (with correspondent relationships with New York banks) and four credit institutions provide credit for investment and commercial transactions.

TAXES AND TARIFFS

A value-added tax applies and profits are taxed at rates varying between 5% and 35%. There are three different incentive schedules for investors. The mining investment code provides special customs and fiscal privileges for mining companies during both the exploration and production stages. Only after the existence of extractable mineral deposits is proven may the holder of the exploration license obtain a mining license or concession allowing total exemption from customs fees on raw materials, components, and equipment necessary for production. The license holder also enjoys a seven year exemption from other taxes.

Burkina Faso's customs fees are based on goods ad valorem (CIF plus fees and commissions) and include a 5% customs fee, a variable import fiscal duty (DFI) and a variable value-added tax based on the type of goods. The government may also subsidize the importation of certain basic products such as rice and sugar by decreasing custom duties.

BUSINESS ACTIVITY

AGRICULTURE
Peanuts, shea nuts, sesame, cotton, sorghum, millet, corn, rice, livestock.

INDUSTRIES
Cotton lint, beverages, agricultural processing, soap, cigarettes, textiles, gold.

NATURAL RESOURCES
Manganese, limestone, marble, gold, antimony, copper, nickel, bauxite, lead, phosphates, zinc, silver.

EXPORTS
$395 million (2005 est.): cotton, animal products, gold.

IMPORTS
$992 million (2005 est.): machinery, food products, petroleum.

MAJOR TRADING PARTNERS
China, Côte d'Ivoire, France, Singapore, Togo.

Doing Business with Burkina Faso

▶ **Investment**

Tax exemptions apply to investments in mining and other sectors and an investment code guarantees foreign investors the right to transfer any funds associated with an investment, including dividends, receipts from liquidation, assets, and salaries. Transfers are authorized in the original currency of the investment. Gold mining and diamond exploration are priority areas. Foreign and domestic investors are treated equally. The Ministry of Industry, Commerce, and Mines approves all new investments on the recommendation of the national investment commission.

▶ **Trade**

Telecommunications and computer equipment, pharmaceuticals, and used clothing are areas where US exporters have managed to capture a share of the market. A local agent/distributor is not required by law but can be helpful. There is a market for wheat, yellow corn, semolina, and rice. Most trade restrictions have been removed and tariffs have been steadily reduced.

▶ **Trade finance**

Burkina is eligible for foreign credit insurance assistance through Eximbank programs and is a member of the Multilateral Investment Guarantee Agency.

▶ **Selling to the government**

Road, dam and other construction projects are at times awarded to local companies in partnership with foreign firms. Purchases by state-owned utilities are done on tender.

▶ **Exchange controls**

Transfer of all funds associated with an investment, including dividends, receipts from liquidation, assets, and salaries is allowed without delay.

▶ **Partnerships**

There is a limited number of business people available with the practical experience and financial capacity needed to form a successful partnership There are several Burkinabé joint ventures in the mining sector involving foreign companies.

▶ **Establishing a presence**

Wholly owned foreign ownership in companies is allowed. Proposed foreign businesses operations are, however, subject to a screening process to ensure full compliance with local laws.

▶ **Project financing**

Burkina Faso is eligible for OPIC programs and the potential exists for direct loans and loan guarantees from the World Bank, the European Union and the African Development Bank.

▶ **Labor**

There is a scarcity of skilled workers, mainly in management, and in the engineering and the electrical trades. Burkinabé workers have a reputation for industriousness and loyalty. A code guaranteeing worker's rights is administered by a labor court. There is a well organized trade union movement. Employers must advise workers at least 30 days prior to termination and except in cases of theft or flagrant neglect of duty they have the right to termination benefits.

▶ **Legal rights**

Basic property rights are protected. In a few cases where the government deems expropriation necessary, compensation must be paid in advance. Since 1960, there have only been three cases: In 1968, the electric company (Safelec) was nationalized; in 1970 Comacico-Benin and SECM, film making and distribution companies, were taken over by the state; and in 1980, a manufacturer of ammunition, Carvolt, was expropriated. If an attempt at settlement of a dispute between the government and an investor fails, arbitration is prescribed. Burkina belongs to the African Intellectual Property Organization as well as the World Intellectual Property Organization. A local attorney and/or notary public may be required when securing or closing a contract.

▶ **Business climate**

Business is almost exclusively conducted in French but adequate translation services are available. There is a small but dynamic Chamber of Commerce, which conducts feasibility studies and training, develops business links, and organizes trade shows. It also serves as a bridge between government authorities and business associations. All matters regarding investments and import-export regulations and procedures are handled by the Ministry of Commerce, Industry and Crafts. Most sales and distribution are conducted from the major cities of Ouagadougou and Bobo-Dioulasso. The main commercial banks and insurance companies have, however, branches in secondary urban areas.

BURUNDI

LIKE NEIGHBORING RWANDA, BURUNDI TOOK CENTER STAGE IN THE MID-1990S FOR THE WRONG REASONS. SITUATED IN THE SCENIC GREAT LAKES REGION OF AFRICA, THIS LAND-LOCKED, RESOURCE POOR FORMER BELGIAN COLONY HAS BEEN THE SCENE OF SOME OF THE MODERN WORLD'S WORST CARNAGE. THE ASSASSINATION IN 1993 OF BURUNDI'S FIRST DEMOCRATICALLY ELECTED PRESIDENT TRIGGERED WIDESPREAD ETHNIC VIOLENCE BETWEEN HUTU AND TUTSI FACTIONS CAUSING MORE THAN 200,000 TO PERISH. THE MOUNTING COST IN HUMAN LIVES WAS ACCOMPANIED BY WORSEN-ING ECONOMIC CONDITIONS. AN INTERNATIONALLY BROKERED POWER-SHARING AGREEMENT BETWEEN THE TUTSI-DOMINATED GOVERNMENT AND THE HUTU REBELS IN 2003 PAVE THE WAY FOR A FREELY ELECTED HUTU MAJORITY GOVERNMENT AND THE OPPORTUNITY TO REBUILD.

COUNTRY PROFILE

The Republic of Burundi is situated in the high rainfall region bordering Lake Tanganyika. Most of the people are Rundi or Barundi, comprising the Bantu Hutu (Bahutu) peoples (85%) and Nilotic Tutsi (Batutsi) (15%). The Twa (Batwa), descendants of the early Pygmy population, number only in the thousands. The majority of both Tutsi and Hutu are Christians—overwhelmingly Roman Catholic. Kirundi and French are official languages and Swahili is widely spoken.

HISTORY

The simple version of history has the Tutsi (Nilotic) cattle breeders arriving in the area from the 15th Century and subjugating the Hutu in-habitants. In reality, the situation is much more complex as boundaries of race and class became less distinct over the years as a result of inter-mingling. Some put part of the blame for the racial animosity that led to the recent mass-scale killings on the shoulders of German and Belgian colonial rulers who pitched the Hutu against Tutsi for their own gain. When Burundi and neighbor-ing Rwanda were incorporated into German East Africa in 1899, they had been kingdoms for several centuries headed by mwamis (kings). After Germany's defeat in World War I these na-tions were transferred to Belgium under the joint name of Ruanda-Urundi. They were, however, "separated at birth" when they gained their inde-pendence in 1962. In 1972, after an abortive coup attempt, between 200,000 and 400,000 Hutus were killed in Burundi and about 200,000 fled the country. Following elections in 1993, a Hutu assumed the presidency for the first time. He was assassinated by the Tutsi-dominated army after only 100 days in office, triggering widespread ethnic violence between the Tutsi and Hutu. Over 200,000 Burundians perished during the ensuing conflict lasting more than a decade. In 1995, the Hutu-led Front pour la démocratie au Burundi (Front for the Democracy in Burundi) (FRODEBU)

197

FAST FACTS

Pres. Pierre Nkurunziza
Born: 18 December 1963
Since August 2005

© IRIN

POLITICAL

Head of State	Pres. Pierre Nkurunziza
Ruling party	CNDD-FDD
Main opposition	FRODEBU & UPRONA
Independence	1 July 1962
National capital	Bujumbura
Official languages	French & Kirundi

PHYSICAL

Total area	10,747 sq. miles
	27,830 sq. km.
	(± Maryland)
Arable land	45% of land area
Coastline	Landlocked

POPULATION

Total	8 million
Av. yearly growth	3.7%
Population/sq. mile	563
Urbanized population	0.8 million
Adult literacy	51.6%

ECONOMY

Currency	Burundi franc (FBu)(US$1:996.74)
GDP (real)	$730 million
GDP growth rate	1.1%
GDP per capita[1]	$106
GDP (ppp)[2]	$5.7 billion
GDP per cap. (ppp)	$700
Inflation rate	8.5%
Exports	$52 million
Imports	$200 million
External debt	$1.2 billion
Unemployment	N/A

1. Atlas method.
2. See page 175 for an explanation of purchasing power parity (ppp).

and the Tutsi-dominated opposition Union pour le progrès national (Union of National Progress) (UPRONA), formed a coalition government under Hutu president Sylvestre Ntibantunganya, but unrest continued. In September 1996, Major Pierre Buyoya, a former Tutsi president, staged a coup, toppled the Hutu-run government and assumed the leadership. In accordance with a transition agreement Buyoya stepped down as president after 18 months in favor of his Hutu deputy, Domitien Ndayizeye. An internationally brokered power-sharing agreement between the government and the Hutu rebels paved the way for elections in July 2005 that swept Pierre Nkurunziza, leader of the Hutu-dominated Conseil national pour la defense de la democratie-Forces pour la defense de la democratie (CNDD-FDD) into power as president.

GOVERNMENT

A bicameral parliament consists of the National Assembly with 100 seats (60% Hutu, 40% Tutsi and at least 30% reserved for women) and a Senate with 54 seats. In the July 2005 Assembly election the CNDD-FDD won 59 of the 100 contested seats against 25 for FRODEBU and 10 for UPRONA. Together with 5 of the 18 additional seats apportioned on an ethnic and gender basis, the ruling party finished with a total of 64 out of a total 118 seats.

ECONOMIC POLICY

Before the massacres and instability following the assassination of Burundi's first Hutu president in 1993, the country had already been among the poorest in the world. Since then the economy shrunk and today more than half of the population live in extreme poverty. During the years of crisis management there was little time left for restructuring and rehabilitating the economy.

SECTORS

Some 90% of the population practice subsistence agriculture. Coffee, tea and cotton are grown for export, while subsistence crops include cassava, bananas, sweet potatoes, pulses, maize, sorghum, yams and peanuts. Cattle rearing and fishing along Lake Tanganyika are also important sources of food. Substantial nickel deposits (about 5% of world reserves) and vanadium are not being mined at present; neither are known reserves of oil, uranium and phosphates. Gold and tungsten are mined on a small scale. Manufacturing involves beer brewing, soft drinks, cigarettes, coffee and tea.

PRIVATIZATION

There were efforts to privatize the deeply indebted water and electricity state enterprises, but these and other restructuring plans are on hold.

TRADE

Coffee accounts for 80% of foreign exchange earnings. Other major export items are tea, cotton and hides.

INVESTMENT

RTZ and BHP have postponed their nickel exploration while others have suspended activity in gold and vanadium mining.

FINANCIAL SECTOR

International banking transactions can be carried out through the Banque de la République du Burundi, the Banque Commerciale du Burundi and the Banque Burundaise pour le Commerce et l'Investissement. The banking sector suffered mass withdrawals in 1994.

BUSINESS ACTIVITY

AGRICULTURE
Coffee, cotton, tea, corn, sorghum. potatoes, bananas, manioc, beef, milk, hides.

INDUSTRIES
Light consumer goods such as blankets, shoes, soap, components assembly, public works construction, food processing.

NATURAL RESOURCES
Nickel, uranium, rare earth oxides, peat, cobalt, copper, unexploited platinum, vanadium, and gold.

EXPORTS
$52 million (2005 est.): coffee, tea, cotton, hides.

IMPORTS
$200 million (2005 est.): capital goods, petroleum products, foodstuffs, consumer goods.

MAJOR TRADING PARTNERS
Germany, Belgium, Switzerland, US, Tanzania, Uganda, China.

DOING BUSINESS WITH BURUNDI

▶ INVESTMENT

Even though minerals such as nickel, vanadium and phosphate have attracted foreign interest, no one is making a serious move until Burundi manages to establish stability and provide security for foreign entrepreneurs.

▶ TRADE

Foreigners who offer goods are advised to appoint an experienced agent, even though it is not legally required. A sizeable portion of the country's basic needs are handled through purchases by donor countries.

▶ SELLING TO THE GOVERNMENT

The purchase of petroleum, a major import item, is supervised by the Ministry of Industry.

▶ INVESTMENT

Burundi maintains strict control over its supplies of hard currency, all of which are held by the Central Bank. Repatriating profits requires permission from the Central Bank. The conversion of Burundi Francs to dollars often a lengthy and cumbersome undertaking.

▶ PROJECT FINANCE

International development assistance is at a virtual halt, apart from humanitarian relief efforts. Financing is not available from OPIC or other known international bodies.

▶ PROJECT FINANCE

The majority of the workforce consists of illiterate and semi-literate displaced farmers. Unionized employees, especially in the urban areas, earn somewhat more than the minimum wage which stood at $0.40 per day in the cities of Bujumbura and Gitega and $0.35 in the rest of the country. Many schools have been destroyed in the civil war, leading to lower rates of student enrollment and a limited pool of educated potential employees.

▶ BUSINESS CLIMATE

French and Kirundi are official languages and are widely used in business. Relatively few people speak English.

CAMEROON

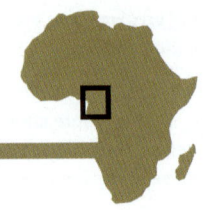

CAMEROON'S ECONOMY IS THE MOST DIVERSIFIED IN CENTRAL AFRICA AND MAKES UP MORE THAN HALF OF THE TOTAL GNP OF THE CENTRAL AFRICAN ECONOMIC AND MONETARY COMMUNITY (CEMAC). ITS ABUNDANT NATURAL RESOURCES, A FAVORABLE CLIMATE, AND WELL-EDUCATED WORK FORCE MAKE IT ONE OF AFRICA'S POTENTIALLY MOST COMPETITIVE ECONOMIES. APART FROM ITS OWN OIL RESOURCES CAMEROON ALSO LARGELY BENEFITS FROM THE RECENTLY COMPLETED PIPELINE TRANSPORTING OIL FOR EXPORT FROM THE DOBA FIELD IN CHAD TO KRIBI. APART FROM ADDITIONAL REVENUES THE PIPELINE SERVES TO STIMULATE FOREIGN INVESTMENT IN CAMEROON IN RELATED INDUSTRIES. THE COUNTRY HAS SUCCESSFULLY COMPLETED SEVERAL IMF AND WORLD BANK PROGRAMS TO SPUR BUSINESS DEVELOPMENT AND ATTRACT INVETSMENT FROM ABROAD.

COUNTRY PROFILE

The Republic of Cameroon is situated on a plateau rising to 1,500 m in the Adamawa Mountains. Mount Cameroon is one of a series of volcanoes running southward, into the ocean, and northward, to Bamenda. In the rain forests of the south an equatorial climate prevails while the fertile soil of the western volcanic zone allows cultivation of a variety of tropical crops. There are more than 200 language groups. The largest single group is the Bamileke. Other major peoples include the Fulani, the Chadic, and the Bantu-speaking Fang. The northern Fulani and Chadic are mainly Muslim, while those in the west and south are predominantly Christian, though many still adhere to traditional ethnic beliefs.

HISTORY

Cameroon is part of the original home of the Bantu cultural grouping who migrated east and south into the countries now known as the Central African Republic, Gabon and Congo. Little was known about the territory until the arrival of the Portuguese in 1472. Explorer Fernando Po named the Wuri River Rio dos Camarões (shrimp or prawn) after large crustaceans found at its mouth. This evolved into the country's present name, Cameroon. During the following three centuries several other European nations and American traders operated along the Cameroon coast. In 1884, it became the German protectorate of Kamerun,

but after the First World War the League of Nations allocated 80% of the territory to France (French Cameroun) and the remaining 20%, consisting of two separate areas along the Nigerian border, to

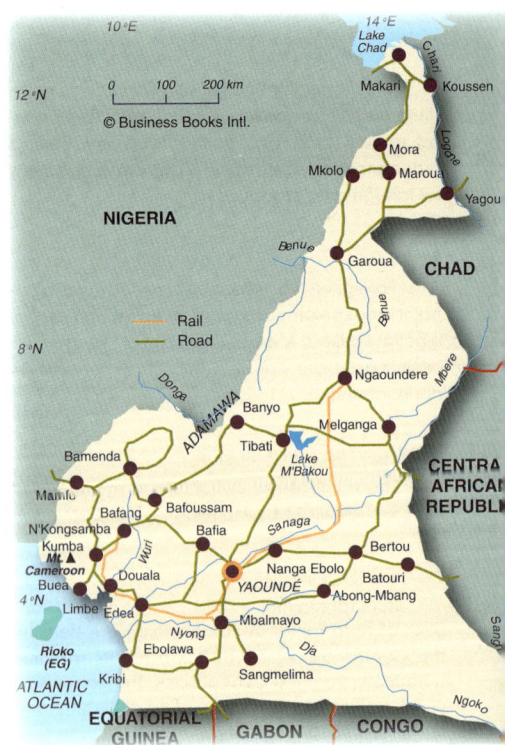

the British as Northern and Southern Cameroons. After a protracted insurgency led by the Bamileke, French Cameroun gained its independence in 1960 under President Ahmadou Ahidjo who adopted single-party rule. In 1982 Ahidjo resigned on grounds of ill health and handed power over to Prime Minister Paul Biya. A war of words between the two former allies led to a trial and a death sentence in absentia for Ahidjo, found guilty of subversion. In March 1992 Biya won reelection in disputed multiparty elections. He was reelected in 1997 and in 2004.

BAKASSI PENINSULA

Parts of the British Cameroons opted to join newly-independent Cameroon in 1960 while others voted to merge with Nigeria. In August 2006, Nigeria, under pressure from UN Secretary General Kofi Annan, honored a ruling by the International Court of Justice and ceded the northern part of the Bakassi peninsula to Cameroon. This ended a decades long row over ownership of the territory. The southern section of the peninsula known as West Atabong and Akwabana will remain under Nigerian administrative control for another two years, giving the mainly Nigerian population of the strip of land that juts into the oil-rich Gulf of Guinea the time to decide to opt for Cameroonian sovereignty or evacuate to Nigeria.

GOVERNMENT

Cameroon has a strong central government dominated by the President, elected for a seven year term, renewable only once. The president appoints the prime minister and cabinet. The 180-member unicameral National Assembly is elected every five years. In the 2002 election Biya's Rassemblement démocratique du Peuple Camerounais (RDPC) in coalition with the Cameroon People's Democratic Movement (CDPM) captured 149 seats. The Front Social Démocratique forms the main opposition with 22 seats. Most of the 150 registered opposition parties have yet to win a seat.

ECONOMIC POLICY

The IMF, World Bank and Paris Club have instituted programs to help reinvigorate Cameroon's economy. However, economic growth continues to be inhibited by a large inefficient parastatal sector, excessive public sector employment, growing defense and internal security expenditures, and by the Government's inability to collect internal revenues effectively, especially

FAST FACTS

Pres. Paul Biya
Born: February 13, 1933
Since 1982

Picture: Esso Chad

POLITICAL

Head of State	Pres. Paul Biya
Ruling Party	RDPC/CPDM
Main Opposition	SDF
Independence	20 May 1960
National capital	Yaoundé
Official languages	English & French

PHYSICAL

Total area	475,422 sq. km.
	183,560 sq. miles
	(± California)
Arable land	15% of land area
Coastline	248 miles/400 km

POPULATION

Total	17.3 million
Av. yearly growth	2.04%
Population/sq. mile	84
Urban population	8.8 million
Adult literacy	79%

ECONOMY

Currency	CFA franc
	(CFAF)(US$1=559.44)
GDP (real)	$15.35 billion
GDP growth rate	2.8%
GDP per capita[1]	$1,035
GDP (ppp)[2]	$40.83 billion
GDP per cap. (ppp)	$2,400
Inflation rate	2%
Exports	$3.24 billion
Imports	$2.5 billion
External debt	$9.2 billion
Unemployment	30%

1. Atlas method.
2. See page 175 for an explanation of purchasing power parity (ppp).

in economically important pro-opposition regions. Cameroon has, however, conformed to a triennial economic program and undertook a number of reforms to reduce its own stake in the economy and promote private sector development.

SECTORS

Although agriculture is the dominant sector and employs about three-quarters of the labor force, Cameroon has one of the few comparatively diversified economies in sub-Saharan Africa. Cocoa is the main cash crop—Cameroon is the world's fifth largest producer—followed by coffee, cotton, tobacco, rubber, palm oil, sugar and bananas. It is the fifth largest producer of petroleum in sub-Sahara Africa. A consortium including ChevronTexaco and ExxonMobil constructed a pipeline to carry petroleum from Chad to Kribi in Cameroon. Unexploited mineral wealth includes bauxite, cobalt, chromium, gold, iron, nickel, sapphires, tin, titanium, uranium, and limestone. Cameroon has the largest tropical rain forest after the Democratic Republic of Congo and produces tropical wood (ebony, mahogany, and iroko) both for export and the local industry. During good rainfall years the country is largely self-sufficient in foodstuffs.

PRIVATIZATION

Cameroon is in the midst of a privatization process that will eliminate all public sector monopolies, except for aluminum. Privatized to date are, among others, CAMSUCO (national sugar company), SOCAPALM (the palm oil complex), the CDC (agricultural plantation complex), BICEC (a state-owned bank) and SOCAR (insurance company). Parastatals that are still scheduled for privatization include the national airliner (CAMAIR), the telecommunication companies (CAMTEL and CAMTEL-MOBILE), and the national insurance retirement fund (CNPS).

TRADE

Petroleum and gas account for 33% of Cameroon's exports, tropical wood (24%), and aluminum 5.5%. Other exports are coffee, cocoa, cotton, rubber, timber, bananas and pineapples. In 1998 the US supplied 8% of the total imports, making Cameroon its seventh largest customer in Sub-Saharan Africa. US sales include bauxite for an aluminum smelting plant as large local bauxite deposits (the 5th largest worldwide) are too expensive to mine. Other major imports from the US are wheat and flour, petroleum coke and pitch additives for aluminum smelting, used clothing and gross lot discounted and discontinued consumer products.

INVESTMENT

France is the leading investor. Construction of the multinational $1.5 billion Chad/Cameroon pipeline should, however, lead to larger US participation. Apart from long-standing investments in oil production, US firms are involved in security services, oral care and hygiene products manufacturing, and fresh fruit production.

FINANCIAL SECTOR

There are nine commercial banks under control of the Banque des Etats de l'Afrique Centrale (BEAC), a common central bank also serving the five other member countries of the Central African sub-region and regulated by the French government. Cameroon has no securities market or bond market but the Banque Nationale de Paris has been mandated to draw up a model for a small, screen-based securities market for the Central African franc zone.

TAXES & TARIFFS

In the mid-nineties Cameroon implemented a new Regional Reform Program, including tax reform. The new code reduced the number of taxes applied to imports.

BUSINESS ACTIVITY

AGRICULTURE
Coffee, cocoa, cotton, rubber, bananas, oilseed, grains, root starches, livestock, timber.

INDUSTRIES
Petroleum production and refining, food processing, consumer goods, textiles, timber.

NATURAL RESOURCES
Petroleum, bauxite, iron ore, timber, hydropower.

EXPORTS
$3.24 billion (2005 est.): crude oil and petroleum products, lumber, cocoa beans, aluminum, coffee, cotton.

IMPORTS
$2.5 billion (2005 est.): machines and electrical equipment, fuel, food.

MAJOR TRADING PARTNERS
Spain, France, Italy, Nigeria, Belgium, US.

DOING BUSINESS WITH CAMEROON

▶ INVESTMENT

A new code simplified foreign investment and introduced financial incentives coupled with minimal eligibility/performance requirements. Equity ownership is subject to limitation only in small and medium size enterprises (SMEs) where a 35% local ownership is required. Privatization in agriculture, reinsurance, banking, telecommunications, water and electrical utilities, rubber production, and transportation has opened up new opportunities. The Industrial Free Zone creates conditions for investors to operate virtually outside the country's established legal and regulatory systems but requires that 80% of the product be sold outside Cameroon.

▶ TRADE

Cameroon is a favored base for foreign trade with Central Africa. Products with potential include fertilizer, used clothing, heavy machinery and material for forestry, transport and road construction, pipeline construction and related services such as security and communications, computer, electronic equipment, and aircraft parts. Local agents with established links to wholesalers and market knowledge are often the best way into this competitive market. Apart from retail outlets operated by large international oil companies and international car rental companies, franchising is limited.

▶ TRADE FINANCE

Eximbank finances US goods and services sold to Cameroon. Exporters usually rely on irrevocable, confirmed letters of credit.

▶ SELLING TO THE GOVERNMENT

Government procurement is handled by the *Direction Générale des Grands Travaux* (DGTC) or Public Works Directorate. Local companies are allowed preferential price margins on all state procurement and development projects. Direct purchases are often made through domestic middlemen who require cash up front on behalf of their foreign clients. Foreign participation in government- subsidized R&D is restricted to programs beyond the technical capability of local firms.

▶ EXCHANGE CONTROLS

The currency continues to be pegged to the French franc, ensured by the French Treasury, and remains readily convertible. Dividends, return of capital, interest and principal on foreign debt, lease payments, royalties and management fees, and returns on liquidation may all be remitted abroad.

▶ PARTNERSHIP

Foreign firms are free to join with any local entity of their choosing in any form desired. Most foreigners obtain expert local counsel when entering into joint ventures and licensing arrangements.

▶ ESTABLISHING A PRESENCE

The Investment Code Management Unit was established in 1991 to assist foreign and domestic business start-ups. It provides investment authorization and a variety of other services through a network of official correspondents in all the relevant ministries. The law requires at least a 35% local ownership for enterprises under the Small and Medium-Size Enterprise (SME) regime.

▶ PROJECT FINANCE

OPIC underwrites viable projects and Cameroon is a member of the Multilateral Investment Guarantee Agency. The World Bank and African Development Bank are further sources of financing.

▶ LABOR

Even though Cameroon has a high literacy rate and a relatively well-educated labor force most of the unemployed are unskilled and nontechnical laborers. The labor code removed government control over layoffs and firings, and reduced official involvement in labor unions.

▶ LEGAL RIGHTS

The IMF and the World Bank, through their structural adjustment oversight, are assisting Cameroon in the reform of its judicial system. Cameroon accepts binding international arbitration of investment disputes and is a member of the International Center for the Settlement of Investment Disputes. It is also the headquarters for the 14-nation West African intellectual Property Organization or *Organisation Africaine de la Propriété Intellectuelle (OAPI)* and is a signatory of the Paris Convention on Industrial Property and the Universal Copyright Convention.

▶ BUSINESS CLIMATE

Cameroon has the largest private sector in French-speaking Central Africa. English is also widely spoken in a business community that does not necessarily conform to western practices. Local business people will first try to "get to know" a potential partner before venturing into concrete discussions. Punctuality is not the norm and patience and persistence are vital.

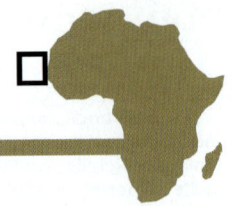

CAPE VERDE

CAPE VERDE CONSISTS OF A GROUP OF ISLANDS STRATEGICALLY LOCATED OFF AFRICA'S WEST COAST. IT DEPENDS LARGELY ON INCOME FROM SERVICES TO FOREIGN SHIPPING AND AIRLINES, REMITTANCES FROM SOME 700,000 CAPE VERDEAN ÉMIGRÉS AND FOREIGN AID. SINCE OPENING ITS ECONOMY TO THE OUTSIDE WORLD, HOWEVER, THE ISLAND GROUP NATION HAS ATTRACTED FOREIGN INVESTMENT IN LIGHT MANUFACTURING, TOURISM, FISHING, TRANSPORTATION AND COMMUNICATIONS. FOREIGN FIRMS ARE BEGINNING TO TAKE ADVANTAGE OF CAPE VERDE'S UNDERUTILIZED QUOTAS IN THE US AND EUROPEAN MARKETS BY ESTABLISHING MANUFACTURING AND ASSEMBLY PLANTS IN ITS EXPORT FREE ZONES.

COUNTRY PROFILE

The Republic of Cape Verde consists of ten windswept Atlantic islands about 500 km west of Dakar. The largest is São Tiago (992 sq. km) and the smallest, Santa Lucia (34 sq. km). Mt. Fogo (2,829 m) is an active volcano island that last erupted in 1995. The islands lie in the North Atlantic high pressure belt, are poor in natural resources and prone to droughts and high temperatures. Afro-Europeans make up 71% of the population and the rest are African. Whites account for about 1% of the total. An estimated 700,000 Cape Verdeans are living and working abroad, most of them sending regular remittances to the 420,000 remaining on the islands. Portuguese is the official language, but the vernacular is Crioulo (Creole), derived from Portuguese and West African languages.

tuguese and the imported slaves from Western Africa. The Cape Verde islands remained obscure until 1975 when they achieved independence from Portugal under President Aristides Pereira of the African Party for the Independence of Guinea and Cape Verde (PAICV). Pereira turned the islands into a one-party state with a centrally controlled economy. Under pressure from the Movement for the Democracy (MPD) led by Carlos Veiga, Cape Verde was eventually transformed into a multi-party democracy in 1990. The following

HISTORY

The islands were uninhabited when Portuguese mariners discovered them during their voyages in search of a sea route around Africa. The first Portuguese governor, appointed in 1462, was based at Ribeira Grande on Sao Antiago, the largest of the islands. A Creole population resulted from intermingling between the Por-

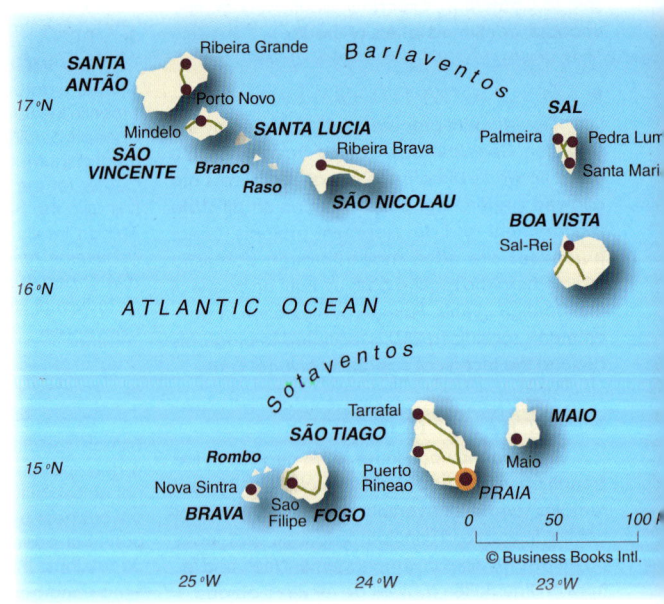

year, the MPD won and Veiga took over as prime minister. A former supreme court judge, Antonio Mascarenhas Monteiro, won the presidential election. The MPD was returned to power with a larger majority in the general elections held in December 1995, but in March 2001 Pedro Pires was inaugurated as president after beating his rival, Carlos Veiga. He was reelected in February 2006, once again defeating Veiga.

GOVERNMENT

The President, elected for 5 years, has limited powers as real authority rests with the Prime Minister, elected by the unicameral 72-member National Assembly. In January 2006, José Maria Pereira Neves was reappointed Prime Minister as leader of the Partido Africano da Independência de Cabo Verde (PAICV) which defeated the Movimento para Democratia (MPD) and several smaller parties by capturing 41 seats.

ECONOMIC POLICY

After years of state control, the new government adopted a development strategy in the early nineties based on market-oriented policies, including an ambitious privatization program. It showed a strong commitment to the implementation of sound macroeconomic and structural reforms and the development of institutions and an infrastructure. Despite slow progress in some sectors, Cape Verde's economic reform policies appear to be paying off, as new businesses are being created, private investment projects are implemented, especially in the tourism sector, construction is booming, and the business community is eager to explore new import markets. Financial and economic legislation has been revised and the government's role in the economy has shifted from a participant in the economy to being a promoter and regulator. Cape Verde's policies have been endorsed and supported by the World Bank, the IMF and many multilateral and bilateral donors, including the US.

SECTORS

The islands suffers from a lack of natural resources coupled with serious water shortages resulting from recurrent droughts. Fishing (mainly tuna and shellfish) is an important activity in the Atlantic ocean economic zone with 28,350 sq. miles (734,265 sq. km.) assigned exclusively to Cape Verde. With only one third of a potential 50,000 tons of fish products per year exploited due to the lack of adequate technology for deep

FAST FACTS

Prime Minister José Maria Neves
Born: August 20, 1943
Since 2001

POLITICAL

Head of State	Pres. Pedro Verona Rodrigues Pires
Prime Minister	José Maria Neves
Ruling Party	PAICV
Main Opposition	MPD
Independence	5 July 1975
National capital	Praia
Official language	Portuguese

PHYSICAL

Total area	1,557 sq. miles
	4,030 sq. km.
	(± Rhode Island)
Arable land	10% of land area
Coastline	600 miles/965 km

POPULATION

Total	420,980
Av. yearly growth	0.64%
Population/sq. mile	258
Urban population	300,000
Adult literacy	76.6%

ECONOMY

Currency	Cape Verde escudo (US$1=94.37)
GDP (real)	$1.13 billion
GDP growth rate	5.5%
GDP per capita[1]	$2,074
GDP (ppp)[2]	$2.99 billion
GDP per cap. (ppp)	$6,200
Inflation rate	0.4%
Exports	$73.35 million
Imports	$500 million
External debt	$325 million
Unemployment	21%

1. *Atlas method.*
2. *See page 175 for an explanation of purchasing power parity (ppp).*

sea fishing, this sector holds great potential. Agriculture can be practiced on only about one-fifth of the total area and meets about 10% of local consumption needs. Cape Verde emigrant communities in New England and Europe provide a continuous inflow of foreign exchange and other informal assistance to relatives back home. The economy is largely service-oriented with commerce, transport, tourism, and public services accounting for 66% of GDP. The dry, tropical climate, diverse terrain, warm, clear waters and beautiful, deserted beaches provide ample resources for growing tourism. An international airport on the island of Sal is used as a refueling stop by international air carriers. About 30% of traffic through the airport is cargo moving between Europe and South America. Traffic between the islands is by air and ferry. Mining is confined to pozzolana (a volcanic substance used for cement) and the production of salt, on Sal, through evaporation.

PRIVATIZATION

In the late nineties Cape Verde started privatizing as part of a five-year World Bank-funded program. Several state-owned enterprises have since been privatized, including three hotels, the national telecommunications company, Cabo Verde Telecom, and the oil distribution company, Enacol. Two commercial banks, an insurance company, the state-run power supply company and the Cape Verdean port authority are on the block.

TRADE

Cape Verde depends almost completely on imports to meet its basic consumer needs and for industrial inputs. Portugal is Cape Verde's most important trading partner and accounts for almost half of the total trade. In 1998 the US supplied 5.6 % of Cape Verde's imports. Non-factor services to international maritime and air transport top the list of foreign currency earners, followed by bananas, lobster and fresh and frozen fish.

INVESTMENT

More than 100 investment projects totaling about a half billion dollars have been licensed. In 1998 alone, a total of $233 million in foreign investment was approved—74% in tourism. Most foreign direct investment came from Portugal, Italy, Spain and other European countries. Recently US and Asian investors have also been targeted by the Cape Verdean foreign investment promotion agency, PROMEX.

FINANCIAL SECTOR

The World Bank has been assisting the government of Cape Verde to restructure its financial sector. The first step was to split the Bank of Cape Verde into a central and a commercial bank. The Stock Market of Cape Verde (BVC) was launched in March 1999 with six listed companies. The financial sector includes four commercial banks (two foreign-owned), two insurance companies and a venture capital company created to promote development of the private sector.

TAXES & TARIFFS

Special tax incentives are extended to firms exporting their entire output from free zones and a 100% tax exemption applies to all dividends earned during the first five years from operations started with foreign capital. Import tariffs have been streamlined.

EXPATRIATES

US-Cape Verdean contacts date from the early 19th Century when the New England whaling industry was at its peak. Today, substantial Cape Verde-American communities live in Massachusetts and Rhode Island. Cape Verde's large trade deficit is in part financed by remittances from expatriates and foreign aid.

BUSINESS ACTIVITY

AGRICULTURE
Bananas, corn, beans, sweet potatoes, sugar cane, coffee, peanuts, fish.

INDUSTRIES
Food and beverages, fish processing, shoes and garments, salt mining, ship repair.

NATURAL RESOURCES
Salt, basalt rock, pozzuolana (volcanic ash used to produce hydraulic cement), limestone, kaolin, fish.

EXPORTS
$73.35 million (2005 est.): shoes, garments, fish, bananas, hides.

IMPORTS
$500 million (2005 est.): foodstuffs, consumer goods, industrial products, transport equipment.

MAJOR TRADING PARTNERS
Spain, Portugal, Germany, France, Brazil, Italy, Netherlands, US.

Doing Business with Cape Verde

▶ INVESTMENT

A competitive incentive package is offered through the Center for Tourism, Investment and Exports Promotion (PROMEX) which acts as a one-stop shop for foreign investors. While favoring free zone enterprises geared to exports, these incentives also apply in large part to other investments based on infusion of foreign capital. Investors establishing export-driven operations are in many instances assured of generous preferential access to the markets of Europe, West Africa and the United States. Apart from light manufacturing, fishing and tourism offer opportunities.

▶ TRADE

There is great receptivity for foreign goods, especially items from Portugal which enjoys strong cultural and linguistic links. The smallness of the market and lack of credit have inhibited trade development but the growing need for high-cost items required in the expansion of the country's airports, fishing fleets, telecommunications systems and other infrastructural projects are of special interest to foreign suppliers.

▶ TRADE FINANCE

The US Department of Agriculture's Commodity Credit Corporation (CCC) administers the Export Credit Guarantee program (GSM-102) providing financing for sales of US agricultural products. Other agencies that provide financing and insurance programs are the International Finance Corporation, the Overseas Private Investment Corporation, Eximbank and the US Small Business Administration.

▶ SELLING TO THE GOVERNMENT

Government procurement is by tender and typically financed by a multilateral lending institutions such as the World Bank or the African Development Bank. Recent major projects include the building of a longer runway at the international airport of Sal, a new runway at Praia and the modernization of Sao Vicente's airport. Other plans involve harbor improvements and modernization of telecommunications.

▶ EXCHANGE CONTROLS

Under current law, revenues and profits, capital gains, and loan repayments may be transferred overseas within 60, 90, and 30 days, respectively, after submission of an application to the Bank of Cape Verde (BCV). The BCV pays interest on all transfers where waiting periods exceed 30 days.

Transfers are at times delayed when requests involve large sums which might affect Cape Verde's balance of payments. In some instances, the government might opt to make the transfer in installments.

▶ ESTABLISHING A PRESENCE

Joint ventures are allowed and encouraged in fisheries, airlines and telecommunications. Apart from these partnerships, foreigners have the option of establishing a branch, a limited liability company or a full corporation. Franchising is limited.

▶ FINANCING PROJECTS

Multilateral Investment Guarantee Agency and Overseas Private Investment Corporation programs apply. The US Trade and Development Agency, the World Bank and the African Development Bank provide funding for feasibility studies and other investment planning services. Bank credit is available to foreign investors under the same conditions as those for national investors. The private sector has access to credit instruments such as loans, letters of credit and lines of credit. There are clear legal guidelines for accounting but they are not totally consistent with international norms.

▶ LABOR

With an unemployment rate of about 28% labor is readily available, much of it unskilled. Technical, managerial and professional talent is difficult to find. The recently revised labor code makes work contracts more flexible. There is no set minimum wage and prevailing levels are around $0.70 per hour.

▶ LEGAL RIGHTS

Disputes between foreign investors and the government are settled either through a single referee or an arbitration commission. Referees may be foreigners of a different nationality than the parties involved in the dispute. Final appeals can be made to the International Center of Settlement of Investment Disputes (ICSID). There have not been any such disputes in recent years. Since 1990 Cape Verde has had copyright laws and it is a signatory to several treaties providing protection.

▶ BUSINESS CLIMATE

Business practices and customs follow the Portuguese model. While Portuguese is spoken in most business circles, English is gaining wider acceptance and some French is spoken as well.

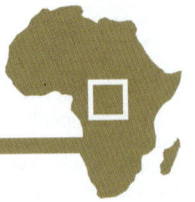

CENTRAL AFRICAN REPUBLIC

THE CENTRAL AFRICAN REPUBLIC (CAR) IS, AS ITS NAME INDICATES, AT THE CENTER OF THE AFRICAN CONTINENT. IT IS A SPARSELY POPULATED COUNTRY, WELL ENDOWED WITH NATURAL RESOURCES. ITS REMOTENESS FROM THE NEAREST SEAPORTS IS A DRAWBACK. PLAGUED IN THE PAST BY SLAVERY, COLONIAL NEGLECT AND BRUTAL TYRANTS, THE CAR HAS SOMEHOW MANAGED TO NURTURE AND STRENGTHEN THE FRAGILE DEMOCRACY INTRODUCED IN 1993 WHEN IT HELD ITS FIRST FREE ELECTIONS. TEMPORARILY UNDER TRANSITIONAL RULE WHEN PRESIDENT ANGE-FÉLIX PATASSÉ WAS OUSTED IN A COUP BY FRANÇOIS BOZIZÉ IN 2003, CAR RETURNED TO CIVILIAN RULE AFTER ELECTIONS IN 2005. CAR IS ACTIVELY COURTING FOREIGN INVESTORS, ESPECIALLY IN DIVERSIFIED MINING TO AUGMENT ITS INCOME FROM DIAMONDS AND GOLD.

COUNTRY PROFILE

The Central African Republic is a landlocked and sparsely populated undulating plateau. During the rainy season much of the southeast is impassable as several rivers overflow into the Ubangi, the great tributary of the Congo River. Vast parts of the northern and eastern regions have been set aside for nature conservation. There are two major ethnic groups: the river peoples (Yakoma and Mabaka) and the savannah peoples (such as the Sara). Sango is widely spoken and used in broadcasting. More than two-thirds of the total population are Christians, though many still profess traditional ethnic beliefs.

HISTORY

The slave trade, especially during the 17th and 18th centuries, had a massive impact on the old kingdoms in this region, decimating their populations. By the turn of the 19th Century the French established themselves at Bangui and founded the colony of Ubangi-Chari (named after two major rivers). Local resistance to excesses by French companies who administered the territory culminated in the Kongo Wara wars from 1928 until 1931. In 1960 CAR achieved independence under the one party rule of President David Dacko. Five years later his cousin, sergeant Jean-Bédel Bokassa, seized power, declared himself president in 1972 and ultimately crowned himself emperor five years later. In 1979, Bokassa's brutal rule came to an end when French troops reinstated Dacko. Two years later Dacko was once again ousted in a military coup, this time by Gen. André Kolingba. In 1993 internal and international pressures forced Kolingba to hold a multi-parry presidential election. He lost to Ange-Félix Patassé, who once

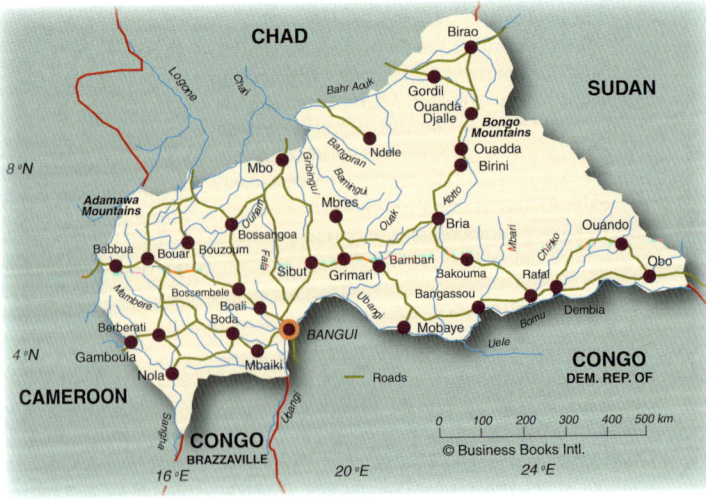

served in Bokassa's cabinet. Patassé was reelected in September 1999, defeating Kolingba and several other candidates. Patassé's rule was plagued by unrest and African forces and the UN Mission in the Central African Republic (MINURCA) were called in to help maintain stability until March 2003, when Patassé was ousted in a coup by François Bozizé. In the May 2005 election Bozizé easily defeated Martin Ziguélé, a former prime minister, in presidential elections.

GOVERNMENT

Under the 1995 constitution the President is elected for a maximum of two 6-year terms. It provides for a bicameral legislature consisting of a 109 member National Assembly, elected for 5 years, and a nominated Economic and Regional Council. In 2005 the Convergence "Kwa na Kwa" (KNK) coalition, supported by Bozizé, won 42 seats against 11 by the Mouvement pour la Libération du Peuple Centrafricain (MLPC). Independents and smaller parties took the rest.

ECONOMIC POLICY

The government has agreed to a framework for economic reform, including the privatization of key parastatals under an IMF-approved Extended Structure Adjustment Facility (ESAF). The country's landlocked position, poor infrastructure and largely unskilled work force have, however, placed constraints on developemnt and economic growth. Grants from France and the international community meet humanitarian needs in part.

SECTORS

The agricultural sector in CAR contributes some 55% of the GDP and employs an estimated 80% of the labor force. Key primary food crops include bananas, cocoa beans, coffee and sugar cane. Meat products range from beef, chicken, goat meat and mutton to pork. The CAR is almost self-sufficient in food and has the potential of becoming a net exporter. Export crops are cotton, coffee, cattle, organic material and tobacco leaves. Mining largely involves alluvial diamonds and gold, together contributing about 4% of the nation's gross domestic product. Key industries are diamond mining, sawmills, breweries, textiles, footwear, and assembly of bicycles and motorcycles.

PRIVATIZATION

Privatization of state enterprises had just begun when the civil unrest broke out in 1996 and has since been significantly delayed. A 49%

FAST FACTS

Pres. François Bozizé
Born: 1946
Since March 2003

POLITICAL

Head of State	Pres. François Bozizé
Ruling Party	KNK
Major Opposition	MPLC
Independence	13 August 1960
National capital	Bangui
Official language	French

PHYSICAL

Total area	241,313 sq. miles 622,980 sq. km. (2 x New Mexico)
Arable land	3% of land area

POPULATION

Total	4.3 million
Av. yearly growth	1.53%
Population/sq. mile	15
Urban population	1.7 million
Adult literacy	51%

ECONOMY

Currency	CFA franc (CFAF)(US$1=559.44)
GDP (real)	$1.46 billion
GDP growth rate	2.2%
GDP per capita[1]	$342
GDP (ppp)[2]	$4.78 billion
GDP per cap. (ppp)	$1,100
Inflation rate	3.6%
Exports	$131 million
Imports	$203 million
External debt	$1.06 billion
Unemployment	8%

1. *Atlas method.*
2. *See page 175 for an explanation of purchasing power parity (ppp).*

share of the national telecommunications operator, Socatel has been sold .

INVESTMENT

Foreign direct investment is primarily concentrated in the diamond mining, gold and timber sectors.

TRADE

France continues to be the major trade partner while the US, Japan, and Iran are significant suppliers of products such processed foods, pharmaceuticals, consumer goods, industrial products, vehicles, and petroleum products.

FINANCIAL SECTOR

Banking in the CAR is under control of the French-controlled Banque des Etats de l'Afrique Centrale (BEAC), which regulates five Francophone countries in the Central African sub-region.

TAXES AND TARIFFS

General corporate income tax is 40%. Agricultural and consumer cooperatives are exempt from income tax.

BUSINESS ACTIVITY

AGRICULTURE
Cotton, coffee, tobacco, manioc, yams, millet, corn, bananas, timber.

INDUSTRIES
Diamond mining, sawmills, breweries, textiles, footwear, bicycles and motorcycles.

NATURAL RESOURCES
Diamonds, uranium, timber, gold, oil.

EXPORTS
$131 million (est. 2005): diamonds, timber, tobacco, coffee, cotton, yams, bananas.

IMPORTS
$203 million (est. 2005): food, textiles, petroleum products, machinery, electrical equipment, motor vehicles, chemicals, consumer goods, industrial products.

MAJOR TRADING PARTNERS
Belgium, France, Italy, Spain, China, France, Cameroon, Netherlands, Japan, US.

DOING BUSINESS WITH CENTRAL AFRICAN REPUBLIC

▶ INVESTMENT

Several American firms have expressed interest in mechanizing the largely manual diamond sector and getting involved in the mining and exploration of gold, copper, iron ore, tin, uranium and zinc. The mining industry is regulated by the Ministry of Energy, Mines, Geology and Water Resources. The government has invited foreign participation in the underdeveloped telecommunications sector by freeing up value added network services and partially lifting restrictions on cellular services development. The CAR shows good potential for foreign involvement in ecotourism in its rain forest and savanna regions. Tentative steps have been taken by foreign entrepreneurs to develop facilities in areas such as the primeval rain forest, Dzanga-Sangha National Park, in the southwestern region of the country.

▶ TRADE

Even though there is a strong interest in American goods, US exporters should expect tough competition from France with which the CAR has maintained strong commercial ties. Importers of consumer items and personal vehicles have expressed an interest in US goods, but logistic problems tend to impede sales and distribution.

▶ SELLING TO THE GOVERNMENT

In selling to the government foreign firms usually concentrate on projects financed by donors.

▶ EXCHANGE CONTROLS

Capital, profits and dividends can be freely transferred. The transfer of more than CFA 500,000 requires permission from the Ministry of Finance.

▶ PARTNERSHIPS

As tax and customs laws may be more strictly enforced against foreigners, it is useful to have a local partner to negotiate the complex web of regulations required to establish a business.

▶ LABOR

The workforce is largely unskilled.

▶ LEGAL RIGHTS

Foreign investors are assured of equal treatment under law which guarantees freedom from expropriation and nationalization, barring special circumstances, and freedom from political or economic interference.

▶ BUSINESS CLIMATE

Business is mostly conducted in French.

CHAD

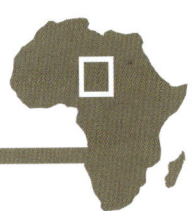

LANDLOCKED CHAD IS AFRICA'S FIFTH LARGEST COUNTRY AND ONE OF ITS POOREST. THIS, HOWEVER, IS LIKELY TO CHANGE AS IT CONTINUES TO DEMONSTRATE MACROECONOMIC STABILITY, CAPACITY BUILDING, DEMOCRATIC REFORM AND SOCIAL PROGRESS. A 665 MILE/1,070 KM PIPELINE COMPLETED IN 2004 THAT CARRIES OIL FROM CHAD'S DOBA BASIN TO THE PORT OF KRIBI IN CAMEROON HAS BEGUN TO STIMULATE GROWTH AND BOOST INCOME. IN THE NEXT DECADE OIL IS EXPECTED TO TRANSFORM CHAD FROM A COUNTRY LARGELY DEPENDENT ON AGRICULTURAL EXPORTS, SUBSISTENCE CROPS AND LIVESTOCK TO A MANUFACTURING AND MINING BASE. THE PIPELINE HAS OPENED UP NEW OPPORTUNITIES FOR FOREIGN INVESTORS, NOT ONLY IN PETROLEUM-RELATED INDUSTRIES BUT IN A RANGE OF OTHER MANUFACTURING AND SERVICE AREAS. CHAD ALSO HAS SUBSTANTIAL DEPOSITS OF GOLD, MARBLE AND NATRON.

COUNTRY PROFILE

The landlocked Republic of Chad is the fifth largest country in Africa. Its capital, N'Djamena, is situated near the confluence of the country's only two rivers, the Chari and the Logone, which flow from the south into Lake Chad. There are sharply contrasting climatic zones varying from wet savannah in the south to arid Sahara Desert conditions in the north. Except for scattered Arab-speaking and Chadic groups, most of the peoples are of Nilo-Saharan origin, comprising the Bagirmi and the Sara of the south, the Maba in the Waddai region, and the Kanuri in the Sahara region. The desert peoples also include the Zaghawa along the eastern border, and the Tubu of the Tibesti Mountains. French and Arabic are official languages but some English is spoken, apart from 100 local languages. More than half the country is Muslim and the rest is divided evenly between Christianity and traditional African religions.

HISTORY

Artifacts dating back to 5000 BC have been discovered at burial sites in the Sahel and Southern Sahara regions, inhabited by nomadic Negroid people, many of whom turned to the Muslim faith as early as the 10th Century. Towards the end of the 19th Century, converted Christians from the south sided with French troops against the north. In 1910 Chad was incorporated into French Equatorial Africa. In 1957 the Chadians formed their first elected government and a year later voted to become a self-governing member of the French Community. The territory became

211

FAST FACTS

Pres. Idriss Déby
Born: 1952
Since 1990

Picture: Esso Chad

POLITICAL

Head of State	Pres. Idriss Déby
Ruling Party	MPS
Major Opposition	RDP, FAR
Independence	11 August 1960
National capital	N'Djamena
Official languages	French & Arabic

PHYSICAL

Total area	495,752 sq. miles
	1,284,000 sq. km.
	(3 x California)
Arable land	3% of land area

POPULATION

Total	9.94 million
Av. yearly growth	2.93%
Population/sq. mile	17
Urban population	2.3 million
Adult literacy	47.5%

ECONOMY

Currency	CFA franc
	(CFAF) (US$1=559.44)
GDP (real)	$4.8 billion
GDP growth rate	6%
GDP per capita[1]	$536
GDP (ppp)[2]	$14.79 billion
GDP per cap. (ppp)	$1,500
Inflation rate	3%
Exports	$3.02 billion
Imports	$749.1 million
External debt	$1.5 billion
Unemployment	N/A

1. Atlas method.
2. See page 175 for an explanation of
   purchasing power parity (ppp).

independent on 11 August 1960 with southerner Francois Tombalbaye as its first president. Two years later, in response to growing internal unrest, he banned the opposition. Muslim opponents formed the Chad Liberation Front (Frolinat) and took control of the north. French assistance to Tombalbaye was countered by Libyan financial and military aid to Frolinat. After the withdrawal of the French military in 1972, Libya laid claim to and annexed the Aozou Strip in northern Chad. Tombalbaye perished during a military coup in April 1975, setting off a series of destabilizing events that prompted incursions by Libyan, Nigerian and French troops. In 1990, former army chief Idriss Déby finally deposed the French-favored ruler, Hissene Habre, declared himself president and announced his commitment to a multiparty system. In 1994 the International Court of Justice ruled in Chad's favor in the Aozou dispute, forcing Libya to withdraw. Déby emerged as the winner in the presidential election of 1996 and was reelected in 2001 and again in May 2006. In 2005 new rebel groups emerged in western Sudan and made incursions into eastern Chad.

GOVERNMENT

The 155-seat unicameral National Assembly is elected to serve four years. In the April 2002 elections Pres. Déby's Mouvement patriotique du Salut (MPS), won 110 seats followed in distant second and third place by the Rassemblement pour la Démocratie et le Progrès (RDP) (12 seats) and the Front des Forces d'Action pour la République (FAR) (9 seats). In a June 2005 referendum the population voted in favor of replacing the Senate with an Economic, Social, and Cultural Council and scrapping term limits on the presidency.

ECONOMIC POLICY

The government has begun to disengage itself from key sectors of the economy, has liberalized pricing, and is promoting competition. Chad's return of internal security and a successful Geneva donors' conference prompted a number of international business representatives to make exploratory visits to Chad. By far the most important venture to date is the oil extraction project in southern Chad that came on stream in 2003. Beginning in late 2000, the Doba Basin oil project has brought in $3.7 billion in foreign direct investment from a consortium led by two US oil companies. In 2006 President Deby found himself in a dispute with ChevronTexaco and ExxonMobil over alleged failure on the part of the corporations to pay taxes due on the oil revenues.

SECTORS

Growth in some sectors has been constrained by Chad's lack of outlets to the sea. There are no railways and the roads are inadequate. Despite growth in the oil sector agriculture still accounts for 80% of the work force. Cotton is cultivated in the south and livestock in the north. Food crops include sorghum, millet, dry beans, sesame, potatoes, rice and maize. The only minerals extracted in quantity are soda and rock salt but there are known reserves of chromium, tungsten, titanium, iron ore, wolfram, gold, uranium and tin. The exploitation of oil deposits at Doba in the south after the construction of a 665 mile/1,070-km pipeline across Cameroon to an offshore tanker terminal at the Atlantic port of Kribi has stimulated industrial activity way beyond the current cotton processing and small scale food, textiles, brewing, tobacco, and leather plants.

PRIVATIZATION

There has been steady progress towards privatization. The Banque Meridien BIAO Tchad (BMBT-BIAT) and l'Office National Hydraulique Pastoral et Villageois (ONHPV) have already been reconstructed. Slated for privatization are SONASUT (sugar monopoly), STEE (water and electricity), TIT (international telecommunications), ONPT (post office/telecommunications), Air Chad, and Cotontchad (cotton monopoly).

INVESTMENT

Foreign direct investment represents more than half of the total capital in Chadian enterprises. As a result of historical ties, France leads the way with an estimated 50-60% of the total. Other significant investors are the Benelux countries, Italy, Taiwan, US, Japan, Saudi-Arabia, and Libya. In 2004, a consortium including ChevronTexaco, ExxonMobil and Malaysia's Petronas completed a pipeline from the Doba basin to the coast of Cameroon. At a construction cost of $3.7 billion production is currently at about 225,000 bbl/day—an expected total of 2 billion barrels over its 30-year life.

TRADE

Cotton is the most important cash crop, accounting for about 90% of export revenues. Gum Arabic, groundnuts, sesame, sugar cane and tobacco are additional cash crops. Livestock is a source of traditional wealth and exported either on the hoof or as frozen meat, hides and skins. Mineral exports include soda and rock salt (mainly to Nigeria) and natron, used in the preservation of meat and in tanning. Once the pipeline project to Cameroon is completed oil is certain to overtake other exports in importance. Major imports include machinery and transportation equipment, industrial goods, petroleum products, and consumer goods.

FINANCIAL SECTOR

As a member of Communautè Financiére Africaine (CFA) zone, Chad belongs to the regional central bank, Banque des Etats de l'Afrique Centrale (BEAC), which controls distribution of its money and the transfer of funds. There are five commercial banks in Chad, some with US correspondent relationships.

TAXES AND TARIFFS

The corporate tax rate is 45% and a turnover tax of 15% applies to all services and products. Additional revenues in 1998 are expected from the newly-installed Impot General Liberatoire (IGL), a tax levied on small business and the informal sector. As a member of the Central African Regional Customs Union (UDEAC), Chad has reformed import and value-added taxes.

BUSINESS ACTIVITY

AGRICULTURE
Cotton, sorghum, millet, peanuts, rice, potatoes, manioc, cattle, sheep, goats, camels.

INDUSTRIES
Cotton textiles, meat packing, beer brewing, natron, kaolin (sodium carbonate), soap, cigarettes, construction materials.

NATURAL RESOURCES
Petroleum, uranium, natron, kaolin, fish.

EXPORTS
$3.02 billion (est. 2005): oil, cotton, cattle, textiles, gum arabic.

IMPORTS
$749.1 million (est. 2005): machinery and transportation equipment, industrial goods, petroleum products, foodstuffs, textiles.

MAJOR TRADING PARTNERS
US, China, France, Cameroon, Portugal, Nerthelands, Nigeria, Saudi Arabia.

DOING BUSINESS WITH CHAD

► **INVESTMENT**

ExxonMobil affiliate, Esso Chad—leading a consortium including Chevron and Petronas—constructed a 665 miles (1,070 km) oil pipeline from the Doba basin in Chad to Kribi in Cameroon at a cost of $3.5 billion. This massive development opened up significant opportunities for foreign firms in finance, construction, oil-related industries and telecommunications. Chad's mineral reserves, including gold, marble and natron, have also attracted interest from investors. Livestock, still largely unexploited, present opportunities in meat and dairy production, leather, glue, fertilizer and other products. Spirulina (blue-green algae) in Lake Chad, shea trees, sesame seed oil, and a need for solar and wind power are other potential areas of investment. Privatization opens up further areas for foreign private participation. While currently uneconomic as a result of poor infrastructure, deposits of copper, silver, zinc and other metals hold future promise. Tax incentives apply to most investment.

► **TRADE**

Imports include pharmaceutical products, flour milling products, malt, starchy food gluten, industrial chemicals, organic and non-organic, cellulose acetates, tire tubes, new and used tires for buses and trucks, paper products, grease-proof paper, rags, used and new textiles and shoes, steel, cable and tubes, tools and hardware, compressor parts, pumps, and air conditioners. There is a growing need for electric power systems; construction, mining, and agriculture machinery; telecommunications equipment and services; and food processing and packaging equipment.

► **TRADE FINANCE**

Eximbank has financed projects for ventures in the past. Short- to medium-term trade financing can also be obtained from the commercial banks and longer term arrangements through multilateral lending institutions such as the World Bank, African Development Bank, the *Fonds Europeen de Development* (FED), and the Islamic Development Bank.

► **SELLING TO THE GOVERNMENT**

Government tenders are published in the local press. The Minister of Finance and Economy together with his staff act as the National Authorization Office (NAO), selecting tenders on behalf of the relevant ministries. Large procurements are usually financed by the multilateral lending institutions.

► **EXCHANGE CONTROLS**

There are no restrictions on the transfer of funds. As a member of the Central African Regional Customs Union (UDEAC) and the regional monetary union (CEMAC), Chad uses the CFA franc, supported by France at a fixed value.

► **PARTNERSHIPS**

Foreign firms have entered into joint venture opportunities in the textile, agricultural and transportation sectors.

► **ESTABLISHING A PRESENCE**

Structuring can be in terms of a limited liability company (*Société à Responsabilité Limitée*—SARL) or a *Corporation Societe Anonyme* (SA) with at least seven shareholders. Both have to be registered with a number of state agencies before authorization is granted by the Ministry of Commerce.

► **FINANCING PROJECTS**

Major development projects are funded by multilateral donors such as the World Bank and African Development Bank. Foreign investors might be able to obtain financing on the local market but credit allotments are limited in range and lending criteria are rigid.

► **LABOR**

Over 80 percent of the workforce is engaged in unpaid subsistence farming, herding and fishing. Unionized labor has no ties to the government and a new labor code has been drawn up in conjunction with the World Bank. Mandatory allowances to workers include transportation, health indemnity, bonuses, and vacation pay.

► **LEGAL RIGHTS**

Law is based on the French Napoleonic Code and Chadian customary law. Chad is a member of the Cameroon-based West African Intellectual Property Rights Organization but due to administrative limitations protection against copyright infringements is not guaranteed.

► **BUSINESS CLIMATE**

There is local tendency to take time developing a broad base of understanding and mutual trust during personal contact before proceeding with serious business discussions. When visiting Chad, it is advisable to have corporate and business materials available in French.

COMOROS

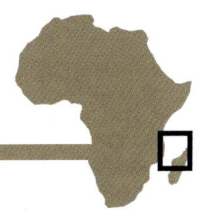

CONSISTING OF FOUR MAJOR AND A NUMBER OF MINOR ISLANDS IN THE INDIAN OCEAN EAST OF MOZAMBIQUE, THE COMOROS ARCHIPELAGO HAS BEEN STRUGGLING TO ATTAIN POLITICAL STABILITY AND ECONOMIC GROWTH SINCE ITS INDEPENDENCE IN 1975. COMOROS SUFFERS FROM LIMITED NATURAL RESOURCES AND A POPULATION TORN BY ANCIENT DIVISIONS. SINCE 1997 THE COMORIAN FEDERAL STATE HAS BEEN THREATENED WITH SECESSION BY THE ISLANDS OF ANJOUAN AND MOHÉLI AND ENDURED SOME 20 COUPS OR ATTEMPTED COUPS. EFFORTS CONTINUE TO STABILIZE THE POLITICAL SITUATION WITH THE HELP OF THE AFRICAN UNION AND OTHER INTERNATIONAL ORGANIZATIONS, AND TO MAKE THE ISLANDS MORE ATTRACTIVE FOR MUCH-NEEDED FOREIGN ECONOMIC INVOLVEMENT.

COUNTRY PROFILE

The four main islands and islets of the Comoros Islamic Federal Republic are scattered like stepping stones across the northern end of the Mozambique Channel, a stretch of Indian Ocean between the African coast and Madagascar. Three of the islands, Grande Comore (Ngazidja), Anjouan (Ndzuani) and Moheli (Mwali), constitute the federal republic, while the fourth, Mayotte (Maore) is a disputed French territory. These islands are the summits of a submerged volcanic ridge. Mount Karthala (2,040 m) on Grande Comore has the largest live crater in the world. The climate on all the islands is tropical, hot and humid, with abundant rainfall in most places. More than 100,000 Comorians live in France. The island population is mainly of Arab, African (Swahili) and Malagasy origin. Arabic and French are the official languages but Kiswahili is the common tongue. Most Comorians are Sunni Muslims.

HISTORY

Originally part of an extensive trade network in the northern Indian Ocean, these islands became known as Comoros—a corruption of the name Jazair al-Komr (Islands of the Moon) given by Arab mariners. A thousand years ago Ndzuani (Anjouan) was settled by Arabs and Shirazi (Persian) Muslims, replete with slaves. Since 1912 the Comoros had been administered as a colony by the French from Madagascar. In 1946 it was separated and in 1961 granted limited self-government. In 1974, when Comoros voted for independence, Mayotte, with its Christian majority, voted against joining the other largely Islamic islands and opted for continued French rule. The first post independence president, Ahmed Abdallah, was ousted after less than a month in office and replaced by a young populist, Ali Solihi. Since then coups, attempted coups and mercenary incursions

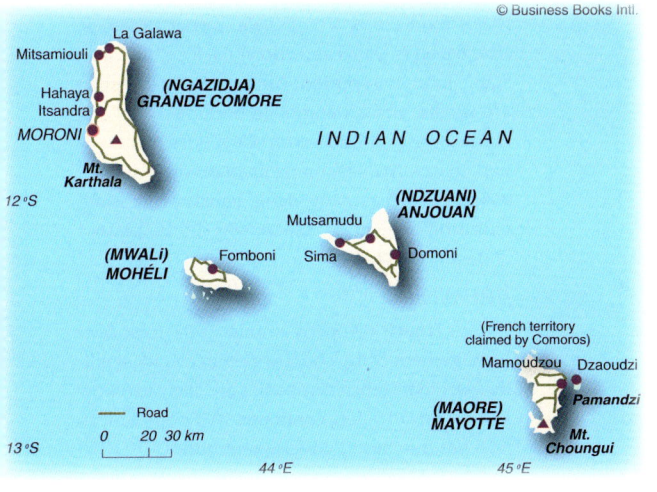

215

FAST FACTS

Pres. Ahmed Sambi
Born: 5 June 1958
Since 2006

UNDPI

POLITICAL

Head of State	Pres. Ahmed Sambi
Independence	6 July 1975
National capital	Moroni
Official languages	Arabic & French

PHYSICAL

Total area	838 sq. miles
	2,170 sq. km.
	(12 x Washington, DC)
Arable land	35%
Territorial sea	12 nautical miles

POPULATION

Total	690,900
Av. yearly growth	2.87%
Population/sq. mile	838
Urban population	300,000
Adult literacy	65.6%

ECONOMY

Currency	Comoron franc
	(CF) (US$1=419.54)
GDP (real)	$402 million
GDP growth rate	3%
GDP per capita[1]	$481
GDP (ppp)[2]	$441 million
GDP per cap. (ppp)	$600
Inflation rate	3.5%
Exports	$34 million
Imports	$115 million
External debt	$232 million
Unemployment	20%

1. *Atlas method.*
2. *See page 175 for an explanation of purchasing power parity (ppp).*

have been part and parcel of the nation's political life. Elected in 1996, President Mohammed Taki died in November 1998 under suspicious circumstances and was succeeded by the president of the High Court, Tadjidine Ben Said Massoude. He was in turn replaced in 1999 in the latest of 20 coups since independence in 1975, engineered by Col. Azali Assoumani, who headed a military government until 2002. Under severe outside pressure Assoumani and other combatants signed a new constitution in March 2002, providing for elections. In June 2002 Assoumani became federal president by virtue of his election to the post of president of the Grand Comoros island. After the May 2006 elections he was succeeded by Ahmed Abdallah Sambi.

GOVERNMENT

In terms of its March 2002 constitution, the three islands—Grand Comoros (Ngazidja), Anjouan and Mohéli—each elects its own president. The federal presidency rotates every four years between the three islands. In May 2006 Pres. Sambi, the newly elected president of Anjouan, succeeded Assoumani of Grand Comoros as president.

ECONOMIC POLICY

In the early nineties Comoros embarked on free market reforms under a structural adjustment program supported by the World Bank and the IMF. However, the islands seem likely to depend on outside aid for the foreseeable future.

SECTORS

Agriculture,—including fishing, hunting, and forestry—is the leading sector, contributing 40% to GDP and employing 80% of the work force. Major food crops are cassava, sweet potatoes, rice, bananas, yams and coconuts. Rice, the main staple food, is imported. The principal cash crops are vanilla, ylang-ylang oil (a perfume base) and cloves, mostly produced on plantations owned by expatriates. Manufacturing involves distillation of essences such as ylang ylang, vanilla processing, extrusion of plant oils, soap, soft drinks, plastics and woodwork.

PRIVATIZATION

A French company in mid-1997 took over management of the country's ailing electrical utility and other French companies are likely to follow suit as privatization continues. A South African firm has purchased government hotels.

INVESTMENT

Efforts by the government to attract foreign investment have been marred by political instability. South Africa is considered to be the prime candidate for investment capital.

TRADE

Vanilla, cloves and ylang-ylang are major exports. France, Germany, and the United States are major buyers and France, Pakistan, South Africa, the United Arab Emirates and Kenya are the major suppliers of goods. Rice accounts for the bulk of the imports. Remittances from more than 150,000 Comorians living overseas are another important source of foreign currency.

FINANCIAL SECTOR

Comoros is a member of the Communauté financière africaine The Banque Nationale de Paris Intercontinentale is the country's only international financial institution. Increased foreign support is needed to help Comoros meet its goal of an annual 4% growth in GDP.

TAXES AND TARIFFS

The corporate income tax rate is 40%. There is a 15% tax on distributed dividends.

BUSINESS ACTIVITY

AGRICULTURE
Vanilla, cloves, perfume essences, copra, coconuts, bananas, cassava (tapioca).

INDUSTRIES
Tourism, perfume distillation, textiles, furniture, jewelry, construction materials, soft drinks.

EXPORTS
$34 million (est. 2005): ylang-ylang, cloves, perfume oil, copra.

IMPORTS
$115 million (est. 2005): rice and other foodstuffs, consumer goods, petroleum products, cement, transport equipment.

MAJOR TRADING PARTNERS
France, Singapore, Japan, Germany, South Africa, US, Netherlands, Kenya, Singapore, Pakistan, Belgium, UAE.

DOING BUSINESS WITH COMOROS

▶ INVESTMENT

The government has encouraged foreign investment by offering a number of special tax and other incentives. Opportunities for profitable trade and investment will, however, remain underutilized until Comoros resolves its deep-seated political problems and follows through with much needed economic reforms. Telecommunications, road construction, fishing and tourism are promising potential future areas for investment once longer term stability is restored.

▶ TRADE

The US can be competitive in supplying items such as medical equipment and supplies, cellular telephone systems and solar energy units, once the political and economic climate improves. The Japanese have helped fund a satellite facility for Comoros which should stimulate growth in the communications sector and create a demand for equipment. Current commerce between the United States and Comoros is limited.

▶ EXCHANGE CONTROLS

The government allows transfer of capital, profits and dividends.

▶ LABOR

Unemployment and underemployment are widespread. The low educational level of the labor force contributes to a subsistence level of economic activity, high unemployment, and a heavy dependence on foreign grants and technical assistance.

▶ BUSINESS CLIMATE

French is the language of business and daily life in Comoros, although some Arabic and Swahili are spoken. Comoros is a Muslim country, and visitors should observe conservative norms of dress and behavior.

CONGO, DEM. REP.

AS AFRICA'S THIRD LARGEST COUNTRY, IN SIZE THE EQUIVALENT OF WESTERN EUROPE, RICHLY ENDOWED WITH MINERAL AND OTHER NATURAL RESOURCES, THE DEMOCRATIC REPUBLIC OF CONGO (DRC) OR CONGO (KINSHASA) HAS THE POTENTIAL TO BECOME ONE OF THE CONTINENT'S MOST PROSPEROUS. HOWEVER, UNTIL PEACE AND STABILITY ARE RESTORED AND EFFECTIVE ECONOMIC REFORMS INTRODUCED IT SEEMS DESTINED TO BE LITTLE MORE THAN THE RENAMED RAVAGED CONTINUATION OF MOBUTU'S ZAIRE. IN JULY AND OCTOBER 2006 THE DRC HELD ITS FIRST ELECTIONS IN 45 YEARS—DECLARED BY THE UNITED NATIONS, WHO SUPERVISED THIS LANDMARK EVENT, AS ITS LARGEST AND MOST COMPLEX TASK TO DATE. ALTHOUGH VIOLENCE MARRED THE PROCEEDINGS THERE IS HOPE THAT IT MIGHT LEAD TO GREATER STABILITY IN THE LONG RUN.

COUNTRY PROFILE

The Democratic Republic of Congo—commonly referred to as Congo Kinshasa to prevent confusion with the neighboring Republic of Congo or Congo Brazzaville—is Africa's third largest country after Sudan and Algeria. The entire Congo Basin is well watered and dense rainforests extend along the Congo River and its tributaries. The eastern border is fringed with mountains overlooking a series of lakes including Albert, Edward, Kivu and Tanganyika. Roughly 80% of the country's inhabitants speak Bantu languages, ranging from the predominant Kongo to the Mongo, the Tumba and Lulua. The remainder, concentrated along the northern border, belong to the Adamawan Ubangian and Sudanic linguistic families. Kiswahili is widely spoken in the eastern parts of the country and in Shaba. More than 75% of the population adhere to Christianity.

HISTORY

Some 3,000 years ago the original hunter-gatherer Pygmies in the Congo Basin were joined by land-tilling Bantu speaking peoples from the north and northeast. Building on the ex-

plorations of American journalist Henry Morton Stanley in the 1870s, Belgian King Leopold I assembled an international consortium of bankers to exploit the Congo's natural resources. At the Berlin Conference of 1884-1885 the European powers recognized Leopold's claim to this vast region. Following widespread public concern over inhumane labor practices in the Congo, the Belgian government took over the administration

218

of the territory in 1908. In 1960, when Belgium granted independence to an ill-prepared colony, a power struggle ensued, fueled in part by the big powers. Brief appearances by Joseph Kasavubu, Moise Tshombe and Patrice Lumumba was followed by Col. Joseph- Desiré Mobutu who exercised autocratic rule over Zaire, as he called the country, for more than three decades. An ailing Mobutu was ousted by Laurent Desiré Kabila and his Alliance of Democratic Forces for the Liberation of Congo-Zaire (ADFL) in 1997 with the support of the Rwandan and Ugandan governments. Kabila renamed Zaire the Democratic Republic of Congo (DRC) but little changed. A new insurrection by disillusioned former compatriots in the northeast, backed by Rwanda and Uganda, prompted Angolan, Namibian and Zimbabwean troops to come to Kabila's aid. In January 2001, Joseph Kabila became president after his father's assassination by a disgruntled bodyguard. In July 2003, under outside pressure, Kabila swore in as vice presidents in his cabinet Jean-Pierre Bemba of the Uganda-backed Congolese Liberation Movement and Azarias Ruberwa of the Rwanda-allied Congolese Rally for Democracy as well as Abdoulaye Yeroda Nbombasi, allied to Kabila, and Arthur Z'Ahidi Ngoma, a member of the country's unarmed political opposition. In the 2006 election—lasting from July until November—held under UN auspices with tight security, Kabila emerged the victor over Bemba. Despite threats from Bemba supporters to take to the streets the election is seen as an important step toward ending a conflict which has cost 4 million lives through fighting and attendant hunger and disease—the most lethal since World War II.

GOVERNMENT

Neither Kabila's *Parti du peuple pour la reconstruction et la démocratie* (PPRD) with its 111 seats nor former Vice-President Jean-Pierre Bemba's *Mouvement pour la libération du Congo* (MLC) party with its 64 seats managed to win an outright majority in the 500 seat legislature. A coalition is expected to be formed.

ECONOMIC POLICY

The government has reopened relations with international financial institutions. Implementing reforms and a measure of transparency and economic stability were accomplished. Cited as priorities are the revitalization of the mining, agricultural and transport sectors in terms of a multi-billion recovery plan.

FAST FACTS

Pres. Joseph Kabila
Born: 1972
Since 2001

UN/DPI

POLITICAL

Head of State	Pres. Joseph Kabila
Major parties	PPRD & MLC
Independence	30 June 1960
National capital	Kinshasa
Official language	French

PHYSICAL

Total area	905,568 sq. miles 2,345,410 sq. km. (¼ of US)
Arable land	3%
Coastline	23 miles/37 km

POPULATION

Total	62.7 million
Av. yearly growth	3.07%
Population/sq. mile	57
Urban population	18.4 million
Adult literacy	65.5%

ECONOMY

Currency	Congolese franc (US$1=464)
GDP (real)	$7.32 billion
GDP growth rate	6.5%
GDP per capita[1]	$120
GDP (ppp)[2]	$40.67 billion
GDP per cap. (ppp)	$700
Inflation rate	9%
Exports	$1.1 billion
Imports	$1.3 billion
External debt	$10.6 billion
Unemployment	N/A

1. *Atlas method.*
2. *See page 175 for an explanation of purchasing power parity (ppp).*

219

SECTORS

Arable land is plentiful and inland waters contain abundant supplies of fish. DRC was the world's largest producer of cobalt, the second largest of industrial diamonds and the fourth largest of copper. Diamonds are largely retrieved from alluvial and kimberlite deposits. Crude oil production is small compared to other Sub-Saharan African oil producers, but output from its small offshore fields remained steady during the 1990s and continues to serve as a reliable source of revenues. Due to extensive smuggling gold production is estimated to be much higher than quantities reflected in official statistics. The country has a hydroelectric potential of 100,000 megawatts (MW) or 13% of the world's total. Manufacturing is concentrated in Kinshasa and the mining centers of Shaba and ranges from brewing, food processing and textiles to vehicle assembly.

PRIVATIZATION

At the peak of the Mobutu-driven nationalization more than 140 enterprises belonged to the state. Since then, several were liquidated, privatized, or replaced by new ones. Today there are 116 of which 56 are fully publicly owned and 60 with mixed ownership.

INVESTMENT

In recent years, foreign investments were mostly concentrated in transportation, chemical products and pharmaceuticals, wood, food processing, mining, and services. The largest US investment is in oil with ChevronTexaco in the lead. Belgian-owned firms are prominent as minority owners in several major parastatal firms. Lebanese, Chinese, South Asian and South African business enterprises have a growing economic influence and French interest is reviving. The diamond industry is controlled by the state-owned Societe Miniere de Bakwanga (Miba), which markets its diamonds through Sediza, a subsidiary of the international De Beers Central Selling Organization.

TRADE

Copper, cobalt, coffee, petroleum, and diamonds account for most of the country's foreign exchange earnings. In the mid-1990s diamonds contributed nearly half of export earnings while copper and cobalt contributed 20%. The US (22%) is, after the Benelux countries (43%), the biggest buyer of Congolese products. As a supplier to the DRC the US ranks 7th behind South Africa, Belgium, France, Zambia, Kenya and Germany.

FINANCIAL SECTOR

The banking system comprises the central bank, twelve commercial banks and a development bank—the Société Financière de developpement (SOFIDE). There are five other financial intermediaries, a postal checking system and 19 credit cooperatives. Most commercial banks maintain correspondent arrangements with banks operating in the US.

TAXES AND TARIFFS

Corporate tax is 40% of income, capital gains and branch profits. Foreign investments valued between $200,000 and $10 million (local currency equivalent) receive extensive tax concessions on profits and dividends.

FOREIGN PRESENCE

Over the years the country's size, population, economic potential, resources and location have made it attractive to Western business, apart from official strategic considerations during the Cold War. Many foreign firms that withdrew amidst civil disorder and an economic downturn are returning.

BUSINESS ACTIVITY

AGRICULTURE
Coffee, sugar, palm oil, rubber, tea, quinine, cassava, bananas, root crops, corn, fruit, wood products.

INDUSTRIES
Mining, mineral processing, consumer products, cement, diamonds.

NATURAL RESOURCES
Copper, cobalt, cadmium, petroleum, industrial and gem diamonds, gold, silver, zinc, manganese, tin, germanium, uranium, radium, bauxite, iron ore, coal, hydropower potential, timber.

EXPORTS
$1.1 billion (est. 2005): diamonds, copper, coffee, cobalt, crude oil.

IMPORTS
$1.3 billion (est. 2005): foodstuffs, mining and other machinery, transport equipment, fuel.

MAJOR TRADING PARTNERS
Belgium, US, South Africa, France, Chile, Japan, China, Finland, Zambia, Kenya.

Doing Business with the DRC

INVESTMENT

With the exception of the minerals extraction sector, the government neither requires nor seeks participation in foreign investments. There is minimal screening of foreign investment. A bilateral investment treaty (BIT) has been in place with the US since 1989, guaranteeing reciprocal rights and privileges to each country's investors. A *Zone Franche d'Inga* (ZOFI) was established to attract potential investors, especially heavy industry users of energy.

TRADE

Export opportunities exist in used clothing, telecommunications and computer equipment, refrigeration and air conditioning equipment, electrical generators and distribution equipment, pharmaceuticals, aircraft and related equipment, cosmetics, four-wheel drive passenger vehicles, commercial trucks, mining, construction, agricultural, and forestry equipment, and food products such as rice, wheat, dried milk products, processed tomato products, canned meat and fish, and poultry. Trained professionals without regular employment offer a range of services from the complex to the mundane, including translating and interpreting, setting up appointments with key officials, following-up with local businesses, arranging accommodation and transportation, and facilitating passage through DROC's notoriously slow airports.

TRADE FINANCE

Although hard-currency accounts are available at commercial banks, most businesses avoid them because of high maintenance costs. International transfers and transfers between various regions of the country are frequently done by direct agreement between businesses. Local banks sometimes serve as matchmakers.

SELLING TO THE GOVERNMENT

Due to political unrest and a drop in revenues, government procurement is currently in a state of flux.

EXCHANGE CONTROL

The transfer of dividends and other funds associated with investments is allowed but licenses are required for all transactions in foreign exchange, including import payments.

ESTABLISHING A PRESENCE

A branch office or sales subsidiary may be a useful method of representation where a large ongoing market exists or frequent contacts are required. Sometimes exporters rely on a group of firms selling complementary items by establishing a jointly owned sales subsidiary. There are five possibilities: *Société Privée à Responsibilité Limitée* (SPRL)— a limited liability company that combines the character of a partnership and a corporation; *Société Privée à Responsabilité Limitée* (SARL) — a joint stock company; *Société Cooperative* (SC)— where each member has a single vote; *Société en Nom Collectif* (SNC)—a simple partnership; and the *Société en Commandité Simple* (SCS)—a limited partnership.

FINANCING PROJECTS

DROC is a member of the World Bank's Multilateral Investment Guarantee Agency, which offers insurance to new foreign investments against foreign exchange risk, expropriation and civil unrest.

LABOR

Even though a large urban population provides a ready pool of available labor—some with high school and university education—skilled industrial labor is in short supply. Minimum wages are set on a regional basis by the government for all workers in private enterprise. Strict labor laws can make termination of employees difficult. Outside the major cities, large companies often become involved in providing infrastructure including roads, schools, and hospitals. As foreign undertakings mature, the government expects the number of expatriates employed to diminish.

LEGAL RIGHTS

Although arbitrary seizure of property was a problem during the early months of the Kabila regime, the government has brought the practice under control in recent months. DROC is a member of the World Intellectual Property Organization and the Paris Convention for the Protection of Industrial Property. However, enforcement of IPR regulations has been lax due to bureaucratic disarray. The complexities of DROC law make the hiring of local legal professionals necessary.

BUSINESS CLIMATE

French is the business language and little English is spoken. European traditions of social etiquette apply. A suit or coat and tie (for men) and a business suit (for women) are appropriate for business appointments or meetings with officials.

# CONGO, REP. OF

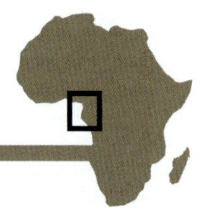

THE REPUBLIC OF CONGO OR CONGO (BRAZZAVILLE) IS SUB-SAHARAN AFRICA'S FOURTH LARGEST OIL PRODUCER (AFTER NIGERIA, ANGOLA, AND GABON). MOST OF ITS REMAINING ESTIMATED PROVEN RESERVES OF 1.5 BILLION BARRELS IS OFFSHORE, MAKING IT HEAVILY DEPENDENT ON FOREIGN EXPERTISE AND TECHNOLOGY. FOREIGN COMPANIES ARE HEAVILY ENGAGED IN THE EXPLORATION AND PRODUCTION OF OIL AND GAS AND AS SUPPLIERS OF EQUIPMENT AND MACHINERY. ETHNIC RIVALRY AND POLITICAL UNREST HAS NOT DISRUPTED THIS VITAL SECTOR BUT PROMPTED POTENTIAL INVESTORS IN OTHER SECTORS TO PUT THEIR PLANS ON HOLD.

COUNTRY PROFILE

The Republic of Congo (commonly referred to as Congo Brazzaville to distinguish it from the Democratic Republic of Congo or Congo Kinshasa) lies within the catchment areas of the Congo and Ubangi rivers. The climate is tropical. The population is Bantu-speaking with the Kongo, Teke and Mboshi forming 85% of the total. About 45% are Christians.

HISTORY

Some 600 years ago when the Bantu-speaking people moved into the region it was inhabited by Pygmies. Towards the end of the 15th Century Portuguese merchant mariners established relations with the Kongo kingdom at the mouth of the Congo river and conducted slave trade until it was abolished in the 19th Century. French colonization began in the late 19th Century when Count Savorgnan de Brazza signed a treaty with the chief of the Batekes, Makoko. In 1910 Congo became part of French Equatorial Africa and in 1960 gained its independence under Pres. Fulbert Youlou. After several coups Col. Denis Sassou-Nguesso took control in 1979 and established a one-party regime. In 1993, Pascal Lissouba won the presidency but his party failed to obtain an absolute majority. A four month civil war erupted which led to the large-scale destruction of Brazzaville. In 1997 Lissouba's fragile coalition government came to an end when Sassou-Nguesso took control with the help of Angolan forces. At the end of 1999 a peace agreement was signed between Sassou-Nguesso, from the north, and the rebels representing the populous south. Continuing conflict led to another peace accord in March 2003. In 2002 Nguesso, backed by the Democratic and Patriotic Forces (FDP), was reaffirmed as president for a seven year term by an overwhelming majority.

© Business Books Intl.

CENTRAL AFRICAN REP.

CAMEROON

EQ. GUINEA

Souanke
Dja
Ngabala
Sembe
Lioesso
Ouesso
Dongou
Implondo
Epena
Ubangi
2°N
Sangha
Kandeko
Likouala aux Herbes

Equator

Likouala
Kelle
Makoua
Owando
Kouyou
Ewo
Oyo
GABON
Gamboma
Mossaka
Congo
2°S

Mbinda
Bambama
Ngo
Mpouya
Banda
Djambala
Zanaga
Mpe
Ngabe
DEM. REP. OF CONGO
Kibango
Sibiti
Odziba
4°S

Mayombe Mts.
Nzambi
Madingo-Kayes
Loango
Pointe Noire
Madingou
Loubomo
Mindouli
Boko
BRAZZAVILLE

Rail
Roads

0 50 100 150 200 250 300 km

ATLANTIC OCEAN

2°E   14°E   16°E   18°E

GOVERNMENT

The present constitution, adopted after a referendum held in March 1992, provides for Parliament with two chambers—a 137-member Assemblée Nationale (National Assembly) elected for five years and a 66-member Sénat (Senate), also serving five year terms. In the June 2002 election the alliance Democratic and Patriotic Forces (FDP) won outright control of the Assembly with 83 seats. The FDP also have a plurality in the Senate after winning 56 seats in the July 2002 election.

ECONOMIC POLICY

Economic reforms have been undertaken with the support of the World Bank, IMF and other international organizations. Pres. Sassou-Nguesso has publicly expressed his intentions to move ahead with further reforms and to implement privatization. Progress was, however, slowed by the resumption of armed conflict in December 1998. The most recent peace agreement has kindled new hope.

SECTORS

The economy presents a mixture of village agriculture and handicrafts, an industrial sector based largely on oil, support services, and a government characterized by budget problems and overstaffing. The main food crops are maize, cassava, rice and yams; the main cash crops are cocoa, coffee, sugar and palm oil. With its more than 90 bridges and 12 tunnels, the over 500 km stretch of Congo-Ocean Railway, built in the colonial era, is not only an engineering feat but provides a vital link in the transport system of equatorial Africa. The railway starts at Pointe Noire with its modern deep-water harbor, opened in 1939 and still regarded as one of the best equipped in Africa. After Nigeria and Cameroon, Congo is the third largest gas resource base in Sub-Saharan Africa. Pointe Noire, Congo's economic and petroleum capital, has not been directly affected by the insecurity elsewhere in the country.

PRIVATIZATION

In April 1998, the Congolese government established a new national petroleum company, the Société Nationale des Pétroles du Congo (SNPC), to market Congo's crude oil and to assume all upstream functions of the former state-owned company, Hydro-Congo. Privatization of Hydro-Congo's downstream operations has been underway since 1997 with Elf and Shell as major participants. Prior to the 1997 civil war, Congo's

FAST FACTS

Pres. Denis Sassou-
Nguesso
Born: 1943
Since 1997

POLITICAL

Head State	Pres. Denis Sassou-Nguesso
Ruling coalition	FDP
Independence	15 August 1960
National capital	Brazzaville
Official language	French

PHYSICAL

Total area	132,046 sq. miles
	342,000 sq. km.
	(± Montana)
Arable land	0.5%
Coastline	105 miles/169 km

POPULATION

Total	3.7 million
Av. yearly growth	2.6%
Population/sq. mile	21
Urban population	2.1 million
Adult literacy	53.8%

ECONOMY

Currency	CFA franc (CFAF)(US$1: 559.44)
GDP (real)	$4.69 billion
GDP growth rate	8%
GDP per capita[1]	$1,465
GDP (ppp)[2]	$4.63 billion
GDP per cap. (ppp)	$1,300
Inflation rate	2.2%
Exports	$2.2 billion
Imports	$806.5 million
External debt	$5 billion
Unemployment	N/A

1. *Atlas method.*
2. *See page 175 for an explanation of purchasing power parity (ppp).*

national utility, Société Nationale d'Electricité (SNE), was one of the several government entities considered for privatization.

INVESTMENT

Elf Aquitaine (Elf) holds a dominant position in exploration, production, and refining with Italy's ENI-Agip playing an important secondary role. US firms engaged in offshore exploration and production include ChevronTexaco, CMS/Nomeco, and ExxonMobil.

TRADE

Oil accounts for 70% of the Congolese government's revenue and 85% of Congo's exports. It is the 15th largest supplier of crude to the United States.

TAXES AND TARIFFS

Corporate income tax and capital gains are taxed at 45%. A 20% tax is levied on dividends. Import duties range from 15% on primary and capital goods to 50% on some consumer goods.

BUSINESS ACTIVITY

AGRICULTURE
Cassava, sugar, rice, corn, peanuts, vegetables, coffee, cocoa, forest products.

INDUSTRIES
Petroleum extraction, cement, lumbering, brewing, sugar milling, palm oil, soap, cigarettes.

NATURAL RESOURCES
Petroleum, timber, potash, lead, zinc, uranium, copper, phosphates, natural gas.

EXPORTS
$2.2 billion (est. 2005): petroleum products, lumber, plywood, sugar, cocoa, coffee, diamonds.

IMPORTS
$806.5 million (2005): capital equipment, construction materials, foodstuffs.

MAJOR TRADING PARTNERS
China, US, Belgium, Italy, France, Germany, Netherlands, Taiwan.

DOING BUSINESS WITH THE CONGO

▶ INVESTMENT

The success of deepwater exploration off the coast of the Congo and neighboring Cabinda (Angola) has sparked renewed interest in these areas. Hydrocarbon legislation enacted in 1994 offers production-sharing agreements (PSAs) to foreign oil companies in partnership with the national oil company, SNPC. Contractors finance all investment and recover their expenditure when the production begins. In 1995, foreign companies were given the option of converting existing exploration and production joint venture contracts to PSAs and since then all major operators in Congo have signed up. Other sectors of interest to foreign investors are forestry, mining, agriculture, pharmaceuticals, and construction.

▶ TRADE

Major imports by Congo include heavy machinery, vehicles, business equipment, clothing, pharmaceuticals, consumer goods, and foodstuffs. US exports are inhibited in part by high transport costs, a cumbersome local bureaucracy, and lack of established networks between US and Congolese traders. The French, with extensive local knowledge and an on-the-ground presence have the edge.

▶ EXCHANGE CONTROLS

As a member of the franc zone, the Congo shares the BEAC as a central bank with neighboring central African states.

▶ ESTABLISHING A PRESENCE

A center for business enterprises (known by its French acronym, CFE) assists foreigners who wish to establish themselves in the Congo.

▶ FINANCING PROJECTS

The International Finance Corporation was a major lender to the N'Kossa offshore project. Most of the financing for projects in the growing oil and gas sector is, however, arranged by the major oil companies themselves.

▶ LABOR

A new labor code aims at making the country more investor-friendly.

▶ BUSINESS CLIMATE

Conducting business in the Congo requires a knowledge of French. Business customs conform to the European model as a result of years of French influence in the region.

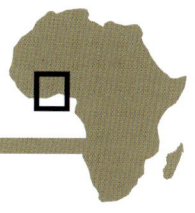

CÔTE D'IVOIRE

COCOA EXPORTS COUPLED WITH AMPLE FOREIGN INVESTMENT AND CLOSE TIES TO FRANCE HELPED CÔTE D'IVOIRE BECOME ONE OF THE MOST PROSPEROUS NATIONS IN THE WEST AFRICAN REGION. CÔTE D'IVOIRE IS NOT ONLY THE WORLD'S LARGEST PRODUCER OF COCOA. IT IS ALSO A SIGNIFICANT EXPORTER OF COFFEE, FOREST PRODUCTS, COTTON, RUBBER, BANANAS, PINEAPPLES, AND PALM OIL. A RELATIVELY WELL-DEVELOPED INFRASTRUCTURE AND A SOPHISTICATED FINANCIAL SECTOR HAVE PROMPTED SEVERAL FOREIGN FIRMS TO ESTABLISH THEIR REGIONAL HEADQUARTERS IN CÔTE D'IVOIRE. RECENT POLITICAL TURMOIL HAS, HOWEVER, IMPACTED NEGATIVELY ON THE COUNTRY.

COUNTRY PROFILE

The Republic of Côte d'Ivoire forms a low plateau less than 500 m. above sea level, bordered in the west by the Nimba mountains stretching northwards to the confluence of the Sassandra, the Red and the White Bandama, and the Komoe rivers. Rainfall along the coast averages 2,000 mm. per year and gradually decreases northward, to around 1,000 mm. The Baoule dominates with 23% of the total population, followed by the Bete (18%), the Senoufou (15%), and Malinke (11%). The country has an immigrant and expatriate population of over 2 million. More than 120,000 Lebanese are mostly engaged in business and French expatriates number around 50,000. French is the official language. About 38% of the population are Muslim, especially in the north, and 28% Christian, mainly in the southeast.

HISTORY

First settled by the Kru and subsequently the Mande-speaking people (including the Muslim Malinke) and the Kwa, Côte d'Ivoire came into French orbit in the 1840s. Forts were built along the coast to facilitate ivory and slave trade. The colony of Côte d'Ivoire was established in 1893 and French colonists, encouraged by the colonial government, began with cocoa and coffee cultivation on large estates with the help of forced labor. In the 1930s a Baoulé medical officer, Félix Houphouet Boigny, took up the cause of black farmers. The name Boigny, which was added to signify "irresistible force," proved prophetic. In 1960 Houphouet Boigny became the executive President of newly independent Côte d'Ivoire and for the next 30 years exercised one party rule. In the country's first free elections in 1990 he was reelected by a margin of 82%. Houphouet Boigny died on 7 December 1993, at the age of 88 and was succeeded by the speaker of the National Assembly, Henri Konan Bédié. On 24 December 1999, Bédié and his elected government were deposed in

FAST FACTS

Pres. Laurent Gbagbo
Born: May 31, 1945
Since 2000

POLITICAL

Head of State	Pres. Laurent Gbagbo
Ruling Party	FPI
Main opposition	PDCI-RDA
Independence	7 August 1960
National capital	Yamoussoukro[3]
Official language	French

PHYSICAL

Total area	124,502 sq. miles
	322,460 sq. km.
	(± New Mexico)
Arable land	9%
Coastline	320 miles/515 km

POPULATION

Total	17.65 million
Av. yearly growth	2.03%
Population/sq. mile	128
Urban population	7.9 million
Adult literacy	50.9%

ECONOMY

Currency	CFA franc
	(CFAF)(US$1=559.44)
GDP (real)	$16.57 billion
GDP growth rate	-1%
GDP per capita[1]	$891
GDP (ppp)[2]	$28.52 billion
GDP per cap. (ppp)	$1,600
Inflation rate	3.9%
Exports	$6.49 billion
Imports	$4.76 billion
External debt	$11.81 billion
Unemployment	13%

1. Atlas method.
2. See page 175 for an explanation of purchasing power parity (ppp).
3. Abidjan is the administrative capital.

a military coup led by former army chief of staff General Robert Guei who promised to stay in power only "to sweep the house clean." Instead he decided to run for president in the October 2000 elections. After declaring himself the winner in what was considered to be a rigged race, Guei was forced by public outcry to step down in favor of his main rival, Laurent Gbagbo. A failed coup split Côte d'Ivoire between a rebel-held north and government-controlled south in September 2002. Since then a number of militia groups have sprung up in the south, claiming to have taken up arms to defend their towns and villages against the rebel forces. By October 2006 more than 750,000 people have been displaced by the conflict, many in need of humanitarian assistance. President Gbagbo has been critical of UN mediation efforts and the inability of the 8,000-strong UN peace-keeping mission (UNOCI) and 2,000 French troops to disarm the combatants. Elections scheduled for October 2006 are likely to be postponed.

GOVERNMENT

The constitution provides for an executive president elected by popular vote for a 5-year term. He appoints a Prime Minister, who in turn selects the Council of Ministers. The 225-member Assemblée Nationale is also elected for 5 years. In December 2002 Gbagbo's Front Populaire Ivorienne (FPI) narrowly defeated the Parti Démocratique de la Côte d'Ivoire (PDCI-RDA) by gaining 96 seats against 94. The Rassemblement des républicains (RDR) boycotted the election.

ECONOMIC POLICY

From the outset Pres. Houphouet-Boigny's government followed conservative and pragmatic pro-Western policies, with emphasis on economic growth rather than wealth redistribution. During the first 20 years following independence the economy grew at an average annual rate of 7.5%. A severe drop in the price of cocoa and coffee in the eighties saddled the country with a large external debt and prompted it to take steps to diversify the economy. The government's strategy has four goals: export diversification, encouraging crops other than coffee and cocoa; encouraging extractive industries; and reinforcement of the services sector.

SECTORS

More than 33% of the GDP activity is in agriculture, forestry or fishing. Côte d'Ivoire is the world's leading exporter of cocoa and a significant producer of cotton, coffee, sugar and rubber. In recent years there has been considerable expansion into the cultivation and export of mangoes, cashews, flowers and silk. New mining and petroleum codes were enacted in the mid-nineties to encourage foreign exploration of gold and nickel and offshore oil production. Mining plays a small role in the economy but oil has been extracted from offshore fields since the late 1970s. The country has considerable largely unexploited iron ore, bauxite and manganese deposits. Manufacturing revolves mostly around the processing of agricultural, forestry and petroleum products, and textiles, chemicals and import substitution. Tropical weather and a well-developed infrastructure make tourism a promising sector.

PRIVATIZATION

Most of the 60 state-owned enterprises earmarked in an ambitious privatization program in the early nineties have been privatized. Projects include restructuring of the telecommunications company, a vegetable-oil producer, the country's leading hotel, an electricity company, the state oil refinery and the national airline.

INVESTMENT

Foreign firms have focused largely on mining and oil exploration. Contracts have been concluded with Canadian, Australian and South African mining houses, focusing largely on gold and, in one instance, nickel. Offshore oil and gas exploration and production drew interest from US, Canadian and European firms. France, however, continues to be the most important foreign investor, accounting for more than half of the total. Attracted by Côte d'Ivoire's track record of political stability until 1999, its liberal investment code, and convertible currency, some 50 US companies have invested about $1 billion. Following the liberalization of cocoa and coffee exports, US-based Cargill and other commodity trading multinationals have invested in both local processing and the export of raw cocoa beans.

TRADE

Côte d'Ivoire is the world's leading exporter of cocoa beans, contributing over 30% of the world's output. It ranks third in Africa in the export of coffee beans, after Ethiopia and Uganda, and is the leading sugar cane producer in West Africa. The country competes with Mali and Nigeria for first place in West Africa as producer of cotton lint

and with Nigeria as a supplier of tobacco leaves. Rice and meat are imported despite significant local production. Imports—primarily from France, Nigeria, the US, Ghana, and Germany—range from industrial inputs to transportation equipment, food and beverages, fuel and lubricants to consumer goods.

FINANCIAL SECTOR

Côte d'Ivoire is a member of the Communauté Financière Africaine (CFA), a financial grouping of Francophone African countries and belongs to the Union Economique et Monétaire de l'Afrique de l'Ouest (UEMOA). The BCEAO, located in Dakar, is the central bank for UEMOA members and the French Treasury guarantees convertibility of its currency. There are 15 commercial banks, regional stock exchange, and over 30 insurance companies. The African Development Bank is headquartered in Abidjan.

TAXES AND TARIFFS

Corporate, capital gains and branch tax rates are 35%. There are several exempt categories for companies developing industrial or agricultural enterprises. The value added tax rate was reduced to 20% from 25% and the weighted average duty rate has been reduced from 43% to 33%.

BUSINESS ACTIVITY

AGRICULTURE
Coffee, cocoa beans, bananas, palm kernels, corn, rice, manioc, sweet potatoes, sugar, cotton, rubber, timber.

INDUSTRIES
Foodstuffs, beverages, wood products, oil refining, automobile assembly, textiles, fertilizer, construction materials, electricity.

NATURAL RESOURCES
Petroleum, diamonds, manganese, iron ore, cobalt, bauxite, copper.

EXPORTS
$5.12 billion (est. 2005): cocoa, coffee, tropical woods, petroleum, cotton, bananas, pineapples, palm oil, fish.

IMPORTS
$4.76 billion (est. 2005): food, consumer and capital goods, fuel, transport equipment.

MAJOR TRADING PARTNERS
France, Netherlands, US, Italy, Nigeria, Singapore, Panama.

Doing Business with Côte d'Ivoire

▶ Investment

Investors who establish themselves in regions outside Abidjan are entitled to an 8-year tax exemption instead of 5 years. Companies seeking priority enterprise status, eligible for these tax holidays and other benefits, might be required to purchase Ivorian products. The *Centre de Promotion des Investissements en Côte d'Ivoire* (CEPICI) serves as a "one-stop-shop" for foreign investors, helping them to find suitable opportunities and serving as a link with the public sector. Investments from outside the Franc Zone must be approved by the external finance and credit office of the Ministry of Economy and Finance. Apart from privatization and the relaxation of state monopolies, a variety of opportunities exists in projects such as waste water and solid waste collection networks in regional cities, the connection of the Mali-Côte d'Ivoire and the Guinea-Côte d'Ivoire electrical grids, and the Abidjan-Ghana expressway, many on a BOT (Build-Own-Transfer) basis.

▶ Trade

Opportunities exist in high value food products, paper products, telecommunications, computers and software, consumer electronics and agricultural, irrigation, mining, construction, air-conditioning, refrigeration, medical, security, and power generation equipment, as well as textile, forestry and woodworking machinery, and cosmetics, toiletries, pharmaceutical and health care products. In the past 5 years, several oil and gas projects have come into production creating a need for field equipment.

▶ Trade finance

Eximbank financing is available. Competitive credit terms are important considerations in purchasing decisions.

▶ Selling to the government

The Ivorian Government periodically issues procurement tenders in local newspapers and sometimes in international media. The *Bureau National d'Etudes Techniques et de Developpement* (BNETD) usually acts on behalf of other ministries in projects financed by the World Bank and the African Development Bank.

▶ Exchange controls

By law all exchange transactions relating to foreign countries must be handled by authorized banks. Foreign exchange for import payments must be purchased either on the date of settlement specified in the commercial contract or at the time the required down payment is made. French Franc-based transactions are the easiest and more common.

▶ Partnerships

Many foreign firms rely on local partners or agents. An increasing number of Ivorians who trained abroad are available as partners.

▶ Establishing a presence

The CEPICI assists foreign firms with formalities such as registration, incorporation, and the modification or dissolution of a local entity. The four most common forms of business are *Association et Participation* (Joint Venture); *Succursale* (Foreign Branch), a *Société à Responsabilité Limitée* (Limited Liability Company); and *Société Anonyme* (Stock Corporation).

▶ Financing projects

The Overseas Private Investment Corporation offers loans, loan guarantees and insurance products to US investors. The US Trade and Development Agency finances feasibility studies and the World Bank and the African Development Bank support government procurement. Côte d'Ivoire is a member of the Multilateral Investment Guarantee Agency.

▶ Labor

Unskilled labor is readily available but clerical, technical, managerial, and professional talent is more difficult to find. Wage rates are relatively high by regional standards.

▶ Legal rights

A new arbitration tribunal has been established under the auspices of the Chamber of Commerce. Côte d'Ivoire is a member of the international center for the settlement of investment disputes (ICSID) and a party to the Paris Convention and the African Intellectual Property Organization (OAPI), which recently adopted revisions to conform to the WTO agreement on trade-related intellectual property issues (TRIPS).

▶ Business climate

Business customs in Côte d'Ivoire are decidedly European. French is the official language and prevalent in business. Academic titles and degrees are frequently used by members of the expatriate community or those who received their schooling abroad.

DJIBOUTI

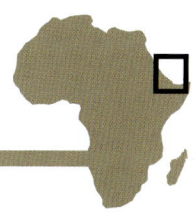

As one of the smallest countries on the African continent and with limited natural resources, Djibouti is largely dependent on its service sector. Its strategic location at the mouth of the Red Sea makes it a convenient transshipment point for goods entering or leaving the East African Highlands. It provides a rail link from Djibouti harbor to Ethiopia's Addis Ababa as well as telecommunication cable connections between Northern Europe and Asia. The government is actively seeking to redress the problem of recurrent deficits by encouraging foreign involvement in mining, shipping and services. Djibouti is host to several thousand French military personnel and allows the US naval and air defense access.

COUNTRY PROFILE

The Republic of Djibouti is a small country at the juncture of the Red Sea and the Gulf of Aden, slightly larger than Swaziland and The Gambia. It consists mainly of a volcanic rock-strewn desert interrupted by patches of arable land, salt lakes and pans, and has high temperatures, high humidity and a low annual rainfall. Its population consists largely of the Issa Somali clan. There is also a strong Afar minority. Both groups are Muslim Cushitic-speaking peoples with a traditionally nomadic lifestyle. The small but influential Arab element comes mainly from Yemen and the expatriate community is mostly French, some of them refugees from Somalia. More than two thirds of the population live in the port city of Djibouti.

HISTORY

Around the 3rd Century B.C. Arabs migrated to what is today Djibouti. Their descendants, the Afars or Danakil people, were joined a century later by the Issas who migrated from southern Ethiopia. Both the Afar and the Issa were nomadic livestock herders who spoke related Cushitic languages and adopted the Muslim faith. Portuguese and Turkish slave traders in the region were eventually followed by the French, British and Italians who competed for control of the sea route through the Red Sea and the Suez Canal. The French prevailed. From 1888, they developed the port of Djibouti on the southern side of the Gulf of Aden and in 1917 connected it by means of a 480 mile (780 km) railway to Addis Ababa in Ethiopia. In 1958 the Afar voted to remain a self-governing part of France in a referendum boycotted by most of the Issas. The same happened in 1967 when the French Territory of the Afars and Issas was granted responsible self-government and renamed French Somaliland. The quest for national unity was, however, stimulated by the territorial claims made on the territory by the independent Somali Republic to the south. In a third referendum in March 1977,

FAST FACTS

Pres. Ismail Omar
Guelleh
Born: 1947
Since 1999

POLITICAL

Head of State	Pres. Ismail Omar Guelleh
Ruling Party	UMP Coalition
Main opposition	FRUD
Independence	27 June 1977
National capital	Djibouti
Official language	French & Arabic

PHYSICAL

Total area	8,494 sq. miles
	22,000 sq. km.
	(± Massachussetts)
Arable land	0.04%
Coastline	314 km

POPULATION

Total	703,000
Av. yearly growth	2.02%
Population/sq. mile	51
Urban population	600,000
Adult literacy	67.9%

ECONOMY

Currency	Djiboutian franc (DF) (US$1=173.68)
GDP (real)	$625 million
GDP growth rate	3.5%
GDP per capita[1]	$883
GDP (ppp)[2]	$619 million
GDP per cap. (ppp)	$1,300
Inflation rate	2%
Exports	$250 million
Imports	$987 million
External debt	$366 million
Unemployment	50%

1. Atlas method.
2. See page 175 for an explanation of purchasing power parity (ppp).

the electorate voted overwhelmingly in favor of independence. A senior Issa politician, Hassan Gouled Aptidon, became executive president of the Republic of Djibouti, a single party state. In September 1992 the voters adopted a multiparty constitution and in April 1999 Aptidon finally stepped aside opening the door for Ismail Omar Guelleh to be elected president. He was reelected in April 2005, unopposed.

GOVERNMENT

The 1992 Constitution provides for a president elected for a maximum of two 6-year terms. It is customary for the prime minister to be appointed from the Afar minority. The National Assembly has 33 seats assigned for Issa and 32 for the Afar. In the January 2003 a three party coalition in support of the president, the Union pour la Majorité Présidentielle (UMP), captured all 65 seats.

ECONOMIC POLICY

Djibouti's economy has been weakened by battles against Afar rebels during the 1990s. In March 2000 they signed a peace accord with the new government. In October 1995 the entire country was declared a free export zone to encourage foreign involvement.

SECTORS

With few natural resources and little industry, Djibouti is largely dependent on foreign assistance to finance development and buttress its balance of payments. The agricultural sector in Djibouti contributes only 3.5% of the GDP but employs an estimated 75% of the people. The service sector constitutes 76.0% of GDP. Djibouti serves as both a transit port for the region and an international transshipment and refueling center. The Djibouti port facility and the railroad that links it to Addis Ababa account for most of the economic activity. The port, the heart of the country's economy, is well equipped. Its container facilities have been greatly expanded but are increasingly being challenged by improved facilities at Saudi Arabia's Jeddah harbor and Ethiopia's Assab port. The country will soon host a state-of-the-art submarine cable link running from Northern Europe to East Asia. At least ten international airlines use the airport at Djibouti as a stopover. An oil refinery was built in 1990. A small fishing industry is being developed. Surveys have indicated the presence of a few minerals such as copper, gypsum and sulfur, but as yet none of them are mined commercially.

Manufacturing is limited to small-scale concerns. The principal source of energy is thermal plants. An expatriate community contributes significantly economically.

PRIVATIZATION

Recent attempts at privatization of state enterprises have met with some response from potential investors.

INVESTMENT

Djibouti has had limited success in attracting foreign investment. Although efforts were made to reduce restrictions on foreign investors, recent warfare and harsh environmental conditions in the region have deterred investors.

TRADE

Exports consisting of cattle, refined sugar, crude organic material, fish, hides and skins, and coffee are mostly transshipments from Ethiopia. A large portion of Djibouti's imports are destined for Ethiopia, Somalia and other neighboring regions.

FINANCIAL SECTOR

A sophisticated private banking service in place. With its almost unrestricted commercial and financial sectors, Djibouti is actively courting offshore banking and insurance firms.

TAXES AND TARIFFS

The corporate income, capital gains, and branch tax rates are 20%. There is a 10% withholding tax on dividends for nonresidents. Residents are exempt from the withholding tax on dividends and interest.

BUSINESS ACTIVITY

AGRICULTURE
Fruit, vegetables, goats, sheep, camels.

INDUSTRIES
Limited to a few small-scale enterprises such as dairy products and mineral-water bottling.

NATURAL RESOURCES
Geothermal areas.

EXPORTS
$250 million (2004): hides and skins, coffee (in transit).

IMPORTS
$987 million (2004): food, beverages, transport equipment, chemicals, petroleum products.

MAJOR TRADING PARTNERS
Saudi Arabia, Ethiopia, Somalia, India, Yemen, France, Italy, China, Japan.

DOING BUSINESS WITH DJIBOUTI

▶ INVESTMENT
Shipping and other port-related activities are seen as prime candidates for investment. The country also shows potential for geothermal and solar energy production. There are small known gold deposits as well as diatomite, geothermal fluids, mineral salts, gypsum, perlite, pumice, and possibly petroleum. Oil interest focuses on the southern region and the offshore area along the Gulf of Aden. Djibouti is trying to lure offshore banking with its liberal economic regime.

▶ TRADE
Merchandise exports of local origin are insignificant and almost all food requirements and consumer goods have to be imported. Djibouti's well-equipped harbor is a transshipment point for products to and form Ethiopia by rail. It is also used by both French and US naval ships.

▶ EXCHANGE CONTROLS
The currency, the Djibouti franc, is pegged to the dollar and is freely convertible. There are no foreign exchange restrictions.

▶ LABOR
An unemployment rate of 40% to 50% continues to be a major problem. Skilled labor is, however, relatively expensive.

▶ BUSINESS CLIMATE
The business practices are Middle Eastern and the language French.

EGYPT

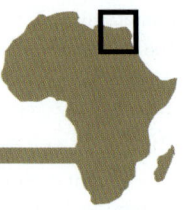

AS THE MOST POPULOUS ARAB COUNTRY, EGYPT IS BOTH AFRICAN AND MIDDLE EASTERN. SOME TEN MILLION OF EGYPT'S TOTAL POPULATION OF MORE THAN 78 MILLION HAVE DEVELOPED WESTERN CONSUMPTION PATTERNS AND EVEN AMONG THE POOR MAJORITY CONSUMER TASTE IS RAPIDLY CHANGING THUS EXPANDING THE POTENTIAL FOR IMPORTED GOODS. BECAUSE OF ITS STRATEGIC POSITION IN THE REGION, EGYPT CONTINUES TO RECEIVE STRONG DONOR SUPPORT, INCLUDING ABOUT SUBSTANTIAL US ECONOMIC AND MILITARY ASSISTANCE, A GOOD PORTION RETURNS IN ORDERS FOR AMERICAN PRODUCTS. DESPITE INFREQUENT FUNDAMENTALIST ACTS OF TERROR, EGYPT ENJOYS POLITICAL STABILITY AND ITS ECONOMY HAS MADE GREAT STRIDES INTEGRATING INTO THE GLOBAL MARKET.

COUNTRY PROFILE

The Arab Republic of Egypt is today as dependent on the river Nile as it was in the days of the pharaohs. Agriculture centers around the valley of the Nile. Even though they speak Arabic, Egyptians are not Arabs but a mixture of peoples tracing their ancestry back to the Nubians, Berbers, mixed Arab-Berber groups and Europeans. About 90% are Muslim and 6% Christian Copts, apart from Roman Catholic, Protestant and Jewish minorities.

HISTORY

Today Egypt has virtually the same borders as those that existed during the time of the pharaohs. First conquered in 332 BC by Alexander the Great it passed on to Roman control in 31 BC. In 639 Muslims from Arabia conquered Egypt and transformed it into an Arabic-speaking Muslim country. Extended Turkish rule, a brief French presence under Napoleon, and finally a British caretaker rule led to the recognition of a sovereign, independent state under King Fuad on 28 February 1922. Violent protests against continued British military presence at the Suez Canal in the

1950s led to a bloodless coup. King Farouk was replaced by Colonel Gamal Abdel Nasser who ruled until his death in 1970. He was succeeded in 1970 by his deputy, Anwar Sadat, who signed the Camp David Peace Accords in 1979 and was assassinated two years later by members of the Islamic Jihad organization. Sadat was succeeded by his deputy, General Hosni Mubarak.

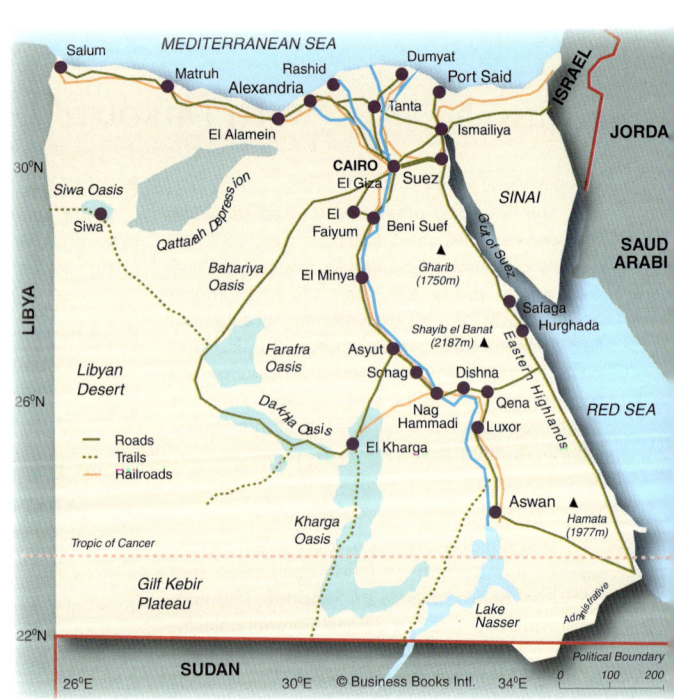

GOVERNMENT

Until 2005 the president was appointed by a two-thirds majority of the People's Assembly (Majlis al-Sha'ab) and confirmed by referendum. President Hosni Mubarak was for the first time under a new rule adopted by referendum elected by popular vote to a fifth six year term in September 2005. In the bicameral parliament all but ten nominated members of the 454-seat People's Assembly are directly elected for a five-year term while the Mailis al-Shura or Advisory Council consists of 176 elected members and 88 apointed by the president. The Hizb al Dimuqratiyah al Wataniyah (HDW) (National Democratic Party—NDP) has dominated the Assembly since its establishment in 1978. It won 311 seats in the November 2005 election against a splintered opposition including the New Wafd Partry (NWP), Tagammu and a large number of independents.

ECONOMIC POLICY

Egypt maintains a market economy with the state sector accounting for 30 percent of GDP and the private sector 70 percent. Continued decentralization has stimulated growth. Legislation has been passed to increase private sector activity and allow greater foreign participation. Privatization in key areas such as insurance, banking, and telecommunications are underway. A reduction in 2005 of personal and corporate tax rates, reduction of energy subsidies and further privatization measures by the government has led to a boom on the stock market and GDP growth of nearly 5%.

PRIVATIZATION

Since January 1996 serious steps have been taken toward selling off state-owned enterprises. The basis has been laid for expanded participation by the private sector and foreign investors in the banking and insurance sectors. Private investment in key infrastructure areas has increased significantly. All future power generation projects will be constructed on a build-own-operate-transfer (BOOT) basis. The government has sold cellular phone concessions and has opened airports, ports, and port services to private investors.

SECTORS

Tourism and the Suez Canal account for 32% of GDP and 35% of the total earnings from goods and services. The oil and gas sector account for about 7% of Egypt's GDP and 34% of its exports. Agriculture's share of the GDP has fallen.from 20% in 1987 to 15% in 2005 but it still accounts

FAST FACTS

Pres. Hosni Mubarak
Born: May 4, 1929
Since 1981

POLITICAL

Head of State	Pres. Hosni Mubarak
Prime Minister	Ahmed Nazif
Ruling Party	HDW or NDP
Main Opposition	NWP
Independence	1922
National capital	Cairo
Official language	Arabic

PHYSICAL

Total area	386,666 sq. miles
	1,001,450 sq. km.
	(3 x New Mexico)
Arable land	3%
Coastline	1,522 miles/2,450 km

POPULATION

Total	78.9 million
Av. yearly growth	1.75%
Population/sq. mile	177
Urban population	31.6
Adult literacy	57.7%

ECONOMY

Currency	Pound (£E)
	(US$1=5.75)
GDP (real)	$92.6 billion
GDP growth rate	4.9%
GDP per capita[1]	$1,228
GDP (ppp)[2]	$303.5 billion
GDP per cap. (ppp)	$3,900
Inflation rate	4.9%
Exports	$14.33 billion
Imports	$24.1 billion
External debt	$35.26 billion
Unemployment	9.5%

1. Atlas method.
2. See page 175 for an explanation of
   purchasing power parity (ppp).

for 32% of the work force. Current oil production is 700,000 bbl/day.

TRADING

Despite productivity gains since the mid-1980s, Egypt remains one of the world's largest food importers. It is also a significant importer of oil and gas field machinery, military equipment, automotive parts, construction and medical equipment, telecommunications equipment, packaging and paper material and, more recently, environmental equipment and materials. Egypt is the largest single market worldwide for American wheat and a significant importer of other agricultural commodities, machinery, and equipment. Currently, the U.S. is Egypt's largest bilateral trading partner. Crude oil and petroleum products, cotton, textiles, metal products, chemicals are important merchandise exports but tourism remains a major foreign exchange earner.

INVESTMENT

The U.S. is the second largest investor in Egypt, after the United Kingdom. Roughly two-thirds of total U.S. investment is in the oil and gas sector, but also includes investment in areas such as consumer goods, automobile production, and financial services. The US Department of Commerce calculated the stock of U.S. FDI as of the end of 2003 at $3.53 billion, Other major investing countries include France, Italy, and several Arab countries. Given its strategic position in the region, Egypt continues to benefit from strong donor support. The U.S. Government has worked closely with Egypt on its economic reform program, and is its largest bilateral aid donor. U.S. non-military economic assistance to Egypt in 2004 was approximately $575 million. Privatization and new customs reforms should help encourage investment.

FINANCIAL SECTOR

Banks are supervised by the central bank of Egypt. There are 61 banks in Egypt, 22 of them joint ventures with foreign participation. Egypt does not limit foreign equity participation in local banks and several foreign banks have majority shares in Egyptian banks, while other foreign banks are registered as branches of the parent bank (rather than subsidiaries). The government , in its belief that there are too many banks, has not issued a new banking license in at least ten years and announced it plans to reduce the number of banks in Egypt to 21. In February 2005 the market capitalization of the Cairo and Alexandria Stock Exchange (CASE) was 46.5 billion with 983 listed companies. European and U.S. mutual funds now include Egyptian stocks, and 52 local issues are included in the International Finance Corporation's general index. The government continues to introduce measures to bring Egypt's capital market closer to international standards. Companies listed on the CASE are required to apply international accounting and disclosure standards.

TAXES AND TARIFFS

Since the early nineties, under an economic reform program developed in conjunction with the IMF and the World Bank, Egypt has reduced its tariff rates. The 2003 establishment of the Model Customs and Tax Center (MCTC) helped modernize customs and tax administration in Egypt. The Cairo-based MCTC is a "one-stop shop" where taxpayers registered in Greater Cairo can settle income taxes, sales taxes and customs for goods passing through any of Egypt's ports. A similar customs center was established in Alexandria in 2005. Customs procedures remain, however, quite cumbersome and subjective when it comes to identifying whether a commodity fits in one tariff category or another.

BUSINESS ACTIVITY

AGRICULTURE
Cotton, rice, corn, wheat, beans, fruit, vegetables, cattle, water buffalo, sheep, goats, fish.

INDUSTRIES
Textiles, food processing, tourism, chemicals, petroleum, construction, cement, metals.

NATURAL RESOURCES
Petroleum, natural gas, iron ore, phosphates, manganese, limestone, gypsum, talc, asbestos, lead, zinc.

EXPORTS
$14.33 billion (est. 2005): crude oil and petroleum products, cotton yarn, raw cotton, textiles, metal products, chemicals.

IMPORTS
$24.1 billion (est. 2005): machinery and equipment, food, fertilizers, wood products, durable consumer goods, capital goods,

MAJOR TRADING PARTNERS
US, Italy, UK, China, France, Germany, Spain, Saudi Arabia, UK.

DOING BUSINESS WITH EGYPT

▶ INVESTMENT

As a result of the government's privatization program, the private sector's role has steadily expanded in key sectors such as metals (aluminum, iron, and steel), petrochemicals, cement, automobiles, textiles, consumer electronics, and pharmaceuticals. The government has made development of high technology a priority and seeks to attract export-oriented manufacturing firms. Generous tax and other incentives are offered. Franchising of fast-food restaurants and clothing stores is a growing business in Egypt.

▶ TRADE

The huge US favorable trade balance with Egypt is ample proof of the possibilities existing beyond the supply of military equipment funded largely by US government grants. Wheat and other agricultural products, medical equipment, computers, construction equipment and a whole range of consumer goods are imported. Foreign firms can sell directly within Egypt as long as they register, but most rely on domestic companies for wholesale and retail distribution.

▶ TRADE FINANCE

Apart from Eximbank facilities, USDA/FAS operates an Export Credit Guarantee Program for Egyptian private sector importers of US food and agricultural commodities. USAID/Egypt sponsors a Private Sector Commodity Import Program (CIP) that makes dollars available to Egyptian private sector importers through some 22 Egyptian banks.

▶ SELLING TO THE GOVERNMENT

Egyptian procurement is either done with national budgetary funds or by using aid funds from USAID or other donors. In the case of USAID-funded procurement, project announcements are made in the US "Commerce Business Daily," published in Chicago. US military aid finances most of Egypt's big-ticket defense procurements. Only registered commercial agents can work on tenders. Government employees are judged on their ability to squeeze the final penny from the lowest bidder—a practice commonly referred to in Arabic as "momarsa."

▶ EXCHANGE CONTROLS

The Foreign Exchange Law of May 1994 allows individuals and legal entities to retain and transfer foreign exchange abroad and entitles banks to conduct foreign exchange transactions.

▶ PARTNERSHIPS

In most sectors foreigners are allowed any measure of shareholding in a partnership, ranging from a few percentage points to close to 100 percent.

▶ ESTABLISHING A PRESENCE

There are several choices, depending on the nature and size of the intended business. Some companies, which intend to conduct market research in scientific, technical or consulting fields, might resort to representative offices funded entirely by remittances from abroad and not subject to Egyptian tax. Oil, construction, and consulting firms often rely on branch offices.

▶ PROJECT FINANCING

OPIC and US TDA support US investment. Egypt is currently included in the International Finance Corporation index for emerging markets and there has been an increase in corporate bonds issued by private sector companies.

▶ LABOR

The abundance of labor has led to low prevailing wages and the use of labor-intensive technologies. Workers may join trade unions but are not required to do so.

▶ LEGAL RIGHTS

The government guarantees against nationalization. The US-Egypt Bilateral Investment Treaty also protects against expropriation and provides for nonbinding, third party arbitration in investment disputes. Even though Egypt is a signatory of several international IPR treaties, the US Trade Representative felt obliged to place Egypt on a priority watch list in April 1998—a designation retained through 1999. In the meantime, the US assisted Egyptian authorities in their efforts to increase intellectual property rights (IPR) protection, primarily through USAID programs.

▶ BUSINESS CLIMATE

Egyptians with whom foreigners do business are typically trilingual (English-French-Arabic), well-traveled individuals who pride themselves on seeking out good deals at decent prices. The Egyptian market is a complex and highly competitive one and an Egyptian agent is frequently essential. Be prepared to bargain. Negotiations are bound by an unspoken culture that assumes that there is not any final, best price that cannot be reduced.

235

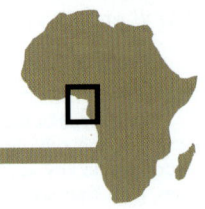

EQUATORIAL GUINEA

ONCE LARGELY DEPENDENT ON COCOA AND COFFEE, EQUATORIAL GUINEA HAS HAD THE WORLD'S FASTEST GROWING ECONOMY IN RECENT YEARS, LARGELY AS A RESULT OF OFFSHORE OIL DISCOVERIES. REFERRED TO BY SOME AS THE "KUWAIT OF AFRICA" TROPICAL EQUATORIAL GUINEA HAS BECOME THE THIRD LARGEST OIL PRODUCING COUNTRY IN SUB-SAHARAN AFRICA. FORESTRY, FARMING, AND FISHING CONTINUE TO BE IMPORTANT COMPONENTS OF GDP. THE GOVERNMENT HAS DECLARED ITS INTENTION TO REINVEST SOME OIL REVENUE INTO AGRICULTURE TO HELP SUBSISTENCE FARMERS. DESPITE THE WINDFALL FROM OIL IMPROVEMENT OF LIVING STANDARDS AMONG THE GENERAL POPULATION HAS BEEN MODEST.

COUNTRY PROFILE

The Republic of Equatorial Guinea covers an area roughly the size of Hawaii, consisting of widely scattered regions—Rio Muni or Mbini on the mainland (which constitutes 92% of the total land area), Bioko island (with 22% of the population and the capital of Malabo), tiny Annobon Island, some 650 km to the south, and the islets of Corsico and Elobey off the mainland estuary. Some 80% of nearly a half million Equato-Guineans live in Mbini—about 150 km wide and extending 200 km inland. Its equatorial climate supports extensive rainforests where mahogany and okoume are grown. Some 125 miles (200 km) from Mbini is Bioko (formerly known as Fernando Po Island), which forms part of a submerged volcanic mountain range with exposed points as far as Annobon Island to the south and Mt. Cameroon to the north. The Bantu-speaking Fang is the largest group in Mbini while the original inhabitants of Bioko Island are the Bubi and the Fernandino—the latter descendants of former slaves whose Krio language has become the lingua franca. Annobon is inhabited by a fishing community of mixed origin. Both French and Spanish are official languages. Most people in the mainland region profess ethnic faiths, but Bioko Island is overwhelmingly Roman Catholic.

HISTORY

In the 1470s the Portuguese reached Fernando Po (later renamed Bioko) and three other tropical islands in the Gulf of Guinea. Bubi hostil-

ity and Bioko's hot, humid climate prompted the Portuguese to concentrate on the deserted islands of Sao Tome, Principe and tiny Annobon further south. In 1778 Portugal bartered Bioko and Annobon to Spain for territory in South America. Until 1858, when the Spanish finally took possession, the British leased Bioko as a naval base for anti-slavery operations. The British developed the port of Clarence, renamed Santa Isabel by the Spanish. Today its known as Malabo, the capital of Equatorial Guinea. Rescued slaves who chose to remain are today known as the Fernandinos. They spoke pidgin English that evolved into Krio. In the 1880s, Spain added a slither of territory on the mainland to its island possessions, named it Rio Muni (today's Mbini) and formed Spanish Guinea. In response to pressures from so-called emancipados, the colony was granted independence on 12 October 1968 under Pres. Macias Nguema who led a decade-long campaign of terror resulting in the death of 20,000 people. One-third of the total population of 300,000 sought asylum in neighboring countries. Cubans and North Koreans helped to keep Macias in power and the Soviet Union was allowed to exploit fish resources from a fishing-cum-military base on Bioko Island. In the process Macias drove one of Africa's most prosperous colonies into bankruptcy. On 3 August 1979, the chief of the army, Lt.-Col. Teodoro Obiang Nguema Mbasogo, replaced his uncle by force, took immediate steps to stabilize the country and cultivated relations with Western donor countries and organizations. He was elected president for a 7-year term in June 1989 and reelected in 1996 and December 2002. The president has almost total control over the political system.

GOVERNMENT

The present Constitution, endorsed by referendum on 16 November 1991, provides for a multiparty system. The President, vested with executive powers, is elected by the voters for 7-year terms and appoints the Prime Minister who heads the government and appoints the Council of Ministers. The 100-member House of People's Representatives serves a 5 year term. In the 2004 election Obiang's Partido Democratieo de Guinea Ecuatorial (PDGE) won 98 seats. The Convergencia para la Democracia Social (Convergence for a Social Democracy) (CPDS) holds 2 seats. This unicameral parliament has very little power since the constitution vests all authority in the presidency.

FAST FACTS

Pres. Teodoro Obiang
Nguema Mbasogo
Born: 1942
Since 1979
© UN/DPI

POLITICAL

Head of State	Pres. Teodoro Obiang Nguema Mbasogo
Ruling Party	PDGE
Main Opposition	UP
Independence	12 October 1968
National capital	Malabo
Official languages	Spanish & French

PHYSICAL

Total area	10,830 sq. miles 28,050 sq. km. (± Maryland)
Arable land	5%
Coastline	184 miles/296 km

POPULATION

Total	540,100
Av. yearly growth	2.05%
Population/sq. mile	44
Urban population	300,000
Adult literacy	85.7%

ECONOMY

Currency	CFA franc (CFAF)(US$1=559.44)
GDP (real)	$7.64 billion
GDP growth rate	18.6%
GDP per capita[1]	$12,742
GDP (ppp)[2]	$25.7 billion
GDP per cap. (ppp)	$50,200
Inflation rate	5%
Exports	$6.73 billion
Imports	$1.86 billion
External debt	$248 million
Unemployment	30%

1. Atlas method.
2. See page 175 for an explanation of purchasing power parity (ppp).

ECONOMIC POLICY

At independence in 1968, Equatorial Guinea's per capita income was one of the highest in Africa. It dropped to one of the lowest after a decade of mismanagement under the Macias regime. The new government liberalizing the economy to some extent and privatized some state enterprises to create a favorable investment climate. Since the late nineties Equatorial Guinea has had the world's fastest growing economy, largely as a result of new oil discoveries. There are long-term incentives for job creation, training, promotion of non-traditional exports, support of development projects and indigenous capital participation, freedom to repatriate profits, exemption from certain taxes and capital and other benefits. Investors, especially in the fast growing oil sector, are given ample scope by a government keen to lure foreigners. Not much of this newfound wealth has trickled down to the general population. Equatorial Guinea has sought a "shadow" fiscal management agreement with the World Bank.

SECTORS

Limited oil production began in 1991 and since the discovery of major additional oil reserves off Bioko Island in 1995 Equatorial Guinea has been referred to by some as the "Kuwait of Africa." It is currently producing approximately 420,000 bbl/day. Other sectors with good potential include fishing, timber, tourism, and mining. There are modest deposits of iron ore, lead, zinc, manganese, uranium, tantalum and molybdenum. Good prospects also exist in agriculture with cocoa, coffee, palm oil, bananas and coconuts as major crops. Deep water port facilities serve as convenient outlets for neighboring countries. The small, isolated island of Annobon lies in a 314,000-square kilometer exclusive maritime economic zone amid some of the Atlantic's richest fishing grounds.

PRIVATIZATION

A decision was taken to privatize the distribution of petroleum products in the country. Private investors have been co-opted to increase electrical capacity and parastatals and public enterprises have been earmarked for privatization in the agro-industry (cocoa), transport (airline, shipping and maritime transport), public utilities (electricity, water and telecommunications) and several other sectors.

INVESTMENT

The US is a major investor in oil and gas operations in Equatorial Guinea but Spain as the former colonial power maintains a sizeable portion of the holdings in the country.

TRADE

Spain, France, Italy, Cameroon, Nigeria and the US are important suppliers of food, petroleum products, automobiles, machinery, and iron and steel. The US, Cameroon and Côte d'Ivoire are major buyers of oil and fuels and the Netherlands, Spain, Germany, France and Italy top the list of purchasers of cocoa, timber and coffee.

FINANCIAL SECTOR

Interest rates are set by the regional central bank (BEAC), monitored and regulated by the French Government. There are two commercial banks regulated by the Banking Commission for Central African States (COBAC)— an affiliate of a Cameroonian bank and another affiliate of a French bank.

TAXES AND TARIFFS

A flat tax of 6.25 % applies to all petroleum revenues. Generalized preferential tariffs apply to goods being shipped to other CEMAC countries. The number of taxes applied to imports was reduced from over seven to four and the overall rate from a maximum 47 % to a maximum 12 % on the most heavily taxed imports. Custom's assessments were simplified.

BUSINESS ACTIVITY

AGRICULTURE
Coffee, cocoa, rice, yams, cassava (tapioca), bananas, palm oil nuts, manioc, livestock, timber.

INDUSTRIES
Petroleum, fishing, sawmilling, natural gas.

NATURAL RESOURCES
Timber, petroleum, small unexploited deposits of gold, manganese, uranium.

EXPORTS
$6.73 billion (est. 2004): petroleum, timber cocoa, methanol.

IMPORTS
$1.86 billion (est. 2005): petroleum, food, beverages, clothing, machinery.

MAJOR TRADING PARTNERS
US, China, Taiwan, Japan, Italy, Spain, UK.

DOING BUSINESS WITH EQUATORIAL GUINEA

▶ INVESTMENT

The investment code allows repatriation of profits and offers tax and other incentives for job creation, training, the promotion of non-traditional exports, and the support of development projects. Investments in non-traditional products in rural areas are favored. Foreign investment is not subject to screening and foreign equity ownership is not restricted. The government is offering attractive terms to foreign entrepreneurs willing to explore and exploit the country's mineral wealth. Fisheries, salting, livestock feeds, cocoa paste, palm oil, transportation and communications, water purification and sanitation, and power and energy have been identified as priority areas for investment.

▶ TRADE

Apart from oil production equipment, airplanes, watercraft, heavy road and logging equipment, construction materials, agricultural inputs such as fertilizers and equipment, foodstuffs, used clothing and shoes offer sales opportunities. Foreign firms are advised to obtain the services of agents with local knowledge. There are few franchise operations in Equatorial Guinea but international oil companies might soon be able to retail petroleum products, currently limited to Total, the government's partner.

▶ TRADE FINANCE

Importers and exporters use internationally accepted methods of settlement. Foreign firms sometimes grant credits of 180 days for consumer goods and 24 months for small machinery and equipment but an irrevocable, confirmed letter of credit is standard practice.

▶ SELLING TO THE GOVERNMENT

Programs financed jointly by international financial institutions and the Government are open to unrestricted competition. Privatization of specific industries might in future present opportunities in the transport sector (both the national airline and the national shipping corporation), and in public utilities (water, electricity and telecommunications).

▶ EXCHANGE CONTROLS

Foreign exchange controls are enforced primarily for statistical purposes and to enable the Ministry of Finance to certify that remittances conform with established regulations. Authorizations for foreign transfers are routinely granted.

▶ PARTNERSHIPS

Partnerships in certain areas are mandatory as local entrepreneurs have exclusive rights in the manufacture of arms, explosives and other weapons, the gathering, treatment and storing of toxic, dangerous and radioactive materials or waste products and the production of alcoholic beverages excluding beer.

▶ FINANCING PROJECTS

The World Bank's resident representative in Yaoundé, Cameroon, and its affiliate, the International Finance Corporation's regional offices in Douala also handles applications from Equatorial Guinea. The African Development Bank Group has been involved in the country and OPIC operates in the country. The International Development Association has on occasion provided loans for projects involving foreigners.

▶ LABOR

Unemployment is difficult to quantify in a developing economy where so many of the citizens are toiling the land or underemployed in rural areas but the UN Development Program has estimated it to be as high as 88 %. A Spanish company (FTF-First Training and Finance) was contracted by the government to regulate labor supplies, initially for the petroleum industry, but subsequently for other sectors.

▶ LEGAL RIGHTS

Foreign and domestic investors are provided with guarantees that comply with international norms. Trademark enforcement is weak as Equatorial Guinea is not a member of the 14nation West African intellectual property organization, *Organisation Africaine de la Propriété Intellectuelle.* Equatorial Guinea does, however, accept binding international arbitration of investment disputes with foreign investors and is a member of the International Center for the Settlement of Investment Disputes. It is also a signatory to the Convention on the Recognition and Enforcement of Foreign Arbitral Awards.

▶ BUSINESS CLIMATE

The business community closely follows Spanish customs and the language most often used is Spanish, with some French. Equato-Guineans insist on getting to know a potential partner before starting concrete discussions.

ERITREA

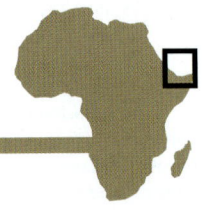

ERITREA, AFRICA'S YOUNGEST NATION, GAINED ITS FREEDOM FROM ETHIOPIA IN 1991 AFTER A 30-YEAR WAR OF LIBERATION AND ACHIEVED STATEHOOD AFTER A REFERENDUM IN 1993. IT TRIUMPHED OVER TREMENDOUS ODDS IN A STRUGGLE THAT REDUCED SUBSTANTIAL PARTS OF A ONCE FAIRLY PROSPEROUS COUNTRY TO ASHES. RECOVERY WAS IMPEDED BY A BORDER WAR WITH ETHIOPIA THAT ERUPTED IN 1998 AND ENDED WITH A UN-SPONSORED PEACE AGREEMENT IN DECEMBER 2000. ERITREA HAS LIBERALIZED ITS ECONOMY AND WITH THE HELP OF FOREIGN INVESTMENT MADE REMARKABLE PROGRESS WHILE A UN PEACEKEEPING FORCE CONTINUES TO MONITOR THE TEMPORARY SECURITY ZONE ON ITS BORDER WITH ETHIOPIA.

COUNTRY PROFILE

As an extension of Ethiopia's mountains, the Eritrean highlands form a steep escarpment, overlooking a narrow coastal plain. With an annual rainfall of 500-1,000 mm the escarpment is the most productive agricultural region. The Tekeze river forms part of the border with Ethiopia and drains into the Nile. The Danakil Depression (130 m below sea level) is one of the hottest places on earth. Nomadic livestock herders occupy the coastal plain. Eritrea's economic zone in the Red Sea includes more than 350 islands of various shapes and sizes, fringed by coral reefs, with a total land area of 515 sq. miles (1,335 sq km). Eritrea's people are of Ethio-Semitic, Cushitic and Nilotic origin. The main language is Tigrinya, spoken by the Tigray—the principal Ethio-Semitic group. Cushitic groups live on both sides of the border with Sudan in the northwest. The Afar (a.k.a. the Adal or Danakil) roam the southern coastal strip. English is the most widely spoken European language. The Tigray are predominantly Christian, belonging to the Eritrean Orthodox Church. There are sizeable minorities of other Christian denominations and Muslims.

HISTORY

Eritrea used to be part of the ancient Ethiopian empire built around Axum (Aksum). During the 4th Century AD Ethiopia's emperors converted to Christianity and established the Ethiopian Orthodox Church throughout the realm. From about the 8th Century Axum went into decline. When Emperor Menelik II came to power at the turn of the 19th Century and founded a new capital, Addis Ababa (the new flower) to replace Asmara (the flower), the Tigray in the north revolted. In 1889, Menelik ceded to Italy the northern and

240

northeastern fringes of his empire in the hope of satisfying Rome's territorial ambitions. The Italian colony of Eritrea—a name derived from Mare Erythraeum, the old Roman designation for the Red Sea—was adopted in 1890. After a humiliating defeat when they tried to expand their influence south into Ethiopia, the Italians concentrated on colonizing Eritrea. In 1936 Italy finally conquered Ethiopia and ruled over both colonies until 1941 when the Allied forces defeated Mussolini's troops and returned Ethiopian emperor Haile Selassie to the thrown. Selassie pressed for the re-incorporation of Eritrea into its "motherland." In 1952 the UN General Assembly decided Eritrea should become an autonomous state federated with Ethiopia. Barely ten years later, however, Emperor Haile Selassie abrogated the federation, dissolved Eritrea's national assembly and absorbed the country as Ethiopia's 14th province. Various liberation movements became active and eventually the Eritrean People's Liberation Front (EPLF) won Eritrea's independence in May 1993. The EPLF leader, Isaias Afwerki was appointed interim president. He is still in power. Since its independence, Eritrea and Ethiopia have disagreed about the exact demarcation of their borders and in May 1998 border clashes began. It erupted into a war lasting until the beginning of 2000 that resulted in the loss of tens of thousands of lives on both sides and depleted state coffers. A cease-fire was signed in June 2000 and a peace agreement concluded later in the year. The UN agreed to provide peace-keeping troops to patrol the buffer zone.

GOVERNMENT

The Constitution adopted in May 1997 provided for an executive President elected for a maximum of two 5-year terms and a 104-member National Assembly (Hagerawi Baito)—60 appointed and 44 representing the members of the Central Committee of the People's Front for Democracy and Justice (PFDJ). The PFDJ, formerly known as the Eritrean People's Liberation Front (EPLF) has ruled the country since independence. Elections scheduled for December 2001 were postponed indefinitely.

ECONOMIC POLICY

The government is actively seeking foreign private investment and partnerships with international donors. In coordination with the World Bank and the IMF it developed a liberal macroeconomic policy with an investment code that offers signifi-

FAST FACTS

Pres. Isaias Afwerki
Born: 1946
Since 1993

POLITICAL
Head of State	Pres. Isaias Afwerki
Ruling party	PFDJ
Independence	24 May 1993
National capital	Asmara
Working languages[4]	Tigriñya, Arabic and English

PHYSICAL
Total area	47,742 sq. miles
	124,320 sq. km.
	(± Pennsyvania)
Arable land	4.95% of land area
Coastline	1388 miles/2,234 km
	(incl. Red Sea islands)

POPULATION
Total	4.79 million[3]
Av. yearly growth	2.47%
Population/sq. mile	90
Urban population	900,000
Adult literacy	58.6%

ECONOMY
Currency	Nafka (US$1=15.00)
GDP (real)	$1.24 billion
GDP growth rate	2%
GDP per capita[1]	$240
GDP (ppp)[2]	$4.47 billion
GDP per cap. (ppp)	$1,000
Inflation rate	15%
Exports	$33.58 million
Imports	$676.5 million
External debt	$311 million
Unemployment	N/A

1. Atlas method.
2. See page 175 for an explanation of purchasing power parity (ppp).
3. Not including 0.5 million refugees awaiting repatriation.
4. Eritrea does not have an official language.

cant incentives to foreign investors. The border dispute with Ethiopia has substantially impacted the Eritrean economy. Even during the war Eritrea has developed new roads and repaired damaged ones and since the peace agreement was signed doubled its efforts to rebuild.

SECTORS

Like the economies of many other African nations Eritrea's is largely dependent on subsistence agriculture. Around 60% of the population is engaged in or relies on crop cultivation and livestock raising. Agriculture and fishing account for about half the national product (GDP) and two-thirds of exports. Main crops are teff, millet, wheat, sesame, sorghum, barley, vegetables, pulses, cotton, fruit and coffee. Fishing waters offer sardine, anchovy, shrimp and lobster in abundance. Eritrea has deposits of salt and other minerals such as basalt, limestone, marble, granite, sands, silicates, gold, silver, copper, nickel, zinc, chrome, sulphur and potash. Prospecting is underway for oil and gas. Eritrea's substantial mineral deposits are largely unexplored as a consequence of the war with Ethiopia. Eritrea is estimated to have some 14,000 kilograms of total gold reserves. Western observers also have noted Eritrea's excellent potential for quarrying ornamental marble and granite. Some 10 mining companies (including Canadian and South African firms) had obtained licenses to prospect for different minerals. The presence of hundreds of thousands of land mines in Eritrea, particularly along the border with Ethiopia, presents a serious impediment to future development of the mining sector. In 2003 industry accounted for 25.3 percent of gross domestic product. Major products include processed food and dairy products, alcoholic beverages, glass, leather goods, marble, textiles, and salt.

PRIVATIZATION

Privatization is planned for most of Eritrea's 42 state-owned enterprises, industries and hotels. A dozen public enterprises have been privatized so far—including a dairy factory, a brewery, and a corrugated iron sheet factory—some in the form of public-private partnerships and others through outright sale to foreign or local investors.

INVESTMENT

No precise country breakdown of foreign direct investment statistics is available. Apart from the United States other major investors include South Korea, Italy, and China.

TRADE

Multilateral lenders who have been impressed with the government's fiscal discipline, despite the recently concluded border war, readily provided financing for imports needed for reconstruction and development. Principal sources for imports consisting largely of machinery, petroleum products, food and manufactured goods are Malaysia, Italy, Egypt India, Japan and Germany. Principal buyers, mostly of unfinished raw materials, textiles and livestock include Ireland, Us, Italy and Turkey.

FINANCIAL SECTOR

A housing and commerce bank, an agriculture and industry development bank and the commercial bank of Eritrea operate alongside the central bank of Eritrea. The central bank of Eritrea, though a government entity, operates independently from the ministry of finance. Eritrea allows foreign banks to operate in the country.

TAXES AND TARIFFS

Tariffs ranging from 2% to 50% have been imposed on essential goods such as capital equipment, industrial inputs, pharmaceuticals, school supplies, books, food, livestock, and seed. On luxury goods, liquor, tobacco, prepared foods (particularly those that compete with domestic products), automobiles, and electronic equipment the tariff is between 50% and 200%.

BUSINESS ACTIVITY

AGRICULTURE
Sorghums, lentils, vegetables, maize, cotton, tobacco, coffee, sisal, livestock, fish.

INDUSTRIES
Food processing, beverages, clothing and textiles.

NATURAL RESOURCES
Gold, potash, zinc, copper, salt, potential of oil and natural gas, fish.

EXPORTS
$33.58 million (est. 2005): livestock, sorghum, textiles, food, small manufactures.

IMPORTS
$676.5 million (est. 2005): processed goods, machinery, petroleum products.,

MAJOR TRADING PARTNERS
Malaysia, Ireland, Italy, US, Egypt, Japan, Turkey, China, Germany, India.

Doing Business with Eritrea

Investment

Investment policy gives domestic and foreign investors equal access to land, utilities, and other production units in all sectors of the economy except domestic retail and wholesale trade and import agencies. A variety of tax and export incentives are extended to investors, especially those involved in relatively depressed areas. Foreign firms are encouraged to participate in the privatization process where, in some cases, the government has favored partnership agreements over outright sales. Among the target areas for foreign investment are fishing, offshore oil and gas exploration, mining, tourism, the development of alternative energy sources such as thermal, wind, and solar, as well as construction enterprises to repair roads, bridges, airports, and railways, rehabilitate port facilities, improve water and sewage networks, and build houses and office and industrial sites.

Trade

Energy, mining, agribusiness, construction, telecommunications, transportation, tourism, heavy equipment, light industry, and marine resources offer significant opportunities for trade. There is a constant shortage of heavy construction equipment and a demand for agricultural and mining equipment. Suppliers of used equipment may find a ready market in a country with the reputation of being able to keep anything running. (During their war for independence the Eritreans thrived on Soviet style vehicles captured from their Ethiopian opponents). There is an expanding English speaking middle class with an appetite for Western consumer products.

Trade finance

Nearly all import financing is done on a letter of credit basis. There are two banks in Eritrea authorized to issue LCs—the commercial bank of Eritrea and the housing and commerce bank.

Selling to the government

Many government purchases are associated with donor financed projects and are subject to bidding and procurement rules of the donors. There is no central procurement office and each ministry handles its own needs. The tenders are open to public bidding and advertised in the local papers. Major governmental infrastructure projects, including road, airport, harbor and hospital construction, create an ongoing need for foreign equipment, expertise and materials.

Exchange controls

The national bank of Eritrea has adopted a free-floating exchange rate. Foreign investors are allowed to remit profits and dividends, principal and interest on foreign loans, and fees related to technology transfer as well as the proceeds from the sale of liquidation of assets.

Partnerships

The government encourages joint ventures with foreign firms, especially in mining and the privatization of state-owned businesses. Franchising is a relatively new concept but former expatriate Eritreans tend to be good candidates as licensing partners.

Establishing a presence

A business licensing office has been established as a one-stop shop to short-circuit procedures. Private entities, both domestic and foreign, have the right to establish, acquire, own, and dispose of most forms of business enterprise but companies affiliated with the ruling party, the People's Front for Democracy and Justice (PFDJ) enjoy certain advantages over other firms.

Financing projects

The Overseas Private Investment Corporation offers risk insurance and loans to US investors. Eritrea is a member of the Multilateral Investment Guarantee Agency.

Labor

Eritrea has an inexpensive but industrious and disciplined workforce but skilled manpower in certain fields is hard to obtain. All workers in public and private enterprise are members of the national confederation of Eritrean workers.

Legal rights

Foreign investors may choose to submit disputes to local settlement under the laws of Eritrea, in terms of The Hague convention or by presenting its case to the Eritrea investment center. Eritrea also abides by the International Convention on the Settlement of Investment Disputes. There are currently no formal mechanism to protect intellectual property rights, patents, and copyrights.

Business climate

Business customs are Western and English. Italian and Arabic are widely spoken. Everyone in the business community seems to know each other and considerable value is placed on character.

ETHIOPIA

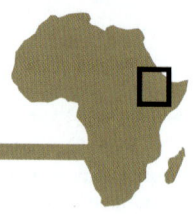

THE LAND OF KINGS AND LEGENDS, ETHIOPIA IS THE OLDEST INDEPENDENT COUNTRY IN AFRICA AND THE ORIGINAL HOME OF COFFEE. IT HAS BEEN UNDER COLONIAL RULE ONLY FOR A BRIEF PERIOD DURING ITALIAN OCCUPATION FROM 1936 UNTIL 1941. POLITICAL AND ECONOMIC REFORMS AND THE CONCLUSION OF A COSTLY WAR AGAINST ERITREA SHOULD ENABLE IT TO MAKE ECONOMIC PROGRESS. ETHIOPIA NOT ONLY HOLDS THE PROMISE OF BECOMING A SIGNIFICANT EXPORTER ONCE IT HAS FULLY UTILIZED ITS RESOURCES BUT AS AFRICA'S THIRD MOST POPULOUS COUNTRY—AFTER NIGERIA AND EGYPT—COULD DEVELOP INTO A MAJOR MARKET FOR FOREIGN PRODUCTS AS PER CAPITA INCOMES RISE. THE NEW GOVERNMENT HAS INTRODUCED ECONOMIC REFORMS TO LURE FOREIGN INVESTORS.

COUNTRY PROFILE

More than half of the Federal Democratic Republic of Ethiopia is at high altitudes. Its highest point, Ras Dashen (4,620 m) is Africa's fourth highest mountain. The national capital, Addis Ababa, is 2,450 m above sea level. The mountainous region is bisected by the Great Rift Valley. South of Addis Ababa a chain of freshwater and salt lakes extends along the valley floor to Lake Turkana at the country's southwestern corner. Numerous large rivers, including the Blue Nile, flow from east to west towards the Nile Basin. The highest rainfall (over 1,000 mm) occurs in the west and southwest. Ethiopian society is a mixture of Caucasoid and Negroid peoples. The three principal groups are the Ethiopian Semites, the Cushites and the Omotic cluster of peoples and tongues, with two subgroups, the Amhara and the Oromo, accounting for 70% of the total population. A much smaller group, the Tigray, speaking Tigrinya, inhabits the far northern highlands and extends across the border into Eritrea. Half the population are Orthodox Christians, 35% are Muslims and the remainder adhere to ethnic beliefs.

HISTORY

Early mixing between the Cushitic, Omotic and Nilotic Negroid peoples produced a racially mixed population in ancient Ethiopia. From about 800 BC there was an influx of Semitic peoples from Saba (now Yemen) across the Red Sea into the highlands of present-day Eritrea and northern Ethiopia. The name Ethiopia (a Greek name meaning "land of dark people") began to apply to the empire centered around the city of Axum. In 333 AD Ethiopian Emperor Ezana was converted to Christianity and, by the 14th and 15th centuries when this territory was surrounded by Muslim regions, tales were told in Europe about the mysterious Christian kingdom of Prester John. Emperor Menelik II came to power at the turn of the nineteenth century and founded a new capital,

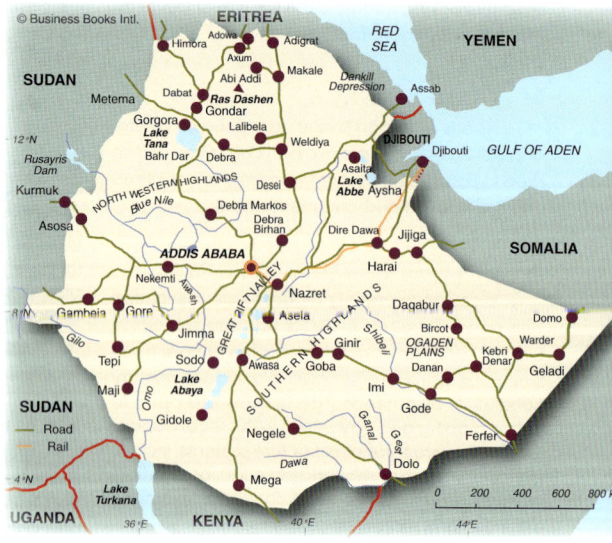

Addis Ababa, to replace Asmara as the capital. Shortly after his ascension to the throne in 1889, Emperor Menelik ceded to Italy the northern and northeastern fringes of his empire to placate Rome but the Italians still tried to incorporate Ethiopia, suffering a humiliating defeat. In 1936 Italy extended its rule over Ethiopia as well and in 1941, with Mussolini's defeat by the Allied forces, Emperor Haile Selassie was restored to the throne. At his insistence that Eritrea be rejoined to the "motherland" the UN General Assembly made it an autonomous state within an Ethiopian federation. In 1962 Selassie abrogated the federation and absorbed the country as Ethiopia's 14th province. Setbacks in the ensuing war with Eritrea and internal dissension led to the imprisonment and alleged strangling in jail of Haile Selassie in 1974. His successor, Major Mengistu Haile Mariam, introduced a Soviet-style regime—known as the Dergue—which led to the killing of 100,000 opponents. In 1991 the brutal 14-year dictatorship ended when the Tigray-led Ethiopian People's Revolutionary Democratic Front (EPRDF) marched into Addis Ababa. Mengistu fled, making way for Meles Zenawi who was reconfirmed as executive prime minister in the first multiparty elections in 1995 and again in 2000 and 2005. Girma Wolde-Giyorgis was elected president in 2001.

GOVERNMENT

The 1994 constitution provides for a bicameral parliament consisting of a 117-member upper chamber (Council of the Federation) and 527-member lower chamber (Council of People's Representatives). A President is elected by both houses for a 6-year term but power rests in the Prime Minister, chosen by the majority party in the Council of People's Representatives. In the May 2005 election Zenawi's ruling Ethiopian People's Revolutionary Democratic Front (EPRDF) coalition won 327 seats to stay in power albeit it with a substantially reduced majority. The opposition Coalition for Unity and Democracy (CUD) won 109 and United Ethiopian Democratic Forces (UEDF) 52, giving them a significant voice.

ECONOMIC POLICY

Since its return to civilian rule in 1991, Ethiopia has established new relationships with international financial institutions and secured funding from the World Bank for economic recovery and reconstruction and implementing structural adjustment programs with the International Monetary Fund (IMF). In 2002 the government produced a

FAST FACTS

Prime Minister
Meles Zenawi
Born: May 9, 1955
Since 1995

POLITICAL

Head of State	Pres. Girma Wolde-Giyorgis
Prime Minister	Meles Zenawi
Ruling Party	EPRDF
Main opposition	CUD, UEDF
Independence	2,000 years
National capital	Addis Ababa
Official language	Amharic

PHYSICAL

Total area	435,184 sq. miles
	1,127,127 sq. km.
	(2 x Texas)
Arable land	11% of land area
Coastline	Landlocked

POPULATION

Total	74.8 million
Av. yearly growth	2.31%
Population/sq. mile	143
Urban population	12 million
Adult literacy	42.7%

ECONOMY

Currency	Birr (BR)
	(US$1=8.72)
GDP (real)	$8.8 billion
GDP growth rate	8.9%
GDP per capita[1]	$143
GDP (ppp)[2]	$62.88 billion
GDP per cap. (ppp)	$900
Inflation rate	11.6%
Exports	$612 million
Imports	$2.7 billion
External debt	$5.1 billion
Unemployment	N/A

1. Atlas method.
2. See page 175 for an explanation of purchasing power parity (ppp).

five-year framework to guide economic development, reform, and poverty reduction. It received $3.6 billion in support from the international donor institutions for the period from mid-2002 to mid-2005. Under these programs, Ethiopia has made substantial progress in shifting expenditures from defense to social and economic sectors and in reforming its banking system.

SECTORS

Agriculture accounts for more than half of GDP, more than 60% of foreign earnings and over 80% of total employment. Coffee exports, averaging more than $150 million a year, are crucial to the economy. Cotton and sugar are other major cash crops and food crops include cereals, particularly teff, maize, and sorghum. Ethiopia's cattle population of around 30 million head is by far the largest in Africa, yet commercial slaughtering (2.3 million head annually) is lower than that of South Africa, with a much smaller human and cattle population. Mineral resources include appreciable reserves of natural gas (in the eastern region), gold, copper, zinc, potash and iron ore. Manufacturing is largely in processed foods, consumer goods and textiles for the home market, and hides for export, handicrafts and leather. Tourism is seen as a growth industry in this country with its cultural diversity, mountains, lakes, rivers, ancient cities.

PRIVATIZATION

Since the nineties when the government started selling state-owned enterprises, 180 entities have been privatized, including the Pepsi Cola and Coca-Cola bottling plants. In the agricultural sector most marketing boards have been abolished, enabling farmers to sell their crops to the highest bidder. Coffee marketing has also been opened to competition.

INVESTMENT

As of 1998 the Ethiopian Investment Authority approved 163 foreign investment projects with total projected capital investment of $1.2 billion— 90 wholly foreign-owned and 73 joint ventures. Ethiopia's major foreign investors include Saudi Arabia, South Korea, Kuwait, the US and Italy. Still, foreign investment by private firms in Ethiopia is quite low. In 2003 the government promulgated new regulations to stimulate foreign investment, among them a lowering of the required investment minimum by foreign firms from $500,000 to $100,000. Some sectors, such as banking, remain wholly or partially off-limits.

TRADE

Primary exports are coffee, hides and skins, sesame seeds, pulses, chat, live animals, honey and beeswax, and fruits and vegetables. Coffee (arabica) is by far the most important export commodity, constituting about two-thirds of exports by value. Main imports are semi-finished goods, crude petroleum and petroleum products, transport and industrial capital goods, medical and pharmaceutical products, motor vehicles, civil and military aircraft, raw materials, and agricultural machinery and equipment.

FINANCIAL SECTOR

There are six private banks and seven private insurance companies. The National Bank of Ethiopia (NBE) regulates credit and exchange. Foreign banking is not permitted but most commercial banks have correspondent relations.

TAXES AND TARIFFS

Customs duties have been reduced on a wide range of imports. The government plans to reduce the maximum rate to 30%.

LOCAL TIME

Ethiopia uses the Julian calendar, which is divided into 12 months of 30 days each and a 13th month of five or six days at the end of the year. The Ethiopian calendar is 7 years and 8 months behind the Gregorian calendar.

BUSINESS ACTIVITY

AGRICULTURE
Cereals, pulses, coffee, oilseed, sugar cane, potatoes, hides, cattle, sheep, goats.

INDUSTRIES
Food processing, beverages, textiles, chemicals, metals processing, cement.

NATURAL RESOURCES
Small reserves of gold, platinum, copper, potash, natural gas.

EXPORTS
$612 million (est. 2005): coffee, leather products, gold, oilseed, live animals.

IMPORTS
$2.7 billion (est. 2005): food and live animals, petroleum and petroleum products, chemicals, machinery, motor vehicles and aircraft.

MAJOR TRADING PARTNERS
Japan, Italy, Djibouti, Saudi Arabia, US, Germany, China.

DOING BUSINESS WITH ETHIOPIA

▶ INVESTMENT

Investors in relatively underdeveloped regions of Ethiopia are eligible for exemption from income tax for up to five years. With the lowest telephone line density in Africa and plans to award a series of contracts to expand services, telecommunications offers good potential. Foreign firms are excluded from the domestic banking, insurance services, high volume air transport or freight services, forwarding and shipping agency services, rail transport services, and non-courier postal services. Foreigners are welcomed to participate in privatization but in some instances the government promotes joint ventures with Ethiopian private concerns rather than outright sales.

▶ TRADE

The country's main imports include motor vehicles, petroleum products, civil and military aircraft, spare parts, construction equipment, medical and pharmaceutical products, agricultural and industrial chemicals, agricultural machinery, fertilizers, irrigation equipment, and food grains. The government requires that all imports be channeled through Ethiopian nationals registered with the government as official import or distribution agents. Ethiopia maintains restrictions and taxes on the export of coffee and chat and regulates the sale of petroleum products.

▶ TRADE FINANCE

The Ethiopian government relies on grants and external borrowing on highly concessionary terms to finance the external current account deficit.

▶ SELLING TO THE GOVERNMENT

Road building, telecommunications development and other infrastructural projects are open for international competitive bidding and are funded by either the Ethiopian government or major international financial institutions such as the International Development Association of the World Bank and the African Development Fund.

▶ EXCHANGE CONTROLS

All foreign exchange transactions must be carried out through authorized dealers under the control of the National Bank. Foreign investors may freely remit profits and dividends, principal and interest on foreign loans, fees related to technology transfer, proceeds from liquidation of assets or transfer of shares, and funds required for debt service or other international payments.

▶ PARTNERSHIPS

Foreign investors are encouraged to go into joint ventures especially where there is the prospect of technology transfer, improvement of the country's foreign exchange position, utilization and development of natural and human resources and added value in various economic sectors.

▶ ESTABLISHING A PRESENCE

Both foreign and domestic private entities have the right to establish, acquire, own, and dispose of most forms of business enterprises. State-owned enterprises have, however, considerable *de facto* advantages over private firms when it comes to cutting red tape, access to credit and swift customs clearance.

▶ FINANCING PROJECTS

The Overseas Private Investment Corporation offers risk insurance and loans to US investors. Ethiopia is also a member of the Multilateral Investment Guarantee Agency. Capital is sometimes available from the International Development Association of the World Bank or the African Development Bank for roads, energy, health and education projects . The International Finance Corporation also offers some equity financing.

▶ LABOR

Labor is readily available and inexpensive, but skilled manpower is scarce. About 300,000 workers are members of unions and approximately 40% of the urban workforce is unemployed.

▶ LEGAL RIGHTS

There has been no expropriation since the transitional government replaced the Mengistu rule. Disputes arising out of foreign investment may be submitted to a competent Ethiopian court or to international arbitration. There are no regulations for the registration of patents and copyrights. Some protection can be secured through registration of trademarks at the Ministry of Trade and Industry and the publication of cautionary notices in local newspapers.

▶ BUSINESS CLIMATE

While Amharic is spoken throughout the country and Oromiffa and Tigrinya also widely used, English is the second official language and understood in most business circles. Ethiopians are universally addressed by first name even in formal situations.

GABON

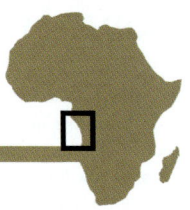

GABON IS ONE OF SUB-SAHARAN AFRICA'S WEALTHIEST COUNTRIES AND A MAJOR SUPPLIER OF OIL TO THE UNITED STATES. IT IS ALSO A SIGNIFICANT EXPORTER OF MANGANESE AND TIMBER. GABON IS SEEN AS HAVING THE POTENTIAL OF BECOMING A REGIONAL HUB FOR SERVICES TO OTHER COUNTRIES IN THE REGION. THERE IS AN ACTIVE RECRUITMENT OF FOREIGN INVESTORS AND PRIVATIZATION HAS OPENED UP OPPORTUNITIES IN TRANSPORT, TELECOMMUNICATIONS AND MANUFACTURING. THE DISCOVERY OF A RANGE OF STRATEGIC MINERALS HAS STIMULATED INTEREST IN THIS SECTOR, AS WELL.

COUNTRY PROFILE

The Republic of Gabon is a small equatorial country of rivers, estuaries and lagoons. Most of Gabon lies in the basin of the Ogoue river and its main tributary, the N'Gounie. The Ogoue is navigable from its delta to Booue, some 300 km upstream. The interior plateau rises to 1,300 m at the southern Chaillu Mountains on the Congo border and the northern Crystal Mountains reaching into Equatorial Guinea. Equatorial forest covers three quarters of the land surface. The climate is hot and humid. The majority of the Bantu-speaking peoples are Fang and there are sizeable minorities of Mbeti, Tsogo, Njabi, Shira, Teke, Omyene, Mpongwe Punu. One-tenth of the population are expatriates from neighboring countries and France. The majority is Christian, due in part to the efforts of the famous Dr. Albert Schweitzer who spent most of his adult life in his missionary leper hospital at Lambarene on the Ogoue River. French is the official language.

HISTORY

The earliest inhabitants of the Gabonese jungles were small bands of Pygmies or Babinga. Some 600 years ago Bantu-speaking peoples from the north started settling the coastal areas. They moved to the interior during the 16th Century. The Portuguese established contact in 1472 and were followed by Dutch, British and French who traded in slaves, ivory and precious tropical woods with the coastal kingdoms. The French established a fortified settlement on the Gabon estuary which evolved into Libreville, a community for liberated slaves. At the urging of explorer Count Pierre Savorgnan de Brazza, the areas known as Gabon and the Middle Congo

were occupied by France in 1886. In 1910 part of Gabon was incorporated into French Equatorial Africa but a year later the northern parts of Gabon and Congo Brazzaville were ceded by treaty to German Cameroon. They were returned to the French after World War I and in 1960 a unified Gabon became an independent republic. When its first president, Leon M'Ba, died in 1967 Vice-President Albert Bernard Bongo took over and continued his pre-decessor's one-man rule until 1992 when he was obliged to call general elections in response to strong internal student and worker pressures. (After his conversion to Islam in 1973, Bongo changed his given names, Albert Bernard to El Hadji Omar). In 1993 Bongo was elected president in a disputed election. He was re-elected in 1998 and again in 2005 for another seven year term, making him one of the longest-serving heads of state in the world.

GOVERNMENT

An executive President is directly elected by the voters for 7-year terms. He appoints the Prime Minister and the Council of Ministers. The bicameral legislature consists of a 91-member Senate (Sénat), elected for six years, and a 120-member National Assembly or Assemblée Nationale, elected for 5-year terms. In 2003 President Omar Bongo's Parti démocratique gabonais (PDG) won a majority in the Senate over Rassemblement National des Bûcherons (RNB) or National Rally of Woodcutters and several minor parties. In the 2001 election the PDG gained a landslide victory over the RNB and a few other smaller parties by capturing 88 of the 120 seats in the National Assembly.

ECONOMIC POLICY

Recent reforms in coordination with the World Bank aim to build a stronger and more diversified economy and reduce debt through privatization and diversification. The government has stepped up its efforts to attract foreign skills and technology to assist in the effort. Privatization is underway.

SECTORS

The economy is dominated by the oil sector, which accounts for about half of GDP and government revenue, sixty percent of gross investment, and over three quarters of merchandise exports. With oil production of 268,900 bbl/day from both offshore and onshore wells, Gabon is Africa's third largest oil producer. After oil, timber and man-

FAST FACTS

Pres. El Hadj
Omar Bongo
Born: Dec. 30, 1935
Since 1967

POLITICAL

Head of State	Pres. El Hadj Omar Bongo
Ruling Party	PDG
Main Opposition	RNB
Independence	17 August 1960
National capital	Libreville
Official language	French

PHYSICAL

Total area	103,347 sq. miles
	267,670 sq. km.
	(± Colorado)
Arable land	1.26% of land area
Coastline	550 miles/885 km

POPULATION

Total	1.42 million
Av. yearly growth	2.13%
Population/sq. mile	12
Urban population	1.2 million
Adult literacy	63.2%

ECONOMY

Currency	CFA franc (CFAF)(UD$1: 559.44)
GDP (real)	$6.7 billion
GDP growth rate	2.1%
GDP per capita[1]	$6.153
GDP (ppp)[2]	$9.5 billion
GDP per cap. (ppp)	$6,800
Inflation rate	-0.1%
Exports	$5.8 billion
Imports	$1.5 billion
External debt	$3.9 billion
Unemployment	21%

1. *Atlas method.*
2. *See page 175 for an explanation of purchasing power parity (ppp).*

ganese are major foreign currency earners. The government is encouraging investors to develop value added operations in the timber industry as less than 10% of the logs are currently locally processed. Okoume, a soft mahogany, represents 75% of wood production. The remainder consists of a large variety of exotic hardwoods. Gabon is Africa's second largest producer of manganese after South Africa and the fourth largest uranium source (after Niger, South Africa and Namibia). High-grade iron ore is still largely unexploited and there is scope for small-scale gold mining. Agriculture, livestock and fishing make up a little less than 8% of GDP. The principal food crops are cassava, maize, manioc, fruit and vegetables. Palm oil, cocoa, coffee, sugar cane, cotton and rubber are cultivated for export. Industry, including energy and construction, accounts for only 10% of GDP and consists of the SOGARA oil refinery in Port Gentil, a cement plant, paint factory and the processing of sugar, flour, beer, cigarettes and bread. The telecommunications system is one of the most advanced in Africa.

PRIVATIZATION

Privatization is underway in various sectors. Targets include the Trans-Gabonese railway (OC-TRA), the state electricity and water monopoly (SEEG), and the telecommunications monopoly, Office des Postes et Télécommu-nications du Gabon (OPT). Experienced international consultants have been engaged to help evaluate needs and to manage tenders.

INVESTMENT

With the help of their government, French firms manage to maintain an edge over competitors from other countries. US firms are most active in the petroleum sector but in recent years some have started focusing on fisheries, port development, transport, and light industry. Spain, Germany, Italy, and Britain are also significant players.

TRADE

Until oil was discovered, tropical timber was the main export item. Today timer products account for only 10% of exports compared with petroleum's 80% share and around 10% for uranium and manganese. The US buys about two-thirds of Gabon's oil (averaging $1.5 billion per year), as well as minerals and timber. US sales to Gabon consist largely of petroleum-related machinery and other heavy equipment.

FINANCIAL SECTOR

French banks dominate in a relatively sophisticated system offering full corporate banking services. Gabon is a member of the French franc zone. The BEAC, headquartered in Yaoundé, issues currency and controls liquidity within the zone. There is no stock exchange.

TAXES AND TARIFFS

Although there have been tariff disputes over the importation of exploration equipment in the past, there are few barriers in the crude oil sector where most of US firms are involved. Normally equipment used in the crude oil sector—such as seismic boats and drilling equipment—enters on a duty free basis. Customs duties apply to virtually all other imported goods. An 18% value-added tax is levied on companies with revenues exceeding $400,000.

FOREIGN PRESENCE

Since its independence Gabon has been pro-West and has maintained a strong relationship with the United States and Europe. American manufacturers have been involved in the installation of 13 earth stations for the domestic satellite network and the establishment of a cellular communications system.

BUSINESS ACTIVITY

AGRICULTURE
Cocoa, coffee, sugar, palm oil, rubber, cattle, okoume (tropical softwood), fish.

INDUSTRIES
Food and beverage, textiles, lumbering, plywood, cement, petroleum, extraction and refining, manganese, uranium, gold, chemicals, ship repair.

NATURAL RESOURCES
Petroleum, manganese, uranium.

EXPORTS
$5.8 billion (est. 2005): crude oil, timber, manganese, uranium.

IMPORTS
$1.5 billion (est. 2005): machinery and equipment, foodstuffs, chemicals, construction materials.

MAJOR TRADING PARTNERS
US, China, France, Netherlands, Cameroon, Trinidad & Tobago.

Doing Business with Gabon

INVESTMENT

Apart from ongoing opportunities in the petroleum sector, Gabon offers considerable scope in mining of alkaline, niobium, titanium, gold, diamonds and phosphates. Privatization opens up new investment opportunities to foreigners in transport, telecommunications and manufacturing, involving parastatals such as Air Gabon, the Trans-Gabonese railway (OCTRA), the national post and telecommunications authority (OPT), the sugar monopoly (SOSUHO) and the oil refinery (SOGARA). There is also an active recruitment of investment in wood processing, light industries, fisheries and port development.

TRADE

The largest portion of foreign sales to Gabon relates to petroleum exploration and mining equipment, as well as other heavy machinery. Major local mining operations—manganese (COMILOG), uranium (COMUF) and phosphate (SOMIMO)—maintain large inventories of US cranes, drag lines, trucks and tractors. Foreign manufacturers have also developed a share in the growing market for state-of-the-art equipment in the telecommunications sector. Gabon is a net food importer.

TRADE FINANCE

Credit is provided through six commercial banks and payment is usually by irrevocable letters of credit. A parastatal funded by the African Development Bank helps finance purchases by small and medium-sized firms owned by Gabonese nationals.

SELLING TO THE GOVERNMENT

In the past a poor payment record discouraged the Eximbank and other overseas agencies from extending credit to the government. As Gabon gets its house in order and better utilizes its substantial petroleum revenues this is bound to change. For the present, however, firms are advised to ensure that funds have been set aside in the official budget for specific items when they make the deal.

EXCHANGE CONTROLS

There are no restrictions on foreign capital and funds may be transferred freely for commercial transactions through regular banking channels. Funds can be transferred with minimal formality within the franc zone (including to France) and repatriation of capital is not subject to onerous restrictions.

PARTNERSHIPS

Joint ventures and licensing are limited but will increase as Gabon's proceeds with privatization. Both US and European soft drinks and beers are produced in Gabon under license.

ESTABLISHING A PRESENCE

To open a branch, applications must be filed with the Ministry of Commerce, the Tax Office of the Ministry of Finance, and the Social Security Office (*Caisse Nationale de Sécurité Sociale*—CNSS). The process can take up to three months and local legal assistance is advisable. Gabonese law allows foreign and local firms to operate as branches constituted locally as limited corporations, *Sociétés à Responsabilité Limitée* (SARL), or corporations, *Sociétés Anonymes* (SA).

FINANCING PROJECTS

Gabon is a member of the Multilateral Investment Guarantee Agency. OPIC involvement has been minimal.

LABOR

Some 20% of Gabon's population are alien Africans active in the informal sector as well as in low and high skill jobs in the formal sector. A serious shortage of Gabonese managers compels firms to recruit non-Gabonese Africans and the Department of Labor reluctantly authorizes such employment, mindful of the objective of the National Employment Commission to replace these expatriates with qualified Gabonese citizens. Labor unions and confederations are active.

LEGAL RIGHTS

There have been no instances of expropriation or nationalization of foreign firms. In some cases the government has mediated settlements of commercial or labor disputes on terms more favorable to foreign firms than those offered by the courts. Gabon is a member of the African Intellectual Property Office (OAPI) based in Yaoundé, Cameroon, and its courts enforce property rights. Registration is handled by the Ministry of Commerce.

BUSINESS CLIMATE

Experience has shown that to be successful an overseas firm needs tenacious, Frenchspeaking representatives who make repeated visits to potential customers. Personal contact and a knowledge of the territory are important. French is the only language of commerce.

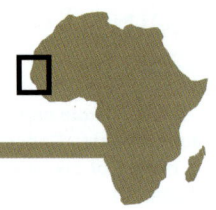

GAMBIA, THE

IN 1996, THE GAMBIA EXCHANGED MILITARY FOR CIVILIAN RULE AND LIBERALIZED ITS ECONOMY. MOST OF THE POPULATION DEPEND ON CROPS AND LIVESTOCK FOR THEIR LIVELIHOOD. SMALL SCALE MANUFACTURING INVOLVES PROCESSING PEANUTS, FISH AND HIDES. AS THE SMALLEST COUNTRY ON THE AFRICAN CONTINENT, THIS SLITHER OF LAND ALONG THE GAMBIA RIVER JUTTING INTO THE HEART OF SENEGAL HAS FOUND A NICHE IN TOURISM AND AS A TRADING POST BETWEEN WEST AFRICA AND THE WORLD. REEXPORTING FORMS A MAJOR PART OF THE COUNTRY'S ECONOMIC ACTIVITY. CONSTRUCTION PROJECTS AND TOURISM HAVE DRAWN FOREIGN PARTICIPANTS TO THIS FORMER BRITISH COLONY. THE GAMBIA, HOWEVER, CONTINUES TO RELY HEAVILY ON BILATERAL AND MULTILATERAL AID AS WELL AS IMF TECHNICAL ADVICE AND ASSISTANCE.

COUNTRY PROFILE

The Republic of The Gambia meanders for 470 km along the banks of one of Africa's most navigable rivers, the Gambia, into Senegal. The capital and main port of Banjul is built on a small peninsula on the south bank of a large, lake-like estuary. Beautiful beaches and warm coastal waters are the main tourist attractions. The climate is hot and humid. Ethnic groups comprise the Mande, including the rural Mandinka, and the Atlantic peoples, including the Wolof. English is the official language but Wolof is spoken in the towns and Mandinka in rural areas. About 85% of the population are Muslim. There is also a sizeable Christian minority.

HISTORY

From the 13th Century the Wolof, Malinke and Fulani peoples settled in the region. Portuguese mariners explored the waters of the Gambia river in the 1450s reaching far into the interior. In 1651, the Duchy of Courland (today's Latvia) took possession of islands in the river and small tracts of land alongside, notably Banjul and St. Andrew (now James Island), starting the first organized European settlement on the African mainland south of the Sahara. (The Cape of Good Hope was settled by the Dutch in the following year). In 1681 the French founded an enclave at Albredabut and during the 17th Century Gambia was occupied by various English merchant companies. From the 17th to the 18th Centuries Gambia was at the center of the slave trade and in 1888 it was declared a British colony. Dawda Jawara, the leader of the People's Progressive Party, led Gambia to independence in 1965. For a few years in the 1980s, Sir Dawda acted as vice-president of Senegambia, an experimental union with surrounding Senegal. After its dissolution he and his party again won elections in 1987 and 1992 but in July 1994 Dawda Jawara was ousted in a bloodless military coup by Lieut. Yaya Jammeh. In September 1996 Jammeh was elected president over three other candidates and

© Business Books

He was reelected in October 2001 and again in September 2006. A landslide victory in the latter despite opposition speculation that he might lose gave rise to charges of irregularities..

GOVERNMENT

The National Assembly has 48 members elected for a five year term and 5 appointed members. In January 2002 Jammeh's Alliance for Patriotic Reorientation and Construction (APRC) scored a landslide victory with 45 seats against 3 for the People's Democratic Organization for Independence and Socialism (PDOIS).

ECONOMIC POLICY

The government launched an economic development program under the banner "Vision 2020—The Gambia Incorporated" to capitalize further on a macroeconomic framework put in place with the help of successive IMF and World Bank structural adjustment programs.

SECTORS

The Gambia has no significant mineral or natural resources. A limited agricultual base accounts for 23% of gross domestic product (GDP) and employs 75% of the labor force. Peanuts represent 5.3% of GDP, other crops 8.3%, livestock 4.4%, and fishing 1.8%. Food crops include rice, maize, millet, sorghum, cassava and pulses. Industry contributes 12% of GDP. Manufacturing involves groundnut and fish processing, brewing, footwear, perfume, cement and brick production. Known mineral deposits include kaolin, tin, ilmenite, zircon and rutile. The country has had considerable success in developing its tourist industry, which contributes about 12% of GNP.

TRADE

India is The Gambia's major export market, accounting for more than 37%. China is its major supplier, followed by Senegal, Côte d'Ivoire and Brazil. The Gambia is an important entrepot for goods distributed to neighboring countries. However, a government-imposed preshipment inspection plan and currency instability has had a negative impact on The Gambia as a reexport base.

INVESTMENT

Growth sectors include construction, tourism, transportation, and to a limited degree, agriculture crop production and fisheries. Schools, roads, hospitals, a new airport terminal building, a new national television station (the first in The

FAST FACTS

Pres. Yaya A.J.J Jammeh
Born: May 25, 1965
Since 1994

POLITICAL

Head of State	Pres. Yaya Jammeh
Ruling Party	APRC
Main Opposition	PDOIS
Independence	18 February 1965
National capital	Banjul
Official language	English

PHYSICAL

Total area	4,361 sq. miles
	11,295 sq. km.
	(2 x Delaware)
Arable land	25% of land area
Coastline	50 miles/80 km

POPULATION

Total	1.64 million
Av. yearly growth	2.98%
Population/sq. mile	334
Urban population	400,000
Adult literacy	40.1%

ECONOMY

Currency	Dalasi (D)
	(US$1=28.75)
GDP (real)	$429 million
GDP growth rate	5.5%
GDP per capita[1]	$302
GDP (ppp)[2]	$3.02 billion
GDP per cap. (ppp)	$1,900
Inflation rate	8.8%
Exports	$140.3 million
Imports	$197 million
External debt	$628 million
Unemployment	N/A

1. *Atlas method.*
2. *See page 175 for an explanation of purchasing power parity (ppp).*

Business activity

Gambia), and Arch 22, a tourist attraction, have been built in recent years. The tourism sector continues to attract private sector investment. Despite announced plans to this effect, privatization of key parastatals has been slow in materializing. The seizure of a private peanut firm, Alimenta, has eliminated the largest buyer of Gambian groundnuts.

FINANCIAL SECTOR

Foreign exchange earnings are too small to pay for the country's imports, leaving it heavily dependent on bilateral and multilateral aid to cover the deficit. Foreign aid contributes 80% of the government's revenue.

TAXES & TARIFFS

The corporate tax rate has been reduced from 50% to 35 % in January 1996 for companies producing properly audited returns. There is a capital gains tax and customs levies on international trade based on the CIF as well as ad valorem value of imports. A flat 10% sales tax applies to all goods and services.

DOING BUSINESS WITH THE GAMBIA

▶ **INVESTMENT**

Designated as priority sectors for investment are manufacturing, agriculture, livestock, fisheries, forestry, mining and quarrying, tourism, and support services such as air cargo, transportation, banking and finance. Investments in these sectors qualify for exemption from customs duty and sales tax on imported capital goods and construction materials as well as special land lease arrangements. Investment incentives need to be negotiated up front. A one-stop office simplifies the establishment of foreign enterprises in The Gambia.

▶ **TRADE**

Most trade restrictions in the form of quotas, licensing, or other restrictive instruments of commerce have been removed.

▶ **EXCHANGE CONTROLS**

There are no exchange controls in effect. Profits and dividends from registered nonresident investments can be transferred without any restriction.

▶ **ESTABLISHING A PRESENCE**

Under the Companies Act, foreigners may establish public or private companies either un-

limited or limited in terms of shares or guarantees. Incorporation simply requires a memorandum and articles of association and registration is swift.

▶ **PROJECT FINANCE**

The Gambia is a member of the Multilateral Investment Guarantee Agency.

▶ **LABOR**

With a relatively high unemployment rate and less than 40% of the population literate, semi-skilled and unskilled workers are readily available.

▶ **LEGAL RIGHTS**

There are constitutional safeguards for the payment of adequate compensation in case of property acquisition or nationalization and the right to appeal to the Supreme Court. This generally positive record was marred by a January 1999 state takeover of the Gambia Groundnut Corporation, a subsidiary of the Swiss-based Alimenta group.

▶ **BUSINESS CLIMATE**

The business language is English but French is also spoken as a result of The Gambia's close relationship with Senegal and Côte d'Ivoire.

GHANA

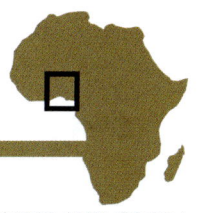

GHANA IS WELL ENDOWED WITH NATURAL RESOURCES. GOLD, TIMBER AND COCOA ARE MAJOR FOREIGN EXCHANGE EARNERS AND ENABLE GHANA TO RANK AMONG THE WEALTHIER NATIONS IN THE REGION. EVEN THOUGH IT HAS ROUGHLY TWICE THE PER CAPITA INCOME OF THE POORER NATIONS OF WEST AFRICA, GHANA REMAINS HEAVILY DEPENDENT ON INTERNATIONAL FINANCIAL AND TECHNICAL ASSISTANCE. SUBSISTENCE FARMING STILL ACCOUNTS FOR ABOUT A THIRD OF GDP AND PROVIDES EMPLOYMENT FOR MORE THAN HALF OF THE WORK FORCE. ECONOMIC REFORMS HAVE CREATED A FAVORABLE BUSINESS ENVIRONMENT FOR THE PRIVATE SECTOR.

COUNTRY PROFILE

The Republic of Ghana lies on a low plateau ranging between 500 and 1,000 ft. (150 to 300 m) above sea level. The Volta River feeds off its White and Black tributaries and has been dammed at Akosombo to form the vast Lake Volta stretching 250 miles (400 km) inland and covers 3.5% of the land area. English is the official language, but 75 native languages and dialects are also spoken. The Akan cultural group (consisting of the Asante, Fante, and Brong) forms 40% of the population. About 38% adhere to ethnic beliefs while Christianity (43%) dominates in the south and the Muslim faith (12%) remains strong in the far north.

HISTORY

Gold first attracted European exploration along what became known as the Gold Coast. In 1482 the Portuguese built the first fort at Elmina (The Mine). The Dutch, French, British and Germans followed. From the 16th until the 19th Century trade in gold was overshadowed by the slave trade. During this period the Asante people gained dominance and prompted weaker tribes such as the Fante to seek British protection. Britain took control and abolished slavery from the mid-19th Century. The British colony, Gold Coast, together with the former UN trust territory, British Togoland, was granted independence as Ghana in 1957, under the leadership of Kwame Nkrumah. After he was ousted in 1966, Nkrumah's military successors—Generals Joseph Ankrah, Kofi Busia, Ignatius Acheompong and Frederick Akkuffo—perpetuated one party rule. Inflation soared and corruption went unchecked. In 1979 a young Flight Lieutenant, Jerry Rawlings, seized power and installed Hilla Limann as president. In 1981 Rawlings seized power again. As head of the Provisional National Defense Council (PNDC) he abolished the constitution and jailed Limann. In 1992 a multiparty system was adopted and a presidential election held, which Rawlings won easily. He won reelection in 1996 but in December 2000 his deputy in the New Democratic Party

255

FAST FACTS

Pres. John Agyekum
Kufuor
Born: Dec. 8, 1938
Since 2000

POLITICAL

Head of State	Pres. John Agyekum Kufuor
Ruling Party	NPP
Main Opposition	NDC
Independence	6 March 1957
National capital	Accra
Official language	English

PHYSICAL

Total area	92,010 sq. miles
	238,305 sq. km.
	(± Oregon)
Arable land	16% of land area
Coastline	335 miles/539 km

POPULATION

Total	22.4 million
Av. yearly growth	2.07%
Population/sq. mile	212
Urban population	10.1 million
Adult literacy	74.8%

ECONOMY

Currency	Cedi
	(US$1=9,090)
GDP (real)	$9.4 billion
GDP growth rate	4.3%
GDP per capita[1]	$537
GDP (ppp)[2]	$48.27 billion
GDP per cap. (ppp)	$2,500
Inflation rate	15.1%
Exports	$2.91 billion
Imports	$4.27 billion
External debt	$7.4 billion
Unemployment	20%

1. Atlas method.
2. See page 175 for an explanation of purchasing power parity (ppp).

(NDC), John Evans Atta Mills, was defeated in his bid for the presidency by John Agyekum Kufuor of the New Patriotic Party (NPP). Kufuor was re-elected in December 2004.

GOVERNMENT

The President holds executive power and legislative power is vested in the 200-member National Assembly, both elected for four year terms. In the December 2004 elections John Kufuor's New Patriotic Party (NPP) defeated the ruling National Democratic Congress (NDC) with 128 seats against 94. Minor opposition parties are the People's National Convention (PNC) with 4 seats and the Convention People's Party (CPP) with 3 seats. There is one independent.

ECONOMIC POLICY

Even though Ghana stands out as one of the more successful economies in West Africa it remains heavily dependent on international finance and technical assistance. It embarked on an economic recovery program funded with low-interest loans from the IMF and World Bank affiliates. Drastic cuts in government expenditure were implemented, as well as a balanced budget, currency devaluation, reduction of the state's role in the economy and the encouragement of free enterprise. In 2002, Ghana opted for debt relief under the Heavily Indebted Poor Country (HIPC) program. Receipts from the gold sector helped sustain a healthy growth rate in recent years.

PRIVATIZATION

The Government has accelerated its program of divestiture of state owned enterprises and rehabilitation of roads, ports and the telecommunication systems, and facilitated private sector participation in the power industry. Through public-private partnerships and joint ventures in commercially viable Ghanaian power utilities the state-owned entities transform themselves and assumed a leadership role in the development of the proposed West Africa Power Pool. More than sixty state enterprises had been divested, while thirty-four were liquidated and another thirty privatized. In a heavily oversubscribed sale of its share in Ashanti Goldfields, the government earned $320 million. The Ghanaian government also sold most of its shares in Standard Chartered Bank (Ghana), Accra Breweries, Equity Insurance, Guinness Ghana, Kumasi Breweries, Pioneer Tobacco and Unilever (Ghana). The government is continuing with this divestiture of state-owned enterprises and reducing its direct role in the economy.

SECTORS

Ghana has large deposits of gold, diamonds, bauxite and manganese, as well as sizeable forests and arable land. It has a good potential in hydro-electric power. Agriculture is the most important economic sector. Ghana is among the world's largest exporters of cocoa. Timber is another major foreign currency earner. Crops grown for sale to local agro-industries include sugar, cotton, oil palms and rubber. Subsistence crops are rice, maize, sorghum, millet, groundnuts, yams and fruit. Mining is the second largest earner of foreign exchange. Gold tops the list with diamonds and manganese gaining in importance. Manufacturing remains relatively modest. Apart from a large aluminum smelter, most other industrial activity revolves around agro-business such as the processing of cocoa and beer brewing.

TRADING

Ghana's largest overall trading partner is the United Kingdom, followed by the United States, Netherlands, Nigeria and China. Nigeria is, however, the largest importer of Ghanaian goods, followed by China, the US and the United Kingdom.

INVESTMENT

Foreign direct investment is aggressively pursued by the Ghanaian government in an effort to stimulate growth as donor assistance is expected to diminish. Foreign investment in Ghana is mostly in mining and manufacturing. The United Kingdom is the largest investor with direct investments exceeding $750 million, much of it attributable to Lonrho's 41% stake in Ashanti Goldfields Corporation. US investments are largely in mining and foods and are expected to rise as there have been expressions of interest by American companies in the acquisition of state-owned communications and manufacturing firms earmarked for divestiture. There are significant investments by other foreign nationals through the government's privatization program. Norwegian investors are part owners of the state's Ghana Cement Works (GHACEM). Ghana Telecom is operated by the state in partnership with Telecom Malaysia. South African companies have become active in the mining sector. The private sector can

now source equity and loans through venture capital companies and equity through the Ghana Stock Exchange.

FINANCIAL SECTOR

The Central Bank oversees 11 commercial banks, 5 merchant banks and over 100 rural banks. In recent years, however, several state-owned banks have been privatized. Nonbank financial institutions (NBFIs) include a Stock Exchange, 21 insurance companies, the Social Security and National Insurance Trust (SSNIT), two discount houses, the Home Finance Company, numerous building societies, a venture capital company, a unit trust and 5 leasing companies.

TAXES AND TARIFFS

Economic reforms have created a new business environment for the private sector. They include removal of price controls, the lowering of the corporate tax, sales tax and excise tax, removal of controls on interest rates, bank charges and credit allocation. The corporate income tax rate is 35%, except for income derived from nontraditional exports (8%) and hotels (25%). A 10-year tax holiday applies to enterprises in the export processing zones. Foreign nationals pay a flat tax of 35%, irrespective of their income level. manufactured commodities.

BUSINESS ACTIVITY

AGRICULTURE
Cocoa, coffee, rice, cassava (tapioca), peanuts, corn, shear nuts, bananas, timber.

INDUSTRIES
Mining, lumbering, light manufacturing, aluminum smelting, food processing.

NATURAL RESOURCES
Gold, timber, industrial diamonds, bauxite, manganese, fish, rubber.

EXPORTS
$2.91 billion (est. 2005): gold, cocoa, timber, tuna, bauxite, aluminum, manganese ore, diamonds.

IMPORTS
$4.27 billion (2004 est.): capital equipment, petroleum, consumer goods, food, intermediate goods.

MAJOR TRADING PARTNERS
UK, Netherlands, US, Nigeria, China, Belgium, France, South Africa.

Doing Business with Ghana

▶ **Investment**

Ghana's telecommunications sector and roads need repair and expansion and deregulation opened up this field for foreign investment. Gold mining remains the focus of growth and exploration by foreign mining companies continues. The Ghana Investment Promotion Center Act of 1994 extends incentives to foreign investors, including tax holidays, accelerated depreciation, locational privileges and other inducements.

▶ **Trade**

Food processing and packaging equipment, telecommunications equipment, secondhand clothing and motor vehicles, mining machinery, construction and earth-moving equipment, computers and peripherals as well as hotel and restaurant equipment offer opportunities for exporters. The channels of distribution available to foreign suppliers of goods and services in Ghana are wholesalers, retail outlets, and agents or distributors.

▶ **Trade finance**

Traditional trade finance instruments such as letters of credit, collections, and funds transfers are available to the exporter. USDA credit guarantee programs provide access to financing for imports of wheat, rice, feed grains, vegetable oil, protein meal, dairy products, as well as agricultural equipment.

▶ **Selling to the government**

The Ghana Supply Commission (GSC) handles procurement on behalf of the government and its agencies. Procurement is typically financed by a multilateral lending institution such as the World Bank, the African Development Bank or the International Finance Corporation.

▶ **Exchange Control**

The government of Ghana has moved away from exchange controls and has permitted the establishment of Foreign Exchange Bureaus. The cedi can now be readily exchanged for foreign currency.

▶ **Partnerships**

The Ghanaian Investment Code provides legislative encouragement for joint venture activities. The government guarantees transfers of capital, profits and dividends.

▶ **Establishing a presence**

Foreigners intending to invest in Ghana should first contact the Ghana Investment Promotion Center (GIPC), a one-stop shop for economic, commercial and investment information. The minimum required equity for foreign investors is $10,000 in joint ventures or $50,000 for enterprises wholly owned by foreign nationals. Trading companies either wholly or partly owned by non-Ghanaians require a minimum foreign equity of $300,000 and employment of at least 10 locals.

▶ **Project financing**

Private sector projects in Ghana might qualify for International Finance Corporation assistance and, in the case of US firms, Overseas Private Investment Corporation loans, loan guarantees and insurance. All the programs of the Eximbank apply. The US Trade and Development Agency finances feasibility studies.

▶ **Labor**

Ghana has a large pool of inexpensive, unskilled labor. Even though there is no legal requirement to involve labor in management deliberations, joint consultative committees involving management and labor are common.

▶ **Legal rights**

Ghana follows British common law and recognizes the right of foreign and domestic private entities to own and operate business enterprises. Ghana is a member of the World Intellectual Property Organization and the English-speaking African Regional Industrial Property Organization (ESARIPO). In 1996, the Ghana Arbitration Center was established to strengthen the legal framework for the protection of commercial and economic interests.

▶ **Business climate**

English is the official language and is used in most business transactions. Normally Ghanaian businessmen wear business suits during working hours and resort to traditional attire for social functions. Often, however, they may also be found in traditional attire during business hours. Businesswomen wear African attire during business hours as well as for social functions.

GUINEA

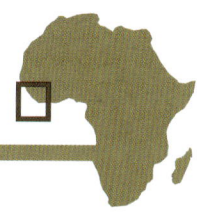

GUINEA'S ECONOMY HAS BEEN RECONSTRUCTED SINCE 1984 WHEN THE SO-
CIALIST DICTATORSHIP OF SÉKOU TOURÉ CAME TO AN END. WHILE THE INFORMAL
SECTOR RESPONSE TO THE MORE LIBERAL ECONOMIC POLICIES INTRODUCED BY
TOURÉ'S SUCCESSOR, GENERAL LASANA CONTÉ, HAS BEEN IMPRESSIVE, INTERNATIONAL
TRADE, AGRICULTURAL PRODUCTION, AND MANUFACTURING HAVE SHOWED SLOWER
PROGRESS. POOR PHYSICAL AND INSTITUTIONAL INFRASTRUCTURE, AN ERRATIC AND
UNPREDICTABLE JUDICIAL SYSTEM, AND CORRUPT PRACTICES CONTRIBUTED TO THE
WEAK FORMAL SECTOR RESPONSE. PRESIDENT CONTÉ HAS PROMISED MAJOR ECO-
NOMIC REFORMS, INCLUDING FINANCIAL AND JUDICIAL REFORM, REDUCTION OF
PUBLIC EXPENDITURES, AND IMPROVED REVENUE COLLECTION. THE COUNTRY IS RICH
IN MINERALS AND FERTILE LAND AND HAS BY ALL ACCOUNTS THE POTENTIAL TO BE
RELATIVELY PROSPEROUS.

COUNTRY PROFILE

The Republic of Guinea is a kidney-shaped country with a coastline marked by shallow estuaries and mangrove swamps. Apart from French, the official language, several native languages are spoken. The Ful (or Fulani), inhabiting the Futa Jallon Highlands, is the largest single group but collectively the Mande people (comprising the Baga, Nalu, Kisi and Landuma) form the majority. Guinea is largely Muslim with less than 2% Christians, mostly Roman Catholic.

HISTORY

Portuguese explorers arrived in the second half of the 15th Century. Though not a major slave trading region, the Los Islands near Conakry were used as slave depots. After the Portuguese came the British and eventually the French, who gained possession of the territory in 1884. Under the leadership of a trade union leader, Sékou Touré, Guinea voted in a 1958 referendum to reject an offer by France of autonomy within the French Community. The French granted Guinea independence and withdrew all assistance and personnel. Touré's socialist dictatorship led to economic decay and the emigration of close to 1 million citizens. After Touré's death in 1984, Gen. Lansana Conté seized power. In 1992 a multi-party system was introduced and Conté retained the presidency. He was reelected in 1998 and again in 2003.

GOVERNMENT

In terms of the new constitution both the president and a 114-seat unicameral National Assembly are elected for five year terms. In June 2002 Conté's Party for Unity

259

Fast Facts

Pres. Lansana Conté
Born: 1934
Since 1984

POLITICAL

Head of State	Pres. Lansana Conté
Ruling Party	PUP
Main opposition	UPR
Independence	2 October 1958
National capital	Conakry
Official language	French

PHYSICAL

Total area	94,925 sq. miles
	245,857 sq. km.
	(± Oregon)
Arable land	3.6% of land area
Coastline	199 miles/320 km

POPULATION

Total	9.7 million
Av. yearly growth	2.63%
Population/sq. mile	79
Urban population	3.2 million
Adult literacy	36%

ECONOMY

Currency	Guinea franc
	(GNF)(US$1=4,120)
GDP (real)	$3.57 billion
GDP growth rate	2%
GDP per capita[1]	$350
GDP (ppp)[2]	$18.99 billion
GDP per cap. (ppp)	$2,000
Inflation rate	25%
Exports	$612.1 million
Imports	$680 million
External debt	$3.46 billion
Unemployment	N/A

1. Atlas method.
2. See page 175 for an explanation of
   purchasing power parity (ppp).

and Progress (PUP) won 85 seats against 20 for the main opposition, the Union for Progress and Renewal (UPR)—the other 9 split between several smaller parties.

ECONOMIC POLICY

In 1984 President Conté inherited a country impoverished by his predecessor's socialist-driven policies. He launched an ambitious program of reform, aimed at dismantling the 24-year-old centralized, state-run economy. Measures were adopted to create a market economy and open the country to trade and investment from outside. Significant progress has been made in downsizing and improving the performance of the public sector, the regulatory environment, liberalizing the price controls, exchange and trade system, and increasing the efficiency of the tax collection.

PRIVATIZATION

The government is gradually disengaging from productive and commercial activities. A comprehensive program was introduced. Plans are afoot to sell the state's 49% stake in the country's largest bauxite mining company, Compagnie des Bauxites de Guinee (CBG). Although there were several publicized investment failures in 1996 and 1997 (mainly due to corruption and poor management), reforms and privatization efforts in the energy sector are bound to create opportunities for foreign investment. Water and electricity production grew significantly. A significant increase in energy production followed the completion of the hydroelectric site at Garafiri. The French and Canadians are primary investors in the energy sector.

SECTORS

Guinea has major mineral, hydropower and agricutural resources. Even though only 3% of the land is under cultivation, agriculture accounts for about one-third of the GDP and provides work for three-quarters of the labor force. Coffee is the most important export crop. Bananas, cotton, pineapples, palm oil, groundnuts and citrus fruits are also grown. Forestry shows considerable potential. Mining remains the most dynamic sector and accounts for most of Guinea's export earnings. The country's bauxite reserves, estimated at 20 billion tons, constitute the world's largest. Guinea is the world's second largest supplier of bauxite and ranks third in aluminum production. Apart from aluminum smelting, the manufacturing sector is small and mostly geared to the local market.

TRADING

Guinea remains largely dependent on mineral exports. Mining receipts account for about three-quarters of the country's foreign exchange earnings. In spite of the growth of its domestic agriculture, The country is, however, a large importer of agricultural products, tobacco, and alcoholic and non-alcoholic beverages. Flour imports originate largely in France with some Belgian contribution. Principal sugar suppliers include France, Belgium, and Italy. Guinea has no free trade or export processing zones or warehouses, but a temporary license to conduct free trade transactions can be obtained with special permission from the Ministry of Finance.

INVESTMENT

Full foreign ownership is permitted in commercial, industrial, mining, agricultural and service sectors. Industries that are restricted from having a majority of foreign ownership are radio, television, and newspapers. The government currently controls, owns, and operates the electronic media, although in 2005, President Conte signed a decree establishing the process for private ownership of broadcast media. France is Guinea's strongest traditional economic partner and provides extensive development assistance. French businesses are active in a variety of sectors including banking, insurance, shipping, communications, construction, agricultural export, and manufacturing. Canadians and Belgians also have a strong local presence. Malaysians began investing in Guinea in telecommunications and banking and shown interest in construction, tourism and agriculture. Lebanese traders are involved in real estate, small manufacturing enterprises, and telecommunications, supermarkets, wholesale food, and electronics. Outside of the mining sector, foreign-aid projects continue to provide the largest source of business opportunities for expatriate firms and are critical driving forces in developing Guinea's infrastructure. Priority areas are education, health, agricultural marketing, rural road construction, and rural enterprise development. During the past few years, USAID has supported the construction of over 1,000 km of rural roads in Guinea. Recurrent fighting along Guinea's borders with Liberia and Sierra Leone, accompanied by large-scale refugee movements, has had a negative impact on investor's confidence.

FINANCIAL SECTOR

The banking system is being reconstructed with the assistance of the IMF and the World Bank. Guinea is, however, not receiving multialteral aid as both the IMF and World Bank has ceased such assistance in 2003.

TAXES AND TARIFFS

In 1994, through a variety of income and import tax increases, the burden on international businesses increased significantly. International financial experts in Conakry criticized this step as one that diminished the level of compensation to investors in Guinea's poor infrastructure and difficult work environment. In 1996 an 18% value added tax (VAT) was introduced on all items except exports, international transportation, and certain basic food items. Since 1998, the government has focused on improving tax administration and collection to increase revenues from non-mining sources. Guinea has a flat import tax rate of 33% on most items. Public investment projects and donor organizations are exempted. A surtax of between 20% and 70% is imposed on luxury items, such as vehicles, alcohol and tobacco. In 1996, the government appointed a Swiss company, SGS, to manage customs.

BUSINESS ACTIVITY

AGRICULTURE
Rice, coffee, pineapples, palm kernels, cassava (tapioca), bananas, sweet potatoes, cattle, sheep, goats, timber.

INDUSTRIES
Bauxite, gold, diamonds, alumina refining, light manufacturing, agricultural processing.

NATURAL RESOURCES
Bauxite, iron ore, diamonds, gold.

EXPORTS
$612.1 million (est. 2004): Bauxite, alumina, diamonds, gold, coffee, fish, agricultural products.

IMPORTS
$680 million (est. 2005): petroleum products, metals, machinery, transport equipment, textiles, grain and other foodstuffs.

MAJOR TRADING PARTNERS
Russia, US, China, Belgium, Ireland, Spain, France, Côte d'Ivoire, Italy, Germany.

Doing Business with Guinea

► INVESTMENT

Privatization in the telecommunications, banking and energy sectors has opened up new areas for foreign investment. Under the auspices of The United Nations Development Program and the United Nations Industrial Development Organization Guinea listed over 100 private and public investment projects, totaling more than $150 million in the agriculture, fishing, industry, and public works sectors. Other targeted sectors include mining, manufacturing, transportation, and energy. Investing is simplified by the Office of Private Investment Promotion (OPIP), a one-stop business registration office, centralizing the administrative, legal, fiscal, and other formalities.

► TRADE

Apart from agricultural products, good prospects for exports to Guinea are machinery and equipment, petroleum products, construction/semi-finished material, industry/manufacturing, telecommunications and hi-tech equipment (computers, soft/hardware), and consumer goods (canned/dry supermarket goods, textiles, cosmetics, used clothing, alcoholic and other beverages, and tobacco products). Expansion of telecommunication and Internet services should increase the demand for cellular phones, relay towers, and switches.

► TRADE FINANCE

Guinea qualifies for three US Department of Agriculture export promotion programs: the dairy export incentive program, a GSM-102 credit program, and a wheat export enhancement program.

► SELLING TO THE GOVERNMENT

Donor countries and institutions usually stipulate the bidding rules for foreign-financed public investment projects. The AGCP (Guinean Central Procurement Agency) handles projects/contracts over one million dollars. The Public Market (*Marché Publique*) handles projects/contracts under one million dollars.

► EXCHANGE CONTROL

All initial capital investments and earnings generated can be converted and repatriated, but only 50% of Guinean capital can be converted or transferred.

► PARTNERSHIP AND PRESENCE

The US Embassy commercial officer, local Chamber of Commerce, the Employers' Association, and Guinean Offices of Investment Promotion are all useful points of contact for business people contemplating establishing a presence. No franchises currently exist in Guinea.

► PROJECT FINANCING

The African Development Bank's private sector window in Abidjan has funding available for development-oriented business projects. The Overseas Private Investment Corporation will also accept applications for investment projects in Guinea. The US Trade and Development Agency assists in the financing of feasibility studies.

► LABOR

Labor is ample but there is a critical shortage of skilled managers and administrators with private sector experience. Employers no longer need to go through the labor office to hire or fire an employee, and there is no obligation to employ only Guineans. The labor code legalizes labor unions and the right to collective bargaining.

► LEGAL RIGHTS

The legal, regulatory, and accounting systems are based upon French civil law but are not always applied uniformly or transparently. While Guinea's laws are designed to promote free enterprise and competition, senior government officials have publicly acknowledged shortcomings due to corruption and lack of training. The government has committed itself to strengthening the judicial and legal institutions to attract more foreign investment and improve economic conditions. The establishment of an independent Arbitration Court is specifically aimed at protecting foreign business people from corruption within the judicial system. Guinea is a member of the African Intellectual Property Organization comprised of 15 African countries and the World Intellectual Property Organization. The country is in the process of modifying its intellectual property right laws to bring them up to international standards.

► BUSINESS CLIMATE

Most Guineans are Muslim, and Islam plays a major role in shaping the customs and habits of the local business culture. Foreigners should be familiar with the basic tenets of Islam to facilitate business dealings. Friendship and trust are very important and it takes time to build a successful working relationship. Patience and face-to-face contact are requirements for successful business.

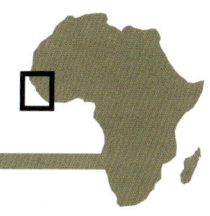

GUINEA-BISSAU

GUINEA-BISSAU COUNTS AMONG THE WORLD'S TEN POOREST COUNTRIES. AS THE WORLD'S SIXTH LARGEST PRODUCER GUINEA-BISSAU RELIES HEAVILY ON THE EXPORT OF CASHEW NUTS, AS WELL AS PEANUTS, PALM KERNELS AND TIMBER. THESE PRODUCTS COULD BE ECLIPSED BY THE MINING OF PHOSPHATE AND OTHER MINERALS AND THE EXPLOITATION OF PETROLEUM. SO FAR HIGH COST AND LACK OF INFRASTRUCTURE HAVE, HOWEVER, DISCOURAGED POTENTIAL FOREIGN INVESTORS IN MINING BUT OFFSHORE OIL PROSPECTING HAS STARTED. THE DOMESTIC ECONOMY RELIES HEAVILY ON FISHING AND FARMING, WITH RICE AS A MAJOR CROP.

COUNTRY PROFILE

The Republic of Guinea-Bissau consists mostly of low-lying marshland. The name of its capital, Bissau, is included in its name to distinguish it from its larger neighbor, Guinea. Its coastline is interrupted by meandering rivers, wide estuaries and adjoined by 18 islands known as the Bijagos (Bissagos) Archipelago. The climate is tropical, hot and wet. Rainfall in the north ranges between 1,000 and 2,000 mm. Within a relatively small area, Guinea-Bissau contains an ethnically diverse population consisting of seven significant cultural groups alongside the dominant Balanta. There is a sizable expatriate community of Portuguese, Syrian and Lebanese traders, most of them involved in commerce. The majority of Guinea-Bissau's inhabitants adheres to traditional ethnic beliefs while one-third is Muslim and about ten percent Christian. Portuguese is the official language but several native tongues are spoken as well as French, mostly in business circles.

HISTORY

In the 13th Century Guinea-Bissau was part of the Kingdom of Gabu in ancient Mali. During the 15th Century Portugal built forts along the coast and engaged in slave trade with the rulers of the region. Rios de Guine, (as it was called then) was administered by the Portuguese from Cape Verde until 1879 when it became a separate colony. After the abolition of slavery, groundnut cultivation became the mainstay of the economy. At the Berlin Conference in 1885, Portuguese Guinea was formally recognized by the European powers. By the 1950s the Balanta and other coastal peoples joined with Cape Verdean dissidents to form the Partido Africano da Independência da Guiné é Cabo Verde (PAIGC) and engaged in an armed struggle against the Portuguese rulers. In September 1974 when the Portuguese army overthrew

SENEGAL
Pirada
Sao Domingos
Ingore
Farim
Mansaba
Gabu
Geba
Cacheu
rela
Cacheu
Sao
Vicente
Bissora
Geba
Bafata
Canchungo
Bula
Mansoa
Mansoa
Babadinca
Ciao
Safirn
BISSAU
Xime
Jeta
Fulacunda
Beli
Pecize
Xitole
Boe
Corubal
Sao Joao
Caravela
Formosa
Bolama
Buba
— Road
uipelago dos Bijagos
Bubaque
Roxa
Catio
Uno
GUINEA
Orango
Cacine
ATLANTIC OCEAN
0   50   100   150 km
usiness Books Intl.
16°W
15°W
14°W

FAST FACTS

Pres. João
Bernardo Vieira
Born: April 27, 1939
Since October 2005
© IRIN

POLITICAL

Head of State	Pres. João Bernardo Vieira
Ruling Party	PAIGC
Main Opposition	PRS
Independence	24 September 1973
National capital	Bissau
Official language	Portuguese

PHYSICAL

Total area	13,945 sq. miles 36,120 sq. km. (3 x Connecticut)
Arable land	11% of land area
Coastline	217 miles/350 km

POPULATION

Total	1.4 million
Av. yearly growth	2.07%
Population/sq. mile	92
Urban population	600,000
Adult literacy	42.4%

ECONOMY

Currency	CFA franc (CFAF)(US$1=559.44)
GDP (real)	$280 million
GDP growth rate	2.3%
GDP per capita[1]	$189
GDP (ppp)[2]	$1.19 billion
GDP per cap. (ppp)[3]	$800
Inflation rate	4%
Exports	$116 million
Imports	$176 million
External debt	$941.5 million
Unemployment	N/A

1. Atlas method.
2. See page 175 for an explanation of purchasing power parity (ppp).

the Caetano dictatorship in Lisbon, Guinea-Bissau was the first of the five Portuguese African territories to achieve independence. Its first ruler, Pres. Luiz Cabral, was deposed by the military veteran prime minister João Bernardo "Nino" Vieira in 1980 who remained in power until 2000 when he was defeated at the polls by Kumba Ialá. After several refusals to call elections Ialá was toppled in a bloodless coup in September 2003 by Gen. Verissimo Correla Seabra. After a caretaker period with the interim appointed Pres. Henrique Rosa at the helm, a presidential election was held in July 2005. Vieira won the presidential election and returned to power.

GOVERNMENT

In terms of the constitution the president is elected by popular vote for a 5-year term, has executive power and appoints the Prime Minister and the Council of Ministers. Members of the 102-member unicameral People's National Assembly are elected for 4-years. In the March 2004 Assembly elections the PAIGC won 45 seats against 35 for the Partido para a Renovaçao Social (PRS), 17 for the United Social Democratic party (PUSD) and 3 for smaller parties. Carlos Gomes, as leader of the majority party, assumed the premiership.

ECONOMIC POLICY

The country's structural adjustment program involving trade reform and price liberalization helped it to attain one of the highest growth rates in Sub-Saharan Africa for almost a decade until 1998, when progress was disrupted by civil strife and most gains wiped out. The government is working together with the World Bank and IMF to implement reforms and promote growth.

SECTORS

Agriculture, fisheries and forestry account for about 90% of employment, an estimated 50% of GDP, and about three-quarters of export revenues. Even though cashew nuts and groundnuts are major export crops, most agriculture consists of subsistence food production and the raising of livestock in the higher-lying areas. High cost has impeded the development of phosphate and other minderal resoruces but petroleum exploration is continuing and promises to become a significant foreign exchange earner. A tightening of government spending under World Bank, IMF and UNDP auspices and the development of the private sector have stimulated some growth.

PRIVATIZATION

A new investment law was adopted to facilitate private participation in all key sectors. A privatization council appointed to oversee the restructuring of state-owned businesses resumed its activity after the restoration of peace.

INVESTMENT

Offshore oil was discovered in 1958 near Guinea-Bissau's border with Senegal but it took until the 1980s to obtain funding from the World Bank for a seismic survey. Exploration agreements signed with foreign oil companies were held up by a border dispute with Senegal. In the nineties an agreement was reached which entitled Senegal to 85% of the petroleum and mineral resources in the disputed area.

TRADE

At about three quarters of export revenue, cashew nuts are the major foreign exchange earner. The downstream petroleum industry is largely dependent on refined petroleum products imported from neighboring countries.

FINANCIAL SECTOR

Guinea-Bissau joined the West African Monetary Union (WAEMU) in 1997 and incorporated its central bank into the Central Bank of West Africa (BCEAO).

TAXES AND TARIFFS

Comprehensive tax reform was adopted in with the introduction of a generalized sales tax, review of customs tariffs and the reform of excise taxes.

BUSINESS ACTIVITY

AGRICULTURE
Rice, corn, beans, cassava (tapioca), cashew nuts, peanuts, palm kernels, cotton, timber, fish.

INDUSTRIES
Agricultural products processing, beer, soft drinks.

NATURAL RESOURCES
Fish, timber, phosphates, bauxite, unexploited deposists of petroleum.

EXPORTS
$116 million (est. 2005): cashews, peanuts, palm kernels, sawn lumber, shrimp.

IMPORTS
$176 million (est. 2005): foodstuffs, transport equipment, petroleum products, machinery and equipment.

MAJOR TRADING PARTNERS
India, Senegal, Italy, Nigeria, Portugal, Ecuador.

DOING BUSINESS WITH GUINEA-BISSAU

▶ INVESTMENT

Since 1993 when it reached a settlement in an offshore territorial dispute with Senegal, Guinea Bissau has placed 4 offshore blocks on offer. The government is also actively seeking foreign participation in the development of its underutilized fish and timber sectors. In mining there is also good potential for exploration and exploitation. Guinea-Bissau's considerable hydropower potential is another area that attracts the attention of foreign investors. Railroad repair and other infrastructure projects are in the offing.

▶ TRADE

Substantial quantities of rice are being imported. Once further developed, the country's fish and timber resources could be of special interest to foreign importers. Gasoline and kerosene form a significant portion of the country's import needs.

▶ SELLING TO THE GOVERNMENT

Future business with the government will most likely be in petroleum equipment, timber and mining machinery, road and rail construction equipment and rolling stock. Procurement, distribution and marketing of fuel products are carried out by the state owned oil company, *Distribudora de Combustiveis e Lubrificantes* (DICOL) together with the Portuguese oil company, Petrogal.

▶ EXCHANGE CONTROLS

As a member of the West African Monetary Union (WAMU), Guinea Bissau offers currency convertibility and applies few controls.

▶ BUSINESS CLIMATE

Although Portuguese is the official language, French is widely used. Customs in the business community are French-European.

KENYA

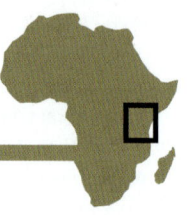

KENYA SERVES AS A REGIONAL HUB FOR TRADE AND FINANCE IN EAST AFRICA. FOR SOME TIME GROWTH HAS BEEN IMPEDED BY TO MUCH RELIANCE ON PRIMARY GOODS AND CORRUPTION. SINCE 2003 CONSIDERABLE PROGRESS WAS MADE UNDER THE NEW GOVERNMENT IN COMBATING CORRUPTION AND ENCOURAGING DONOR SUPPORT. RECENT REFORMS AND MARKET DEREGULATION ARE ALSO EXPECTED TO FURTHER STIMULATE INTEREST AMONG FOREIGN INVESTORS. THERE HAS BEEN INCREASED FOREIGN PARTICIPATION IN KENYA'S CAPITAL MARKETS AFTER THE LIBERALIZATION OF FOREIGN EXCHANGE FLOWS.

COUNTRY PROFILE

The Republic of Kenya is bisected by the Great Rift Valley extending from Lake Turkana in the north to Lake Natron on the Tanzanian border. There are some 20 national parks, including Masai Mara (adjoining Tanzania's Serengeti park), Amboseli and Tsavo. The equator runs across the foothills of snow-capped Mount Kenya (17,057 ft/5,199 m), Africa's second highest mountain. Three quarters of the population consist of Bantu-speaking peoples (Kikuyu, Luhya and Kamba) while the remainder are Nilotic (Luo, Maasai or Masai, Samburu, Turkana and Kalenjin). Other minority groups include the Indian, Arab and European expatriates. English and Swahili are official languages. About three-quarters of the population is Christian while the rest adhere to ethnic beliefs.

HISTORY

The discovery of fossilized remains of human-like beings and Stone Age relics from archaeological sites in Kenya gave rise to the belief that this region might well be the cradle of humanity. Paleontologists estimate that people may first have inhabited Kenya 2 million years ago. The Nilotic people expanded southward during the beginning of Christian era into western Kenya where they absorbed the Cushitic and Omotic communities. They were joined by the Bantu-speaking peoples and in the 10th Century Muslim merchants began to develop ports and trading stations along the coast. Portuguese explorer Vasco da Gama was the first European to drop anchor at Mombasa in 1498. The region became a British protectorate in 1890 and a crown colony in 1920. In 1905

Nairobi, strategically located halfway along the newly completed railway to Lake Victoria, became the capital of the British East Africa. To the chagrin of the locals, white settlers had occupied almost all the prime agricultural land by the 1950s. Discontented with the slow progress towards meaningful land reform and political change, the Kikuyu-dominated Mau Mau movement under the leadership of Jomo Kenyatta engaged in a drawn-out, costly struggle. Independence was granted

by Britain in 1963 and Kenyatta was elected president as leader of the Kenya African national Union (KANU). In 1978 when Kenyatta died, he was succeeded by Vice-President Daniel arap Moi, a member of the minority Kalenjin group, chosen as a compromise candidate by the Kikuyu-dominated KANU to promote unity. From 1964 until 1992, when President Moi, under severe pressure, called elections, KANU exercised single party control over Kenya. Moi was reelected in 1992 and 1998 and stepped down in 2003. In the December 2003 presidential election KANU's new candidate, Uhuru Kenyatta (son of the legendary Jomo Kenyatta), was defeated by Emilio Mwai Kibaki of the National Rainbow Coalition (NARC). Kibaki captured 62.2% of the popular vote against 31.3% for Kenyatta, while several other candidates drew minor support.

GOVERNMENT

An executive President is elected for a maximum of two 5-year terms. In the National Assembly 210 members are elected by popular vote, 12 are appointed and 2 are ex officio members. In the December 2003 election Kibaki's NARC gained 132 seats against KANU's 68. The Forum for the Restoration of Democracy-People (FORD P) finished third with 15 seats.

ECONOMIC POLICY

In the wake of an economic downturn after 30 years of sustained growth, the government embarked on a substantive reform program, dismantling foreign exchange controls, allowing a free-floating exchange rate, removing import licensing, and liberalizing marketing and decontrolling prices. Privatization and tax reform are vital ingredients. In July 2000 the World Bank resumed loans to Kenya, ending a three year suspension; then halted lending a year later when the Moi government failed to introduce anti-corruption measures. When Pres. Kibaki came to power in 2003 with the promise to root out corruption loans and donor support were restored.

SECTORS

Agriculture provides employment to 75% of the workforce and accounts for about 30% of GDP and 50% of merchandise export value. Kenya is among the world's leading exporters of tea and coffee (mostly high-grade arabica). It is the world's largest supplier of pyrethrum, a natural insecticide. It also exports cut flowers, vegetables and fruit, cotton, sugar, pineapples, sisal, hides and skins.

FAST FACTS

Pres. Emilio
Mwai Kibaki
Born: 15 Nov. 1931
Since 2003

POLITICAL

Head of State	Pres. Emilio Mwai Kibaki
Ruling Party	NARC
Main Opposition	kanu
Independence	12 December 1963
National capital	Nairobi
Official languages	English & Swahili

PHYSICAL

Total area	224,960 sq. miles 582,650 sq. km. (2 x Nevada)
Arable land	8% of land area
Coastline	333 miles/536 km

POPULATION

Total	34.7 million
Av. yearly growth	2.57%
Population/sq. mile	135
Urban population	13.7 million
Adult literacy	85.1%

ECONOMY

Currency	Kenyan shillings (KSh)(US$1=75.42)
GDP (real)	$16.11 billion
GDP growth rate	5.2%
GDP per capita[1]	$556
GDP (ppp)[2]	$37.15 billion
GDP per cap. (ppp)	$1,100
Inflation rate	10.3%
Exports	$3.17 billion
Imports	$5.13 billion
External debt	$7.3 billion
Unemployment	40%

1. Atlas method.
2. See page 175 for an explanation of purchasing power parity (ppp).

The country is self-sufficient in maize, the major staple food. Soda ash is mined and large deposits of titanium and zircon have been discovered along the coast. Other minerals include fluorspar, salt, limestone and precious stones. Manufacturing includes beverages, tobacco, textiles, electric and electronic appliances, metal products, food products, petroleum products, machinery, glass, cement, pulp and paper products, sugar and confectionery. Relying on its ample wildlife and numerous game reserves, tourism has become one of Kenya's major sources of foreign exchange. Regular visits by British royalty and famous personalities, Hollywood productions such as Mount Kilimanjaro, The Macomber Affair and Out of Africa and the writings of Robert Ruark, Ernest Hemingway and others have made this country a popular destination for safari enthusiasts.

PRIVATIZATION

In the first eight years of a privatization program that started in the nineties Kenya divested from more than 160 public enterprises. The container terminal operations at Mombasa harbor and the airport operations are privatized.

INVESTMENT

More than 200 foreign companies are registered in Kenya—most of them from the United Kingdom, Germany, and the US—and engaged in the manufacturing of products ranging from shoes to pharmaceuticals, petroleum products to beverages, foodstuffs, vehicles and automobiles. About 75 US companies are involved with an estimated $300 million in investment. Established in 1954, the Nairobi Stock Exchange (NSE) is the oldest and largest Exchange in East and Central Africa, providing the opportunity for foreign investors to participate in the local financial market.

TRADE

About 40% of Kenya's exports (especially manufactured products and re-exported petroleum) go to COMESA countries. The European Union (including the UK) is Kenya's main supplier and second largest export market. However, in recent years South Africa has become a major source, while Kenya's exports to South Africa have shown substantial growth. US exports to Kenya include wheat, aircraft, fertilizer, soybean oil, and aircraft parts. Tea exports, Kenya's largest single foreign exchange earner, netted $520 million in 1998. Tourism, catering on an average to 700,000 visitors per year, is second, and coffee third.

FINANCIAL SECTOR

Kenya has a well-developed financial sector comprising 48 licensed national and internationally-affiliated banks, 11 non-bank financial institutions, 4 building societies, 2 mortgage finance companies and 48 foreign exchange bureaus. Several major foreign banks offer a full range of services. The Capital Markets Authority regulates the stock market and the brokerage firms. More than sixty firms are listed on the Nairobi Stock Exchange (NSE)—established in 1954 and a compliant member of the African Stock Exchanges Assocation (ASEA). It is a fully computerized facility with an electronic central depository system (CDS) in operation.

TAXES AND TARIFFS

The taxation system has been streamlined and modernized and rates were lowered in recent years. The maximum individual marginal tax rate has been reduced from 65% to 32.5% and the company tax rate was cut from 45% to 32.5%. Kenya progressively reduced its number of customs duty bands (including the zero rate) from 8 to 4 and the maximum tariff rate dropped from 45% to 25%. Still, the government adopted a more protectionist tariff regime in 1999.

BUSINESS ACTIVITY

AGRICULTURE
Coffee, tea, corn, wheat, sugar cane, fruit, vegetables, dairy products, beef, pork, poultry, eggs.

INDUSTRIES
Small-scale consumer goods (plastic, furniture, batteries, textiles, soap, cigarettes, flour), agricultural products processing, oil refining, cement, tourism.

NATURAL RESOURCES
Gold, limestone, soda ash, salt barytes, rubies, fluorspar, garnets, wildlife.

EXPORTS
$3.17 billion (est. 2005): tea, coffee, petroleum products, fish, horticultural products.

IMPORTS
$5.13 billion (est. 2005): machinery and transportation equipment, consumer goods, petroleum products.

MAJOR TRADING PARTNERS
Uganda, South Africa, Tanzania, UK, US, UAE, Netherlands, Japan, China, India, Saudi Arabia.

Doing Business with Kenya

► INVESTMENT

Investment opportunities exist in tourism, agriculture (including ostrich and crocodile farming), and the manufacturing of electronics, plastics, chemicals, pharmaceuticals and engine parts. Foreign manufacturers are encouraged to use Kenya as a base to access and penetrate the larger East and Central African market. Special incentives are extended to factories in Export Processing Zones. Incentives offered to investors in the manufacturing and hotel sectors include tax breaks on the cost of buildings and capital machinery. The Investment Promotion Center provides a one-stop entry. As privatization proceeds new opportunities are offered in infrastructure development.

► TRADE

There is a growing need for equipment relating to power generation, telecommunications, road building and food processing. A US firm has been successful in selling solar panels. Since the reduction of duties and VAT on computers, US and other foreign suppliers have been enjoying a healthy growth. US exporters who do not manufacture or assemble locally usually rely on local distributors with a thorough knowledge not only of the Kenyan but the regional market. Other than Coca-Cola, franchising has not been particularly successful.

► TRADE FINANCE

The US Eximbank is open to short- and medium-term financing for government and private sector entities in Kenya. Several banks and specialized financial institutions finance Kenyan exporters and importers.

► SELLING TO THE GOVERNMENT

Extensive road and rail repair with funding from the World Bank, African Development Bank, and other multilateral and bilateral sources should provide ample opportunity for foreign construction and engineering firms.

► EXCHANGE CONTROLS

The Exchange Control Act has been repealed and there are no restrictions on converting or transferring funds associated with an investment or trade.

► PARTNERSHIPS

Unlike franchising, joint ventures and licensing are common as they combine local marketing expertise with foreign manufacturing competence.

► ESTABLISHING A PRESENCE

To establish a presence, foreign firms merely need to register with the Kenyan Registrar of Companies. Incorporation of a company in Kenya as a subsidiary of a foreign entity is more complicated and usually requires the services of a local attorney.

► FINANCING PROJECTS

The Overseas Private Investment Corporation provides services to US investors. Kenya is also a member of the Multilateral Investment Guarantee Agency. Apart from the World Bank, IFC and African Development Bank, the Industrial Development Bank (IDB)—a Kenyan government-funded financial institution—provides medium and long term loan finance.

► LABOR

Women constitute more than 25% of the work force in finance, insurance, and other business services and over 29% in public administration and agriculture. Some textile factories are almost exclusively staffed by women. The informal sector, known as *jua kali*, employs about 64% of all workers and accounts for about 90% of all new jobs outside the agricultural small holdings. Kenyan law provides safeguards and benefits for workers and spells out mechanisms and procedures to address complaints relating to worker rights. Wage scales for 12 different categories of employees are stipulated. Often benefits include housing and transportation.

► LEGAL RIGHTS

The Foreign Investment Protection Act protects investors against expropriation. There is also legislation to control monopolies and restrictive trade practices. Patents, trademarks and trade secrets are the responsibility of the Kenya Industrial Property Office in the Ministry of Research, Technical Training and Technology. Copyrights are handled by the Attorney General's office. Kenya is a member of several international and regional intellectual property conventions.

► BUSINESS CLIMATE

Business executives are relatively informal and open to new ideas. The use of first names at an early stage of a business relationship is acceptable. Friendship and mutual trust are highly valued. English is spoken across the country.

LESOTHO

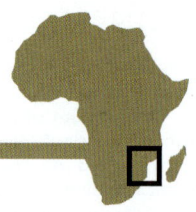

THE SMALL MOUNTAINOUS KINGDOM OF LESOTHO IS ENTIRELY SURROUNDED BY
SOUTH AFRICA ON WHICH MANY OF ITS CITIZENS HAVE TRADITIONALLY DEPENDED FOR
LABOR, ESPECIALLY IN THE GOLD MINES. THE SALE OF WATER TO ITS LARGE NEIGHBOR
AS THE MASSIVE LESOTHO HIGHLANDS PROJECT ENTERS ITS FINAL PHASE, IS COM-
PENSATING IN PART FOR AN EROSION OF JOB OPPORTUNITIES IN SOUTH AFRICA. THE
DOMESTIC ECONOMY IS STILL LARGELY DEPENDENT ON SUBSISTENCE FARMING EVEN
THOUGH THE EMPHASIS HAS STARTED TO SHIFT TO MANUFACTURING FOR EXPORT
TO SOUTH AFRICA AND OTHER COUNTRIES WHERE LESOTHO ENJOYS DUTY-FREE
PRIVILEGES.

COUNTRY PROFILE

The terrain of the small, mountainous Kingdom of Lesotho has been likened to Switzerland
and Andorra. Altitudes in the eastern half exceed
2,440 m and peaks in the northeast and along
the Drakensberg mountains go beyond 3,350 m.
Thabana Ntlenyana (3,482 m) in this range is the
highest point in Southern Africa. Lesotho receives
heavy rainfall (averaging 1,900 mm) and winter
snow. Water is the country's most valuable natural
asset. Lesotho has one of Africa's most homogeneous populations, consisting almost exclusively
of Basotho. More than 90% are Christians,
of whom about 45% belong to the Roman
Catholic Church and the rest to various
Protestant denominations. English is the
official language but Sesotho is widely
spoken.

HISTORY

In the 19th Century King Moshoeshoe
I brought together a number of splinter
groups in this mountainous stronghold,
giving birth to the Basotho nation. It was
in reality a kingdom made up of refugees
from the fierce tribal wars in neighboring regions. Through smart military and
diplomatic strategies Moshoeshoe managed to keep his enemies at bay until he
was challenged by the Dutch-descended
Boers who established their own Orange
Free State Republic alongside his kingdom
and then started making territorial claims.

War ensued that led to the defeat of the Basotho
at Thaba Bosiu. Moshoeshoe was forced to cede
some of his best land to the Boers. Fearing further
intrusion from the Boer republic the king asked
for British protection. It was annexed to the British
Cape Colony in 1871 but in 1884 it was restored
to direct control by the British Crown. Lesotho
functioned as the so-called Basutoland Protectorate until 1966, when it regained its independence.
It functioned as a multiparty democracy until
1986—most of these years under Chief Lebowa

270

Jonathan, a descendant of Moshoeshoe—when a military regime took power. The country returned to an elective political system in 1993 as a constitutional monarchy. Recent years have seen considerable political intrigue, an abortive coup attempt and unrest that necessitated the intervention of South African and Botswana forces to maintain the status quo. These troops left in March 1999 after peace was restored. King Letsie III has ruled since the death of his father, King Moshoeshoe II, in 1996. Prime Minister Pakalitha Mosisili heads the government as leader of the dominant Lesotho Congress for Democracy (LCD).

GOVERNMENT

Lesotho is a constitutional monarchy with real authority vested in the Prime Minister as the leader of the strongest party. A 120-member National Assembly is elected for a 5 year terms. The Senate is made up of 33 Principal Chiefs, descendants of the chiefs originally appointed by King Moshoeshoe I. In May 2002, Prime Minister Mosisili's LCD won 77 Assembly seats. The Basotholand National Party (BNP) took 21 seats and several smaller parties make up the rest of the opposition.

ECONOMIC POLICY

Despite impressive gains in recent years, the government still faces severe and growing unemployment and underemployment in some areas as cutbacks in the South African mining sector continue to eliminate job opportunities for expatriate workers. Since 1988 reform policies have been aimed at flexibility and efficiency in tax collection, deregulation of the agricultural markets, and privatization.

SECTORS

Agriculture employs a quarter of the workforce. Subsistence farming—mainly animal husbandry and maize cultivation—is the predominant activity, with wool and mohair as major exports. Other crops include wheat, sorghum, beans and sunflower oil. Since 1990, the contribution of the industrial sector to GDP has increased from 34 per cent to more than 45 percent. It provides employment for a quarter of the workforce. Most of the activity is in labor-intensive small to medium-sized clothing, footwear and textile enterprises. Limited mining operations consist largely of artesian digging for diamonds. There are, however, reserves of uranium, iron ore, lead and peat. Tourism is a growing sector. Lesotho's

FAST FACTS

King Letsie III
Born: July 17, 1963
Since 1996

POLITICAL

Head of State	King Letsie III
Prime Minister	Pakalitha Mosisili (1998)
Ruling Party	LCD
Main Opposition	BNP
Independence	4 October 1966
National capital	Maseru
Official languages	English & Sesotho

PHYSICAL

Total area	11,718 sq. miles
	30,350 sq. km.
	(± Maryland)
Arable land	11% of land area
Coastline	Landlocked

POPULATION

Total	2 million
Av. yearly growth	-0.46%
Population/sq. mile	183
Urban population	300,000
Adult literacy	84.8%

ECONOMY

Currency	Loti (US$1=6.75)
GDP (real)	$1.36 billion
GDP growth rate	0.8%
GDP per capita[1]	$817
GDP (ppp)[2]	$5.12 billion
GDP per cap. (ppp)	$2,500
Inflation rate	4.7%
Exports	$602.8 million
Imports	$1.16 billion
External debt	$735 million
Unemployment	45%

1. Atlas method.
2. See page 175 for an explanation of purchasing power parity (ppp).

single most important asset is the Lesotho Highlands Water Project (LHWP) which entered its final
phase of construction. Delivering water from the
highlands of Lesotho to South Africa's Vaal River
system and generating hydropower for Lesotho,
the project is Africa's largest. Water from the highlands has already started to flow to South Africa's
thirsty Pretoria Witwatersrand Vereeniging (PWV)
industrial complex and at full capacity the LHWP
is expected to contribute an estimated 5% of GDP.
The project is expected to be completed in 2020
at a final cost of $8 billion..

PRIVATIZATION

With the assistance and advice of the World
Bank, Lesotho planned to spin off at least four
parastatals per year. The process has, however,
been proceeding at a slower pace. Since 1997
less than 10 of the 31 companies slated for
privatization have been sold. One of the first to
be spun off was Lesotho Airways and the most
recent involved Lesotho Bank, when a private
South African bank purchased a 70% share. There
is speculation that the Lesotho Telecommunications Corporation (LTC) and the Lesotho Electric
Company (LEC) may soon be on the block.

INVESTMENT

Lesotho has had considerable success in
diversifying its traditional export base by moving into the production of textiles and electrical
goods, footwear, radios and television sets with
the help of foreign entrepreneurs, mostly from
Europe, South Africa, Hong Kong, Singapore
and Taiwan. The Lesotho Highlands Water Project
(LHWP) represents major involvement by foreign
firms from Europe, South Africa, Hong Kong,
Singapore and Taiwan, as well as the US. Two
Canadian mining companies, Messina Diamond
Corp. and Diamond Works, have taken options
on diamond exploration.

TRADE

Most of Lesotho's exports go to other SADC
countries. Fifty percent of its imports originate
from the region, primarily from South Africa.
However, 40% of its exports find markets in
North America. Export growth has been strong
in livestock, leather products, furniture, and garments—the latter produced for the most part by
Taiwanese-owned factories. Its textile industry has
largely benefited from the trade benefits extended
by the United States under the Africa Growth and
Opportunity Act (AGOA)

FINANCIAL SECTOR

Lesotho is a member of the South African
Common Monetary Area (CMA) and its currency,
the Loti (plural Moloti) is at parity with the South
African rand. It is therefore easily convertible for
business transactions. Three local banking groups
have branches throughout the country and two
international banks have entered the market. The
Lesotho Agricultural Development Bank (LADB)
serves the agricultural sector.

TAXES AND TARIFFS

Subsidiaries and branches of foreign companies are taxed at a rate of 35% on profit. Manufacturers are taxed at 15% and entitled to incentive
breaks on personnel training and a variety of
other items. As a member of the South African
Customs Union (SACU), Lesotho's import tariffs
and trading regime are determined collectively
with other member states. Customs regulations
allow temporary importation of raw materials on
a duty-free basis.

FOREIGN PRESENCE

Foreign companies handle most of their
business with Lesotho from South African-based
branches and subsidiaries as they incur no duties
on crossborder transactions.

BUSINESS ACTIVITY

AGRICULTURE
**Corn, wheat, pulses, sorghum, barley,
livestock.**

INDUSTRIES
**Food, beverages, textiles, handicrafts, con-
struction, tourism.**

NATURAL RESOURCES
**Water, agricultural and grazing land, some
diamonds and other minerals.**

EXPORTS
**$602.8 million (est. 2005): manufactures
(clothing, footwear, road vehicles), wool
and mohair, food and live animals.**

IMPORTS
**$1.16 billion (est. 2005): food, building
materials, vehicles, machinery, medicines,
petroleum products.**

MAJOR TRADING PARTNERS
US, Canada, UK, South Africa.

Doing Business with Lesotho

▶ INVESTMENT

As the principal government investment agency, the Lesotho National Development Corporation (LNDC) assists with loans, serviced sites, training grants and work permits. New factories are allowed duty-free importation of raw materials and components and effective export processing zone status anywhere in the country. A non-repayable skills training grant covers 75% of the wage bill during the initial training period at newly-established manufacturers. Loan finance is provided by the LNDC for projects which can demonstrate long-term economic viability and sometimes it will take equity in new developments considered to be in the national interest. Continuing privatization provides new opportunities.

▶ TRADE

Imports include agricultural products, pharmaceuticals, iron tubes and pipes, metalwork and office machinery. As the Lesotho Highlands Water Project (LHWP) enters its second phase there is a continuing need for construction equipment and engineering services. The consumer market is relatively small but several foreign companies have taken advantage of Lesotho's extensive preferential trade privileges in southern Africa, Europe and elsewhere by establishing export-oriented factories and assembly points.

▶ TRADE FINANCE

The customary irrevocable letter of credit is supported by a sophisticated private banking system.

▶ SELLING TO THE GOVERNMENT

Purchases of heavy equipment and engineering services by the LHWP are handled independently in accordance with internationally-accepted tendering procedures. There are several other government projects where outside donors control tenders. To date, for example, the World Bank assists with projects in agriculture, infrastructure, health, population, education, water, and land management and conservation.

▶ EXCHANGE CONTROLS

As a member of the Common Monetary Area (CMA) Lesotho applies the same controls as South Africa, Swaziland and Namibia. Although closely monitored, the transfer of funds for trade and investment purposes and the repatriation of profits and dividends present no serious problem.

▶ PARTNERSHIPS

The Lesotho-South Africa treaty governing the LHWP stipulates that all foreign companies working on this multi-billion dollar project must enter into joint ventures with local firms. In all other operations foreign investors, have the option of either involving local partners or setting up on their own.

▶ ESTABLISHING A PRESENCE

The LNDC serves as a one-stop shop for any foreign firm that wishes to establish an office, a branch or a manufacturing plant in the country. The process is relatively uncomplicated and does not take long.

▶ FINANCING PROJECTS

The World Bank, the International Development Association and the International Finance Corporation have been financing projects seen as vital to the national interest. Lesotho is a founding member of the Multilateral Investment Guarantee Agency. The LNDC provides loan finance for up to 15 years.

▶ LABOR

The formal sector work force has a high literacy rate and an aptitude for new skills. Training grants are extended to new factories for up to 50% of the payroll. Wages are considerably lower than in neighboring South Africa. While this can be an advantage it also poses the danger of turnover as workers are lured to higher incomes across the border.

▶ LEGAL RIGHTS

Lesotho has no history of expropriation or nationalization of private property. It is a member of the International Center for the Settlement of Disputes. Like South Africa, Lesotho's legal system is based on Roman Dutch law. Intellectual Property rights are protected under laws drafted in cooperation with the World Intellectual property Organization . Lesotho is a signatory to the convention on the settlement of investment disputes between states.

▶ BUSINESS CLIMATE

The business environment shows a strong British influence and can be likened to that of neighboring South Africa. It is, however, customary to approach serious business at a slow and deliberate pace. English is widely spoken in both business and social circles.

 # LIBERIA

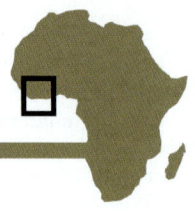

AFRICA'S OLDEST REPUBLIC, ESTABLISHED MORE THAN TWO CENTURIES AGO BY FREED AMERICAN SLAVES, LIBERIA SUFFERED FROM YEARS OF TURMOIL CAUSED BY TRIBAL STRIFE AND EXACERBATED BY THE INTRUSION OF KINSMEN FROM NEIGHBORING STATES. HOPES OF RECOVERY WHEN CHARLES TAYLOR BECAME PRESIDENT IN JULY 1997 IN AN ELECTION DECLARED FREE AND FAIR BY FOREIGN OBSERVERS, WERE DASHED AS HE ABUSED HIS POWERS AND CIVIL WAR RESUMED. IN AUGUST 2003 TAYLOR WAS FORCED TO STEP DOWN AND GO INTO EXILE AND 2005 DR. ELLEN JOHNSON-SIRLEAF BECAME AFRICA'S FIRST HEAD OF STATE WHEN SHE WON A HOTLY CONTESTED ELECTION AGAINST WORLD SOCCER STAR GEORGE WEAH. THE NEW GOVERNMENT HAS AGGRESSIVELY PURSUED FOREIGN INVESTORS TO REINVIGORATE THE ECONOMY.

COUNTRY PROFILE

The Republic of Liberia has a hot and humid monsoon climate lasting from April to November. The coastline is straight, with shallow, mangrove-fringed lagoons and no natural harbors. The land rises from the broad coastal plain to a plateau and high mountain ranges on the northern borders. Diamonds are extracted from the river valleys and timber and rubber from the forests. Some 30 indigenous groups belong to three cultural or linguistic groupings—the Mandé and Atlantic Mel in the northern half of the country and the Kru (or Kruan) in the southern half of the country. The Liberians of African-American lineage, who dominated the country's politics from the 1820s to 1980, account for only 5% of the total population and are concentrated around Monrovia and other coastal centers. There are also small groups of Lebanese and Ful (Fulani) in these cities and towns. English is the official language but a Creole version referred to as Merico or Liberian English is the mother tongue of the Americo-Liberians. More than 70% of the population profess ethnic religious beliefs, 20% practice the Muslim faith and 10% are Christians.

HISTORY

A thousand years ago the territory now known as Liberia was occupied by the Mandé, Kru and Atlantic Mel-speaking peoples from the north and east and in the mid-15th Century the coastal towns were conducting a flourishing slave trade with European merchants. Modern Liberia (derived from the Latin liber or freedom) was the creation of the American Colonization Society (ACS) founded in 1816 to encourage the return of freed slaves to Africa, similar to a program organized by the British in Sierra Leone. Over a period of 40 years some 12,000 slaves were voluntarily resettled. The original constitution denied indigenous Liberians equal rights with these American emigrants and their descendants. With

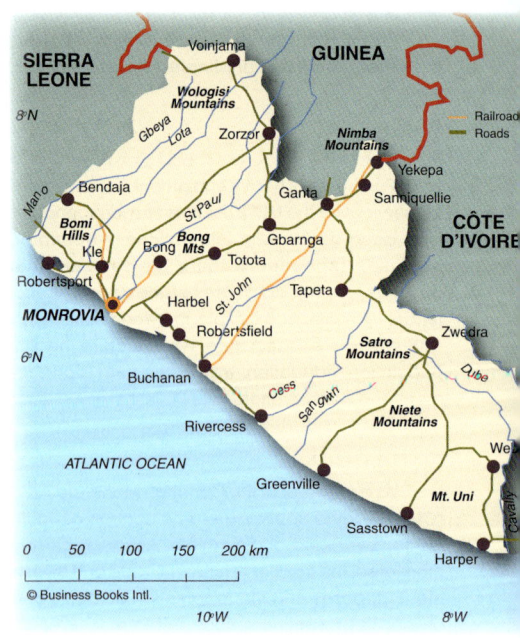

modest assistance from the US government, Monrovia, named after President James Monroe, and other settlements such as Robertsport, Buchanan, Greenville and Harper, were established. On 26 July 1847 Liberia declared itself a sovereign and independent republic. Though the government at Monrovia claimed to rule all the people along the Liberian coast and for some distance inland, effective administration was limited to the coast where the settlers and their descendants lived. It was only since 1920 that real progress was made towards opening up the interior with the help of a 43 mile (69 km) railroad from Monrovia to the Bomi Hills. American influence remained strong. The US dollar was then, and still is, the preferred currency. Firestone rubber company was the first major investor. President William Tubman, a descendant of the African American settlers, served seven consecutive terms and his successor, William Tolbert, ruled from 1971 to 1980, when he was killed by Master Sergeant Samuel Doe, self-styled leader of the National Democratic Party of Liberia (NDPL). A devastating civil war raged from 1989 until 1996. In accordance with the Abuja Accord the warring Liberian factions agreed to participate in elections during July 1997. Charles Taylor's National Patriotic Front of Liberia won in an election declared free and fair by foreign observers, including former US President Jimmy Carter. Soon faced with renewed insurgency by, among others, Liberians United for Reconciliation and Democracy (LURD), Taylor resorted to force and involved himself in destabilizing neighboring Sierra Leone and Guinea. In August 2003, Taylor was forced to go into exile in Nigeria and was replaced by Deputy President Moses Blah who in turn stepped down in favor of entrepreneur Gyude Bryant who promised free elections. The presence of a West African peacekeeping force helped maintain some measure of stability until the November 2005 presidential elections. Harvard graduate and former World Bank official, Dr. Ellen Johnson-Sirleaf, defeated world soccer star George Weah to become Africa's first female head of state. Weah's Congress for Democratic Change (CDC) captured a majority in the legislature with Johnson-Sirleaf's United Party forming the main opposition.

ECONOMIC POLICY

Civil war and official mismanagement have seriously impaired Liberia's economy. Much of the infrastructure around Monrovia has been

FAST FACTS

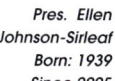
Pres. Ellen
Johnson-Sirleaf
Born: 1939
Since 2005

POLITICAL

Head of State	Pres. Ellen Johnson-Sirleaf
Independence	26 July 1847
Ruling party	CDC
Main opposition	UP
National capital	Monrovia
Official languages	English

PHYSICAL

Total area	43,000 sq. miles
	111,370 sq. km.
	(± Tennessee)
Arable land	4% of land area
Coastline	360 miles/579 km

POPULATION

Total	3.04 million
Av. yearly growth	4.91%
Population/sq. mile	74
Urban population	1.7 million
Adult literacy	57.5%

ECONOMY

Currency	Liberian dollar (L$) (US$1=50)
GDP (real)	$357 million
GDP growth rate	8%
GDP per capita[1]	$1,000
GDP (ppp)[2]	$2.76 billion
GDP per cap. (ppp)	$1,000
Inflation rate	15%
Exports	$910 million
Imports	$4.8 billion
External debt	$3.2 billion
Unemployment	85%

1. Atlas method.
2. See page 175 for an explanation of
   purchasing power parity (ppp).

destroyed in the war while international trade sanctions imposed against the Taylor government prevented the country from marketing diamonds and timber on the open world markets. During this long civil strife GDP fell by 10% a year as production halted at mining and rubber installations and the single oil refinery was forced to shut down. Numerous businessmen left the country, siphoning off capital and causing a serious brain drain. Only the registration of foreign merchant vessels under the Liberian flag continued operating smoothly from a small Washington office. Abundant natural resources should make Liberia a good candidate for increased foreign involvement once order is restored and a stable government established.

SECTORS

More than two-thirds of Liberia's workforce is dependent on agriculture. Rubber is the principal cash crop and provided 28% of export revenue before the war. Starting with Firestone many years ago, significant rubber plantations are still foreign-owned even though smallholders are today responsible for over half the total production. Coffee and cocoa are grown for export while palm oil is mainly produced for the domestic market. Food crops include rice, cassava and vegetables. Commercial ocean fishing concentrates on shrimp. Iron ore is the premier mining activity and normally accounts for 55% of all exports. In some years, however, the value of diamond sales exceeds that of iron ore. There are known deposits of bauxite, manganese, columbite, uranium, tantalite, copper, tin, lead, and zinc. Manufacturing is confined mainly to textiles, food processing, wood products, cement and chemicals.

UN BAN

In 2001 the United Nations imposed sanctions on Liberian diamonds, along with an arms embargo and a travel ban on government officials in an effort to dissuade the Taylor government from supporting rebel insurgents in Sierra Leone. In the spring of 2003, Taylor was indicted by the Special Court for Sierra Leone (SCSL) on war crimes charges. It remains to be seen whether the former Liberian president would be extradited to stand trial from his current safe haven in Nigeria.

PRIVATIZATION

Despite public declarations in favor of a free market system the Taylor government continued granting monopolies in rice, gasoline, and cement

imports and production. Future plans are on hold as Liberia attempts to establish order.

TRADE

Major exports from Liberia include diamonds, iron ore, rubber, timber and coffee, while exports consists of mostly of fuels and lubricants, chemicals, machinery and transport equipment, manufactured goods, and rice and other foodstuffs. During the seven year civil war leading up to the 1997 election, trade was curtailed and skewed as the fighting factions apportioned assets for their own gain and traded informally in iron ore and diamonds from areas under their control. Rubber exports resumed and full and proper channels were established for trade in diamonds, iron and other minerals after Taylor's assumption of power but have seen been disrupted since by renewed unrest.

INVESTMENT

In 1925 the US Firestone Rubber Company became a major foreign player in Liberia when it obtained a 99-year lease on 1 million acres of forest near Monrovia. For decades Firestone was the country's largest employer. It branched into a number of other financial and commercial areas, but rubber remained its major export until the 1950s when iron ore production gained dominance.

BUSINESS ACTIVITY

AGRICULTURE
Rubber, coffee, cocoa, rice, cassava (tapioca), palm oil, sugar cane, bananas, sheep goats, timber.

INDUSTRIES
Rubber and palm oil processing, diamonds.

NATURAL RESOURCES
Iron ore, timber, diamonds, gold.

EXPORTS
$910 million (est. 2005): diamonds, iron ore, rubber, timber, coffee, cocoa.

IMPORTS
$4.8 billion (est. 2005): fuel, chemicals, machinery, transportation equipment, manufactured goods, foodstuffs.

MAJOR TRADING PARTNERS
US, Belgium, Denmark, South Korea, Spain, Japan, Singapore, Germany, Croatia.

FINANCIAL SECTOR

Currently, banks in Liberia operate only as a repository for funds. A fee is charged to receive a wire transfer, to make a deposit or withdrawal, or to cash checks. Banks do not pay interest or make loans.

TAXES AND TARIFFS

Duties on imported goods range from 2.5% to 25%. The higher rate applies to luxury items such as electronic equipment, clothes, and alcoholic beverages.

SPECIAL TIES

Special ties between the US and Liberia date back to its creation in the 1820s. This close relationship continues to be tested by the human rights abuses, corruption and lawlessness. The US government continues, however, to finance projects through its Agency for International Development (USAID) and has been under severe pressure to step in and help its "stepchild" African state restore stability after Charles Taylor's forced departure.

DOING BUSINESS WITH LIBERIA

▶ INVESTMENT

A National Investment Commission was established to grant incentives to foreign investment, some in the form of monopolies in areas such as rice and gasoline importation. This practice has served to stifle further foreign interest. Also still in force is the 1975 "Liberianization" law that prohibits foreign ownership of businesses such as travel agencies, retail gasoline stations, and beer and soft drink distributorships. Investors also have to cope with a myriad of ministries and agencies, conflicting rules and regulations, and bureaucratic red tape. To build investor confidenece the Governance and Economic Management Action Plan (GEMAP) was created, aimed at ensuring transparent revenue collection and allocation.

▶ TRADE

Relatively cheap products such as used clothing, used cars, and used equipment offer trade prospects. There is also is a demand for US consumer goods such as toiletries, hair products, and other personal care items. It is expected that the market for pesticides and chemical fertilizers should improve as post-conflict Liberia returns to full production in the agricultural sector.

▶ SELLING TO THE GOVERNMENT

As economic conditions improve, the Liberian government is likely to become a significant market. New infrastructural projects will create a need for foreign supplies and services.

▶ EXCHANGE CONTROLS

There is no difficulty obtaining Liberian currency at the unofficial rate and there are no restrictions on converting or transferring investment funds.

▶ ESTABLISHING A PRESENCE

Foreign firms considering establishing an office are strongly advised to retain the services of a local attorney. They should also take cognizance of a law that mandates that Liberian nationals should be employed at all levels, including upper management.

▶ PROJECT FINANCING

Liberia does not participate in OPIC or other investment insurance programs. Foreign investors will also find it difficult obtain credit on the local market.

▶ LABOR

A considerable number of skilled professionals emigrated during the civil war. There is, however, no shortage of unskilled and semiskilled labor in Liberia. Unofficial unemployment figures are as high as 85%. Current law requires that Liberian nationals should be employed at all levels and the Ministry of Labor has on occasion held up work permits for expatriates and intervened in disputes between investors and their Liberian employees.

▶ LEGAL RIGHTS

Liberia's judiciary has at times been subjected to political, social, familial, and financial pressures. Currently several US firms are in litigation over the expropriation of property during the seven-year civil conflict. In past cases the government has been accused of settling such claims at well below market value.

LIBYA

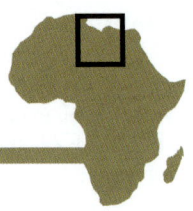

TOP QUALITY OIL RESERVES—THE LARGEST ON THE AFRICAN CONTINENT COUPLED WITH A RELATIVELY SMALL POPULATION—ENABLE LIBYA TO BE AMONG THE TOP ON THE AFRICAN CONTINENT IN PER CAPITA INCOME. UN SANCTIONS INTRODUCED IN 1992 AGAINST LIBYA IN THE WAKE OF THE TERRORIST BOMBING OF US AND A FRENCH COMMERCIAL AIRLINERS WERE LIFTED IN SEPTEMBER 2003 AFTER MUAMMAR QADDAFI ACCEPTED RESPONSIBILITY AND PAID COMPENSATION TO THE FAMILIES OF VICTIMS. HOWEVER, US SANCTIONS PROHIBITING US-LIBYAN BUSINESS REMAINED IN PLACE UNTIL APRIL 2004 WHEN THE BUSH ADMINISTRATION LIFTED MOST RESTRICTIONS AND OPENED THE WAY FOR INVESTMENT AND COMMERCIAL ACTIVITIES. CERTAIN CONTROLS ON US EXPORTS TO LIBYA ARE, HOWEVER, STILL MAINTAINED.

COUNTRY PROFILE

The Great Socialist People's Libyan Arab Jamahiriya sits on a vast plateau. The Tripolitania region, centered around Tripoli has a Mediterranean climate. To the south is the dryer Jefara Plateau and in the east the high escarpment of Cyrenaica, with Benghazi at its hub. Sabha, Kufra and Jofra are clusters of oases, with extensive croplands under irrigation. The predominantly Arab and Muslim population speak Western Arabic dialects. There are various Berber and Tuareg minorities around Tripoli and at oases in the desert.

Its dominance ended in 1942 when the German-Italian Axis was defeated in the Western Desert. The British took Tripolitania and Cyrenaica and the French occupied the Fezzan. In 1951 Libya became independent under King Idris. Wealth followed the discovery of oil in 1960 and led to corruption and discontent. On 1 September 1969, a 28-year-old army captain, Muammar Qaddafi, seized power. Eight years later he formed a monolithic General People's Congress and renamed the country, the Great Socialist People's Libyan Arab Jamahiriya.

HISTORY

The first inhabitants of Libya were Berber tribes. Ancient Libya was invaded by Phoenicians, Numidians, Greeks, Romans, Vandals and Byzantines, followed in 648 by Arabs and the Turks in 1551. Both Tripolitania and Cyrenaica became part of the Ottoman Empire. Tripolitania became one of the outposts for the Barbary pirates who exacted "tribute" payments from merchant ships in the Mediterranean. This practice led to a four year war between the Pasha of Tripoli and the US ending in a peace treaty in June 1805, exempting US ships from this "tribute." Before World War II Italy took control of the coastal towns while the Turks ruled the interior. After the war, the Italians began to pacify the country.

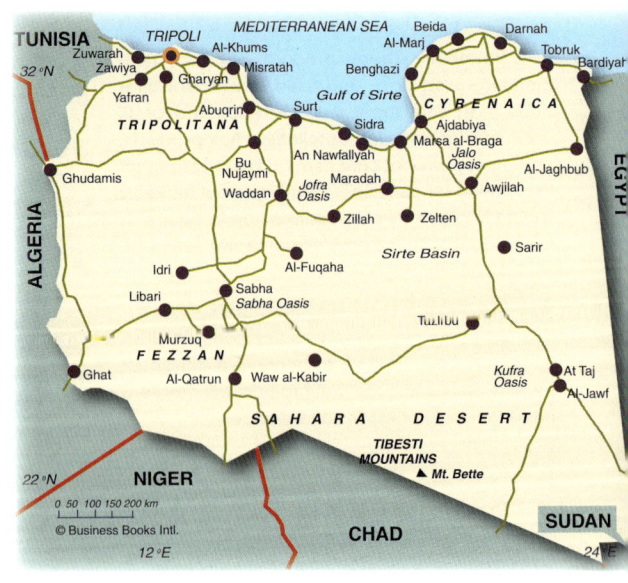

Government

Since March 1977 Libya has been ruled according to the tenets of Qaddafi's Third Universal Theory enunciated in his Green Book. The electorate is divided into some 1,500 People's Congresses, each electing 13-member People's Committees (local governments) which in turn send two members each to a General People's Congress (national legislature), that meets briefly once a year. The General People's Congress elects the General Secretariat (the highest executive body) and the General People's Committee (cabinet). In 1977 Muammar Qaddafi was elected Revolutionary Leader and head of state.

Economic policy

Oil revenues and a small population give Libya one of the highest per capita incomes in Africa, but, as in the case of several other oil producers, there is considerable inequality in actual incomes. Non-oil manufacturing and construction sectors have expanded from largely processing agricultural products to include the production of petrochemicals, iron, steel, and aluminum and currently account for about 20% of GDP. Agriculture constitutes only 5% of GDP but employs 18% of the labor force. The Great Manmade River project, designed to move water to the coast from aquifers deep in the Sahara, has absorbed some 10% of Libya's annual public expenditure and is almost completed. Another major plan involves rail links with Egypt and Tunisia. Libya has applied for membership of the World Trade Organization, reduced state subsidies and implemented privatization but it still has some way to go in transforming and modernizing its state-driven socialist economy.

Privatization

In the late 1980s the centrally planned (socialist) economy began to be opened up for free enterprise in an effort to counter the effect of lower oil prices and sanctions. A few economic and social services formerly performed by the state are now handled by private enterprise.

Sectors

Petroleum production accounts for between 30% and 40% of GDP; construction 11%; public services and administration 12%; transportation and communication 5%; manufacturing 5%; and agriculture 4%. Less than 2% of the country is arable. There are deposits of iron, potassium, magnesium, sulphur, gypsum and phosphate. In

Fast Facts

Col. Muammar
Qaddafi
Born: 1945
Since 1969

POLITICAL

Head of State	Col. Muammar Qaddafi
Ruling Party	Arab Socialist Union
Independence	24 December 1951
National capital	Tripoli
Official language	Arabic

PHYSICAL

Total area	679,359 sq. miles 1,759,540 sq. km. (± Alaska)
Arable land	1% of land area
Coastline	1,100 miles/1,770 km

POPULATION

Total	5.9 million
Av. yearly growth	2.3%
Population/sq. mile	8
Urban population	5 million
Adult literacy	82.6%

ECONOMY

Currency	Libyan Dinar (LD) (US$1=1.36)
GDP (real)	$31.49 billion
GDP growth rate	8.5%
GDP per capita[1]	$6,365
GDP (ppp)[2]	$65.79 billion
GDP per cap. (ppp)	$6,700
Inflation rate	3.4%
Exports	$30.79 billion
Imports	$10.82 billion
External debt	$4.27 billion
Unemployment	30%

1. *Atlas method.*
2. *See page 175 for an explanation of purchasing power parity (ppp).*

the 1970s huge investments were made in import substituting factories and refineries for the liquefaction of natural gas and the processing of other petrochemicals, the manufacture of iron, steel industries and concrete piping and auto assembly.

TRADE

Petroleum exports account for about 95% of Libya's foreign hard currency earnings and 60% of the public sector wages. The government claims that UN sanctions during the nineties have cost the country more than $24 billion in revenues. The state-owned National Oil Corporation maintains a virtual monopoly over the marketing of all Libyan oil and gas. State enterprises also control most manufacturing, agriculture and trade outside the petroleum sector. Poor soils and an unfavorable climate limit agricultural output and Libya currently imports about 75% of its food requirements. There is the potential for a large increase in Libyan gas exports to Europe. Major trading partners are Italy, Germany, United Kingdom, Spain, South Korea and France.

INVESTMENT

Since 1968, Libya's oil industry has been run by the state-owned National Oil Corporation (NOC) along with a number of smaller subsidiary companies. The leading foreign oil producer in Libya is Italy's Agip-ENI, operating in the country since 1959. Two US oil companies—Exxon and Mobil—withdrew from Libya in 1982, following a US trade embargo in 1981. Five other US companies—Amarada Hess, Conoco, Grace Petroleum, Marathon, and Occidental—remained active in Libya until 1986, when the Reagan administration ordered all US firms to cease activities against a state charged with sponsoring terrorism. US oil companies have been returning to Libya since the US government lifted of sanctions in 2004.

LOCKERBIE

Relations between Libya and the US and its western partners reached an all-time low following the "Lockerbie Affair" in December 1988 when all 259 passengers aboard Pan Am flight 103 died in an explosion over Lockerbie in Scotland—an event blamed by London and Washington on two Libyan nationals. Qaddafi's refusal to extradite the two suspects led to the imposition of mandatory economic sanctions against Libya by the UN Security Council on 31 March 1992. The US formulated its own sanctions under the Iran and Libya Sanctions Act. The effect of sanctions on the

Libyan economy is seen to have forced Qaddafi to seeking a way out of the impasse by extraditing the suspects for trial in The Hague. This led to the suspension of UN sanctions and the reestablishment of economic and diplomatic relations by most nations, excluding the US. Early in 2001, one of the two accused, Abdel Baset Ali Mohmed Al-Megrahi, was convicted and sentenced to twenty years in a Scottish jail. After accepting responsibility for Pan Am 103 and making payments to the families of the victims of both Pan Am 103 and a UTA flight downed over Niger in 1989, UN sanctions were finally lifted by the UN Security Council in 2003. The Council voted 13-0 in favor with the US and France abstaining. Apart from a relaxation in restrictions on the trade of a few items—including pharmaceuticals—the US kept its embargo in place until April 2004 when the Bush administration lifted most US sanctions. This was in response to Libya's commitment to open its weapons programs to international inspectors and to dismantle its weapons of mass destruction. Today most US commercial business, investment and trade with Libya is possible, but certain controls on exports are maintained in accordance with the State Department's State Sponsors of Terrorism list that still classifies Libya as a state sponsor of terrorism.

BUSINESS ACTIVITY

AGRICULTURE
Wheat, barley, olives, dates, citrus, vegetables, peanuts, beef, eggs.

INDUSTRIES
Petroleum, food processing, textiles, handicrafts, cement.

NATURAL RESOURCES
Petroleum, natural gas, gypsum.

EXPORTS
$30.79 billion (est. 2005): Crude oil, refined petroleum products, natural gas.

IMPORTS
$10.82 billion (est. 2005): machinery, transport equipment, manufactured goods, food.

MAJOR TRADING PARTNERS
Italy, Germany, US, South Korea, Spain, France, Turkey, China, Greece, UK, Tunisia.

Doing Business with Libya

▶ INVESTMENT

Since the lifting of UN sanctions the overseas focus has been on the development of several dormant oil exploration and production projects. Continued expansion of gas production remains a high priority in Libya. The National Oil Corporation is offering concessions to foreign partners. Libya has had no railroad in operation since 1965, as all previous systems were dismantled. Current plans are to construct a 890 mile (1,435 km) standard gauge line from the Tunisian frontier to Tripoli and Misratah, continuing inland to Sabha, the center of a mineral-rich area, as well as another that will link Tobruk with As Sallum in Egypt.

▶ TRADE

Since the lifting of UN sanctions Libya has resumed purchases of oil industry equipment. Latest trade figures show a growing market in food and live animals, manufactured goods, machinery and equipment and chemicals. Most purchasing is done by the government and foreign currency payments, even in the case of private sector purchases, are state-monitored and controlled. The National Oil Corporation prefers to sell crude to refiners under long-term contracts and very little Libyan oil finds its way onto the spot market.

▶ TRADE FINANCE

Since April 1999 Libya has been eligible for international export credit guarantees and risk assurance. In the past commodity imports have been purchased by confirmed letters of credit at standard terms. Despite occasional administrative delays, Libya has maintained a good payment record in the past.

▶ SELLING TO THE GOVERNMENT

Most sales to Libya are in fact to the government. State agencies hold monopolies on a broad range of products. For example, pharmaceuticals—one of the areas where US firms are once again allowed to trade—are purchased at public tender by the Medical Supply Organization. In several other areas the Export-Import Board allocates foreign exchange for the importation of specific products by state or even to private enterprises. Libya is a major purchaser of agricultural products and US producers of wheat, barley and other products are expected to gain largely after sanctions were lifted. There are constant modifications and a local expert is needed to keep potential exporters current. Equipment for the National Oil Corporation and its subsidiaries is largely sourced through a central purchasing agency in London.

▶ EXCHANGE CONTROLS

Controls apply. Even though the government has declared the intention to unify the official and parallel market exchange rates, a large differential persists.

▶ PARTNERSHIP

To ensure that overseas interests were not subject to the asset freeze imposed by UN sanctions in the early nineties, Libyan holdings, both outright and in partnership with foreign firms, went out of their way to obfuscate and disguise their partnerships. Since the lifting of sanctions, the Libyan authorities have actively sought new partnerships.

▶ ESTABLISHING A PRESENCE

Since the final departure of its oil companies in 1986, the US has not had any formal links with Libya. The return of US business has been actively sought after the lifting of sanctions.

▶ PROJECT FINANCING

Despite occasional instances of administrative delays, Libya has maintained a good payment record on foreign service contracts. Although international financing has become available after the lifting of UN sanctions, Libya is not likely to be a candidate for major loans. The government is expected to continue shying away from long-term debt in its endeavors to maintain a balanced financial position in foreign transactions.

▶ LABOR

A constraint is imposed on the economy by the shortage of skilled and unskilled labor. The country relies on a large contingent of foreign technicians and about a million migrant manual workers from Egypt and other neighboring countries. Most Libyan workers are absorbed by an extensive state bureaucracy. In 1990, some 70% of all Libyan salaried workers were on the state's payroll.

▶ BUSINESS CLIMATE

Even though Arabic is the official language and often the only one spoken by officials, both English and Italian are widely used in the business community. Local representatives are essential to establish a long-term presence and make inroads.

MADAGASCAR

THE WORLD'S FOURTH LARGEST ISLAND, MADAGASCAR, IS EMERGING FROM SEVERAL YEARS OF NEGLECT AND BEGINNING TO ATTRACT THE ATTENTION OF INVESTORS WITH ITS AMPLE SUPPLY OF NATURAL RESOURCES, LABOR, AND AN ECOSYSTEM WITH GREAT POTENTIAL FOR TOURISM. THE GOVERNMENT, IN COOPERATION WITH THE IMF AND WORLD BANK, REDUCED BUDGET DEFICITS, CORRECTED THE OVERVALUATION OF THE CURRENCY AND REMOVED TRADE BARRIERS. IN RECENT YEARS, FOREIGN INVESTORS HAVE BEEN TAKING A CLOSER LOOK AT THIS INDIAN OCEAN ISLAND, SAID BY EXPERTS TO HAVE FORMED PART OF THE MAIN AFRICAN CONTINENT IN PREHISTORIC TIMES. AGRICULTURE, FISHING AND FORESTRY, ARE THE MAIN COMPONENTS OF THE ECONOMY.

COUNTRY PROFILE

The Republic of Madagascar (known as the Malagasy Republic from 1959 to 1975 and as the Democratic Republic of Madagascar from 1975 until 1992) is situated 400 miles off the east coast of Africa. It is the world's fourth largest island after Greenland, New Guinea and Borneo, and nearly twice the size of the British Isles, measuring 1,570 km from north to south and 570 km at its widest. The highest point is the volcanic Mt. Tsaratanana (2,876 m) in the far north. The east coast is hot and humid, the central highlands around Antananarivo temperate, and the savanna regions in the southwest, arid. There are 18 ethnic groups of Malay-Polynesian, African and Arab origin. The Merina highlanders are the largest group, followed by the coastal Betsimisisaraka. Later arrivals include French, Comorians, Indians and Chinese. More than half the population follow traditional tribal beliefs brought from Borneo. The remainder are mostly Christians apart from a few Muslims.

HISTORY

The Malagasy are of mixed Malayo-Indonesian and African-Arab ancestry. Settled originally around the 10th Century by Borneo mariners who arrived in outrigger canoes, the island was first claimed by the Portuguese early in the 16th Century. They named it Madagascar after a reference to such an island in the writings of Marco Polo. After destroying existing Arab settlements on the island, the Portuguese were displaced by the French. Towards the end of the 19th Century

the island was formally handed over to France by the British in return for a free hand in Egypt and Zanzibar. After several uprisings, a referendum called by France in 1958 showed Madagascans

overwhelmingly in favor of independence within the French community. In 1959, pro-French Philibert Tsiranana became the first president. He was ousted in May 1973 in an army coup led by Maj. Gen. Gabriel Ramantsoa. Admiral Didier Ratsiraka, who was named president in June 1975, nationalized banks, insurance companies, shipping companies, the oil refinery and a leading foreign trading company. In response to riots following his reelection in 1989 under suspicious circumstances, Pres. Ratsiraka agreed to share power with Albert Zafy. In the 1993 election Zafy won the presidency only to be impeached by parliament for abusing his constitutional powers during an economic crisis. He was defeated in the 1996 presidential election by Ratsiraka with a narrow margin. Seeking reelection in December 2001, Ratsiraka was defeated by Marc Ravalomanana who drew 51.5% of the overall vote against his 35.9%. Ratsiraka, however, refused to step down, claiming that his opponent did not score an outright majority. In June 2002, after months of stalemate and violence between supporters of the two contestants the High Constitutional Court declared Ravalomanana the winner.

GOVERNMENT

The executive President serves four-year terms and appoints the Council of Ministers. The bicameral Parliament comprises a 90-member Senate, consisting of indirectly elected and appointed members, and the National Assembly whose 160 members are elected on a basis of proportional representation for 4 years. In December 2002 election the I Love Madagascar party (*Tiako I Madagasikara-TIM*) won 103 seats. Its closest rival, the National Union (*Firaisankinam-Pirenena-FP*) got 22 seats. The rest of the seats were split between four other parties and independents.

ECONOMIC POLICY

The Malagasy government began to implement market-oriented reforms in the mid-nineties. Under a program directed by the World Bank and IMF it liberalized exchange, trade, and price systems; eliminated restrictions in key economic sectors, such as petroleum, food, and transportation; and began to tighten fiscal and monetary policies. The country has been on a steady albeit slow growth pattern with the exception of 2002 when the political crisis triggeered a 12% drop in GDP in a single year. A broadening of the tax base and strengthening of tax administration achieved

FAST FACTS

Pres. Marc Ravalomanana 2002

© UN/DPI

POLITICAL

Head of State	Pres. Marc Ravalomanana
Ruling Party	TIM
Main Opposition	FP
Independence	26 June 1960
National capital	Antananarivo
Official languages	Malagasy & French

PHYSICAL

Total area	226,657 sq. miles
	587,042 sq. km
	(2 x Arizona)
Arable land	5% of land area
Coastline	3000 miles/4,828 km

POPULATION

Total	18.6 million
Av. yearly growth	3.03%
Population/sq. mile	68
Urban population	5 million
Adult literacy	68.9%

ECONOMY

Currency	Malagasy Ariary
	MGA (US$1=9,050.23)
GDP (real)	$4.7 billion
GDP growth rate	5.1%
GDP per capita[1]	$275
GDP (ppp)[2]	$16.36 billion
GDP per cap. (ppp)	$900
Inflation rate	15%
Exports	$951 million
Imports	$1.4 billion
External debt	$4.6 billion
Unemployment	23%

1. *Atlas method.*
2. *See page 175 for an explanation of purchasing power parity (ppp).*

a major increase in revenues and a reduction in deficits. Returning confidence boosted domestic financial savings and investment. Real GDP growth of almost 4% in 1998 (an increase of more than 1% of GDP per capita) resulted from increased foreign investment, especially in export zone manufacturing and tourism. Poverty reduction and combating corruption have been priorities in the formulation of economic policy in recent years.

SECTORS

Agriculture, including fishing and forestry, is the mainstay of the economy, accounting for 32% of GDP. Major capital-intensive industries are oil refining, fertilizer and cement production, textile manufacturing and the processing of agricultural products. Madagascar is the world's 10th largest chrome producer. Prospecting by US and European companies since the 1970s has led to the discovery of small deposits of oil and gas. Madagascar also has substantial reserves of high quality chrome ore, graphite, mica, bauxite and iron ore as well as small deposits of uranium, quartz, monazite, garnet, amethyst, ilmenite, zircon and titanium. Tourism is a growing sector and expected to become a major foreign exchange earner.

PRIVATIZATION

In the course of the privatization of the public bank, BFV, its nonperforming loans were transferred to a debt workout unit (SOFIRE), which is responsible for continuing the recovery effort. The second public bank (BTM) was offered for sale in 1998. The petroleum company (SOLIMA) was also put up for sale. Forty other state enterprises are earmarked for sale, including the national carrier, Air Madagascar.

TRADE

Agriculture, including fishing and forestry, contributes 70% of export earnings. Minerals, with chromium in the lead, form about 5% of exports. Other export items include iron ore, graphite, mica, and bauxite.

INVESTMENT

France is the leading foreign investor, followed by Hong Kong, Singapore, Germany and Italy. Some 125 foreign companies are involved in the island's Export Processing Zones (EPZ). Offshore fishing and shrimp farming have also developed into significant foreign exchange earners in recent years, attracting both Japanese and European investors. The discovery of important

deposits of sapphires in the north and the south of the country has attracted investors from the United States, Thailand, Indonesia, Israel and Europe. A US firm, Telecel, is involved in the modernization of Madagascar's telecommunications system. The Iridium system is on sale in the country. The local Internet service has grown considerably since 1998 when 10 service providers were licensed.

FINANCIAL SECTOR

The banking system comprises six commercial banks, of which several are under foreign control. Union Commercial Bank (UCB) and State Bank of Mauritius (SBM) are branches of Mauritian parent companies of the same name. The former state bank BFV was purchased by the French bank Société Générale, and BTM bank is in the process of privatization. For private banks, financial statements are required that are in compliance with international standards.

TAXES AND TARIFFS

The government started to reorganize its tax department and improve coordination between revenue-collecting units, based on a plan developed with the assistance of the IMF.

BUSINESS ACTIVITY

AGRICULTURE
Coffee, vanilla, sugar cane, cloves, cocoa, rice, cassava (tapioca), beans, bananas, peanuts, livestock.

INDUSTRIES
Meat processing, soap, breweries, tanneries, sugar, textiles, glassware, cement, automobile assembly, paper, petroleum, tourism.

NATURAL RESOURCES
Graphite, chromite, coal, bauxite, salt, quartz, tar sands, semiprecious stones, mica, fish.

EXPORTS
$951 million (est.2005): coffee, vanilla, cloves, shellfish, sugar, petroleum products, cotton.

IMPORTS
$1.4 billion (est. 2005): capital goods, petroleum, consumer goods, food.

MAJOR TRADING PARTNERS
France, US, Japan, Germany, South Africa, Hong Kong, Mauritius, China, Iran.

Doing Business with Madagascar

► INVESTMENT

A "*guichet unique*" or one-stop office coordinates new investment proposals. In recent years the government has dismantled some of the regulatory and tax constraints impeding foreign investment, especially in the energy, mining, hydrocarbon, telecommunication, and air transportation sectors. Other areas with good investment potential include hotels and other tourist facilities, aquaculture, and apparel manufacturing. An Export Processing Zone (EPZ) is a major area for foreign direct investment.

► TRADE

Manufacturers of telecommunications, mining and petroleum extraction equipment, road-building and repair machinery, automotive spare parts, lubricants, hardware and civil aviation equipment will be able to sell in Madagascar as the country's development and reconstruction programs unfold. A need for wheat, flour and edible oils in a liberalized market offers further potential for exporters. Import licenses are not needed except for a few strategic items. Telecommunications items, however, do require prescreening to ensure compatibility.

► TRADE FINANCE

Eximbank has introduced a new program to assist US trade with Madagascar. Local credit is available to exporters of traditional agricultural products such as vanilla, coffee, cocoa and cloves at relatively high interest rates.

► SELLING TO THE GOVERNMENT

Tenders for government-funded projects are usually announced in official and local journals or on radio and television. Normally these bids are handled in a transparent fashion although on occasion international bids have been awarded to favored local suppliers without explanation. Lack of transparency does not, however, appear to have affected the privatization process where public bidding has generally been open and foreign investors have been welcomed.

► EXCHANGE CONTROLS

Exchange controls were eliminated in 1996 and there are no restrictions on converting or transferring funds associated with a foreign investment, including remittances of investment capital, earnings, loan repayments, and lease payments into foreign currency at a legal market clearing rate.

► PARTNERSHIP

Local partners are helpful in finding a way through a bureaucratic maze requiring from investors a series of permits from several government ministries. The Malagasy partner is likely be a minority shareholder.

► ESTABLISHING A PRESENCE

In 1996, in a drastic departure from its socialist past, Madagascar adopted laws allowing for the first time not only local private interests but foreigners the freedom to establish, acquire, and dispose of business interests.

► PROJECT FINANCE

On March 31, 1998, OPIC and Madagascar signed a bilateral Investment Incentive Agreement. Madagascar is a member of the Multilateral Investment Guarantee Agency. The World Bank and the African Development Bank have also financed a variety of infrastructure projects.

► LABOR

There is widespread unemployment and wage rates in the country are among the lowest in the world. Malagasy workers are easily trained and skills are readily available in areas such as textiles, knitting, and clothing assembly.

► LEGAL RIGHTS

Madagascar is busy restoring foreign trust after the seizure by its socialist government in the 1970s of property owned by foreign oil companies to create SOLIMA, the state oil company. The expropriation claims of some of the affected companies have been settled. Today the government is committed to a system of arbitration for commercial conflicts under a new arbitration law. Madagascar is a member of the World Intellectual Property Organization and has two offices for IPR protection: OMAPI, *Office Malgache de la Propriété industrielle* (Malagasy Office for Industrial Property) and OMDA, *Office Malgache des Droits d'Auteurs* (Malagasy Office for Copyrights).

► BUSINESS CLIMATE

Malagasy people are culturally reserved. The concept of sales service and customer support is relatively new to the island and is primarily practiced by distributors of computers and automobiles. Retailers of most consumer goods rarely accept returns. French is the language of business but a substantial number of people also speak English.

MALAWI

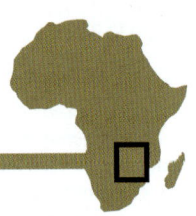

LANDLOCKED MALAWI IS ONE OF THE MOST DENSELY POPULATED COUNTRIES ON THE AFRICAN CONTINENT. WITH SOME OF THE CONTINENT'S MOST FERTILE SOIL AND AMPLE RAINFALL, IT RELIES HEAVILY ON AGRICULTURAL PRODUCTS SUCH AS TOBACCO, TEA AND SUGAR. RECENT REFORMS AIMED AT LIBERALIZING AND DIVERSIFYING THE ECONOMY HAVE LED TO HIGHER GROWTH RATES, REDUCTION OF DEFICITS, AND LOWER INFLATION. REMOVAL OF GOVERNMENT CONTROLS AND PRIVATIZATION ARE EXPECTED TO ATTRACT A HIGHER DEGREE OF FOREIGN DIRECT INVESTMENT AND EXPERTISE NOT ONLY IN AGRICULTURE BUT ALSO ITS LARGELY UNDEVELOPED MINING SECTOR. PRIVATIZATION HAS INVOLVED SEVERAL FOREIGN PURCHASES IN RECENT YEARS. EXPORT PROCESSING ZONES OFFER TARIFF-FREE ACCESS TO NEIGHBORING COUNTRIES AND QUOTA PRIVILEGES TO OVERSEAS MARKETS.

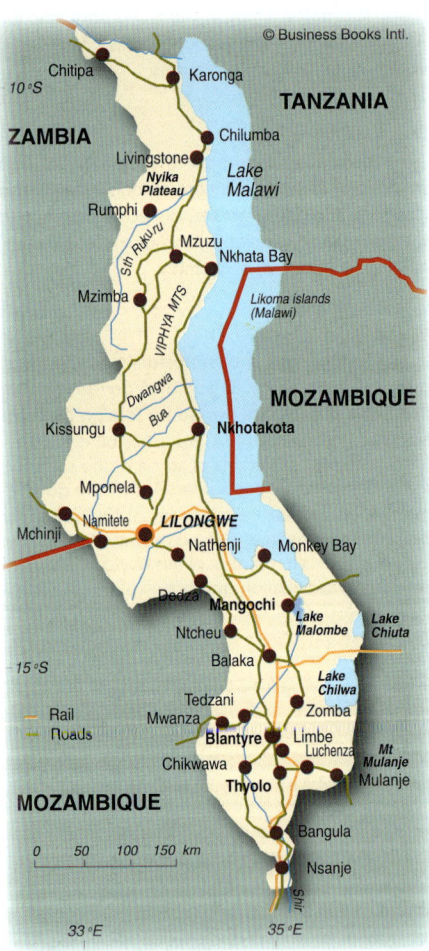

COUNTRY PROFILE

The landlocked Republic of Malawi stretches for 840 km along the fertile western and southern sides of Africa's third largest lake—Lake Malawi. The country's width varies between 80 and 160 km. Lake Malawi and the much smaller Malombe, Chiuta and Chilwa lakes take up 20% of the total area. The Shire River, a tributary of the Zambezi, feeds into the Malawi and Malombe lakes while the Shire Highlands, which peak at Mount Mulanje (3,050 m), overlook the country's principal tea-growing region. Further to the north are the Viphya Mountains and the Nyika Plateau. The climate is temperate, with high rainfall and moist savanna woodland vegetation in the high-lying areas and dry savanna along the lakes. The closely related Chewa and Nyanja ethnic groups account for about half of the total population. Other significant groups in the south are the Lomwe, Yao, and Ngoni and in the north the Tumbuka, Tonga and Nkhonde. English and Chichewa are official languages. More than half of the population is Christian with the remainder split evenly between the Muslim faith and their own ethnic beliefs.

HISTORY

Lake Malawi was named after the 16th Century Maravi empire that extended to the Indian Ocean and comprised peoples such as the Chewa, Nyanja, Nyasa, Nsenga, Phiri and Zimba, who broke away from the Lunda-Luba kingdom in the southern Congo Basin. There was early contact with Portuguese along the Mozambican coast and Arab traders who settled along the coast of modern-day Tanzania. David Livingstone first visited Lake Malawi in 1859 and was followed by other missionaries and a group of Glasgow businessmen, who set up the African Lakes Company and established Blantyre—named after David Livingstone's Scottish birthplace—that became the territory's largest urban center. In 1891 Malawi (then known as Nyasaland) became a British colony and in 1953 it was incorporated into the Federation of Rhodesia and Nyasaland together with Northern Rhodesia (Zambia) and Southern Rhodesia (Zimbabwe). Dr. Hastings Banda—who qualified as a medical doctor in both the US and Scotland—led the opposition against this federation and ultimately forced the British in 1962 to grant independence to the new state of Malawi. In the 1970s, over objections from the OAU, President Banda established diplomatic relations with apartheid South Africa and accepted considerable financial and technical assistance, including the funding and construction of the new capital at Lilongwe to replace Blantyre. In 1994 an aging and ailing Banda was pressured into holding the first free elections since independence. Banda and his ruling Malawi Congress Party were swept from office by the United Democratic Front (UDF). Muslim businessman Bakili Muluzi became president and was reelected in 1999. In 2004 Bingu wa Mutharika, Economic Minister in Muluzi's cabinet was nominated to represent the UDF. Dr. Wa Mutharika won a hotly contested race to become president in May 2004.

GOVERNMENT

The executive President and Vice President are elected on one ballot by popular vote for 5-year terms. The 192-member National Assembly is also elected for 5-year terms. In the May 2004 election the Malawi Congress Party (MCP) won 60 seats against 49 for the United Democratic Front (UDF), 16 for the Mgwirizano Coalition and 28 split between smaller parties.

ECONOMIC POLICY

Economic structural adjustment programs have been applied with the help of the World Bank, International Monetary Fund, and other donors since 1981. As a former UN Director for Trade and Development Finance for Africa and Secretary-general of the Common Market for Eastern and Southern Africa (COMESA), Dr. Wa

FAST FACTS

Pres. Bingu
wa Mutharika
Born: February 27, 1934
Since 2004

© UN/DPI

POLITICAL

Head of State	Pres. Bingu wa Mutharika
Ruling Party	UDF
Main Opposition	MCP
Independence	6 July 1964
National capital	Lilongwe
Official languages	English & Chichewa

PHYSICAL

Total area	45,745 sq. miles
	118,480 sq. km.
	(± Pennsylvania)
Arable land	23% of land area
Coastline	Landlocked

POPULATION

Total	13 million
Av. yearly growth	2.38%
Population/sq. mile	170
Urban population	2.2 million
Adult literacy	62.7%

ECONOMY

Currency	Malawian kwacha (MK) (US$1=123.56)
GDP (real)	$1.98 billion
GDP growth rate	-3%
GDP per capita[1]	$154
GDP (ppp)[2]	$7.5 billion
GDP per cap. (ppp)	$600
Inflation rate	15.4%
Exports	$364 million
Imports	$645 million
External debt	$3.29 billion
Unemployment	N/A

1. Atlas method.
2. See page 175 for an explanation of purchasing power parity (ppp).

Mutharika is expected to trim over-spending and the bloated bureaucracy of his predecessor. Heavily aid-dependent, Malawi needs to reassure multilateral donors to qualify for soft loans and grants. In 2000 Malawi was approved for relief under the Heavily Indebted Poor Countries (HIPC) program. Poverty, improvements in agriculture, unemployment, and the HIV/AIDS epidemic are ongoing issues. Under the current government Malawi's fiscal policy performance has been impressive. Severe droughts in 2005 and 2006 have hampered growth.

SECTORS

Fertile soil and ample rainfall form the basis of a thriving agricultural sector that employs nearly half of the workforce and directly or indirectly supports an estimated 85% of the population. Smallholders grow food crops such as maize, potatoes, groundnuts, cassava and plantains, and keep livestock. Estate farmers account largely for the major export crops such as tobacco, tea and sugar. Both fishing and forestry are being developed and coal is mined on a scale sufficient to supply the country's domestic needs. Limestone is extracted for cement production. Major bauxite deposits at Mount Mulanje are not mined due to prohibitive transportation costs. Manufacturing largely involves agricultural processing and includes tea factories, sugar refineries, cotton gins, tobacco plants, sawmills and plywood manufacturers, oil and grain mills, abattoirs and cold storage plants. Other manufacturing includes textiles, footwear, cement, fertilizer, soap, and matches. Lake Malawi and the various national parks are tourist attractions.

PRIVATIZATION

Foreigners are allowed to participate in all phases of the privatization program but in some cases nationals are given preferential treatment ranging from discounted share prices to subsidized credits. These concessions are extended to locals on condition that the shares or assets be retained for at least two years.

INVESTMENT

The Malawi Investment Promotion Agency puts private foreign direct investment at an amount of about $10 million per year. Understandably, this level is considered insufficient to complement local private and public sector investment and new investment is aggressively pursued through promotional programs abroad.

TRADE

Major overall trading partners are South Africa, Zimbabwe, UK, Japan and Germany. The US, UK, South Africa, Japan, and Germany are the largest purchasers. With a 60% share of the total, tobacco tops the list of exports.

FINANCIAL SECTOR

Malawi has a sound banking sector, monitored and regulated by the Reserve Bank of Malawi (RBM). There are five full-service commercial banks of which the largest two—the NBM and CBM—are state-owned. As of June 25, 1999, 1,159.01 million shares with a market capitalization of some $170 million were traded on the Malawi Stock Exchange.

TAXES AND TARIFFS

There are efforts to reduce or eliminate various tariff and non-tariff barriers. In 1998, the Government removed export taxes on tobacco, sugar, tea and coffee. Duties of 10% and 15% on industrial machines, designated raw materials, and intermediate goods were reduced to 5% and 10%, respectively. In July 1999 the maximum import tariff rate was lowered from 30% to 25% and customs duty on aviation fuel was eliminated.

BUSINESS ACTIVITY

AGRICULTURE
Tobacco, sugar cane, cotton, tea, corn, potatoes, cassava (tapioca), sorghum, pulses, cattle, goats.

INDUSTRIES
Tea, tobacco, sugar, sawmill products, cement, consumer goods.

NATURAL RESOURCES
Limestone, uranium, coal, bauxite.

EXPORTS
$364 million (est. 2004): tobacco, tea, sugar, coffee, peanuts, wood products.

IMPORTS
$645 million (est. 2004): food, petroleum products, semimanufactures, consumer goods, transportation equipment.

MAJOR TRADING PARTNERS
US, South Africa, Germany, Japan, UK, Netherlands, Mozambique, India, Zambia. Zimbabwe.

Doing Business with Malawi

▶ Investment

Investment incentives include duty-free importation of raw materials for manufacturing industry, and tax holidays. There are several export processing zones (EPZs) that offer tariff free access into South Africa as well as quota privileges for textiles and sugar in the European Union and the US. Manufacturers also enjoy export advantages to neighboring countries such as Zambia, Tanzania, Congo (Kinshasa). Agriculture is the sector where Malawi competes most successfully internationally and there is a concerted effort to find alternatives to tobacco growing with its uncertain future.

▶ Trade

There is a growing Malawi market for computers, peripherals and software. Used clothing, equipment and vehicles are major imports. Product distribution in Malawi can be problematic as some rural areas become inaccessible during the rainy season from November to April. Infrastructural and community programs sponsored by USAID, the World Bank, and the African Development Bank present opportunities for the sale of materials, equipment, and expertise.

▶ Trade Finance

Overseas purchases are financed primarily through secured letters of credit. Short-term export finance Eximbank insurance is available to US exporters.

▶ Selling to the government

The government issues tender notices for supplies and services in local and international publications 15 to 90 days in advance. Completed bids accompanied by the required deposit are submitted to Malawi Government Central Tender Board (MGCTB) and opened in the presence of bidders or their representatives. As Malawi upgrades its transport and telecommunications systems, major purchases and service contracts are imminent.

▶ Exchange controls

There are no restrictions on remittance of foreign investment funds (including capital, profits, loan repayment and lease repayment) as long as it was originally sourced from abroad and registered with the Reserve Bank of Malawi (RBM).

▶ Partnerships

Joint ventures are allowed under the Partnership Act. The amount and shareholding are not regulated but joint ventures must be licensed by the Registrar General in the Ministry of Justice.

▶ Establishing a presence

Foreign businesses are allowed to establish themselves either through a subsidiary, branch, franchise, joint venture, or licensing relationship. Currently, US subsidiary or affiliate US companies operate in the agro-industry (mostly tobacco), computers and office equipment, and petroleum products. MIPA, as well as organizations such as the Malawi Chamber of Commerce and Industry, the Malawi Development Corporation (MDC), and the Malawi Export Promotion Council (MEPC) all assist foreign firms with registration.

▶ Financing projects

Malawi has had an OPIC investment guarantee agreement since 1967 and is a signatory to the Multilateral Investment Guarantee Agency. The World Bank's International Development Agency, the African Development Bank, and USAID are principal donors.

▶ Labor

Unskilled labor is readily available but skilled staff is scarce. Union membership is still low and there is a general lack of awareness of worker rights and benefits. Only 13% of the formal sector workforce belongs to unions.

▶ Legal rights

The legal system is based on British common law. The courts accept and enforce foreign court judgments that are registered in accordance with established legal procedures. Malawi is a member of the International Center for Settlement of Investment Disputes and accepts international arbitration of investment disputes. Malawi is a member of the World Intellectual Property Organization, the Berne Convention, and the Universal Copyright Convention. The Copyright Society of Malawi (COSOMA) administers the Copyright Act and the Registrar General administers the Patent and Trademarks Act and oversees the protection of industrial intellectual property rights.

▶ Business climate

Malawians are courteous and easygoing in business. Their approach shows the strong influence of the British. It is a small country where most prominent business people know each other well.

MALI

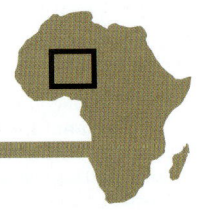

ECONOMIC ACTIVITY IN LANDLOCKED MALI DEPENDS LARGELY ON FARMING AND FISHING ALONG THE NIGER RIVER THAT MEANDERS THROUGH THE DESERT. IN THE NINETEENTH CENTURY EXPLORERS BRAVED THE DIFFICULT ROUTE TO TIMBUKTU IN SEARCH OF LEGENDARY GOLD-PAVED STREETS THAT TURNED OUT TO BE A FIGMENT OF THE IMAGINATION. TODAY, HOWEVER, MALI IS AFRICA'S FOURTH LARGEST GOLD PRODUCER AND BOTH SOUTH AFRICAN AND CANADIAN MINING COMPANIES ARE EXPLORING FOR MORE. IN 1992 A LONG PERIOD OF POST-INDEPENDENCE AUTOCRACY BENT ON SOCIALISM MADE WAY FOR A DEMOCRATICALLY ELECTED GOVERNMENT AND ECONOMIC REFORM POLICIES SUPPORTED BY INTERNATIONAL AGENCIES. THE COUNTRY IS ACTIVELY SEEKING FOREIGN PARTICIPATION TO HELP BOOST AGRICULTURAL PRODUCTION AND DEVELOP MINING PROSPECTS.

COUNTRY PROFILE

Most of landlocked Republic of Mali consists of monotonous plains, less than 500 m above sea level. The more than 4,000 km long Niger river flows northeast from Guinea through the heart of Mali into the Sahara desert. Between the towns of Ségu and Timbuktu it branches into lakes and swamps forming the Masina Delta. Both the Niger and its tributary, the Bani, are vital for transport and irrigation. In the summer moist maritime winds move in from the Gulf of Guinea and in winter the dry harmattan blows from the Sahara Desert in the north. The Sahel Belt, bordering the desert, extends from Senegal and Mauritania through Mali. Mandé-speaking peoples, consisting of the Bambara, Malinké (Manding or Mandinka) and Soninké, account for half the population. Other significant groups include the Ful (or Fulani), the Senufo, the Dogon, and the Songhai. The nomadic Tuareg are concentrated around the scattered oases of the Sahara to the north of Timbuktu and Gao and speak Berber. About 80% of the population are Muslim and the rest is split between Christianity and ethnic beliefs. French has official status and Bambara is the lingua franca.

HISTORY

The advent of the camel as a means of transport across the desert some 1,800 years ago stimulated trade between Mediterranean Africa and ancient Mali, a creation of a Mandé group, the Malinké. The Malinké empire ruled regions of Mali from the 12th to the 16th Century while the Songhai empire reigned over the Timbuktu-Gao region in the 15th Century. Originally explorers braved the arduous route inland in search of the legendary golden riches of Timbuktu, only to discover that the tales were heavily inflated. Morocco conquered Timbuktu in 1591 and controlled it for two centuries. In the

© Business Books Intl.

late 19th Century the French set out from their colony in Senegal to establish a colonial empire that would stretch to the Red Sea. With their claims validated at the 1885 Berlin Conference, the French applied a combination of diplomacy and military force to overpower several Sahelian states, including Mali. As French Soudan it was first incorporated into French West Africa and afterwards given joint independence with Senegal in the Federation of Mali. Shortly after independence in 1960, the federation split up and French Soudan became Mali. The first Malian president, Modibo Keita, opted for a one-party state, severed ties with France, introduced socialist policies and sought assistance from the Soviet Union. In 1968 the Keita dictatorship was overthrown by Lieutenant Moussa Traoré who retained one-man rule while adopting some free-market policies. Violent repression of pro-democracy forces prompted Lt.-Col. Amadou Toumani Touré to depose Traoré and facilitate the country's first free elections in 1992. Alpha Konaré won the presidential election and was reelected in 1997 for a second term. In May 2002 Amadou Touré returned to power by gaining 64.4% of the popular vote in a race against Soumaila Cissé.

GOVERNMENT

The 1992 constitution provides for an executive President, elected for a five year term. The President appoints the Council of Ministers and the Prime Minister. The 160-member unicameral *Assemblée Nationale* (National Assembly) also serves for a 5-year term. In the July 2002 election a multi-party coalition under the umbrella of Espoir 2002 (Spirit 2002) gained 66 seats against 51 for the *Alliance pour la République et la démocratie* (ARD). Malians from abroad won 13 seats and several other parties ten or less.

ECONOMIC POLICY

With 65% of its land area desert or semi-desert and an unequal distribution of income, Mali counts among the world's poorest countries. Since 1992 the emphasis has been on free trade and private enterprise, promoted in cooperation with the IMF, World Bank, and bilateral donors, including the United States. Strict adherence to IMF guidelines has stimulated foreign investment and enabled Mali to become the second largest cotton producer in Africa. Mali's successful implementation of the IMF-recomemended struc tural adjustment programs and a drastic devaluation

FAST FACTS

Pres. Amadou
Tomani Touré
Born: 1948
Since 2002

POLITICAL

Head of State	Pres. Amadou Tomani Touré
Prime Minister	Ahmed Hamani
Ruling Party	Espoir 2002
Main Opposition	ARD
Independence	22 September 1960
National capital	Bamako
Official languages	French

PHYSICAL

Total area	478,764 sq. miles
	1.24 million sq. km.
	(2 x Texas)
Arable land	3.8% of land area
Coastline	Landlocked

POPULATION

Total	11.7 million
Av. yearly growth	2.63%
Population/sq. mile	22
Urban population	4.7 million
Adult literacy	46.4%

ECONOMY

Currency	CFA franc (CFAF)(US$1=559.44)
GDP (real)	$5.4 billion
GDP growth rate	6%
GDP per capita[1]	$379
GDP (ppp)[2]	$13.56 billion
GDP per cap. (ppp)	$1,200
Inflation rate	4.5%
Exports	$323 million
Imports	$1.86 billion
External debt	$2.8 billion
Unemployment	14.6%

1. *Atlas method.*
2. *See page 175 for an explanation of purchasing power parity (ppp).*

of the CFA franc have led to a strong 5% average economic growth since the mid-nineties. Export taxes, import duties, and price controls have been reduced or eliminated and a new investment code adopted. Landlocked Mali remains vulnerable to unrest in neighboring countries both as far as trade routes and worker remittances are concerned.

SECTORS

Even though only 3% of the total land area is arable more than 80% of the people make a living in agriculture, accounting for half of Mali's GDP. Some 10% still live a nomadic life. Mali is Africa's fourth largest and Sub-Saharan Africa's largest producer of cotton. Other cash crops are groundnuts, sugar cane and rice. Food crops include millet, sorghum and maize. Livestock is responsible for half of the agricultural sector's activity. The country is self-sufficient in freshwater fish and a significant exporter. Gold mining has become an important contributor to GDP and has attracted considerable foreign interest, including the leading mining producers in South Africa. Mali also has deposits of bauxite, iron ore and tin. Prospecting is underway for petroleum, copper, lithium and diamonds. Manufacturing is mainly confined to small-scale agricultural processing for domestic consumption and export. Other industries include soft drinks, textiles, soaps, plastics, cigarettes, cement, bricks, and agricultural tools and equipment.

PRIVATIZATION

Around 90% of all production is still in the hands of state enterprises, but privatization is continuing. A US firm won an international bid to purchase the state-owned tannery.

INVESTMENT

Foreign direct investment in Mali's manufacturing sector is modest but growing. Canadian and South African mining houses have become prominent players in the gold mining sector while the French are dominant in cotton production, food processing, and petroleum retailing—a sector where Exxon/Mobil has also been a significant player for some time.

TRADE

Mali is the largest producer and exporter of cotton in Sub-Saharan Africa. Gold accounts for one third of its foreign exchange earnings. Although the French dominate the automobile and consumer goods market, North American, Asian, and other African nations are steadily gaining. Côte d'Ivoire and Senegal supply a whole range of essential consumer goods. Exports of US goods to Mali were estimated at $26 million in 1998.

FINANCIAL SECTOR

As a member of UEMOA, Mali's banking system is regulated from the regional central bank in Dakar, Senegal. Commercial banks enjoy considerable liquidity but tend to invest in Western capital markets instead of local enterprises. The ongoing privatization program is expected to make the local market more attractive. In 1994, the government started issuing treasury bonds that carry tax advantages for investors. Companies in Mali are expected to list on the UEMOA stock exchange.

TAXES AND TARIFFS

Except for a 3% levy on cotton and gold, taxes on exports were eliminated in 1990. Import duties on some goods were reduced or eliminated in 1994. The tax system remains complicated and in the view of some outsiders needs further overhaul to make it more attractive for foreign investors.

BUSINESS ACTIVITY

AGRICULTURE
Cotton, millet, rice, corn, vegetables, peanuts, cattle, sheep, goats.

INDUSTRIES
Minor local consumer goods production, food processing, construction, phosphate and gold mining.

NATURAL RESOURCES
Gold, phosphates, kaolin, salt, limestone, uranium, bauxite, iron ore, manganese, tin, unexploited copper deposits.

EXPORTS
$323 million (2004): cotton, gold, livestock.

IMPORTS
$1.86 billion (2004): machinery and equipment, construction materials, petroleum, foodstuffs, textiles.

MAJOR TRADING PARTNERS
Thailand, Italy, China, Pakistan, Brazil, Côte d'Ivoire, France, Taiwan, India, Senegal.

Doing Business with Mali

▶ Investment

The investment code favors investment in export-oriented and labor-intensive businesses. The mining code encourages investments in medium and small mining enterprises and allows two year exploration permits free of charge. The investment, mining, and commercial codes all offer duty-free importation of capital equipment, tax advantages for new ventures in priority industries and repatriation of profits and capital. Foreign investors go through the same one-stop screening process as domestic investors. Criteria for approval include the size of capital investment, the potential for added value, and the level of job creation. Any company that exports at least 80% of its production is entitled to tax-free status.

▶ Trade

Mali imports petroleum products, chemicals, vehicles, machinery, processed foods, pharmaceutical products, used clothing, cosmetics, electronics, telecommunications equipment, mining equipment, and most manufactured items. Most exporters to Mali make use of local agents or distributors.

▶ Trade finance

Payment is usually by irrevocable letters of credit. US investors in Mali enjoy short and medium term Eximbank coverage.

▶ Selling to the government

Significant government purchases usually involve programs sponsored by international agencies and donors such as USAID. These procurement contracts offer opportunities for foreign suppliers of agricultural, construction, irrigation, computer, and telecommunications equipment and services. Bidding rules are normally set by the donors.

▶ Exchange controls

Although there are no restrictions or limits on the repatriation of capital or profits, the regional central bank requires that all remittances be channeled through it, together with supporting commercial documents.

▶ Partnerships

Several overseas investors in the manufacturing and service sector have opted for partnerships or joint ventures. Such arrangements are encouraged but not required by the government. In the case of joint ventures involving the government, its share is limited to 20%.

▶ Establishing a presence

Establishing a presence requires a one-stop procedure (*guichet unique*). Manufacturers apply at the National Directorate of Industries and Trading Companies and at the National Directorate of Economic Affairs. The Chamber of Commerce and Industry assists in the process and registration takes on an average between 30-45 days. Foreign investors are allowed full ownership. They are also permitted to purchase shares in privatized parastatal and other domestic companies.

▶ Financing projects

Mali is eligible for Overseas Private Investment Corporation financing and insurance programs. It is a member of the World Bank's Multilateral Investment Guarantee Agency.

▶ Labor

Skilled workers laid off by the state and college and high school graduates without employment prospects are available in the job market. Workers have the right to belong to unions and although a warning notice is not required, mediation is generally sought before workers resort to striking. Although not mandatory, firms often find it useful to liaise with official labor inspectors—especially when hiring and firing.

▶ Legal rights

In rare instances of expropriation of property the Malian government has done so in accordance with international law. The investment code allows a foreign company which signs an agreement with the government to refer to international arbitration in cases where the local courts are unable to resolve disputes in a satisfactory manner. Mali is a member of the International Center for the Settlement of Investment Disputes and New York Convention of 1958 on the recognition and enforcement of foreign arbitrage awards. The *Direction Nationale des Industries* implements copyright and patent protection. Mali is a signatory to the WTO TRIPS agreement. Intellectual property right infringement has not been a serious problem.

▶ Business climate

Very little English is spoken in the French-oriented business community. Malians place great emphasis on protocol and courtesy and discussions normally start with an extensive exchange of pleasantries. Although most Malians are Muslim and do not drink, smoke, or eat pork, they usually do not object to foreigners doing so.

293

MAURITANIA

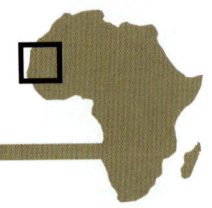

MAKING THE MOST OF ITS RESOURCES DESPITE LARGE STRETCHES OF DESERT AND THE WORLD'S THIRD LOWEST POPULATION DENSITY AFTER NAMIBIA AND MONGOLIA, MAURITANIA HAS MADE NOTABLE PROGRESS IN RECENT YEARS. EXTENSIVE IRON ORE DEPOSITS ACCOUNT FOR NEARLY 40% OF TOTAL EXPORTS. A NEW INVESTMENT CODE WIDENED THE SCOPE FOR FOREIGN PARTICIPATION IN KEY SECTORS SUCH AS MINING, FISHING AND AGRICULTURE. THERE IS PROSPECTING FOR MINERAL RESOURCES, IN-CLUDING OIL AND GOLD. PRIVATIZATION IS EXPECTED TO ATTRACT LARGER INFLOWS OF CAPITAL AND SPUR ECONOMIC GROWTH AND DEVELOPMENT.

COUNTRY PROFILE

More than 70% of the Islamic Republic of Mauritania consists of the Sahara Desert. Both the desert and the Sahel regions rise from monotonous coastal plains in the west to a low plateau eastward and northward, exceeding heights of 500 m above sea level at the iron-bearing hills around Fderik and Zouerate. Only the southernmost strip, along the northern bank of the Senegal River receives sufficient rainfall (up to 800 mm) for intensive crop cultivation. Most Mauritanians are descendants of Berbers and Arab immigrants, but black groups such as the Wolof, Tukulor, and Soninke and the nomadic Tajakant and Regeihat are present in significant numbers. Hassaniya Arabic, which had enjoyed equal status with French since 1967, became the only official language in 1991. The Mandé languages of the Soninké, Fula and Wolof are also recognized as national languages and used in schools. French is still widely spoken in commerce. The Muslim faith prevails.

HISTORY

Mauritania was first inhabited by black peoples and Berbers. From the 7th Century, following the advent of the Arabs in Northern Africa, the Berbers in the region were converted to the Islamic faith and they in turn proselytized the Tukulor and other black communities in the Sahel region. As was the case in Morocco, Arab and Berber intermixing led to the emergence of Moors (derived from the Latin

Mauri or French *Maures*) who viewed themselves as al-Bidan (white) as opposed to their al-Sudan (black) neighbors. Portuguese slave traders established a base on Arguin Island (Tidra) from 1443. The French took over the region in the 1930s. In 1960, over strenuous opposition from Morocco, which laid claim to the territory, Mauritania became independent under President Moktar Ould Daddah (son-in-law of French president Charles de Gaulle). Ould Daddah's party had won all the seats in a 1959 general election. In 1976 Spain ceded Spanish (Western) Sahara on a 50/50 basis to Morocco and Mauritania. The Polisario guer-

rillas, who sought independence for Western Sahara, attacked targets in Mauritania, drawing it into a protracted and costly war. In 1997, in the midst of growing opposition to this unpopular war, Ould Daddah was ousted by Lt-Col. Khouna Ould Haidalla, who assumed the presidency and appointed Col. Maaouiya Ould Sid'Ahmed Taya as his prime minister. Mauritania dropped its territorial claims, leaving the way clear for Morocco to expand its influence over all of Western Sahara. In 1984 Taya assumed the presidency. He exercised autocratic rule until 1992 when his *Parti Républicain Démocratique et Social* (PRDS), or Social and Democratic Party, won in free elections. Tension between the Moorish and black non-Moorish groups has eased since the restrictions on political parties were lifted after the adoption of a new democratic constitution at a referendum in 1991. Pres. Taya was reelected in 1997 and again in November 2003 but subsequently deposed in a bloodless military coup by Col. Ely Ould Mohamed Vall in August 2005. Pres. Vall promised to have democratric and free elections after an interim period of two years. Until then the country—troubled by tensions among its black population and the different Moor (Arab-Berber) factions—is to be controlled by an autocratic government.

GOVERNMENT

The 1991 Constitution provides for an executive President elected by popular vote for six year terms. He appoints the Prime Minister and Council of Ministers. A bicameral parliament consists of a 56-member Senate or Majlis al-Shuyukh elected by municipal leaders for six years, and a 81-member National Assembly *(Al Jamiya al-Wataniyah)* elected by popular vote every five years. Winning 64 seats in the Assembly elections of October 2001, the Democratic and Social Republican Party (PRDS) maintains an overwhelming majority over its nearest rival, the *Action pour Changement* (Action for Change)(AC) with only 4 seats. The PRDS holds 52 of the 56 Senate seats.

ECONOMIC POLICY

The government has successfully implemented an IMF and World Bank-sponsored structural adjustment program. Reforms include privatization and restructuring of the banking sector, liberalization of the exchange rate system, and reduction of trade and investment barriers. These reforms resulted in an increase in real GDP (in local currency) during the nineties . But they did not

FAST FACTS

*Pres. Ely Ould
Mohamed Vall
Born: 1952
Since 2005*

POLITICAL

Head of State	Pres. Ely Ould Mohamed Vall
Ruling Party	PRDS
Main Opposition	AC
Independence	28 November 1960
National capital	Nouakchott
Official languages	Hasaniya Arabic

PHYSICAL

Total area	397,964 sq. miles 1,030,700 sq. km. (3 x Arizona)
Arable land	0.48%
Coastline	469 miles/754 km

POPULATION

Total	3.18 million
Av. yearly growth	2.88%
Population/sq. mile	7
Urban population	2 million
Adult literacy	41.7%

ECONOMY

Currency	Ouguiya (UM) (US$1=277.05)
GDP (real)	$1.35 million
GDP growth rate	5.5%
GDP per capita[1]	$594
GDP (ppp)[2]	$6.9 billion
GDP per cap. (ppp)	$2,200
Inflation rate	7%
Exports	$784 million
Imports	$1.12 billion
External debt	$2.5 billion
Unemployment	20%

1. *Atlas method.*
2. *See page 175 for an explanation of purchasing power parity (ppp).*

come without a certain measure of political risk. A new investment code approved in December 2001 widened the scope for direct foreign investment in key sectors. The Taya government's restructuring programs have at times provoked strong protests. Mauritania qualified for debt relief under the Heavily Indebted Poor Countries (HIPC) initiative.

SECTORS

The economy depends largely on the mining of iron and copper ore and fishing in the Atlantic. Less than 3% of Mauritania is cultivable and only one-fifth of its food crop requirements is produced locally. Imported cereals supplement the locally-grown food crops consisting mainly of millet, sorghum, maize, rice and vegetables. Livestock (cattle, sheep, goats and camels) account for about 15% of GDP or three-quarters of the total agriculture production. Only 10% of the working-age population is employed in the formal sector of the economy. Mauritania's coastal waters are among the richest fishing areas in the world but indiscriminate fishing by foriegners threatens to deplete this source of income. Marine fishing around Nouadhibou contributes 5% of GDP. Joint-venture companies are responsible for about 95% of output, most of it processed locally. At an estimated 6 billion tons, Mauritania's iron ore reserves are among the largest in the world. Other mineral resources include gold, copper, phosphates, sulphur, gypsum and uranium. The US is an important provider of equipment to the mining sector. Development is hampered by large-scale deforestation, over-exploitation of fishing grounds and a chronic water shortage. In 2001 exploratory drilling 80 km offshore indicated potential profitable oil extraction and production is estimated at 75,000 bbl/day in an area estimated to have a reserve of 1 billion barrels.

PRIVATIZATION

The telecommunications, electricity, and air transport companies are being privatized.

INVESTMENT

Foreign investment dried up during ethnic clashes between 1989 and 1991 but resumed modestly towards the mid-1990s after the government introduced new incentives. Foreign investors include firms from the US, France, Saudi Arabia, China, Belgium, Australia and Ireland in areas such as petroleum, mining, food processing, banking, fishing and manufacturing.

TRADE

With 58% of the total, iron ore is the country's leading export earner, followed by fishing, which accounts for 38% of the total. Mauritania imports almost all its food, machinery and consumer needs, including foodstuffs, vehicles and spare parts, petroleum products, building materials, mining equipment, telecommunications equipment, electronics, cosmetics and most other manufactured items. French, Spanish and Asian goods dominate the market but there is a growing demand for US-made items.

FINANCIAL SECTOR

Banking supervision has been strengthened to encourage development of an interbank market and to ensure solvency. There are five commercial banks and about 30 exchange offices in Mauritania. The Central Bank fixes the exchange rate for the ouguiya through a basket of currencies of principal trading partners.

TAXES AND TARIFFS

Recent laws focus on a more efficient and simplified revenue collection system coupled with lower rates. Still, import duties remain relatively heavy as rates vary from 9% to as high as 43%. Value Added Tax (VAT) rates on imported goods are divided into two categories: 5% for essential and 14% for non-essential goods. VAT is not applied to exported goods.

BUSINESS ACTIVITY

AGRICULTURE
Dates, millet, sorghum, root crops, cattle, sheep, fish products.

INDUSTRIES
Fish processing, mining of iron ore and gypsum.

NATURAL RESOURCES
Copper, iron ore, gypsum, fish, phosphate.

EXPORTS
$784 million (est. 2005): fish and fish products, iron ore, gold.

IMPORTS
$1.12 million (2004): foodstuffs, consumer goods, petroleum products, capital goods.

MAJOR TRADING PARTNERS
Japan, Italy, France, UK, US, Germany, Belgium, Spain, Russia, China.

Doing Business with Mauritania

▶ **INVESTMENT**

Incentives are offered to investors in small- and medium-sized enterprises and export-oriented manufacturing utilizing local manpower and raw materials in areas outside of Nouakchott and Nouadhibou. Government priorities range from re-organization of the fishing sector to gold and other mineral prospecting, increased water supply and improved irrigation systems to rural road construction and rehabilitation, and telecommunications expansion to increased electricity generation.

▶ **TRADE**

Three market segments are considered to be prime prospects for US exporters: foodstuffs (especially wheat, flour, rice, powdered milk, and canned food), mining equipment (machinery and trucks), and telecommunications. Foreign firms have also been successful in supplying fishing gear, wind and solar energy equipment, pharmaceutical and medical products, computers and software, cosmetics, toiletries, and oil and clothing.

▶ **TRADE FINANCE**

Most imports are by irrevocable and confirmed letters of credit issued by local banks. Some Mauritanian importers hold bank accounts abroad and pay for imports without involving their local bank. The Foreign Credit Insurance Association (FCIA) insures purchases by the state mining company, SNIM.

▶ **SELLING TO THE GOVERNMENT**

Purchases are usually by tenders (*avis d'appel d'offres*) but direct negotiations are common in small transactions involving local suppliers. Major projects are often guaranteed and controlled by international donors. The Central Procurement Board (*Commission Centrale des Marchés*) monitors all government procurement.

▶ **EXCHANGE CONTROLS**

The foreign exchange system has been liberalized, and repatriation of dividends and capital as well as payments for overseas goods and services are possible through commercial banks without prior approval from the Central Bank.

▶ **PARTNERSHIPS**

The government offers a wide range of incentives to encourage partnership arrangements. Current joint ventures are primarily with other Arab countries in the mineral, fishing, and banking sectors.

▶ **ESTABLISHING A PRESENCE**

An official investment agency (*Guichet Unique de l'Investissement*) and the Mauritanian Chamber of Commerce and Industry offer assistance and advice to foreigners who wish to establish an office. Even though procedures can be handled without a local lawyer, foreign investors with long-term plans usually retain one to ensure strict compliance from the outset.

▶ **FINANCING PROJECTS**

Mauritania relies for about 85% of its project funding on loans from The African Development Bank, IMF, and European Investment Bank, and the Islamic Bank.

▶ **LABOR**

Even though unemployment is high among high school and college graduates, there is a shortage of factory-skilled workers and managerial staff in all sectors, with the possible exception of mining. Workers are free to associate with and establish unions at local and national levels. Work stoppages are rare. Foreign firms are normally at liberty to hire any number of expatriates, except in areas such as industrial fishing where crews are required to have five Mauritanians per vessel.

▶ **LEGAL RIGHTS**

Since Mauritania's independence, there has only been one case of nationalization when in 1974 the government took over a mining company from a majority French partner. It paid a mutually agreed sum in compensation. Disagreements over investment issues are settled in the courts or in terms of arbitration procedures in conformance with the rules of the World Bank. Mauritania is a member of the African Intellectual Property Organization, the Paris, Berne and Hague conventions and the World Intellectual Property Organization.

▶ **BUSINESS CLIMATE**

A working knowledge of French or Arabic is an advantage but interpreters are readily available. As a Muslim country, consumption of alcohol and pork is taboo. A handshake is customary when initiating and closing a business meeting but it should be remembered that some conservative Muslim men will not shake a woman's hand.

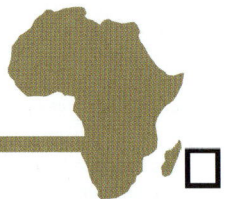

MAURITIUS

WHEN MAURITIUS BECAME INDEPENDENT IN 1968, THIS SMALL ISLAND COUNTRY IN THE INDIAN OCEAN WAS AN UNDERDEVELOPED SINGLE CROP COMMUNITY. SINCE THEN IT BRANCHED OUT FROM SUGAR INTO SEVERAL OTHER SECTORS AND RAISED ITS PER CAPITA INCOME TO THE SECOND HIGHEST IN AFRICA. WHILE SUGAR CANE STILL COVERS MORE THAN NINETY PERCENT OF THE CULTIVATED LAND AREA AND ACCOUNTS FOR 25% OF EXPORT EARNINGS, THE EMPHASIS TODAY IS ON BANKING AND THE IN-FORMATION INDUSTRY. MAURITIUS HAS ATTRACTED MORE THAN NINE THOUSAND OFFSHORE ENTITIES. TEXTILES AND TOURISM HAVE BECOME SIGNIFICANT SECTORS.

COUNTRY PROFILE

The Republic of Mauritius comprises the main island and a much smaller Rodrigues Island, about 500 km northeast, as well as two dependencies, the virtually uninhabited Cargados Carajos (600 km north), and Agalega, with a few hundred inhabitants (1,200 km north). It also lays claim to the uninhabited French island of Tromelin (500 km north) and the British Chagos Islands about halfway to Sri Lanka. The Chagos group includes Diego Garcia, used as an American military communications base. Mauritius itself measures about 58 km by 47 km and has a subtropical climate, beaches, coral reefs and scenery that at-tract thousands of upscale tourists. Its inhabitants trace their ancestry to three continents—Africa, Asia and Europe. The Indian group (Hindu and Muslim) accounts for 69% while citizens of mixed Afro-European origin (Creoles) constitute 27%. Education levels and health standards are high. About 52 percent of the population is Hindu and 16 percent Muslim.

HISTORY

The Dutch first came to this island in 1638 and named it Mauritius (after the Dutch leader, Mauritz of Nassau). They made way for the French in 1715, who renamed it Isle de France, stayed until 1810 and lost it to the British, who reinstated the name Mauritius. Indentured Hindu workers were brought from India to work on sugar estates. Their descendants are in the majority, followed by Creoles (of mixed, predominantly African slave origin), Muslim Indians, Chinese and a few Euro-peans. The Creole population gave birth to a lan-guage based on the French, Malagasy and African languages, which became the lingua franca of the island. Mauritius received its independence under the British crown in 1968 and became a Republic in 1992. Continuous political squabbles, splits and shifting alliances do not seem to have derailed a climate of continuity and stability. Prime Minister Navin Ramgoolam headed an unstable coalition government for 5 years before being ousted at the polls by an opposition alliance in September 2000. Sir Anerood Jugnauth, leader of the *Move-ment Socialiste Miltant* or Militant Socialist Move-ment (MSM), served as prime minister for 3 years

before handing over to his coalition partner, Paul Bérenger, of the *Mouvement Militant Mauricien* (MMM). In the 2005 National Assembly elections, the opposition Social Alliance (AS) spearheaded by Navin Ramgoolam's Mauritius Labour Party (MLP) defeated the incumbent Mauritian Militant Movement-Mauritian Socialist Movement (MMM-MSM). This enabled Ramgoolam to regain the premiership in a truly democratic and transparent fashion.

GOVERNMENT

Both the president and the prime minister, who heads the government, are elected for 5 years. The unicameral National Assembly, elected by the voters for 5-year terms, has 62 members plus an additional maximum of eight seats allocated to the "best losers"—the unsuccessful candidates with the largest number of votes. After the 2005 election the Social Alliance (AS), led by the Mauritius Labour Party (MLP), finished with 42 seats against 24 for the Mauritian Militant Movement-Mauritian Socialist Movement (MMM-MSM).

ECONOMIC POLICY

Starting with a monocrop, impoverished island nation some 30 years ago, Mauritius has earned the top spot among African countries on the UN Human Development Index. Today it is a diversified economy, relying not only on exports of sugar, but textiles and services such as tourism and financial and offshore business. Mauritius has attracted more than 9,000 offshore entities, mostly aimed at commerce in India and South Africa. Investment in the banking sector alone has generated $1 billion. The country, however, faces new challenges as both sugar and textiles are losing their preferential access to major markets in Europe and the US. It has compensated by taking full advantage of the Africa Growth and Opportunity Act (AGOA) for textile exports to the US. The emphasis is on productivity and turning some of its most companies into multinationals. The aim is to make Mauritius a regional trade and financial center. Impressive annual economic growth has resulted in more equitable income distribution, increased life expectancy, lowered infant mortality and improved infrastructure.

PRIVATIZATION

The government's share of GDP is modest but it still controls key sectors. The State Trading Corporation regulates imports of rice, flour, petro-

FAST FACTS

Navinchandra Ramgoolam
Born: July 13, 1947
Since 2005

© UN/DPI

POLITICAL

Head of State	Pres. Anerood Jugnauth
Prime Minister	Navinchandra Ramgoolam
Ruling Coalition	AS
Main Opposition	MMM/MSM
Independence	12 March 1968
National capital	Port Louis
Official languages	English & French

PHYSICAL

Total area	788 sq. miles 2,040 sq. km. (11 x Washington DC)
Arable land	50% of land area
Coastline	110 miles/177 km

POPULATION

Total	1.24 million
Av. yearly growth	0.82%
Population/sq. mile	1,499
Urban population	500,000
Adult literacy	85.6%

ECONOMY

Currency	Mauritian Rupee (MauR) (US$1=30.10)
GDP (real)	$6.68 billion
GDP growth rate	3%
GDP per capita[1]	$5,131
GDP (ppp)[2]	$13.1 billion
GDP per cap. (ppp)	$13,100
Inflation rate	5%
Exports	$1.9 billion
Imports	$2.5 billion
External debt	$3.2 billion
Unemployment	9.6%

1. *Atlas method.*
2. *See page 175 for an explanation of purchasing power parity (ppp).*

leum products, and cement, and the Agricultural Marketing Board the importation of potatoes, onions and spices. Slated for privatization are trade monopolies, telecommunications, banking and broadcasting entities.

SECTORS

Initially heavily dependent on sugar, Mauritius has developed a strong manufacturing and tourism sector in the past few decades. Agriculture's share of GDP shrank to 9%, while manufacturing's contribution rose to 23%. Sugar, however, remains the basis of the economy. It is grown on about half the total land area and employs 14% of the labor force. Apart from high-value textiles, local manufactures include pharmaceuticals, publishing, software, light engineering, and jewelry. Tourism is the third pillar on which the Mauritian economy rests, accounting for 5% of GDP and providing direct and indirect employment for some 50,000 people. Offshore banking has become a major source of income.

TRADE

Sugar and textiles together with a variety of light manufactures account for most of the country's exports. Other significant exports are tea and cut flowers. Mauritius imports three-quarters of its food, especially rice, a staple food. The US is Mauritius' third largest market but it ranks 13th in terms of exports to Mauritius, well behind South Africa, France, India, and the United Kingdom. The US and Singapore are leading suppliers of computers. Main imported raw materials are textile yarn and fabrics (55%), cotton, wool and synthetic fibers (6%), and chemicals (4%). Caterpillar and John Deere are major suppliers of derocking machinery for sugar farms, followed by a few European manufacturers. The US also leads in supplying pivot irrigation systems for these estates.

INVESTMENT

Foreign direct investment fell sharply since the early 1980s when many Hong Kong firms, the leading investors in textile manufacturing, relocated. There are a few US investors in the Export Processing Zone (mostly diamond cutting/polishing and garment manufacturing). Most recent foreign direct investment has gone into information technology, printing and publishing, pharmaceuticals, light engineering, high-quality garments, and jewelry. India, UK, France, Germany and South Africa are leading investors.

FINANCIAL SECTOR

A sophisticated banking system comprises 10 commercial banks (seven foreign-owned) and 10 financial intermediaries, including the Development Bank of Mauritius, the State Investment Corporation, the Mauritius Leasing Company (a joint private-public venture), as well as two private leasing companies. There are seven offshore banks and 4,600 non-banking off-shore companies providing insurance, funds management, aircraft leasing, consultancy, and data processing. The Stock Exchange of Mauritius has 45 listed companies (including two foreign) and an over-the-counter market with 60 companies. Capitalization is close to $2 billion. The Bank of Mauritius oversees domestic and offshore banks and implements monetary policies. Much of the country's offshore business involves US investment in India, channeled through Mauritius for tax reasons.

TAXES & TARIFFS

Tax incentives allow for a corporate rate of 15% instead of the normal 35%. Companies in the Mauritius Freeport are fully exempted. There is no withholding tax on dividends and no tax on capital gains. Mauritius operates a two-tiered system that allows imports from certain countries, including the US, preferential duties ranging between 0% and 80%. A VAT of 10% percent is payable by importers.

BUSINESS ACTIVITY

AGRICULTURE
Sugar cane, tea, corn, potatoes, bananas, pulses, cattle, goats, fish.

INDUSTRIES
Food processing (largely sugar milling), textiles, clothing, chemicals, metal products, transport equipment, nonelectrical machinery, tourism.

NATURAL RESOURCES
Arable land, fish.

EXPORTS
$2.01 billion (2004 est.): clothing, textiles, sugar, cut flowers, molasses.

IMPORTS
$2.24 billion (2004 est.): manufactured goods, capital equipment, foodstuffs, petroleum products, chemicals.

MAJOR TRADING PARTNERS
UK, France, US, Germany, Italy, South Africa, India, Italy, Hong Kong.

DOING BUSINESS WITH MAURITIUS

▶ INVESTMENT

Tax concessions and other incentives are offered in Export Processing Zones scattered around the island. Textiles and apparel account for 80% of EPZ exports, but there has been diversification into the manufacture of watches, electronic measuring instruments, jewelry, leather goods, toys, and optical goods. The Mauritius Export Development and Investment Authority assists investors and promotes exports. Generous incentives are also available to foreign companies operating from the Mauritius Freeport in transshipment and reexportation, offshore banking and other financial services, light manufacturing, and information technology. The authorities encourage both local and foreign private investment in major infrastructure projects ranging from energy to roads and airport construction.

▶ TRADE

There is growing interest in foreign technology, especially in telecommunications, computers, software, and farm machinery. Opportunities also exist in restaurant and food-processing equipment and design consulting. The government controls prices and markups on items such as rice, flour, cement, cooking gas, infant milk powder, cheese, fertilizer, frozen fish, iron and steel bars, and petroleum products. Major expansion of both traditional and nontraditional sources of energy such as electricity from bagasse and wind power-created demand for turbo-alternators, boilers, machinery to handle bagasse, coal and ash, and associated electrical equipment. There is an ongoing need for machinery and irrigation systems.

▶ TRADE FINANCE

Mauritius qualifies for the full range of Eximbank loans extended to US exporters. The government-controlled Development Bank of Mauritius provides loans to large and medium-sized industrial enterprises and manages various concessionary lending schemes for small-scale enterprises.

▶ SELLING TO THE GOVERNMENT

Infrastructure projects such as airport and port development, energy, telecommunications, health, sewage, road and dam construction, and computerization offer opportunities .

▶ EXCHANGE CONTROLS

There are no exchange control regulations and dividends and royalties are freely repatriated.

▶ PARTNERSHIP

Joint ventures are rare except in architecture, construction and civil engineering projects. Several Mauritian firms, however, manufacture foreign products under license.

▶ ESTABLISHING A PRESENCE

Foreigners usually opt for a limited company or a branch. It is common procedure to nominate two residents to form the company and transfer the shares to the foreign investor after approval. A foreign investor in export-oriented manufacturing is permitted 100% equity, but the government encourages local participation. Foreign participation may be limited to 49% in investments serving the domestic market, and is generally not encouraged in areas where Mauritius has already mastered the technology.

▶ PROJECT FINANCING

Mauritius is eligible for OPIC programs and major infrastructure projects are financed by the World Bank, the African Development Bank, the European Investment Bank/European Development Fund, the Kuwait Fund, and the Arab Bank for Economic Development in Africa.

▶ LABOR

It is not difficult to recruit workers with basic secondary education and some technical training. There is, however, a shortage of skills in financial services and management, especially human resource management. Labor-management relations are generally good and unions account for less than 25 percent of the workforce.

▶ LEGAL RIGHTS

The legal system, based on both the Napoleonic code and British common law, protects property, patents and trademarks. Mauritius is a member of the World Intellectual Property Organization and party to the Paris and Bern Conventions for the Protection of Industrial Property and the Universal Copyright Convention. Its copyright law is in conformity with WTO's Trade Related Aspects of Intellectual Property Rights (TRIPS).

▶ BUSINESS CLIMATE

Business customs are Western. For men, normal business wear is a suit. Lunches and cocktail receptions are common business events. International mail, telephone, fax and e-mail services are reliable. The official language is English but French and Creole are used in everyday life.

MOROCCO

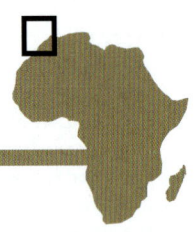

As the African country closest to Europe, Morocco's economic fate is closely tied to markets across the Mediterranean Sea. Separated from Spain by the 13 kilometer Strait of Gibraltar, most of Morocco's trade is directed towards the European Union but there is a concerted effort to expand business relations with the United States. Despite diversity and the lingering Western Sahara dispute, Morocco is one of the most stable countries in the Arab world, due largely to the efforts of the late King Hassan, a consummate politician, and his successor, King Mohammed VI. It has the largest phosphate reserves in the world, a thriving agricultural sector, rich fisheries, a sizeable tourist industry, and a growing manufacturing sector. Since the early 1980s Morocco has pursued an economic reform program that has led to rising per capita incomes, lower inflation, and smaller deficits.

COUNTRY PROFILE

The Kingdom of Morocco is part of a region dominated by the Atlas Mountains that extends into Algeria and Tunisia. The port city of Ceuta at Morocco's northernmost point is Spanish territory, as is Mellila further east. Mount Toubkal in the High Atlas is 13,670 ft (4,165 m) above sea level and snow-capped during much of the year. The much lower Anti-Atlas mountains stretch into in the desert borderlands with large clusters of oases. Between the Atlantic coast and the mountain ranges is fertile agricultural land. Earthquakes sometimes occur and in 1960 one razed Agadir, causing the death of some 15,000 people. About 60% of the population is of Arab and mixed Arabo-Berber origin and speak Arabic, while the remainder still converse in various Berber dialects. Arabic is the official language but French is widely used in business, government and education. Many people in the far north speak Spanish. Islam is the state religion and but there are about 100,000 Christians, mainly Roman Catholic, and several thousand Jews.

HISTORY

When the Phoenicians started trading with the region it was already occupied by people of caucasoid origin. These Africans were called barbarians by the ancient Greeks and Romans and the name Berber is probably derived from barberoi (Greek) or barbari (Latin). Arab-Muslim conquerors in the course of the 7th Century succeeded in converting many Berbers to Islam. Marriages between Arab warriors and Berber women started

a process of assimilation. In 1492 the Christians in Spain and Portugal finally overpowered the Moors and caused a considerable migration to Morocco of Muslims and Jews. Following their victory, the Spaniards and Portuguese seized most of the ports along the Maghreb coast. Ceuta and Tanger were already under Portuguese control and Melilla became a Spanish stronghold. In 1684 the city of Tanger, which had been donated to the English by the Portuguese, was reoccupied by the Moroccans. However, Spain held on to Melilla and to Ceuta, which it had acquired from the Portuguese as well. In 1912 France took possession of the larger (central) part of Morocco, with all its important cities, and later that year ceded to Spain two territories to the north and south including Ceuta and Melilla and Rio de Oro (later to become known as the Spanish or Western Sahara). The nationalist opposition in Morocco defeated a combined Franco-Spanish force of over 250,000 in 1926 and forced France to grant it self-government in 1956. Spain had to cede all its possessions except Ceuta, Melilla, Ifni and Spanish Sahara. As the neighboring states (Algeria, Mauritania and Mali) became independent, Morocco claimed, on historic grounds, parts of their territory, as well as the entire Spanish Sahara. King Mohammed V ruled from 1957 until his death in 1961. He was succeeded by his son Mulay Hassan II who ruled until his death in 1999. King Hassan was followed to the throne by his heir, King Mohammed VI.

GOVERNMENT

The current constitution, dating back to 1972, combines limited democracy with strong, virtually unlimited royal authority. As head of state, the king may introduce and veto legislation, dissolve the legislature and rule by decree. He appoints the Prime Minister and the cabinet. After the 2002 election Driss Jettou was appointed Prime Minister. The bicameral parliament consists of the 270-member *Majlis al-Mustasharin* or Assembly of Counselors elected for a nine year term by local councils, professional organizations, and labor syndicates, and the *Majlis al-Nuwab*—a 325 seat lower house or Assembly of Representatives elected by for five years by popular vote. The *Rassemblement National des Indépendents* or National Rally of Independents (RNI) dominates the Chamber of Counsellors with 42 seats, followed by the *Mouvement Démocratique et Social* or Social Democratic Movement (MDS) with 33. In the September 2002 election the *Union Socialiste*

FAST FACTS

King Mohammed VI
Born: August 12, 1963
Since 1999

POLITICAL

Head of State	King Mohammed VI
Prime Minister	Driss Jettou
Ruling Party	USFP
Opposition parties	RNI, UC, MDS
Independence	2 March 1956
National capital	Rabat
Official language	Arabic

PHYSICAL

Total area	172,413 sq. miles
	446,550 sq. km.
	(± California)
Arable land	20% of land area
Coastline	1,140 miles/1,835 km

POPULATION

Total	33.24 million
Av. yearly growth	1.55%
Population/sq. mile	175
Urban population	18.5 million
Adult literacy	51.7%

ECONOMY

Currency	Moroccan dirham (DH) (US$1=9.28)
GDP (real)	$51.94 billion
GDP growth rate	1.8%
GDP per capita[1]	$1,661
GDP (ppp)[2]	$138.3 billion
GDP per cap. (ppp)[3]	$4,200
Inflation rate	1%
Exports	$9.47 billion
Imports	$18.15 billion
External debt	$15.61 billion
Unemployment	11%

1. Atlas method.
2. See page 175 for an explanation of purchasing power parity (ppp).

303

des Forces Populaires (USFP) won 50 seats in the Assembly of Representatives, followed by the *Istiqial/Parti d'Independence* with 48 seats. The rest of the seats are split up between twenty different parties.

ECONOMIC POLICY

IMF-style economic reform measures, including fiscal caution and privatization, are in place. Even though its economic policies brought stability unemployment remains a concern. Morocco has agreed to the creation by 2010 of a free trade area with the EU which will force Moroccan producers to become more amenable to foreign partnerships. In 2004 the government signed a free trade agreement with the United States and implemented large scale privatization projects—including the sale of government shares in the state-owned bank telecommunications company—to boost foreign direct investment. The Free Trade agreement went into effect in January 2006.

SECTORS

Agriculture, fishing and forestry employ about 35% of the working population, account for 15% of GDP and contribute about 25% of the country's export revenues. At 21% a comparatively high proportion of the total area is arable and utilized by large-scale commercial farmers, producing citrus and wine—apart from numerous peasant smallholders. The principal food crops are wheat, barley, maize and vegetables. Sugar cane, sugar beet, olives and cotton are major industrial crops but the principal agricultural exports are citrus, tomatoes, canned fruit, vegetables and wine. The country is self-sufficient in livestock production, mainly sheep. Canned fish and fresh fish, including shellfish, account for around 14% of total exports. Together with Western Sahara, Morocco accounts for 75% of the world's known phosphate reserves and is, after Russia and the US, the world's third largest producer. Other mineral resources include silver, zinc, copper, fluorine, lead, barite, and iron.

PRIVATIZATION

Since 1992 when it launched its privatization program, Morocco has sold about half of its 114 state enterprises. Sugar plants, hotels, and banks were privatized. A 35% interest in the state telecommunications monopoly, Maroc Telecom, was sold to France's Vivendi Universal for $2.7 billion. Royal Air Maroc is due for partial privatization,

INVESTMENT

Foreign investment has grown considerably since privatization started and the government opened infrastructural projects to private participation.

TRADE

The export of phosphates and derivatives accounts for over a quarter of the total. Morocco is a net exporter of fruits and vegetables, but a net importer of cereals. Textile and clothing comprise 70% of all manufactured exports.

FINANCIAL SECTOR

There are 12 major banks, five government-owned specialized financial institutions, some 15 credit agencies and 10 leasing companies. Insurance companies, pension funds, and a stock market are the other components of a modern, well developed financial sector. The Casablanca stock exchange enjoyed a recent revival after new laws made it more efficient.

TAXES AND TARIFFS

Most imports are subject to customs duties to a maximum of 35%, apart from a surcharge of between 10% and 15%. A value-added tax (TVA) of between 7% and 19% applies.

BUSINESS ACTIVITY

AGRICULTURE
Barley, wheat, citrus, wine, vegetables, olives, livestock.

INDUSTRIES
Phosphate rock mining and processing, food processing, leather goods, textiles, construction, tourism.

NATURAL RESOURCES
Phosphates, iron ore, zinc, fish, salt, lead, manganese.

EXPORTS
$9.47 billion (est. 2005): food and beverages, semiprocessed goods, consumer goods, phosphates, clothing, petroleum products.

IMPORTS
$18.15 billion (est. 2005): crude petroleum, textile fabric, transistors, plastics.

MAJOR TRADING PARTNERS
France, Spain, UK, China, Germany, Italy, Saudi Arabia.

DOING BUSINESS WITH MOROCCO

INVESTMENT

Apart from agricultural land and a few sectors still reserved for the state such as phosphate mining, air and rail transport, and public utilities, foreign participation is strongly encouraged. Under Morocco's privatization program most of these restricted areas are expected to be opened up. A Moroccanization decree limiting foreign ownership in the petroleum refining and distribution sector was repealed and allowed, among others, Mobil Oil to buy back the government's 50 percent share of its local subsidiary. There are no foreign investor performance requirements and incentives apply. In the building of power plants, telephone network expansion and other infrastructural developments the government relies largely on foreign entrepreneurs.

TRADE

The favored port of entry is Casablanca and foreign manufacturers and exporters are represented in the market either through their own affiliate branch office or by authorized agent/distributors who import, install and service the equipment. There seems to be ample scope in the fast food sector. Additional franchising opportunities include hotels and motels, automotive parts and services, dry cleaning business equipment and services. Among the top prospects for sales are water distribution equipment, electrical power systems, pollution control, mining, medical and telecommunications equipment, computers and software, and architectural, engineering, tourism and other services. Agricultural needs range from large quantities of wheat to vegetable oil, sugar, and cotton.

TRADE FINANCE

Local financing is available for Moroccan investors and importers, but real interest rates are high by overseas standards. Most Moroccan imports are by irrevocable confirmed letters but intense competition at times requires attractive payment terms. The Eximbank provides assistance to US exporters and the US Department of Agriculture extends credit guarantee programs.

SELLING TO THE GOVERNMENT

While government purchases are at times directly negotiated, tenders are common. So-called medium and major projects are open to international firms while minor ones are reserved for locals. Major projects are often guaranteed by an international financial entity.

EXCHANGE CONTROLS

Foreign exchange is available through the commercial banks upon presentation of documents for the repatriation of dividends and capital by foreign investors, for remittances by foreign residents, and for payments for foreign technical assistance, royalties and licenses.

PARTNERSHIPS

There is growing local interest joint ventures and at latest count 1,500 have been operating in the manufacturing sector, mostly with French, Spanish and German partners.

ESTABLISHING A PRESENCE

To form a local company foreigners merely need to file documents with the Secretariat of the Court of First Instance.

FINANCING PROJECTS

In most instances project financing comes from the World Bank, the African Development Bank, the European Investment Bank, the Kuwaiti Fund, the Saudi Fund and the Abu Dhabi Fund.

LABOR

Workers are free to form and join unions but only about 6% of Morocco's nine million workers are unionized, mostly in the public sector. Collective bargaining has, however, been a long-standing tradition in some parts of the economy, notably heavy industry.

LEGAL RIGHTS

The law protects and facilitates acquisition and disposition of property rights, including intellectual property rights. Morocco is a member of the World Intellectual Property Organization and party to the Berne copyright, Paris industrial property, and universal copyright conventions. Still dating from the era of French and Spanish protectorates is the requirement that patent and trademark applications to be filed in both Casablanca and Tangier. Morocco is a member of the International Center for the Settlement of Investment Disputes and a party to the 1958 convention on the recognition and enforcement of foreign arbitrary awards.

BUSINESS CLIMATE

Morocco is a Muslim country and business meetings are best avoided on Friday. Although Arabic is the official language, French is widely used.

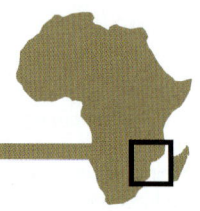

MOZAMBIQUE

ONCE PLAGUED BY INTERNAL STRIFE AND FAILED SOCIALIST POLICIES MOZAM-
BIQUE CHANGED ITS FORTUNES IN RECENT YEARS THROUGH POLITICAL STABILITY AND
SOUND ECONOMIC POLICIES THAT LURED FOREIGN INVESTMENT. IMPORTANT FISCAL
REFORMS AND THE INTRODUCTION OF VALUE-ADDED TAX BOOSTED STATE REVENUES.
A MAJOR ALUMINUM SMELTER, TITANIUM EXTRACTION AND TEXTILE MANUFACTURING
ARE AMONG THE FOREIGN-DRIVEN PROJECTS THAT STIMULATED GROWTH. MOZAM-
BIQUE, HOWEVER, CONTINUES TO DEPEND ON FOREIGN ASSISTANCE FOR MUCH OF
ITS ANNUAL BUDGET.

COUNTRY PROFILE

Much of the Republic of Mozambique consists of a coastal plain and lowland less than 500
m above sea level. The Zambezi River is the largest
of 25 rivers in the region. The climate is hot and
humid, with temperatures and rainfall rising to
the north. Most of the people are Bantu-speaking.
The Makua and Lomwe account for 40%
of the total. Other inhabitants range from
the Yao, Makonde, Sena, Chewa, Shona,
to the Tsonga, and Shangaan. Minority
groups such as the mestizos (people of
mixed descent), Indians and whites—Portuguese and a growing number of South
Africans—are prominent in the economy.
Portuguese is the official language, but
English is widely spoken in business and
professional circles.

HISTORY

In ancient times northern Mozambique formed part of the trade network
in slaves, gold and ivory between Arabs
and Persians and the Bantu kingdom of
Mwene Mutapa. Intermarriage between
these merchants and their African slaves
gave rise to a distinct Swahili culture. Portuguese involvement started in 1498 when
Vasco da Gama reached Mozambique
Island. By 1510 the Portuguese had control
of all the former Arab sultanates on the
east African coast. Portugal participated
in the partitioning of Africa among the
European powers in the last two decades
of the 19th Century and Mozambique took
its present shape on the map in 1890.

Mozambique was ruled as an overseas Portuguese
province. In 1964 the Frente da Libertação de
Moçambique or Liberation Front of Mozambique
(Frelimo), led by Dr. Eduardo Mondlane, began
an armed revolt against the Portuguese rulers.
The struggle was continued after his death in

© Business Books Intl.

1969 by Samora Moises Machel. After a military coup in Portugal in 1974, a peace agreement was concluded and on 25 June 1975, 470 years of Portuguese rule ended. Machel became president of an independent Mozambique. Asset-stripping by the fleeing Portuguese, Marxist-Leninist centralization and nationalization, and a paralyzing and five year civil war against the Resistencia Nacional Moçambicana or Mozambican National Resistance (Renamo) contributed to the country's rapid economic decay. In October 1986 President Machel was killed when his aircraft crashed. Following the collapse of the Soviet Union, Machel's successor, President Joaquim Alberto Chissano, turned to the West and post-apartheid South Africa to jump start the economy. A general peace agreement between Frelimo and Renamo led to the adoption of a new democratic constitution in 1994. In November 1995, Mozambique was the first non-former-British colony to become a member of the Commonwealth. In 2005 Chissano was succeeded as head of state by businessman Armando Guebuza.

GOVERNMENT

Under the new constitution, both the president and the 250-member unicameral Assembly, or the Assembleia da República, are elected for 5-year terms. In the December 2004 elections Frelimo presidential candidate Armando Guebuza gained 64 percent of the popular vote, defeating Afonso Dhlakama of Renamo. With 160 seats Frelimo maintained a majority in the Assembly over Renamo and its and its coalition partners with their 90 seats.

ECONOMIC POLICY

At independence Mozambique was one of the world's poorest countries. Socialist mismanagement and civil war exacerbated the situation. In the nineties the failed Marxist policies were abandoned in favor of free market practices. Mozambique's creditors decided to write off most of its debt. Foreign debt was further reduced by rescheduling and forgiveness under the IMF's Heavily Indebted Poor Countries (HIPC) and Enhanced HIPC initiatives. Privatization is proceeding well. Outside investors are reacting positively to the improved climate in Mozambique. Early in 2000, Mozambique experienced a severe setback as devastating floods not only took a heavy toll in human lives but washed away much of its impressive economic gains. Despite impressive

FAST FACTS

Pres. Armando
Guebuza
Born: January 20, 1943
Since 2005

© SADC Review

POLITICAL

Head of State	Pres. Armando Guebuza
Ruling Party	Frelimo
Main Opposition	Renamo
Independence	25 June 1975
National capital	Maputo
Official language	Portuguese

PHYSICAL

Total area	302,737 sq. miles
	784,090 sq. km.
	(±2 x California)
Arable land	5.1% of land area
Coastline	1,535 miles/2,470 km

POPULATION

Total	19.69 million
Av. yearly growth	1.38%
Population/sq. mile	19
Urban population	7.4 million
Adult literacy	47.8%

ECONOMY

Currency	Metical (Mt)
	(US$1=28,180)
GDP (real)	$5.73 billion
GDP growth rate	7%
GDP per capita[1]	$345
GDP (ppp)[2]	$26.03 billion
GDP per cap. (ppp)	$1,300
Inflation rate	6.5%
Exports	$1.69 billion
Imports	$2.04 billion
External debt	$5.45 billion
Unemployment	21%

1. *Atlas method.*
2. *See page 175 for an explanation of purchasing power parity (ppp).*

307

growth in recent years Mozambieque remains dependent on foreign assistance for part of its budget. The majority of the population is still below the poverty line.

SECTORS

Agriculture is the mainstay of the economy, employing up to 60% of the workforce, mainly in subsistence farming. Principal cash crops are cashew nuts, tea, sugar, sisal, cotton, copra and oil seeds. Maize is the main subsistence crop, but cassava, millet, sorghum, groundnuts, beans and rice are also grown. The country has a rich variety of minerals including large deposits of iron and bauxite ore and coal, tantalite (used in the electronics industry and for special steels) and pegmatite (a source of tantalite), beryl, mica, bismuth and semiprecious stones. Along the coast are also titanium-bearing beach sands. Plans are underway to develop the large natural gas fields at Pande, west of Inhambane, and in the Buzi swamps, near Beira. Manufacturing includes food processing and industrial crops, fertilizer, agricultural implements, cement, textiles, beverages, ceramics, wood processing, tires, and radios. Pristine beaches and national wildlife parks are important assets and tourism is a growing sector. Once extensive civil war damage is repaired, Cahora Bassa Dam on the Zambezi—Africa's largest hydropower station after the Aswan High in Egypt—will be capable of supplying not only in the needs of Mozambique but those of its neighbors.

PRIVATIZATION

Over 900 state-owned enterprises have been sold including a cement plant, flour mills, breweries, commercial agriculture operations, cashew processing plants, and fishing and trading companies. The management of coal, sugar, citrus, and container terminals at ports has been entrusted to private consortia. In most of these transactions, there was substantial foreign participation. As a final step to privatizing the financial sector, two of the country's largest state-owned banks have been sold.

INVESTMENT

Just under $4 billion in foreign direct investment has been registered during the past five years. South Africa surpassed Britain and Portugal as the most important source of investment after its Industrial Development Corporation (IDC) became an active participant in large projects such as the Mozal plant. Several major US firms have

also become involved. These projects, along with the toll road under construction from South Africa and the upgrading of the port of Maputo should provide the impetus for further investment along what has been dubbed the Maputo Development Corridor.

TRADE

Exports consist largely of cashews, sugar, cotton, and other agricultural commodities, textiles, seafood, and minerals. Sales of electric power, natural gas and related products, as well as tourism, are expected to the chronic negative current account balance.

FINANCIAL SECTOR

Nowhere is the dramatic effect of recent reforms more apparent than in the banking system. The Banco de Mozambique, which acted as both the central bank and the major commercial bank in the past has been replaced by a separate central bank and a number of private banks.

TAXES AND TARIFFS

The corporate income, capital gains and branch tax rates in Mozambique are 35% for agricultural companies, 40% for industrial companies, and 45% for all others. A withholding tax of 18% applies to dividends, 5% to interest.

BUSINESS ACTIVITY

AGRICULTURE
Cotton, cashew nuts, sugar cane, tea, cassava (tapioca), corn, rice, tropical fruit, beef, poultry.

INDUSTRIES
Food, beverages, chemicals (fertilizer, soap, paints), petroleum products, textiles, cement, glass, asbestos, tobacco.

NATURAL RESOURCES
Coal, titanium, natural gas.

EXPORTS
$1.69 billion (est. 2005): aluminum, bulk electricity, prawns, cashews, cotton, sugar, copra, citrus.

IMPORTS
$2.04 billion (est. 2005): food, clothing, machinery, metal products, chemicals, fuel.

MAJOR TRADING PARTNERS
South Africa, Belgium, Spain, Netherlands, Italy, Germany, Australia, China.

Doing Business with Mozambique

▶ INVESTMENT

The Investment Promotion Center (CPI) offers a variety of tax incentives according to regions and the type of investment. Specific performance requirements are built into mining concessions and management contracts and sometimes into the sale of state-owned entities. Approval for investment follows automatically in 10 days if no objections are voiced by the relevant ministries, provincial governor (for investments under $100,000), or the Minister of Planning and Finance (in the case of investments under $100 million). The Council of Ministers must review investments over $100 million as well as those involving large tracts of land. Legislation supports the creation of "Industrial Free Zones." There are good opportunities in energy, mining, fishing, timber, tourism, agriculture and manufacturing of inexpensive goods.

▶ TRADE

Trade opportunities exist in the energy, mining, fishing, timber, tourism, and agriculture (cashews, cotton, and sugar) sectors. There is a growing demand for construction, telecommunications, agricultural, plastic, food processing and packaging and fishing equipment. Planned new projects such as an aluminum smelter, natural gas pipelines, a direct reduced iron and steel plant, and new mineral sands processing are bound to increase the demand for engineering and construction equipment and expertise. Wheat, rice, and edible oils are imported in reasonably large quantities.

▶ TRADE FINANCE

Eximbank provides short-, medium-, and long-term financing to US exporters. The US Trade and Development Agency assists with feasibility studies and reverse trade missions.

▶ SELLING TO THE GOVERNMENT

Major government purchases might be subject to the procurement rules set by international donors as Mozambique often relies on outside financial support. It is, however, necessary for bidders to establish personal contacts within the government and to keep abreast of frequent changes in the procurement process.

▶ EXCHANGE CONTROLS

Repatriation of profits and repayment of offshore loans are allowed. Investment laws guarantee foreign investors the right to remit loan repayments, dividends, profits and invested capital .

▶ PARTNERSHIPS

Joint ventures are encouraged by the government and can help ease potential problems with regulatory issues and red tape. The government itself favors partnerships with foreign firms in privatization deals.

▶ ESTABLISHING A PRESENCE

The official Investment Promotion Center (CPI) has developed a package of services to assist foreign investors with this process.

▶ FINANCING PROJECTS

OPIC has an Investment Incentive Agreement in place. Mozambique is also a member of the Multilateral Investment Guarantee Agency. Some major projects are financed by the World Bank, the African Development Bank, and donor agencies such as USAID. The International Finance Corporation and the Commonwealth Development Corporation provide medium-term loans and equity finance in Mozambique. The US government-sponsored $100 million Southern African Enterprise Development Fund (SAEDF) assists Mozambican entrepreneurs out of its Johannesburg offices.

▶ LABOR

Most working Mozambicans derive income from more than one activity, and grow corn and vegetables on small parcels of land for personal consumption. Labor unions, created during the socialist years, are gradually asserting their independence from the ruling Frelimo Party.

▶ LEGAL RIGHTS

The government grants land-use concessions for periods of up to 50 years with options to renew. Foreign investors have recourse to arbitration through the UNCITRAL (United Nations Commission on International Trade Law) model. The government has also acceded to the New York Convention on the Recognition and Enforcement of Foreign Arbitral Awards. Mozambique has signed the Bern Convention on International Copyrights, as well as the New York and Paris Conventions. Intellectual property right infringement is not considered a significant problem.

▶ BUSINESS CLIMATE

Portuguese is widely spoken but the use of English is growing in business circles. The business community in Maputo is small enough for most to know each other .

309

NAMIBIA

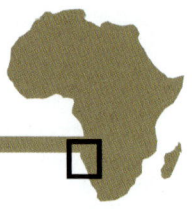

DESPITE ITS SPARSE POPULATION AND LACK OF RAINFALL, NAMIBIA SEEMS POISED TO BECOME A CONVENIENT GATEWAY TO THE GROWING SOUTHERN AFRICAN REGIONAL MARKET. GOOD INFRASTRUCTURE AND AN EFFICIENT, DEEP-WATER PORT AT WALVIS BAY, COUPLED WITH A STRONG MINING AND AGRICULTURAL BASE, MAKE NAMIBIA A GOOD CANDIDATE FOR INVESTMENT AND FUTURE TRADE. IN ITS EFFORT TO BRING PREVIOUSLY-DISADVANTAGED NAMIBIANS INTO THE ECONOMIC MAINSTREAM VIA PRIVATE SECTOR COMMERCIAL DEVELOPMENT, THE NAMIBIAN GOVERNMENT IS ACTIVELY COURTING FOREIGN INVESTORS. SINCE INDEPENDENCE, PERSONAL AND CORPORATE TAX RATES HAVE BEEN CUT TO IMPROVE THE BUSINESS CLIMATE.

COUNTRY PROFILE

The Republic of Namibia consists of three regions running from north to south: the Namib Desert along the coast, the great escarpment which reaches its highest elevation at the Auas mountains near Windhoek, and the semi-arid Kalahari Basin continuing into Botswana and South Africa. Average annual rainfall for the country is only 270 mm—about 70% of the land is classified as arid and 22% as desert. Underground water sources sustain large herds of cattle on the northern savanna pastures and sheep, including karakul, on the desert scrub in the south. Wildlife abounds and is protected in a number of nature reserves and wilderness areas. The three Bantu-speaking groups—the Ovambo, Kavango and Herero—account for about two-thirds of the population. Whites comprise about 5 percent of the total. Even though English is the official language, Afrikaans is widely spoken, as well as some German. More than 90% of the population is Christian.

HISTORY

The San and Nama or Khoikhoi peoples were already in the region 500 years ago when Ovambo and Kavango groups migrated south from present-day Angola. In the 19th Century German merchants settled in the territory around the British possession of Walvis Bay. German forces moved inland to claim what became known as German West

Africa, almost annihilating the Herero and the Nama in the process. During the First World War South Africa defeated the Germans in the territory and in 1919 the League of Nations confirmed its control over the mandate of South West Africa (SWA). South African attempts after the Second World War to incorporate the territory instead of submitting it to the control of the newly-formed UN Trusteeship Council led to a lengthy political struggle in the UN. The South West African Peoples Organization (SWAPO), under leadership of Sam Daniel Shafiishuna Nujoma, resorted to arms in

1966 after the International Court of Justice gave a ruling favorable to the South African government. In 1988, a US-inspired peace agreement ended hostilities on the northern border where South Africa was engaged in a protracted battle with Cuban and Angolan MPLA troops, assisted by SWAPO commandos. SWAPO emerged as the victor in an election held in 1989 under supervision of a UN Transitional Assistance Group (UNTAG) and on 21 March 1990, Nujoma was sworn in as president of independent Namibia and reelected several times until he stepped down in 2005. He was succeeded by Hifikepunye Pohamba as leader of SWAPO and as president after the November 2004 election, where he scored a landslide victory.

GOVERNMENT

The executive President is elected for a 5-year term. He appoints the Prime Minister and other cabinet ministers. The 78-member National Assembly is also elected for 5 years on a party-list proportional basis, while the 26-member National Council—elected every six years by the Regional Councils—serves as an upper house. In 2004 Swapo captured 55 seats in the National Assembly against 5 for the Congress of Democrats (COD) and 4 for Democratic Turnhalle Alliance (DTA). There are also a few smaller parties represented.

ECONOMIC POLICY

There is considerable state involvement in sectors such as postal services, telecommunications, development banking, electricity and water supply, transport, and agricultural commodity marketing. The government has advocated an interventionist role in major infrastructure projects or "high risk ventures" where the private sector is reluctant to participate. At the same time, it has adopted a free market-based investment code with wide-ranging incentives to encourage private sector involvement. The goal is to diversify the economy away from heavy dependence on diamonds, uranium, and base metals. Outstanding external debt is among the lowest in Africa, helped by South African President Nelson Mandela's decision in 1995 to write off $200 million owed to South Africa.

SECTORS

Heavily dependent on this sector, Namibia ranks among the top 20 mining countries in the world. It is the fourth largest exporter in Africa of nonfuel minerals. Currently mining accounts for 20% of its GDP. Namibia is a major producer of

FAST FACTS

Pres. Hifikepunye Pohamba
Born: August 8, 1935
Since 2005

POLITICAL

Head of State	Pres. Hifikepunye Pohamba
Ruling Party	Swapo
Main Opposition	COD & DTA
Independence	21 March 1990
National capital	Windhoek
Official language	English

PHYSICAL

Total area	318,694 sq. miles 825,418 sq. km. (½ x Alaska)
Arable land	1%
Coastline	977 miles/1,572 km

POPULATION

Total	2.04 million
Av. yearly growth	0.59%
Population/sq. mile	6
Urban population	700,000
Adult literacy	84%

ECONOMY

Currency	Namibian dollar (N$) (US$1=6.75)
GDP (real)	$4.98 billion
GDP growth rate	3.5%
GDP per capita[1]	$3,124
GDP (ppp)[2]	$14.23 billion
GDP per cap. (ppp)	$7,000
Inflation rate	2.3%
Exports	$2.04 billion
Imports	$2.35 billion
External debt	$712.9 million
Unemployment	35%

1. *Atlas method.*
2. *See page 175 for an explanation of purchasing power parity (ppp).*

uranium, pyrites, cadmium, arsenic, gold, silver, fluorspar, and semi-precious stones, but gem quality diamonds are the country's largest generator of foreign exchange. The mining sector, however, employs only about 3% of the population with most of the population still dependent on subsistence agriculture. Even though the agricultural sector forms only 11.7% of Namibia's GDP, 70% of the population depend on it. Cattle raising is predominant in the central and northern regions, while karakul sheep, goat, and ostrich are raised in the south. Pilchard, hake, horse mackerel, anchovy and rock lobster are the main catches off the Namibian coast, rated among the world's richest fishing grounds. The primary industrial activity in the country (excluding mining) is meat and fish processing. The tourism industry is currently 7% of GDP. Large offshore natural gas reserves have been discovered. Tourism is a growing sector.

PRIVATIZATION

Even though the state continues to control key economic sectors such as electricity, telephones, water, the national airline and the railway, it is moving towards private sector-led growth, Despite strong union opposition, it is proceeding with privatization of select state-owned companies, with minority shares reserved for black empowerment groups.

INVESTMENT

The five major foreign investor countries in Namibia are South Africa, Germany, Britain, the US and Malaysia. Namibia obtained a stake in the diamond industry previously monopolized by De Beers in 1994 when it struck an agreement with the company that gave the state a 50 percent share of the new entity, NAMDEB. Diamond output was boosted further through offshore mining by the UK-based Namibian Minerals Corporation. Other mining opportunities such as the Australian owned Haib copper prospect in the far south are among recent areas of focus. Shell has identified a promising gas field offshore that could make the country a significant energy exporter in the next century.

TRADE

Exports consist largely of gem-quality diamonds, uranium, base metals, cattle, karakul hides and fish. Namibia's export earnings exceed 50% of the GDP. Imports are similarly high. Around 85% of Namibia's imports originate in or transit through South Africa. Normally Namibia imports

about half of its cereal requirements and during drought periods food shortages become a majro problem in the rural regions.

FINANCIAL SECTOR

The Bank of Namibia has formal authority over the country's foreign exchange dealings. Namibia enjoys good creditworthiness in international financial circles, and is eligible to draw on the resources of the IMF, the World Bank, and the African Development Bank. Commercial banks provide comprehensive domestic and international services. The Namibian Stock Exchange (NSE), which relies in part on double listings of major South African firms, is the second largest African stock market in terms of value of shares listed. The Namibian economy is closely linked to that of South Africa and its dollar is pegged to the SA rand.

TAXES AND TARIFFS

The corporate tax rate in Namibia is 35% but special breaks are offered as incentives to manufacturers establishing themselves in designated regions where development and job creation are needed. A general sales tax of 8% is levied at the point of final sale. This tax is applied to all products, including those imported through the Southern African Customs Union (SACU).

BUSINESS ACTIVITY

AGRICULTURE
Millet, sorghum, peanuts, livestock, fish.

INDUSTRIES
Meat packing, fish processing, dairy products, mining (diamond, lead, zinc, tin, silver, tungesten, uranium, copper).

NATURAL RESOURCES
Diamonds, copper, uranium, gold, lead, tin, lithium, cadmium, zinc, salt, vanadium, natural gas, fish, suspected deposits of oil, coal, iron ore.

EXPORTS
$2.04 billion (est. 2005): diamonds, copper, gold, zinc, lead, uranium, cattle, processed fish, karakul skins

IMPORTS
$2.35 billion (est. 2005): foodstuffs, petroleum products and fuel, machinery and equipment, chemicals.

MAJOR TRADING PARTNERS
South Africa, US.

Doing Business with Namibia

▶ Investment

An Investment Center within the Ministry of Trade and Industry assists foreign investors. Investment and tax incentives are available for new and existing manufacturing firms, and an Export Processing Zone (EPZ) has been set up at the port of Walvis Bay. A well-developed infrastructure in Namibia is a good asset for prospective foreign investors looking at Namibia as a gateway to the Southern Africa region. The fishing, tourism, manufacturing, mining, water and energy sectors offer prospects for development and expansion by foreign entrepreneurs.

▶ Trade

Namibia, with its solid managerial and physical infrastructure, provides a useful springboard to the central and southern African markets. Useful areas for exporters are agricultural equipment and chemicals, consumer food products, and telecommunications equipment. South African and German-linked concerns dominate the marketing and distribution networks and many of the product line markets.

▶ Trade finance

The Eximbank provides insurance and guarantees for US exporters to Namibia. The US Department of Agriculture provides credit guarantees for up to three years for qualifying exports.

▶ Selling to the government

Government purchases are usually by tender. Often Namibian government needs are too modest to interest the larger US supplier, but there are notable exceptions. In an effort to diversify sources of supply, the government contracted in late 1996 with Detroit-based Barden International to supply more than 800 General Motors vehicles to its motor pool. Barden invested about $15 million in right-hand drive conversion at a plant in Windhoek.

▶ Exchange controls

Under the CMA Agreement, the South African rand is also legal tender and exchange controls are similar to those applied in South Africa.

▶ Partnerships

The government sometimes allocates business rights to Namibian companies on more favorable terms. For example, in the fishing sector joint ventures with Namibian concession holders are obviously the best route for foreigners.

▶ Establishing a presence

A presence may be in the form of a public or private company, branch of a foreign company, partnership, joint venture, or as a sole trader. A branch of a foreign company must register within 21 days of establishing itself in Namibia. Namibian accountants and auditors should be engaged to ensure strict adherence to local tax and labor laws.

▶ Financing projects

The Overseas Private Investment Corporation provides funding and political risk insurance to qualified US investors. Namibia is also a member of the Multilateral Investment Guarantee Agency. Local commercial banks provide project financing in agriculture, commercial fishing, tourism, housing, minerals and mining.

▶ Labor

There is a large pool of qualified workers in varying professions but a shortage of highly skilled personnel. A special tax deduction of up to 25% is extended to manufacturing companies that provide technical training. The government will also reimburse companies for costs directly related to employee training under approved conditions. Most workers belong to trade unions. The NUNW, an affiliate of the ruling SWAPO party, represents the workers of seven affiliated trade unions. Wage rates of $200 per month and a 45 hour work week are common. Overtime pay plus annual and maternity leave are standard.

▶ Legal rights

Namibia's legal system is based on Roman-Dutch law. The Foreign Investment Act protects investors against expropriation and stipulates steps for the settlement of disputes by international arbitration. The local court system provides an effective means to enforce property and contractual rights. An independent, transparent legal system protects and facilitates acquisition and disposition of property rights. The issue of intellectual property is understood and generally respected by most companies operating in Namibia and, unlike some other developing countries, IPR infringement is not a major problem.

▶ Business climate

Business customs are similar to those practiced in neighboring South Africa. Most business with foreigners is conducted in English but among the locals Afrikaans and German are also spoken.

NIGER

THE NIGER RIVER FLOWING THROUGH SAHEL TERRAIN IS AS MUCH OF A LIFELINE FOR NIGER AS THE NILE IS FOR SUDAN AND EGYPT—BOTH AS A SOURCE OF WATER AND A MEANS OF TRANSPORT. WITH SOME OF THE WORLD'S LARGEST RESERVES A SLOWDOWN IN WORLD MARKET FOR URANIUM HAS SEVERELY DAMAGED THIS LAND-LOCKED COUNTRY'S ECONOMY. THE CURRENT EMPHASIS IS ON EXPLORATION AND DEVELOPMENT OF ALTERNATIVE MINERAL RESOURCES AND THE EXPANSION OF ITS AGRICULTURAL BASE WITH THE HELP OF FOREIGN INVESTORS. FOREIGN FIRMS HAVE BEEN FOCUSING ON GOLD, COAL AND OIL. DRASTIC ECONOMIC REFORMS HAVE BEEN INTRODUCED TO MAKE THE COUNTRY MORE INVESTOR-FRIENDLY.

COUNTRY PROFILE

The Republic of Niger covers a plateau less than 500 m (1,640 ft) high reaching northwards into the Sahara Desert. In the central region the partly volcanic Air Mountains rise to 1,800 m (6,000 ft) above sea level. The perennial Niger River meanders for about 500 km (310 miles) through the southwestern tip of the country. During the flood season from July to September it is navigable by smaller boat and provides irrigation along its banks. The Hausa people extending across the Nigerian border form the largest cultural group, accounting for more than half of Niger's population. The closely related Songhai and Zarma (or Djerma), concentrated along the Niger River, account for about a quarter of the population. These groups and the smaller Kanuri, Daza and Teda factions speak Nilo-Saharan languages. About 10% of the population are Fulani (or Ful) and 3% Tuareg. Over 85% of the population are Muslims, but among some ethnic faiths still prevail.

HISTORY

The nomadic Tuaregs were the first inhabitants of this Sahara region. They were followed by the Hausa (14th Century), the Zerma (17th Century), the Goboir (18th Century) and the Fulani. About 1,000 years ago, Arab traders first made contact with the Hausa in the Sahel region and introduced them to the Muslim faith. The Hausa were subjugated by Songhai around 1500 but regained their independence in 1591. In 1806 Mungo Park, the first European to reach this remote region, encountered Hausa, Songhai, Fulani and Tuareg. In 1903 the French created colonies in the Sahel and southern Sahara, extending from Senegal through French Sudan (Mali) and Upper Volta (Burkina Faso) to Niger. Due to stiff resistance from the Tuareg and Kanuri peoples, France's conquest of Niger was not finalized until 1922. Niger was granted independence in 1960 under Hamani Diori who drove out Marxist rivals headed by his cousin Djibo Bakary. In 1974, Diori was overthrown by

Col. Seyni Kountché who invited back Bakary and others and included them in a new government of national unity. When Kountché died in 1987 he was succeeded by Colonel Ali Saibou who solidified one-party rule under the Mouvement National de la Société de Devéloppement or National Movement for the Development Society (MNSD). He in turn lost to Mahamane Ousmane and the Alliance des Forces du Changement (AFC) in free elections in 1993. Ousmane was ousted in a coup by Ibrahim Baré Mainassara in 1996. Baré, considered corrupt and ineffective as a leader, was assassinated in April 1999 and succeeded by Pres. Mamadou Tandja, who was subsequently reaffirmed in his post in free elections in 1999 and 2004. There is a ceasefire in effect between Tuareg rebel movements and the government but these nomadic, impoverished descendants of the Berbers and Arabs maintain a fiercely insular culture and show little affinity for the black African majority in Niger.

GOVERNMENT

The 1996 Constitution calls for a president to be elected for a 5-year term and a bicameral National Assembly with one 83-seat chamber elected by popular vote for five years and the other yet to be determined. In the 2004 election President Tandja's National Movement for a Developing Society-Nassara (MNSD-Nassara) won 47 seats against 25 for the Nigerien Party for Democracy and Socialism-Tarayya (PNDS-Tarayya) and its allies. The Democratic and Social Convention-Rahama (CDS-Rahama) came third with 22 seats.

ECONOMIC POLICY

The government is committed to reform of the economy by implementing of a structural adjustment program (SAP) together with the World Bank and IMF. Since the uranium-led boom of the seventies ended, the economy stagnated and new investment practically dried up. Current efforts are to encourage foreign investors to explore alternative mineral sources. In December 2000 Niger qualified for enhanced debt relief under the Highly Indebted Poor Countries (HIPC) program. This led to a significant reduction of annual debt service obligations. Nearly half of the national budget depends on foreign donor resoruces.

SECTORS

The economy is largely based on subsistence farming and uranium mining. Over 80% of the

FAST FACTS

Pres. Mamadou Tandja
Born: 1938
Since 1999

UNDPI

POLITICAL

Head of State	Pres. Mamadou Tandja
Ruling Parties	MNSD-Nassara
Main Opposition	PNDS-Tarayya
Independence	3 August 1960
National capital	Niamey
Official language	French

PHYSICAL

Total area	489,189 sq. miles
	1,267,000 sq. km.
	(2 x Texas)
Arable land	3.5% of land area
Coastline	Landlocked

POPULATION

Total	12.5 million
Av. yearly growth	2.92%
Population/sq. mile	21
Urban population	3 million
Adult literacy	17.6%

ECONOMY

Currency	CFA Franc (CFAF)(US$1=559.44)
GDP (real)	$3.4 billion
GDP growth rate	4.5%
GDP per capita[1]	$217
GDP (ppp)[2]	$11.28 billion
GDP per cap. (ppp)	$900
Inflation rate	0.2%
Exports	$222 million
Imports	$588 million
External debt	$2.1 billion
Unemployment	N/A

1. Atlas method.
2. See page 175 for an explanation of purchasing power parity (ppp).

economically active people depend on subsistence crop growing. Less than 3% of the land is arable, including the irrigated areas along the Niger River, where food and cash crops such as millet, sorghum, cassava, rice and cowpeas are grown. Livestock (mainly cattle) are sold to neighboring countries, and hides and skins overseas. Niger has, after South Africa, the largest uranium reserves in Africa. Despite a recent slight recovery foreign exchange earnings from this mineral has shrunk as the world market declined considerably from its peak in the eighties. Other minerals in reasonable quantity include tin-bearing casserite ore, phosphates, molybdenum, coal and salt. Foreign firms are involved in exploration for gold along the border with Burkina Faso and oil in the Lake Chad region. Manufacturing comprises sugar refining, brewing, cotton ginning, tanning, rice milling, and small-scale production of cement, metals, textiles, plastics, soft drinks and construction materials.

PRIVATIZATION

Although the government has shown a receptiveness to foreign acquisition of privatized parastatals, the process has been slow.

INVESTMENT

The uranium bust of the early 1980s has led to the withdrawal of French and several other European firms. In the eighties ExxonMobil (in partnership with Elf-Aquitaine) discovered oil in southeastern Niger near Lake Chad while Hunt Oil Company concentrated on the northeastern Djado plateau. Other US firms have shown an interest in gold mining and telecommunications but most of the current investment in Niger is French. Coal mining is another area of interest.

TRADE

Uranium which contributed around 40% of the export revenue in the boom years, today accounts for merely 8%. Devaluation of the CFA franc helped to boost exports of livestock, cowpeas, onions, and cotton. There is also an effort to fill the void with any of a range of proven and still to be explored gold, oil, phosphates, molybdenum, coal and salt reserves. Even though Niger currently shows deficits on its trade balance, the long-term outlook is for a modest surplus.

FINANCIAL SECTOR

There is one large international bank, the Meridien-BIAO, which serves as a regional institution and has close connections with the French banking system. Smaller banks include the Banque Commerciale du Niger (BCN), jointly owned by the governments of Niger and Libya. All these banks offer an array of financial instruments including letters of credit and short- and long-term loans.

TAXES AND TARIFFS

Despite continuing efforts to make the tax laws more transparent, investors find it prudent to spell out such details beforehand in contractual arrangements with the government. Import duties go as high as 66%. Value added taxes of between 10 and 24% and a 4% tax on profits apply.

ASSISTANCE

While France remains a major donor, aid has also been coming from the US and various multilateral sources. In the eighties when an estimated 2 million people were in danger of starvation in Niger, 200,000 tons of imported food (largely from the US) helped avert the famine. The USAID has been involved in a number of programs aimed at promoting political and democratic reform while the US Department of Defense has extended assistance with military training.

BUSINESS ACTIVITY

AGRICULTURE
Cowpeas, cotton, peanuts, millet, sorghum, cassava (tapioca), rice, cattle, sheeps, goats, camels, donkeys, horses, poultry.

INDUSTRIES
Cement, brick, textiles, food processing, chemicals, slaughterhouses, light industries, uranium mining.

NATURAL RESOURCES
Uranium, coal, iron ore, tin, phosphates, gold, petroleum.

EXPORTS
$222 million (2004): uranium ore, livestock products, cowpeas, onions.

IMPORTS
$588 million (2004): consumer goods, machinery, vehicles and parts, petroleum, cereals, foodstuffs.

MAJOR TRADING PARTNERS
US, France, Nigeria, Switzerland, Côte d'Ivoire, China, Italy, Spain, Germany, Belgium, French Polynesia.

DOING BUSINESS WITH NIGER

▶ INVESTMENT

Incentives offered to investors include tax holidays, duty-free importing, subsidized energy and assistance in setting up industrial sites. There are no screening or local ownership requirements but a clear preference for labor-intensive operations exists. The government is actively seeking investment in energy production, mineral exploration and mining, agriculture, food processing, forestry, fishing, low-cost housing, construction, handicrafts, hotels, schools, health centers and transportation. Gold, coal and oil are three mining sectors where US companies have been noticeable in recent years. The planned modernization of the telecommunications system is expected to become an area of keen competition between US and other firms with know-how and equipment.

▶ TRADE

Overseas suppliers usually approach Niger as part of a larger West African market and supply goods and services via neighboring states. Among the proven markets for US goods are computers and related products, telecommunications equipment, vehicles (especially four-wheel drive), machinery, office equipment, pharmaceuticals (particularly generic drugs), heavy construction and earth-moving equipment, and coal-fired electrical generating equipment.

▶ TRADE FINANCE

The cost of local credit is high and the most common form of payment remains irrevocable letters of credit. Eximbank extends financing to US exporters.

▶ SELLING TO THE GOVERNMENT

Aside from donor-financed development projects requiring engineering consulting services, technical assistance, agricultural planning, and specialized equipment, recent government purchases ranged from generic drugs to four-wheel drive vehicles. A local agent may be helpful in the process.

▶ EXCHANGE CONTROLS

Niger is a member of the Franc zone and its currency is fully convertible into French francs. Investment capital and earnings on invested capital—dividends, interest, loan and lease payments, royalties, and fees—are usually transferred to and from Niger through French banks. There are no restrictions on payments and transfers.

▶ ESTABLISHING A PRESENCE

Private entities can freely establish, acquire, and dispose of interests in business enterprises. Attempts have been made to cut red tape and authorization for investment is guaranteed within three months of the date of application. For those unfamiliar with French law, on which Niger bases its own system, the advice of a local attorney is recommended.

▶ FINANCING PROJECTS

The OPIC investment guarantee program has applied since 1962 but there has been little activity on this front.

▶ LABOR

There is a shortage of professionals as more than half of the 65,000 salaried, formal sector workers are employed in the public sector. Even though wages are low the government considers organized labor a key "social" partner in running and developing the country. Labor-management relations are generally good but there have been instances where the National Federation of Labor Unions (USTN) has practically shut down the country with general strikes as part of politically-inspired protests.

▶ LEGAL RIGHTS

Niger has an independent court system which respects and protects property and commercial rights. The investment code guarantees against acts of nationalization or expropriation except when deemed to be in the public interest. There is provision for the settlement of disputes and indemnification either by local arbitration or through the International Center for Settlement of Disputes on Investments. Niger is a member of the West African Intellectual Property Organization (OAPI) and a signatory to the Paris Convention for the Protection of Industrial Property. It is also a member of World Intellectual Property Organization and a signatory to the Universal Copyright Convention.

▶ BUSINESS CLIMATE

The culture is largely Muslim and business is conducted in a calm and deliberate fashion. Rushing the deal is not only considered unseemly but is often self-defeating The official language is French and the services of an interpreter might be necessary to prevent misunderstandings.

NIGERIA

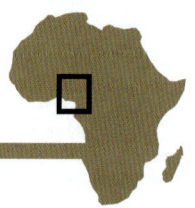

WITH 131 MILLION PEOPLE, NIGERIA IS AFRICA'S MOST POPULOUS NATION. ITS ECONOMY IS SECOND IN SIZE ONLY TO SOUTH AFRICA'S. IT IS THE CONTINENT'S MAJOR OIL PRODUCER AND THE FIFTH LARGEST SUPPLIER OF CRUDE TO THE UNITED STATES. UNDER ITS NEW RULERS THERE ARE CONCERTED EFFORTS TO HAVE NIGERIA'S RICHES TRICKLE DOWN TO THE BROADER POPULATION AND RECTIFY THE INEQUITIES OF PAST DICTATORSHIPS. THE COUNTRY OFFERS INVESTORS A LOW-COST LABOR POOL, ABUNDANT NATURAL RESOURCES, AND BY FAR THE LARGEST DOMESTIC MARKET ON THE CONTINENT. NIGERIA'S RETURN TO DEMOCRACY REOPENED ONE OF AFRICA'S MAJOR MARKETS FOR OVERSEAS BUSINESS. AMERICAN, EUROPEAN AND ASIAN INVESTORS HAVE NOT BEEN SLOW IN TAKING ADVANTAGE AS EVIDENCED IN IMPRESSIVE RECENT FOREIGN DIRECT INVESTMENT NOT ONLY IN THE OIL SECTOR BUT MANUFACTURING AND TELECOMMUNICATIONS INDUSTRY.

COUNTRY PROFILE

Nigeria is the largest of several West African countries on the Gulf of Guinea. The Niger and Benue rivers flow through a Y-shaped delta into the Gulf of Guinea. The Hausa-Fulani, mostly Muslim, dominate in the north while the Ibo are in the majority in the southwestern part of the country. Major cities, apart from Lagos with a population of 9 million, are Abuja (the capital), Kano, Port Harcourt, and Kaduna. About 50% of Nigeria's population is Muslim, 40% Christian and the rest adhere to ethnic religions.

HISTORY

Old kingdoms were flourishing when Portuguese mariners first visited the shores of Nigeria in 1472. In 1914 they were united in one British colony and on 1 October 1960 Nigeria gained its independence. The 40 years since were marred by a series of coups and a major civil war. The Biafra War broke out in May 1967 when the Ibo-controlled Eastern Regional legislature proclaimed an "independent" republic and took up arms to defend itself. Hundreds of thousands of people were killed in a struggle which, despite support from some African and Western countries, ended in defeat for Biafra in January 1970. Following another abortive attempt at installing a democratically-elected government in 1993, General Sani Abacha took charge. In 1995 the execution by the Abacha regime of nine political prisoners,

including the renowned writer Ken Saro-Wiwa, led to Nigeria's temporary suspension from the Commonwealth and the imposition of sanctions. Following Abacha's death in 1998, four separate elections culminated in the establishment of local, state and federal governments and the swearing in of Olusegun Obasanjo as president in May 1999. He was re-elected in April 2003.

GOVERNMENT

The 1999 constitution introduced a western decentralized form of government. The President is elected by popular vote for a maximum of two 4-year terms and appoints the cabinet or Federal Executive Council. On a federal basis a 109-member Senate and a 360-seat House of Representatives are elected to serve for 4 year terms. Each of the country's 36 states elects its own legislature and a governor. In April 2003 Obasanjo's People's Democratic Party (PDP) captured 223 House and 76 Senate seats against the All Nigeria People's Party (ANPP) with 96 and 27, and the Alliance for Democracy's (AD) 34 and 6, respectively.

ECONOMIC POLICY

Since the replacement of the Abacha regime concerted efforts have been made to root out corruption, improve the dilapidated infrastructure, privatize state-run industries and promote export-led growth. With oil prices likely to remain high in the foreseeable future, the new government has the potential of reinvigorating the economy and promote greater wealth distribution. After Nigeria's return to democratic rule in 1999, the US and other major industrial nations normalized relations that had chilled during the Abacha era. Recently, Nigeria has started implementing IMF reforms. Market-oriented reforms include modernization of the banking system, curbing inflation by resisting excessive wage demands and elimination of regional disputes over oil income share. Paris Club approval of a debt relief agreement aims at eliminating $30 billion of Nigeria's $37 billion foreign debt. Under the terms of this deal Nigeria is required to first repay $12 billion in arrears to its bilateral creditors. The National Economic Empowerment Development Strategy—styled after the IMF's Poverty Reduction and Growth Facility—was formed to tighten fiscal and monetary management.

PRIVATIZATION

There are plans to privatize most of Nigeria's state-owned companies. First, 13 banks, state-run

FAST FACTS

Pres. Olusegun
Aremu Obasanjo
Born: March 6, 1937
Since 1999

POLITICAL

Head of State	Pres. Matthew Olusegun Fajinmi Aremu Obasanjo
Ruling Party	PDP
Main Opposition	ANPP
Independence	1 October 1960
National capital	Abuja
Official language	English

PHYSICAL

Total area	356,557 sq. miles 923,768sq. km. (2 x California)
Arable land	31% of land area
Coastline	530 miles/853 km

POPULATION

Total	131.86 million
Av. yearly growth	2.38%
Population/sq. mile	480
Urban population	62.9 million
Adult literacy	68%

ECONOMY

Currency	Naira (N) (US$1=130.25)
GDP (real)	$77.33 billion
GDP growth rate	6.2%
GDP per capita[1]	$720
GDP (ppp)[2]	$174.1 billion
GDP per cap. (ppp)	$1,400
Inflation rate	13.5%
Exports	$52.16 billion
Imports	$25.95 billion
External debt	$37 billion
Unemployment	N/A

1. Atlas method.
2. See page 175 for an explanation of purchasing power parity (ppp).

cement companies and oil marketing companies, already listed on the Nigerian Stock Exchange, were to be sold. In the second phase, all the state's interest in hotels, automotive plants and similar industries will be sold. In the third stage the Nigeria Electric Production Authority (NEPA), Nigeria Telecommunications Limited (NITEL), oil refineries, and the state-owned National Fertilizer Company of Nigeria (NAFCON) were to be privatized. In 2003 the government started deregulating fuel prices and announced the privatization of Nigeria's four state-owned oil refineries.

SECTORS

Some 70 percent of the population is engaged in agriculture. In the south, rubber trees, oil palm and cocoa are cultivated for export and in the north groundnuts, cotton and cattle. Currently the agricultural sector accounts for 40 percent of the GDP. Nigeria has, however, slipped in recent years from being a net exporter to becoming a major importer of agricultural products. Petroleum continues to power the Nigerian economy, accounting for almost all of the country's foreign exchange earnings. The current government is attempting to move away from this over-independence on the lucrative and capital-intensive oil sector. Despite some diversification in recent years manufacturing still consists largely of import substituting products. Other manufacturing activities include iron and steel and fertilizer production, and automobile assembly.

TRADING

Nigeria is currently the fifth largest importer of US wheat. Its oil export revenues accounted for 95 percent of total exports with the US purchasing anout half of the total. Other substantial American exports to Nigeria include computers and software, medical equipment, automotive parts, cosmetics, textiles and fabrics. Nigeria is the fifth largest supplier of crude oil to the US after Saudi Arabia, Canada, Venezuela and Mexico.

INVESTMENT

Since 1999, foreign companies, particularly in the oil and gas sector, have been looking at new or expanded investments in Nigeria. Abundant oil reserves have kept the economy afloat and once again hold the key to the future. Total US foreign direct investment in Nigeria is estimated at around $4 billion, largely in the petroleum sector. A newly planned Export Processing Zone (EPZ) at Port Harcourt aims at attracting foreign investments in the manufacturing sector. Incentives have also been approved to encourage investment in downstream oil and gas processing and marketing. The privatization of state-owned properties is expected to diversify and intensify foreign investment.

FINANCIAL SECTOR

The Central Bank of Nigeria (CBN) monitors the banking system to ensure compliance with monetary, credit, and foreign exchange guidelines. There are 89 commercial and merchant banks, 67 of them classified as healthy. There are also a number of finance houses and mortgage and community banks throughout the country. Some 200 companies are listed on the Lagos (formerly Nigerian) Stock Exchange, in operation since 1961.

TAXES AND TARIFFS

Nigeria's corporate tax is a flat 30%. In the case of certain small-scale enterprises involved in agricultural production, mining and manufacturing, a rate of 20% applies. Import taxes range from 5% to 60%.

BUSINESS ACTIVITY

AGRICULTURE
Cocoa, peanuts, palm oil, corn, rice, sorghum, millet, cassava (tapioca), yams, rubber, cattle, sheep, goats, pigs, timber, fish.

INDUSTRIES
Crude oil, coal, tin, columbite, palm oil, peanuts, cotton, rubber, wood, hides and skins, textiles, cement and other construction materials, food products, footwear, chemicals, fertilizer, printing, ceramics, steel.

NATURAL RESOURCES
Petroleum, tin, columbite, iron ore, coal, limestone, lead, zinc, natural gas.

EXPORTS
$52.16 billion (est. 2005): petroleum and petroleum products, cocoa, rubber.

IMPORTS
$25.95 billion (est. 2005): machinery, chemicals, transportation equipment, manufactured goods, food, live animals.

MAJOR TRADING PARTNERS
US, China, UK, Spain, France, Netherlands, Brazil.

DOING BUSINESS WITH NIGERIA

▶ INVESTMENT

The new government in 1999 signaled its intention to make Nigeria investor-friendly and to encourage foreign participation. Its privatization program should present foreign investors with new opportunities in oil exploration, banking, hotels, and automotive parts manufacturing. Plans to install 3 million telephone lines per year will require foreign private sector participation will be required.

▶ TRADE

Oil and gasfield machinery will continue to be prime import items. There is a growing market for computers, cellular phone sets, transmission and switching and other telecommunications equipment. Other prime items include medical supplies, pharmaceuticals, textiles, and wheat and used cars and buses. The demand for earthmoving and roadbuilding machinery will increase as road reconstruction begins.

▶ TRADE FINANCE

In July 1999 Eximbank returned to Nigeria with a $100 million pilot program, once again making medium-term financing available to US exporters. The Nigerian Export-Import Bank (NEXIM) was established in 1991 to assist banks to provide pre- and post-shipment financing in local currency to support non-oil exports.

▶ SELLING TO THE GOVERNMENT

Nigeria buys products and services through a "tender board" composed of senior government officials, sometimes together with local consultants or foreign firms represented in Nigeria. *The Central Bank of Nigeria (CBN) does not buy products and services for the government or its agencies and purported inquiries and business proposals emanating from the CBN on behalf of the Nigerian government or any of its agencies should be disregarded as scams.*

▶ EXCHANGE CONTROLS

Foreign exchange control applies. All applications must be channeled through selected banks to the Central Bank of Nigeria (CBN).

▶ PARTNERSHIPS

Establishment of a joint venture is in itself not sufficient to constitute a legal entity. A foreign firm may, however, participate as a shareholder in a local company incorporated as a joint venture.

▶ ESTABLISHING A PRESENCE

Foreign firms are not allowed to operate through a branch office but obliged to establish a place of business and incorporate to conduct business in Nigeria. A local presence can also be established on the basis of equity participation, joint ventures, an arrangement for the provision of technical services to a Nigerian company, or the purchase of securities in existing Nigerian companies. All foreign companies must register with the NIPC to obtain a business permit.

▶ PROJECT FINANCING

Overseas Private Investment Corporation programs are available to US ventures in Nigeria. The US Trade and Development Agency extends funding for feasibility studies. Financing can also be obtained through any of the local commercial, merchant or industrial banks and, to a limited extent, from insurance companies, building and property development companies, pension funds and institutional investors.

▶ LABOR

Nigeria has a large, English-speaking workforce, generally better educated and skilled than elsewhere on the continent. Any nonagricultural firm with more than 50 workers must recognize trade unions and deduct dues for union members. Collective bargaining is common.

▶ LEGAL RIGHTS

The legal system is fashioned after English Common law. Nigeria is a signatory to the major world agreements on Intellectual Property Protection and a member of the World Intellectual Property Organization. The government's Patents and Design Decree of 1970 and Trademark Act of 1965 regulate the registration of patents and trademarks.

▶ BUSINESS CLIMATE

English is widely spoken. Visitors should make their contacts well before departure for Nigeria. *A fraudulent practice that has received wide publicity is known as "419." It involves an offer to transfer large sums of money with promises of commissions after up-front payments are made by the potential victim. While remaining on their guard against such practices, foreign citizens should also be aware that these scams do not represent the Nigerian business community at large. Scam attempts should be reported to the nearest Nigerian embassy.*

RWANDA

THE 1994 GENOCIDE DECIMATED RWANDA, DAMAGED ITS FRAGILE ECONOMIC BASE, SEVERELY IMPOVERISHED THE REMAINING POPULATION, AND ERODED THE COUNTRY'S ABILITY TO ATTRACT PRIVATE AND EXTERNAL INVESTMENT. THIS TRAGIC SETBACK CAME ON THE HEELS OF AN ECONOMIC DOWNTURN IN THE 1980s AS THE WORLD PRICE OF COFFEE PLUNGED. SINCE PEACE WAS RESTORED RWANDA HAS, HOWEVER, MADE SIGNIFICANT PROGRESS IN STABILIZING AND REHABILITATING ITS ECONOMY—GDP HAS REBOUNDED, AND INFLATION HAS BEEN CURBED. CURRENTLY THE EMPHASIS IS ON DIVERSIFICATION AWAY FROM COFFEE AND TEA TOWARDS MINING AND TOURISM.

COUNTRY PROFILE

In the west the Republic of Rwanda borders on Lake Kivu. On its eastern border with Tanzania it shares marshy lakes along the Kagera River. The climate is tropical with rainfall ranging between 800 and 1,400 mm (32 and 55 inches). Much of the terrain is covered with lush vegetation. Conservation regions include well-known game parks such as Akagera National Park and *Parc National des Volcans* where the mountain gorilla and other endangered species are found. Most inhabitants are Banyarwanda, of whom 80% are Hutu and the rest Tutsi. They speak Kinyarwanda which, together with French and English, is an official language. Most Rwandans are Christians.

HISTORY

The original inhabitants of Rwanda were the Pygmies or Twa, today numbering barely 1% of the total population. The simple version of history has the Tutsi (Nilotic) cattle breeders arriving in the area from the 15th Century and subjugating the Hutu inhabitants. In reality, the situation is much more complex as boundaries of race and class became less distinct over the years as a result of intermingling. Some put part of the blame for the racial animosity that led to the recent mass-scale killings on the shoulders of German and Belgian colonial rulers who pitched the Hutu against Tutsi for their own gain. When Burundi and neighboring Rwanda were

incorporated into German East Africa in 1899, they had been kingdoms for several centuries headed by *mwamis* (kings). After Germany's defeat in World War I these nations were transferred to Belgium under the joint name of Ruanda-Urundi. They were, however, "separated at birth" when they gained their independence in 1962. After periodic outbursts of violence, conciliation between Hutu and Tutsi leaders finally seemed to be in the making when Pres. Juvenal Habyarimana, under international and domestic pressure, began reforms in 1994. The reform process was, however, short-lived as Habyarimana perished in an aircraft

downed by a rocket near Kigali on 6 April 1994, along with the president of neighboring Burundi. The next day, the Rwandan government mobilized the country's ethnic Hutu majority in a genocide against the Tutsi and moderate Hutus, a campaign that claimed over 800,000 lives. Maj. Gen. Paul Kagame and his Tutsi-dominated multi-ethnic *Front Patriotique Rwandais* or Rwanda Patriotic Front (FPR) invaded from Uganda and defeated the Rwanda regime in July 1994. Shortly afterwards, Kagame was appointed Vice President and Defense Minister, and in March 2000 he was sworn in as President. The FPR formed a coalition government with Paul Kagame as a Tutsi serving as president and Bernard Makuza, leader of the Hutu-dominated *Mouvement Démocratique Républicain* or Republican Democratic Movement (MDR), appointed prime minister. Although much of the country is now at peace, members of the former regime continue their efforts to destabilize the northwest area of the countryfrom a base in the neighboring Democratic Republic of Congo. Pres. Kgama was reaffirmed in his post by an overwhelming majority in the August 2003 election. He retained Makuza in his post as prime minister.

GOVERNMENT

The president is elected by popular vote for a seven year term. The bicameral parliament consists of a 26-seat Senate with an 8-year term (12 members elected by local councils, 8 appointed by the president, 4 by the Political Organizations Forum and 2 by institutrions of higher learning) and an 80-seat Chamber of Deputies with a 5-year term (53 elected by popular vote, 24 women elected by local bodies, and 3 selected by youth and disability organzations). In the September 2003 election Kagame's Tutsi-dominated FPR won 40 of the 53 popular seats against 7 for the Hutu-dominated *Parti Social-Démocrate* or Social Democratic Party (PSD) and 6 for the *Parti Libéral* or Liberal Party (PL).

ECONOMIC POLICY

Rwanda is at the same time the most densely populated and one of the poorest countries in Africa. Despite the ravages of civil war and the 1994 genocide it has made great strides towards recovery. The government has implemented with the help of the IMF structural reforms, focusing on improving the civil service, privatization, reducing tariffs, and the restructuring of banks.

FAST FACTS

Pres. Paul Kagame
Born: October 1957
Since 2000

POLITICAL

Head of State	Pres. Paul Kagame
Prime Minister	Bernard Makuza
Majority party	FPR
Other parties	PSD & PL
Independence	1 July 1962
National capital	Kigali
Off. languages	Kinyarwanda, French & English

PHYSICAL

Total area	10,170 sq. miles
	26,340 sq. km.
	(± Maryland)
Arable land	40% of land area
Coastline	Landlocked

POPULATION

Total	8.6 million
Av. yearly growth	2.43%
Population/sq. mile	711
Urban population	1.9 million
Adult literacy	70.4%

ECONOMY

Currency	Rwandan franc
	(RF)(US$1=537.06)
GDP (real)	$1.8 billion
GDP growth rate	5.2%
GDP per capita[1]	$231
GDP (ppp)[2]	$12.65 billion
GDP per cap. (ppp)	$1,500
Inflation rate	8%
Exports	$98 million
Imports	$243 million
External debt	$1.4 billion
Unemployment	N/A

1. *Atlas method.*
2. *See page 175 for an explanation of purchasing power parity (ppp).*

SECTORS

Agriculture is the mainstay of the economy and the largest employer, with coffee and tea as major cash crops. Other export crops are pyrethrum and quinquina. The fishing potential of the lakes is underutilized and forestation programs have come to a standstill. Casserite (tin), wolfram, beryl, colombo-tantalite and gold are mined on a small scale. Large deposits of methane gas under Lake Kivu remain underexploited.

PRIVATIZATION

Privatization started in the late nineties. About half of the 46 enterprises earmarked have been restructured and another 18 were ceded to the private sector. Foreign investment is in commercial establishments, tea, coffee, and tourism.

TRADE

Coffee and tea account for about 85% of total export revenues. Most consumer products are imported from neighboring countries and Europe.

BUSINESS ACTIVITY

AGRICULTURE
Coffee, tea, pyrethrum , bananas, beans, sorghum, potatoes, livestock.

INDUSTRIES
Cement, agricultural processing, beverages, soap, furniture, shoes, plastic goods, textiles, cigarettes.

NATURAL RESOURCES
Gold, casseterite (tin ore), wolframite (tungsten ore), natural gas, hydropower.

EXPORTS
$98 million (est. 2005): coffee, tea, hides, tin ore.

IMPORTS
$243 million (est. 2005): foodstuffs, machinery and equipment, steel, petroleum products, construction material.

MAJOR TRADING PARTNERS
Indonesia, Germany, China, Germany, Kenya, Uganda, Belgium.

DOING BUSINESS WITH RWANDA

► INVESTMENT

With the passage of an investment code and creation of a one-stop investment promotion agency, Rwanda hopes to attract foreign direct investment. Tax breaks are offered to new firms as well as expatriate employees. While the tea and coffee sectors remain prime targets for investment, privatization will also open up the telecommunications, energy and water supply sectors for foreign participation.

► TRADE

There is also a growing demand for used clothing, 4-wheel drive vehicles, trucks, communications and computer equipment, cosmetics, and consultant services.

► TRADE FINANCE

Unless orders are placed by international agencies, irrevocable letters of credit are the standard mode of payment.

► SELLING TO THE GOVERNMENT

A tender board handles procurement and sets guidelines and policies. It is involved in purchases by all government departments and international donors.

► EXCHANGE CONTROLS

Controls have been relaxed and commercial banks are able to assist in the transfer of overseas payments of profits and dividends.

► FINANCING PROJECTS

In 1996, humanitarian relief began to shift to reconstruction and development assistance. Rehabilitation and expansion of road, water, health and educational facilities and agricultural projects involve overseas funding. The World Bank, the UN Development Program, the European Development Fund and various countries provide aid.

► LABOR

Four prewar independent trade unions are back in operation. The largest union, CESTRAR, was created in the early nineties as a government institution but has since become fully independent. Minimum wage and social security regulations are in force.

► BUSINESS CLIMATE

Business in Rwanda is conducted in both English and French. There is a strong desire to expand relations with US firms and in sophisticated circles a taste for American goods.

SÃO TOMÉ & PRÍNCIPE

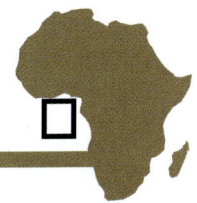

COMPRISING TWO SMALL FORMER PORTUGUESE ISLANDS OFF THE WEST AFRICAN COAST, THE STATE OF SÃO TOMÉ AND PRINCIPÉ IS LOCATED IN THE OIL-RICH GULF OF GUINEA, OFF THE COAST OF NIGERIA, AFRICA'S LARGEST OIL PRODUCER. THE TWO COUNTRIES ARE CLOSELY LINKED BY A JOINT OIL EXPLOITATION PACT. THE ISLANDS, HEAVILY DEPENDENT ON FOREIGN AID SINCE THEIR INDEPENDENCE IN 1975, SIT ON TOP A POTENTIAL OIL BONANZA ESTIMATED AT OVER A BILLION BARRELS OF CRUDE. IN THE MEANTIME ECONOMIC CHANGES AIM AT MAKING THE ISLANDS LESS DEPENDENT ON A SINGLE CASH CROP, COCOA.

COUNTRY PROFILE

The island country of São Tomé and Príncipe comprises two extinct volcanic islands and four rocky islets about 300 km off the coast of Gabon. The larger island, São Tomé, located on the equator, rises at its peak to over 2,000 m (6,500 ft). The eastern slopes are covered with cocoa plantations and smallholdings cut out of dense rainforest. To the north, Príncipe rises to 948 m (3,100 ft) above the sea. The climate of both islands is equatorial Annual rainfall decreases from 5,000 mm (197 inches) on the southwestern slopes of the islands to 1,000 mm (39 inches) on their northeastern sides. Society on both islands is fairly homogeneous, consisting largely of native-born descendants of the early Portuguese settlers and African slaves. There are also a number of Chinese, Cape Verdeans, Mozambicans and Angolans. Portuguese is the official language, but the more common lingua franca is Portuguese Crioulo (Creole). Most are Roman Catholic.

HISTORY

The island of São Tomé was discovered by Portuguese mariners in 1478 and granted to Portugal's crown prince, together with its sister island, Príncipe (Prince). After the prince's accession to the throne as Joao II, he encouraged settlement of the uninhabited islands to expand the Portuguese presence in this region and promote trade with Africa. The settlers imported slaves from the mainland and a mixed Afro-European population emerged who spoke a creole language based on Portuguese and various African languages. In the face of fierce competition from Brazil, sugar was replaced by cocoa as the main crop. In 1975 the *Movimiento de Libertaçao de São Tomé e Príncipe* or Movement for the Liberation of São Tomé and Príncipe (MLSTP) under the leadership of Manuel Pinto da Costa, led the islands to independence. Under pressure from foreign donors in the late 1980s, the MLSTP government began to

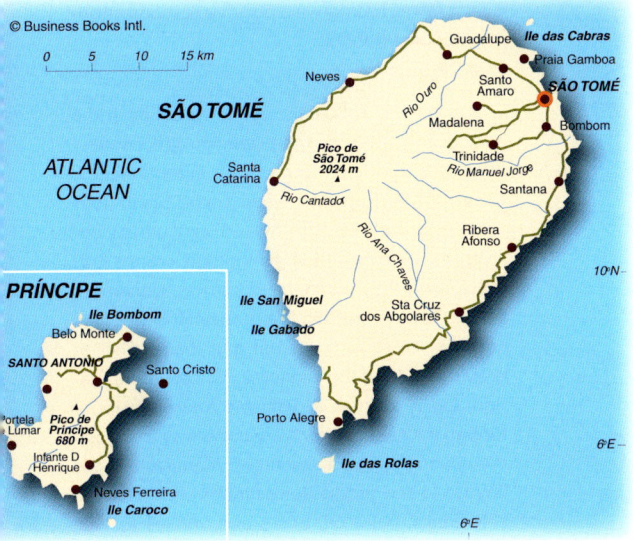

FAST FACTS

Pres. Fradique
de Menezes
Born: 1942
Since 2001

liberalize the economy and removed the ban on opposition parties. It was voted out of office in 1990 but returned victorious in 1994 when the interim government failed to cope with economic problems. Miguel Trovoada, who returned from exile to win the presidency in 1991, was reelected in 1996. In July 2001 Fradique de Menezes of the *Acçao Democrática Independente* or Independent Democratic Action (ADI) won the presidency. In July 2003 his government survived a military coup when Major Fernando "Cobo" Pereira and his rebel soldiers caved in under pressure from the African Union, released their captives and returned to their barracks. Pres. de Menezes was reelected in July 2006.

GOVERNMENT

An executive President is elected for a maximum of two 5-year terms and appoints the Prime Minister. The 55-member unicameral National Assembly is elected for a 4-year term. In the 2006 election the *Partido de Convergência Democrática-Grupa de Reflexão* (Force for Change Democratic Movement/Democratic Convergence Party) (MDFM-PCD) won 23 seats against 19 for the MLSTP, and 12 for the ADI.

ECONOMIC POLICY

After a period of economic decline and chronic deficits, São Tomé and Príncipe, together with the IMF, implemented vigorous adjustment measures. It still depends on concessional aid and benefited from $200 million in debt relief under the Highly Indebted Poor Countries (HIPC) program. Its successful implementation of structural reforms has drawn a positive response from international donors.

SECTORS

Since the 1800s, the economy of São Tomé and Principé was based on plantation agriculture—first sugar and later cocoa. After independence, control of Portuguese-owned cocoa plantations passed to various state-owned agricultural enterprises. The second-largest export crop is coffee, followed by copra, palm kernels, cinnamon, pepper and breadfruit. The principal food crops are taro, cassava, breadfruit and maize. Fishing employs 10% of the economically active population and is seen as a valuable future earner of foreign exchange. Efforts are underway to exploit the country's timber resources. Manufacturing is limited to the production of items such as soap, soft drinks, palm oil, bricks and textiles as well as timber processing. The island's beaches and tropical environment offer good tourism potential. Considerable additional income is expected from the exploitation of São Tomé and Príncipe's offshore oil resources in the Gulf of Guinea a 60/40 split arrangement with Nigeria.

PRIVATIZATION

The government has been turning over management of the parastatals, as well as the agricultural, commercial, banking, and tourism sectors, to the private sector. The focus has been on restructuring of the state-run agricultural and industrial sectors. Agricultural privatization involving several cocoa estates has met with mixed success due to a lack of domestic capital.

INVESTMENT

Private investment is expected to grow from 18.4% of GDP in 1998 to 45% of GDP in 2002. Two American oil companies, ExxonMobil and Environmental Remediation Holding Corporation, have begun oil exploration activities in São Tomé's recently delineated exclusive economic deep water zone.

TRADE

The dominant crop on São Tomé is cocoa, representing about 98% of exports. Other export crops include copra, palm kernels, and coffee. Netherlands and Belgium are major trading partners.

BUSINESS ACTIVITY

AGRICULTURE
Cocoa, coconuts, palm kernels, copra, cinnamon, pepper, coffee, bananas, papayas, beans, poultry, fish.

INDUSTRIES
Light construction, textiles, soap, beer, fish processing, timber.

EXPORTS
$8 million (est. 2005): cocoa, coffee, copra, palm oil.

IMPORTS
$38 million (est. 2005): machinery and electrical equipment, food products, petroleum products.

MAJOR TRADING PARTNERS
Netherlands, Belgium, Germany, Portugal, US, UK.

FINANCIAL SECTOR

The authorities have set a relatively high reserve requirement ratio of 22% and the government's counterpart funds were transferred to the Central Bank, enhancing liquidity in the banking system. The collection of proceeds from privatization and the sale of oil exploration concessions contributed to government liquidity.

DOING BUSINESS WITH SÃO TOMÉ & PRÍNCIPE

▶ INVESTMENT

An aggressive pursuit of potential foreign investors has met with limited success. The task is complicated by the small size and relative isolation of the islands, remaining foreign exchange controls, and low productivity and human resource development. There are attempts to stimulate interest abroad not only in tropical agriculture, but in areas such as tourism, industrial fishing, and manufacturing in a regional free trade zone. Expectations are that São Tomé and Principé, situated in the oil-rich Gulf of Guinea near Nigeria, will strike petroleum in large quantity and join other nations in the region who built new economies on such bonanzas. In 1993, the government announced plans to designate a free trade zone to attract offshore investors and stimulate development of the country's shipping and manufacturing sectors.

▶ TRADE

Even though priority is given to the development of food crops in an effort to reduce the large food import bill, the islands are still heavily reliant on foreign sources. In the 1990s foodstuffs accounted on average for about 35% of total imports.

▶ FINANCING PROJECTS

The government relies on foreign assistance from various donors. The UN Development Program, the World Bank, the European Union, and the African Development Bank have all at different stages financed projects.

▶ LABOR

The local workforce is largely involved in agricultural activity. Lack of employment has led to an exodus of workseekers abroad.

SENEGAL

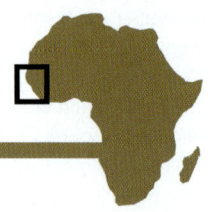

HISTORICALLY SENEGAL AND ITS CAPITAL, DAKAR, SERVED AS THE GATEWAY TO WEST AFRICA. ALTHOUGH ITS INDUSTRIAL AND COMMERCIAL BASE IS SMALLER THAN THAT OF RIVAL CÔTE D'IVOIRE, IT IS EQUIPPED WITH ONE OF AFRICA'S MOST EFFICIENT AND MODERN INFRASTRUCTURES AND POPULATED BY A SOPHISTICATED PEOPLE WITH AN INTERNATIONAL, DISTINCTLY FRENCH, OUTLOOK. SENEGAL HAS MET ALL IMF BENCHMARKS IN ITS MACROECONOMIC PROGRAM. A DECENT SUPPLY OF MINERALS COUPLED WITH A COSMOPOLITAN ENVIRONMENT HAVE ATTRACTED MANY EUROPEAN AND—MORE RECENTLY— AN INCREASING NUMBER OF AMERICAN ENTREPRENEURS. HOWEVER, SENEGAL STILL RELIES ON OUTSIDE DONOR ASSISTANCE.

COUNTRY PROFILE

The Republic of Senegal consists largely of a low plateau between 100-200 m above sea level. Three perennial rivers flow through the region—the Senegal, Gambia and Casamance. All three open up in large deltas or estuaries, replete with expansive beaches, national parks and tourist resorts. The Senegalese Peninsula with its ample rainfall was appropriately named Cape Verde or Green Cape. The Wolof in the northwest are the largest ethnic group and account for about 40% of the total population. Their language is a lingua franca in Senegal along with French, the official tongue. Other significant groups include the Serer, Tukulor, Ful (or Fulani), Mandé and a large Mauritanian (Moorish) community. More than 90% adhere to the Muslim faith but there is a small Christian minority in Dakar. Ethnic beliefs survive.

HISTORY

The earliest evidence of civilization in this region are mysterious circles of huge stone columns (megaliths) in the vicinity of the Gambia and Saloum rivers. The inhabitants of modern Senegal and The Gambia are descendants of Negroid peoples who settled some 1,400 years ago. From 1445 Portuguese mariners traded with the Wolof and Serer kingdoms but in 1588 they were driven out by the Dutch. Ultimately the French gained dominance from their settlement on St. Louis Island in the estuary of the Senegal, capturing Rufisque and Gorée Island, which served as slave trading posts until the abolition of this trade in the first half of the 19th Century. Millions of Africans were shipped from Gorée to the New World during the 1700s. Eventually these coastal centers and Dakar became integral parts of France, electing their own deputies to the National Assembly. France not only annexed Senegal, but used the colony as a base for further expansion eastward. A Catholic poet-politician, Léopold Sedar Senghor, led Senegal to independence in 1960 and exercised

virtual one-man rule until his voluntary retirement in 1981 when he stepped down in favor of his prime minister, Abdou Diouf. During his term as president, Diouf witnessed the creation in 1982 together with The Gambia, of the Confederation of Senegambia as well as its breakup in 1989. In the presidential election of March 2000, Diouf, as leader of the *Parti Socialiste du Sénégal* or Socialist Party of Senegal (PS), was defeated at the polls and succeeded as president by Abdou-laye Wade, representing the *Parti Démocratique Sénégalais* or Senegalese Democratic Party (PDS). Wade inherited an ongoing problem posed by the secessionist *Mouvement des forces democratiques de Casamance* (MFDC), led by the Rev. Augustin Diamacoune in southern Senegal.

GOVERNMENT

The executive President is directly elected by the voters for a term of five years, renewable once. (When Pres. Wade was elected in 2000, the term was seven years). He appoints the Prime Minister who forms the cabinet. The 120-member unicameral National Assembly (*Assemblée Natio-nale*) is elected for five years. In the April 2001 election the SOPI Coalition comprising President Wade's PDS and a half dozen smaller parties captured 89 seats in the Assembly. The Alliance of Forces for Progress (AFP) won 11 seats and the Socialist Party (PS) 10. The other 10 seats were split between smaller parties. Although elections were scheduled for 2006 it was decided to post-pone it to 2007 to coincide with the presidential elections..

ECONOMIC POLICY

With an ambitious economic reform pro-gram started in the nineties Senegal has met all IMF benchmarks and macroeconomic indicators show a respectable performance with a real growth in GDP averaging 5% between 1995 and 2003. Inflation has also been pushed down sig-nificantly. There has been an increasing emphasis on measures to attract private sector investment after completion of the first phase of economic liberalization. Private activity currently accounts for 82% of the country's GDP. Hiwever, Senegal still relies on on outside donor assistance and under the IMF's Highly Indebted Poor Countries (HIPC) debt relief program will have two-thirds of its bi-lateral multilateral, bilateral and private sector debt eliminated. Senegal is working towards greater regional integration with its neighbors.

FAST FACTS

Pres. Abdoulaye Wade
Born: May 29, 1926
Since 2000

POLITICAL

Head of State	Pres. Abdoulaye Wade
Ruling Party	SOPI (Coalition)
Main Opposition	AFP & PS
Independence	4 April 1960
National capital	Dakar
Official language	French

PHYSICAL

Total area	75,749 sq. miles
	196,190 sq. km.
	(± South Dakota)
Arable land	12% of land area
Coastline	330 miles/531 km

POPULATION

Total	11.98 million
Av. yearly growth	2.34%
Population/sq. mile	131
Urban population	5.4 million
Adult literacy	40.2%

ECONOMY

Currency	CFA franc (CFAF)(US$1=559.44)
GDP (real)	$7.97 billion
GDP growth rate	6.1%
GDP per capita[1]	$717
GDP (ppp)[2]	$20.53 billion
GDP per cap. (ppp)	$1,800
Inflation rate	1.7%
Exports	$1.53 billion
Imports	$2.4 billion
External debt	$3.5 billion
Unemployment	48%

1. *Atlas method.*
2. *See page 175 for an explanation of purchasing power parity (ppp).*

SECTORS

The economy remains heavily dependent on agriculture that employs about 75% of the working population and accounts for over one-fifth of GDP. Groundnuts, cotton and sugar are major cash crops. Staple foods are millet, sorghum, maize and rice. Livestock is raised across the country. Fresh and canned marine fish is the principal export and involves some 10% of the working population. Even though the mining sector accounts for less than 2% of GDP, exports of phosphate rock, phosphate acid and fertilizers contribute more than 25% of foreign earnings. There are large unexploited iron ore and limited gold reserves. Titanium, zirconium and rutile are mined south of the Cape Verde Peninsula. Natural gas from offshore wells fuel a power station near Dakar and modest oil deposits off the Casamance coast are still to be exploited. Food processing, textiles, chemicals and petroleum products, plastics, paint, soap and pharmaceuticals are manufactured.

PRIVATIZATION

Privatization is considered key to attracting foreign investment. Eighteen enterprises were earmarked for restructuring, including the state-owned telecommunications company, a peanut oil processor, the national power utility, the railroad company and several hotels. There is a desire on the part of the government to continue influencing the direction of these large entities by retaining a stake. A subsidiary of France Telecom was allowed to purchase a one-third share in SONATEL while the government insisted on retaining 51% control over the power utility SENELEC.

INVESTMENT

Among the US firms involved in Senegal are GTI (in a build, own, operate and transfer—BOOT—power project), Motorola (developing paging systems), and Senelec (a factory for fuel-efficient lights and refrigerators). As privatization offers new opportunities, other foreign firms are expected to challenge the historic dominance of the French in the industrial sector. Irish and Canadian companies are involved in gas exploration while South African and Australian firms have become involved in gold and other mining operations.

TRADE

Fresh and canned marine fish is the principal export, contributing over 30% of export revenue. Senegal is the largest exporter of groundnuts on the continent and the fifth largest exporter of phosphates. Major imports include crude and refined petroleum products, machinery, electrical appliances, rice, grain, lubricants, and dairy products. France remains Senegal's largest trading partner, followed by India, Germany, Nigeria, and the US. Principal exports from the US, which maintains a surplus, are rice, wheat, and other agricultural commodities, as well as petroleum products, computer equipment, used clothing, and cosmetics. Tourism is also a major foreign exchange earner .

FINANCIAL SECTOR

Senegal shares the Banque Central Des Etats de L'Afrique de L'Ouest (BCEAO), or Central Bank of West African States, with other members of the CFA franc zone. In the wake of a serious banking crisis in the 1980s, significant reforms were introduced. Five stronger banks emerged with greater liquidity, tighter controls and a full range of services.

TAXES AND TARIFFS

Corporate income tax is levied at 33.33%. Payroll taxes are 3% for national salaries and 6% for expatriate salaries. A value-added tax (VAT) of 20% is charged for most goods. Some services are taxed at a reduced rate of 12.5%.

BUSINESS ACTIVITY

AGRICULTURE
Peanuts, millet, corn, sorghum, rice, cotton, tomatoes, green vegetables, cattle, poultry, pigs, fish.

INDUSTRIES
Agricultural and fish processing, phosphate mining, fertilizer production, petroleum refining, construction materials.

NATURAL RESOURCES
Fish, phosphate, iron ore.

EXPORTS
$1.53 billion (est. 2005): fish, groundnuts (peanuts), petroleum products, phosphates, cotton.

IMPORTS
$2.4 billion (est. 2005): food and beverages, consumer goods, capital goods, petroleum products.

MAJOR TRADING PARTNERS
France, India, Nigeria, US, Mali, Cameroon, Guinea-Bissau, The Gambia, Italy, Thailand.

Doing Business with Senegal

► INVESTMENT

The Dakar Industrial Free Zone (DIFZ) is an industrial park dedicated primarily to export-oriented and labor-intensive manufacturing. Investors in the DIFZ and other designated areas enjoy tax-free status and duty-free entry of raw materials and components. Foreign investors need to register at a central one-stop facility to qualify for these and other incentives. The emphasis is on investment outside the Dakar region, small- and medium-sized enterprises and sectors such as agriculture, fishing, manufacturing, mineral extraction, and tourism. US investors are engaged in hotel renovation programs on the historic slave site, Gorée Island, off the coast of Dakar. Majority Senegalese ownership is a requirement in food production and fishing projects and most enterprises are obliged to employ a certain number of local workers.

► TRADE

Although Senegal has until now offered a relatively limited market for US products, the liberalization of the economy, freer access for imports, and new developments in power generation and in telecommunications are expected to broaden the scope. Best deals in the past were in agricultural commodities, mining, tourism, information technology, and used clothing. There is a strong growth in the computer market and products ranging from air conditioners to cosmetics. US and other importers have concentrated on groundnuts and phosphates from Senegal. Distribution is mostly through large French-owned or Lebanese firms.

► TRADE FINANCE

Irrevocable letters of credit are the preferred form of payment. Local financing is tight.

► SELLING TO THE GOVERNMENT

Both in privatization deals and major government purchases foreign firms are invited to present bids. Procurement of goods and services with the help of multilateral funds is in accordance with international rules for competitive bidding. In recent years, major government contracts involved telecommunications, energy and water projects.

► EXCHANGE CONTROLS

Senegal's currency, the CFA Franc, is freely convertible into French francs at a fixed rate. Foreign investors are guaranteed repatriation of profits and capital. Transactions are channeled through authorized banks, the postal administration, or the regional central bank, the BCEAO.

► PARTNERSHIPS

In major privatization deals involving telecommunications, energy projects and the like, the government insists on being a partner with foreign private investors. It is also actively promoting joint ventures between foreign and domestic entrepreneurs in certain sectors of the economy.

► ESTABLISHING A PRESENCE

There is provision for several types of companies, including general partnerships, limited liability companies (LLC), public limited companies (PLC), and joint venture enterprises. Incorporation costs are moderate. Copies of all agency agreements between foreign principals and local distributors or agents must be submitted to the Department of Internal Trade and Prices for final approval.

► FINANCING PROJECTS

The Overseas Private Investment Corporation provides insurance and assistance to US investors. Several international agencies are involved in major projects.

► LABOR

There is a reasonable availability of unskilled and semi-skilled labor but investors with a need for specialized skills need to factor in expenditure for training purposes.

► LEGAL RIGHTS

Property rights are protected and there are no known cases of expropriation involving US or other overseas firms. Senegal is a member of the Cameroon-based African Intellectual Property Organization or *Office African et Malagache de la Propiété Industrielle* (OAMPI), which safeguards trademarks, patents, and industrial designs among its members. It is also a member of the Paris Convention for the Protection of Industrial Property and the Berne Convention for the Protection of Literary and Artistic Works.. Trademarks are filed through the Central Office and granted protection by OAMPI for 20 years, renewable indefinitely.

► BUSINESS CLIMATE

The business culture has a decidedly French flavor. Still, usage of English is growing as efforts intensify to lure larger investment from the United States, Britain and countries such as South Africa and Australia.

SEYCHELLES

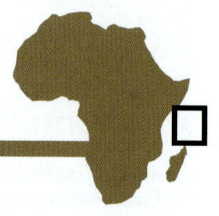

INCOME FROM TOURISM HAS HELPED AFRICA'S SMALLEST STATE, SEYCHELLES, TO RANK NEAR THE TOP IN AFRICA IN TERMS OF GNP PER CAPITA. SINCE ITS INDEPENDENCE IN SEVENTIES THE PER CAPITA OUTPUT OF THIS INDIAN OCEAN ARCHIPELAGO HAS INCREASED SEVENFOLD. ALREADY A CROSSROAD FOR SEA AND AIR TRAVELERS AND FREIGHT SHIPPING, THE MULTI-ISLAND NATION IS AIMS TO BECOME A MAJOR OFFSHORE BANKING AND INSURANCE CENTER BY OFFERING FACILITIES COMPARABLE TO PLACES LIKE THE BAHAMAS. INVESTOR-FRIENDLY REFORMS AND PRIVATIZATION HAVE LURED INVESTMENT IN FISHING AND MANUFACTURING FROM THE US AND EUROPE. A TUNA PROCESSING PLANT PARTLY OWNED AND OPERATED BY A US FIRM IS THE BIGGEST SINGLE EMPLOYER ON THE ISLANDS.

COUNTRY PROFILE

The Republic of Seychelles comprises 115 small islands scattered over an area of about 1.3 million sq. km (0.5 million sq. miles) in the Indian Ocean, just south of the equator some 1,600 km (1,000 miles) east of Mombasa. The main island, Mahe, about 27 km (17 miles) long and 8 km (5 miles) at its widest, is the largest of 40 non-volcanic Inner Islands formed by granite rock, renowned for their unique flora and fauna. The outlying islands consist of nine archipelagos, including coralline atolls and groups of volcanic islands. The Aldabra, Farquhar and Desroches island groups are all included in the Republic of Seychelles. Most Seychellians are of mixed descent, primarily African and European. French-Kreol is the lingua franca and an official language, together with English. The population is predominantly Christian.

HISTORY

The Seychelles were uninhabited when the British East India Company discovered the archipelago in 1609. It soon became a haven for pirates. The islands were claimed by the French in 1756 and administered as part of the colony of Mauritius. In the Peace Treaty of Paris in 1814 the French signed over

Séchelles to the British who anglisized the name to its current spelling. The Seychelles islands gained independence in 1976 under a coalition government headed by Sir James Mancham, leader of the *Mouvement Seychellois pour la Democratie* or Seychelles Democratic Party (DP), as president, and Marxist nationalist, France Albert René of the *Front Progressiste du Peuple Seychellois or* Progressive Front of the Seychelles Peoples Progressive Front (SPPF) as prime minister. In 1977 while Mancham was abroad, René overthrew him and set up a one-party pro-Soviet state. (The American space agency's radar station which paid a substantial rent, was allowed to stay).

In 1992, in the wake of

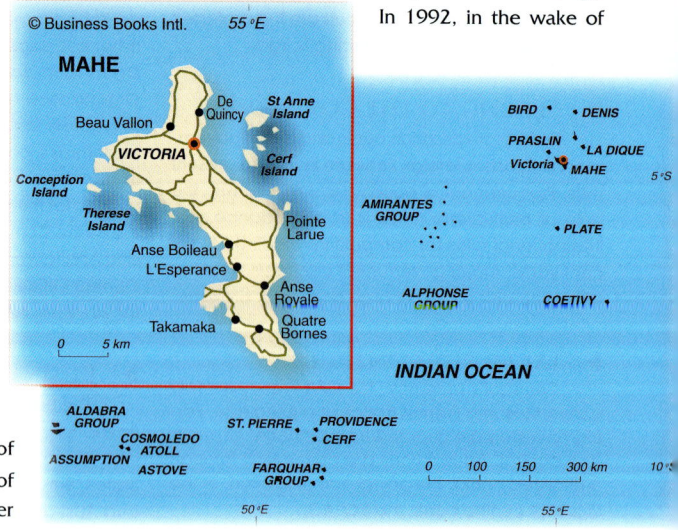

© Business Books Intl.   55 °E

MAHE

Beau Vallon
De Quincy
St Anne Island
VICTORIA
Conception Island
Cerf Island
Therese Island
Pointe Larue
Anse Boileau
L'Esperance
Anse Royale
Takamaka
Quatre Bornes
0   5 km

BIRD   • DENIS
PRASLIN   • LA DIQUE
Victoria   MAHE   5 °S
AMIRANTES GROUP
• PLATE
ALPHONSE GROUP   COETIVY •

INDIAN OCEAN

ALDABRA GROUP
COSMOLEDO ATOLL
ASSUMPTION
ASTOVE
ST. PIERRE •   PROVIDENCE
• CERF
FARQUHAR GROUP •
0   100   150   300 km   10 °S
50 °E   55 °E

Soviet Union's demise, René lifted restrictions on opposition parties and won handsomely. He was reelected president in 1998 and 2001. On 14 April 2004 René stepped down and Vice President James Michel was sworn in as president.

GOVERNMENT

An executive President is elected by popular vote for a 5-year term and appoints a Council of Ministers. A unicameral 34-seat National Assembly, or *Assemblée Nationale,* consists of 25 elected seats and 9 appointed on a proportional basis to parties that won 9% or more of the popular vote. In December 2002 the SPPF captured 23 seats against 11 for the centrist Seychelles National Party (SNP).

ECONOMIC POLICY

Despite reforms to attract foreign investors, the government still plays accounts for 40% of GDP. Seychelles has undertaken an intensive review of its economic policies.

SECTORS

Tourism and tuna fishing are major sectors apart from agriculture and small-scale manufacturing. Tourism employs 30% of the workforce and accounts for more than 70% of the foreign currency earnings. There are official attempts to shift the emphasis towards farming, fishing and light manufacturing. A fully equipped international airport on Mahe island not only handles an inward tourist flow but serves as a stopover on international routes. Victoria has the deepest port in the Indian Ocean and serves as a major fish and freight transshipment point.

PRIVATIZATION

Privatization has created new investment opportunities. A celebrated case is the partial purchase several years ago by a subsidiary of US-based Heinz of a state-owned tuna plant.

INVESTMENT

Foreign investment in recent years was largely in telecommunications, tourism and manufacturing. Recent expansion has turned the tuna-processing plant owned and operated by Heinz in partnership with the government into the largest employer on the islands.

TRADE

Leading foreign exchange earners are tourism and fishing, largely geared to exporting canned tuna, fish, and frozen shrimp and prawns. Recently tea has been added to its exports.

FAST FACTS

Pres. James
Alix Michel
Born: August 18, 1944
Since 2004

POLITICAL

Head of State	Pres. James Alix Michel
Ruling Party	SPPF
Main Opposition	SNP
Independence	29 June 1976
National capital	Victoria
Official languages	English & French-Kreol

PHYSICAL

Total area	175 sq. miles
	455 sq. km.
	(2½ x Washington DC)
Arable land	2% of land area
Coastline	305 miles/492 km

POPULATION

Total	81,540
Av. yearly growth	0.43%
Population/sq. mile	453
Urban population	40,000
Adult literacy	58%

ECONOMY

Currency	Seychelles Rupee (SRe)(US$1=5.19)
GDP (real)	$722 million
GDP growth rate	-3%
GDP per capita[1]	$8,659
GDP (ppp)[2]	$626 million
GDP per cap. (ppp)	$7,800
Inflation rate	1.6%
Exports	$312 million
Imports	$460 million
External debt	$508 million
Unemployment	N/A

1. *Atlas method.*
2. *See page 175 for an explanation of purchasing power parity (ppp).*

FINANCIAL SECTOR

Four international banks maintain branches in the Seychelles. Corporate tax, withholding tax on dividends and interests, wealth tax, capital gains tax, customs duties, stamp duty, and exchange controls have been waived for offshore investors. The Insurance Act, modeled on similar legislation in Singapore, makes provision for the licensing of offshore insurance companies. Like Mauritius, Seychelles is aggressively courting offshore banking business.

TAXES AND TARIFFS

Investors are exempted from withholding tax on dividends, personal income tax, and wealth tax. Some trade regulations, however, are still restrictive and at variance with WTO standards. Imports usually require government approval in one form or another and price controls apply to imports.

BUSINESS ACTIVITY

AGRICULTURE
Coconuts, cinnamon, vanilla, sweet potatoes, cassava (tapioca), bananas, broiler chickens, tuna fish.

INDUSTRIES
Fishing, tourism, processing of coconuts and vanilla, coir (coconut fiber),rope, boat building, printing, furniture, beverages.

EXPORTS
$312 million (est. 2005): fish, cinnamon, bark, copra, petroleum products (reexports).

IMPORTS
$460 million (est. 2005): manufactured goods, food, petroleum products, machinery and equipment, chemicals.

MAJOR TRADING PARTNERS
France, UK, Saudi Arabia, Germany, South Africa, Singapore, Spain, Italy.

DOING BUSINESS WITH SEYCHELLES

▶ INVESTMENT

Several government organizations have been established to assist potential foreign investors. A one-stop shop, the Seychelles International Business Authority (SIBA), is largely preoccupied with the registration of offshore companies and promoting the Seychelles as a hub in the Indian Ocean region while the Seychelles International Trade Zone concentrates on tax-exempt, export-oriented operations in the zone. The greatest potential for US investors is in tourism, fisheries, light manufacturing and infrastructure. There is growing foreign interest in newly created opportunities for secure and confidential offshore banking and insurance facilities.

▶ TRADE

Marketing of products is inhibited by a lack of adequate foreign exchange and the government policy of restricting non-essential imports.

▶ TRADE FINANCE

The foreign exchange shortage is one of the main obstacles to doing business in the Seychelles.

▶ SELLING TO THE GOVERNMENT

The state-owned Seychelles Marketing Board has a monopoly on the importation of essential products such as rice, sugar and dairy products.

▶ FINANCING PROJECTS

Major infrastructure investments are typically financed by bilateral donors such as France, Kuwait and China and multilateral agencies such as the World Bank, the European Development Bank and the African Development Bank.

▶ LEGAL RIGHTS

By its own admission, the Seychelles is not sufficiently equipped by law to provide intellectual property protection. Steps are underway to tighten the laws and improve monitoring.

▶ LABOR

The local workforce is easily adaptable to manufacturing and service sector tasks. In the fishing sector, there is a wealth of talent.

▶ BUSINESS CLIMATE

Business is conducted at a an easy pace in either English, French or Creole. Seychellians are quite informal and casual dress is the norm even at the senior government and company levels.

SIERRA LEONE

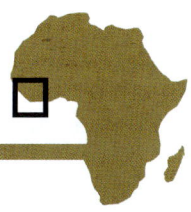

IN RECENT YEARS, THIS PROMISING FORMER BRITISH PROTECTORATE SUFFERED HEAVILY AS RIVAL FORCES ENGAGED IN FIERCE FIGHTING. SUBSTANTIAL MINERAL, AGRICULTURAL AND FISHING RESOURCES IN SIERRA LEONE REMAIN UNDERUTILIZED AS POTENTIAL FOREIGN INVESTORS STEER CLEAR. INTERRUPTION IN THE MINING OF DIAMONDS, BAUXITE AND RUTILE HAS PRACTICALLY DRIED UP THE FLOW OF FOREIGN CURRENCY AND THE MASS EXODUS OF PROFESSIONALS FROM SIERRA LEONE IS CONTINUING. THE GOVERNMENT IS SLOWLY REESTABLISHING ORDER AFTER A COSTLY DECADE-LONG CIVIL WAR.

COUNTRY PROFILE

The Republic of Sierra Leone is a country of many rivers perched on a mountainous peninsula. From the coast the land rises gradually to the Loma and Tingi mountains near the northern border. As the capital of a country with an average rainfall of between 79 and 197 inches (2,000 and 5,000 mm) per year, Freetown is one of the world's wettest cities. Rainforest covers much of the terrain. The Temne and Mende are major groups, There are substantial Creole (or Krio) and Lebanese minorities. English is the official language, but Krio, an English-based Creole language, is the lingua franca.

HISTORY

The Bulom people were the first to settle in the region, followed by the Mende and the Temme in the 15th Century and the Fulani. In the middle of the 15th Century, Portuguese mariners began to sail up the broad mouth of the Sierra Leone River in search of fresh water. They named the mountainous peninsula, Serra Lyoa and traded in gold, ivory and slaves. During the last half of the 16th Century a Mende warrior people invaded the region and subjugated the local communities. Towards the end of the 18th Century liberated slaves from North America sponsored by private British patrons found a province in Sierra Leone. In 1808 Britain turned the capital, Freetown, into a naval base to enforce the abolition of slavery and in 1896 declared a protectorate over the interior to prevent it from falling into French hands. After the discovery of gold, diamonds, iron ore, bauxite and rutile, the colony experienced considerable economic growth. Since Dr. Milton Margai and his Sierra Leone People's Party (SLPP) led Sierra Leone to independence in 1961, the colony has experienced more than its fair share of coups and counter-coups. On 25 May 1997, the democratically-elected government of President Ahmad Tejan Kabbah was overthrown by a disgruntled coalition of personnel of the Armed Forces Revolutionary Council (AFRC) and the Revolutionary United Front (RUF) under the command of Major Johnny Paul Koroma. In 1998 Kabbah was reinstated by

335

FAST FACTS

Pres. Ahmad
Tejan Kabbah
Born: February16, 1932
Since1996

© P Anderson

POLITICAL

Head of State	Pres. Ahmad Tejan Kabbah
Ruling Party	SLPP
Main Opposition	APC
Independence	27 April 1961
Capital	Freetown
Official languages	English

PHYSICAL

Total area	27,698 sq. miles
	71,740 sq. km.
	(± South Carolina)
Arable land	7% of land area
Coastline	250 miles/402 km

POPULATION

Total	6 million
Av. yearly growth	2.3%
Population/sq. mile	187
Urban population	2.1 million
Adult literacy	29.6%

ECONOMY

Currency	Leone (Le)
	(US$1=2,352)
GDP (real)	$1.13 billion
GDP growth rate	6.3%
GNP per capita[1]	$211
GDP (ppp)[2]	$4.92 billion
GDP per cap. (ppp)	$800
Inflation rate	1%
Exports	$185 million
Imports	$531 million
External debt	$1.6 billion
Unemployment	N/A

1. Atlas method.
2. See page 175 for an explanation of purchasing power parity (ppp).

the Economic Community of West African States Cease-Fire Monitoring Group (ECOMOG). In January 1999, renewed fighting broke out between the AFRC/RUF and ECOMOG troops, bringing commerce to a standstill. Until May 2002 sufficient stability was restored to enable Sierra Leone to have its first free postwar presidential election. Tejan Kabbah won more than 70% of the popular vote, defeating four other candidates, including Johnny Koroma, and Pallo Bangura, the rebel-allied candidate who substituted for his jailed associate, Foday Sankoh. The new government faces the challenge of rebuilding infrastructure in a decade-long war that cost the lives of tens of thousands and left 2 million (one-third of the population) homeless.

GOVERNMENT

The current constitution provides for an executive President, directly elected for a maximum of two 4-year terms. The 124-member House of Representatives serves for a 5-year term—112 are elected on a proportional basis and 12 seats are for representatives of the traditional chiefs. In May 2002 Kabbah's Sierra Leone People's Party (SLPP) won 83 seats against 22 for the All People's Congress (APC).

ECONOMIC POLICY

The IMF introduced an enhanced structural adjustment facility in the nineties. The International Finance Corporation, assisted with financing. Sierra Leone's recovery depends to a large extent on the ability of the government to maintain peace and assistance from overseas donors.

SECTORS

Agriculture, mostly on smallholdings, provides a livelihood for about 70% of the population. Rice is grown by most farmers, but despite government efforts to promote self-sufficiency, increasing quantities have to be imported. Other food crops include maize, cassava, sweet potatoes and sorghum. The major export crops are coffee, cocoa, palm kernels and ginger. Fishing is a growing industry with oysters and shrimp as major products. Diamonds are mined in alluvial fields around the eastern towns of Koidu-Sefadu and Kenema by numerous individual diggers and a government-controlled corporation. Rutile (titanium dioxide) mined in the sands on Sherbro Island has overtaken diamonds as the principal export. Sierra Leone is currently the world's second largest producer of this mineral, an essential ingredient in paints. Bauxite ore, which has overtaken diamond mining in importance, has resumed after the new government took control. Manufacturing is largely concentrated around the porcessing of raw materials and light industry aimed at the domestic consumer market.

INVESTMENT

Foreign investment, mostly British, is largely concentrated in the mining sector. Output in diamond mining is expected to increase once stability returns.

TRADE

Diamonds have for many years been the principal export, but in recent years rutile accounted for over 40% of export earnings, followed by bauxite ore and diamonds.

FINANCIAL SECTOR

Private foreign exchange bureaus operate freely, bank accounts in foreign currencies are available, and interest rates fairly reflect market conditions. Banking and tax laws are being reformed.

BUSINESS ACTIVITY

AGRICULTURE
Rice, coffee, cocoa, palm kernels, palm oil, peanuts, poultry, cattle, sheep, pigs, fish.

INDUSTRIES
Mining (diamonds), small-scale manufacturing (beverages, textiles, cigarettes, footwear), petroleum refining.

NATURAL RESOURCES
Diamonds, bauxite, iron ore.

EXPORTS
$185 million (est. 2005): diamonds, rutile, cocoa, coffee, fish.

IMPORTS
$531 million (est. 2005): foodstuffs, machinery and equipment, fuel and lubricants.

MAJOR TRADING PARTNERS
Belgium, Germany, Côte d'Ivoire, US, UK, Belgium, Luxembourg, South Africa, China, Netherlands.

DOING BUSINESS WITH SIERRA LEONE

▶ INVESTMENT

For security reasons most foreigners pass on the considerable potential in this troubled country as rebels continue to operate in the mineral-rich northern and eastern portions of the country. While fighting has caused suspension of most mineral operations, foreign entrepreneurs are expected back as soon as stability can be restored. In the past the mineral industry accounted for 20% of the nation's gross domestic product, 80% to 90% of export earnings, and employed almost 15% of the total workforce, primarily in rural areas. There are opportunities in the mining of bauxite, cassiterite, clays, columbite, diamonds, gold, iron ore, kaolin, lignite, platinum, dimension stone, and tantalite.

▶ TRADE

Reconstruction and repair of roads, schools, hospitals, airports and telecommunications connections, largely with the help of donor funding, are areas where foreigners are bound to play a meaningful role in the future. Some projects have already been initiated with the help of funding from international donor agencies. Sales of food, clothing and other supplies at this time are mostly to humanitarian and specialized agencies that will insist on giveaway pricing to augment donations. Once Sierra Leone has regained its equilibrium it should again become a small but vibrant market for a wide range of consumer goods.

▶ EXCHANGE CONTROLS

The foreign exchange rate is market-determined. Private foreign exchange bureaus operate freely and bank accounts in foreign currencies are allowed.

▶ FINANCING PROJECTS

Sierra Leone has been a MIGA member since 1996 and has pending applications with the institution for projects in agribusiness, mining and telecommunications. World Bank activities have focused on sectoral programs and projects in the agriculture, education, infrastructure, and health sectors. The IFC's portfolio as of July 31, 1998 totalled $5.2 million (in Sierra Rutile).

SOMALIA

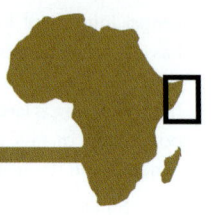

FOREIGN BUSINESS WITH SOMALIA REMAINS ON HOLD AS THE STRUGGLE BE-
TWEEN THE FIGHTING FACTIONS CONTINUES. ECONOMIC PROGRESS HAS STALLED IN
MOST PARTS OF THE COUNTRY IN THE WAKE OF THE UNREST AND INSTABILITY THAT
FOLLOWED THE FALL OF THE MILITARY REGIME IN 1991. AFTER FAILED ATTEMPTS BY
US AND UN MILITARY FORCES TO IMPOSE A SETTLEMENT WHILE OVERSEEING THE
DISTRIBUTION OF INTERNATIONAL FOOD AND OTHER HUMANITARIAN AID, SOMALIA
HAS BEEN LEFT LARGELY TO ITS OWN DEVICES SINCE THE MID-1990S. A TRANSITIONAL
GOVERNMENT STILL FACES STRONG OPPOSITION FROM RIVAL FACTIONS IN THEIR
EFFORTS TO REUNITE THE BREAKAWAY REPUBLIC OF SOMALILAND IN THE CENTRAL
REGION AND PUNTLAND STATE WITH A CENTRAL AUTHORITY IN MOGADISHU.

COUNTRY PROFILE

The largely inoperative Somali Democratic
Republic has a rhino-horn shaped coastline of
more than 3,000 km (1,684 miles)—the longest
in Africa—which earned it the designation, Horn
of Africa. The Ras Hafun peninsula, to the south
of Cape Guardafui at the Horn's tip, is the African
continent's most easterly point. Ethiopia cuts
into Somalia, virtually dividing it into northern
Somalia (the former British Somaliland)
and southern Somalia (formerly Italian
Somaliland). In the north a steep escarpment rises inland from a narrow coastline
towards Ethiopia. The south consists
largely of monotonous plains below 500
m (1,650 ft) and the region adjoining the
Juba and Shibeli rivers provides grazing
for livestock. About half of the largely
homogenous population is nomadic and
the other half evenly divided between
settled farming regions of Juba-Shebeh
and the towns. Islam is the prevailing
faith and most Somalians speak Somali,
which, together with Arabic, is an official
language. English and Italian are the main
European languages.

origin such as the Berbers and the ancient Egyptians and Nubians. About 1,500 years ago Negroid
peoples arrived from the west and in the course
of time extensive intermixing occurred. Arab and
Persian merchant mariners founded the port of
Mogadishu in the 10th Century and subsequently
Merca, Brava, Kismayu, Lamu, Kilwa and other
settlements further to the south. First the Hawiya

HISTORY

While early civilizations were flourishing in the lower Nile Valley several
thousand years ago, there was a migration
southward into this region. Most of these
early settlers were Cushites of caucasoid

338

Cushite clan near Mogadishu and in the ensuing years most others adopted the Muslim faith. In the 16th Century the area bordering the Gulf of Aden was part of the Turkish Ottoman empire. The Portuguese controlled the coastal centers in the south but were driven out early in the 18th Century by the Omani Arabs who gained control of the coast from Zanzibar and Mombasa to Mogadishu. Through all this activity the Somali peoples remained divided. At the height of the colonial era at turn of the 19th Century the Somalis were ruled by three European powers—France, Britain and Italy—and Ethiopia, in five separate regions. By mutual agreement, Italian and British Somaliland were united and given their independence as the united Republic of Somalia in 1960, while French Somaliland became the independent Republic of Djibouti in 1977. Somalis continue to live in Kenya's North-West Frontier province and in Ethiopia's Ogaden desert. After a brief period of democracy, the Republic of Somalia fell under the power of General Mohammed Siad Barre, who nationalized the economy as part of his economically disastrous policy of "scientific socialism."

RECENT DEVELOPMENTS

In 1977 Barre attempted to distract attention from his domestic failures by sending army units to help Somali rebels trying to take over Ethiopia's Ogaden with the help of Cuban troops An estimated one million ethnic Somalis sought refuge in Somalia from war and droughts. In 1991 the Majerteen and Hawiye clans formed the United Somali Congress (USC) and forced Barre to flee. Once in control of Mogadishu, the USC found itself split between two warlords, triggering another internal battle. Intervention by US and UN troops to enforce a peace and oversee the delivery of international food and medical supplies to refugees saved numerous lives but ended in political failure. The fighting resumed in 1995 after the foreign forces evacuated. In the early nineties Somaliland (primarily former British Somaliland) seceded from Somalia. So did Puntland in the northeast along the Horn of Africa. While both lay claim to greater stability than the rest of the country neither has been recognized internationally.

GOVERNMENT

In August 2000 a Somalia parliament was convened in neighboring Djibouti to elect a new president, Abdulkassim Salat Hassan. Despite recognition of this transitional government by several neighboring countries, Somali warlords in

FAST FACTS

Pres. Abdullahi
Yusuf Ahmed
Born: Dec. 15,1934
Since 2004

POLITICAL

Head of State	Abdullahi Yusuf Ahmed
Prime Minister	Ali Mohamed Ghedi
Independence	1 July 1960
Capital	Mogadishu
Official language	Somali

PHYSICAL

Total area	246,200 sq. miles 637,660 sq. km. (± Texas)
Arable land	2% of land area
Coastline	1,880 miles/3,025 km

POPULATION

Total	8.86 million
Av. yearly growth	2.85%
Population/sq. mile	29
Urban population	3.9 million
Adult literacy	37.8%

ECONOMY

Currency	Somali shilling (US$1=1,842)
GDP (real)	N/A
GDP growth rate	2.4%
GDP per capita[1]	N/A
GDP (ppp)[2]	$4.6 billion
GDP per cap. (ppp)	$600
Inflation rate	N/A
Exports	$241 million
Imports	$576 million
External debt	$3 billion

1. Atlas method.
2. See page 175 for an explanation of purchasing power parity (ppp).

Mogadishu and the breakaway regions of Somaliand and Puntland did not. In October 2004, after a further two years of negotiations in neighboring Kenya, an interim-parliament—the Transitional Federal Parliament—elected Abdullahi Yusuf, a military strongman and president of the Somali semi-autonomous region of Puntland, president of Somalia. Unlike his predecessors who have emerged from similar peace initiatives, Yusuf was recognized by most of Somalia's warlords. He appointed Ali Mohamed Ghedi as prime minister to strengthen his base in the capital, Mogadishu. Yusuf 's daunting task is to lead this chaotic country towards new elections under a new constitution in five years' time. The Transitional Federal Government has been challenged by the Union of Islamic Courts (IUC) from its stronghold in Magadishu. The IUC includes some hard-line Jihadi Islamists in its ranks.

ECONOMIC POLICY

The continuing power struggle in and around the former capital, Mogadishu, and along the routes of communication has severely impeded serious economic planning.

SECTORS

A large section of the population consists of nomads who depend on livestock for their livelihood. Agriculture accounts for about two-thirds of GDP. The major cash crop is bananas. Also grown are cotton, sugar cane, sorghum and maize. Northern Somalia is the world's largest source of incense and myrrh. With the longest coastline in Africa, Somalia's fishing industry is relatively undeveloped. Mining is confined to the commercial extraction of salt and gypsum but there are reserves of iron ore, uranium, beryl and columbite. Somalia has the world's largest reserves of gypsum hydrite. Despite the continuing anarchy the country's service sector continues to grow. Modagishu offers a variety of goods ranging from exotic imported foods to the newest electronic gadgets— as well as Africa's lowest international wireless call rates.

BUSINESS ACTIVITY

AGRICULTURE
Bananas, sorghum, corn, sugar cane, mangoes, sesame seeds, beans, cattle, sheep, goats, fish.

INDUSTRIES
Small industries, including sugar refining, textiles , petroleum refining (shut down).

NATURAL RESOURCES
Uranium.

EXPORTS
$241 million (2004): livestock, bananas, hides, fish, charcoal, scrap metal.

IMPORTS
$576 million (2004): manufactures, petroleum products, foodstuffs, construction materials.

MAJOR TRADING PARTNERS
UAE, Djibouti, Kenya, Yemen, Brazil, Oman, Bahrain, India.

DOING BUSINESS WITH SOMALIA

▶ INVESTMENT

Once peace is restored, foreign activity in oil exploration and mining is bound to follow. A large number of minerals have been discovered, including gold, gypsum, iron ore, kynite, lead barite, limestone piezo-quartz, tin, sepiolite titaniferous sand, and uranium. To date, only limestone and gypsum deposits have been exploited commercially. The recovery of gas reserves in the Ogaden region of Ethiopia and oil across the Red Sea in North and South Yemen spurred interest in Somalia on the part of Chevron, Conoco, Exxon Mobil and others. Since the disintegration of Somalia most of this activity ceased but the self-proclaimed Somaliland Republic has recently indicated that oil prospecting contracts signed by the former government of united Somalia in its region would be honored. Telecommunications and fishing are future prospects.

▶ TRADE

The only potential sales to most of Somalia at this stage are in food and other supplies to UN and other agencies involved in relief programs.

▶ FINANCING

Most of Somalia's international financing consist of humanitarian assistance and disaster relief with UN agencies and some NGO programs involved.

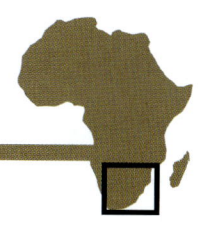

SOUTH AFRICA

RATED BY THE UN AS ONE OF THE WORLD'S 26 INDUSTRIALIZED NATIONS AND BY THE US COMMERCE DEPARTMENT AS ONE OF A FEW SELECT BIG EMERGING MARKETS (BEMS), SOUTH AFRICA OFFERS GREAT POTENTIAL FOR EXPORTERS AND INVESTORS WITH THE RIGHT PRODUCTS, RESOURCES AND COMMITMENT. SOUTH AFRICA HAS A SUBSTANTIAL AND SOPHISTICATED MARKET WITH SIGNIFICANT GROWTH POTENTIAL, WELL-DEVELOPED FINANCIAL INSTITUTIONS AND CAPITAL MARKETS, FIRST-RATE COMMUNICATION AND TRANSPORT LINKS AND READILY AVAILABLE ELECTRICAL POWER AND RAW MATERIALS. IT OFFERS EASY ACCESS NOT ONLY TO NEIGHBORING MARKETS BUT ELSEWHERE IN AFRICA. IN AREAS SUCH AS MINING, INFORMATION TECHNOLOGY, PAPER PRODUCTION AND BEVERAGES SOUTH AFRICAN COMPANIES HAVE BECOME MAJOR INTERNATIONAL PLAYERS.

COUNTRY PROFILE

The Republic of South Africa at the southern tip of the African continent comprises 1,219,090 sq. km. or 470,893 sq. miles (including two island possessions more than 1,920 km/1,193 miles southeast of Cape Town—Prince Edward and Marion. The country is within the subtropical high pressure belt and wide expanses of ocean have a moderating influence on the climate. More than 76% of the population is of black African heritage; some 12.7% whites; 8.5% Colored; and 2.5% East Indian. Two-thirds of black South Africa belongs to the Nguni group and speak Xhosa, Zulu, Swazi and Ndebele. The rest belongs to the South, North and West Sotho (Tswana), the Tsonga, and the Venda. The Coloreds are a mixed race and Indians are the descendants of indentured laborers brought to Natal by Britain in the 1860s to work on sugar plantations. Forebears of the Afrikaners and English-speaking whites came from the Netherlands, France and Britain in the 17th and early 19th centuries, and, more recently, Germany, Portugal, Italy, Greece and other European countries. There is also a sizeable Chinese community. Next to English and Afrikaans, nine major Bantu languages enjoy official status. South African society is predominantly Christian but there are also sizeable minorities of Muslims, Jews and Hindu.

HISTORY

The region is said to have been occupied by small nomadic groups of San or Bushmen hunter-gatherers 100,000 years ago. Some 2,000 years

Map Legend:
- Rail
- Highways

Kilometers 0 — 480
Miles 0 — 300

ZIMBABWE
BOTSWANA
NAMIBIA
MOZAMBIQUE
SWAZILAND
LESOTHO

Messina
Louis Trichardt
Palaborwa
Pietersburg
Kruger National Park
Skukuza
Kalahari Gemsbok Park
Mafikeng
PRETORIA
Nelspruit
Vereeniging
Johannesburg
Klerksdorp
Sishen
Kroonstad
Hluluwe Park
Upington
Welkom
Kimberley
Ladysmith
Richards Bay
Alexander Bay
BLOEMFONTEIN
Pietermaritzburg
Port Nolloth
Kenhardt
De Aar
Aliwal North
Durban
Springbok
Victoria West
Middelburg
Port Shepstone
ATLANTIC OCEAN
Calvinia
Umtata
Vanrhynsdorp
Cradock
Bisho
Port St. Johns
Saldanha
Beaufort West
Worcester
Graaff Reinet
East London
CAPE TOWN
Cape Point
Mossel Bay
Knysna
Port Elizabeth
Cape Agulhas
Bredasdorp
INDIAN OCEAN

24°S
24°E
28°E
32°E
20°E

© Business Books Intl.

341

FAST FACTS

Pres. Thabo Mbeki
Born: June 18, 1942
Since 1999

POLITICAL

Head of State	Pres. Thabo Mvuyelwa Mbeki
Ruling Party	ANC
Main Opposition	Democratic Alliance
Independence	31 May 1910
Freedom Day	27 April 1994
Capitals	Pretoria Cape Town, Bloemfontein
Official languages	English & 10 others

PHYSICAL

Total area	470,691 sq. miles 1,219,090 sq. km. (2 x Texas)
Arable land	12% of land area
Coastline	1,738 miles/2,798 km

POPULATION

Total	44.19 million
Av. yearly growth	-0.4%
Population/sq. mile	92
Urban population	26.2 million
Adult literacy	86.4%

ECONOMY

Currency	Rand (R)(US$1=6.75)
GDP (real)	$187.3 billion
GDP growth rate	4.9%
GDP per capita[1]	$5,075
GDP (ppp)[2]	$533.2 billion
GDP per cap. (ppp)	$12,000
Inflation rate	4%
Exports	$50.9 billion
Imports	$52.97 billion
External debt	$29.97 billion
Unemployment	26.6%

1. *Atlas method.*
2. *See page 175 for an explanation of purchasing power parity (ppp).*

ago they were gradually displaced by the pastoral Khoi or Hottentot and 1,500 years ago migrant Bantu entered the region from the north-central part of the continent. Portuguese explorer Bartholomeu Dias was the first European to set foot on South African soil in August 1487. It was, however, only on 6 April 1652 that a small group of Dutch under command of Jan van Riebeeck of the Dutch East India Company settled at the Cape. In 1689 they were joined by French Huguenots who developed the settlement into a notable wine producer. Britain took control of the Cape in 1806. The new British settlers aligned themselves with the Dutch frontiersmen. However, relations between the British authorities and the Boers (farmers)—as these descendants of the original Dutch and French settlers called themselves—were strained. The Boers trekked north and established their own independent Republics of the Transvaal and the Orange Free State. After their defeat by Britain in the Anglo-Boer War of 1899-1902 both Boer Republics were ruled from Westminster for eight years until 31 May 1910 when, together with the Cape and Natal colonies, they received independence as part of the Union of South Africa. Until 1994 the country was ruled by a succession of white governments applying segregation in one form or another. Beginning in 1912 the African National Congress (ANC) represented much of the disenfranchised black majority. In 1960s, the ANC abandoned its non-violent stance at the insistence of leaders such as Nelson Mandela, Walter Sisulu and Govan Mbeki. With most of these leaders later convicted and jailed at Robben Island, the ANC continued its struggle from abroad. The decision in 1990 by President F.W. de Klerk to scrap apartheid and negotiate a new South Africa with Mandela and his comrades led to the first free elections on 24 April 1994. The ANC won and Nelson Mandela became president. After his retirement in 1999, Deputy President Thabo Mbeki led the ANC to victory and assumed the presidency. He scored another major victory in 2004.

GOVERNMENT

Parliament consists of a National Assembly with 400 members elected on a proportional basis, and a National Council of Provinces (NCOP), consisting of 54 permanent members and 36 special delegates representing provincial interests. The President, formally elected by the National Assembly, is both the Head of State and leads the Cabinet. He serves for a maximum of two five year terms. Each of the nine provinces has its own legislature of between 30 and 80 members and is headed by a premier representing the majority party. In the April 2004 election the ANC captured almost 70% in the national parliament with 279 seats against 50 for the largely white Democratic Alliance led by Tony Leon and 28 for the Inkatha Freedom Party (IFP) headed by Zulu Chief Mangosuthu Buthelezi. The New National Party (NNP), as the successor of the once dominant National Party of the apartheid era, managed to capture less than 2% of the popular vote for 7 seats. A few months later the leadership finally disbanded the party and joined the ANC. Smaller parties include the United Democratic Movement (UDM) (9), Independent Democrats (7), the *Vryheidsfront* (Freedom Front) (6), the United Christian-Democratic Party (UCDP) (3), and the Pan African Congress of Azania (PAC) with 3 seats.

ECONOMIC POLICY

The South African government sees its broad goals as the creation of a strong, dynamic and balanced economy; the elimination of poverty; meeting the basic needs of every South African; development of human resources; protection against racial or gender discrimination in hiring, promotion or training; the development of a prosperous and balanced regional economy in southern Africa; and integration into the world economy. Its Growth, Employment and Redistribution (GEAR) macroeconomic strategy set specific goals in all spheres of economic activity, ranging from gross domestic product growth to budget deficits, interest rates, inflation and job creation. Even though the country has fallen short in terms of GDP growth and job creation, it held its own on inflation and deficit targets. The government continues to receive good ratings from Moody's, Standard & Poors, Fitch and other rating agencies.

SECTORS

South Africa has a modern, well-diversified economy. Agriculture contributes about 4.5% of the gross domestic product (GDP) and accounts for 13% of the total employment. Mining and mineral process-

ing—even though they have been outstripped by manufacturing in recent years—remain vital to the economy. They still make an 8% direct contribution to GDP and employ more than half a million. South Africa's mineral wealth is found in diverse geological formations. The Witwatersrand Basin around Johannesburg yields 98% of South Africa's gold output while the Bushveld Complex, spanning the North-West and Mpumalanga provinces, contains the world's largest reserves of platinum group minerals (PGMs), chromium, vanadium, nickel, fluorspar and andalusite, apart from substantial supplies of antimony, asbestos, diamonds, coal, fluorspar, phosphates, iron ore, lead, zinc, uranium, vermiculite and zirconium. Both South Africa's fishing and forestry industries have developed into key economic players on the domestic scene and important currency earners. The sophistication of its manufacturing industry places South Africa in the company of the world's thirty top industrial nations. Nearly 32% of GDP is derived from secondary industry and policy-mak-

Red carpet at the SA Parliament for UN Secretary General Kofi Annan in 2006

UNDPI

343

ers are devoting particular attention to sound, accelerated development of this sector. South Africa manufactures a wide range of consumer goods, including food products, textiles, footwear and clothing, metal and chemical products, and paper and paper products. The production of capital goods such as machinery, transport and electrical equipment is also expanding. In 1997, manufacturing, electricity, gas, water and construction contributed almost a third of the nation's total GDP, compared to agriculture's 4.5% and mining's 7.8%. South Africa's modern and extensive transport system places it in the company of top industrialized nations. A number of countries in southern Africa use this network to move their imports and exports. In the past the government has assisted strategic undertakings with subsidies and preferential treatment, including ADE (diesel engines), SASOL (synthetic fuels and petrochemicals), IDC (Industrial Development Corporation), CSIR (Scientific and Industrial Research), Mossgas, the Strategic Fuel Fund, and Soekor (oil and gas exploration). Since the mid-nineties, however, the trend has been to privatize.

PRIVATIZATION

Under a "National Framework Agreement" (NFA), government, business, and labor agreed to a substantial program of restructuring and privatization of state assets. Partially or fully privatized so far are the Airports Company, six radio stations of the state-owned SA Broadcasting Corporation, Telkom (the national telecommunications company), and South African Airways (SAA). The two biggest deals to date are the sale of 30% percent of Telkom SA to a consortium of SBC Communications of the US and Telekom Malaysia for $1,261 million and the sale of 20% of SAA to Swissair for $230 million. Deals in the offing involve an additional stake in Telkom and the restructuring of Denel (a defense contractor), Eskom (a power utility), and Transnet (the country's major transport group). So far the government has managed to overcome opposition from the strong trade unions movement, COSATU, and the South African Communist Party.

INVESTMENT

The US tops the list of major foreign investors including Britain, Malaysia , Germany and Japan with. In the megadeal section, the US telecommunications giant SBC Communications ranks a close second on the FDI list to Malaysia's

Petronas. Dow Chemicals, Coca-Cola, IBM, Salem, Goodyear, Duracell, Ford and McDonalds are other big US investors. Main sectors for investment are telecommunications, energy and oil, automobile manufacturing, food and beverages, chemicals and plastics and mining. Dow Chemical's takeover of Sentrachem for $850 million in the late nineties is the largest single outright purchase of a South African private company in recent years. During the past six years, however, direct investment abroad by South African multinational firms has outpaced FDI inflows. South Africa has also become the largest source of investment not only in neighboring SADC nations but much of the rest of Africa.

TRADE

Significant trading partners are the US, United Kingdom, Germany,Japan, Italy and France. The U.S. and South Africa signed a Trade and Investment Framework Agreement (TIFA)—the first in Sub-Saharan Africa. The US is a major supplier of wheat and rice to South Africa and accounts for more than 10% of the country's total agricultural imports. The US also has a significant share of the growing market for high technology equipment, computers and software, and machinery. As a result of the liberalization of its economy, South Africa's ratio of trade in goods and services to gross domestic product increased from to 65%.

ECONOMIC EMPOWERMENT

Increasingly both foreign and local companies are seeking Black Economic Empowerment partners to secure good working relationship with other entrepreneurs in the private sector and to secure approval in lucrative government tenders. In terms of the Broad-Based Black Economic Empowerment Act of 2003 companies doing business with the government are obliged to promote black advancement in business. Black equity in public companies was estimated at 9.4% in 2002 compared with 3.9% in 1997 and was virtually non-existent before 1994. The number of previously disadvantaged individuals (PDIs) on the boards of public companies grew from 14 (1.2%) in 1992 to 438 (13%) in 2002. The overall goal is to attain a black share in the economy of between 25 and 30% in 2014. The various sectors of industry in South Africa are setting their own targets in accordance with their own specific needs. In the mining, petroleum, maritime, tourism and financial sector charters declared so far set an average target of 25% black ownership in the next decade. The government has been at great pains to try and reassure multinationals that they are not required to give away shares to BEE partners to do business in South Africa. All BEE deals, the government insists, should take place at market value or at most a 10 percent discount. It is evident, however, that any company that does not conform to BEE practices drastically reduces its chances of doing business in South Africa.

FINANCIAL SECTOR

The South African Reserve Bank (SARB) oversees a world-class banking system comprising 56 fully licensed institutions and 60 representative offices of foreign banks. The JSE Securities Exchange is Africa's largest and ranked 18th worldwide in terms of market capitalization in 2003 with 426 companies valued at close to $268 billion. Trading volume of $102 billion placed it 23 worldwide. The JSE offers screen trading through its Johannesburg Equities Trading (JET) system. Its Share TRAnsactions Totally Electronic (STRATE) system eliminates paper transactions by making settlement and the transfer of ownership of scrip possible through electronic book entry. The JSE accounts for more than 93% of the total portfolio equity flows into Sub-Saharan Africa. In 1995 the JSE began permitting banks and foreign firms to join its registry. Foreign trade accounts for a sizeable portion of the daily volume.

SOPHISTICATION

The level of sophistication of South Africa can best be judged by looking at the size of the top one hundred companies and tracing the success that its private sector has had in capturing world market share not only in mining and minerals but manufacturing and information technology. Notable among these are Sappi, which leads the world in the production of fine coated paper and dissolving pulp. Headquartered in Johannesburg, with manufacturing operations in eight countries on three continents and customers in more than a hundred countries, Sappi is listed on both the London and New York Stock Exchanges. Other South African giants include South African Breweries which ranks second worldwide and operates breweries in the US, Africa and Europe, and Anglo American and Billiton that dominate mining around the globe. South Africa's Datatec and Didata that have become world players in information technology.

KEY PARTNERS

The Development Bank of Southern Africa (DBSA) works with donors and partners at international, national and regional levels on targeted infrastructural and strategic developments. It is playing an increasingly important role in the Southern African Development Community (SADC). The state-run Industrial Development Corporation is another potential partner for investors who seek to establish manufacturing plants in South Africa. The IDC gets involved with startups and disengages once the undertaking is up and running. In the past it has stood midwife to many a major industrial undertaking in the country.

TAXES & TARIFFS

With the exception of mining companies which are subject to special rates, the corporate tax rate is 30%. A secondary tax on companies (STC) is imposed at a rate of 12.5% on the net dividends and withholding taxes are levied on interest and royalties paid to non-residents. A 14% value-added tax (VAT) applies on all sales. Exports are zero-rated, and no VAT is payable on imported capital goods.

BUSINESS ACTIVITY

AGRICULTURE
Corn, wheat, sugar cane, fruit, vegetables, beef, poultry, mutton, wool, diary products.

INDUSTRIES
Mining (world's largest producer of platinum, gold, chromium), automobile assembly, metalworking, machinery, textiles, iron and steel, chemicals, fertilizer, foodstuffs.

NATURAL RESOURCES
Gold, diamonds, platinum, uranium, coal, iron ore, phosphates, manganese.

EXPORTS
$50.9 billion (est. 2005): gold, diamonds, other minerals and metals, food, chemicals, manufactured goods.

IMPORTS
$52.97 billion (est. 2005): machinery, transport equipment, chemicals, petroleum products, textiles, scientific instruments.

MAJOR TRADING PARTNERS
US, UK, Germany, Italy, Japan, France, China, Saudi Arabia, Iran.

DOING BUSINESS WITH SOUTH AFRICA

▶ INVESTMENT

Since 1994 steps have been taken to make South Africa more attractive to foreign investment by reducing import tariffs and subsidies to local firms; eliminating discriminatory non-resident shareholders tax; removing remaining limits on hard currency repatriation; reducing by half secondary tax on corporate dividends; lowering the corporate tax rate on earnings to 30 percent; and allowing foreign investors 100 percent ownership. Foreign investors are not screened or subjected to performance or other special requirements. The government, however, encourages investments that will strengthen, expand, or enhance technology in various industries.

Foreign firms are entitled to the same export incentive programs, tax allowances and other trade regulations applicable to domestic enterprises. As the Government pushes ahead with plans to attract strategic equity partners for its large parastatal organizations, there is an increased sensitivity to the concerns of foreign investors. In terms of Black Economic Empowerment goals investors are well advised to partner with local previous disadvantaged individuals (PDIs)—black, Colored and Indian—as it will enhance their chances of qualifying for lucrative government contracts. In fact, most local private companies tend to require a good measure of black economic empowerment in dealing with other enterprises. This is simply good business. Incentives and assistance are available to both locals and foreigners under the Small/Medium Manufacturing Development Program (SMMDP). Major areas for investment have been in telecommunications, energy and oil, motor and components, food and beverages, chemicals and plastics, mining, manufacturing and hotels. A Government program of Spatial Development Initiatives (SDIs) has enhanced investment opportunities outside the major industrial centers. An official agency, Investment South Africa (ISA), provides information and assistance to prospective investors, helps identify opportunities, and assists them in finding joint venture partners and obtaining technology and capital. Franchising is an established practice. The Department of Trade and Industry must approve manufacturing royalties.

▶ TRADE

Rapid development and expansion of telecommunications, large new pollution and waste management systems, increased use of computers and high technology devices, modernization of airports, the introduction of managed health care

and a growing market for security systems are only a few areas where American products have found ready acceptance in recent years. The US remains a major exporter of agricultural products and current estimates indicate that for the medium term South Africa will continue to rely in part on imports to meet its food needs. Principal imports for include wheat, corn, rice, vegetable oils and a variety of consumer-oriented food products. Prospective exporters to South Africa from industrial nations find that this country replicates on a smaller scale their own domestic market, both in product preference and marketing methods.

At the same time, US importers have been able to purchase sophisticated local manufactures and sold them back into the US market at handsome profits. Lately the rapidly growing tourism sector has provided a market for US suppliers of information systems, marketing, design, architecture, finance and management planning. E-commerce is expected to play a significant role in future business. South Africa is an extremely competitive marketplace and it is essential that exporters provide adequate servicing, spare parts, and components, as well as qualified personnel capable of handling inquiries. It is common to appoint a single agent or distributor capable of providing national coverage either through a single office or a network of branch offices and outlets. South Africa is an ideal springboard for trading with the 13 other countries of the Southern African Development Community (SADC) and the neighboring members of the South African Customs Union (SACU).

▶ TRADE FINANCE

All Eximbank programs are available to US exporters of goods and services to South Africa. South Africa's sophisticated financial sector provides overdraft facilities and short- to long-term credit. Key areas of business for foreign banks include trade finance, letters of credit, foreign exchange activities and services to offshore investors.

▶ SELLING TO THE GOVERNMENT

Not only the central government but nine provincial governments and hundreds of local authorities present a market for overseas suppliers of sophisticated goods and services. Government purchasing is done through competitive bidding on tenders published in the State Tender Bulletin and some of the leading newspapers. A local agent is needed to act on behalf of foreign bidders. When selling to the government, consideration should be given to the government's goal to expand black participation in the economy. Even though there are no set rules pressure is growing to include "set-asides" for black businesses. In doing business with South Africa a foreign enterprise should seriously consider black partners. In some large-scale infrastructural projects a Black Economic Empowerment (BEE) partner is mandatory. The government's Industrial Participation Program (IPP) mandates a countertrade/offset package for all state and parastatal purchases of goods, services, and lease contracts above $10 million. Under this program, bidders on governmental and parastatal contracts must submit an industrial participation package worth 30 percent of the imported content value. The bidder has seven years to fulfill this obligation.

▶ EXCHANGE CONTROLS

Exchange controls are administered by the South African Reserve Bank's (SARB) Exchange Control Department through commercial banks that are authorized to deal in foreign currency. In March 1997, the Finance Ministry started to relax foreign exchange controls. Royalties, software license fees, and certain other remittances to non-residents still require the approval of the SARB.

▶ LEGAL RIGHTS

An independent judiciary allows full recourse without political interference in disputes over property or any other facet of business. Patents may be registered for 20 years and trademarks for 10 years, renewable for an additional 10 years. While South African IPR laws and regulations are largely TRIPS-compliant, there is still concern over copyright piracy and trademark counterfeiting and the US is working with the government to find ways of reducing infractions.

▶ PARTNERSHIPS

In looking for partners, foreign firms have a range of choices between sophisticated large, medium-sized and smaller entities. Often the choice is determined by prevailing politics which favor black enterprise participation in government contracts. The government has leaned towards Private Public Partnerships (PPPs) in some projects, inviting foreign firms to enter in a joint venture with the authorities. It also makes good sense for foreigners with designs on the regional SADC market and other areas of Africa to join forces with South African firms with extensive local knowledge.

▶ ESTABLISHING A PRESENCE

South Africa's Companies Act provides for clear, transparent regulations concerning the establishment and operation of businesses. Foreign investments are organized under the same rules and regulations as domestic firms with one exception: overseas companies may opt to operate as "external companies" which do not pay tax on undistributed profits. Share capital duty is based instead on the shares of the parent firm. Foreigners may normally buy into local firms without limitation, either by acquiring shares or assets. There is no record of any expropriation or nationalization of American or any other foreign investment in South Africa.

▶ FINANCING PROJECTS

The Development Bank of Southern Africa and the Industrial Development Corporation assist in the financing of projects involving local partners. The Overseas Private Investment Corporation backs and insures US projects in South Africa. The US Trade and Development Agency funds feasibility studies, consultancies, training programs, and other project planning services in the area. Under current exchange controls foreigners need special permission to borrow locally as part of an effort to prevent excessive "gearing" through local financing. The World Bank's International Finance Corporation has established the Africa Enterprise Fund (AEF) to finance projects ranging from $100,000 to $1.5 million at market interest rates.

▶ LABOR

The government has promised to review labor legislation in response to complaints that the South African labor market is over-regulated. Unemployment rates are highest among black South Africans (29%), followed by Coloreds (16%), Indian (10%), and Whites (4%). Nearly 35% of the workers belong to unions . The strongest among them, the 1.8 million member Congress of South African Trade Unions (COSATU), is a full partner in the ANC governing alliance. Even though strike activity has declined sharply under the ANC-led government, COSATU and others have not been slow at using mass stayaways for political purposes.

▶ BUSINESS CLIMATE

Business customs in South Africa are similar to those in the US and Western Europe. South African business people tend to dress conservatively and those of the old school make every effort to be on time for appointments. Even though English dominates, business ignores Afrikaans at its own peril, especially if it is consumer-oriented. There is a level of language sensitivity among Afrikaners that prompts most local firms and many foreign entities to advertise and print their literature in both languages.

SUDAN

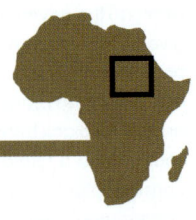

THE MINERAL AND AGRICULTURAL POTENTIAL IN AFRICA'S LARGEST COUNTRY, SUDAN, REMAINS LARGELY UNTAPPED AS FOREIGN INVESTORS AWAIT A RESOLUTION TO THE ONGOING INTERNAL STRIFE. SINCE 2004 SUDAN FOUND ITSELF UNDER PRESSURE FROM THE MAJOR POWERS AND THE UN TO STOP "GENOCIDE" IN THE DARFUR REGION. AS LONG AS IT REMAINS AT WAR WITH ITSELF, SUDAN WILL HAVE TO DEFER ITS DREAMS OF BECOMING THE BREADBASKET OF AFRICA AND THE MIDDLE EAST THROUGH LARGE SCALE IRRIGATION OF FERTILE LAND ALONG THE NILE AND ITS TRIBUTARIES. THERE HAS, HOWEVER, BEEN CONSIDERABLE FOREIGN ACTIVITY IN OIL AND MINERALS.

COUNTRY PROFILE

The Republic of Sudan spans more than 2,000 km (1,243 miles) from north to south along the Sahel Belt on the fringe of the Sahara Desert. The Arabs named the territory the territory *bilad al-sudan*—land of the blacks. Except for a few peaks such as Mount Kinyeti (3,187 m/10,456 ft) on the Ugandan border and Mount Marra (3,070 m/10,072 ft)) on its border with Chad, Sudan consists largely of plains below 1,000 m/3,280 ft). The White and Blue Nile tributaries join in Sudan to form the world's longest waterway as it flows north into Egypt. All three of the continent's major linguistic supergroupings —Afroasiatic, Nilo-Saharan and Niger-Congo—are present. More than 70% of the population is Muslim, mostly in the north. There are substantial numbers of Christians in the south. Arabic is the official language.

HISTORY

In ancient times the stretch of desert along the Nile drew Negroid people from the south and Caucasoids from the north. Based at Meroe, Nubian civilization reached its zenith in the third and second centuries BC. Sudan became an Anglo-Egyptian condominium in 1899 and gained its independence in 1956. It has been plagued since by ethnic and religious strife between the Arab Muslim rulers and largely black Christian population in Darfur region. In 2004 the United Nations focused on what the US termed genocide in Darfur. International pressure led to peace talks between the Khartoum government and the southern Sudan People's Liberation Army (SPLMA).

In July 2005 the joint appearance in Khartoum of rebel leader John Garang as Vice President of Sudan's new Government of National Unity, and Omer Hassan Al-Bashir, the President of Sudan, seemed to herald an end to the war. Hopes were dashed when Garang died a few weeks later in a helicopter crash on his way back from a visit to Uganda. Riots broke out and hostilities between the SPLA and the government forces resumed, continuing a battle that took nearly two million

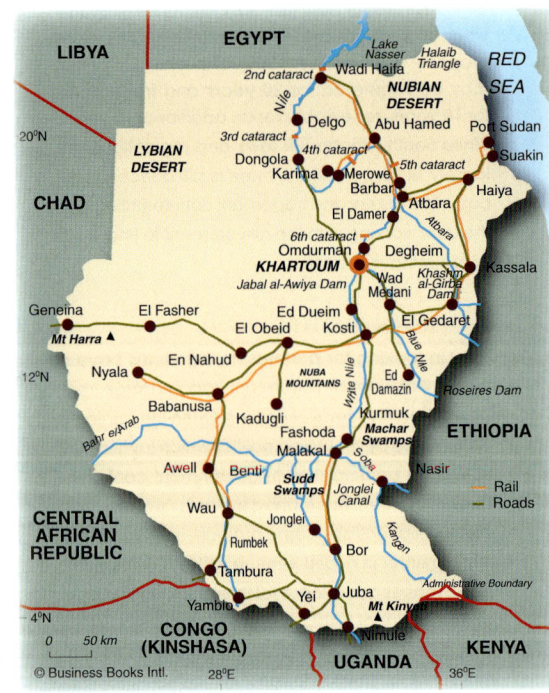

lives and left millions displaced. Darfur still remains a burning issue at the United Nations and a resolution was still not in sight at end 2006.

GOVERNMENT

A nonparty system that evolved from military rule allows for an elected executive President serving 5-year terms. He appoints vice presidents and the Council of Ministers. The 360-member National Assembly (Majlis Watani) serves 4-year terms—270 members are elected and other seats filled by presidential appointees. Of the elected seats 35 are reserved for women, 26 members for university graduates and 29 for representatives of trade unions. President Omar al-Bashir, elected in 1996, disbanded parliament three years later and declared a state of emergency. Elections were again held in December 2000 but boycotted by most opposition parties. Bashir's National Congress Party (NCP) claimed 355 of the 360 seats.

ECONOMIC POLICY

Sudan reached agreement with the IMF on a reform program aimed at streamlining investment procedures, promoting privatization, eliminating most of the non-targeted consumer subsidies, and liberalizing the foreign trade and exchange regimes. It has managed to make impressive strides in turning around an ailing economy with sound economic policies and infrastructural improvements. The government has managed to stabilize the currency.

SECTORS

Two-thirds the population depend on crop farming or grazing. With the help of several major water projects, Sudan accounts for 16% of Africa's total irrigated land. Food crops include sorghum, wheat, peanuts, dates, yams, sugar cane, and a variety of fruits and vegetables. Cotton for export is grown in the region between the Blue and White Niles. Sudan accounts for about four-fifths of the world's supply of gum Arabic and is the largest producer of sesame seeds. There is fishing along the rivers and the coast. A recently completed pipeline carries oil for export to Port Sudan. The increased oil production has given the economy a boost, enabling Sudan to show a trade surplus for the first time in recent history in 1999. Small amounts of chromium, manganese, and mica are produced. Other minerals with potential include gold, magnesite, and salt. Manufacturing involves processing of agricultural products, textile, paper mills, sugar and consumer goods.

FAST FACTS

Pres. Omar
Hassan al-Bashir
Born: January 1, 1944
Since 1989

POLITICAL

Head State	Pres. Omar Hassan al-Bashir
Ruling Party	NCP
Independence	1 January 1956
National capital	Khartoum
Official languages	Arabic

PHYSICAL

Total area	967,494 sq. miles 2,505,810 sq. km. (¼ USA)
Arable land	6.8% of land area
Coastline	530 miles/853 km

POPULATION

Total	41.24 million
Av. yearly growth	2.55%
Population/sq. mile	36
Urban population	14.3 million
Adult literacy	61%

ECONOMY

Currency	Sudanese dinar (US$1=233.33)
GDP (real)	$22.75 billion
GDP growth rate	7%
GDP per capita[1]	$776
GDP (ppp)[2]	$85.65 billion
GDP per cap. (ppp)	$2,100
Inflation rate	9%
Exports	$6.98 billion
Imports	$5.03 billion
External debt	$27.34 billion
Unemployment	18.7%

1. Atlas method.
2. See page 175 for an explanation of purchasing power parity (ppp).

PRIVATIZATION

The government has mapped out a privatization strategy and partnered with foreign oil companies in the development of oil resources.

INVESTMENT

Foreign investment focuses largely on oil exploration and exploitation in the southern region. In February 1984 Chevron suspended operations following attacks by the SPLA and in March 1990 sold its interest in the Abu Jarra field and left, leaving the field to Swedish, Malaysian, Dutch, Canadian, Saudi, Iranian and Chinese suitors, and Sudan's Sudapet. There is some US involvement in sugar cane and cotton.

TRADE

Most of Sudan's export revenues come from cotton lint and cottonseed. Other major exports are gum Arabic, sorghum, peanuts, and sesame seeds. This is bound to change as oil exports increase.

BUSINESS ACTIVITY

AGRICULTURE
Cotton, groundnuts (peanuts), sorghum, millet, wheat, gum arabic, sesame, sheep.

INDUSTRIES
Cotton ginning, textiles, cement, edible oils, sugar, soap distilling, shoes, petroleum.

NATURAL RESOURCES
Crude oil, some iron ore, copper, chrome, industrial metals, gold, uranium.

EXPORTS
$6.98 billion (est. 2005): petroleum, cotton, sesame, livestock, meat, gum arabic, sugar.

IMPORTS
$5.03 billion (est. 2005): foodstuffs, manufactured goods, refinery and transport equipment, chemicals, textiles, medicines.

MAJOR TRADING PARTNERS
China, Saudi Arabia, Germany, Japan, UAE.

DOING BUSINESS WITH SUDAN

▶ INVESTMENT

In February 2000, acting on reports of government atrocities against the local population around the newly built pipeline to Port Sudan, the US Treasury imposed sanctions on the Greater Nile Oil Project, the consortium set up to exploit the oil. China, aggressively seeking oil and other raw materials in Africa, has more than picked up the slack. China first established a presence in the unexploited Muglad oilfields of southern Sudan 10 years ago. Now it imports 50% of the region's crude oil, and 13 of the 15 most important foreign companies operating in Sudan are Chinese, from the China National Petroleum Corporation to the Zhongyuan Petroleum Corporation. More than 80% of all available concessions in oil exploration has been allotted to international companies. There is an ongoing effort to involve foreign firms in iron ore, manganese, magnesite, silver, gold, chromium ore, gypsum, mica, zinc, tungsten, copper and uranium mining. High grade deposits of gold have, however, been discovered in the Red Sea Hills, with reserves estimated at 100 tons. The expansion of Sudan's hydroelectric station at Roseires on the Blue Nile and a projected new station the 4th cataract are planned in conjunction with foreign partners.

▶ TRADE

Sudan offers opportunities to exporters of machinery, transportation equipment, metal goods, and textiles.

▶ SELLING TO THE GOVERNMENT

The $400 million Roseires dam extension project and a hydroelectric project, the Al Hamdab hydroelectric dam, provided construction contracts with foreign loan funding.

▶ FINANCING PROJECTS

There has been some progress toward normalizing Sudan's relations with international and regional financial institutions.

▶ LABOR

Most of the work force is engaged in agricultural or pastoral occupations. Some 1.75 million workers belonged to the principal trade union federation, the Sudan Workers Trade Unions Federation, until it was banned after the 1989 coup.

▶ LEGAL RIGHTS

Sudan's judicial system comprises a civil branch that handles most cases and an Islamic branch dealing exclusively with personal and family matters.

▶ BUSINESS CLIMATE

The government enforces strict adherence to the Muslim faith and the business environment conforms.

350

SWAZILAND

THE KINGDOM OF SWAZILAND—THE SECOND SMALLEST COUNTRY ON THE AF-
RICAN MAINLAND AFTER THE GAMBIA—HAS ENJOYED STEADY ECONOMIC GROWTH
THROUGH FREE MARKET POLICIES THAT ATTRACTED SIZEABLE FOREIGN INVESTMENT
FROM NEIGHBORING SOUTH AFRICA AND ABROAD. THE MONARCHY HAS BEEN UNDER
CONSIDERABLE PRESSURE FROM WITHIN AND OUTSIDE TO UNBAN POLITICAL PARTIES
AND ALLOW TRUE DEMOCRACY. WHILE PROGRESS ON THE POLITICAL FRONT MIGHT
BE SLOW, SWAZILAND CONTINUES TO STAY AMONG THE LEADERS ON THE CONTINENT
AS FAR AS ECONOMIC REFORMS ARE CONCERNED. THIS, TOGETHER WITH A GOOD
MEASURE OF STABILITY, PRESENT AN ENVIRONMENT CONDUCIVE TO INVESTMENT
AND FREE TRADE.

COUNTRY PROFILE

The Kingdom of Swaziland is a stamp-sized
country squeezed between the Drakensberg and
Lebombo mountains and bordered by South
Africa and Mozambique. Rainfall is highest in the
elevated region (more than 1,000 mm/39 inches)
and lowest in its so-called lowveld (less than 750
mm/30 inches). Four large rivers flowing from
South Africa—the Komati, Mbuluzi, Great Usutu
and Ngwavuma—provide irrigation. Several nature reserves and game sanctuaries combined
with a temperate climate, spectacular scenery

and Swazi cultural life, attract visitors. More than
80% of the population are Swazi belonging to the
Nguni-speaking peoples. Most are Christians and
English and siSwati are official languages.

HISTORY

Late in the 16th Century the Embo-Nguni
people moved into southern Africa and settled in
what is today southern Mozambique. Towards the
middle of the 18th Century, King Ngwane III led
the Dlamini and related clans across the Lebombo
Mountains into Swaziland. Culminating
with the rule of King Mswati the Dlamini
clan extended their power over an area
much larger than modern Swaziland and
became known as the amaSwati or Swazi.
In 1846 white migrants from the Cape
Colony laid claim to a large portion, insisting that Mswati II had ceded it to them
by treaty. Swazi denials were fruitless and
the kingdom continued to shrink. In 1895
Swaziland came under the administrative control of President Paul Kruger's
Transvaal Republic. The Anglo-Boer War
of 1899-1902 brought this arrangement
to an end and in 1903 Britain took over.
In 1968 Swaziland's independence was
restored under King Sobhuza who ruled
as an absolute monarch until his death
in 1982. Several of Sobhuza's 67 sons
from marriages to 100 wives engaged
in a power struggle which was eventu-

© Business Books Intl.

SOUTH AFRICA

Komatipoort
Bulembu (Havelock)
Hhohho
Tjaneni
Piggs Peak
Namaacha
Mhlume
MAPUTO
Ngwenya
MBABANE
Ezulwini
Mpaka
Goba
Mhalambanyatsi
Lobamba
Manzini
Sitela
Bhunya
Matsapa
MOZAMBIQUE
Sipofaneni
Mankayane
Big Bend
Sitobela
Hlatikulu
Nsoko
Nhlangano
Hluti
Mahamba
Lavumisa
SOUTH AFRICA
Golela
Drakensberg Mts
Lebombo Mts
INDIAN OCEAN
Rail
Road
50 km
31°E
32°E

FAST FACTS

King Mswati III
Born: April 19, 1968
Since1985

POLITICAL

Head of State	King Mswati III
Prime Minister	Absolom Themba Dlamini
Ruling Party	Elections on a non-party basis
Independence	6 September 1968
National capital	Mbabane
Official languages	English & siSwati

PHYSICAL

Total area	6,703 sq. miles 17,360 sq. km. (± New Jersey)
Arable land	11% of land area
Coastline	Landlocked

POPULATION

Total	1.14 million
Av. yearly growth	-0.23%
Population/sq. mile	162
Urban population	300,000
Adult literacy	81.6%

ECONOMY

Currency	Lilangeni (E) (US$1=6.75)
GDP (real)	$2.12 billion
GDP growth rate	1.8%
GDP per capita[1]	$2,601
GDP (ppp)[2]	$5.66 billion
GDP per cap. (ppp)	$5,000
Inflation rate	4%
Exports	$1.99 billion
Imports	$2.15 billion
External debt	$357 million
Unemployment	40%

1. Atlas method.
2. See page 175 for an explanation of purchasing power parity (ppp).

ally resolved when King Mswati III took to the throne in 1986. King Mswati has reintroduced Swaziland's old, non-party political system of Tinkhundlas—a collection of chiefdoms serving as constituencies.

GOVERNMENT

Swaziland is a modified traditional monarchy ruled by King Mswati III together with an appointed prime minister. An advisory 5-year term Parliament or *Libandla* consists of 30-seat Senate (10 members elected by the House of Assembly and 20 appointed) and the 65-seat House of Assembly (10 appointed by the monarch and 55 elected by popular vote). Political parties are banned and balloting is done on a nonparty basis and candidates are nominated by the local council of each constituency. The last election was held in 2003. The king can veto any law passed by the legislature and at times rules by decree.

ECONOMIC POLICY

With a modern infrastructure, Swaziland has attained one of the largest per capita manufacturing sectors in Africa. The government aims at further development of a modern export-oriented sector producing side-by-side with a traditional subsistence sector producing for local consumption. Swaziland's economy compares favorably with most of Africa but even though the government has taken the right steps to encourage further investment it has been, in the view of some critics, slow in responding to international pressures to introduce labor reforms. Privatization of some sectors previously dominated by the state is underway. King Mswati has taken the lead in facing up to the dangers of HIV/AIDS, which has become a major threat to the nation. It recently surpassed Botswana as the couyntry woith the world's highest known rates of infection. Apart from active campaigns to promote awareness, the king has ordered his subjects to follow his own example and that of his seven wives by undergoing routine AIDS tests.

SECTORS

More than 10% of the population is directly dependent on the sugar industry— the country's single largest employer and leading exporter. Other important crops are cotton, maize, tobacco, rice, vegetables, citrus fruits and pineapples. Swaziland has Africa's largest manmade forest covering 7% of the country's total land area and earning valuable foreign currency through the sale of wood and pulp. Iron ore, asbestos, industrial-quality diamonds and coal are being exploited. Until the late 1980s when diversification spawned textiles, footwear, beverages, sweets and beer processing, four-fifths of the industrial sector depended largely on the processing of agricultural and forestry products, sugar, cotton and meat. Tourism plays an important role in the economy.

PRIVATIZATION

The Swazi Post and Telecommunications Corporation (SPTC) is among the key state enterprises earmarked for privatization. Joint venture partners are sought for Royal Swazi National Airways and the building of a new terminal at Matsapa International Airport.

INVESTMENT

Foreign direct investment has long been a vital element in an economy favorably disposed towards outsiders. During years of sanctions against the apartheid regime in South Africa, foreign firms found a convenient escape across the border in Swaziland. With sanctions something of the past, Swaziland has continued to lure foreign entrepreneurs, among them leading South African beer, and paper and pulp conglomerates. The Central Bank does not track foreign direct investment (FDI) by sector or country but statistics indicate a preponderance of South African firms, accounting on average for 45% of the total annual inflow. British firms are second followed by the Taiwanese. There have also been modest inflows from the US, Denmark, the Netherlands, and Germany.

TRADE

South Africa—a fellow member of the South African Customs Union—accounts for 80% of Swaziland's imports and 50% of its exports. Sugar is a major export item but there has in recent years been a strong growth in the export of electronic appliances, textiles, and processed food. Swaziland experiences a large trade deficit with South Africa and has been trying to compensate for this by expanding its trade with the rest of the world. It has managed a comfortable surplus in recent years. It is likely that trade liberalization measures within the SACU and the Southern African Development Community (SADC) will lessen Swaziland's heavy dependence on South Africa. Customs duties from the Southern African Customs Union and remittances from Swazi workers in South Africa contribute largely to the economy.

FINANCIAL SECTOR

There are four commercial banks monitored by the Central Bank of Swaziland. The government-owned Swaziland Development and Savings Bank was liquidated in June 1995 and is being restructured. An exchange was established in July 1990 by Sibusiso Dlamini, a former World Bank executive who became Swaziland's prime minister, to enable ordinary Swazis to become stakeholders in their economy. It remains closely tied to the South African market and operates under similar conditions.

TAXES AND TARIFFS

Companies are taxed at 37.5% rate on profits derived from a Swaziland source. Three provisional tax payments are made and the balance is payable or refundable at the close of the tax year. Dividends are exempt from company tax but subject to a non-resident shareholders tax of 12.5% to 15%. Sales tax at 12% or 20% is charged on certain transactions, imported goods, and the sale of locally-manufactured goods and services. Interest on borrowings abroad (subject to prior approval of the Central Bank) may be remitted subject to provision for a non-resident tax on interest of 10%.

BUSINESS ACTIVITY

AGRICULTURE
Sugar cane, cotton, maize, tobacco, rice, citrus, pineapples, corn, sorghum, peanuts cattle, goats, sheep.

INDUSTRIES
Mining (coal and asbestos), wood pulp, sugar, soft drink concentrates.

NATURAL RESOURCES
Diamonds, asbestos.

EXPORTS
$1.99 billion (est. 2005): soft drink concentrates, sugar, wood pulp, cotton yarn, citrus and canned fruit, refrigerators.

IMPORTS
$2.15 billion (est. 2005): motor vehicles, machinery, transport equipment, foodstuffs, petroleum products, chemicals.

MAJOR TRADING PARTNERS
South Africa, EU, Mozambique, North Korea, Japan, UK, Singapore, US.

DOING BUSINESS WITH SWAZILAND

INVESTMENT

Four industrial areas have been set aside for special development. The principal estate is at Matsapha between Mbabane and Manzini, offering easy rail and road access to the ports of Durban and Port Richards in South Africa and Maputo in Mozambique. Incentives include tax allowances for new and existing businesses and, in the case of pioneering enterprises that bring unique operations and skills, a tax holiday of five years. Far from discriminating against foreigners, the government has been accused at times of favoring expatriate business over local entrepreneurs. In some instances overseas entrepreneurs have been able to avail themselves of government-financed research programs. Opportunities exist in sugar, wood pulp, timber, citrus, canned fruit and the manufacturing of textiles, electrical and electronic goods.

TRADE

Many foreign firms opt for assembly and distribution points in South Africa to sell computers and software, telecommunications equipment, and a range of consumer goods in Swaziland and other smaller markets in the SACU. The sugar, wood pulp, and fruit industries have in the past offered good markets for US sales of harvesting, loading, weeding, fertilizing, and irrigation equipment. The upgrading of the infrastructure continues to create demands for air traffic control and other airport equipment, road building machinery, and rolling stock for the railroads and trucks.

TRADE FINANCE

Export financing is available through Eximbank. Irrevocable letters of credit are common practice.

SELLING TO THE GOVERNMENT

Sometimes the government gives preferential treatment to local tenders. A large proportion of government contracts are filled by South African and other southern African companies. Privatization of the fixed line system, hydroelectric projects, low- and middle-income housing and railroad construction are projects where foreign participation is actively sought.

EXCHANGE CONTROLS

As a member of the Common Monetary Area, Swaziland permits repatriation of profits and dividends (after a withholding tax of 15%) upon application to the Central Bank. There are no exchange regulations affecting transactions within the CMA.

PARTNERSHIPS

US firms are noticeable in the franchising of fast food restaurants and retail stores, usually established as an extension of their South African network. In recent years, however, Swazi entrepreneurs have been insisting on cutting their own deals directly with US firms instead of going through South Africa.

ESTABLISHING A PRESENCE

Registration of either a wholly-owned foreign enterprise or a joint venture takes approximately two weeks and is usually carried out by local attorneys and accounting firms. Business sites for industrial operations are available from the Ministry of Enterprise and Employment and the Swaziland Industrial Development Corporation (SIDC).

FINANCING PROJECTS

The Overseas Private Investment Corporation, the US Trade and Development Guarantee Agency, and the Multilateral International Guarantee Agency are active in Swaziland. Project financing for infrastructure development is available through the World Bank and African Development Bank.

LABOR

An estimated 10% of the work force is employed in South Africa. Relations between organized labor and government have been strained over political issues in the past few years. After the banning of political parties, labor unions have taken on the role of activists.

LEGAL RIGHTS

Although a dual legal system comprising Roman-Dutch and customary law is a source of confusion to some foreigners, it is generally administered in a fair and reasonably swift manner. There are also traditional royal courts where the king as supreme authority adjudicates in disputes. Swaziland is in the process of tightening its patent and copyright legislation. Under new legislation, the government relies on technical assistance from the African Regional Industrial Property Organization in Harare and coverage has been extended to pharmaceutical and agricultural chemical products. An updated Copyright Act is styled after that of the World Intellectual Property Rights Organization .

BUSINESS CLIMATE

The business culture shows a strong British and South African influence.

TANZANIA

ALTHOUGH RENOWNED FOR ITS POLITICAL STABILITY, TANZANIA SUFFERED SE-
VERELY FROM THREE DECADES OF DECAY UNDER A CENTRALIZED SOCIALIST ECONOMY.
IT PROCEEDED ON THE ROAD TO RECOVERY WITH THE ELECTION OF A CAPITALIST-
MINDED DEMOCRATIC GOVERNMENT IN THE MID-NINETIES. CONSIDERING THE
DEGREE TO WHICH THIS POTENTIALLY PROSPEROUS NATION WAS ALLOWED TO SLIP
DURING THE SOCIALIST ONE-PARTY REGIME OF THE LATE PRESIDENT JULES NYERERE,
THE CHALLENGE IS QUITE FORMIDABLE. ENCOURAGING PROGRESS IN INFRASTRUC-
TURE REBUILDING AND PRIVATIZATION WITH THE HELP OF FOREIGN CAPITAL AND
EXPERTISE HAS, HOWEVER, PLACED TANZANIA AMONG THE BRIGHT PROSPECTS ON
THE CONTINENT.

COUNTRY PROFILE

The United Republic of Tanzania is a land of lakes and offshore islands. It includes the southern half of Lake Victoria, most of the eastern half of Lake Tanganyika [at depths of 1,433 m (4,700 ft) the world's deepest after Russia's Lake Baikal] and borders on Lake Malawi in the south. Its offshore areas include the densely populated spice islands of Zanzibar and Pemba and the fishing resort, Mafia Island. In the north is Africa's highest mountain, snow-capped Mount Kilimanjaro (5,896 m/19,344 ft). Rainfall inland averages 750 mm (29.5 inches). The coastal region and the islands of Zanzibar and Pemba share a humid tropical climate. The savanna plains of mainland Tanzania support a rich and diverse wildlife in at least 12 national parks, 10 game reserves and various other conservation areas. There are 120 Bantu-speaking groups, none of them large enough to dominate the rest. There are also a number of non-Bantu groups speaking Maasai, Cushitic and Khoisan languages. Influential Arab and Indian minorities reside in the coastal centers and on Zanzibar and Pemba. The 60% who do not adhere to ethnic beliefs are evenly split between Christianity and Islam. Swahili and English are official languages.

HISTORY

The discovery of the remains of the Australopithecus hominid family in Tanzania's Olduvai Gorge supports claims that this region gave birth to humanity. About 3,000 years ago Khoisan peoples entered the region, followed by caucasoid Cushites and Negroid Nilotes from the north. As long as 2000 years ago traders from Egypt (Greeks and Romans), Axum (Ethiopians), Arabia, the Persian Gulf, India and Indonesia visited the shores and around 500 AD the Bantu-speaking peoples

FAST FACTS

Pres. Jakaya Kikwete
Born: October 7, 1950
Since 2005

UNDPI

POLITICAL

Head of State	Pres. Jakaya Kikwete
Ruling Party	CCM
Main Opposition	CUF
Independence	26 April 1964
National capital	Dar es Salaam/ Dodoma[3]
Official languages	English & Swahili

PHYSICAL

Total area	364,900 sq. miles
	945,090 sq. km.
	(2 x California)
Arable land	4.5% of land area
Coastline	885 miles/1,424 km

POPULATION

Total	37.45 million
Av. yearly growth	1.83%
Population/sq. mile	97
Urban population	14.4 million
Adult literacy	78.2%

ECONOMY

Currency	Tanzanian shilling (TSh) (U$1=1,1625)
GDP (real)	$12.12 billion
GDP growth rate	6%
GDP per capita[1]	$318
GDP (ppp)[2]	$27.07 billion
GDP per cap. (ppp)	$700
Inflation rate	4.3%
Exports	$1.58 billion
Imports	$2.39 billion
External debt	$8.18 billion
Unemployment	N/A

1. Atlas method.
2. See page 175 for an explanation of purchasing power parity (ppp)
3. The National Assembly is in Dodoma but many government offices remain in the original capital, Dar-es-Salaam.

moved in from the great lakes. Portuguese explorers reached the coastal regions in 1500 and held some control until the 17th Century. Most strongholds established by the Portuguese fell into Arab hands by the early 19th Century. In 1840 Sayyid Said, the Imam of Muscat (Oman), took up residence on Zanzibar Island and established a sultanate that spanned over the entire coastal belt and associated islands of present-day Tanzania and Kenya. Homegrown spices, slaves, and ivory from the mainland were traded in Zanzibar, which eventually became a base from where the likes of Livingstone and Stanley explored. In 1871 American journalist Henry Stanley went from Zanzibar to look for Livingstone and found him at the slave depot of Ujiji (close to Kigoma) on Lake Tanganyika, using the memorable phrase, "Dr. Livingstone, I presume?" A German East African Protectorate formed in 1891 included Tanganyika and its coastal belt (formerly part of the Zanzibar Sultanate), as well as the kingdoms of Ruanda and Rundi. After Germany's defeat in World War I, Tanganyika was handed over to Britain and Ruanda-Urundi to Belgium. The Zanzibar Protectorate remained a separate sultanate under British rule. Julius Nyerere and his Tanganyika African National Union (TANU) gained independence for Tanganyika in 1961. Three years later it joined with Zanzibar in the United Republic of Tanzania and Zanzibar. Over the next 30 years Nyerere's socialist communes (ujaama) led to economic disaster. In 1984 he was succeeded by his vice president, Ali Hassan Mwinyi, who introduced some changes and in 1995 newly-elected President Benjamin Mkapa set Tanzania firmly on the road to reform. In December 2005 Mkapa was succeeded as president by Jakaya Kikwete who captured 80% of the popular vote against two opponents.

GOVERNMENT

The executive President and the Vice President of the Republic of Tanzania are directly elected by the voters for a 5-year term. Zanzibar elects its own president to handle internal affairs on the island. The unicameral 274-seat National Assembly or *Bunge* also serves for 5 years—232 members are elected by popular vote, 37 seats allocated to women nominated by the president, and five seats reserved for representatives of the Zanzibar House of Representatives. In the 2005 election Pres. Kikwete's *Chama Cha Mapinduzi* (CCM) or Revolutionary State Party captured 206 seats against the 19 won by the *Chama*

Cha Wananchi or Civic United Front (CUF). The *Chama Cha Demokrasia na Maendeleo* (Party of Democracy and Development) (CHADEMA) won 5 seats.

ECONOMIC POLICY

Tanzania has been consolidating and strengthening the tentative steps taken since 1985 to reverse the disastrous socialist policies of the past. With the assistance of the IMF, economic reforms were implemented, including cuts in state expenditure, reduction of the civil service, devaluation of the currency, privatization of state corporations and removal of price controls. Growth rates rose to a healthy 6% and inflation was drastically curbed. Bilateral donors have contributed funds to assist in the refurbishing of Tanzania's dilapidated infrastructure.

SECTORS

Even though topography limists the clutivation of crops to 4% of the total land area agriculture employs about three quarters of the working population. Together with fishing and forestry it contributes around 55% of GDP. The principal cash crops on the mainland are coffee and cotton, followed by cashew nuts, tobacco, tea and sisal. On the islands of Zanzibar and Pemba, cloves, copra, tobacco, vanilla, peppermint, rubber and seaweed are produced. Maize, millet, sorghum, cassava, rice and bananas are the main food crops. Fishing involves marine activity around the islands and freshwater catches in Lake Victoria and Lake Tanganyika. The cattle population of over 13 million is the fourth largest in Africa. Added recently to well-established supplies of gemstones such as diamonds, rubies, sapphires and a variety of semi-precious stones are discoveries of gold, nickel, copper and cobalt. There are also confirmed reserves of phosphates, graphite, uranium, niobium, titanium, vanadium and natural gas. Tourism is a major industry.

PRIVATIZATION

Most of the 150 state properties privatized are medium-sized manufacturing enterprises and trading companies. The government is, however, committed to restructuring major public utilities in telecommunications, power, water and sewerage and transport.

INVESTMENT

Since Tanzania established its Investment Promotion Center in 1990, it has approved more than a thousand projects worth some $3 billion involving investors from Britain, Germany, Italy, Thailand, India, Canada, South Africa and the US. Sectors that have attracted most of the foreign capital are manufacturing, tourism, agriculture, fisheries and mining.

TRADE

Coffee, cotton and tourism are major foreign exchange earners together with diamonds and a variety of other minerals. The US share of Tanzania's imports is modest but growing.

FINANCIAL SECTOR

After nearly 25 years of government monopoly, legislation was passed in August 1991 to allow private banks back into Tanzania. Banking reforms since have encoujraged private sector growth and investment.

TAXES AND TARIFFS

Steps are underway to harmonize differing tariff rates on the mainland and in Zanzibar. In 1995, the government introduced a uniform tax of 5% on imported capital goods, thereby rationalizing (and encouraging) investment across the board.

BUSINESS ACTIVITY

AGRICULTURE
Coffee, sisal, tea, cotton, pyrethrum (insecticide made from chrysanthemums), cashew nuts, tobacco, cloves (Zanzibar), corn, wheat, cassava (tapioca), bananas, fruit, vegetables , cattle, sheep, goats.

INDUSTRIES
Primarily agricultural processing (sugar, beer, cigarettes, sisal twine), diamond and gold mining, oil refining, shoes, cement, textiles, wood products, fertilizer, salt, tourism.

NATURAL RESOURCES
Hydroelectric potential, phosphates, iron and coal.

EXPORTS
$1.58 billion (est. 2005): coffee, manufactured goods, cotton, cashew nuts, minerals, tobacco, sisal.

IMPORTS
$2.39 billion (est.2005): consumer goods, machinery and transportation equipment, industrial raw materials, crude oil.

MAJOR TRADING PARTNERS
China, India, South Africa, UAE, Germany, Japan, Netherlands, Kenya, UK, Belgium, Zambia, Bahrain.

Doing Business with Tanzania

▶ Investment

The Tanzania Investment Center (TIC) seeks out, directs and assists foreign investment. In designated priority areas investors are entitled to generous incentives. Opportunities range from large infrastructural projects to smaller industrial developments. Through foreign participation, internal air charter services have increased from five to more than twenty. Road reconstruction and tourism are other areas targeted by foreign investors. Foreign firms have teamed up with locals in the mining of gemstones, gold, ferrous metals and petroleum and gas exploration.

▶ Trade

Trade opportunities exist in industrial equipment, textiles and used clothing, telecommunication equipment, aircraft and parts, computers and software, corn, and soy bean and wheat, much of the latter destined for refugees from the troubled Great Lakes area who spilled across the border into Tanzania. There are a number of bonded warehouses in Dar es Salaam which serve as transit points for shipments to Uganda, Rwanda, Burundi, the Democratic Republic of Congo, Zambia, and Malawi.

▶ Trade finance

An irrevocable letter of credit confirmed by an outside bank is normal practice. Local financing is available, usually at high interest rates, while a parastatal insurance company provides cover against loss, damage and destruction.

▶ Selling to the government

Procurement is by tender boards although in certain unspecified instances the government purchases on a direct basis. Tenders are usually issued at the beginning of each calendar year. Sometimes international donor agencies help set the requirements and the rules.

▶ Exchange controls

Although Tanzania continues to be plagued by intermittent shortages of foreign exchange, the advent of exchange bureaus has made it easier to transfer profits, dividends and other investment returns.

▶ Partnerships

Several local firms rely on franchising arrangements with US firms, an arrangement that is expected to grow in popularity as Tanzania progresses into a free enterprise environment. Privatization also presents increased opportunities

for joint ventures and licensing arrangements. The use of local legal advice might be necessary to ensure that both parties in such arrangements are on the same page as misunderstandings sometimes arise due to cultural differences.

▶ Establishing a presence

In establishing a presence, foreign firms have the choice of entering into a joint venture with a local firm or creating a wholly-owned subsidiary. Both are reasonably easy to set up, especially with local legal advice and the assistance of the TIC.

▶ Financing projects

The Overseas Private Investment Corporation supports US investors. Project financing is also available from institutions such as the World Bank, Tanzania Development Finance Co. Ltd, Tanzania Investment Bank, Tanzania Venture Capital Fund, East African Development Bank, African Development Bank and the International Finance Corporation.

▶ Labor

Although labor is plentiful in Tanzania, it is largely unskilled. The few jobless but highly educated Tanzanians often lack managerial experience and need further training.

▶ Legal rights

While property rights, including intellectual property, are protected by law, enforcement might be lacking in some instances. The establishment of commercial courts is expected to expedite cases involving commercial disputes. Still, many of the antiquated provisions dating from the colonial and post-independence socialist era still need to be revised. After a long history of expropriation which culminated in 1973 with the nationalization of several European firms, Tanzania has in recent times maintained a clean record on this score. Tanzania is a member of both the International Center for Settlement of Investment Disputes and Multilateral Investment Guarantee Agency.

▶ Business Climate

Strong traces of European influences in the business community and a fluency in English might be deceptive. Americans are advised to ensure complete understanding on important issues when entering into agreements. In most cases it does help to engage a local legal adviser with past experience in international business negotiations.

TOGO

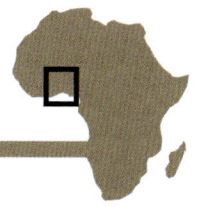

TOGO'S CAPITAL, LOMÉ, WAS ONCE THE HUB OF A REGIONAL ECONOMY BUT IN RECENT YEARS IT HAS BEEN SERIOUSLY CHALLENGED BY POLITICAL AND ECONOMIC DIFFICULTIES AND DEVELOPMENTS IN NEIGHBORING STATES. IN EFFORTS TO REGAIN ITS PROMINENCE, TOGO IS RELYING ON A SUPERIOR PORT AND AIRPORT, HIGH QUALITY TELECOMMUNICATIONS, ONE OF THE MOST LIBERAL TRADE REGIMES IN THE REGION, AND AN EXPERIENCED, VIBRANT BUSINESS COMMUNITY. KNOWN FOR ITS COFFEE, COTTON AND COCOA, AS WELL AS LARGE SUPPLIES OF PHOSPHATE, TOGO ALSO OFFERS AMPLE OPPORTUNITY FOR ENTREPRENEURS INTERESTED IN MANUFACTURING FOR EXPORT.

COUNTRY PROFILE

The Republic of Togo extends about 540 km (335 miles) inland from a narrow, 56 km (35 mile) coastline along the Bight of Benin in the Gulf of Guinea. Sandy barrier beaches separate a chain of lagoons and lakes, including Lake Togo, from the sea. Most of the land lies below 500 m (1640 ft). The southern two-thirds of the country is drained by the Mono River, flowing from the Atakora Mountains. Vegetation varies from moist savanna, oil palm plantations and patches of dense forest in the south, to dry savanna in the northern lower rainfall areas. The Ewe, including the Mina and other related groups, account for about 45% of the total population. The Kabre (Kabye), Fulani, Mande and the Gurma make up the rest. Both Ewe and Kabre have the status of national languages and are taught in the schools. The voodoo (vodun) religion is prevalent in the coastal regions of Togo and Benin from where it spread during the slave trade era to the Caribbean and the Americas. Christians and Muslims number less than half of the population.

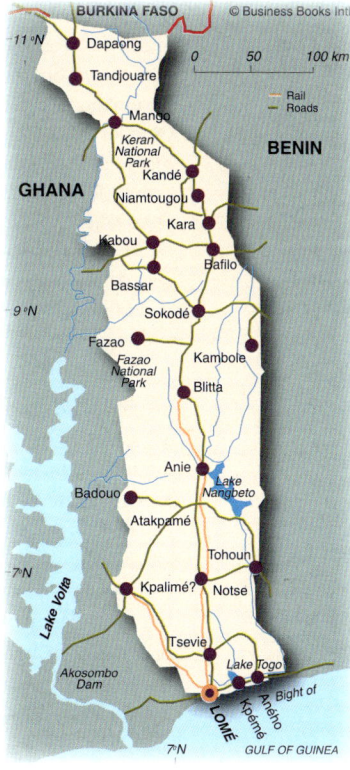

HISTORY

The Voltaic peoples and the Kwa were the earliest known inhabitants. Unlike its neighbors, ancient Togo was not an area of kingdoms but settled by refugees from the strong neighboring military states. When European traders visited these shores towards the end of the 15th Century the Ewe and the Mina were already entrenched on the coastlands and the Kabre established in the north. In the late 1880s, while the British and the French were focusing on other parts of the so-called Slave Coast, the Germans took the land of the Ewe and the Kabre by treaty. Togoland's borders were finally fixed in 1897. Although their rule was as authoritarian as that of other colonial governments, Germany turned Togoland into a model colony with good roads and railways and a well-equipped harbor at Lomé. After Germany's defeat in World War I, Togo was split into two parts. The western section was placed under British administration and the larger eastern part given to the French. A UN referendum in the mid-forties in both territories—largely boycotted by the Ewe—decided against

FAST FACTS

Pres. Faure
Gnassingbé
Born: Jun. 6, 1966
Since 2005

POLITICAL

Head/State	Pres. Faure Gnassingbé
Ruling Party	RPT
Main Opposition	RSDD
Independence	27 April 1960
National capital	Lomé
Official languages	French

PHYSICAL

Total area	21,926 sq. miles
	56,790 sq. km.
	(± West Virginia)
Arable land	46% of land area
Coastline	35 miles/56 km

POPULATION

Total	5.55 million
Av. yearly growth	2.72%
Population/sq. mile	229
Urban population	1.9 million
Adult literacy	60.9%

ECONOMY

Currency	CFA franc (CFAF) (U$1:559.44)
GDP (real)	$1.99 billion
GDP growth rate	1%
GDP per capita[1]	$354
GDP (ppp)[2]	$8.9 billion
GDP per cap. (ppp)	$1,700
Inflation rate	6%
Exports	$768 million
Imports	$1.05 billion
External debt	$2 billion
Unemployment	N/A

1. Atlas method.
2. See page 175 for an explanation of purchasing power parity (ppp).

reunification and when the Gold Coast became the independent state of Ghana in March 1957 it included British Togoland. French Togoland became the independent Republic of Togo in 1960. In 1967 the government led by the Polish-descended Nicolas Grunitzky was overthrown in a bloodless coup by Kabre army colonel Etienne Eyadema. After a few months of interim rule by a newly constituted National Reconciliation Committee Eyadema, took over as President Gnassingbé Eyadema's autocratic rule was initially marked by rapid economic growth but the 1980s were fraught with decay. Internal pressures and a threat by France to withhold economic assistance persuaded Gnassingbé to lift restrictions on opposition parties in April 1991. Gnassingbé Eyadema remained in power until his death in 2005. Parliament subsequently appointed his son, Faure, to succeed him to the post of president. After strong objections from the African Union he stepped down and called and election. Faure Gnassingbé won 60% of the popular vote over his main rival, Emmanuel Akitani Bob's 38%.

GOVERNMENT

The Constitution adopted after the 1992 referendum provides for an executive President directly elected for a term of five years, renewable once. The President appoints the Prime Minister from the majority party in the 81-member National Assembly, also elected for 5-year terms. In the October 2002 election Gnassingbé's *Rassemblement du Peuple Togolais or Rally of the Togolese People* (RPT) won 72 seats against 3 for the *Rassemblement pour le Soutien de la Démocratie et du Développement* (RSDD) or Rally for Democracy and Development. Several smaller parties captured two or one seats.

ECONOMIC POLICY

For the past decade the government has implemented economic reform measures with the assistance of the World Bank and IMF, encouraging foreign investment and trying to balance its budget. Current structural adjustment programs stress privatization and liquidation of state-owned enterprises, withdrawal of the government from commodity marketing and agricultural inputs, the streamlining of government operations, and promotion of both administrative and judicial transparency. Near term prospects are for good as increased transparency and fiscal responsibility encourages foreign involvement.

SECTORS

Agriculture employs about 80% of the working population and contributes 35% of the GDP. The main export crop is cotton, followed by coffee, cocoa, palm kernels and shea nuts. The three Cs—cocoa, coffee and cotton—currently accounts for 40% of the country's export earnings. Sugar cane and groundnuts are also grown. The country is largely self-sufficient with food crops such as rice, sorghum, millet, yams, cassava, vegetables and tropical fruit but basic foodstuffs are still imported. Livestock is important in the northern savanna regions. There is small-scale marine fishing and limited forestry. Mining activity concentrates on phosphates which account for more than a third of export earnings. Limestone, marble and salt are extracted and there are known reserves of iron ore, bauxite, dolomite and chromite. Manufacturing involves beverages, footwear, textiles and plastics. Togo has a flow of tourists from Europe.

PRIVATIZATION

The government has been working with the World Bank setting as future benchmarks the privatization of phosphate mining and telecommunications. The ginning of cotton has already been opened to private firms competing with SOTOCO, a restructured parastatal, and the agricultural commodity marketing monopoly was liquidated. Some 20 private firms have been granted marketing licenses for coffee and cocoa. The state pharmaceutical sales company lost its monopoly, allowing private competitors to enter the market with a wide range of generic drugs.

INVESTMENT

Both privatization and the establishment of export promotion zones (EPZs) have drawn foreign direct investors. In recent years foreign firms have purchased from the government an oil refinery, dairy, cement plant, brewery, spaghetti factory, flour mill, and an edible oil refinery. Toward the end of 1999 there were more than 30 firms from the US, Denmark, Germany, Norway, and Hong Kong active in Togo's EPZs, manufacturing, assembling and distributing cement, textiles, leather goods, automobiles, and petroleum products.

TRADE

Togo's major agricultural export crops are coffee, cocoa, and cotton but phosphates tops the list in terms of total foreign exchange earnings. Primary customers are France, Canada, South Africa, and the Philippines, followed by Greece, Poland, Brazil, and the US. The well-established modern harbor of Lomé serves as a convenient entry point for trade with the surrounding region. It is estimated that much more than the 30% of imports officially designated for re-export cross the border in informal trade.

FINANCIAL SECTOR

Over the years Togo developed an efficient, modern banking system to support its role as regional trading center. After the economic and political crisis years a review of the financial sector—undertaken together with the World Bank—has led to restructuring and recapitalization. However, Togo still has some way to go before it regains its reputation or position as a regional banking center. All major banks maintain correspondent relationships with US banks.

TAXES AND TARIFFS

Good progress was made towards simplifying and streamlining the tax system. The value-added tax has been unified at 18%. Import tariffs are to be set in accordance with an external tariff regime for WAEMU members. Togo has one of the most liberal tariff regimes in the CFA zone.

BUSINESS ACTIVITY

AGRICULTURE
Coffee, cocoa, cotton, yams, cassava (tapioca), corn, beans, rice, millet, sorghum, livestock, fish.

INDUSTRIES
Phosphate mining, agricultural processing, cement, handicrafts, textiles, beverages.

NATURAL RESOURCES
Marble, phosphate, limestone.

EXPORTS
$768 million (est. 2005): cotton, phosphates, coffee, cocoa, re-exports.

IMPORTS
$1.05 billion (est. 2005): machinery and equipment, consumer goods, petroleum products.

MAJOR TRADING PARTNERS
Burkina Faso, Benin, Ghana, China, Mali, India, Netherlands, UK, France.

DOING BUSINESS WITH TOGO

▶ INVESTMENT

The recently resumed privatization process is expected to attract foreign direct investment in energy, telecommunications, banking, and hotels. Togo has distinguished itself throughout the 1980s as an investor-friendly, western-oriented country but foreign interest waned during the period of political unrest. The government is trying to restore the investment levels of the past in areas such as agriculture, manufacturing, mining, and tourism. Applications are evaluated by the Planning Ministry in consultation with the National Investment Commission, which sets conditions once approved. The process takes about a month. Investors can obtain EPZ status in two designated zones entitling them to a less restrictive labor code, foreign currency-denominated accounts and tax advantages.

▶ TRADE

Togo offers a limited domestic market but a good potential in its traditional role as a transshipment point to neighboring countries. Imports include used clothing and shoes, computer equipment, cosmetic products, and wheat and meat, but as privatization proceeds the need for telecommunications and power generation equipment is expected to grow. Togo operates a free port .

▶ TRADE FINANCE

Normally irrevocable letters of credit are used. Eximbank facilitates trade. Some of the larger trade prospects involve development projects funded by the World Bank, the West African Development Bank, and the African Development Bank.

▶ SELLING TO THE GOVERNMENT

Plans to develop self-reliance in power generation and improve telecommunication will require large-scale purchases of services and equipment. Tenders will most likely be handled by the international and individual country donor agencies.

▶ EXCHANGE CONTROLS

There are no restrictions on the transfer of funds to other West African franc zone countries or to France but the transfer of funds elsewhere requires Finance Ministry approval.

▶ PARTNERSHIPS

Even though Togolese business people eagerly pursue partnerships with American and other foreign firms, most of them offer local expertise and management instead of funding. The government encourages joint ventures. Although a few US firms, including Coca-Cola, rely on licensing agreements, franchising is limited.

▶ ESTABLISHING A PRESENCE

Establishing an office in Togo is in theory relatively simple, but administrative obstacles and delays are common. If there are expatriate managers they must obtain residence permits. The authorization to open an office comes from the Ministry of Commerce. Companies also need to register with the Commercial Court and the Togolese Chamber of Commerce at a minimal fee. The final step is the purchasing of an importer's card from the Ministry of Commerce, at about $150 per year.

▶ FINANCING PROJECTS

Multilateral institutions involved in funding projects in Togo include the African Development Bank, the ECOWAS fund, the West African Development Bank, and the World Bank.

▶ LABOR

There is a large pool of qualified university graduates and unskilled workers but a shortage of workers with technical skills and practical experience. Separate wage scales are negotiated by employers, workers, and the government for industry, construction, public works, commerce, and banking. Although several labor confederations have combined forces to negotiate more effectively with the government and business, they have had limited impact.

▶ LEGAL RIGHTS

The investment code provides for the resolution of investment disputes involving foreigners under bilateral agreements with various governments or prearranged conciliation and arbitration procedures between the interested parties. Togo is a member of the International Center for the Settlement of Investment Disputes. Lack of transparency and predictability of the judiciary in the enforcement of property rights is being addressed in conjunction with the World Bank.

▶ BUSINESS CLIMATE

French is the language of business and so is the culture itself. While foreigners without a working knowledge of French might have problems conversing, deal-making should not be a problem for those who have operated in the European market. There is no shortage of professional interpreters.

TUNISIA

TUNISIA—AFRICA'S NORTHERNMOST COUNTRY—HAS ENJOYED MODERNIZATION, STABILITY AND RELATIVE PROSPERITY OVER A LONG PERIOD AND IS ARGUABLY THE MOST COHESIVE AND PROGRESSIVE SOCIETY IN THE MAGHREB REGION. WOMEN HAVE BEEN LIBERATED IN WHAT IS THE OLDEST MUSLIM STRONGHOLD ON THE CONTINENT. METRO RAILWAYS RUN ACROSS THE SITES OF ANCIENT CITIES. ITS FORMER SOCIALIST GOVERNMENT SPAWNED A MARKET-ORIENTATED ECONOMY. THIS MIDDLE-INCOME COUNTRY OFFERS A GOOD POTENTIAL FOR FOREIGN ENTREPRENEURS NOT ONLY AS A MARKET IN ITSELF BUT TO SERVE AS A CONVENIENT SPRINGBOARD TO THE EU WITH WHICH TUNISIA HAS A FREE TRADE AGREEMENT. TUNISIA IS EXPECTED TO LIFT ALL REMAINING TRADE BARRIERS WITH THE EU IN 2007.

COUNTRY PROFILE

The Republic of Tunisia, on the western side of the great Gulf of Sirte, is the smallest country in North Africa with the largest proportion of arable land. Its northern portion enjoys a Mediterranean climate with winter rainfall varying from at least 400 to over 1,000 mm (16 to 39 inches). The country's only perennial river is the Medjerda, opening into wide coastal plains around the city of Tunis. Apart from a small Berber presence, Tunisians are largely descendants of migrants who in Carthaginian times made this crossroads region their home. Their culture is predominantly Arab and the Muslim faith prevails. French is widely spoken and taught in schools.

HISTORY

More than 3,000 years ago the Phoenicians established trading posts in the region and, according to legend, in 814 BC a group of exiles under the leadership of Princess Dido fled from Tyre (in present-day Lebanon) and founded Carthage (the New City). Carthaginian colonizers in Sicily and Spain encountered Roman opposition and became embroiled in a protracted struggle known as the Punic Wars which lasted from 264 until 146 BC when Carthage was finally defeated and razed. The Romans called their conquered territory Africa, a name probably derived from Afrig (Arab: Ifriqiya), the name also given to the Berber group living to south of Carthage. Carthage was rebuilt by Julius Caesar and became an important center for Christianity in the Roman empire. Except for an interval of Vandal rule from 439-533, Carthage remained part of the Roman Empire until 669 when the Arabs invaded. After the Arabs took control of the region which they called the Maghreb, they virtually annihilated Carthage and founded the new city of Tunis. In Tunisia, as

Map labels

MEDITERRANEAN SEA

Ras ben Sekka • Bizerte
Mateur • Gulf of Tunis • Cape Bon
Tabarka
37°N
TUNIS
Ghardimaou • Beja • La Goulette • Kelibia
Mejez el Bab • Nabeul • Hammamet
El Kef
Teboursouk Mts • Dahmeni • Gulf of Hammamet
Dorsal Mts • Sousse • Mastir
Karouan • M'Saken
El Jem • Mahda
Kasserine • Sid Saad • Ksour Essaf
35°N • Gulf of Sirte
Meknassy • Sfax • Kerkkenna Isles
Shott Garsa • Gafsa
Metlaoui • La Skhira • Gulf of Gabes
Tozeur • Shott Fedjadj
Netta • Kebili • Gabes • Houmt Souk • Jerba island
33°N • Shott Djerid • Medenine • Zarzis • Rass Ajdir
SAHARA DESERT • Chenini • Ben Guerdane • Tatouine
Bir Aouin
Dehiba
Al Borma
ALGERIA
LIBYA
Rail
Roads
0 50 100 150 km
8°E   10°E   © Business Books Intl.

FAST FACTS

Pres. Zine El Abidine
Ben Ali
Born: September 3, 1936
Since 1989

POLITICAL

Head of State	Pres. Zine El Abidine Ben Ali
Prime Minister	Hamed Karoui
Ruling Party	RCD
Main Opposition	MDS
Independence	20 March 1956
National capital	Tunis
Official languages	Arabic

PHYSICAL

Total area	63,170 sq. miles 163,610 sq. km. (± Georgia)
Arable land	18% of land area
Coastline	713 miles/1,148 km

POPULATION

Total	10.18 million
Av. yearly growth	0.99%
Population/sq. mile	152
Urban population	6.5 million
Adult literacy	74.2%

ECONOMY

Currency	Tunisian dinar (TD) (U$1=1.37)
GDP (real)	$30.94 billion
GDP growth rate	4.3%
GDP per capita[1]	$2,906
GDP (ppp)[2]	$83.54 billion
GDP per cap.(ppp)	$7,100
Inflation rate	2.1%
Exports	$10.3 billion
Imports	$12.06 billion
External debt	$16.09 billion
Unemployment	14.2%

1. Atlas method.
2. See page 175 for an explanation of purchasing power parity (ppp).

elsewhere in the Mahgreb region, Berbers assimilated with the Arab rulers and adopted their faith. Tunisia became part of the Ottoman Empire in 1570. France invaded Tunisia in 1881 and ruled it as a protectorate until 1956 when a freedom movement under Habib Bourguiba finally forced it to grant independence. First as prime minister and afterwards as president-for-life, Bourguiba stayed in office until the age of 84 in 1989 when he was declared physically and mentally unfit by a panel of medical doctors. The life-presidency was subsequently abolished and an age limit of 70 years introduced. He was succeeded as president by Zine El Abidine Ben Ali who was reelected in October 2004 by an overwhelming margin of 94.5% over his closest rival, Mohamed Bouchiha, who only managed to draw 3.8% of the popular vote. By his election Ben Ali overrode the two term stipulation in the constitution adopted in the wake of Bourguiba's long tenure.

GOVERNMENT

In terms of the constitution an executive President is elected for a maximum of two 5-year terms, appoints the Prime Minister and heads the Cabinet. The bicameral parliament consists of the 189-seat Maijlis al-Nuwaab or Chamber of Deputies elected by popular vote for 5 years and the 126-seat Chamber of Advisors, serving a six year term—85 elected by municipalities, trade unions and other professional associations and the rest appointed by the president. In the 2004 election President Ben Ali's *Rassemblement Constitutionelle et Démocratique* (RCD) or Constitutional Democratic Rally won 152 of the 182 seats in the Chamber of Deputies while the *Mouvement des démocrates socialistes* or Movement of Socialist Democrats (MDS) captured 14 seats. The rest of the seats were split among four smaller parties.

ECONOMIC POLICY

Progressive policies and solid economic planning have helped to raise living standards in recent years. Privatization has proceeded slowly and involved mostly smaller enterprises. Broader privatization and the rmoval of trade barriers are sseen as a key to further accelerate growth. Tunisia has implemented two structural adjustment programs (SAPs) together, with the IMF and managed, after a long period of post-independence socialist economic stagnation, to boost GDP growth to, cutting inflation and dramatically increasing exports.

SECTORS

Tunisia has a diverse economy. Despite its modest natural resources, it has made impressive economic strides. Agriculture, fishing and forestry provide employment to a third of the workforce. One-third of the cultivated land is under olive trees, making Tunisia one of the largest producers and exporters of olive oil in the world. Tunisia is, after Morocco, the largest producer of phosphates in North Africa but the quality of the rock is poor and extraction is largely geared towards the production of fertilizer. Tunisia is one Africa's smaller oil producers, managing a modest export after supplying its domestic needs. The recent discovery of the Miskar gasfield in the Gulf of Gabes will make the country self-sufficient in natural gas and enable it to become a significant exporter. Iron ore, zinc, lead, aluminium fluoride and salt are mined. Textiles and leather goods account for about 85% of manufactured exports, with mechanical and electrical goods and chemicals growing industries. Some four million tourists (mainly from Germany and other European countries) visit the beaches, oases and historic sites each year.

PRIVATIZATION

Only the smaller among 189 public enterprises identified for privatization have been sold. Mindful of labor opposition, the government has been moving slowly. A 20% share was sold in Tunis Air and two cement plants and several semi-public firms were privatized through offerings on the stock exchange and direct sales. The tender for Tunisia's first private build-own-operate (BOO) power generation was awarded to an American-led consortium. Broader privatization is seen as a necessary step for private sector growth.

INVESTMENT

As much as 75% of foreign direct investment (FDI) has been in the energy sector, largely in petroleum exploration and development. There is, however, a growing interest in manufacturing and official statistics list some 1,600 companies fully or partially owned by foreigners. France is the largest single source of foreign investment, followed by Italy, Germany, Belgium, Switzerland and the United Kingdom. Over the past five years, however, the US has been the third-largest source of FDI and recent developments in the energy industry are expected to bolster that position further.

TRADE

Textiles and tourism are major foreign currency earners, followed by hydrocarbons, agricultural products, phosphates and chemicals. The European Union represents 80% of total trade.

FINANCIAL SECTOR

The banking system is a mixture of private and state-owned institutions comprising 13 commercial banks, 8 development banks, one savings bank, 5 portfolio management institutions, 8 leasing companies, 8 offshore banks, and 2 merchant banks. The government is still a controlling shareholder in most of these banks which are regulated by the Central Bank of Tunisia. The financial markets, consisting of a semi-privatized stock exchange and a number of bond and stock funds, showed impressive growth. To encourage firms to list on the exchange, the government introduced tax incentives, reducing the corporate tax rate from 35 to 20 percent for companies with at least 30% of their shares traded on the exchange.

TAXES AND TARIFFS

In 2007 Tunisia will form a free trade area with the EU and lift remaining protective barriers. The first phase of tariff reduction and elimination of quantitative import restrictions envisaged in the EU agreement was completed in 1996.

BUSINESS ACTIVITY

AGRICULTURE
Olives, dates, oranges, almonds, grain, sugar beets, grapes, poultry, beef, dairy products.

INDUSTRIES
Petroleum, mining (particularly phosphate and iron ore), tourism, textiles, footwear, food, beverages.

NATURAL RESOURCES
Petroleum, phosphate, iron ore.

EXPORTS
$10.3 billion (est. 2005): hydrocarbons, textiles, agricultural products, phosphates, chemicals, mechanical goods.

IMPORTS
$12.86 billion (est. 2005): machinery, hydrocarbons, food, consumer goods, textiles.

MAJOR TRADING PARTNERS
France, Italy, Germany, Spain, Libya.

DOING BUSINESS WITH TUNISIA

▶ INVESTMENT

A broad range of incentives for foreign investors includes tax relief, reduced tariffs on imported capital goods, and depreciation schedules for production equipment. Companies exporting at least 80% of their production enjoy a ten-year tax holiday. Additional incentives are available to attract investment in designated depressed areas and in sectors such as health, education, training, transportation, environmental protection, waste treatment, and research and development in technological fields. The best investment opportunities are in the infrastructure improvement (hydrocarbons, power generation, transportation, telecommunications) or in offshore, export-oriented, labor-intensive industries such as textiles and light manufacturing. Tunisia has two free trade zones—one at Bizerte and the other at Zarzis—offering tax and customs duty exemptions to manufacturers.

▶ TRADE

The best prospects for exporters are in agricultural products such as wheat, barley, livestock and meat, agricultural equipment, and luxury and durable goods. It is customary to rely on local agents and distributors. Exclusive distribution contracts are, however, forbidden by law.

▶ TRADE FINANCE

Most transactions are by irrevocable letters of credit. Reputable importers usually have no problem in obtaining the necessary financing from local bank. For US exporters Eximbank financing and insurance are available.

▶ SELLING TO THE GOVERNMENT

Government purchases are usually by tender published in the local media and sometimes in selected foreign journals. Factors that might influence the selection of bids are their contribution to the local economy and employment, the level of transfer of skills or technology, and impact on the balance of trade. US bidders have typically been stronger on price and technology while European firms have offered better financing packages and links to the local economy. Depending on the size and complexity of the project, the decision-making procedure can take several months. Decisions on major projects might even require the approval of the Chamber of Deputies, which goes into session for only about half of the year. Performance bonds of between one and ten percent are common on government contracts.

▶ EXCHANGE CONTROLS

Central bank authorization is needed for some foreign exchange transactions.

▶ PARTNERSHIPS

Even though there are examples of successful US joint ventures, many businesses are family-owned and often resist outside management. The government has blocked several proposed partnerships in department stores and restaurants.

▶ ESTABLISHING A PRESENCE

Registering an office of a foreign company in Tunisia is relatively simple. The Foreign Investment Promotion Agency (FIPA) offers a one-stop shop to investors and it generally takes about two weeks to complete the process. When it involves fisheries, tourism, transportation, communications, and other specified sectors it might take longer as government approval is needed. Foreign investors are permitted to purchase up to 49% of the shares in resident firms.

▶ FINANCING PROJECTS

OPIC provides political risk insurance and other services while the World Bank and African Development Bank support projects relating to the environment, privatization, road construction, dams and irrigation.

▶ LABOR

About 15% of the workforce belongs to the national labor confederation, the General Union of Tunisian Workers (UGTT). Working conditions are established through triennial collective bargaining agreements between the UGTT and the National Employers Association (UTICA). Tunisian law limits the number of expatriate employees per company.

▶ LEGAL RIGHTS

To ensure enforcement, foreign firms must register their trademarks and industrial designs with the Tunisian Institute for Standardization and Intellectual Property (INNORPI). Tunisia is a member of the World Intellectual Property Organization, and has signed the agreement on the protection of patents and trademarks.

▶ BUSINESS CLIMATE

Tunisia is a relatively open society that sees itself as a bridge between the European and Arab worlds. Although the official language is Arabic, French is widely spoken.

UGANDA

EMERGING UNDER NEW RULE IN 1987 FROM A LONG PERIOD OF MISMANAGE-
MENT AND POLITICAL UPHEAVAL, UGANDA HAS SINCE UNDERGONE AN IMPRESSIVE
TURNAROUND. THE UGANDAN GOVERNMENT HAS SHOWN A SINGULAR COMMITMENT
TO ECONOMIC REFORM IN LINE WITH IMF SUGGESTIONS AND A DETERMINATION TO
ATTRACT FOREIGN INVESTORS AND TRADERS THROUGH PRIVATIZATION AND OTHER
INCENTIVES. IT HAS SUBSTANTIAL NATURAL RESOURCES INCLUDING COPPER AND CO-
BALT. SOIL IS FERTILE AND RAINFALL REGULAR. AGRICULTURE IS THE MOST IMPORTANT
SECTOR AND EMPLOYS OVER 80% OF THE WORKFORCE. COFFEE ACCOUNTS FOR THE
BULK OF UGANDA'S EXPORT REVENUES.

COUNTRY PROFILE

The Republic of Uganda is situated north of Lake Victoria and consists largely of prime agricultural land. The equator cuts across the northern shores of this lake. The Victoria Nile links Lake Victoria with Lake Kyoga and Lake Albert. Much of the country is covered by moist woodland savanna, with large tracts of equatorial forest. There are 10 national parks and a number of other game and forest reserves. The largest population groups are of Nilotic origin. The Bantu-speaking people account for 20%. English is the official language, but, as elsewhere in Eastern Africa, Swahili is the lingua franca. Some 75% of the population are Christians, with Roman Catholics in the majority. Many people, mostly in the north, have ethnic beliefs.

HISTORY

About 500 BC Bantu-speaking peoples migrated to the area now known as Uganda. By the 14th Century there were three dominant kingdoms in the region—the Buganda, Bunyoro and Ankole. In the 19th Century explorers such as Richard Burton and Robert Livingstone found Uganda settled by the Nilotic peoples in the north and Bantu in the south, including the Baganda, from whom the country derived its name. In the 1890s Britain in a deal with Germany took possession of Uganda and Kenya while Germany apportioned Tanganyika (Tanzania) for itself. Independence from Britain in 1962 was followed by several decades of turmoil. Milton Obote seized power with the help of the second-in-command of the army, Colonel Idi Amin, and took Uganda down the road of nationalization before he was ousted in 1971 by Amin. Considered by many as one of Africa's most brutal leaders ever, Amin expelled the large Asian (mainly Indian) community and carried out massive purges resulting in the death of thousands. After exiled Ugandans with the help of neighboring Tanzania toppled Amin, Obote bounced back by winning a presidential election in 1980. This time he pursued liberal IMF-style economic policies to obtain aid from western donors and the

FAST FACTS

Pres. Yoweri Kaguta
Museveni
Born: 1944
Since 1986

POLITICAL

Head of State	Pres. Yoweri Kaguta Museveni
Ruling Party	NRM
Main Opposition	FDC
Independence	9 October 1962
National capital	Kampala
Official language	English

PHYSICAL

Total area	93,065 sq. miles 241,038 sq. km. (± Oregon)
Arable land	26% of land area
Coastline	Landlocked

POPULATION

Total	28.2 million
Av. yearly growth	3.37%
Population/sq. mile	255
Urban population	3.4 million
Adult literacy	70%

ECONOMY

Currency	Ugandan shilling (Ush)(US$=1,845)
GDP (real)	$7.9 billion
GDP growth rate	4%
GDP per capita[1]	$294
GDP (ppp)[2]	$48.7 billion
GDP per cap. (ppp)	$1,800
Inflation rate	8.1%
Exports	$768 million
Imports	$1.6 billion
External debt	$4.97 billion
Unemployment	N/A

1. Atlas method.
2. See page 175 for an explanation of purchasing power parity (ppp).

economy perked up slightly until another coup in 1985 led to further instability. In 1986 a rebel army led by Yoweri Museveni, leader of the National Resistance Movement (NRM), took control. President. Museveni banned rallies by other political groups and invited his opponents to join the NRM. He was reelected for the third time in 2006. The Lord's Resistance Army has been engaged in an armed rebellion against the Ugandan government in one of Africa's longest-running conflicts. Led by Joseph Kony, who proclaims himself a spirit medium who wishes to establish a state based on his unique interpretation of the Acholi religious syncretism and Biblical millenarianism, the LRA have been accused of widespread human rights violations. While efforts are ongoing toi broker a ceasefire agreement with the rebels the International Criminal Court has issued warrants for the arrest of the LRA leadership.

GOVERNMENT

A new 1995 constitution provided for a strong executive President, to be elected every five years, but with significant requirements for parliamentary approval of presidential actions. The National Assembly has a total of 319 members serving a 5-year term—215 elected in single seat constituencies; an additional 69 reserved for women representatives; and 15 indirect or nominated seats—including 10 for army representatives and 10 for *ex officio* members. In a referendum in June 2005 an overhelming majority of voters supported the re-instatement of multiparty politics over the non-party system introduced by Museveni when he first assumed power in 1986. In the first mutli-party election in February 2006 Pres. Museveni's National Resistance Movement (NRM) captured 205 seats against 37 for its nearest rival, the Forum for Democratic Change (FDC).

ECONOMIC POLICY

Museveni has had remarkable success in lifting Uganda out of the ruins left by Amin and Obote. Uganda signed a loan program with the IMF and implemented reforms. It attained higher growth rates, lowered the budget deficit and inflation, and dismantled price controls and state monopolies. The civil service payroll was drastically reduced. Growth in sectors such as manufacturing, mining, transport, communications, and construction led to a doubling of the size of the economy since the late eighties. Improved economic conditions and government assurances led to the return of a number of Indian-Ugandan entrepreneurs who were exiled during the Amin and Obote regimes. In 2000 Uganda qualified for enhanced Highly Indebted Poor Countries (HIPC) and Paris Club debt relief worth $1.5 billion Uganda has taken among African nations the fight against HIV/AIDS by reducing the rate of new infections through an intensive public health campaign.

SECTORS

Agriculture and fishing are the mainstay of the economy, employing more than 80% of the working population and contributing about 44% of GDP. The country has long been famous for its robusta coffee, grown around Mount Elgon and in the foothills of the Ruwenzori Mountains. Other cash crops are cotton, tea, tobacco and sugar cane. The main food crops are plantains, cassava, millet, maize, rice, beans and groundnuts. Commercial cattle and dairy farming is undertaken in the southwest. Freshwater fish from the country's many lakes meets a high proportion of the population's protein needs and is also exported. Mining has been neglected for some time, but a revival is underway. There are extensive copper and iron ore reserves and hitherto less viable deposits of tungsten, tin, phosphates, columbo-tantalite, beryl, bismuth and limestone. Manufacturing revolves largely around food processing and import-substituting items such as textiles, cement, soap, plastics and metal products. Tourism has become a growth industry in recent years.

PRIVATIZATION

The government has committed itself to privatization but the program has been marred by several failed deals, a lack of transparency, and rampant asset stripping. Latest on the list of entities to be privatized is the Uganda Electricity Board (UEB).

TRADE

Agricultural production, with coffee as a major component, represents the major portion of Uganda's export earnings. Other agricultural exports include flowers, vanilla, silk, cotton, tobacco and tea.

INVESTMENT

Most investors are companies and individuals with experience in Uganda or elsewhere in Africa. They include British and Indian firms, as well as growing numbers of Kenyan and South African entities. There has been significant foreign investment in the past two years in the beverage industry by Coca-Cola, South African Breweries and Guinness.

FINANCIAL SECTOR

The Bank of Uganda (BOU) monitors 18 commercial banks and two development banks. A deposit insurance fund with contributions from the government and banks is in place to protect depositors. A stock exchange was established on 6 June 1997 by the Uganda Securities Exchange (USE) Ltd.—a company formed by licensed broker/dealers and investment advisers.

TAXES & TARIFFS

Resident companies and foreign branches of companies are taxed at a 30% rate. Dividends are subject to withholding tax at a 20% rate for residents and 15% for nonresidents. Management fees, dividends, royalties and interest paid to nonresidents may be remitted to non-resident shareholders with the approval of the Bank of Uganda and are subject to a 15% withholding tax. Businesses with annual revenues of more than $35,000 are subject to a 17% VAT. To reduce costs and increase competitiveness, all 30% import duties have been reduced to 15%. Excise surcharges are set at 10%.

BUSINESS ACTIVITY

AGRICULTURE
Coffee, tea, cotton, tobacco, cassava (tapioca), potatoes, corn, millet, pulses, beef, goat meat, milk, poultry.

INDUSTRIES
Sugar, brewing, tobacco, cotton, textiles, cement.

NATURAL RESOURCES
Copper, gold, cobalt, limestone, salt.

EXPORTS
$768 million (est. 2005): coffee, gold, fish and fish products, cotton, tea, corn.

IMPORTS
$1.3 billion (est.2005): transportation equipment, petroleum, medical supplies, iron and steel.

MAJOR TRADING PARTNERS
Kenya, Belgium, South Africa, India, China, UK, US, Germany, France, Rwanda, Netherlands, UAE.

DOING BUSINESS WITH UGANDA

▶ INVESTMENT

Food processing, livestock, tourism, infrastructure, and transportation, import substitution, light manufacturing, mining, and telecommunications offer prospects for foreign investment. In an effort to revive mining, the government is encouraging foreigners to exploit deposits of copper, cobalt, gold, tin, tungsten, and oil. Accelerated depreciation incentives are offered. Acquisition, takeovers and greenfield investments are permitted.

▶ TRADE

A small but growing middle class offers a ready market for quality consumer goods but new products often have to compete with used goods, especially in automobiles and clothing. The Uganda Manufacturers Association (UMA) and the Ugandan National Chamber of Commerce and Industry offer assistance to local agents and distributors.

▶ TRADE FINANCE

Eximbank provides short- to medium-term loans for US exporters. The Bank of Uganda supports export credit guarantees by commercial banks. Letters of credit and other standard instruments are also used. Sellers are advised to collect as much as possible of the price in cash and to collateralize all loans in cases where buyers are unknown.

▶ SELLING TO THE GOVERNMENT

The Central Tender Board controls tenders and advertises in the newspapers or sends invitations to organizations in Kampala. SWIPCO, a US-based company, is responsible for auditing all procurement of $50,000 and above by Ugandan ministries and parastatals.

▶ FOREIGN EXCHANGE

Foreign exchange, based on a market-determined exchange rate, can be freely purchased. The Investment Code of 1991 allows foreign exchange remittances with respect to transfer of foreign technologies. There are no foreign exchange controls affecting legitimate trade.

▶ PARTNERSHIP

There are no restrictions on foreign ventures with local investors.

▶ ESTABLISHING A PRESENCE

The Uganda Investment Authority (UIA) offers advice on registry, licensing, immigration, tax, and customs matters, and sublicenses and permits. Foreign investors may form wholly-owned companies or joint ventures with local investors. There is no minimum equity capital requirement for companies. A branch of a foreign company may operate in Uganda if it registers with the Registrar of Companies and delivers to the Registrar a certified copy of the Memorandum and Articles of Association.

▶ PROJECT FINANCING

Most development projects are funded by outside donors who often give preference to purchases from companies based in their own country. In March 1998, Uganda signed an agreement allowing OPIC to broaden the scope of its activities. Local banks are generally weak and hesitant lenders.

▶ LABOR

The private sector resorts to on-the-job training of unskilled and semiskilled workers to compensate for a shortage of skilled workers. Unions are relatively weak and labor unrest is rare. Employers must contribute an amount equal to 10% of the employee's gross salary to the National Social Security Fund (NSSF). Monthly salaries range from $60 to $140 for unskilled labor, $160 to $270 for skilled labor, and $350 to $670 for a junior manager.

▶ LEGAL RIGHTS

The law allows expropriation for public purposes through a transparent process and investors are guaranteed fair market value compensation within 12 months. The leadership has repeatedly reaffirmed Uganda's resolve that private property will never again be arbitrarily expropriated as it was in the dreaded Amin era. Instead, Uganda is in the process of returning land expropriated at the time, mostly from the Indian population. Commercial laws are based on the British mode. The Registrar of Patents awards patents for an initial period of 15 years, with a possible five-year extension. Uganda is a member of the International Center for the Settlement of Investment Disputes and opened a commercial court in August 1996.

▶ BUSINESS CLIMATE

Business decisions are often made by consensus. Initial business meetings are focused more on people's backgrounds and families than the business on hand. It is not uncommon for Ugandans to arrive late and for meetings to run over their scheduled time. Most business is conducted in English.

ZAMBIA

TRANSITION TO MULTIPARTY DEMOCRACY IN THE EARLY NINETIES ENABLED LAND-LOCKED ZAMBIA TO CHANGE ITS FORTUNES THROUGH DRASTIC ECONOMIC REFORMS AND A PRIVATIZATION PROGRAM. DESPITE DEPRESSED MINERAL PRICES INHIBITING GROWTH, LIBERALIZATION AND DIVERSIFICATION OF ITS ECONOMY HELPED SET ZAMBIA ON A FIRM ROAD TO RECOVERY. ZAMBIA REMAINS LARGELY DEPENDENT ON COPPER, COBALT, ZINC AND LEAD. PRIVATIZATION OF STATE-OWNED MINES HAS INCREASED FOREIGN HOLDINGS AND PRODUCTIVITY AND INCREASED OVERSEAS INTEREST IN A VARIETY OF OTHER SECTORS LED TO FURTHER GROWTH. ZAMBIA CONTINUES TO IMPLEMENT INTERNATIONALLY ENDORSED POVERTY REDUCTION PROGRAMS.

COUNTRY PROFILE

The landlocked Republic of Zambia shares boundaries with eight other countries. It is part of the high African plateau averaging more than 1,000 m (3,280 ft) and rising towards the north-eastern Muchinga Mountains. Most of the country consists of savanna terrain. The Bantu-speaking population comprises more than 70 ethnic groups with the Bemba dominant in the northeastern Copperbelt region, the Nyanja in the east and around Lusaka, the Tonga in the south and the Lozi in the west. English is the official language. About two-thirds of the people are Christians and the rest profess traditional ethnic beliefs.

HISTORY

Paleontologists claim that humans inhabited the region between one and two million years ago. During the 15th Century the Luba, Lunda (Kazembe), Bemba (Chitimukulu) and Lozi (Barotse) kingdoms flourished in the region stretching from Shaba (in Congo Kinshasa) to Zambia. They were joined in 1840 by fugitives from upheavals in the Zulu kingdom in South Africa. By the 1880s, driven by his dream of a British Empire from the Cape to Cairo, Cecil John Rhodes and his British South Africa Company (BSA) claimed the region. In 1924 Northern Rhodesia, as it was known, was transferred to the British government and in the late 1920s the discovery of vast copper reserves lured mining moguls from Britain, South Africa and America and thousands of white settlers. In 1953 Northern Rhodesia (over strong objections from its inhabitants) was linked together with Nyasaland (later Malawi) and Southern Rhodesia in a white-ruled Federation of Rhodesia and Nyasaland. Agitation by Northern Rhodesia's Kenneth Kaunda and his United National Independence Party (UNIP) and Dr Hastings Banda of Nyasaland led to the dissolution of the Federation in 1963. In October 1964 President Kaunda led Zambia to independence. He consolidated his rule by banning the opposition and nationalizing the copper mines and other assets. In 1991, the relaxation of

FAST FACTS

Pres. Levy Patrick
Mwanawasa
Born: 3 Sept. 1948
Since 2002

POLITICAL

Head/State	Pres. Levy Patrick Mwanawasa
Ruling Party	MMD
Main Opposition	UPND
Independence	24 October 1964
National capital	Lusaka
Official languages	English

PHYSICAL

Total area	290,583 sq. miles 752,610 sq. km. (± Texas)
Arable land	7% of land area
Coastline	Landlocked

POPULATION

Total	11.5 million
Av. yearly growth	2.11%
Population/sq. mile	33
Urban population	4 million
Adult literacy	80%

ECONOMY

Currency	Zambian kwacha (ZK) (US$1=4,082)
GDP (real)	$5.35 billion
GDP growth rate	4.6%
GDP per capita[1]	$581
GDP (ppp)[2]	$10.59 billion
GDP per cap. (ppp)	$900
Inflation rate	18.3%
Exports	$1.94 billion
Imports	$1.93 billion
External debt	$4.6 billion
Unemployment	50%

1. Atlas method.
2. See page 175 for an explanation of purchasing power parity (ppp).

the ban propelled trade union leader and head of the Movement for Multiparty Democracy (MMD), Frederick Chiluba, to victory against Kaunda at the polls. He restored democracy and instituted drastic economic reforms. Chiluba was reelected in November 1996 and after completion of his second five year term stepped down. He was succeeded after the 2001 presidential election by Levy Mwanawasa of the MMD. In the September 2006 election he was reelected when he garnered 43 percent of the popular vote against populist rival Michael Sata's 30 percent. Sata's pledges to evict foreign investors and expressions of admiration for the policies of Zimbabwe's President Robert Mugabe were of great concern to foreign investors.

GOVERNMENT

Under the constitution an executive President is elected by popular vote for a maximum of two 5-year terms. He presides over a cabinet appointed by the majority party in the 159-seat National Assembly, also elected for 5 years. In the December 2001 election the MMD won 68 seats against 48 for the UPND.

ECONOMIC POLICY

Since 1991 Zambia has moved aggressively towards a freer investor-friendly economy by removing price controls, reducing tariffs and privatizing. Tight fiscal and monetary policies coupled with democratic governance have resulted in renewed balance of payments support from donors and helped restore foreign investor confidence. In 1998 the government and IMF reached agreement on a second Enhanced Structural Adjustment Facility. The Mwanawasa market-opening economic policies drew support from the US, the World Bank and other donor and lending institutions who agreed to cancel nearly all of Zambia's $7.2 billion foreign debt.

SECTORS

Zambia has six times as much agricultural land as Zimbabwe but only 20% of it is cultivated. Currently agriculture employs about 40% of the workforce, largely on a subsistence basis. Cash crops include tobacco, seed cotton, coffee, fresh flowers and groundnuts. The main food crops are maize, rice, sorghum, millet, soy beans and wheat. Livestock farming is largely under control of small-scale farmers in the southern and western provinces. There is a reasonably large fresh fishing sector and half of the land area is forest, providing fuel wood and timber for mining and industrial use. The economy depends primarily on the copper industry. The country fell into heavy debt as copper prices plunged in the 1970s and 1980s but rebounded with a resurgence of the metal on the world markets—more than doubling in price in 2006. Zambia is the second largest producer after Congo (Kinshasa) of cobalt and also exports lead and zinc. Its gemstones, especially emeralds, remain largely unexploited. Over one-third of its manufacturing output consists of processed food and beverages. Other major products include textiles, chemicals and metal products. Zambia has good tourist potential and shares with Zimbabwe popular attractions such as Victoria Falls and Lake Kariba. Zambia is becoming increasingly popular as a destination for safari enthusiasists. Recently, oil was discovered in the Northern provinces of Zambezi and Chavuma, near the border with Angola. Zambia has been the chief beneficiary of Zimbabwe's economic and political crisis, diverting much of the tourism traffic, manufacturing business and international investment traditionally destined for its neighbor.

PRIVATIZATION

Most of Zambia's 330 parastatal companies have been privatized since the early nineties, including a major brewery, bakery, farms, several hotels, a mill and the copper mining conglomerate Zambia Consolidated Copper Mines (ZCCM). Among the other state enterprises slated for privatization are the telecommunications parastatal (ZAMTEL), Nitrogen Chemical of Zambia (NCZ), Zambia State Insurance Corporation (ZSIC), Zambia Postal Services Corporation (ZAMPOST), Zambia Electricity Supply Corporation (ZESCO) and Zambia Railways (ZR). Heavily indebted Zambia Airways could not find a buyer and was closed down.

INVESTMENT

Large-scale privatization and the freeing up of sectors previously reserved for government monopoly has boosted foreign direct investment over the past ten years. Among the megadeals were the selling of the large state copper mining giant ZCCM to South Africa's Anglo American. Manufacturing operations have sprung up, involving several American investors.

TRADE

Zambia derives about 80% of its export earnings and about half of its government tax revenue

from copper. The mining and marketing of copper, cobalt, lead and zinc are handled by the recently privatized Zambia Consolidated Copper Mines (ZCCM). Diversification efforts are underway to help expand the export share of tourism, agricultural products and manufactured goods.

FINANCIAL SECTOR

The financial sector experienced rapid growth since 1992 as a result of the liberalization of banking, insurance, the removal of controls on interest rates, and the easing (and eventual elimination) of capital controls. Today there are 15 banks—6 of them foreign-owned subsidiaries, 7 belonging to local investors, 1 to the government and 1 under joint ownership of the Zambian and Indian governments. The banking sector is supervised by the central bank, the Bank of Zambia. The Lusaka Stock Exchange (LSE) trades shares of a few major companies.

TAXES AND TARIFFS

The government introduced some tariff protection in 1999. Duty-free goods include mining and agricultural machinery, medicines, pharmaceuticals, veterinary and medical equipment, chemicals, fertilizers, and seeds. Other goods fall into one of three tariff bands: 5% on selected raw materials and capital equipment, 15% on intermediate goods, and 25% on final products.

BUSINESS ACTIVITY

AGRICULTURE
Corn, sorghum, rice, peanuts, sunflower seed, tobacco, cotton, sugarcane, cassva (tapioca), cattle, goats, pigs, poultry, beef, pork.

INDUSTRIES
Copper mining and processing, construction, foodstuffs, beverages, chemicals, textiles, fertilizer.

NATURAL RESOURCES
Copper, zinc, lead, cobalt, coal.

EXPORTS
$1.94 billion (est. 2005): copper, cobalt, zinc, lead, tobacco, cut flowers.

IMPORTS
$1.93 billion (est. 2005): machinery, transportation equipment, foodstuffs, fuel, petroleum products, electricity, fertilizer, clothing.

MAJOR TRADING PARTNERS
South Africa, UAE, Thailand, UK, Switzerland, Tanzania, Zimbabwe, Dem. Rep. of Congo.

Doing Business with Zambia

▶ Investment

The Zambian Investment Center (ZIC) seeks and an investment board screens foreign direct investments. The privatization process is open to foreign bidders and there are no requirements relating to local content, equity, financing, employment or technology transfer. Incentives are offered in regard to investments in rural enterprises, farming, and the manufacturing of non-mineral exports. Companies listed on the Lusaka Stock Exchange qualify for reduced corporate income tax. Mining, tourism, insurance, telecommunications and energy are prime areas of investment.

▶ Trade

Horticultural inputs, veterinary medicines, wheat and corn are significant import items. There is also a growing demand for heavy machinery and construction equipment as Zambia introduces major new infrastructure rehabilitation projects. Franchising is expanding in printing, fast food, postal services, computer/office supplies, telecommunications, education, and business services.

▶ Trade finance

Short-term local borrowing is expensive. Many buyers either undertake their own financing or seek funding outside the country. An irrevocable letter of credit is the most common method of payment. Eximbank programs are available.

▶ Selling to the government

The government has an ongoing need for products and services relating to rehabilitation of the country's railway and road networks, hydroelectric power, mining, and telecommunications. Many of these projects are funded by multilateral lending institutions and bilateral donors and subject in part to their tender requirements. All government purchases are channeled through the National Tender Board.

▶ Exchange controls

There are no controls on the movement of capital in or out of Zambia. Bank accounts may be held in local or foreign currency, and funds are easily transferred or allowed to be held offshore.

▶ Partnerships

In the few instances where franchising arrangements have been made they were done on the basis of British law. Joint ventures and licensing are inhibited by a shortage of local capital.

▶ Establishing a presence

To establish itself in Zambia a foreign firm must register with the Registrar of Companies at the Ministry of Commerce, Trade and Industry. Payment of a fee and submission of the company's charter are required. The minimum nominal capital required is approximately $200 and a registration fee of 2.5% of this startup capital is charged. Certificates of Incorporation are usually issued within 24 hours.

▶ Financing projects

Apart from bilateral and multilateral government agencies, commercial banks and venture capital funds are playing an increasing role in the financing of projects. The Overseas Private Investment Corporation, the International Finance Corporation and the Commonwealth Development Corporation also offer project financing, political risk insurance, and investor services.

▶ Labor

Labor is readily available although companies often have to invest in training to make up for a lack of skills. While the government stipulates preference for locals in positions where qualified, foreign firms are allowed automatic allowed work and residence permits for five expatriate workers when they invest, and more when justified later.

▶ Legal rights

The investment code allows for international arbitration should internal attempts at settlement of a commercial dispute fail. US companies have been successful in getting court rulings enforcing their contracts, even against parastatal companies. Trademark protection is considered adequate and there are fines for revealing business proprietary information. Copyright protection is limited and does not yet cover computer software. Zambia is a signatory to a number of international agreements on patents and intellectual property, including the Paris and Bern Convention and the African Regional Industrial Property Organization (ARIPO), and is a member of the World Intellectual Property Organization.

▶ Business climate

Business customs were shaped and influenced by the British (and Americans) since the end of the 19th century. Visitors who have conducted business in any of Southern Africa's English-speaking countries will find the environment in Zambia quite familiar.

 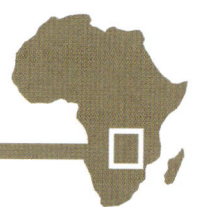

ZIMBABWE

AS ONE OF AFRICA'S MOST SOPHISTICATED COUNTRIES, ZIMBABWE'S ECONOMIC PERFORMANCE HAS BEEN A DISAPPOINTMENT IN RECENT YEARS. INTERNATIONAL OBSERVERS BLAME ITS FAILURE TO LIVE UP TO EXPECTATIONS—DESPITE AMPLE MINERAL AND AGRICULTURAL RESOURCES, A WELL-DEVELOPED INFRASTRUCTURE, ADVANCED FINANCIAL SERVICES AND SOLID MANUFACTURING SECTOR—ON MISGUIDED OFFICIAL POLICIES. AS INTERNAL PRESSURES FOR POLITICAL AND ECONOMIC REFORM CONTINUE, FOREIGN INVESTORS ARE HOLDING BACK AND MANY PROMISING OPPORTUNITIES FOR INVESTMENT AND TRADE EXPANSION ARE LEFT UNTOUCHED. UNEMPLOYEMNT HAS REACHED 80% AND INFLATION, ACCORDING TO PRIVATE SECTOR ESTIMATES, TOPPED 1,200 PERCENT.

COUNTRY PROFILE

The Republic of Zimbabwe is situated on an extension of the South African Highveld Plateau. The Zambezi and Limpopo rivers run along the country's northern and southern borders. At Victoria Falls the Zambezi plunges for 100 m (328 ft) over a width of 1.5 km (1 mile) into a narrow ravine, sending up a spray that earned it the indigenous name of Mosi-oa-Tunya—the "smoke that thunders." Downstream is Kariba Dam, the second largest human-made lake in Africa after Lake Volta in Ghana. Hwange National Park is one of several national parks. Rainfall in the high-veld region averages 800 mm (31.5 inches) and

along the lower regions less than 400 mm (15.7 inches). More than three-quarters of the population are Shona or Mashona. The second largest group is the Ndebele or Matabele, accounting for about 15% of the total. The white population number some 80,000 and Asians around 15,000. English is the official language. Well over half of the population is Christian and the rest adhere to traditional beliefs.

HISTORY

The remains of humans dating back 500,000 years have been discovered in the region. The country traces its history back to about 500 when the city of Great Zimbabwe (house of stone) was developed by the ancestors of the Shona. Around the middle of the 19th Century, the territory was invaded by Ndebele or Matabele migrants from the south. In 1890 Cecil John Rhodes' British South Africa Company (BSA) started a white settlement at Salisbury (today's Harare, the capital of Zimbabwe). The territory was named Rhodesia, after Rhodes, and in 1923 white settlers were given the choice of joining South Africa or becoming a self-governing colony within the British Empire. They opted for the latter. By law the best cropland was reserved for a rapidly-growing white settlement. Joshua Mqabuko Nkomo's Zimbabwe

375

FAST FACTS

Pres. Robert Gabriel
Mugabe
Born: February 21, 1924
Since 1980

POLITICAL

Head of State	Pres. Robert Gabriel Mugabe
Ruling Party	ZANU-PF
Main Opposition	MDC
Independence	18 April 1980
National capital	Harare
Official language	English

PHYSICAL

Total area	150,803 sq. miles
	390,580 sq. km.
	(± Montana)
Arable land	8.3% of land area
Coastline	Landlocked

POPULATION

Total	12.2 million
Av. yearly growth	0.62%
Population/sq. mile	75
Urban population	4.7
Adult literacy	90%

ECONOMY

Currency	Zimbabwean dollar (Z$) (U$1=61,693)
GDP (real)	$3.2 billion
GDP growth rate	-7%
GDP per capita[1]	$445
GDP (ppp)[2]	$28.37 billion
GDP per cap. (ppp)	$2,300
Inflation rate	266.8%[3]
Exports	$1.64 billion
Imports	$2.05 billion
External debt	$5.2 billion
Unemployment	80%

1. Atlas method.
2. See page 175 for an explanation of purchasing power parity (ppp).
3. Official rate. Private sector estimates are much higher.

African Peoples Union (ZAPU) and Robert Gabriel Mugabe's Zimbabwe African National Union (ZANU) led the black protest against this inequity. They resorted to arms in 1965 when Prime Minister Ian Smith and his ruling Rhodesian Front issued a unilateral declaration of independence (UDI). UN-imposed sanctions and a protracted guerilla war on two fronts involving ZAPU and ZANU forced Smith to the negotiating table and in April 1980 Zimbabwe gained independence under Prime Minister (later President) Robert Mugabe. Land resettlement remained a hot political issue with one-third of the country's arable land occupied by 4,000 white farmers. Mugabe's open support for forceful occupation of white farmland by displaced "war veterans" placed him at the center of a storm and the rise of the Movement for Democratic Change (MDC). In March 2002 Mugabe defeated Morgan Tsvangirai of the MDC in a presidential election that was widely condemned by overseas observers as rigged and rife with intimidation. Mugabe has continued pressing for the evacuation of white farmers despite widespread opposition from abroad. The international community has attempted to coerce Mugabe into relaxing restrictions imposed on the opposition.

GOVERNMENT

The 1980 independence constitution was changed in 1987 to eliminate the 20 seats reserved for representatives of white voters and create the post of president, elected by the for a 6-year term. In the March 2005 election the ruling Zimbabwe African National Union-Patriotic Front (ZANU-PF) finished up with 78 seats against 41 for the Movement for Democratic Change (MDC). With 30 seats reserved for government appointees it has achieved a two-thirds majority, enough to alter the constitution. The government barred or failed to invite election observers that were critical of past elections. One seat is held by the Zimbabwe African National Union-Ndonga (ZANU-N). Zimbabwean opposition political parties, churches and civil society groups appear to have taken the first step in forming a broad alliance—dubbed Save Zimbabwe—to confront Mugabe and the ruling ZANU-PF party. Zimbabwe is provisionally set to hold its next presidential elections in 2008.

ECONOMIC POLICY

The National Economic Development Priority Programme (NEDPP) aims to raise US$2.5 billion in cash and investment in mining, manufacturing and agriculture. China has reportedly signed up to NEDPP with a US$1.3 billion finance deal—equivalent to Zimbabwe's total exports—to build coal mines and three thermal power stations in exchange for chrome and other raw materials. Progress is, however, hampered, by price controls, state interference in several sectors and the politically-motivated state-supported violence and invasion of farms. Mugabe's support for the squatters has led to foreign sanctions and economic setbacks. Latest unofficial statistics catalogue the country's economic woes with unemployment topping 80% and inflation at close to 1,200%.

SECTORS

In the past the agricultural sector contributed 20% of GNP and employed about 70% of the total labor force. Some 4,400 large commercial farms, covering 29% of the total land area, used to account for 80% of the country's commercial agricultural output. Maize, wheat, barley, cassava, soy beans, bananas and oranges were popular food crops. There was also a substantial production of cotton, sugar, coffee and beef but tobacco was by far the most important cash crop. Zimbabwe used to account for 17% of the world's total. Serious disruption of established farms have, however, resulted in drastic cutbacks in crops. Mining of gold, chrome, nickel and asbestos provided employment to some 60 000 workers. Other important minerals are coal, copper, iron ore, tin, silver, platinum, phosphate, limestone, cobalt and lithium. The manufacturing sector is dominated by chemicals, metals, textiles, chemicals and minerals.

INVESTMENT

A survey conducted by the Confederation of Zimbabwe Industries (CZI) in the late 1980s indicated that 25% of all industrial concerns had some foreign ownership. Foreign investment accounted for 40% to 50% of the country's industrial output. The latest estimates put the total value of foreign investment at $5 billion, mostly by British and South African interests. Many Zimbabwean companies have relocated to neighbouring Botswana, perceived as the region's most investor-friendly country, and to Zambia. Zimbabwean-run small- and medium-scale business, such as bus and truck operators, funeral parlors, vehicle repair shops and sawmills, have mushroomed in the northern city of Francistown and the satellite towns of Tati and Tonota near Botswana's border with Zim-

babwe. There is a steady influx of Zimbabweans, reportedly 125,000 a month, into Botswana and Zambia. This has created tension between these countries, with Botswana blaming the immigrants for increased crime.

TRADE

In the past tobacco used to be by far the most important cash crop, contributing more than 25% of Zimbabwe's total export revenues. Mining of gold, chrome, nickel and asbestos accounted on average for about 40% of total export earnings. Zimbabwe's largest trading partner is South Africa, followed by China.

FINANCIAL SECTOR

Of the Zim$43 trillion circulating in Zimbabwe in October 2006 only 15% was estimated to be in the formal sector. Some 40% was said to be stashed in people's homes, offices and outside Zimbabwe. Under the Presidential Powers Temporary Measures Currency Revaluation Regulations of 2006, more than $10 trillion in the old currency was seized as part of far-reaching reforms announced by Zimbabawe's Reserve Bank. Individuals and corporations, respectively, were prohibited from having cash in excess of Zim$100 million (US $100,000) in new currency) and Zim$5 billion (US $5 million) as the central bank sought to curtail suspected money laundering.

BUSINESS ACTIVITY

AGRICULTURE
Corn, cotton, tobacco, wheat, coffee, sugar cane, peanuts, cattle, sheep, goats, pigs.

INDUSTRIES
Mining (coal, clay, numerous metallic and non-metallic ores), copper, steel, nickel, tin, wood products, cement, chemicals, fertilizer, clothing and footwear, foodstuffs, beverages.

NATURAL RESOURCES
Gold, copper, chrome, nickel, tin, asbestos.

EXPORTS
$1.64 billion (est. 2005): tobacco, chromium, gold, ferro alloys, cotton, clothing.

IMPORTS
$2.05 billion (est. 2005): machinery and transport equipment, other manufactures, chemicals, fuels.

MAJOR TRADING PARTNERS
South Africa, China, Switzerland, Botswana, Japan, UK, US, Netherlands.

Doing Business with Zimbabwe

▶ Investment

The Zimbabwe Investment Center (ZIC) was created as one-stop shop for potential investors. Incentives for investors include allowances on the purchase of industrial and commercial buildings, implements and machinery, and for training, as well as special mining leases. The government, however, still prefers majority Zimbabwean participation in new investment projects and the degree of local ownership remains an important criterion in the evaluation of investment proposals. Its privatization program announced in late 1998 limits foreign ownership to between 15 and 20%, down from previous levels of 30 to 35%. There are a number of sectors reserved for domestic investors such as horticulture, game, wildlife ranching, forestry, fishing, freight and passenger transport (excluding airlines), and tobacco products. Investing in export processing zones entitles foreigners to a five-year tax holiday and duty-free importation of raw materials and capital equipment.

▶ Trade

There is a market for transportation equipment, construction and farm machinery, computers and peripherals, chemicals and plastics, textile machinery, telecommunications equipment and food products. Exports include ferrochrome, nickel, tobacco, gold, sugar, and clothing.

▶ Trade finance

Eximbank offers facilities to US exporters and financing is also available from local banks at relatively high interest rates.

▶ Selling to the government

There is an increasing demand for equipment related to telecommunications, power generation and road building and repair. Purchases are through tender and sometimes involve multilateral and bilateral financing.

▶ Exchange controls

Foreign investors are allowed to remit all their after-tax profits. The government monitors all capital outflows relating to prospective outward investment and dividend remittances.

▶ Partnerships

Partnership is the preferred form of foreign investment, especially if it advances black economic empowerment. Several US firms have entered the market through franchising agreements relating to consumer goods and services.

▶ Establishing a presence

Approval from the Zimbabwean Investment Center is required in all cases where a new business is established, an existing one expanded, or part or all of a business acquired.

▶ Financing projects

There are investment agreements in place with the Overseas Private Investment Corporation and the World Bank's Multilateral Investment Guarantee Agency. Project financing is also available from two Zimbabwean development banks and a venture capital company.

▶ Labor

Unskilled and semi-skilled labor is readily available but there is a growing shortage of technical skills. The 1985 Labor Relations Act sets strict standards for occupational health and safety, working hours and minimum wage. The Zimbabwe Congress of Trade Unions (ZCTU), the country's umbrella labor organization, consisting of 35 member unions and about 300,000 members, is a powerful advocate for workers.

▶ Legal rights

Zimbabwe's judiciary has a reputation for fairness and independence. The country is a member of the World Intellectual Property Organization but efforts to honor intellectual property ownership and rights are sometimes hampered by ineffective means of enforcement. Recently, remittances for royalties, technical services and management fees have been suspended in some instances due to the severe hard currency shortage. Government buyouts of both foreign investors and commercial farmers since independence have generally been on a mutually agreed basis. Recently, however, the government sanctioned white commercial farmland invasions by "war veterans" without proper compensation, causing a serious dent in foreign investor confidence. Once investors have exhausted local remedies, appeal to private arbitration is allowed in accordance with the rules and procedures of the UN Commission on International Trade Law.

▶ Business climate

Business customs generally follow the British model and are fairly formal. Despite bureaucratic red tape and a lack of transparency in some instances, patient and persistent companies with experienced local representation manage to develop profitable businesses.

WESTERN SAHARA

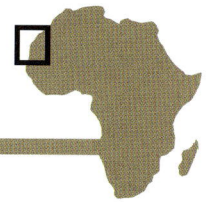

Editor's Note: The situation in Western Sahara is complex. In previous years, our description has displeased either Morocco or Algeria, depending on how it was described. The following represents what we believe to be a factual representation of the situation as it now stands.

AT PRESENT WESTERN SAHARA IS ADMINISTERED BY MOROCCO AS PART OF ITS GREATER SOUTHERN REGION. HOWEVER, THE TERRITORY HAS ALSO BEEN PROCLAIMED THE SAHARAN ARAB DEMOCRATIC REPUBLIC (SADR) BY A GOVERNMENT-IN-EXILE, BASED IN ALGERIA, LED BY MOHAMMED ABDAL-AZIZ. THE POPULATION OF THIS DISPUTED TERRITORY, CURRENTLY UNDER UN OBSERVATION, IS AWAITING A REFERENDUM TO DECIDE WHETHER THEY WISH TO BECOME PART OF MOROCCO OR ESTABLISH AN INDEPENDENT STATE. THE UNITED STATES GOVERNMENT DOES NOT RECOGNIZE EITHER MOROCCAN RULE OVER WESTERN SAHARA OR THE GOVERNMENT-IN-EXILE IN ALGERIA.

As Algeria, Mauritania and Mali became independent, Morocco had laid claims on historic grounds to parts of their territory, as well as the entire Spanish Sahara. The latter claim was pursued forcefully by King Hassan. After a proposed UN referendum on the future of the territory failed to materialize, Western Saharan voters were allowed to participate in Moroccan elections in 1993.

PROFILE

Western Sahara's covers an area of 252,000 km consisting of a low plateau and desert, scattered oases and dry river beds. It shares contested borders with Morocco, Algeria and Mauritania. The climate along the 1,500 km coastline is moderated by the Northern Atlantic Ocean's cold Canaries current. Most of its 220,000 inhabitants (not including thousands of refugees in adjoining lands) are Muslim. They call themselves Saharans or Sadirawi and are of mixed Arabo-Berber origin. The largest group is the northern Tekna, who are preponderantly Berber and related to the inhabitants of southern Morocco. The Regeihat and the Imragen along the coast are nomadic fishermen. Arabic and Berber dialects are widely spoken, apart from a smattering of French and Spanish. More than 80% of the population is concentrated in Al-Aaiun (Laayoune) and settlements along the Saguia al-Hamra Valley in the far north.

ECONOMY

Crop growing, mainly for subsistence, takes place at the numerous oases, and goats, sheep and camels are raised along the coast where the moisture sustains some pasturage. Both the rich offshore fishing waters and vast phosphate deposits at Boukra (Bou Craa) are important economic resources for Morocco. The phosphate rock is transported on a 62 mile (100 km) conveyor belt to the port of Al-Aaiun. The northern region of Western Sahara has greatly benefited from the Moroccan government's large

379

spending on military operations in recent years. In the process, social services, housing and sport facilities, roads, air transport, postal services and telecommunications have been improved. By developing the economy of the region, creating employment opportunities, and improving social services the Moroccan government aims not only at foster goodwill among the locals but also to encourage its own citizens to settle here.

HISTORY

At different stages and even as late as the mid-18th Century a vast region that included present-day Western Sahara, was controlled by different tribal and regional interests. The nomadic desert peoples, however, continued to resist the so-called makhzan or world of government control. In 1884, during the "scramble" for Africa, Spain grabbed a piece of this desert and declared a protectorate over it. When the territory's international borders were finally established, Spain controlled only the coastlands. The discovery of rich phosphate deposits at Boukra in 1963 intensified the resistance to Spanish domination and stimulated a desire for independence among the indigenous inhabitants. Responding to their appeals, the UN General Assembly adopted several resolutions from 1967 to 1973, condemning the Spanish presence in Western Sahara and affirming the right of the Saharans to self-determination. The Frente Popular para la Liberacion de Saguia al-Hamray Rio de Oro (Polisario) was founded in 1973.

TAKEOVER

Under pressure from the Polisario, the UN and Morocco, Spain decided to hold a referendum in Western Sahara on the independence issue. With the referendum still pending, a UN mission reported that the majority of Saharans whom it consulted in the territory were in favor of independence and rejected Morocco's territorial claims. This was interpreted by an infuriated King Hassan as an attempt to influence the outcome of the referendum. Hassan had in the meantime struck a deal with Mauritania to partition Western Sahara between them to counter Algeria in its support of the Polisario. In November 1975 King Hassan responded to the untimely UN interference by mobilizing Moroccans of all political parties and persuasions to stage a massive peaceful march into Western Sahara. In what was known as the Green March, some 350,000 Koran-bearing civilians

obliged Spain to capitulate and evacuate, allowing Moroccan troops to move in. A subsequent tripartite agreement between Spain, Morocco and Mauritania paved the way for a formal partitioning of the area between Morocco and Mauritania in 1976. Morocco claimed the phosphate-rich northern two-thirds of the territory and Mauritania the remainder, including the port of Dakhla. In 1997, Mauritania dropped its territorial claims, leaving the way clear for Morocco to expand its influence over all of Western Sahara.

SADR

In defiance the Polisario proclaimed the Saharan Arab Democratic Republic (SADR) and set up a government-in-exile in Algeria, a move that resulted in severance of diplomatic relations between Morocco and Algeria. Thousands of Polisario supporters followed their leaders into exile, settling around the oasis of Tindouf, not far from Algeria's border with Western Sahara. The Polisario subsequently embarked on a guerrilla war against Morocco and Mauritania. In the 1980s it also managed to obtain recognition for its "independent republic" when a majority of OAU member states conferred membership on the SADR over objections and the eventual resignation from the organization by Morocco. Some 70 UN member states recognize the SADR but lately support among African states has begun to erode.

RECENT DEVELOPMENTS

In recent years relations between Morocco and its neighbors have been improving. Algeria joined with Morocco and several others in the Arab Maghreb Union. A cease-fire agreement between Morocco and the Polisario was concluded on 6 September 1991 and a UN Mission for the Organization of the Referendum in the Sahara (Minurso) was established to oversee Western Sahara until the quarrelling parties agree on the details of a long-awaited referendum.

CHAPTER 8

TRAVEL TIPS AND TRIVIA

TRAVEL TO AFRICA CAN BE COMPLICATED, CUMBERSOME AND SOMETIMES DOWNRIGHT DIFFICULT. OR IT CAN BE SMOOTH, SIMPLE AND SOOTHING. IN PART IT DEPENDS ON WHERE YOU ARE GOING AND WHAT YOU WANT TO DO. BUT MOSTLY IT IS A MATTER OF PROPER PREPARATION AND PRUDENT PREPLANNING. IN THESE PAGES WE OFFER THE TRAVELER A FEW TIPS AND SUGGESTIONS THAT MIGHT MAKE FOR SMOOTHER TRAVEL AND GREATER ENJOYMENT. REGARDLESS OF WHETHER YOU ENCOUNTER A FEW SNAGS ONE THING IS CERTAIN: YOU WILL WANT TO RETURN. AFRICA TENDS TO CLING TO YOUR SOLE AND YOUR SOUL ONCE YOU HAVE STEPPED ON ITS SOIL.

Travel Tips

THESE TRAVEL TIPS ARE MERE GEN-
ERAL GUIDELINES AND TRAVELERS ARE
ADVISED TO CHECK WITH AUTHORITA-
TIVE SOURCES AT EMBASSIES, THEIR OWN
RESPECTIVE GOVERNMENT DEPARTMENTS,
TRAVEL AGENCIES AND AIRLINES BEFORE
THEY START ON THEIR JOURNEY. ARRIV-
ING WITHOUT THE PROPER DOCUMENTA-
TION CAN LEAD TO EMBARRASSING AND
COSTLY EXPERIENCES. INSUFFICIENTLY
DOCUMENTED VISITORS ARE LIABLE TO BE
HELD AT THE PORT OF ENTRY AND SENT
BACK AT THEIR OWN EXPENSE.

ACCOMMODATION

Major international hotel chains such as Mar-
riott, Intercontinental, Hilton and Le Meridien have
established themselves in cities across Africa. There
are also a number of homegrown hotel groups that
offer economy to luxury services. Some countries
grade hotels according to the quality and extent of their
services on a scale of one to five stars. In the past five
years hotels in South Africa have on several occasions
been voted best in the world by readers of Conde Nast
and other travel magazines.

AIR TRAVEL

International links to Africa are provided by a
host of major international airlines and a number of
African carriers. Although most other African nations
have their own national airlines, only few serve intercontinental routes. Major international entry points such as
Johannesburg, Cairo, Dakar, Nairobi, Dar es Salaam,
Addis Ababa, Windhoek, Lagos and Abidjan provide
multiple links to neighboring countries and remote
destinations on the continent,

BUSINESS HOURS

Across the continent the variation in business
hours is minimal. North African countries usually go
for longer lunch breaks and later closings. Foreigners
should not interpret lack of punctuality in some cultures
as a sign of disrespect or disinterest. Keep in mind that
there are Africans who find the Western obsession with
speed and immediacy in conducting business not only
strange but downright rude. Not much can be gained by
insisting on fast decisions in a societies where ample
group discussion and consensus are prerequisites.

CREDIT CARDS

While major credit cards are widely used and
accepted in the larger cities across the continent and
even in remote parts in some countries, it is prudent to
enquire beforehand whether this form of payment is
accepted in any specific part of Africa. In a few countries,
travelers are cautioned against widespread credit card
fraud and might be advised to rely on travelers checks
or cash payments instead.

CAR RENTAL

Multinational car rental firms all have a presence in some but not all African countries—mostly on
a franchise basis. There are also domestic services
but for those who are just passing through and do not
know the country well enough to judge their reliability,
the familiar names might be a better option. Be prepared
to pay heavy insurance rates and do not assumed that
your American Express or other international insurance coverage will be accepted. Also shop around as
rates differ drastically between different operators but
be prepared to pay considerably more than the going

THE MANY FACES OF AFRICA

Burkina Faso

Burundi

Darfur

rate in the United States and some other countries. Keep in mind that outside urban areas roads and driving conditions can present quite a challenge and chauffeur-driven vehicles or public transport should be considered. For obvious reasons, foreigners—unless they are adventurous and amply equipped with water and other supplies—are dissuaded from taking long trips into the desert or African hinterland. Driving in most of the former British colonies is on the left-hand side of the road and in the former French, Spanish, Italian and Portuguese possessions on the right-hand side. There are exceptions, such as former British-ruled Ghana, where driving is on the right.

CLIMATE

Hollywood's Africa conjures up images of people in khaki and pith helmets braving steamy jungles and forbidding deserts. Most visitors will do neither. Safari-goers usually find themselves in savanna terrain where most of the animals live. While the weather in some West African countries might be summed up in terms of hot and humid, most areas present a much more complex weather profile. During summer in South Africa, for instance, travelers find themselves moving between Mediterranean-type weather at the southern coast to subtropical and humid weather on the east coast and dry heat inland. Countries such as Egypt, Algeria, Libya and Tunisia offer pleasant Mediterranean climates on their coast in contrast to searing hot days in the inland desert, followed by cold nights. For a description of climate and weather patterns in individual African countries visit www.worldtravelguide.net/navigate/region/afr.asp. and for a daily updated weather forecast in major African cities visit www.usatoday.com/weather.

CLOTHES

While locals in North African and West African countries wear sensible traditional dress to cope with hot weather, foreigners are often obliged to wear suit and tie to business meetings. Even though the trend is towards greater informality in some countries, this formal dress code largely prevails. Travelers who plan to go on safari outings are should take along a smaller bag for travel to game reserves. The feeder aircraft that serve these routes maintain strict baggage limits, requiring travelers to leave the bulk of their baggage in safekeeping at their hotel or the airport.

EMAIL

Business travelers who rely on email to communicate will find an increasing number of major hotels in the larger African cities offering not only cable and other data transmission connections for laptop carriers but also business centers, replete with computers. Some major hotels have introduced wireless broadband connection for guests with suitably equipped laptops, enabling them to connect anywhere within the hotel. Another growth industry in Africa is Internet cafés. The continent still has some way to go but the pace is picking up towards full connection to the information highway. As elsewhere, email is bound to replace snail mail and faxes as the preferred communication mode.

ELECTRICITY

Consider Africa 220/240 volts AC 50Hz territory—and at a few places power might surge up to 380 volts. There is a whole array of power connections in use, ranging from two and three-prong round to bayonet type plugs. Remote areas and some game parks rely on their own power generation. Some have no electricity at all.

FOOD

Expect on a continent with hundreds of cultures and customs to find a wide choice of local dishes. Middle Eastern fare dominates in North Africa and down south traditional tribal dishes are mixed in with colonial and

Morocco

Tunisia

Western Sahara

other imported cullinary delights from India, Malaysia and Indonesia. For centuries Zanzibar has been an important source for spices. When served uncooked or unprocessed food, such as salads and fruit, call for the same caution as applies in the case of drinking water.

HEALTH

In most African countries a valid yellow fever vaccination certificate is required for travellers over one year of age. Cholera remains a serious risk in some regions. Although largely contained and eradicated in the urban and developed areas of the continent, malaria remains a risk, especially for those touring game park regions. Mefloquine or other medication should be taken on a prophylactic basis and in sometimes mosquito nets and repellents are used at night. Experts caution against swimming in fresh water in some outlying areas as Bilharzia (schistosomiasis) might be present. Hepatitis A, B and E are present and meningococcal meningitis may occur. Leishmaniasis and human trypanosomiasis (sleeping sickness) occur in a few isolated areas. Avoid ticks which spread African tick typhus. Wear shoes to avoid soil-borne parasites. Even though most of these cautionary statements do not apply to city centers but it is better to err on the safe side. When in doubt, call your physician or health department for advice.

MEDIA

In this modern day and age where CNN and other 24-hour news channels are piped into hotel rooms all over the continent, travelers are able to stay on top of the news without understanding the local language. Being conversant in both French and English will, however, enable a visitor to read local papers from Cape to Cairo and understand most of the local TV and radio news broadcasts. Those who have access to the Internet and wish to stay abreast of news developments across the continent should visit www.allafrica.com.

MEDICAL SERVICES

Medical facilities across the continent run the gamut from poor to fair and excellent. At the one end of the spectrum is war-torn Sierra Leone where medical facilities are extremely limited and continuing to decline and at the other South Africa where hospitals are modern and medical staff well trained. (It is in Cape Town where the world's first heart transplant was performed.) Health insurance is recommended and travelers are advised to take an ample supply of their own personal medication along. Insurance is available that provides accident protection and emergency assistance in Africa. Programs for remote areas also include Flying Doctors insurance which facilitates emergency medical evacuation.

MONEY MATTERS

In most African countries the US$ is the preferred currency but in former French and British colonies franc and pounds are widely used. Sometimes additional exchange rate charges can be avoided by using travelers checks. However enticing, black market exchange of foreign into local currency is always a risk and official bureaus at airports, banks or hotels should be used instead. Normally banks offer the best legal rates. In the Democratic Republic of Congo, locals in possession of US dollars are liable to be charged with treason. [For past and current exchange rates see our

PLACES IN AFRICA

Cape Town shopping center

tanle on page 398 and for real-time exchange rates visit *www.gocurrency.com* or ask your bank.

PHOTOGRAPHY

Safarigoers who intend to take first-class pictures of animals will need telephoto lenses even in private game reserves where visitors are afforded the opportunity to see lions, leopards, elephants and others closer up. Africa also presents a treasure house of scenery, cultures and creations where ordinary photographic equipment can produce outstanding results. Photographic stores in major cities stock the products of leading manufacturers. It is prudent, however, to bring along spare custom batteries and other maintenance items.

PUBLIC HOLIDAYS

In North Africa Muslim holidays are observed and in the southern region mostly Christian holidays. In several West African countries where both faiths are practised extensively, both Muslim and Christian holidays are observed. Add in national days, workers' days and a number of other specials and some African countries may have 14 public holidays per year. Others have as few as four. As Muslim festivals are timed according to local sightings of various phases of the moon, there are no fixed dates. Ethiopia and Eritrea still use the Julian calendar, divided into 12 months of 30 days each, and a 13th month of five or six days at the end of the year, resulting on Christmas Day 2001 falling on January 7. The Julian calendar is seven years and eight months behind that of the rest of the world. (For an up-to-date listing of national public holidays in specific African countries visit www.worldtravelguide.net/navigate/region/afr.asp)

PUBLIC TRANSPORT

Most major cities are served by reasonably well-run and reliable taxis. While public transport offers a cheaper way of getting around, buses and trains—with few exceptions—tend to be overcrowded and in some instances downright chaotic.

SECURITY

Seasoned travelers know the potential pitfalls when leaving valuables unattended or strolling down dark and lonely alleys in cities anywhere in the world. While some might marvel at the great sense of decency that prevails in Africa at large, it is advisable to apply the same caution and alertness that one would in large cities anywhere. Hotels have minisafes in bedrooms for personal valuables or alternatively provide safekeeping at the front desk. It should be noted that even though South Africa, for example, ranks alarmingly high on the world's crime charts, comparatively few visitors have been personally affected. In a few isolated regions of Africa, the problem of crime pales in comparison to the brutality and dangers of fierce civil upheaval and war. The US State Department (www.state.gov) provides online travel advisory updates.

SHOPPING

Africa markets itself as the continent of curios. Wood carvings of people, animals and masks come in all sizes, some in dimensions that necessitate shipping. In the latter case it is obviously advisable to purchase from

PICTURES BY SA TOURISM AND LES DE VILLIERS

reputable dealers instead of street vendors. Other items include ivory, gold and silver objects and jewelry, beadwork and weaving. Vendors of animal skins will provide treatment certificates and other documentation required by customs in the US and other countries.   There is a ban on the importation of ivory in several countries. Do not expect to get diamonds or gold items at bargain prices in Africa. Outside the risky black market, prices are controlled. African artists, however, add a special local flavor and charm to their jewelry designs that attract foreign buyers.

SPORT

Travelers with a penchant for sport will find plenty to do or to watch, depending on their preference. Soccer is big throughout the continent and cricket is widespread. Rugby—traditionally played in South Africa, Zimbabawe and Namibia—is gaining ground as far as Morocco. Angling and fishing along the continents coastline or in its major rivers. are popular pastimes for visitors and golf course abound, especially in South Africa where courses designed by the likes of Gary Player, Jack Nicklaus, and Greg Norman supplement century old country clubs. Most clubs ofgfer rental clubs so there is no need to cart along your own equipment. Most hotels have fitness centers.

TELECOMMUNICATIONS

European visitors who are on GSM integrate seamlessly with their own equipment into cellphone networks in several major African countries. US and other visitors who operate on a different mobile system will find convenient stalls and stores at some airports and in major cities where they can rent phones. Cellphone communication has grown at a faster pace in the African continent than anywhere else in the world. Visitors with GSM capable telephones simply purchase and insert a simcard and purchase time as they go along. Calls from hotels are usually subject to a heavy surcharge. Most hotels offer facsimile services.

TRAINS

Train buffs looking for the unusual will find it in several parts of the continent. Kenya's Nairobi to Mombasa train and South Africa's renowned state-of-the -art luxury Blue Train and exquisite Rovos Rail are favorites. Sadly, however, in many parts of the continent railroads have fallen into disrepair.

VISAS

Citizens of the United States, United Kingdom and other European countries, as well as Japan need visas (obtainable at fees ranging from $20 to $100) for travel to most African countries. Exceptions are Botswana, Lesotho, Mauritius, Morocco, Namibia, Senegal, Seychelles, and South Africa, where no visas are required. In Zambia, US and Japanese citizens are not exempted and in Zimbabwe only the British and Canadians are exempted. In some cases a fee is charegd for visas and arrival and departure taxes levied. *[Regulations change and travelers are advised to contact the respective embassies or consulates before embarking on their trip or have their travel agents do so].*

WATER

Even though drinking water in some African countries poses no danger, it is better to err on the safe side. While South Africans, for example, might find it peculiar to see anyone resort to bottled water unless they prefer the taste and don't mind paying extra, drinking water out of the faucet in many other countries borders on being reckless. There may be the risk of diarrhoeal diseases, the dysenteries and various parasitic worm infections in both water and uncooked vegetables or fruit washed in contaminated water. Where there are no signs posted in bathrooms, the rule of thumb is not to drink water from any faucet anywhere before asking the question: "Is the water safe?' While this question might offend some of the locals, most will understand. Most establishments provide guests with bottled water in their rooms.

CALLING CODES

COUNTRY	TO[1]	FROM[2]
Algeria	213	00
Angola	244	00
Benin	229	00
Botswana	267	00
Burkina Faso	226	00
Burundi	257	90
Cameroon	237	00
Cape Verde Islands	238	0
Central African Republic	236	19
Chad	235	15
Comoros	269	10
Congo (Brazzaville)	242	00
Congo (Kinshasa)	243	00
Côte d'Ivoire	225	00
Djibouti	253	00
Egypt	20	00
Equatorial Guinea	240	00
Eritrea	291	00
Ethiopia	251	00
Gabon	241	00
Gambia	220	00
Ghana	233	00
Guinea-Bissau	245	00
Guinea	224	00
Kenya	254	000
Lesotho	266	00
Liberia	231	00
Libya	218	00
Madagascar	261	00
Malawi	265	101
Mali	223	00
Mauritania	222	00
Mauritius	230	00

COUNTRY	TO	FROM
Morocco	212	00
Mozambique	258	00
Namibia	264	09
Niger	227	00
Nigeria	234	009
Rwanda	250	00
São Tomé and Principe	239	00
Senegal	221	00
Seychelles	248	00
Sierra Leone	232	00
Somalia	252	19
South Africa	27	09
Sudan	249	00
Swaziland	268	00
Tanzania & Zanzibar	255	000
Togo	228	00
Tunisia	216	00
Uganda	256	000
Zambia	260	00
Zimbabwe	263	00

OTHER TERRITORIES

COUNTRY	TO	FROM
Diego Garcia	246	00
Mayotte Island	269	10
Réunion Island	262	00
St. Helena	290	01

Source: AT&T

1. The country code to be used when making international calls to a particular African country before dialing the city area code and number. 2. The access code needed to make an outgoing international call from a specific African country or territory before dialing another country and city code and telephone number.

TIME ZONES

Abidjan—GMT, Accra—GMT, Addis Ababa—GMT+3, Algiers—GMT+1, Antananarivo—GMT+3, Asmara—GMT+3, Bamako—GMT, Bangui—GMT+1, Banjul—GMT, Bissau—GMT, Brazzaville—GMT+1, Bujumbura—GMT+3, Cairo—GMT+2, Casablanca—GMT, Conakry—GMT, Dakar—GMT, Dar es Salaam—GMT+3, Djibouti—GMT+3, Freetown—GMT, Gaborone—GMT+2, Harare—GMT+2, Johannesburg—GMT+2, Kampala—GMT+3, Khartoum—GMT+3, Kigali—GMT+3, Kinshasa—GMT+1, Lagos—GMT+1, Libreville—GMT+1, Lilongwe—GMT+2, Lomé—GMT+1, Luanda—GMT+1, Lusaka—GMT+2, Malabo—GMT+1, Maputo—GMT+2, Maseru—GMT+2, Mbabane—GMT+2, Mogadishu—GMT+3, Monrovia GMT, Moroni—GMT+3, Nairobi—GMT+3, N'Djamena—GMT+1, Niamey—GMT+1, Nouakchott—GMT, Ouagadougou—GMT, Port Louis—GMT+4, Porto Novo—GMT+1, Praia—GMT, São Tomé—GMT, Tripoli—GMT+2, Tunis—GMT+1, Victoria—GMT+4, Windhoek—GMT+1, Yaoundé—GMT+1.

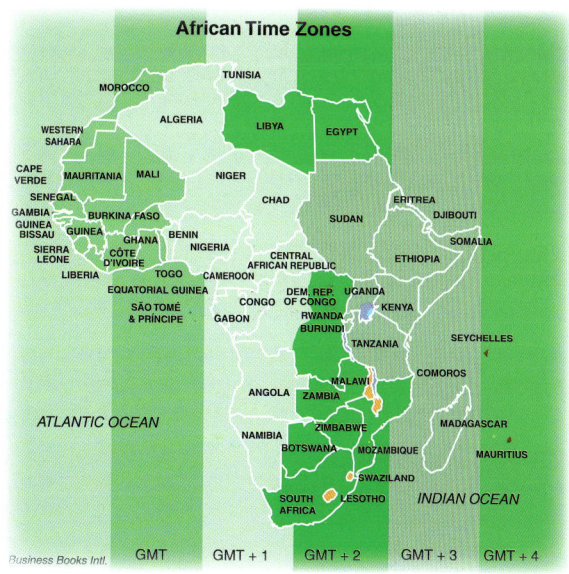

African Time Zones

African Weather - °Fahrenheit & and Rain Days per Month

		JAN	FEB	MAR	APR	MAY	JUN	JUL	AUG	SEP	OCT	NOV	DEC
EGYPT LUXOR	Max	73	78	84	95	104	106	106	106	104	95	84	77
	Min	41	45	52	61	70	73	75	75	72	64	54	46
	Rain	-	-	-	-	-	-	-	-	-	-	-	-
ETHIOPIA ADDIS ABAB	Max	75	75	77	77	77	73	70	70	72	75	73	73
	Min	43	46	48	50	50	48	50	50	48	45	43	41
	Rain	2	5	8	10	10	20	28	27	21	3	2	2
MALI BAMAKO	Max	91	97	102	102	102	93	90	88	90	93	93	91
	Min	60	66	72	75	75	73	72	72	72	72	64	63
	Rain	-	-	-	2	5	10	16	17	12	6	1	-
MOROCCO MARAKESH	Max	64	68	73	78	84	91	100	100	91	82	73	66
	Min	39	43	48	52	57	63	66	68	63	57	48	43
	Rain	7	5	6	6	2	1	1	1	3	4	3	7
TUNISIA TUNIS	Max	57	61	64	70	75	84	90	91	88	77	68	61
	Min	43	45	46	52	55	63	68	70	66	59	52	45
	Rain	8	7	5	2	1	-	-	-	1	3	5	7
BOTSWANA MAUN	Max	89	88	88	88	82	77	77	84	90	95	93	90
	Min	66	66	64	59	50	43	43	48	57	66	66	66
	Rain	8	7	5	2	1	-	-	-	1	3	5	7
KENYA NAIROBI	Max	77	78	77	75	72	70	70	70	75	75	73	73
	Min	53	55	57	57	55	54	52	52	52	55	55	55
	Rain	5	6	11	16	17	9	6	7	6	8	15	11
MADAGASCAR ANTANANARIVO	Max	78	78	78	75	73	70	68	70	73	81	81	81
	Min	61	61	61	57	54	50	48	48	52	54	57	61
	Rain	21	20	17	11	9	9	10	9	7	9	13	20
MALAWI LILONGWE	Max	81	81	81	81	77	73	73	77	81	86	84	82
	Min	63	63	61	57	52	46	45	46	54	59	63	64
	Rain	19	18	13	5	1	-	-	1	1	1	7	15
NAMIBIA WINDHOEK	Max	84	82	81	77	72	68	68	73	77	84	84	86
	Min	63	61	59	55	48	45	43	46	54	59	59	63
	Rain	8	8	8	4	1	-	-	-	-	2	3	6
SOUTH AFRICA CAPE TOWN	Max	78	78	77	72	66	64	63	64	64	70	73	75
	Min	61	61	57	54	48	46	45	46	48	52	55	57
	Rain	3	2	3	6	9	9	10	9	7	5	3	3
SOUTH AFRICA JO'BURG	Max	78	77	75	72	66	63	63	68	73	77	77	79
	Min	57	57	55	50	43	39	39	43	48	54	55	57
	Rain	8	7	5	2	1	-	-	-	1	3	5	7
TANZANIA ARUSHA	Max	82	82	81	77	73	72	72	73	77	81	81	81
	Min	55	57	59	61	59	55	54	54	55	57	57	57
	Rain	12	9	11	7	2	-	-	-	-	1	4	9
UGANDA KABALE	Max	75	75	73	73	73	73	73	73	73	75	73	73
	Min	48	52	52	52	52	48	46	48	52	50	52	50
	Rain	11	13	16	20	16	5	3	8	15	18	19	15

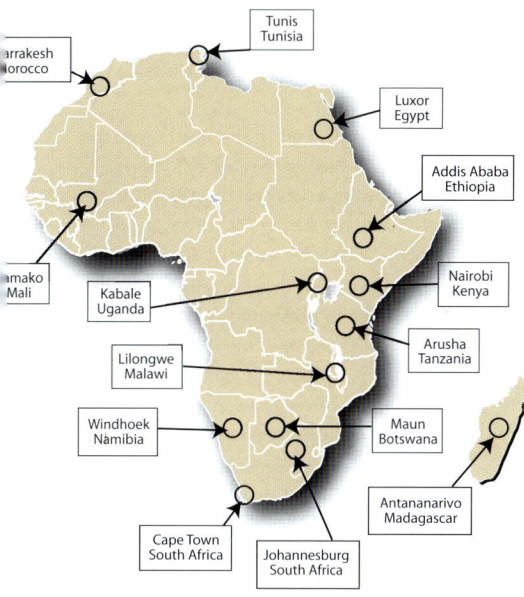

Map labels:
- Tunis, Tunisia
- Marrakesh, Morocco
- Luxor, Egypt
- Addis Ababa, Ethiopia
- Bamako, Mali
- Kabale, Uganda
- Nairobi, Kenya
- Arusha, Tanzania
- Lilongwe, Malawi
- Windhoek, Namibia
- Maun, Botswana
- Antananarivo, Madagascar
- Cape Town, South Africa
- Johannesburg, South Africa

EXCHANGE RATES PER US$1.00

	Currency	Symbol	2005[1]	2006[2]
Algeria	Dinar	DA	72.37	70.79
Angola	New Kwanza	Nkz	81.65	79.90
Benin	CFA Franc	CFAF	559.44	493.23
Botswana	Pula	P	5.68	6.057
Burkina Faso	CFA Franc	CFAF	559.44	493.23
Burundi	Burundi Franc	FBu	996.74	1,032.06
Cameroon	CFA Franc	CFAF	559.44	493.23
Cape Verde	Escudo	C.V. Esc.	94.37	83.1
Cent. Afr. Rep.	CFA Franc	CFAF	559.44	493.23
Chad	CFA Franc	CFAF	559.44	493.23
Comoros	Com. Franc	CF	419.54	370.01
Congo, DR of	Cong. Franc	CDF	464.00	432.00
Congo, Rep.	CFA Franc	CFAF	559.44	493.23
Côte d'Ivoire	CFA Franc	CFAF	559.44	493.23
Djibouti	Djib. Franc	DF	173.68	174.75
Egypt	Eg. Pound	£E	5.75	5.72
Eq. Guinea	CFA Franc	CFAF	559.44	493.23
Eritrea	Nafka	Nfa	15.00	15.00
Ethiopia	Birr	Br	8.72	8.75
Gabon	CFA Franc	CFAF	559.44	493.23
Gambia, The	Dalasi	D	28.75	27.83
Ghana	Cedi	¢	9,090.00	9,151.01
Guinea	Guinea Franc	GNF	4,120	5.556.70
Guinea-Bissau	CFA Franc	CFAF	559.44	493.23
Kenya	Shilling	KSh	75.42	69.64
Lesotho	Loti	L	6.75	7.04
Liberia	Liberian dollar	L$	49.99	49.00
Libya	Libyan Dinar	LD	1.36	1.27
Madagascar	Ariary	MGA	9,050.23	2,015.00
Malawi	Kwacha	MK	123.56	138.89
Mali	CFA Franc	CFAF	559.44	493.23
Mauritania	Ouguiyas	UM	277.05	268.00
Mauritius	Rupee	MauR	30.10	33.04
Morocco	Dirham	DH	9.28	8.39
Mozambique	Metical	Mt	28,180	27.03
Namibia	Namib.dollar	N$	6.75	7.04
Niger	CFA Franc	CFAF	559.44	493.23
Nigeria	Naira	N	130.25	128.34
Rwanda	Rw. Franc	RF	537.06	550.19
São Tomé & P.	Dobra	Db	7,432	6,750
Senegal	CFA Franc	CFAF	559.44	493.23
Seychelles	Rupee	SR	5.19	5.45
Sierra Leone	Leones	Le	2,352	2.95
Somalia	Shilling	SoSh	1,842	1,342
South Africa	Rand	ZAR	6.75	7.04
Sudan	Dinar	SDD	233.33	212.09
Swaziland	Lilangeni	SZL	6.75	7.04
Tanzania	Shilling	TSh	1,162	1,268
Togo	CFA Franc	CFAF	559.44	493.03
Tunisia	Dinar	TD	1.37	1.28
Uganda	Shilling	USh	1,845	1,795
Zambia	Kwacha	ZK	4,082	4,005
Zimbabwe	Zimb. Dollar	Z$	61,693	250.50

1.Exchange rate on November 13, 2005. 2.Exchange rate on December 7, 2006

WHEN TO GO

Business travelers usually do not have the luxury of picking the best time to visit based on weather but the chart on the opposite page should provide a useful guideline to those who do. These are averages based on conditions over several years but no guarantees. Like anywhere else the weather in Africa at times shows total disregard for neat tables and median numbers. Those who visit Africa for pure pleasure should keep in mind that the best time of the year is not necessarily purely a matter of sunshine and warmth. In Southern Africa, for example, the best time to go on safari is during the winter months when the foilage is sparse and the animals more readily seen. But this does not augur well for travelers who have looked forward to enjoying the magnificent beaches.

RUMOURS OF TIMBUCTOU

In 1825 when nineteen year old Oxford student-poet Alfred Tennyson was assigned the task of comparing Timbuktu with the legendary lost civilizations of Atlantis and El Dorado, he asked, rhetorically:

> Is the rumour of thy Timbuctou
>
> A dream as frail as those of ancient Time?

His subsequent lines suggested a place with *"low-built, mudwall'd barbarian settlement."*

Tennyson took his cue from French explorer Rene Caillie who had just returned from Timbuktu to debunk the wondrous tales of a city built on gold. Instead, he found a mud-walled town whose glory had largely faded.

It was a distinguished Moroccan traveler, Leo Africanus, who first stimulated European interest in Timbuktu with the appearance of his History and Description of Africa in 1525—translated into English in 1600. Africanus spoke of a rich king who possessed great treasures in gold with some ingots weighing as much as 1,300 pounds. He found in the city many men of learning and a treasure of books.

By the late fifteenth century Timbuktu or, as some called it, the Queen of the Sudan, had become the educational and commercial center of Western Sudan.

In 1618 a company was formed in London with the expressed purpose of establishing a gold trade with Timbuktu. The first expedition ended in the massacre of all its members along the Gambia River and the second lost its way.

Of the almost fifty Europeans who braved the Sahara desert in an attempt to reach this legendary city in Mali, Englishman Gordon Lang was the first to succeed. He did not survive, however, to tell his story. On his way back he was murdered.

So Caillie was the one to bring back the disappointing tale. In pursuing his goal to reach Timbuktu—that had become "the continual object of all my thoughts"—Caillie traveled as a Muslim to evade the wrath of religious fanatics encountered by other European explorers.

Other explorers followed, including Dr. Heinrich Barth, the scholarly German contemporary and friend of David Livingstone. Barth's accounts of his journey to Timbuktu form part of a five volume set of books (600 pages each) on his Travels in Central Africa. Apart from contributing further to the knowledge of Timbuktu, Barth also lays claim to having "discovered" Agades, a sister city which, in his words, has by "mere accident" not attracted as much attention as Timbuktu.

In its glory days during the fifteenth and sixteenth century, Timbuktu was seen by some as the "gateway to the Sahara desert " and by others as "the most distant place on earth." While the first image rapidly faded as Caillie and others dismantled the golden tales of the past, the second appellation stuck until today. How often do we still hear this expression whenever someone plans to travel to far and remote places: "I am going to Timbuktu."

Caravan approaching Timbuktu—German engraving—1853 (Barth, Travels in Central Africa, 1857)

Diplomatic addresses

African Embassies in the US

ALGERIA
Embassy of the Republic of Algeria
2118 Kalorama Road NW
Washington, DC, 20008
Tel: 202-265-2800 Fax: 202-667-2174

ANGOLA
Embassy of the Republic of Angola
1615 M Street NW, Suite 900
Washington, DC, 20036
Tel: 202-785-1156 Fax: 202-785-1258

BENIN
Embassy of the Republic of Benin
2737 Cathedral Avenue NW
Washington, DC, 20008
Tel: 202-232-6656 Fax: 202-265-1996

BOTSWANA
Embassy of the Republic of Botswana
1533 New Hampshire Ave NW
Washington, DC, 20036
Tel: 202-244-4990 Fax: 202-244-4164

BURKINA FASO
Embassy of Burkina Faso
2340 Massachusetts Avenue NW
Washington, DC, 20008
Tel: 202-332-5577 Fax: 202-667-1882

BURUNDI
Embassy of the Republic of Burundi
2233 Wisconsin Avenue NW, Suite 212
Washington, DC, 20007
Tel: 202-342-2574 Fax: 202-342-2578

CAMEROON
Embassy of the Republic of Cameroon
2349 Massachusetts Ave NW
Washington, DC, 20008
Tel: 202-265-8790 Fax: 202-387-3826

CAPE VERDE
Embassy of the Republic of Cape Verde
3415 Massachusetts Avenue NW
Washington, DC, 20007
Tel: 202-965-6820 Fax: 202-965-1207

CENTRAL AFRICAN REPUBLIC
Embassy of Central African Republic
1618 22nd Street NW
Washington, DC, 20008
Tel: 202-483-7800 Fax: 202-332-9893

CHAD
Embassy of the Republic of Chad
2002 R Street NW
Washington, DC, 20009
Tel: 202-462-4009 Fax: 202-265-1937

COMOROS
Embassy of the Republic of Comoros
420 E. 50th St.
New York, NY, 10022
Tel: 212-972-8010 Fax: 212-983-4712

CONGO [KINSHASA]
Embassy of the Dem. Republic of Congo
1800 New Hampshire Ave NW
Washington, DC, 20009
Tel: 202-234-7690 Fax: 202-234-2609

CONGO [BRAZZAVILLE]
Embassy of the Republic of the Congo
4891 Colorado Avenue NW
Washington, DC, 20011
Tel: 202-726-0825 Fax: 202-726-1860

CÔTE D'IVOIRE
Embassy of the Republic of Cote d'Ivoire
3421 Massachusetts Avenue NW
Washington, DC, 20008
Tel: 202-797-0300 Fax:202-462-9444

DJIBOUTI
Embassy of the Republic of Djibouti
1156 15th Street NW, Suite 515
Washington, DC, 20005
Tel: 202-331-0270 Fax: 202-331-0302

EGYPT
Embassy of the Arab Republic of Egypt
3521 International Court NW
Washington, DC, 20008
Tel: 202-895-5400 Fax: 202-244-5131

EQUATORIAL GUINEA
Embassy of the Republic of Equatorial Guinea
2020 16th Street NW
Washington, DC, 20009
Tel: 202-518-5700 Fax: 202-518-5252

ERITREA
Embassy of the State of Eritrea
1708 New Hampshire Ave NW
Washington, DC, 20009
Tel: 202-319-1991 Fax: 202-319-1304

ETHIOPIA
Embassy of the Fed. Dem. Rep. of Ethiopia
2134 Kalorama Road NW
Washington, DC, 20008
Tel: 202-364-1200 Fax: 202-686-9857

GABON
Embassy of the Gabonese Republic
2034 20th Street NW, Suite 200
Washington, DC, 20009
Tel: 202-797-1000 Fax: 202-332-0668

GAMBIA
Embassy of The Gambia
1155 15th Street NW, Suite 1000
Washington, DC, 20005
Tel: 202-785-1399 Fax: 202-785-1430

GHANA
Embassy of the Republic of Ghana
3512 International Drive NW
Washington, DC, 20008
Tel: 202-686-4520 Fax: 202- 686-4527

GUINEA
Embassy of the Republic of Guinea
2112 Leroy Place NW
Washington, DC, 20008
Tel: 202-483-9420 Fax: 202-483-8688

GUINEA-BISSAU
Embassy of the Republic of Guinea-Bissau
15929 Yukon Lane
Rockville, MD, 20855
Tel: 301-947-3958 Fax: 301-947-3958

KENYA
Embassy of the Republic of Kenya
2249 R Street NW
Washington, DC, 20008
Tel:202-387-6101 Fax:202-462-3829

LESOTHO
Embassy of the Kingdom of Lesotho
2511 Massachusetts Ave NW
Washington, DC, 20008.
Tel: 202-797-5533 Fax: 202-234-6815

LIBERIA
Embassy of the Republic of Liberia
5303 Colorado Avenue NW
Washington, DC, 20011
Tel: 202-723-0437 Fax: 202-723-0436

LIBYA
Libyan Permanent Representative to the UN
309-315 East 48th St
New York, NY, 10017
Tel: 212-752-5775 Fax: 212-593-4787

MADAGASCAR
Embassy of the Republic of Madagascar
2374 Massachusetts Avenue NW
Washington, DC, 20008
Tel: 202-265-5525 Fax: 202-265-3034

MALAWI
Embassy of the Republic of Malawi
2408 Massachusetts Avenue NW
Washington, DC, 20008
Tel: 202-797-1007 Fax:202-265-0976

MALI
Embassy of the Republic of Mali
2130 R Street NW
Washington, DC, 20008
Tel: 202-332-2249 Fax: 202-332-6603

MAURITANIA
Embassy of the Islamic Rep. of Mauritania
2129 Leroy Place NW
Washington, DC, 20008
Tel: 202-232-5700 Fax: 202-319-2623

MAURITIUS
Embassy of Republic of Mauritius
4301 Connecticut Ave NW
Washington, DC, 20008
Tel: 202-244-1491 Fax: 202-966-0983

MOROCCO
Embassy of the Kingdom of Morocco
1601 21st Street NW
Washington, DC, 20009
Tel:202-462-7979 Fax:202-265-0161

MOZAMBIQUE
Embassy of the Republic of Mozambique
1990 M Street NW, Suite 570
Washington, DC, 20036
Tel: 202-293-7146 Fax: 202-835-0245

NAMIBIA
Embassy of the Republic of Namibia
1605 New Hampshire Ave NW
Washington, DC, 20009
Tel: 202-986-0540 Fax: 202-986-0443

NIGER
Embassy of the Republic of Niger
C2204 R Street NW
Washington, DC, 20008
Tel: 202-483-4224

NIGERIA
Embassy of the Federal Rep. of Nigeria
1333 16th Street NW
Washington, DC, 20036
Tel: 202-986-8400 Fax: 202-986-8449

RWANDA
Embassy of the Republic of Rwanda
1714 New Hampshire Ave NW
Washington, DC, 20009
Tel: 202-232-2882 Fax: 202-232-4544

SÃO TOMÉ & PRÍNCIPE
UN Mission of São Tomé & Príncipe
400 Park Ave, 17th Floor
New York, NY, 10022
Tel:212-317-0533 Fax: 212-317-0580

SENEGAL
Embassy of the Republic of Senegal
2112 Wyoming Ave NW
Washington, DC, 20008
Tel: 202-234-0540 Fax: 202-332-6315

SEYCHELLES
UN Mission of the Republic of Seychelles
820 Second Avenue, Suite 900F
New York, NY, 10017
Tel: 212-687-9766 Fax: 212-922-9177

SIERRA LEONE
Embassy of the Republic of Sierra Leone
1701 19th Street NW
Washington, DC, 20009
Tel: 202-939-9261 Fax: 202-483-1793

SOUTH AFRICA
Embassy of the Republic of South Africa
3051 Massachusetts Ave NW
Washington, DC, 20008
Tel: 202-232-4400 Fax: 202-265-1607

SUDAN
Embassy of the Republic of the Sudan
2210 Massachusetts Ave NW
Washington, DC, 20008
Tel: 202-338-8565 Fax: 202-667-2406

SWAZILAND
Embassy of the Kingdom of Swaziland
3400 International Drive NW
Washington, DC, 20008
Tel: 202-234-5002 Fax: 202-234-8254

TANZANIA
Embassy of the United Republic of Tanzania
2139 R Street NW
Washington, DC, 20008
Tel: 202-939-6125 Fax: 202-797-7408

TOGO
Embassy of the Republic of Togo
2208 Massachusetts Avenue NW
Washington, DC, 20008
Tel: 202-234-4212 Fax: 202-232-3190

TUNISIA
Embassy of the Republic of Tunisia
1515 Massachusetts Ave NW
Washington, DC, 20005
Tel: 202-862-1850 Fax: 202-862-1858

UGANDA
Embassy of the Republic of Uganda
5911 16th Street NW
Washington, DC, 20011
Tel: 202-726-7100 Fax: 202-726-1727

ZAMBIA
Embassy of the Republic of Zambia
2419 Massachusetts Ave NW
Washington, DC, 20008
Tel: 202-265-9717 Fax: 202-332-0826

ZIMBABWE
Embassy of the Republic of Zimbabwe
1608 New Hampshire Ave NW
Washington, DC, 20009
Tel: 202-332-7100 Fax: 202-483-9326

US EMBASSIES IN AFRICA

ALGERIA
4 Chemin Cheikh Bachir El-Ibrahimi, Algiers 16000
Tel: [213] (2) 69-12-55 Fax: 69-39-79
Web: us-embassy.eldjazair.net.dz.

ANGOLA
Rua Houari Boumedienne No. 32, Luanda
Tel: [244] (2) 347-028/345-481 Fax: 346-924

BENIN
rue Caporal Bernard Anani, Cotonou 2012
Tel: [229] 30-06-50 Fax: 30-14-39
Web: amemb.coo@intnet.bj.

BOTSWANA
P.O. Box 90, Gaborone
Tel: [267] 353-982 Fax: 356-947
E-mail: usembgab@global.co.za

BURKINA FASO
602 Avenue Raoul Follerau, Ouagadougou 01 B.P. 35
Tel: (226) 30-67-23 Fax: (226) 30-38-90
Web: amembouaga@ouagadougb.us-state.gov/

BURUNDI
Avenue Des Etas-Unis , Bujumbura B.P. 1720
Tel: [257] 22-34-54 Fax: 22-29-26
E-mail: @bujumburab.us-state.gov.

CAMEROON
rue Nachtigal, Yaounde B.P. 817
Tel: (237) 23-40-14 Fax: 23-07-53
Web: yaounde@youndeb.us-state.gov.

CAPE VERDE
Rua Abilio Macedo 81, Praia, C.P. 201
Tel: [238] 61-56-16 Fax: 61-13-55

CENTRAL AFRICAN REPUBLIC
Avenue David Dacko, Bangui B.P. 924
Tel: [236] 61-02-00 Fax: 61-44-94

CHAD
Ave. Felix Eboue, N'Djamena B.P. 413
Tel: [235] (51) 70-09 Fax: 51-56-54
Web: paschallrc@ndjamenab.us-state.gov.

DEM. REPUBLIC OF THE CONGO
310 Avenue des Aviateurs, Kinshasa
Tel: [243] (12) 21804 Fax: (88) 43805

REPUBLIC OF THE CONGO
The Brazzaville Embassy Office
is co-located in Kinshasa
Tel: [243] (88) 43608 Fax: (88) 41036

COTE D'IVOIRE
5 rue Jesse Owens, Abidjan 01 B.P. 1712
Tel: [225] 20-21-09-79 Fax: 20-22-32-59

DJIBOUTI
Plateau du Serpent, Blvd, Djibouti B.P. 185
Tel: [253] 35-39-95 Fax: 35-39-40

EGYPT
8 Kamal el-Din Salah St., Garden City Cairo
Tel: [20] (2) 355-7371 Fax: 357-3200

ERITREA
Franklin D. Roosevelt St, Asmara
Tel: [291] (1) 120004 Fax: 127584

ETHIOPIA
Entoto St. P.O. Box 1014, Addis Ababa
Tel: [251] (1) 550-666 Fax: 551-328
Email: usembassy@telecom.net.et.

GABON
Blvd. de la Mer, Libreville B.P. 4000
Tel: [241] 762-003/4 Fax: 745-507

THE GAMBIA
Fajara, Kairaba Ave, Banjul P.M.B. 19
Tel: (220) 392-856 Fax: 392-475

GHANA
Ring Road East - P.O. Box 194, Accra
Tel: [233] (21) 775-348 Fax: 776-008
Web: http:www.usembassy.org.gh.

GUINEA
rue KA 038, Conakry B.P. 603
Tel: [224] 41-15-20 Fax: 41-15-22
Web: www.eti-bull.net/usembassy

KENYA
Mombasa Road
Nairobi
Tel: [254] (2) 537-800 Fax: 537-810

LESOTHO
P.O. Box 333 , Maseru 100
Tel: [266] 312-666
310-116 Fax: E-mail: amles@lesoff.co.za.

LIBERIA
111 United Nations Dr., Mamba Point Monrovia
Tel: [231] 226-370-380 Fax: 226-148

MADAGASCAR
14 & 16, rue Rainitovo Antsahavola, Antananarivo 101
Tel: [261] (20) 22 21257 Fax: (20) 22 34539

MALAWI
P.O. Box 30016, Lilongwe 3
Tel: [265] 783-166 Fax: 780-471

MALI
rue Rochester NY
Bamako B.P. 34
Tel: [223] 22-54-70 Fax: 223712
Web: ipc@usa.org.ml.

MAURITANIA
rue Abdallaye, Nouakchott B.P. 222
Tel: (222) 25-26-60 Fax: 25-15-92
Web: aemnouak@opt.mr.

MAURITIUS
(Also COMOROS & SEYCHELLES)
Rogers House (4th Fl.) John Kennedy St, Port Louis
Tel: [230] 208-2347 Fax: 208-9534

MOROCCO
2 Ave. de Marrakech , Rabat PSC 74
Tel: [212] (7) 76-22-65 Fax: 76-56-61
Web: http://www.usembassy-morocco.org.ma.

MOZAMBIQUE
Avenida Kenneth Kaunda 193, Maputo
Tel: [258] (1) 49-27-97 Fax: 49-01-14
Web: usacomm@mail.tropical.co.mz

NAMIBIA
Ausplan Building 14 Lossen St. , Windhoek
Tel: [264] (61) 221-601 Fax: 229-792
Web: www.usemb.org.na.

NIGER
rue Des Ambassades, Niamey B.P. 11201
Tel: [227] 72-26-61 Fax: 73-31-67
Email: usemb@intnet.ne.

NIGERIA
2 Walter Carrington Crescent, Victoria Island, Lagos
Tel: [234] (1) 261-0050 Fax: 261-9856

RWANDA
Blvd. de la Revolution, Kigali B.P. 28
Tel: (250) 75601/2/3 Fax: 419-710-9346
Email: amembkigali@hotmail.com.

SIERRA LEONE
Walpole and Siaka Stevens Sts, Freetown
Tel: [232] (22) 226-481 Fax: 225-471

SOUTH AFRICA
877 Pretorius St., Arcadia Pretoria 0083
Tel: [27] (12) 342-1048 Fax: 342-2244

SUDAN
Sharia Ali Abdul Latif, Khartoum
Tel: [249] (11) 774611 Fax: [249] (11) 774137

TANZANIA
140 Msese Road, Kinondoni District, Dar Es Salaam
Tel: [255] (51) 666010-5 Fax: 666701
Web: usembassy-dar2@cats-net.com.

TOGO
rue Pelletier Caventou & rue Vauban, Lome B.P. 852
Tel: [228] 21-29-91 Fax: 21-79-52
Web: ustogo1#cafŽ.tg.

TUNISIA
144 Ave. de la Liberte, Tunis-Belvedere 1002
Tel: [216] (1) 782-566 Fax: 789-719

UGANDA
Parliament Ave, Kampala
Tel: [256] (41) 259792/3/5 Fax: 259794

ZAMBIA
Independence & United Nations Aves, Lusaka
Tel: [260] (1) 250-955 Fax: 252-225

ZIMBABWE
172 Herbert Chitepo Ave, Harare
Tel: [263] (4) 250-593 Fax: 796487
Email: amembzim@africaonline.co.zw.

Index

A

B

C